D1476311

Corporate Insolvency: Employment and Pension Rights

Fourth edition

Corporate Insolvency: Employment and Pension Rights

Fourth edition

David Pollard

Partner

Freshfields Bruckhaus Deringer LLP

Bloomsbury Professional

Bloomsbury Professional Ltd, Maxwelton House, 41–43 Boltro Road, Haywards Heath, West Sussex, RH16 1BJ

First edition: 1994 (Tolley Publishing)
Second edition: 2000 (Butterworths)
Third edition: 2007 (Tottel Publishing)

A CIP Catalogue record for this book is available from the British Library.

ISBN 978 1 84766 307 8

Typeset by Phoenix Photosetting, Chatham, Kent

Printed in Great Britain by CPI Antony Rowe Ltd, Chippenham, Wiltshire

Preface

The aim of this book is to bridge the gap between what have generally been regarded as three separate legal disciplines. Legal practitioners, whether solicitors or barristers, have tended to specialise in one area only, whether it be pensions law, employment law or insolvency law. Each of these areas is covered by its own legal books and literature although the pensions area has, until recently, seen the least by way of legal literature.

This division into distinct specialisations has tended to mean that difficulties can arise at the stage where two or more areas meet. The purpose of this book is to draw out the legal principles applicable where the different legal regimes interact.

Although a brief overview of employment law and insolvency principles is given, the basic law in each of the three areas concerned is dealt with in more depth in other, readily available, works. Instead, this book focuses on the application of the rules relating to corporate insolvency and how they impact on employees and pensions. For example, how is the position of employees affected by the appointment of an insolvency practitioner over their employing company? Who is liable and what priority is given to past or future claims? This simple and everyday question leads to a complex legal analysis.

This book will have succeeded if it brings out the difficulties that can arise in these three areas, and gives practitioners a base on which to answer the questions that arise. Not least, it aims to bring together the statutory and other materials applicable in this area.

As in other areas, the law is becoming more and more complex.

Since the third edition appeared in 2007, there have been continual changes:

- cases on administration expenses

- new powers of the Pensions Regulator

- cases on protective awards

- cases on the new TUPE provisions

- changes to employer debt provisions on pensions

- cases on directors or majority shareholders as employees

This new 4th edition takes account of all these changes.

In practice the legislation is often confusing and unclear.

In some cases this can be the result of the drafter being faced with a rather vague EU Directive (are there any other kinds?) and deciding to follow it (rather than risk mis-interpreting it). I do have some sympathy for this, given the track record of the ECJ in delivering even vaguer 'judgments'.

But in other cases, the problem is a pure UK 'own goal'. Take the re-casting of the employee adoption provisions in administration by the Enterprise Act 2002. The Court of Appeal in *Krasner* castigated the new drafting as being 'on any view … unsatisfactory' and a 'thoroughly unsatisfactory piece of drafting'.

This is not rocket science. There is no good reason why the drafters cannot do better.

Many people have given me useful comments and suggestions. The mistakes, of course, remain my own. Thanks are due to my colleagues at Freshfields Bruckhaus Deringer who gave comments: Dawn Heath, Julia Chirnside, Lara Zellick, Holly Insley, Sarah Swift, Isobel Carruthers, Nick Squire, Alex Fricke, Michael Muenterfering, Josh Gabriel, Paula Volkmer, Dan Schaffer, Harriet Maurice-Williams, Look Chan Ho, Lynn Dunne, Caroline Smith and Talia Carman. Thanks also go to Alex Chiang, Emma Lester and Andrew Taggart. Particular thanks must go to Ken Dierden whose advice ('don't do it') was invaluable.

Last, but by no means least, this book is dedicated to my wife, Louise, and my children, Jessica, Elizabeth and Andrew. Their hope to be able to see me occasionally in the evening and at weekends, instead of losing me to the office, must be close to realisation.

The law is stated as at 1 November 2009.

David Pollard
Freshfields Bruckhaus Deringer LLP
London
1 November 2009
david.pollard@freshfields.com

Abbreviations

Insolvency processes

CVA	Company voluntary arrangement
CVL	Creditors' voluntary liquidation
MVL	Members' voluntary liquidation

Legislation

ARD	Acquired Rights Directive
EPA	Employment Protection Act
EPCA	Employment Protection (Consolidation) Act
ERA	Employment Rights Act
IA	Insolvency Act
ICTA	Income and Corporation Taxes Act
IORP	Directive on Institutions for Occupational Retirement Provision (2003/41/EC)
ITEPA	Income Tax (Earnings and Pensions) Act
MFR	Minimum Funding Requirement
PA	Pensions Act
PSA	Pension Schemes Act
SI	Statutory Instrument
SSF	Scheme Specific Funding (Part 3, PA 2004)
SSPA	Social Security Pensions Act
TULRCA	Trade Union and Labour Relations (Consolidation) Act
TUPE	Transfer of Undertakings (Protection of Employment) Regulations
Employer Debt Regulations	The Occupational Pension Schemes (Employer Debt) Regulations 2005
MFR Regulations	The Occupational Pension Schemes (Minimum Funding Requirement and Actuarial Valuations) Regulations 1996
PPF Entry Rules Regulations	The Pension Protection Fund (Entry Rules) Regulations 2005
Scheme Funding Regulations	The Occupational Pension Schemes (Scheme Funding) Regulations 2005

Courts

CA	Court of Appeal
DC	Divisional Court
EAT	Employment Appeal Tribunal

Abbreviations

ECJ	European Court of Justice
ET	Employment Tribunal
HL	House of Lords (became the Supreme Court from October 2009)
IT	Industrial Tribunal (became the ET from August 1998)
NIRC	National Industrial Relations Court
PC	Privy Council

Judges

C	Chancellor (replaced the Vice-Chancellor from October 2005)
CJ	Chief Justice (High Court)
J	Justice (High Court)
LJ	Lord Justice (Court of Appeal)
MR	Master of the Rolls
V-C	Vice-Chancellor

Other bodies

APL	Association of Pension Lawyers
BAS	Board of Actuarial Standards
BERR	Department for Business, Enterprise & Regulatory Reform (became BIS in June 2009)
BIS	Department for Business, Innovation and Skills (created in June 2009 by a merger of BERR and the Department for Innovation, Universities and Skills)
CAC	Central Arbitration Committee
DSS	Department of Social Security (became the DWP in June 2001)
DTI	Department of Trade and Industry (became BERR in June 2007)
DWP	Department for Work and Pensions
FMLC	Financial Markets Law Committee
HMRC	Her Majesty's Revenue and Customs
IP	Insolvency Practitioner
IT	Independent Trustee
Opra	Occupational Pensions Regulatory Authority (replaced by the Pensions Regulator in April 2005)
PPF	Pension Protection Fund
R3	the Association of Business Recovery Professionals
RPO	Redundancy Payments Office (of the Insolvency Service and part of BERR)
SPI	Society of Practitioners of Insolvency (the SPI is now called "R3" or the 'Association of Business Recovery Professionals')
tPR	the Pensions Regulator

Case references

AC	Appeal Cases
ACLC	Australian Company Law Cases
ACLR	Australian Company Law Reports
All ER	All England Law Reports
ALR	Australian Law Reports
BCC	British Company Cases
BCLC	Butterworths Company Law Cases
BPIR	Bankruptcy and Personal Insolvency Reports
CCPB	Canadian Cases on Pensions and Benefits
Ch	Chancery
CLR	Commonwealth Law Reports (Australian)
CMLR	Common Market Law Reports
DLR	Dominion Law Reports (Canadian)
ECR	European Court Reports
Env LR	Environment Law Reports
Eq	Equity
EWCA	England and Wales, Court of Appeal
EWHC	England and Wales, High Court
FCA	Federal Court of Australia
HCA	High Court of Australia
ICR	Industrial Case Reports
IR	Irish Reports
IRLIB	Industrial Relations Legal Information Bulletin
IRLR	Industrial Relations Law Reports
ITR	Industrial Tribunal Reports
JLR	Jersey Law Reports
KB	King's Bench
NSWLR	New South Wales Law Reports
NZLR	New Zealand Law Reports
NZSC	New Zealand Superannuation Cases
OPLR	Occupational Pensions Law Reports
P&CR	Property and Compensation Reports
PLR	Pensions Law Reports
QB	Queen's Bench
SC	Scottish Cases
SCLR	Scottish Company Law Reports
SCR	Supreme Court Reports (Canada)
STC	Simon's Tax Cases
TLR	Times Law Reports
UKHL	United Kingdom, House of Lords
UKPC	Privy Council
VR	Victorian Reports (Australian)
WLR	Weekly Law Reports
WN	Weekly Notes

See generally the index "Cardiff Index to Legal Abbreviations" (maintained by Cardiff University) at www.legalabbrevs.cardiff.ac.uk.

Useful websites

Websites

Organisation and website	Details
APL: www.apl.org.uk	Association of Pension Lawyers: The APL has a website and most of the papers given at its conferences find their way on to it. But I think you now have to be a member to access them.
Austlii www.austlii.edu.au	Australasian Legal Information Institute: Australian cases (including state courts) and materials
BAILII: www.bailii.org	The newer British Isles equivalent of Austlii. It contains British and Irish case law and legislation, European Union case law, Law Commission reports, and other law-related British and Irish material.
CANLII www.canlii.org/en/index.php	Canadian Legal Information Institute: Canadian cases, including the provinces.
Cardiff Index to Legal Abbreviations www.legalabbrevs.cardiff.ac.uk	Case citation index from Cardiff University
ECJ http://curia.europa.eu/jurisp/ cgi-bin/form.pl?lang=en	Judgments of the European Court of Justice from 1997 (earlier caselaw is also available). The link is to the search form.
Employment Appeal Tribunal www.employmentappeals.gov.uk	Hears appeals from the Employment Tribunal. The ET has jurisdiction in most employment matters and for discrimination cases.
Financial Markets Law Committee www.fmlc.org	Some papers on insolvency issues
Freshfields Bruckhaus Deringer LLP www.freshfields.com	Publications page includes copies of various briefings. Includes many on employment and pensions issues.
HMRC Insolvency Manual www.hmrc.gov.uk/manuals /insmanual	Tax manual on insolvency issues

House of Lords

www.publications.parliament.uk/ pa/ld/ldjudgmt.htm	This page lists Html versions of all House of Lords judgments delivered since 14 November 1996. Not searcheable (but try BAILII).

From October 2009, see the Supreme Court website

Insolvency service
www.insolvency.gov.uk   Insolvency service

Legislation:
Office of Public Sector Information
www.opsi.gov.uk/legislation   This site provides links to the full text of all UK Parliament Public General Acts (from 1988 onwards) and all statutory instruments (from 1987 onwards) as they were originally enacted. For more recent legislation, the explanatory memorandum is also available.

Pensions Ombudsman
www.pensions-ombudsman.org.uk   Includes determinations of the Ombudsman in a searcheable form.

Pensions Regulator
www.thepensionsregulator.gov.uk   Includes various codes of practice and guidance. Also a few decisions of the determinations panel.

Privy Council
www.privy-council.org.uk   Privy Council judgments since 1999 (yes there are still some appeals, notably from the Isle of Man, the various Channel Isles, Jamaica, Mauritius, the Cayman Islands, Bermuda, Gibraltar and Brunei).

R3
www.r3.org.uk/publications   Association of Business Recovery Professionals

Statute Law Database
www.statutelaw.gov.uk   The UK Statute Law Database (SLD) is the official revised edition of the primary legislation of the United Kingdom made available online.

Supreme Court
www.supremecourt.gov.uk/   The Supreme Court took over from the House of Lords in relation to legal appeals from October 2009. Supreme Court decisions are on this website.

Subscription needed:

Justis – UK official law reports (a subscription service)

Westlaw – a full case and legislation service

Lexis Nexis – All England Law Reports etc. A subscription service

Perspective/Pendragon – a commercial site dedicated to pensions. Includes a 'timetravel' option to see what was in force on earlier dates.

Contents

Table of Statutes

Table of Statutory Instruments and Other Material

Table of Overseas Material

Table of Other Material

Table of Cases

F

I

CHAPTER 1

Introduction

1.1   This book deals with the effect under the law of England and Wales of the formal insolvency of a company on its employees and their employment contracts and on their pension rights. The first two chapters are brief general descriptions of the law relating to employment and the insolvency regimes in England and Wales. These are followed by chapters giving a specific analysis of the special effects of such insolvency regimes on the employment relationship.

1.2   Generally, employees will be unsecured creditors of the employer, having the usual rights of a contracting party against the insolvent employer, both to claim for any sums owing at the date of insolvency and in relation to rights connected with on-going obligations on the part of the insolvent employer.

This general position of employees as unsecured creditors or as contracting parties has been modified to an extent by specific statutory intervention for example:

(a)   some employment related claims against the employer are given preferential status in the insolvency – see Chapters 9 and 10;

(b)   some employment related liabilities are, in effect, guaranteed by the state out of the National Insurance Fund – see Chapter 13 (National Insurance Fund);

(c)   where the business of the insolvent employer is continued, the insolvency practitioner needs to deal with liabilities to the employees who continue in the business, particularly where the insolvency practitioner 'adopts' their contract of employment – see Chapters 15 to 18 (Carrying on business);

(d)   where a sale of business by a company in an insolvency process occurs there are special features under TUPE, the Transfer of Undertakings (Protection of Employment) Regulations 2006 – see Chapters 19 to 24;

(e)   PAYE and national insurance obligations – discussed in Chapter 25;

(f)   there are special obligations under the Pensions Acts 1995 and 2004 where the employer has established an occupational pension scheme – see Chapters 27 to 37;

(g)   the impact of overseas employees – see Chapter 40;

(h)   who is connected or associated is relevant in some areas – see Chapter 41

(i)   pre pack administrations raise particular issues – see Chapter 42.

1.3   The law is stated on the materials available as at 1 November 2009.

When the Employment Rights (Dispute Resolution) Act 1998 came into force on 1 August 1998 industrial tribunals were renamed 'employment tribunals' (see s 1). Accordingly, where appropriate, I have used this new term in this book (but retained the term industrial tribunal where this is historically accurate).

CHAPTER 2

Employment law

2.1   The aim of this Chapter is to provide a brief summary of the employ-ment law principles relevant to insolvency situations.

SOURCES OF EMPLOYMENT LAW

2.2   Employment law in England and Wales is a mixture of statutory provi-sion, particularly the Employment Rights Act 1996 (ERA 1996) and common law rights, particularly those arising under the employment contract. There is increased statutory intervention in the employment law field, arising as a result of initiatives being taken within the European Union, particularly those under the Social Charter. Other major employment legislation includes:

(a)   the Trade Union and Labour Relations (Consolidation) Act 1992 (TULRCA 1992) – this consolidates most of the legislation relating to col-lective rights and collective bargaining;

(b)   the Health and Safety at Work etc Act 1974 – dealing with health and safety;

(c)   the Equal Pay Act 1970 and the Sex Discrimination Act 1975 which, together with the Race Relations Act 1976, deal with sex and race discrimination in employment. The Disability Discrimination Act 1995 deals with disability discrimination. Various regulations deal with discrimination in employment on the grounds of religion, sexual orientation, age etc. The Equality Bill cur-rently before Parliament aims to consolidate and extend this legislation;

(d)   the Transfer of Undertakings (Protection of Employment) Regulations 2006 – which deal with the position of employees on a transfer of a business (see further Chapters 20 to 24 below);

(e)   the National Minimum Wage Act 1998 and the Working Time Regulations 1998.

EMPLOYED OR SELF-EMPLOYED?

2.3   The question of whether an individual is employed or self-employed is fundamental as crucial distinctions are drawn in a number of areas between the rights of persons who are employees as against those who are self-employed. The areas where this is relevant include:

(a) the rights conferred by the employment legislation (which often apply only to employees, although some – mainly the discrimination statutes – apply to the more generic 'workers');

(b) the insolvency legislation which makes certain debts owed to employees preferential (see Chapters 9 and 10 below);

(c) the tax treatment of payments to employees which generally differs from the tax treatment of payments to the self-employed. Employees are taxed on employment income (old Schedule E), whereas the self-employed generally pay tax on income from a trade or profession (old Schedule D). Employers are required to deduct tax under the PAYE system on payments to employees but not generally on payments to the self-employed. Similarly, liability for Class 1 national insurance contributions only arises in relation to payments to employees (see Social Security Contributions and Benefits Act 1992, ss 2, 5). Payments to employees are, in effect, exempt from any charge to VAT[1].

1 See eg *Talbot v Revenue & Customs* [2008] UKVAT V20665 (1 May 2008), citing what is now Article 10 of Council Directive 2006/112/EC on the common system of value added tax and the ECJ in *Commission of the European Communities v Kingdom of the Netherlands* (C-235/85) [1987] ECR 1471; [1988] 2 CMLR 921 and *Ayuntamiento de Sevilla v Recaudadores de Tributos de las Zonas Primera y Segunda* (C-202/90) [1993] STC 659; [1991] ECR I-4247; [1994] 1 CMLR 424.

2.4 Where the term 'employee' or 'employment' is defined in a statute, it usually does no more than refer to a contract of service or apprenticeship. See, for example the definition of 'contract of employment' in ERA 1996, s 230(2), the definition of 'employed earner' in the Social Security Contributions and Benefits Act 1992, s 2(1)(a) and the definition of 'employee' in TUPE, the Transfer of Undertakings (Protection of Employment) Regulations 2006, reg 2(1).

For a discussion of the position of directors and controlling shareholders as employees see Chapter 11 below.

Common law tests

2.5 The general common law test for determining whether a particular individual is an employee or is self-employed involves drawing a distinction between a contract for services – where there is no employment relationship and a contract of service – where there is an employment relationship.

2.6 The statutory definitions mentioned in para 2.4 above add little to the general common law test and the courts adopt a similar basis, even in those statutes which do not define the term 'employee' – see, for example, the test used in relation to insolvency in *Re CW & AL Hughes Ltd*[1].

1 [1966] 2 All ER 702 (Plowman J) and paras 9.31 and 13.2 below.

2.7   Deciding whether a particular individual is an employee or is self-employed can be difficult in some cases. Generally, the courts will look at the substance of the relationship and will not necessarily follow any labels the parties have themselves chosen to use. How the parties label their relationship is a relevant, but by no means conclusive, factor in deciding whether a person is employed or self-employed. His or her status is determined by an objective assessment of all the relevant facts – see, for example, *Young & Woods Ltd v West*[1] and *M & P Steelcraft v Ellis*[2].

1 [1980] IRLR 201, CA.
2 [2008] ICR 578; [2008] IRLR 355, EAT.

2.8   In order to determine whether there is a contract of employment rather than a contract for services, a number of factors will be considered by the courts. For example, there must be mutual obligations on both parties – on the employer to provide work and the employee to perform work – see *Nethermere (St Neots) Ltd v Gardiner*[1], *Hellyer Brothers Ltd v McLeod*[2], *Clark v Oxfordshire Health Authority*[3] and the decision of the House of Lords in *Carmichael v National Power plc*[4].

1 [1984] ICR 612, CA.
2 [1987] ICR 526, CA.
3 [1998] IRLR 125, CA.
4 [1999] 4 All ER 897; [1999] 1 WLR 2042; [1999] ICR 1226, HL.

2.9   The answer to the question 'employed or self-employed' can vary depending on the underlying purpose. An individual can be held to be an employee for one purpose (eg unfair dismissal rights) but self-employed for another (eg for tax purposes) – see eg *Airfix Footwear Ltd v Cope*[1]. But usually the result will be the same.

1 [1978] ICR 1210, EAT.

2.10   The courts have from time to time laid down a number of general tests to determine the status of an individual. These are briefly described in paras 2.11 to 2.14 below.

The control test and 'shams'

2.11   A traditional method of deciding the issue was to determine the extent to which the employer could control not only *what* work an employee carries out but also how it is carried out. However, as industrial and technological processes become more sophisticated, skilled employees, for example doctors, pilots and engineers, have more autonomy and control over their working practices and the employer's control is at a minimum with regard to the 'how'.

A provision in the relevant contract giving the person an unfettered right to provide a substitute to do the work points to there not being an employment relationship, absent a 'sham' – the Court of Appeal in *Express & Echo Publications Ltd v Tanton*[1].

As to what will be a sham for these purposes see the EAT (Elias P) in

Consistent Group Ltd v Kalwak[2] and the Court of Appeal in that case. The EAT considered the Court of Appeal reasoning in *Kalwak* in *Redrow Homes (Yorkshire) Ltd v Buckborough*[3] and both *Kalwak* and *Tanton* were further considered by the Court of Appeal in *Protectacoat Firthglow Ltd v Szilagyi*[4]. The most recent case is the decision of the EAT in *MPG Contracts Ltd v England*[5]. See also the discussion by the Court of Appeal in *Neufeld*[6] (see para 11.16 below).

1 [1999] ICR 693, CA.
2 [2007] IRLR 560, EAT; [2008] IRLR 505, CA.
3 [2009] IRLR 34, EAT.
4 [2009] EWCA Civ 98, [2009] IRLR 365, [2009] All ER (D) 208 (Feb), CA. Discussed by A C L Davies in 'Sensible Thinking About Sham Transactions: *Protectacoat Firthglow Ltd v Szilagyi*' (2009) 38 ILJ 318.
5 UKEAT/0488/08, EAT, (2009) 8 May.
6 *Neufeld v Secretary of State for Business, Enterprise and Regulatory Reform* [2009] EWCA Civ 280; [2009] 3 All ER 790; [2009] IRLR 475, CA.

The integration test

2.12 The integration test involves assessing the extent to which the individual is integrated into the business as opposed simply to providing services to the business. This test is not as easy to apply as the control test since control is more easily delineated than integration. This test is perhaps at its most useful in the case of skilled workers who would fail the control test because, being highly skilled, their employer cannot tell them how to work, but who are, nevertheless, to be regarded as part of the organisation (for example, a doctor such as in *Cassidy v Ministry of Health*[1]).

1 [1951] 2 KB 343, CA.

The economic test

2.13 Another means of deciding the issue is to determine whether the individual is performing the services as a person in business 'on his own account'. For example, does he or she provide his or her own equipment, and his or her own helpers? What degree of financial risk does he or she take?

The multiple test

2.14 The multiple test is a more modern approach which denies that any particular test or any particular feature of the work is conclusive. The correct approach is to use these tests as useful guides but to weigh up the facts of the particular case and decide whether the individual is an employee or independent contractor. In *Ready-Mixed Concrete (South East) Ltd v Minister of Pensions and National Insurance*[1] MacKenna J set out three questions to be answered in reaching a decision:

(a) Did the worker undertake to provide his own work and skill in return for remuneration?

(b) Was there a sufficient degree of control to enable the worker fairly to be called an employee?

(c)   Were there any other factors inconsistent with the existence of a contract of service?

1 [1968] 2 QB 497 (MacKenna J). Followed recently by the Court of Appeal in *Neufeld v Secretary of State for Business, Enterprise and Regulatory Reform* [2009] EWCA Civ 280; [2009] 3 All ER 790; [2009] IRLR 475, CA.

Present position

2.15   In *Lee Ting Sang v Chung Chi-Keung*[1], the Privy Council said that the matter had never been better put than by Cooke J in *Market Investigations Ltd v Minister of Social Security*[2]:

> 'The fundamental test to be applied is this: "Is the person who has engaged himself to perform these services performing them as a person in business on his own account?" If the answer to that question is "yes", then the contract is a contract for services. If the answer is "no", then the contract is a contract of service. No exhaustive list has been compiled and perhaps no exhaustive list can be compiled of the considerations which are relevant in determining that question, nor can strict rules be laid down as to the relative weight which the various considerations should carry in particular cases. The most that can be said is that control will no doubt always have to be considered, although it can no longer be regarded as the sole determining factor; and that factors which may be of importance are such matters as whether the man performing the services provides his own equipment, whether he hires his own helpers, what degree of financial risk he takes, what degree of responsibility for investment and management he has, and whether and how far he has an opportunity of profiting from sound management in the performance of his task.'[3]

1 [1990] 2 AC 374, PC.
2 [1969] 2 QB 173, at pages 184 and 185 (Cooke J).
3 See also *Walls v Sinnett* [1987] STC 236 (Vinelott J); *Eaton v Robert Eaton Ltd and Secretary of State for Employment* [1988] IRLR 83, EAT and *Hall v Lorimer* [1994] 1 WLR 209 [1994] STC 23, CA. For more recent cases see *Cheng v Royal Hong Kong Golf Club* [1998] ICR 131, PC; *Carmichael v National Power plc* [1999] 4 All ER 897, HL; *Clark v Oxfordshire Health Authority* [1998] IRLR 125, CA; *Express and Echo Publications Ltd v Tanton* [1999] ICR 693, CA; *Wilson v Circular Distributors* [2006] IRLR 38, EAT; *Castle Construction (Chesterfield) Limited v Revenue and Customs Commissioners* (2008, SpC 723) *Talbot v Revenue & Customs* [2008] UKVAT V20665 (01 May 2008) and the cases mentioned in Chapter 11 (Directors and controlling shareholders as employees) below.

Tax and National Insurance tests

2.16   The test is the same for both income tax and national insurance and it was generally the case that a decision as to an individual's status by one authority would be followed by the other[1]. This is now even more likely since the move, on 1 April 1999, of the functions in relation to the collection of national insurance contributions from the DSS to the Inland Revenue (National Insurance Contributions Office), now the HMRC.

HM Revenue and Customs (HMRC) has published on its website[2] a tool for checking if a person is employed or self-employed. It is called the 'Employment

Status Indicator Tool' (ESI). This requires a series of questions to be answered 'yes' or 'no' before giving an opinion as to status with a reference number.

Employment Status Indicator

The Employment Status Indicator (ESI) tool enables you to check the employment status of an individual or group of workers – that is, whether they are employed or self-employed for tax, National Insurance contributions (NICs) or VAT purposes.

Who can use the tool

The ESI tool is helpful for anyone who takes on workers, such as employers and contractors. (The tool refers to anyone in this position as an engager.) Individual workers can also use the tool to check their employment status.

However, the tool can't be used to check the employment status of some workers:

- company directors and other individuals who hold office

- agency workers

- anyone providing services through an intermediary (sometimes referred to as IR35 arrangements)

How the tool works

The ESI tool is completely anonymous, so no personal details about the worker or engager are requested.

The tool will ask you a series of questions about the working relationship between worker and engager. If you have a contract setting out the terms of the relationship, it will be useful to have it to hand.

When you start using the tool, your enquiry will be assigned a 14-digit ESI reference number (look for it in the top left of the screen). Write this down because you can use it to resume your session later if you don't complete all the questions in one go. The tool automatically saves your progress when you close it, and you have seven days to continue from where you left off.

The ESI result

When you've answered all the questions, the ESI tool will provide an indication of the worker's employment status. You can rely on the ESI outcome as evidence of a worker's status for tax/NICs/VAT purposes if both of the following apply:

> your answers to the ESI questions accurately reflect the terms and conditions under which the worker provides their services

> the ESI has been completed by an engager or their authorised representative (if a worker completes the ESI tool the result is only indicative)

However, you should print or save copies of the 'Enquiry Details' screen and the 'ESI Result screen', bearing the 14-digit ESI reference mentioned above. If the worker's employment status is questioned in the future, HM Revenue & Customs will only be bound by the ESI outcome if these copies can be produced.

---

1 For further guidance see the leaflet published by the two authorities – IR 56/NI39 entitled 'Tax–Employed or Self Employed'. A new factsheet for workers, ES/FS1 was issued in June 2008, replacing part of IR56. See also Chapter 4 of *Taxation of Employments* by Robert Maas (13th edn, Tottel Publishing, 2008).

2 http://www.hmrc.gov.uk/calcs/esi.htm.

2.17   HMRC's Employment Status Manual is also online[1].

The issue can be approached by looking either at whether the individual worker is carrying on a trade (and so self-employed) or is an employee.

The Business Income Manual on HMRC's website at BIM20205[2] lists the 'badges of a trade' (and includes cross references to more detailed information):

- Profit seeking motive.

- The number of transactions.

- The nature of the asset.

- Existence of similar trading transactions or interests.

- Changes to the asset.

- The way the sale was carried out.

- The source of finance.

- Interval of time between purchase and sale.

- Method of acquisition.

HMRC's website[3] discusses the issue of employment status and suggests as follows:

In order to determine the nature of a contract, it is necessary to apply common law principles. The courts have, over the years, laid down some factors and tests that are relevant, which is included in the overview below.

As a general guide as to whether a worker is an employee or self-employed; if the answer is 'Yes' to all of the following questions, then the worker is probably an employee:

- Do they have to do the work themselves?

- Can someone tell them at any time what to do, where to carry out the work or when and how to do it?

- Can they work a set amount of hours?

- Can someone move them from task to task?

- Are they paid by the hour, week, or month?

- Can they get overtime pay or bonus payment?

If the answer is 'Yes' to all of the following questions, it will usually mean that the worker is self-employed:

- Can they hire someone to do the work or engage helpers at their own expense?

- Do they risk their own money?

- Do they provide the main items of equipment they need to do their job, not just the small tools that many employees provide for themselves?

- Do they agree to do a job for a fixed price regardless of how long the job may take?

- Can they decide what work to do, how and when to do the work and where to provide the services?

- Do they regularly work for a number of different people?

- Do they have to correct unsatisfactory work in their own time and at their own expense?

Source: HMRC website

1 http://www.hmrc.gov.uk/manuals/esmmanual/index.htm
2 http://www.hmrc.gov.uk/manuals/bimmanual/BIM20205.htm
3 http://www.hmrc.gov.uk/employment-status/index.htm

Other factors

2.18   Different working practices which are now evolving mean that the various tests devised by the courts, and indeed the guidance issued by HMRC, are less easily applied. Current issues in this field of law involve employees who work at home with electronic communication links. In particular, this may break the link of control between an employer and employee but will not necessarily mean that the individual is not an employee. There is also debate as to whether the practice of job sharing breaks the personal relationship between an employee and employer.

2.19   As a general rule it is easier to determine that someone is self-employed when he or she works for several different employers (although this is not by itself conclusive, see for example *Sidey v Phillips*[1]) but harder to determine that he or she is self-employed when he or she works for just one person. It will be difficult for an appellate court to disturb a finding of fact by the first instance court as to whether or not an individual is or was an employee – see *O'Kelly v Trusthouse Forte plc*[2] and *Lee Ting Sang v Chung Chi-Keung*[3].

Temporary contracts can result in a person becoming an employee – see *McMeechan v Secretary of State for Employment*[4].

1 [1987] STC 87 (Knox J).
2 [1984] QB 90, CA.
3 [1990] 2 AC 374, PC.
4 [1997] ICR 549, CA.

Shams

2.20   Generally the courts will look to the substance of the relationship. The contractual documents will be relevant but may be considered to be a 'sham' (if the parties intention was not to operate in accordance with them) or not to reflect how the position has later changed in reality – see the Court of Appeal in *Protectacoat Firthglow Limited v Szilagyi*[1]. See further Chapter 11 below.

1 [2009] EWCA Civ 98; [2009] IRLR 365, CA. Discussed by A. C. L. Davies in ''Sensible Thinking About Sham Transactions: *Protectacoat Firthglow Ltd v Szilagyi*' (2009) 38 ILJ 318.

Directors

2.21 Difficulties can arise particularly in relation to a director of a company in determining whether he is employed or self-employed (see further Chapter 11 below). Payments made to a director may be considered to be director's fees or, alternatively, may be evidence of an employment relationship. The Department of Employment had indicated (in relation to claims on the National Insurance Fund – see Chapter 13 (National Insurance Fund) below) that it will look for a written contract of employment or a written memorandum as required by the Companies Act 1985, s 318[1] (see for example *Eaton v Robert Eaton Ltd*[2]). If there is no written contract then the Department will consider the substance of the relationship using the following factors (see also claim form RP3).

(a) How many hours were worked per week? Were they fixed and regular?

(b) Were PAYE and earnings related national insurance deductions made?

(c) Was payment regular?

(d) Was there provision for sick pay and annual leave?

(e) What were the pension arrangements?

(f) What were the director's duties?

(g) Was the director subject to control or supervision? If so, by whom and how was it exercised?

(h) Was the director given formal notice? If so, what were its terms?

(i) What was the director's shareholding and did he or she have other business commitments?

The Technical Manual published by the Insolvency Service (and available on the web[3]) comments on the position of Directors in Chapter 76 (Employment Law) as follows (at para 76.3):

> 'Directors – a director is an officer of the company but may also have a contract of service, either an express service agreement or one implied at law. In *Albert J. Parsons & Sons Ltd v Parsons* [1979] ICR 271, the Court of Appeal held that there was no contract of employment in the case of a full-time working director who was paid by director's fees only and had not been treated as employed for national insurance purposes. In *Eaton v Robert Eaton Ltd and the Secretary of State for Employment* [1988] IRLR 83, when it was held that the director was not an employee, the main factors in determining the question were identified as:
>
> a the use of any descriptive term such as managing director,
>
> b whether there was an express contract of employment or a board minute constituting an agreement to employ,
>
> c whether remuneration was by way of salary as opposed to a director's fee,
>
> d whether that remuneration was fixed in advance rather than paid on an ad hoc basis,

  e whether remuneration was by way of entitlement rather than being gratu-
itous, and

  f the function actually performed by the director.'

1 Now CA 2006, s 228.
2 [1988] IRLR 83, EAT.
3 http://www.insolvency.gov.uk/freedomofinformation/technical/TechnicalManual/Ch73-84/
 Chapter76/Chapter76.htm

2.22 Where a director has not drawn a salary, the Department said that it
would normally reject any claim on the National Insurance Fund and require the
director to prove that an employment contract still exists (see, for example,
Eaton v Robert Eaton Ltd[1]).

1 [1988] IRLR 83, EAT.

2.23 The Society of Practitioners of Insolvency (SPI), now R3, issued in
August 1999 Technical Release No 6 dealing with the treatment of directors'
claims as employees in insolvency administration.

2.24 Further more recent case law indicates that one factor that needs to be
considered is whether or not the individual is also a controlling shareholder of
the company. This is not conclusive, but may be a factor – see *Neufeld v
Secretary of State for Business, Enterprise and Regulatory Reform*[1] and further
Chapter 11 (Directors and substantial shareholders as employees) below.

1 [2009] EWCA Civ 280; [2009] 3 All ER 790; [2009] IRLR 475.

CONTRACTUAL TERMINATION CLAIMS

2.25 On termination of employment, an employee may have a claim for
breach of contract by the employer. This can arise where either:

(a) the contract of employment has been expressly terminated by the employer
   without full contractual notice in circumstances where the employee was
   not in breach of contract (or not in a sufficiently serious breach of contract
   to justify dismissal); or

(b) where the employer has broken a fundamental term of the employment contract entitling the employee to consider that he has been constructively dismissed by the employer.

2.26 The usual contractual rules apply both as regards when there has been a
breach of contract by the employer and as to the level of contractual damages
claimable by the employee as a result. Where the contract contains a payment in
lieu of notice provision, the employee may be able to sustain an argument that he
or she is not obliged to mitigate any claim[1].

1 See *Abrahams v Performing Rights Society* [1995] ICR 1028, CA, *Gregory v Wallace* [1998]
 IRLR 387, CA. Contrast *Cerberus Software Ltd v Rowley* [2001] EWCA Civ 78, [2001] ICR 376,
 [2001] IRLR 160, CA and *Zepbrook Ltd v Magnus* (2006) 18 October; UKEAT/0382/06/MAA;
 [2007] All ER (D) 118 (Jan) (EAT).

2.27   In practice, in the situation where the employer has become insolvent, dismissals will usually be either express (eg instigated by the insolvency practitioner) or arise by operation of law (eg where the company is wound up by court order – see Chapter 4 below) or arise because the employer breaches some fundamental term of the contract (eg fails to make payment of wages – see *Western Excavating (ECC) Ltd v Sharp*[1]). Following such termination of employment, the employee will usually, unless termination has been in accordance with his contract of employment (eg with proper notice) have a contractual claim for damages for breach of contract.

1 [1978] QB 761, CA.

Assessing damages for breach of contract

2.28   The following principles are relevant in assessing damages for breach of contract.

(a)   Damages will be assessed by reference to the contractual rights (remuneration and benefits etc) which the employee would have enjoyed over the remaining term of the contract, ie to the date that the contract of employment could first have been terminated lawfully by the employer. In the case of a fixed term contract this will be the period to the end of the fixed term or, in the case of contract determinable by notice, to the expiry of the relevant notice period. Minimum notice periods are laid down in ERA 1996, s 86 and are generally one week's notice for each year of continuous employment (up to a maximum of twelve weeks' notice). It is not possible to reduce the statutory minimum notice period by contractual agreement (ERA 1996, s 203).

(b)   A longer notice period than the statutory minimum can be contained in the contract. If no express notice period is contained in a contract (other than a fixed term contract) then a reasonable notice period (which may be longer than the ERA minimum) will be implied by the courts.

(c)   When assessing the damages claim, the position previously was that only items to which the employee was contractually entitled were taken into account. Benefits which the employer had a discretion as to whether or not to pay (eg a discretionary bonus) were excluded, even if the employee had a reasonable expectation that they would be paid – see *Lavarack v Woods of Colchester Ltd*[1]. This is a difficult area[2]. The impact of the implied duty of trust and confidence is also difficult to foresee – see Timothy Walker J in *Clarke v BET plc*[3] and the Court of Appeal in *Horkulak v Cantor Fitzgerald International*[4] (distinguishing *Lavarack*).

(d)   The value of other benefits should also be included where these are contractual and the employer does not have an option to withdraw them – eg rent free accommodation (*Ivory v Palmer*[5]) and a car or free medical insurance (*Shove v Downs Surgical plc*[6]).

(e)   No damages are awarded for distress and vexation associated with a wrongful dismissal (*Addis v Gramophone Co Ltd*[7], *Bliss v South-East Thames*

13

Regional Health Authority[8] and *Johnson v Unisys Ltd*[9]). Damages may be awarded if a breach of the implied duty of trust and confidence means that the employee's job prospects are reduced as a result (eg if the employer conducted a fraudulent enterprise) so that he or she is less able to obtain fresh employment after termination – see *Malik v BCCI*[10] or for a breach in the run up to dismissal – *Eastwood v Magnox Electric Plc and McCabe v Cornwall CC (joined cases)*[11].

1 [1967] 1 Q.B. 278; [1966] 3 All ER 683, CA.
2 A consistent practice of paying benefits automatically can give rise to an implied contractual right based on 'custom and practice', but not generally if the benefit is always stated to be discretionary. A mere statement that a bonus is discretionary and not contractual can still give rise to contractually enforceable claims – see the EAT in *Small v Boots Co PLC* [2009] IRLR 328, EAT.
   It used to be argued that the position in relation to discretionary benefits could be different as a result of the deduction provisions in Pt II of ERA 1996, (formerly the Wages Act 1986), given the extended definition of 'wages' in s 27 and the decision in *Kent Management Services Ltd v Butterfield* [1992] IRLR 394, EAT. But this now seems unarguable given the decision of the Court of Appeal in *New Century Cleaning Co Ltd v Church* [2000] IRLR 27, CA that the deduction provisions only apply if there is a legal obligation to make the payment – see also *Campbell v Union Carbide* [2002] Emp LR 1267, EAT.
3 [1997] IRLR 348 (Timothy Walker J).
4 [2004] EWCA Civ 1287; [2005] ICR 402; [2004] IRLR 942, CA.
5 [1975] ICR 340, CA.
6 [1984] 1 All ER 7 (Sheen J).
7 [1909] AC 488, HL.
8 [1985] IRLR 308, CA.
9 [2001] UKHL 13, [2003] 1 AC 518, HL.
10 [1998] AC 20, HL.
11 [2004] UKHL 35; [2005] 1 AC 503, HL.

DAMAGES FOR LOSS OF PENSION BENEFITS

2.29   Pension benefits are a difficult area. A right to a particular level of contributions to a money purchase (defined contribution) arrangement will often be contractual.

2.30   In relation to a final salary (defined benefit) scheme, sometimes an express contractual right to particular benefits is given. However, in the absence of an express provision, generally historically such benefits were treated as discretionary and terminable by the employer at any time, so that there was no contractual right to the pension and no right for it to be included in any assessment of damages.

2.31   However, this approach has evolved over time, particularly following the decision of the House of Lords in *Parry v Cleaver*[1] and the impact of statutory preservation (or vesting) of benefits for early leavers (under the Social Security Act 1973 and later statutes).

2.32   It is common for the employer to retain the right in the pension scheme to terminate the scheme and for the employment contract to do no more than refer to membership of a pension scheme being available.

2.33 There are arguments which might lead a court to construe the employment arrangements in such a way that the employer would not have an unfettered right to amend or terminate a pension scheme. This would mean that the loss of pension benefits would be taken into account in a wrongful dismissal claim. Such an analysis could be supported:

(a) by a construction of particular documents or by implying a term into the employment contract to the effect that the pension scheme would not be terminated without the employee's consent; or

(b) by limiting an unfettered power given to the employer as being inconsistent with an implied obligation on the employer not to act to destroy or seriously damage the relationship of trust and confidence between employer and employee – see, for example, *Imperial Group Pension Trust Ltd v Imperial Tobacco Ltd*[2]; or

(c) by holding that a failure to meet the employee's reasonable expectations is contrary to the provisions of the Unfair Contract Terms Act 1977[3], but this seems unlikely following the decisions of the Court of Appeal in *Baker v J E Clark & Co*[4] (UCTA not applicable to trusts) and *Keen v Commerzbank AG*[5] (UCTA not applicable to employment contracts).

1 [1970] AC 1, HL.
2 [1991] 2 All ER 597 (Browne-Wilkinson V-C).
3 For further discussion see the Chapter by the author: '*Pensions*' in *Tolley's Employment Law*.
4 [2006] EWCA Civ 464, [2006] PLR 131, CA.
5 [2006] EWCA Civ 1536, [2007] IRLR 132, CA.

REDUCTIONS IN CONTRACTUAL DAMAGES

2.34 Having established the employee's loss of benefits over the remainder of his notice period, various deductions would apply to any claim brought by the employee for contractual damages as set out below:

(a) there should be a reduction to reflect the requirement on the employee reasonably to mitigate his or her loss – see eg *Fyfe v Scientific Furnishings Ltd*[1];

(b) the claim of the employee should be reduced to reflect the fact that a lump sum would be received in advance of the usual periodic payments of wages or salary. Thus a lump sum payment at the beginning of a notice period should be reduced to reflect the fact that the employee would normally have received the salary payments spread over the notice period (eg weekly or monthly) – see, for example, *Shove v Downs Surgical plc*[2]; and

(c) because compensation payments payable to employees in relation to termination of their employment are not taxable under normal employment income principles (unless the right to such termination payment is contained in the contract of employment itself) the effect is that payment of a lump sum compensation amount gives rise to a benefit to the employee (looking to the net after tax amounts received). Termination payments are generally only taxable under ITEPA 2003, s 401 (formerly ICTA 1988, s 148), but there is a £30,000 exemption under ITEPA 2003, s 403 (formerly ICTA 1988, s 188). The legal position is that the employee should be placed in such a position that he receives the same amount after tax as he would have received after tax had the employment contract continued – see *British Transport Commission v Gourley*[3] and *Shove v Downs Surgical plc*[4].

1 [1989] IRLR 331; [1989] ICR 648, EAT.
2 [1984] 1 All ER 7; [1984] ICR 532 (Sheen J).
3 [1956] AC 185, HL.
4 [1984] 1 All ER 7 (Sheen J). See also *Jones v Global Crossing (UK) Telecommunications Ltd* [2008] All ER (D) 19 (Sep); UKEAT/0145/05/JOJ, EAT.

2.35   These deductions may not apply if there is an express provision providing for a compensatory amount to be paid on termination. See *Abrahams v Performing Rights Society*[1]. Contrast *Cerberus Software Ltd v Rowley*[2] and *Zepbrook Ltd v Magnus*[3].

1 [1995] ICR 1028, [1995] IRLR 486, CA.
2 [2001] EWCA Civ 78; [2001] ICR 376 [2001] IRLR 160, CA.
3 (2006) 18 October; UKEAT/0382/06/MAA; [2007] All ER (D) 118 (Jan), EAT.

2.36   Further details of relevant calculations are contained in Technical Release No 5 issued in August 1999 by the SPI (now R3) on 'Non-preferential claims by employees dismissed without proper notice by insolvent employers' – see www.r3.org.uk/publications.

UNFAIR DISMISSAL

2.37   In addition to any contractual claim that an employee who is dismissed may have, a statutory right for an employee not to be unfairly dismissed is given by ERA 1996, ss 94–134.

2.38   In order for a claim of unfair dismissal to succeed, the employee must first show that he or she has been dismissed (or that a fixed term contract has not been renewed on its expiry). Dismissal can either be express (eg the giving of notice by the employer) or constructive (ie following a fundamental breach of contract by the employer). The test for determining whether or not there has been a constructive dismissal is the same as the contractual test; that is, the employer was guilty of conduct which went to the root of the contract of employment or which showed that the employer no longer intended to be bound by one or more of the essential terms of the contract[1].

1 See *Western Excavating (ECC) v Sharp Ltd* [1978] QB 761, CA and para 2.27 above.

Burden of proof

2.39   Once dismissal (or failure to renew a fixed term contract) has been established, the onus is on the employer (see ERA 1996, s 98) to show:

(a) that the reason (or principal reason) for the dismissal fell within one of the following categories as a reason which:

   (i)   related to the capability or qualifications of the employee for performing work of the kind which he was employed by the employer to do;

   (ii)   related to the conduct of the employee;

   (iii)   was that the employee could not continue to work in the position which he held without contravention (either on his part or on that of his employer) of a duty or restriction imposed by or under an enactment; or

   (iv)   was some other substantial reason such as to justify the dismissal of an employee holding the position which that employee held,

   and

(b) that the employer acted reasonably in the circumstances in treating that reason as a sufficient reason for dismissing the employee.

Qualifying period

2.40   In order to bring a claim for unfair dismissal an employee must usually have been continuously employed (see ERA 1996, ss 210–219) for not less than one year (ERA 1996, s 108).

2.41   This period was reduced from two years, where the effective date of dismissal falls on or after 1 June 1999, by the Unfair Dismissal and Statement of Reasons for Dismissal (Variation of Qualifying Period) Order 1999, SI 1999/1436.

2.42   Before 1995, an employee who was employed for eight hours or more a week but less than sixteen hours a week needed to work for five years or more in order to satisfy the requirement relating to the qualifying period for bringing a claim for unfair dismissal[1]. However this extended qualifying period was removed by the Employment Protection (Part-time Employees) Regulations 1995 (SI 1995/31) following the decision of the House of Lords in *R v Secretary of State for Employment, ex p EOC*[2].

1 EPCA 1978, Sch 13, para 6(1).
2 [1994] IRLR 176, HL.

2.43   There is no qualifying period if dismissal relates to trade union membership (see TULRCA 1992, ss 152, 154). There is also no qualifying period for claims of unlawful discrimination – eg for race, sex or disability discrimination under the Race Relations Act 1976, the Sex Discrimination Act 1975 or the Disability Discrimination Act 1995 (see further paras 8.39 to 8.60 below).

2.44   There is also no qualifying period – see s 108(3):

- for dismissals related to acting on jury service – s 98B, taking family leave (eg pregnancy or maternity leave) – s 99, acting as a trustee of an occupational pension scheme – s 102; or

- in cases where an employee is dismissed after alleging the breach of certain relevant statutory rights by the employer – s 104 – or is acting as an employee representative – s 103.

Compensation for unfair dismissal

2.45   Claims in relation to unfair dismissal are brought in the employment tribunal. If unfair dismissal is established, then an employee has a claim to a basic award and a compensatory award.

2.46   The level of the basic award is calculated as a multiple based on a week's pay (subject to a maximum level of a week's pay of, currently, £350 per week), length of continuous service (subject to a maximum of 20 years) and age of the employee (ERA 1996, ss 119, 227). The multiple is:

- one and a half weeks' pay for each year of employment when the employee is over 40,

- one week's pay for each year between 21 and 40; and

- one-half of a week's pay for each year under 21.

2.47   These age bands were not repealed by the age discrimination laws introduced by the Employment Equality (Age Discrimination) Regulations 2006 (SI 2006/1031), although those regulations did abolish (from 1 October 2006) the upper age limit on unfair dismissal claims that used to apply under ERA, s 119.

The Government takes the view that these bands are objectively justifiable[1] and so in compliance with the obligations under the underlying EU Equality Directive (2000/78/EC). There must be some prospect that the Government's view is wrong – at least one recent ECJ decision has held that a right not to be discriminated against on the grounds of age is fundamental – see *Mangold v Helm*[2]. The concept of objective justification and compliance with the relevant directive is discussed further in the recent ECJ case brought by Heyday on the legality of the age 65 retirement age, *Incorporated Trustees of the National Council on Ageing (Age Concern England) v Secretary of State for Business, Enterprise and Regulatory Reform*[3].

As a matter of English law, redundancy payments based on length of service were upheld by the Court of Appeal in *Rolls-Royce PLC v Unite*[4].

1 See the Final Regulatory Impact Assessment on statutory redundancy pay attached to the explanatory notes to SI 2006/1031 at page 78. See further the statement on 2 March 2006 by the Parliamentary Under-Secretary of State for Trade and Industry (Mr Gerry Sutcliffe) HC Deb 14 July 2008, col 64 and the discussion in House of Commons Research paper 08/87 'Small Business, Insolvency and Redundancy' at pages 52 to 54 (22 November 2008).

2 [2005] ECR I-9981, [2006] IRLR 143, ECJ, but contrast the ECJ decision and Advocate-General's opinion in *Félix Palacios de la Villa v Cortefiel Servicios SA* (C-411/05) [2008] 1 CMLR 16; [2007] IRLR 989.

3 (C-388/07) [2009] All ER (D) 51 (Mar); [2009] IRLR 373, ECJ. The mandatory retirement age provisions in the 2006 Age Regulations were subsequently upheld by Blake J in the High Court, [2009] EWHC 2336.

4 [2009] EWCA Civ 387; [2009] All ER (D) 131 (May); [2009] IRLR 576, CA.

2.48 The compensatory award is such amount as the tribunal considers just and equitable in all the circumstances, having regard to the loss sustained by the employee (ERA 1996, s 123) and is subject to a maximum award of, currently £66,200 (ERA 1996, s 124).

2.49 The maximum level of a week's pay and of a compensatory award is usually increased annually (Employment Relations Act 1999, s 34) with effect from February by a statutory instrument, most recently an Employment Rights (Increase of Limits) Order. Recent changes are listed in the table below.

The Work and Families Act 2006, s 14 gave a one off power to the Secretary of State to make a catch up increase in the level of a week's pay. It was not clear what the adjustment would be or even whether the power would definitely be used. It appeared that the power would be used to implement a commitment made by the government to trade unions in the Warwick Agreement to increase the level of statutory redundancy pay[1].

The 2009 budget included an announcement that the government intends that the limit on statutory redundancy pay would be increased to £380 per week. In June 2009, BERR confirmed that this rise was intended to take effect on 1 October 2009 and would apply to all relevant weekly pay tests – eg including for unfair dismissal and claims on the National Insurance Fund). Having applied this increase, the February 2010 increase in a week's pay would be suspended: this was put into effect by the Work and Families (Increase of Maximum Amount) Order 2009, SI 2009/1903.

Effective date of dismissal on or after	*Compensatory award*	*Week's pay*
1 October 2009	£380 (SI 2009/1903)	£66,200 (no change)
1 February 2009	£350	£66,200 (SI 2008/3055)
1 February 2008	£330	£63,000 (SI 2007/3570)
1 February 2007	£310	£60,600 (SI 2006/3045)
1 February 2006	£290	£58,400 (SI 2005/3352)
1 February 2005	£280	£56,800 (SI 2004/2989)
1 February 2004	£270	£55,000 (SI 2003/3038)
1 February 2003	£260	£53,500 (SI 2002/2927)
1 February 2002	£250	£52,600 (SI 2002/10)
1 February 2001	£240	£51,700 (SI 2001/21)
1 February 2000	£230 (SI 1999/3375)	£50,000 (no change)
25 October 1999	£220 (no change)	£50,000 (ERA 1999, s 34 and SI 1999/2830)
1 April 1998	£220	£12,000 (SI 1998/924)

27 September 1995	£210	£11,300 (SI 1995/1953)
1 June 1993	£205 (no change)	£11,000 (SI 1993/1348)
1 April 1992	£205 (SI 1992/312)	£10,000 (no change)
1 April 1991	£198 (SI 1991/464)	£10,000 (SI 1991/466)
1 April 1990	£184 (SI 1990/384)	£8,925 (no change)
1 April 1989	£172 (SI 1989/526)	£8,925 (SI 1989/527)

1 See House of Commons Research paper 08/87 '*Small Business, Insolvency and Redundancy*' at page 50 (22 November 2008) and Michael Millar, '*Redundancy time-bomb in Work & Families Bill*', Personnel Today, 17 January 2006.

REDUNDANCY

2.50   A statutory right is also given in ERA 1996, ss 135–181 for an employee to claim for a redundancy payment where there is a dismissal by reason of redundancy. ERA 1996, s 139 provides that in order for a dismissal to be by reason of redundancy, the dismissal must be attributable wholly or mainly to:

(a)   the fact that his employer has ceased, or intends to cease, to carry on the business for the purposes of which the employee was employed by him, or has ceased, or intends to cease, to carry on that business in the place where the employee was so employed; or

(b)   the fact that the requirements of that business for employees to carry out work of a particular kind, or for employees to carry out work of a particular kind in the place where he was so employed, have ceased or diminished or are expected to cease or diminish.

2.51   The same definition of redundancy was formerly applied by TULRCA 1992 to ss 188 to 198 of that Act which deal with the obligations imposed on employers to consult with appropriate employee representatives and to notify the Secretary of State where redundancies are proposed (see Chapter 3 below). However, the definition in s 195 of TULRCA 1992 was amended by the Trade Union Reform and Employment Rights Act 1993 (see para 3.16(a) below).

Exclusions from right to redundancy payment

2.52   No right to a redundancy payment under ERA 1996 arises:

(a)   if there is no dismissal (eg where there is a transfer of an undertaking within the Transfer of Undertakings (Protection of Employment) Regulations 2006 (TUPE) – see Chapters 19 to 24 below); or

(b)   if a suitable offer of re-employment is made by the employer (or an associated employer) in certain circumstances (ERA 1996, s 138);

(c)   if the employee has not been continuously employed for two or more years (see ERA 1996, s 155 and para 2.40 above).

Compensation for redundancy

2.53   The level of a redundancy payment is generally approximately the same as the level of the basic award for unfair dismissal and is subject to the same limits on a week's pay (see para 2.49 above).

2.54   Redundancy is a potentially fair reason for a dismissal and as such it is possible that no additional claim for unfair dismissal may arise. However, a dismissal by reason of redundancy may still be unfair if, for example, there has been unfair selection for redundancy or relevant procedures have not been followed.

OTHER STATUTORY RIGHTS

2.55   Various other statutory rights are relevant for the purposes of considering claims by employees on the insolvency of the employer.

Guarantee payments

2.56   ERA 1996, ss 28–35 give employees certain rights to payments when no work is done owing to circumstances beyond the control of the employee. These benefits arise where there is a 'workless day' or 'workless period' as defined in ERA 1996, s 28. Generally, the rights are of most importance to employees who are only paid by the amount of work available, for example those on hourly rates or on piece rates.

Remuneration on suspension on medical grounds

2.57   Rights are also given in ERA 1996, ss 64–70 for an employee to be paid remuneration by his employer while the employee is suspended on medical or maternity grounds. This applies where an employee is suspended on medical grounds as a result of a requirement under an enactment or under a code of practice issued under the Health and Safety at Work etc Act 1974 which is specified in ERA 1996, s 64(3). While an employee is so suspended, he is entitled to be paid remuneration by his employer for up to 26 weeks, subject to complying with various qualifying conditions.

Payments for time off work

2.58   Various sections of ERA 1996, ERA 1999 and TULRCA 1992 also give a right to an employee to be paid during certain time off work. The relevant sections are:

- TULRCA 1992, s 169 (trade union duties),

21

- ERA 1996, ss 52–54 (looking for work or making arrangements for train-ing for future employment when under notice of dismissal by reason of redundancy etc),

- ERA 1996, ss 58–60 (time off to act as trustee of an occupational pension scheme of the employer or to obtain training to so act),

- ERA 1996, ss 61–63 (time off to act as an employee representative under Pt IV of TULRCA 1992 or Tupe 2006 or to be a candidate in an election to become such a representative), and

- ERA 1996, ss 55–57 (ante-natal care).

2.59   There are various other sections containing rights for employees to take time off work, for example to take part in trade union activities (TULRCA 1992, s 170), to look after dependants in some circumstances (eg illness) (ERA 1996, s 57A), and to carry out public duties (ERA 1996, s 50). However, the employee has no right to be paid during these periods of time off.

OCCUPATIONAL PENSION SCHEMES

2.60   The term 'occupational pension scheme' is used throughout the pen-sions legislation (in particular in the Pension Schemes Act ('PSA') 1993 and in the Pensions Acts 1995 and 2004).
    The definition in PSA 1993, s 1 applies in both PA 1995[1] and PA 2004[2].

1 See PA 1995, s 125(5).
2 See PA 2004, s 318(1).

2.61   Before September 2005, the term was defined in s 1 of PSA 1993[1] as follows:

> 'occupational pension scheme' means any scheme or arrangement which is com-prised in one or more instruments or agreements and which has, or is capable of having, effect in relation to one or more descriptions or categories of employment so as to provide benefits, in the form of pensions or otherwise, payable on termi-nation of service, or on death or retirement, to or in respect of earners with qual-ifying service in an employment of any such description or category.

1 Formerly the Social Security Act 1973, s 51(3)(a) and the Social Security Pensions Act 1975, s 66(1).

2.62   This definition is quite wide: it covered not only traditional funded retirement schemes, but also life assurance and small self-administered schemes. It was not limited to schemes with revenue approval or tax registration.

2.63   In a 1999 case, *City & County of Swansea v Johnson*[1], Hart J upheld a decision of the Pensions Ombudsman that an industrial injury scheme was an occupational pension scheme. Hart J held that a local authority regulation pro-viding unquantified injury benefits regardless of length of service was nonetheless an occupational pension scheme. The key to the decision was the Judge's view that 'qualifying service' as used in the definition of occupational pension scheme meant no more than 'such service as qualifies'.

1 [1999] Ch 189 (Hart J). See also the Court of Appeal in *Parlett v Guppys (Bridport) Ltd* [1996] 2 BCLC 34 and in *Westminster City Council v Haywood (No.1)* [1998] Ch 377.

2.64   The *Swansea* case opened up the possibility that permanent health insurance policies (which normally pay out benefits without regard to length of service) constitute occupational pension schemes. The determination of this would likely come down to whether the employee received the benefit after termination of employment. If so, it would fall within the definition of an occupational pension scheme. If the employee technically remains in service while claiming the benefit, it would likely not constitute an occupational pension scheme.

2.65   With effect from 22 September 2005 (the date the IORP Directive came into force) the definition of occupational pension scheme in s 1 of PSA 1993 was amended by s 239 of the Pensions Act 2004 to read as follows:.

'(1)   "occupational pension scheme" means a pension scheme—

(a)   that—

(i)   for the purpose of providing benefits to, or in respect of, people with service in employments of a description, or

(ii)   for that purpose and also for the purpose of providing benefits to, or in respect of, other people,

is established by, or by persons who include, a person to whom subsection (2) applies when the scheme is established or (as the case may be) to whom that subsection would have applied when the scheme was established had that subsection then been in force, and

(b)   that has its main administration in the United Kingdom or outside the member States,

or a pension scheme that is prescribed or is of a prescribed description;

...

(4)   In the definition in subsection (1) of "occupational pension scheme", the reference to a description includes a description framed by reference to an employment being of any of two or more kinds.

(5)   In subsection (1) "pension scheme" (except in the phrases "occupational pension scheme", "personal pension scheme" and "public service pension scheme") means a scheme or other arrangements, comprised in one or more instruments or agreements, having or capable of having effect so as to provide benefits to or in respect of people—

(a)   on retirement,

(b)   on having reached a particular age, or

(c)   on termination of service in an employment.'

2.66   The new definition is in some respects wider than the previous occupational pension scheme definition in PSA 1993. The requirement for benefits to be payable by reference to 'qualifying service' has gone. Instead the scheme must provide benefits 'on retirement, on having reached a particular age, or on termination of service in an employment'. A scheme will be an occupational scheme if it is established for the purpose of providing benefits to or in respect of people in employments in a description (or for such persons and others). This seems to allow a scheme including self-employed people to be an occupational pension scheme[1].

1 Before 6 April 2006, this was not allowed by the Inland Revenue if tax approval was to be obtained for the scheme. But the tax position changed in April 2006 when the pensions tax simplification provisions in the Finance Act 2004 came into force.

2.67   Conversely the definition is narrower in other respects. The new requirement is that the scheme must have its main administration in the United Kingdom or outside the member states. The intention here is that pension schemes that are administered in other EU member states are not regulated by the UK legislation (instead they will be regulated primarily by the authorities in the relevant member state).

2.68   One (probably unintended) side effect of this change is that occupational pension schemes that are administered outside the UK but in another EU member state will not be occupational pension schemes and so covered by the exemption in reg 10 of TUPE 2006 – see Chapter 24 below. Conversely, occupational pension schemes administered outside the EU will still be within the definition (and so within the exemption in reg 10).

Death benefits and occupational schemes

2.69   It is common for occupational pension schemes to include provisions for benefits to be paid following the death of the member/employee. These include payment of lump sum death benefits and pensions to survivors (spouse or dependants of the member).

2.70   The old definition in s 1 of PSA 1993 included an express reference to benefits payable on death. The new definition inserted by PA 2004 does not. But a scheme which provides death benefits will still be an occupational pension scheme if it provides retirement benefits as well.

2.71   But s 255 of the Pensions Act 2004 includes a prohibition on occupational pension schemes having any activities other than 'retirement-benefit activities', defined broadly to mean activities relating to retirement benefits. These are defined in s 255(5) to mean

> ' "retirement benefits" means—
>
> (a)   benefits paid by reference to reaching, or expecting to reach, retirement, and

(b) benefits that are supplementary to benefits within paragraph (a) and that are provided on an ancillary basis—

    (i) in the form of payments on death, disability or termination of employment, or

    (ii) in the form of support payments or services in the case of sickness, poverty or need, or death.'

2.72   In February 2006, the DWP stated that it considers that this prohibition prevents occupational pension schemes from providing death benefits other than as ancillary to the provision of retirement benefits for the particular member. If this interpretation is correct, it will mean that occupational pension schemes will have to cease providing benefits for members only on death (eg life cover only members). Such benefits would need to be provided by a separate scheme (which will not qualify as an occupational pension scheme). The Pensions Regulator has issued guidance on this[1].

1 See http://www.thepensionsregulator.gov.uk/trustees/lumpSumDeathBenefits.

2.73   The definition in s 1 of PSA 1993 is also incorporated by reference in TUPE 2006 – see reg 10(1)(a) and Chapter 24 below.

2.74   Aside from imposing a degree of inconvenience, one side effect of this may be that rights and benefits under such life cover only schemes do pass under TUPE.

2.75   The term 'occupational pension scheme' used to be defined separately (but in a similar way to that under PSA 1993, s 1) in PSA 1993 s 123(3)[1]. This was used in relation to payments out of the National Insurance Fund with regard to unpaid contributions to occupational pension schemes under s 123 of PSA 1993 – see Chapter 13 (National Insurance Fund) below. But this separate definition too was repealed from 22 September 2005 by the Pensions Act 2004 so that the new definition in s 1 of PSA 1993 applies here as well.

1 Formerly EPCA 1978, s 127(3).

2.76   In some statutes the term 'occupational pension' or 'pension scheme' is used but not defined – see for example the provisions relating to liabilities under adopted employment contracts in IA 1986[1].or relating to the definition of an associated person in IA 1986, s 435[2]. In practice it is suggested that the courts are likely to follow the definition in s 1, PSA 1993.

1 See s 44 and para 99 of Sch B1 – discussed in Chapter 18 (Carrying on business) below.
2 See the discussion in *Re Thirty Eight Building Limited* [1999] 1 BCLC 416, discussed at para 6.32 below.

2.77   As mentioned above (see para 2.51), the definition in s 1 of the PSA 1993 (as substituted by PA 2004) is very wide and covers both funded and unfunded schemes and tax registered or unregistered schemes (Revenue approved and unapproved schemes before 6 April 2006 and the changes under the Finance Act 2004). It may be that the definition also covers certain other arrangements set up by employers such as redundancy plans, profit sharing schemes, savings plans and medical plans, etc[1]. Section 33 of the Trade Union Reform and Employment Rights Act 1993 amended reg 7 of TUPE 1981 to clarify the position so that the exclusion in reg 7 did not apply to benefits other than old age, invalidity or survivors' benefits. This has been carried forward as reg 10(2) of TUPE 2006[2].

1 See the decisions discussed at para 2.63 above (on the definition in s 1 before its substitution by PA 2004) of Hart J in *Swansea City Council v Johnson* [1999] Ch 189 and the Court of Appeal in *Parlett v Guppys (Bridport) Ltd* [1996] 2 BCLC 34 and in *Westminster City Council v Haywood (No.1)* [1998] Ch 377.
2 See the ECJ decisions in *Beckmann v Dynamo Whicheloe Macfarlane* [2002] IRLR 578 and *Martin v South Bank University* [2004] IRLR 74 and Chapter 24 below.

CHAPTER 3

Insolvency: consultation with employees

3.1   There are various obligations imposed by legislation on employers to consult with employees or their representatives.

The main ones applicable in an insolvency situation are discussed in this chapter.

REDUNDANCY: CONSULTATION WITH EMPLOYEE REPRESENTATIVES

3.2   Where redundancies are proposed (see para 2.50 above) or other dismissals for a reason not related to the individual concerned[1], there is a statutory obligation on an employer under s 188 of the Trade Union and Labour Relations (Consolidation) Act 1992 (TULRCA 1992)[2], to consult with 'appropriate representatives' ie employee representatives elected by the employees or representatives of recognised trade unions.

The statute does not require agreement to be reached, but consultation must be with a view to reaching agreement with the employee representatives and must include consultation about ways of avoiding the dismissals, reducing the number of employees to be dismissed and mitigating the consequences of the dismissals[3].

The EAT has held that consultation must be about the reasons for the redundancies, as well as their impact – *UK Coal Mining Ltd v National Union of Mineworkers (Northumberland Area)*[4].

1 Eg if there was a dismissal for failure to accept a new general practice or new terms and conditions – see TULRCA 1992, s195 (as substituted by the Trade Union Reform and Employment Rights Act 1993). See para 3.16 below.
2 Formerly the Employment Protection Act 1975, s 99.
3 TULRCA 1992, s188(2).
4 [2008] ICR 163; [2008] IRLR 4, EAT.

3.3   These provisions originally only applied where the employer recognised an independent trade union (as defined in TULRCA 1992, s 178(3)). However, following the decision of the European Court in *Commission v United Kingdom*[1] the provisions of s 188 (and TUPE – see para 3.9 below) were extended[2], in relation to dismissals on or after 1 March 1996, to require the employer to consult either with a trade union or with elected representatives of the affected employees.

1 [1994] ICR 664, ECJ.
2 See the Collective Redundancies and Transfer of Undertakings (Protection of Employment) (Amendment) Regulations 1995, SI 1995/2587.

3.4   A challenge to these changes was rejected by the Divisional Court in R v *Secretary of State, ex p Unison*[1].

1 [1996] ICR 1003, DC.

3.5   Such consultation must begin in good time, with a *minimum* time period of:

- 90 days where 100 or more employees at one establishment are to be dismissed and

- 30 days where 20 or more but less than 100 employees are to be dismissed,

unless there are special circumstances which render such consultation not reasonably practicable – see TULRCA 1992, s 188(7) and paras 7.27 to 7.37 below.

Protective award

3.6   If an employer fails to comply with the obligation under s 188 of TULRCA 1992 then a trade union or employee representative affected has the right, under s 189, to complain to an employment tribunal. The tribunal may make an award, called the 'protective award', not exceeding 90 days' pay.

3.7   For dismissals before 1 November 1999, the maximum used to be 30 days' pay where there were 20 or more and less than 100 employees made redundant, but the maximum was increased to 90 days' pay in all cases for dismissals on or after 1 November 1999[1].

1 See the Collective Redundancies and Transfer of Undertakings (Protection of Employment) (Amendment) Regulations 1999, SI 1999/1925.

3.8   There is no limit to a day's pay for this purpose (unlike the position in relation to most other statutory rights, for example unfair dismissal or individual redundancy – see para 2.49 above).

CONSULTATION UNDER TUPE

3.9   Consultation obligations with trade unions or elected employee representatives also arise under regs 13 and 14 of TUPE 2006 (replacing regs 10 and 11 of TUPE 1981).

3.10   These obligations are similar to those arising under TULRCA 1992, save that the obligation is to consult 'long enough before a relevant transfer to enable consultations to take place' – TUPE 2006, reg 13(2). There is a similar 'special circumstances' defence (see paras 7.27 to 7.37 below).

3.11   The maximum amount of compensation which a tribunal may award for failure to comply with this obligation is 13 weeks' pay – reg 16(3). Again, there is no limit to a week's pay for this purpose.

3.12   The Trade Union Reform and Employment Rights Act 1993 increased the maximum amount of compensation (from two to four weeks' pay) in relation to transfers after 30 August 1993. The maximum rose again, to 13 weeks' pay, for transfers on or after 1 November 1999[1].

1 See the Collective Redundancies and Transfer of Undertakings (Protection of Employment) (Amendment) Regulations 1999, SI 1999/1925.

EC law

3.13   The obligation to consult with trade unions or elected employee representatives arises by virtue of EC Directive 98/59/EC which consolidates Directive 75/129 (as amended by Directive 92/56), the Collective Redundancies Directive. The Directive in fact requires consultation with employee representatives where the employer is contemplating redundancies. This may be at an earlier time than that contained in s 188, which refers to the position where the employer is 'proposing' to carry out redundancies.

3.14   This point has been considered in *Hough v Leyland Daf Ltd*[1,] *Re Hartlebury Printers Ltd*[2], R v *British Coal Corpn, ex p Vardy*[3], *Dewhirst Group v GMB*[4] and *MSF v Refuge Assurance*[5].

1 [1991] IRLR 194 (EAT).
2 [1993] 1 All ER 470 (Morritt J).
3 [1993] IRLR 104 at 106 (DC).
4 [2003] All ER (D) 175 (Dec) (EAT).
5 [2002] IRLR 324 (EAT).

3.15   Following the decision of the ECJ in *Junk v Kuhnel*[1], the EAT held in *Leicestershire County Council v Unison*[2] that it was right to construe the words 'proposing to dismiss' in s 188(1) as meaning 'proposing to give notice of dismissal'.

In *Akavan Erityisalojen Keskusliitto AEK ry v Fujitsu Siemens Computers Oy*[3] the ECJ considered the Collective Redundancies Directive further. The decision gives some support for the view that the UK term 'proposes' may be equivalent to the term "contemplates" used in the Directive.

1 C-188/03, [2005] IRLR 310 (ECJ).
2 [2005] IRLR 920 (EAT) at para 35. The decision of the EAT was upheld by the Court of Appeal [2006] IRLR 810, but it refused to consider the new point on the issue of interpretation of *Junk v Kuhnel*.
3 C–44/08; [2009] All ER (D) 69 (Sep).

3.16 Section 34 of the Trade Union Reform and Employment Rights Act 1993 changed the consultation provisions to bring them more into line with the Collective Redundancies Directive. These changes took effect in relation to dismissals on or after 28 November 1993 (see para 3(12) of SI 1993/1908). In particular:

(a) the definition of redundancies for this purpose (but not otherwise) was changed so that a dismissal is treated as a redundancy if the dismissal is for a 'reason not related to the individual concerned or for a number of reasons all of which are not so related'. This revised definition extends the obligations to cover some dismissals which were not previously treated as redundancies (eg by way of enforcement of a change in working practices). See for example *GMB v MAN Truck & Bus UK Ltd*[1] dealing with a dismissal an re-hire on new terms;

(b) the consultation obligations were extended and need to 'be undertaken by the employer with a view to reaching agreement with the trade union representatives';

(c) it has ceased to be a special circumstance justifying a reduced consultation period (see paras 7.27 ff below) if the failure to consult was based on a failure by a person controlling the employer to provide information (this change was required by EC Directive 92/56 which amended the Collective Redundancies Directive); and

(d) it was previously possible to offset payments actually made by the employer during any protected period (eg pay in lieu of notice) against a protective award under TULRCA 1992, s 190(3) – see *Vosper Thornycroft (UK) Ltd v TGWU*[2]. This section has now been repealed. See further para 14.15 below discussing set-off in claims on the National Insurance Fund and the comments of the House of Lords in *Secretary of State v Mann*[3].

1 [2000] ICR 1101; [2000] IRLR 636, EAT.
2 [1988] ICR 270, EAT.
3 [1999] ICR 898, HL.

COLLECTIVE REDUNDANCIES: DUTY TO NOTIFY SECRETARY OF STATE

3.17 The Secretary of State for Employment must also be notified (on form HR 1) if over 20 employees are to be made redundant over a period of 90 days (TULRCA 1992, s 193). This applies whether or not the employees are represented by a union recognised by the employer.

Failure to notify is a criminal offence (TULRCA 1992, s 194), with the potential for an insolvency practitioner to be liable – see Chapter 8 (Personal liability of insolvency practitioners) below.

There is no duty to notify the Secretary of State in relation to a TUPE transfer (nor is there a criminal offence).

3.18   In *Junk v Kuhnel*[1], the ECJ held that under the Collective Redundancies Directive, consultation (and notice to the Secretary of State) must take place before notice of any dismissal is given. In order to comply with this judgment, with effect on and from 1 October 2006, s 193 of TULRCA 1992 was amended[2] to require the notice to be given to the Secretary of State before any notice was given to terminate employment.

1 C-188/03, [2005] IRLR 310, ECJ.
2 See the Collective Redundancies (Amendment) Regulations 2006, SI 2006/2387.

WORKS COUNCILS

3.19   The Information and Consultation of Employees Regulations 2004 (SI 2004/3426) (the 'ICE Regulations') came into force on 6 April 2005[1]. They apply to undertakings with more than a specified number of employees in the UK (150 from 6 April 2005, 100 from 6 April 2007 and 50 from 6 April 2008). The ICE Regulations enact an EU Directive[2].

1 See Squire, Healy and Broadbent *'Informing and Consulting Employees – the New Law'* (OUP, 2005) and the guidance issued by the DTI in January 2006, now on the BERR website at http://www.berr.gov.uk/files/file25934.pdf.
2 Directive 2002/14/EC.

3.20   Broadly if an appropriate request is made by employees, the employer has an obligation to seek to negotiate an information and consultation procedure (or to rely in some cases on a pre-existing agreement)[1]. If agreement on such a procedure cannot be reached, a standard procedure, involving election of information and consultation representatives, will apply[2]. These representatives are commonly called a 'works council'.

1 ICE Regulations, regs 14 to 16.
2 ICE Regulations, reg 18.

3.21   The standard procedure requires employers to give information to and consult with the works council on various matters[1]. Information must be given to the representatives on:

(a) the recent and probable development of the undertaking's activities and economic situation;

(b) the situation, structure and probable development of employment within the undertaking and on any anticipated threat to employment; and

(c) any decisions likely to result in substantial changes to work organisation or contractual relationships – including collective redundancies or transfers of undertakings.

Consultation must take place about the matters outlined in (b) and (c) above.

1 ICE Regulations, reg 20.

3.22   The full range of situations in which the new obligations apply will become clear only over time, once the Central Arbitration Committee (CAC) starts considering claims about failures to consult (see para 3.34 below). Guidance issued by the DTI in 2006 gave some general factors to consider when deciding whether information and/or consultation obligations could apply, but could not provide definitive guidance on precisely when there will be an obligation to inform or consult.

3.23 Pending caselaw, it is reasonably clear that changes to terms and conditions of employment will trigger a right to consultation. What is less clear is the number of employees that must be affected before consultation is required. The DTI guidance says that no minimum number of employees can be specified, but it is reasonably clear that the greater the number, the more likely it is that there will be a duty to consult. It is to be hoped that employee representatives and the CAC will take a pragmatic approach to what amounts to a collective issue suitable for consultation.

3.24 A transfer of an undertaking or a proposal to make collective redundancies will trigger consultation obligations under the regulations in addition to the existing consultation requirements under TUPE and the collective dismissals legislation (TULRCA).

However, following the initial consultation, the government accepted that it would be undesirable for an employer to have to consult two different bodies of employee representatives about the same issue.

Where the default rules apply under the ICE Regulations, an employer can give information and consultation representatives written notification that it will consult under TUPE or TULRCA as the case may be[1]. It then does not have to consult under the information and consultation regulations as well.

However, the DTI guidance makes it clear that such notification can be given only once the duties under TUPE or TULRCA have been triggered[2]. Employers therefore may need to consult information representatives at an earlier stage about events that could ultimately give rise to another consultation obligation but before that obligation has actually arisen.

Provided the employer notifies employees each time that it consulting separately under the Pension Consultation Regulations 2006 (see para 3.43 below), consultation is not needed under the ICE Regulations about a "listed change" on which the employer is consulting under the Pension Consultation Regulations 2006[3].

1 ICE Regulations, reg 20(5).
2 DTI Guidance (2006), para 63 (pages 56 to 58), now on the BERR website at http://www.berr.gov.uk/files/file25934.pdf.
3 ICE Regulations, reg 17A (inserted by SI 2006/514) and see the DTI Guidance also at para 63.

3.25 Although this is not obvious from the default procedure itself, it appears that a sale of a business by share sale will trigger information and consultation rights. Previously there had been no obligation on an employer to consult where there has been a share sale, as the identity of the employer does not change. In future, advance information and consultation is likely to be required. The extent of the obligation may depend on what the outcome of the share sale is likely to be. If there is no immediate impact on employment, there is an argument that the sale is merely an example of the organisation's development, in which case information but not consultation will be required. If, however, there are to be changes to contractual relations (for example, the harmonisation of terms and conditions of employment) or a threat to employment (for example, redundancies to avoid overstaffing) it is likely that both information and advance consultation will be required – possibly with a view to reaching agreement. This may imply that consultation is needed before a deal is actually signed.

3.26   Information has to be given to representatives at a time that will allow them to conduct an adequate study and, where appropriate, prepare for consultation. No more concrete guidance is given on how much time is needed for an 'adequate study' to take place. Nor is there any indication how often information and consultation should take place, although the DTI guidance suggests that an annual meeting is a minimum requirement, with additional ad hoc meetings as necessary. In practice the frequency will vary depending on the nature of the information to be provided. Employers will need to bear in mind the need to give employee representatives an opportunity to consider the information and (where information is not confidential) discuss it with the employees they represent and with other representatives before meeting the employer to discuss the material.

3.27   The default requirements do not require the employer to pay for 'expert assistance' for the information representatives of the sort that may be given by trade union officials, lawyers or accountants. (There could, of course, be agreement on this matter in a negotiated agreement.) However, the possibility of the representatives seeking to obtain expert assistance should be taken into account in deciding how long the representatives should have to consider the information before they meet the employer's representatives.

3.28   Consultation must take place about the structure and probable development of employment and about any substantial changes that are envisaged. The timing, method and content of the consultation must be 'appropriate'. It must take place on the basis of the information supplied by the employer and of any opinion formed by the representatives. Representatives must be able to meet the appropriate level of management and obtain an opinion from them in response. Consultation in relation to substantial changes has to take place with a view to reaching agreement.

3.29   The thrust of all these requirements indicates that consultation must take place before a final decision is taken and acted upon.

3.30   Consultation must take place about 'anticipatory measures' that are 'envisaged'. The reference to consultation taking place at an appropriate time also points to consultation occurring at a time that gives representatives a chance to have some meaningful input to a discussion. However, as noted previously, an employer is not obliged to obtain the consent of representatives to proposed measures.

3.31   Having said that, there is an obligation on employers and representatives 'to work in a spirit of co-operation and with due regard for their reciprocal rights and obligations' (reg 21). Contrast the obligation in a collective redundancy consultation to consult 'with a view to reaching agreement' – TULRCA 1992, s 188(2).

Impact on insolvency

3.32   The ICE Regulations do not contain any specific provision dealing with what happens when the employer enters formal insolvency. The DTI guidance[1] on the ICE Regulations states:

> '84. Administrators and receivers. Where there is a negotiated agreement, or an employer is subject to the standard information and consultation provisions, the obligation to inform and consult in accordance with that agreement or the standard provisions will continue to apply where a company goes into administration or receivership. The administrator or receiver would be acting on behalf of the employer who will continue to be subject to the obligations in the agreement or the standard provisions. The administrator or receiver must fulfil the employer's obligations, but would not be personally liable for failing to do so. The requirement to inform and consult would also continue to be subject to the provisions allowing confidential information to be subject to a confidentiality restriction in the legitimate interest of the undertaking, or to be withheld where disclosure would seriously harm the functioning of the undertaking or be prejudicial to it.'

1 On the BERR website at http://www.berr.gov.uk/files/file25934.pdf.

Penalties

3.33   Employers face sanctions if they fail to comply with a negotiated agreement or standard information and consultation procedure.

3.34   Information and consultation representatives or (where no representatives have been chosen) individual employees can complain to the CAC about the failure. If the CAC upholds the complaint, it can make an order requiring the employer to take steps to comply with the relevant procedure within a defined period. A complaint to the CAC is the only legal remedy for failure to comply with the ICE Regulations (reg 24).

3.35   The Advisory, Conciliation and Arbitration Service (ACAS) has a statutory power to endeavour to conciliate a complaint before it is determined by the CAC. A CAC decision can be appealed to the Employment Appeal Tribunal (EAT) on points of law.

3.36   Where the CAC has upheld a complaint, a further application can be made to the EAT for the issue of a penalty notice. The EAT must issue a penalty notice unless it is satisfied that the failure was for a reason beyond the employer's control or that there was a reasonable excuse for the failure – reg 22(7). A failure by a controller of the employer (eg a parent company or an insolvency practitioner) to provide relevant information is not a valid excuse – reg 20(6).

3.37 A penalty of up to £75,000, payable to the Secretary of State, can be imposed (reg 23(2)). When determining the level of the penalty, the EAT must take into account the gravity of the employer's failure, the period over which it occurred, the reason for it, the number of employees affected and the total number of employees within the undertaking.

These factors look similar to those applicable under TULRCA and TUPE and will probably be interpreted as being penal based on any failure (rather than any loss suffered). The principles in *Susie Radin Ltd v GMB*[1] seem likely to apply.

1 [2004] IRLR 400, CA and para 21.3 below.

3.38 The ICE regulations do not contain an express 'special circumstances' defence. As mentioned above (and see para 7.27 below), in TUPE and the collective dismissals legislation, an employer can point to special circumstances that rendered it not reasonably practicable for it to comply with its information and consultation obligations. As long as it took such steps as were reasonably practicable, it will have complied with its obligations.

3.39 In practice, this means that in an insolvency situation, it may be possible for the purposes of TUPE and the collective dismissals legislation for an employer to argue (through the insolvency practitioner) that it was not possible to consult employees for the requisite period. As long as such consultation as was reasonably practicable was carried out, no protective award can be made.

3.40 The omission of such a defence from the ICE Regulations is surprising. Presumably, in the relatively rare cases where there are such special circumstances, it will be open to an employer to argue that its failure to inform and consult resulted from a reason beyond its control or amounts to some other reasonable excuse for the failure and that the EAT should accordingly not issue a penalty notice. Alternatively, given that the reasons for a failure must be taken into account by the EAT when determining the amount of the penalty, the existence of genuine special circumstances might result in a lower penalty being issued.

3.41 The making of an order by the CAC has no effect on acts committed or agreements already made by the employer, nor can it prevent or delay any act or agreement the employer is proposing to commit or make – reg 22(9). A business decision therefore cannot be unwound, even if it was not consulted upon.

3.42 It is also clear that employee representatives (who will, in many cases, be union representatives and therefore have union backing) will not be able to obtain an injunction to prevent a particular step being taken by an employer before information and consultation requirements are met. The ICE Regulations expressly state that the only remedy for a failure to comply is by way of a complaint to the CAC – reg 24.

PENSION CONSULTATION – PA 2004, s 259

3.43   From 6 April 2006, the Pensions Act 2004 (PA 2004) has required employers to carry out consultation where they are proposing 'listed' changes to active or prospective members' pension arrangements. Before any decision is made, employers must give at least 60 days notice of the changes (with background information) to all affected members, and consult (ie exchange views) with trade unions or works councils or members' elected representatives[1]. The relevant regulations are notably obscure in various areas.

1 See Squire, 'Informing and consulting over pension scheme changes' (2006) 783 Industrial Relations Law Bulletin 5 (April) and the DWP guidance (March 2006) at www.dwp.gov.uk/publications/dwp/2005/occ_pen_schemes/occ_personal_pens_schemes_regs06.pdf

3.44   This requirement arises under PA 2004, ss 259 to 261 and the Occupational and Personal Pension Schemes (Consultation by Employers and Miscellaneous Amendment) Regulations 2006, SI 2006/349, (the 'Pension Consultation Regulations'). The requirement came into effect on 6 April 2006, the same date as changes were made to s 67 of the Pensions Act 1995 (which deals with changes to accrued rights). The consultation required under ss 259 and 260 differs from that required under s 67.

3.45   The new obligation applies only to changes that affect active (or prospective) members. Changes affecting deferred or pensioner members are not within new regulations (although PA 1995, s 67 limits changes that affect accrued rights).

3.46   The new consultation obligation is in addition to any other consultation requirements, for example under TUPE or the Information and Consultation of Employees Regulations 2004 (the ICE Regulations). As mentioned above (see para 3.24), provided the employer notifies employees each time that it consulting separately under the 2006 Pension Consultation Regulations, consultation is not needed under the ICE Regulations about a "listed change" on which the employer is consulting under the 2006 Pension Consultation Regulations.

3.47   Together the Pensions Act 2004 and the Pension Consultation Regulations 2006 require most employers in relation to occupational or personal pension schemes to consult active and prospective members on proposals to make 'listed changes' (see below) which may affect those members. This applies to changes made by an employer or the trustees or (in the case of a multi-employer scheme) any other person (eg a principal employer or sponsor).

3.48   Consultation must take place before any decision (or series of decisions) to make those changes is made (reg 6). If the proposal to make a listed change is made by a person other than the employer (ie the trustees or managers or, in relation to a multi-employer scheme, a non-employer with power to make a listed change), that person may not make the decision without first notifying each employer and being satisfied that the employer has undertaken the necessary consultation.

3.49   In line with the ICE Regulations 2004, the requirements under the Pension Consultation Regulations had a phased implementation, with employers of more than 150, 100 and 50 employees having to implement them from 6 April 2006, 2007 and 2008 respectively. The limits apply to each employer, regardless of how many employers participate in a multiemployer scheme (either occupational or personal). The test is based on number of employees, not numbers of members of the scheme employed by that employer. The obligations apply regardless of whether or not there is a recognised trade union or works council.

Excluded employers

3.50   Employers entirely excluded from the scope of the Pension Consultation Regulations (regs 4 and 5) are set out below.

Occupational pension schemes

Any employer:

- in relation to a public service scheme;

- in relation to a small scheme with less than 12 members who are each trustees (or where there is an independent trustee – effectively a small self administered scheme (SSAS);

- in relation to a scheme with only one member;

- in relation to an employer-financed retirement benefits scheme; or

- in relation to an overseas scheme (main administration outside the EU) which is not registered with HMRC under the Finance Act 2004.

Personal pension schemes
Any employer in relation to a personal pension scheme where direct payment arrangements exist but no employer contributions fall to be paid towards the scheme.

Listed changes

3.51   The following changes are listed changes (regs 8 and 9) giving rise to a consultation obligation.

Occupational pension schemes

Changes requiring consultation are:

- an increase in the normal pension age for active or prospective members;

- the closure of the scheme to new members (or a class) or for future accrual;

- the removal of the employer's liability to contribute or, in the case of money purchase schemes only, any reduction in employer contributions;

- the increase or introduction of member contributions;

- a change of some or all benefits from defined benefits (DB) to defined contribution (DC);

- a change in the basis for determining the future accrual rate; and

- a reduction of the future accrual rate.

Personal pension schemes

Changes requiring consultation are:

- reduction in or cessation of employer contributions; or

- an increase in member contributions.

Exclusions

3.52   No consultation is required (reg 10) where:

- the active and prospective members of the scheme to whom the listed change relates ('affected members') were notified of the proposal before 6 April 2006;

- (occupational and personal pension schemes) as a result of a consultation on a proposal for cessation of employer contributions there is a further proposal to reduce employer contributions or (occupational schemes only) as a result of a consultation to prevent future accrual, there is a further proposal to reduce the future accrual rate (instead of ceasing altogether) – see reg 6(3) to (7);

- changes made for the purpose of complying with a statutory provision or a determination of the Pensions Regulator;

- changes having no lasting effect on eligibility or benefits (eg administrative changes); and

- changes covered by the provisions of PA 1995, s 67 (as amended by PA 2004). Section 67 restricts amendments in relation to occupational pension schemes that adversely affect accrued rights. There is a separate consultation/notification obligation in s 67 for changes within that provision.

Consultation procedure

3.53   Specified written information must be given to all affected members before the consultation starts (reg 11(2)(b)) and the consultation must start at least 60 days before the proposed effective date of the change – reg 15(4).

3.54   Consultation 'in a spirit of co-operation, taking account the interests of both sides' (reg 15) then must take place with at least one of the following employee representatives (reg 12):

● recognised trade union representatives;

● information and consultation representatives under the ICE Regulations 2004 (who have rights to paid time off, protection from unfair dismissal, etc for the purpose of their functions in the consultation process); or

● representatives elected for the purpose of and in accordance with these pension consultation regulations.

3.55   The ICE Regulations have been amended so that employers are not obliged to consult about the same issues twice under both sets of regulations – see para 3.24 above.

3.56   The specified information (reg 11) is:

● details of the listed change and its likely effects on the scheme and its members (to be accompanied by 'any relevant background information');

● the timescale for implementation; and

● the closing date for responses.

3.57   The information must be clear and comprehensive enough to enable members' representatives to consider and conduct a study of the impact of the proposed change and give views to the employer – reg 11(2)(f).

3.58   The employer must then consider the responses received -reg 16(3) – and, if the listed changes were proposed by a third party (eg the trustees or the principal employer), give them written notification of the responses as soon as reasonably practicable – reg 16(1). The third party must then satisfy itself that consultation was carried out in compliance with the regulations – reg 16(2). If no responses are received, the consultation is deemed complete at the end of the consultation period – reg 15(5).

Penalties

3.59   The exclusive remedy for failure to comply with the Pensions Consultation Regulations as originally enacted was by way of a complaint to the Pensions Regulator: reg 18. If a complaint is made to the Pensions Regulator, no specific sanction was originally specified for a breach of the consultation oblig-ation.

The DWP issued a consultation document[1] in December 2008 on whether it would be appropriate to include power for the Pensions Regulator to impose a civil penalty against the employer for failure (without reasonable excuse) to comply with the pension consultation regulations. This change, adding a new reg 18A, was made with effect on and from 6 April 2009 by the Occupational,

Personal and Stakeholder Pensions (Miscellaneous Amendments) Regulations 2009[2].

The civil penalty looks to be free standing (and not one cross referring to s 10 of the Pensions Act 1995). This seems to mean that the extended liability provisions in s 10 would not apply, so it would not be possible for directors or insolvency practitioners also to be liable – see Chapter 8 (Personal liability of insolvency practitioners) below.

1 See http://www.dwp.gov.uk/consultations/2008/pensions-misc-regs-2009.pdf, at proposed reg 23, envisaging a new reg 18A in the 2006 Pensions Consultation Regulations.
2 SI 2009/615.

3.60 The Pensions Regulator could also issue an improvement notice (under PA 2004, s 13), directing the person in default (whether a trustee or another) to take steps to remedy the contravention. Civil penalties can be imposed on the defaulter (or on a director etc responsible) for failure to take all reasonable steps to secure compliance with such a notice (PA 2004, s 13(8) and (9), applying PA 1995, s 10).

3.61 If any breach of the consultation requirements is material, trustees and employers, etc will be under an obligation to notify the Pensions Regulator of the breach (PA 2004, s 70) – see Chapter 29 (TPR/PPF power to gather information) below on reporting breaches of the law.

3.62 The Pensions Regulator has a limited power to waive or relax any of the requirements of the Pension Consultation Regulations, but can do so only if it is satisfied that this would be 'necessary in order to protect the generality of the interests of the members' (reg 19). The DWP guidance on the Pension Consultation Regulations[1] indicates (at para 47) that

> 'An application should set out reasons why delay in making a change to the pension scheme in accordance with regulations 8 or 9 by the minimum period of 60 days that is required for consultation would be damaging to scheme members' interests. For example: it could be demonstrated that the delay would adversely impact the company's ability to remain solvent. The Regulator may only waive or relax the requirement to consult if it is satisfied that it is necessary to do so in order to protect the interests of the generality of the members of the scheme. In view of the potential urgency to waive or relax the consultation period, Regulation 21 enables the Regulator to apply the special procedures in section 98 of the Pension Act 2004 to any request to waive or relax the consultation period. This requires the Regulator to give a "determination notice".'

1 See http://www.dwp.gov.uk/publications/dwp/2005/occ_pen_schemes/occ_personal_pens_schemes_regs06.pdf.

3.63 In an insolvency situation, this may be a relevant factor (eg if the insolvency practitioner looks to arrange for the company to cease accrual under a pension scheme). But in practice the appointment of an insolvency practitioner (other than as a part of a members' voluntary liquidation) will be a 'relevant event' and so, if there is an eligible scheme, is likely in many cases to trigger an 'assessment period' under PA 2004, s 132 in relation to the Pension Protection Fund (PPF) and hence a cessation of future accrual in any event, under PA 2004, s 133(5) – see Chapter 28 (PPF: Notice obligations on IPs/assessment period) below.

Such a cessation is outside the consultation obligation under the Pensions Consultation Regulations as being 'made for the purpose of complying with a statutory provision' (reg 10).

CHAPTER 4

Insolvency proceedings

GENERAL

4.1   A detailed analysis of the insolvency regimes in England and Wales is beyond the scope of this book. Reference should be made to specialist works. However, a brief description of the insolvency regime is given below.

4.2   The statutory insolvency regime in England and Wales was largely consolidated in the Insolvency Act 1986 (IA 1986) and the accompanying statutory instruments, in particular the Insolvency Rules 1986 (SI 1986/1925 as amended). Major amendments to the insolvency regime were introduced in the Insolvency Act 1985 and consolidated (with most of the relevant provisions from the Bankruptcy Act 1914 and the Companies Act 1985) in the Insolvency Act 1986. This Act mainly came into force on 29 December 1986. The major statutory provisions are now as follows:

(a)   Insolvency Act 1986 – deals with bankruptcies, liquidations, administrations and voluntary arrangements. Receiverships are partly covered by IA 1986 and partly by the Law of Property Act 1925;

(b)   Insolvency Rules 1986 (SI 1986/1925 as amended);

(c)   Law of Property Act 1925 – various provisions relating to receiverships;

(d)   Companies Act 2006[1] – some legislation of importance in an insolvency, in particular s 754 (formerly CA 1985, s 196) (floating charge priority); s 993 (formerly CA 1985, s 458) (criminal offence of fraudulent trading, tracking the civil liability under the IA 1986, s 213, but the criminal liability arising whether or not the company is in liquidation); s 860 (formerly CA 1985, s 395) (registration of charges).

1 The Companies Act 2006 broadly replaced the Companies Act 1985 from 1 October 2009.

Enterprise Act 2002

4.3   The Enterprise Act 2002 significantly amended the Insolvency Act 1986. The changes mainly came into force from 15 September 2003. The main changes were:

- new ways to appoint administrators out of court;

- abolition of administrative receivership, with certain exceptions;

- grandfathering of old floating charges;

- abolition of Crown preference;

- ring-fencing of a proportion of floating charge realisations for unsecured creditors; and

- new set-off provisions in administration.

4.4   Administrations already under way before 15 September 2003 remain subject to the previous legislation (see para 4.37 below).

OPTIONS ON INSOLVENCY

4.5   The UK insolvency regime has been enacted in order to achieve various different (and sometimes conflicting) end results. These include:

(a)   termination of the existence of a corporate body, whether solvent or insolvent (liquidation and some administrations);

(b)   enforcement of security by a creditor (usually under a receivership arrangement);

(c)   breathing space to attempt a company rescue (administrations);

(d)   arrangements between creditors to keep a company going (voluntary arrangements);

(e)   termination of an insolvent undertaking (corporate or individual) and equitable division of the assets amongst creditors (bankruptcy or insolvent liquidation and some administrations).

4.6   These different end results must always be kept in mind when considering the different effects of the various insolvency regimes on employees (and others).

LIQUIDATIONS

4.7   A liquidation involves the termination of the existence of a company (or other corporation). Such a termination may be desired where the company is solvent. In this case the position of creditors is of less concern (by definition, if the company is solvent all creditors will ultimately be paid in full). Conversely, termination of the company may be required because the company is insolvent. In this case the position of creditors will be of more concern, given that they will not be wholly repaid. This distinction is reflected in the greater degree of control and influence given to creditors in an insolvent liquidation. Liquidations may either be voluntary or ordered by the court (compulsory)[1].

1 IA 1986, s 73. Court liquidation is often called 'compulsory' in contrast to a voluntary liquidation, although the term 'compulsory liquidation' is not used in the legislation.

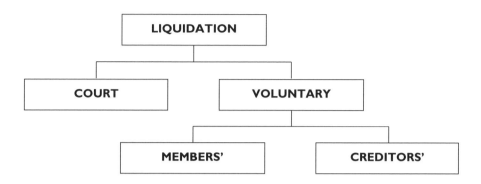

Court liquidations

Petition for a winding up

4.8   Court liquidations are governed primarily by Chapter VI of Part IV (ss 117–162) of IA 1986. Such liquidations require the making of an application to the court (by a winding-up petition) for a winding-up order[1], followed by an order of the court if the conditions for the making of an order have been fulfilled (see below).

If a winding-up order is made, the winding up is deemed to commence on the date the petition was presented[2].

This backdating of the effect of the winding-up will only apply for the purposes of IA 1986. A pensions scheme provision referring to the employer 'going into liquidation' would only be triggered by the making of the winding-up order, not the presentation of the petition – see *Mettoy Pension Trustees Ltd v Evans*[3] and para 39.5 below.

1 IA 1986, s 124.
2 IA 1986, s 129(2), although see s 129(1) and (1A) where there has been a prior winding-up resolution passed or administration application made.
3 [1991] 2 All ER 513 at 544 (Warner J).

Grounds for petition

4.9   The grounds for a petition to the court are set out in the IA 1986, s 122(1). The main grounds are set out in sub-ss (a), (f) and (g) as listed below:

(a)   a special resolution has been passed by the members of the company that the company be wound up by the court – s 122(1)(a);

(b) the company is insolvent – ie it is unable to pay its debts as they fall due ('cash flow insolvent') or its liabilities exceed its assets ('balance sheet insolvent') – s 122(1)(f) (see also s 123); or

(c) that winding up would be 'just and equitable' – s 122(1)(g).

4.10   A petition may be presented by various parties. It is usually presented either by the company or the directors or by a creditor[1]. Pension trustees will count as creditors for this purpose if there is a potential statutory debt under PA 1995, s 75 (see Chapter 34 below). A creditor cannot force a voluntary winding up without the co-operation of the board of directors and his only remedy, if the directors do not co-operate, is to proceed by way of a court winding up.

1 IA 1986, s 124.

4.11   Creditors usually proceed under s 122(1)(f), relying on a statutory demand under s 123(1)(a) in order to show the inability of the company to pay its debts. Section 123(1)(a) deems a company to be unable to pay its debts if a written demand (in the prescribed form) for a sum exceeding £750 has been served and remains unsatisfied.

In addition, the company will be deemed to be unable to pay its debts if it is proved to the satisfaction of the court that the value of the company's assets is less than the amount of its liabilities, taking into account its contingent and prospective liabilities (note also s 123(2) on this point). Factually this can be difficult to show – see for example the decision of Jacob J (in relation to an administration petition) in *Highberry Ltd v Colt Telecom Group Plc (No.2)*[1].

1 [2002] EWHC 2815; [2002] All ER (D) 347 (Dec); [2003] BPIR 324 (Jacob J).

4.12   Court actions against the company are automatically stayed if a winding-up order is made by the court (see IA 1986, s 130 and para 4.46 below). Permission is needed from the court or the liquidator before such actions can be continued or commenced.

Appointment of provisional liquidator

4.13   The court may also, after the presentation of a winding-up petition, appoint a provisional liquidator under IA 1986, s 135. A provisional liquidator will (depending on the terms of the order of appointment) usually take over the management of the company as an interim measure pending the ultimate winding-up order (eg where it is desired to displace the existing management or in order for the company to continue to trade).

Voluntary liquidations

Resolution for winding up

4.14   Voluntary liquidations are primarily governed by Chapters II to IV of Pt VI (ss 84–116) of IA 1986. Under s 84, a company may be wound up voluntarily by a shareholder resolution which is:

(a)   a special resolution; or

(b)   before 1 October 2007, when the changes in CA 2006 applied, an extraordinary resolution (ie 75% in favour, but a meeting need only be called on 14 days' notice – Companies Act 2006, ss 307, 283[1]) to the effect that the company cannot continue its business by reason of its liabilities and that it is advisable to wind up; or

(c)   an ordinary resolution in the (somewhat unusual) position where there is a special provision in the Articles of Association (eg if the company has a fixed term stated in the Articles).

1 Formerly CA 1985, ss 369, 378.

Members' and creditors' voluntary winding up

4.15   A voluntary winding up may be either a members' voluntary winding up or a creditors' voluntary winding up. A voluntary winding up will be a creditors' voluntary winding up unless a declaration of solvency has been sworn by the directors and filed with the Companies Registry[1]. A members' voluntary winding up may be converted to a creditors' winding up if it later becomes apparent that the company is in fact insolvent[2]. A voluntary winding up can also be converted to a court winding up[3].

1 IA 1986, ss 89, 90.
2 IA 1986, ss 95, 96.
3 IA 1986, s 124(5).

4.16   In a members' voluntary winding up, generally control of the winding up remains with the shareholders (eg appointment of liquidator, approval of actions, etc). In a creditors' voluntary winding up control passes to the creditors (eg right to override appointment of liquidator by the members and appointment of liquidation committee to oversee the liquidator).

4.17   The effect of appointment of a liquidator is that the powers of the directors cease (unless empowered to continue by the company or liquidator in a members' voluntary liquidation or the liquidation committee or creditors in a creditors' voluntary liquidation)[1].

1 IA 1986, ss 91(2) and 103.

All liquidations

4.18   In the case of a voluntary winding up, the company must cease to carry on business from the time of passing of the passing of the resolution for winding-up, unless it is necessary for a beneficial winding up[1]. The sanction of the court is needed for the liquidator to continue carrying on business in a court winding-up[2]. See further para 6.6 below.

1 IA 1986, s 87.
2 IA 1986, s 167(1)(a) and Sch 4, para 5.

4.19   The liquidator must gather in the assets of the company out of which the liquidation expenses will be taken. For these purposes company assets will not include assets held on trust or subject to a fixed charge (save for any equity of redemption remaining).

The House of Lords in *Buchler v Talbot: Re Leyland Daf*[1] ruled that the 'company's property' does not include floating charge assets, so that liquidation expenses may not come out of floating charge realisations. However, this decision was effectively reversed by the Companies Act 2006, which from 6 April 2008[2] inserted a new s 176ZA into IA 1986. This new section provides that winding-up expenses will be payable out of floating charge realisations (for liquidations starting after 5 April 2008).

Creditors then prove the amount of their debts as at the date the company went into liquidation (ie the date of the winding-up order or resolution) (Insolvency Rules 1986, rr 4.75(1), 4.76 – see Chapter 16 below). The liquidator realises the assets and distributes them in accordance with the prescribed order, as follows:

(a)   liquidation expenses have priority (IA 1986, ss 115, 156). Insolvency Rules 1986, r 4.218 sets out the order of priority between themselves;

(b)   preferential debts (IA 1986, s 175);

(c)   debts secured by a charge which, as created, was a floating charge (IA 1986, s 251; CA 2006, s 754; CA 1985, s 196);

(d)   ordinary, unsecured debts;

(e)   post-liquidation interest (IA 1986, s 189);

(f)   any deferred claims (Insolvency Rules 1986, r 12.3(2A)).

1 [2004] UKHL 9; [2004] 2 AC 298; [2004] 1 All ER 1289, HL.
2 See Sch 4, Pt 1, para 43(1) to the Companies Act 2006 (Commencement No 5, Transitional Provisions and Savings) Order 2007 (SI 2007/3495, as amended).

4.20   Special rules apply to secured creditors (Insolvency Rules 1986, rr 4.88, 4.95–4.99), foreign currency claims (r 4.91) and contingent or future claims (rr 4.86, 4.94 and 11.13). There are special rules:

●   for the liquidation of partnerships – see the Insolvent Partnerships Order 1994 (SI 1994/2421 as amended); and

●   on the insolvency of some utilities and industries and banks, insurers and other financial institutions..

RECEIVERSHIPS

4.21   The term 'receiver' is used in many differing senses. It is important to be aware of the precise meaning being used in any particular situation.

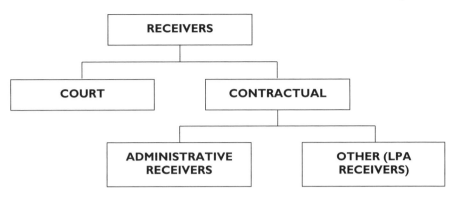

Court receivers

4.22   The appointment of a receiver by the court is an interim measure devised by the courts. In a similar manner to interim injunctions, a receiver is appointed by the court to take charge of property or a company in order to preserve the position pending resolution of some dispute.

Contractual receivers

4.23   These are a contractual device included within security documents (usually fixed and floating charges) as a means of realisation and enforcement of the security by enabling a receiver to be appointed to take charge of the company in a similar manner to court receivers, but without the need for a court order.

4.24   Essentially, the security will provide that the security holder is able to appoint a receiver and manager to receive income and manage the property of the company which has given the security. Obviously, the primary purpose of the appointment of such a receiver and manager is to recover the relevant secured amount. However, the security document will generally provide that the receiver is the agent of the company (so that he is able to manage its assets and continue its business, etc).

4.25   Statutory recognition of a contractual receiver has been given. The Law of Property Act 1925, s 101(1)(iii) implies a power to appoint a receiver (but not a manager) under a mortgage or charge made by deed. Such a receiver cannot (unless there is an express power in the deed), carry on the company's business – see *Richards v Kidderminster Overseers*[1].

1 [1896] 2 Ch 212 (North J).

4.26   Provisions were before 1986 included in the Companies Acts relating to receivers (or receivers and managers) appointed in relation to assets of companies. These were updated and are now generally found in the IA 1986, ss 33–41, 71. It is important to realise that these represent a limited codification of the regime applicable to receivers appointed in relation to security documents. The basic regime in relation to such receivers remains that of enforcement of security by contractual means.

4.27   Generally, where a receiver has been appointed under a floating charge, the receiver will take control of the business and assets of the company (but see the cases cited at para 26.36 below for a discussion of the residual area of competence of the directors). Unsecured creditors (such as employees) will not usually seek to enforce their claims (unless they wish to place the company in liquidation, say in order to contest the validity of the security under which the receiver is appointed) as they know they will rank behind the security.

The receiver's agency to carry on the business of the company will terminate if the company enters liquidation (but the receivership itself remains in effect). Any administrative receiver (see paras 4.28 and 4.29 below) must vacate office must vacate office if the company enters administration[1].

1 IA 1986, s 11 and Sch B1, para 41.

ADMINISTRATIVE RECEIVERS

4.28   This was a new categorisation, introduced in 1986, of certain types of contractual receivers appointed in relation to a company under a floating charge. They must be a receiver or manager of the whole (or substantially the whole) of a company's property – see the definition in IA 1986, s 29(2). They should not be confused with administrators (see para 4.32 below). Not all receivers will be administrative receivers.

Duties and powers of administrative receivers

4.29   Administrative receivers must be insolvency practitioners (see para 4.42 below) and are given certain enhanced duties and powers under the IA 1986, ss 42–49[1]. In particular:

(a)   administrative receivers are under a duty to obtain a statement of affairs from the officers of the company, to report to creditors and to form a creditors' committee (ss 47–49);

(b)   administrative receivers are given the general powers listed in Sch 1 to IA 1986 (unless the security document otherwise provides) (s 42);

(c)   administrative receivers are given power to dispose of charged property in certain circumstances (s 43);

(d)   administrative receivers may not be removed save with an order of the court (s 45).

1 See generally in relation to receivers, Picarda *The Law Relating to Receivers, Managers and Administrators* (Tottel Publishing, 2006).

4.30   With effect on and from 15 September 2003, the ability to appoint an administrative receiver was limited by the Enterprise Act 2002. Subject to limited exceptions, it ceased to be possible to appoint an administrative receiver. Instead a charge holder would need to enforce either by exercising a power of sale (ie without the insolvent company being able to carry on its business) or seek to appoint an administrator. This means that a floating charge holder who cannot appoint an administrative receiver cannot block an appointment of an administrator by appointing an administrative receiver (IA 1986, Sch B1, para 39).

4.31   The exceptions[1] where an administrative receiver can still be appointed after 15 September 2003 are:

- where the security was originally granted before 15 September 2003: and

- some finance structures.

1 See new IA 1986, ss 72A to 72H, inserted by the Enterprise Act 2002.

ADMINISTRATIONS

4.32   Administration[1] is an insolvency procedure which was new when introduced in 1986. It is designed to help in the rescue of companies (ie to avoid liquidation if possible). The reasons for this were:

(a)   liquidation can force the cessation of a continuing business because liquidators have only limited powers to keep the business running (see para 4.18 above). Indeed one reason for an administration may be to avoid the redundancies that would otherwise occur on a liquidation[2];

(b)   an administrative receivership may not have been possible (eg there is no existing security); and

(c)   an administrator is given power to seek some remedies previously only available to a liquidator (eg avoidance of unregistered charges, avoidance of transactions at an undervalue, etc).

1 See generally in relation to administrators, Picarda *The Law Relating to Receivers, Managers and Administrators* (Tottel Publishing, 2006).
2 See *Re Brooke Marine Ltd* [1988] BCLC 546 (Harman J) and *Re Harris Simons Construction Ltd* [1989] 1 WLR 368 (Hoffmann J).

Purpose of administration

4.33   Administration was originally designed as a mechanism to freeze the enforcement of a security or presentation of winding-up petitions, etc. It was intended to give a breathing space for negotiations to take place to see if the company or its business can be saved (or its assets more beneficially realised) without the irrevocable step of a winding up. The governing law for administrations was (before 2003) set out in ss 8 to 27 of IA 1986, but has now been moved (from 15 September 2003) by the Enterprise Act 2002 to Sch B1 to the Insolvency Act 1986. The relevant rules are in Pt 2 of the Insolvency Rules 1986[1], as amended.

4.34 An administration was, before 15 September 2003, only an interim measure. It was followed by liquidation or (if it succeeded) by the return of the company as a going concern or an arrangement with creditors (including a company voluntary arrangement (CVA) under Pt I of IA 1986 or a court scheme of arrangement under the Companies Act 2006, s 895, formerly CA 1985, s 425).

For administrations starting on or after 15 September 2003, IA 1986, Sch B1, para 3 deals with the purpose of an administration as follows:

'3(1)   The administrator of a company must perform his functions with the objective of—

(a)   rescuing the company as a going concern, or

(b)   achieving a better result for the company's creditors as a whole than would be likely if the company were wound up (without first being in administration), or

(c)   realising property in order to make a distribution to one or more secured or preferential creditors.'

Administrators in administrations starting on or after 15 September 2003 have increased powers, including an ability to pay dividends. In practice they may end up terminating the company.

1 SI 1986/1925, as amended.

Appointment of administrator

4.35 Before 15 September 2003, an administrator was appointed by order of the court following a petition presented by a creditor or (more usually, given the requirement to provide various information to support the petition) the directors or the company.

4.36 From 15 September 2003, the changes made by the Enterprise Act 2002 allow an administrator to be appointed out of court as well (although appointment documents are still filed at court).

4.37 The powers of the administrator are now in new Sch B1 to IA 1986. They were previously set out in the IA 1986, s 14 and Sch 1. The old provisions still apply to administrations starting before 15 September 2003 (see SI 2003/2093).

COMPANY VOLUNTARY ARRANGEMENTS (CVAS)

4.38 This was also a new procedure introduced in 1986. The procedure is set out in Pt I of the IA 1986 (and Sch 1A for certain small eligible companies) and Pt 1 of the Insolvency Rules 1986.

Proposal for voluntary arrangement

4.39 A proposal (containing prescribed information) is put forward by the directors (or a liquidator or administrator) to a nominee (who must be a qualified insolvency practitioner). The nominee, if he accepts the prospects of success of the proposal, files a copy with the court and then summons a meeting of the shareholders and creditors. A notice of meeting is accompanied by the proposal and statement of affairs. If the proposal is approved by meetings of the members and creditors, then the proposal binds each person who had notice of the meetings and was entitled to vote (IA 1986, s 5) save that:

(a) the court may overturn the proposal if it is challenged within 28 days on the basis that the creditor is unfairly prejudiced or there has been a material irregularity (s 6); and

(b) there are savings for the position of secured creditors (s 4(3)) and preferential creditors (s 4(4)).

4.40 In the case of a voluntary arrangement for a small company, a moratorium on legal proceedings can apply under Sch A1 to IA 1986 (inserted from 1 January 2003 by IA 2000). Aside from this, there are no provisions staying actions or proceedings while a voluntary arrangement is being approved. If there is a danger of a creditor taking action before approval is given, it would be usual to apply for an administrator to be appointed to give protection during the interim period.

4.41 If the proposal is adopted at the meetings, a supervisor (who may be and usually is the same person as the nominee) is then appointed to carry out the voluntary arrangement[1].

A voluntary arrangement can bind employees. The limitation in section 230, ERA 1996 restricting contracting-out of statutory rights (save in limited circumstances) does not apply to a CVA – *Re Britannia Heat Transfer Limited*[2].

1 IA 1986, s 7.
2 (2007) 21 February (Judge Norris QC). Noted in (2007) 23 Insolvency Law & Practice by James Morgan and Edward Pepperall.

COMMON FEATURES

4.42 Insolvency proceedings contain various common features (despite their differing aims) which are as follows:

(a) management of the company (or of the estate of a bankrupt) is in general (see para 26.36 below for exceptions) taken away from the directors (or bankrupt) and given to an insolvency practitioner (whether a liquidator, administrator, trustee in bankruptcy or administrative receiver);

(b) the relevant office holder (ie liquidator, administrator, administrative receiver, supervisor of a voluntary arrangement or trustee in bankruptcy) must be a qualified insolvency practitioner[1]. Part XIII of IA 1986 (ss 388–398) deals with the qualifications required. An insolvency practitioner will be an accountant (or perhaps, but unusually, a solicitor) who has been specially licensed by the relevant professional body;

(c)   certain powers are granted in common to insolvency practitioners. For instance, IA 1986, ss 233–237 contain certain powers in relation to supplies of utilities and getting control of property, etc. There are also various common implied powers under IA 1986, Schs 1 and 4;

(d)   some powers are given to certain types of insolvency practitioner only. For instance, certain powers are given to liquidators and administrators but not to receivers – for example, avoidance of antecedent charges and transactions (IA 1986, ss 238–246) and avoidance of unregistered charges (Companies Act 2006, ss 860–877)[2].

1   IA 1986, s 230.
2   Formerly Companies Act 1985, ss 395–409.

Position of insolvency practitioner

4.43   In all these insolvency proceedings, the relevant officer appointed to take over management of the affairs of the company or individual will be responsible for carrying out the purposes of the insolvency proceeding. In the case of a liquidation, this purpose will be realising assets and distributing the proceeds to creditors and members. In the case of an administration it will be for the relevant purpose of the administration (eg to preserve the position of the company for an interim period) and in the case of a receivership it will be to realise assets in order to repay the secured debt.

4.44   The insolvency practitioner, in carrying out these duties, commonly acts as agent of the company concerned. So far as the position of an employee (as a creditor and contracting party) is concerned, if the company is insolvent the employee's claims against the company may have little value. Conversely, if the employee (or other creditor) can establish a liability or responsibility on the part of the insolvency practitioner, then the chances of recovery are much enhanced. If this can be established, then either the insolvency practitioner will be personally liable to the employee or any claim may be established as an expense of the insolvency proceeding. Usually such expenses rank ahead of all other claims on the assets of the insolvent company – see Chapter 17 (Carrying on business: Insolvency expenses) below. The effect of this will be to prefer the claim of the employee ahead of even some secured creditors.

4.45   In practice, insolvency practitioners will be more willing to accept that a claim will rank as an insolvency expense than to accept that the insolvency practitioner has personal liability. Although an insolvency practitioner will usually have the right to be indemnified out of the assets of the insolvent company, he will be reluctant to incur possibly unlimited liability to a creditor (such as an employee) when this might not be covered by the relevant assets – see further Chapters 15 to 18 (Carrying on business) below.

CHAPTER 5

Effect of insolvency on legal proceedings and process

5.1   The effect of the commencement of insolvency proceedings or the appointment of an insolvency practitioner in relation to a company on legal proceedings against the company (whether existing or upon the issue of new proceedings) is summarised below.

Court liquidation

5.2   The presentation of a petition to wind up a company does not of itself affect other legal proceedings, but the leave of the court is needed to commence or continue any legal action or proceedings after a winding-up order has been made or a provisional liquidator (see para 4.13 above) appointed[1]. Leave may probably be given retrospectively – see para 5.23 below and *Re Linkrealm Ltd*[2].

1 IA 1986, s 130(2).
2 [1998] BCC 478 (Sir John Vinelott).

Voluntary liquidation

5.3   There is no provision affecting the commencement or continuation of legal proceedings in relation to a company incorporated in England and Wales[1] in voluntary winding up (whether members' or creditors'), although it is possible for the liquidator to seek directions from the court to stay proceedings under the IA 1986, s 112 – see eg *Re Dicksmith (Manufacturing) Ltd*[2].

1 Compare IA 1986, s 113 in relation to companies incorporated in Scotland.
2 [1999] 2 BCLC 686 (Judge Howarth QC).

Receivers

5.4   Legal proceedings against a company are unaffected by it going into receivership (whether administrative or not). In practice, given that the assets of the company will be subject to the charge (now fixed) under which the receiver was appointed, there will usually be little point in bringing or continuing proceedings.

Administrators

5.5   Following the presentation of a petition for an administration order against a company, the leave of the court is required for the commencement or continuation of legal proceedings against the company[1]. This does not apply to the presentation of a winding-up petition or the appointment of an administrative receiver[2].

In an administration starting on or after 15 September 2003, there is a similar interim moratorium where an application for administration has been made or where notice of intention to appoint an administrator has been filed at the court.

1 IA 1986, s 10(1) (pre 2003 administrations), Sch B1, para 44 (post 2003 administrations).
2 IA 1986, s 10(2) (pre 2003 administrations), Sch B1, para 44(7) (post 2003 administrations).

5.6   When a company is in administration[1], IA 1986 Sch B1, para 43(6) provides that:

'(6) No legal process (including legal proceedings, execution, distress and diligence) may be instituted or continued against the company or property of the company except—

(a)   with the consent of the administrator, or

(b)   with the permission of the court.'

For an administration starting before 15 September 2003[2], IA 1986 s 11(3)(d) was to similar effect, stating:

'(d) no other proceedings and no execution or other legal process may be commenced or continued, and no distress may be levied, against the company or its property except with the consent of the administrator or the leave of the court and subject (where the court gives leave) to such terms as aforesaid.'

1 Ie while the appointment of an administrator of the company has effect – see Sch B1, para 1(2)(a) – ie following the making of an administration order or appointment of an administrator.
2 Sch B1, para 43 applies to administrations staring on or after 15 September 2003 IA 1986, s 11(3)(d) continues to apply to administrations started before 15 September 2003.

5.7   Case law before 2003 on the old wording remains relevant. If anything the wording in para 43(6) is clearer than that in s 11(3)(d) in that the term "legal process" does not look to be limited by the term "legal proceedings". See for example the discussion by the EAT in *Carr v British International Helicopters Ltd*[1], discussing *Air Ecosse Ltd v Civil Aviation Authority*[2].

See also the Court of Appeal in *In re Rhondda Waste Disposal Ltd*[3] and in *Winsor v Bloom: In re Railtrack plc (in railway administration)*[4].

1 [1994] 2 BCLC 474, [1994] ICR 18, [1994] IRLR 212, [1993] BCC 855, EAT.
2 1987 SLT 751; (1987) 3 BCC 492, Court of Session (Inner House).
3 [2001] Ch 57, CA.
4 [2002] EWCA Civ 955; [2002] 1 WLR 3002, CA.

5.8   Case law indicates that legal proceedings or legal process requiring leave under para 43(6) will cover:

- criminal proceedings – *R v Dickson*[1] and *In re Rhondda Waste Disposal Ltd*[2];

- proceedings against a third party, but involving the company – *Biosource Technologies Inc v Axis Genetics plc*[3] (proceedings seeking revocation of a patent);

- proceedings in the employment tribunal – *Carr v British International Helicopters Ltd*[4];

- proceedings in an arbitration – *Bristol Airport plc v Powdrill*[5] and see also *Josef Syska (acting as the Administrator of Elektrim SA (in bankruptcy)) and Elektrim SA (in bankruptcy) v Vivendi Universal SA*[6] holding that arbitration proceedings are within the scope of being a "lawsuit pending" for the purposes of articles 4.3(f) and 15 of Council Regulation (EC) No 1346/2000 on Insolvency Proceedings.

1 [1991] BCC 719, CA, a case on the liquidation moratorium under s 130(2).
2 [2001] Ch 57, CA.
3 [2000] 1 BCLC 286; [2000] BCC 943 (Ferris J).
4 [1994] 2 BCLC 474, [1994] ICR 18, [1994] IRLR 212, [1993] BCC 855, EAT.
5 [1990] Ch 744; [1990] 2 All ER 493; [1990] BCLC 585, CA. In the later case of *ETI Euro Telecom International NV v Republic of Bolivia* [2008] EWCA Civ 880, the Court of Appeal held (at para 92) that arbitration was not within the term "proceedings" as used in the Civil Jurisdiction and Judgments Act 1982 (Interim Relief) Order 1997 (SI 1997/302), but that turned on the wording in the underlying Act which referred specifically to arbitration elsewhere.
6 [2008] EWHC 2155 (Comm) (Christopher Clarke J), on appeal [2009] EWCA Civ 677, CA.

5.9   Matters *not* requiring leave seem to include:

- serving notices under a contract, eg a notice making time of the essence, or a notice terminating the contract because of non-performance – *Re Olympia and York Canary Wharf Ltd, American Express Europe Ltd v Adamson*[1];

- an application for an extension of time for registration of a charge under CA 1985, s 404 (now CA 2006, s 873) – *In Re Barrow Borough Transport plc*[2],

- an application by a competitor airline to the Civil Aviation Authority for the revocation of air transport licences held by a company in administration – *Air Ecosse Ltd v Civil Aviation Authority*[3];

- a determination by the Rail Regulator (under s 17 of the Railways Act 1993) was not 'other proceedings' for the purposes of IA 1986, s 11(3)(d), as modified in relation to railway administrators by the Railways Act 1993 (although note that the expression "other proceedings" does not appear in IA 1986, Sch B, para 43) – *Winsor v Bloom: In re Railtrack plc (in railway administration)*[4];

- proceedings by the Traffic Commissioner to revoke a national operators licence (under the Goods Vehicles (Licensing of Operators) Act 1995) held by the company in administration – *Brian Hill Waste Management Ltd v Secretary of State for Transport*[5], although the decision seems to have turned partly on the fact that the relevant regulations envisaged action against an administrator.

- Proceedings against directors of the company or the insolvency practitioners themselves – *Re Rhondda Waste Disposal Ltd*[6].

1 [1993] BCLC 453 (Millett J).
2 [1990] Ch 227; [1989] BCLC 653 (Millett J).
3 1987 SLT 751; (1987) 3 BCC 492, Court of Session (Inner House).
4 [2002] EWCA Civ 955; [2002] 1 WLR 3002, CA.
5 decision of the Transport Tribunal on 30 January 2009, see www.transporttribunal.gov.uk.
6 [2001] Ch 57, CA at para [19].

STAY ON PROCEEDINGS BY THE PENSIONS REGULATOR?

5.10   It can be difficult for the courts to decide how the powers of a statutory regulator intersect with the statutory moratorium and the powers of an insolvency practitioner. If a liquidator or administrator is in place, can the Pensions Regulator still exercise its various statutory powers against the company or are they covered by the various statutory stays?

The two cases most on point here have allowed legal process to continue by a regulator against a company in administration. In *Air Ecosse Ltd v Civil Aviation Authority*[1] it was the Civil Aviation Authority and in *Winsor v Bloom*[2] it was the Rail Regulator. Both cases concerned ongoing use of powers by the relevant regulator in regulating the relevant industry.

1 1987 SLT 751; (1987) 3 BCC 492, Court of Session (Inner House).
2 [2002] EWCA Civ 955; [2002] 1 WLR 3002, CA.

5.11   In the case of the Pensions Regulator, the answer to the question as to whether leave is needed from the court or administrator/liquidator probably depends on what power is being exercised.

If the power is part of the general regulation of an on-going business (perhaps including the pension scheme), this points more towards allowing the Pensions Regulator to continue.

But conversely, if (say) the scheme has been frozen (as it will be if the company is an employer and a PPF assessment period has started) or the claim is against the company as a third party (eg a potential contribution notice against a holding company), then it is less easy to see that the proceedings should continue without leave. This latter case looks to be closer to the position of a contractual claim.

The cases discussed below in relation to other regulators (eg the Rail Regulator or the Civil Aviation Authority) seem mainly concerned with powers exercisable by the relevant regulator in relation to the company in administration while it was still carrying on the relevant business (ie running trains or aircraft). The need for the relevant regulator to be able, on policy grounds, to continue to regulate the company is clear.

Conversely, this is much less obvious in relation to a pension scheme where the only real claims by the Pensions Regulator against an insolvent company (eg as an employer or connected party) are likely to be monetary claims (eg civil penalties or contribution notices).

1 See Chapter 28 (PPF: Assessment Period) below.
2 See Chapter 37 (tPR Moral Hazard Powers) below.

5.12   In *Winsor v Bloom*, the Court of Appeal overturned the decision of the Vice-Chancellor and allowed an appeal by the Rail Regulator. The Court of Appeal held that a determination by the Rail Regulator could be made against a company in railway administration. The consent of the court or the administrators was not needed despite the provisions in s11(3)(d).

Lord Woolf (with whom the other two members of the Court of Appeal agreed) held:

> '5 In his judgment in *Bristol Airport plc v Powdrill* [1990] Ch 744, Sir Nicolas Browne-Wilkinson V-C (in a different context involving section 88 of the Civil Aviation Act 1982) considered the proper approach to the meaning of the critical phrase "other proceedings" in section 11(3)(d) of the 1986 Act. He said, at pp 765-766:
>
> > "In my judgment the natural meaning of the words 'no other proceedings … may be commenced or continued' is that the proceedings in question are either legal proceedings or quasi-legal proceedings such as arbitration. It is true that the word 'proceedings' can, in certain contexts, refer to actions other than legal proceedings, e g proceedings of a meeting … Further, the reference to the 'commencement' and 'continuation' of proceedings indicates that what Parliament had in mind was legal proceedings. The use of the word 'proceedings' in the plural together with the words 'commence' and 'continue' are far more appropriate to legal proceedings (which are normally so described) than to the doing of some act of a more general nature. Again, it is clear that the draftsman when he wished to refer to some activity other than 'proceedings' was well aware of the word 'steps' which he used in section 11(3)(c). The judge took the view that the words 'other proceedings' covered 'every sort of step against the company, its contracts or its property which may be taken and the intention of Parliament by section 11 is to prevent all such, without the leave of the court or the administrators'. In my judgment, however anxious one may be not to thwart the statutory purpose of an administration, the judge's formulation must be too wide. If the word 'proceedings' has this wide meaning, all the other detailed prohibitions in section 11(3) would be unnecessary. Moreover such a construction would introduce great uncertainty as to what constituted commencement or continuation of proceedings … In my judgment, the judge's view would produce an undesirable uncertainty which, in view of my construction of section 11(3)(c), it is unnecessary to introduce into the Act."
>
> 6 Before this court, both Mr Philip Sales on behalf of the Rail Regulator and Mr Gabriel Moss for the railway administrators agreed that this court was bound to follow the approach of Sir Nicolas Browne-Wilkinson V-C and that, in particular, "no other proceedings" for present purposes is to be treated as applying to proceedings which are "either legal proceedings or quasi-legal proceedings such as arbitration.'

Lord Woolf commented later (at para 33):

> 'Notwithstanding the making of the railway administration order, the Rail Regulator's role over the whole rail network and in relation to a company in administration remains the same. Because of his statutory responsibilities, the Rail Regulator is better placed to make an overall assessment of what is in the interests of the rail network than the railway administrators or even the court. I

would regard it as surprising if his supervisory role relating to the running of the railway as a whole should be subject to the control of the administrator or (other than by way of judicial review) the court.'

Lord Woolf went on (at para 35):

'35   In my view, Mr Moss's submission that an application under section 17 of the 1993 Act is very much in the nature of, or analogous to, an arbitration is misconceived. It is inconceivable that an arbitrator would be in a position where he was required to take into account considerations which could be not be in the interests of the parties to the arbitration but third parties namely rail users. The fact that the railway administrators cannot misuse their powers to withhold their consent does not mean that Parliament could have intended them to have powers over the Rail Regulator. It is to turn the Rail Regulator's role on its head to make him subject to the consent of a body, namely the railway administrators, who it is his responsibility to regulate while the administration continues.

36   While the relationship between section 17 and section 18 is inconsistent with the argument of the railway administrators, the position is different once the Rail Regulator has performed his function by making his direction. When it is known what his direction is, then there is no difficulty in making his application for assistance of the court as to the enforcement of that direction by legal proceedings subject to section 11(3)(d) of the 1986 Act.'

5.13   Lord Woolf finished his judgment by noting the decision of the Inner House of the Court of Session in Scotland in *Air Ecosse Ltd v Civil Aviation Authority*:

'Finally, I refer to the decision of the Inner House in *Air Ecosse Ltd v Civil Aviation Authority* (1987) 3 BCC 492. That decision is not binding on us but, as Sir Andrew Morritt V-C acknowledges, the views of the members of the Court of Session are entitled to the greatest respect. However, he considered that the context being considered was very different from that with which we are at present concerned. That may be so, but that case did involve a similar conflict to that which exists here between the role of an administrator and the role of regulator. As a consequence of section 11(3)(d) of the 1986 Act, the Civil Aviation Authority, in that case, was in a similar position to the Rail Regulator, in relation to granting of air transport licences to a company in administration. Mr Sales recognises that parts of that decision have not been followed in this jurisdiction, but submits that the conclusion of the Inner House that it was unlikely that Parliament would have intended to limit the powers that it had conferred on the Civil Aviation Authority by the terms of the 1986 Act is persuasive as to the proper approach to the issue here. I agree. The decision supports my approach to the present situation.'

5.14   **Sea Containers** In June 2007, the Determinations Panel of the Pensions Regulator had to consider the situation of Sea Containers as being in US Chapter 11 proceedings at the time that an FSD was being considered.
The panel commented[1]:

'32   We should add that we consider it wrong to suggest, as Mr Simmonds appeared to do, that the provisions of the 2004 Act which deal with FSDs and

Contribution Notices do not apply in the case of insolvency. We note, in this context, that it is specifically provided that the jurisdiction is exercisable "at any time": see section 45(2)(a) and (b) of the 2004 Act. Moreover, it seems to the Panel that those provisions are likely to be of particular significance in insolvency situations.'

This comment by the Determinations Panel is of course right, but seems not to deal with the point about the stay on proceedings applicable under IA 1986. It seems to me that more than a reference to being able to exercise a power 'at any time' is needed to override the moratorium provisions in IA 1986.

1 See http://www.thepensionsregulator.gov.uk/pdf/DNseaContainers.pdf

5.15   Later, in September 2008 in the US courts, following the issue of a financial support direction (FSD)[1] by the Pensions Regulator against Sea Containers, the US bankruptcy judge had to consider the effect of an FSD made against a company which was in Chapter 11 proceedings in the US.

In *Re Sea Containers et al*[2], Kevin J Carye (a United States Bankruptcy Judge) allowed the FSD claims to be proved in the bankruptcy. He held[1] (at pages 16 and 17)

'After reviewing the history of the Schemes' distress and recognizing that the relationship with TPR has developed in response to that distress, the Court concludes that it is reasonable to calculate the Schemes' claims as though the FSDs are valid. (See Exs. 35, 38, 54, 94, 137, 138, 139.) The Determinations Panel contemplated the impact of the automatic stay on the FSDs, and concluded that they should be issued though it would ultimately be for this Court to approve any proposed funding arrangement. (Ex. 139.) This Court concludes that the mere issuance of the FSDs does not violate the automatic stay, for the FSDs are issued by TPR, a statutorily created entity endeavoring to exercise its regulatory power. The FSDs resulted from communications of concern over funding expressed by the Scheme Trustees, but the Court does not believe that there was an underhanded collaboration between the Trustees and the Schemes at play. Rather, the FSDs reflect that the TPR was fulfilling its statutory objective of ensuring that pension schemes are properly funded and maintained.

Issuance of the FSDs, without more, does not amount to an attempt to collect a debt or assert a claim against the Debtors, but they do provide guidance as to the needs of the Schemes and therefore the pertinent considerations in valuing the Schemes' claims. Accordingly, the FSDs should not be ignored as invalid. Rather, the single, direct claim against SCL in the buyout rate amount that the Settlement proposes is an effective and reasonable manner by which to resolve the various potential claims of the Trustees and satisfy TPR and the Schemes. [footnote 11]

11 Moreover, even if, arguendo, the automatic stay, as a matter of United States' law, applies, the Debtors' legal expert, Jonathan Evans, a London, England barrister, testified without contradiction that, under applicable English law, such pension-related, regulatory proceedings were "exempt" from the automatic stay and would not "be enjoined by an English Court." (Hr'g Tr. May 28, 2008, 72:11-73:9, Tr. Ex. 16, ¶¶ 83-88 at pp. 35-37 (Evans' Expert Report)).'

It is not clear why the view was that the issue of a financial support direction by tPR was not a legal proceeding within the moratorium under IA 1986. In my view it looks pretty clear that such a claim would fall within the category of legal proceedings within IA 1986, s 130(2) (court liquidations) and definitely within the category of legal process within IA 1986, Sch B1, para 43(6) (administrations).

The issue of a financial support direction or contribution notice looks to be a formal legal proceeding similar to (say) an arbitration. The decision of the Pensions Regulator to issue such a notice is taken by the determinations panel at the Regulator (PA 2004, s 10) after that panel has considered submissions. That decision can itself be appealed to the Pensions Regulator Tribunal (PA 2004, s103). An appeal from the Pensions Regulator Tribunal can be made on a point of law to the Court of Appeal (or in Scotland, the Court of Session) – PA 2004, s 104.

Similar rules apply to the award of a civil penalty under PA 1995, s 10 and the other 'reserved regulatory functions' under PA 2004, Sch 2.

Preliminary steps leading up to a formal decision by the determinations panel (eg the issue of a warning notice by the Pensions Regulator) would also seem to fall within the moratorium.

It could be argued that policy reasons should mean that, as a matter of interpretation, the moratorium in IA 1986 should not be considered to apply to the various statutory powers of the Pensions Regulator. But, as stated above (see para 5.11), the better view is that the cases on the Rail Regulator or the Civil Aviation Authority are distinguishable from the position of a regulator such as the Pensions Regulator merely seeking to impose or deal with financial obligations.

As to whether monetary claims or orders issued by the Pensions Regulator are provable in an insolvency, see Chapter 16 (Carrying on business – provable debts) below.

1 See Chapter 37 (tPR Moral Hazard Powers) below.
2 [2008] PLR 413. See www.deb.uscourts.gov/Opinions/2008/seacontainers.06.11156. memorandum.order.pdf.

EMPLOYEE CLAIMS

5.16   In a case in 1993 before an industrial tribunal, *MSF v Parkfield Castings*[1], the tribunal considered that claims by employees for unfair dismissal and protective awards against a company in administration, were not prohibited by s 11(3)(d). The tribunal seems to have considered that the employees were not creditors of the company before any award had been made by a tribunal and, accordingly, fell outside the prohibition on proceedings in the section.

While it may be right that the employees may not be creditors (in the sense of having a provable claim – see Chapter 16 below), there is nothing in the moratorium provisions that limits the moratorium so that it only applies to a creditor – see eg *Biosource Technologies Inc v Axis Genetics plc*[2]

1 (1993) IDS Brief (February) (IT).
2 [2000] 1 BCLC 286; [2000] BCC 943 (Ferris J).

5.17   In 1994 in *Carr v British International Helicopters Ltd*[1], the EAT referred to the *Parkfield Castings* case and held that IT proceedings are within the moratorium. The EAT held that industrial tribunal proceedings are within the statutory moratorium. The EAT commented[2]:

> 'As *Quazi v Quazi* [1979] 3 All ER 987, [1980] AC 744 shows, the word "proceedings" may encompass procedures which fall outwith formal legal, or court, procedures, or proceedings analogous to formal legal proceedings. For the purposes of the present case, however, it is not necessary to extend the meaning of the term so far. It is quite clear that the term 'proceedings' covers not only court procedures but also analogous procedures such as arbitrations. There is, in our view, no reason why procedures before an industrial tribunal, whether initiated by individuals or by organisations, should not fall within the meaning of the term.'

1 [1994] 2 BCLC 474; [1994] ICR 18; [1994] IRLR 212; [1993] BCC 855, EAT.
2 [1994] 2 BCLC 474 at page 482.

5.18   The moratorium therefore applies to employee claims in the employment tribunal. Any other decision would be inconsistent with the decision in *Re Hartlebury Printers Ltd*[1] and the wide ambit of the prohibition held by the Court of Appeal in the case of *In re Rhondda Waste Disposal Ltd*[2].

1 [1993] 1 All ER 470 (Morritt J).
2 [2001] Ch 57, CA.

5.19   The expression 'legal process', as used in s 11(3) (and now in Sch B1, para 43), has also been widely interpreted in *Exchange Travel Agency Ltd v Triton Property Trust plc*[1] and in *Re Olympia and York Canary Wharf Ltd*[2]. The reasoning in these cases is wide enough so that legal process will cover employment tribunal claims.

1 [1991] BCLC 396, (Harman J).
2 [1993] BCLC 453 (Millett J).

5.20   In *Day v Haine*[1] the Court of Appeal held that a protective award (relating to dismissals before the start of the insolvency) was a provable debt, thus in effect confirming that the employees were creditors. This means that it is clear that their claims caught by the prohibition in Sch B1, para 43 (although the moratorium extends beyond just creditors).

1 [2008] EWCA Civ 626; [2008] ICR 1102; [2008] IRLR 642, CA.

GRANT OF LEAVE

5.21   Where the leave of the court is required to commence or continue legal proceedings (ie when the company is in a court liquidation and administration), a case for allowing proceedings to continue must be established (see para 5.25 below).

The leave is usually only granted by the relevant insolvency court – and not, say the employment tribunal. Under IA 1986, s 251, definitions used in the

Companies Acts used to have the same meaning when used in the first group of parts in the Insolvency Act 1986. CA 2006, s 1156[1] defines 'the court' as meaning in England and Wales, the High Court or a county court (in Scotland, the Court of Session or the sheriff court and in Northern Ireland, the High Court).

It seems that any division of the High Court can grant leave and it may be appropriate for the order to be made by the division in which proceedings are pending. In most cases, the more appropriate court will be the court with the conduct of the liquidation or administration.

Judge Anthony Thornton QC commented in *Joinery Plus Ltd v Laing Ltd*[2] that:

> '105   Secondly, the application for leave to commence or continue its claim may be made to the TCC [Technology and Construction Court] by Laing and may be made in these proceedings. This is because the Insolvency Act 1986 requires the leave of the court to be obtained without specifying which court is to grant that leave. The Chancery Guide states that that court should be the Companies Court. This is a statement of practice which, although usually to be followed, is not mandatory and can be overridden if the overriding objective suggests that another court is appropriate. Clearly, in this case, it would be disproportionate in costs to require the parties to apply to the Companies Court during these ongoing adjudication proceedings for leave and I will accede to Laing's application for leave to apply under section 11(3)(d) of the IA.'

See also the comments of the Court of Appeal in *Clarke v Coutts & Co*[3] that there was a wide jurisdiction for courts to give leave (in that case in the context of a bankruptcy and the moratorium in IA 1986, s 252(2)).

This power of another division of the High Court to give leave does not seem to extend to a tribunal (such as the Employment Tribunal).

1 Formerly CA 1985, s 744.
2 [2003] EWHC 439; [2003] All ER (D) 201 (Jan); [2003] BPIR 890 at para [105] (Judge Anthony Thornton QC).
3 [2002] EWCA Civ 943; [2002] BPIR 916; [2002] All ER(D) 98 (Jun), CA at paras [47] to [50].

5.22   Where the court gives permission for a transaction in relation to a company in administration under IA 1986, Sch B1, paragraph 43, it may impose a condition on or a requirement in connection with the transaction – para 43(7).

There is no express power given to an administrator to impose conditions when giving consent. However it seems that an administrator has such power. This seems implicit from the decision of the Court of Appeal in *Re Atlantic Computer Systems plc*[1] and is explicit in *Bristol Airport v Powdrill*[2].

1 [1992] Ch 505,CA.
2 [1990] Ch 744 at page 763C, CA.

Retrospective leave?

5.23   There are several first instance decisions that leave can be given retrospectively (ie after the proceedings etc have been issued) and that the proceedings are not a nullity. See the EAT decision (in an administration case) in *Carr v*

British International Helicopters Ltd[1] and the decision of Lindsay J in the bankruptcy case of *Re Saunders (a bankrupt)*[2]; followed in later bankruptcy and liquidation cases: *Razzaq v Pala*[3] and *Re Linkrealm Ltd*[4]. *Re Saunders* was also cited with apparent approval by the Court of Appeal in *Clarke v Coutts & Co*[5].

1 [1994] 2 BCLC 474, EAT, not following *Wilson v Banner Scaffolding Ltd* (1982) Times, 22 June.
2 [1997] Ch 60; [1997] 3 All ER 992 (Lindsay J), not following *Wilson v Banner Scaffolding Ltd* (1982) Times, 22 June and *Re National Employers Mutual General Insurance Association Ltd (in liq)* [1995] 1 BCLC 232 (Lightman J).
3 [1997] 1 WLR 1336; [1998] BCC 66 (Lightman J).
4 [1998] BCC 478 (Sir John Vinelott).
5 [2002] EWCA Civ 943; [2002] BPIR 916; [2002] All ER (D) 98 (Jun), CA.

5.24   But more recently, in 2006, in *Re Taylor (A Bankrupt); Davenham Trust Plc v CV Distribution (UK) Ltd*[1] Judge Kershaw QC (sitting as a High Court judge) extensively reviewed the authorities, including *Carr v British International Helicopters* and *Re Saunders* and refused to follow them, holding instead that retrospective leave could not be given. Judge Kershaw QC based his decision on the clear wording of the relevant statutes and followed two decisions to similar effect – the Court of Appeal in a 2005 mental health case: *Seal v Chief Constable of South Wales Police*[2] and the Northern Ireland Court of Appeal in a 1963 liquidation case (not cited in *Re Saunders*): *Boyd v Lee Guinness Ltd*[3].

In a later case, *Godfrey v Torpy*[4] Peter Leaver QC (sitting as a deputy judge of the High Court) distinguished *Re Taylor* on the facts and in any event would have followed *Re Saunders* in granting retrospective leave.

1 [2006] EWHC 3029 (Ch); [2007] Ch 150; [2007] 3 All ER 638 (Judge Kershaw QC sitting as a High Court judge).
2 [2005] 1 WLR 3183, CA, later upheld in the House of Lords (Lord Woolf and Baroness Hale dissenting) [2007] UKHL 31, [2007] 4 All ER 177, [2007] 1 WLR 1910, HL.
3 [1963] NI 49, CA (NI).
4 [2007] All ER (D) 181 (Apr) (Peter Leaver QC sitting as a deputy judge of the High Court).

WHEN WILL LEAVE BE GIVEN?

5.25   Where the leave of the court is required to commence or continue legal proceedings (ie court liquidations and administrations), a case for allowing process or proceedings to start or continue must be established.

In a liquidation context, Brightman LJ, giving the judgment of the Court of Appeal in *Re Aro Ltd*[1], said that s 231 of the Companies Act 1948, (the predecessor of IA 1986, s 130(2)), gave the court 'freedom to do what is right and fair in all the circumstances'.

This was followed by the Court of Appeal in *New Cap Reinsurance Corp Ltd v HIH Casualty & General Insurance Ltd*[2].

1 [1980] Ch 196; [1980] 1 All ER 1067, CA.
2 [2002] EWCA Civ 300; [2002] 2 BCLC 228, CA.

5.26   In an administration context, the burden is on the claimant to make out its case and to satisfy the court that it was inequitable for it to be prevented from commencing the intended proceedings – see the Court of Appeal in *Re Atlantic Computer Systems plc*[1].

Judge Anthony Thornton QC commented in *Joinery Plus Ltd v Laing Ltd*[2] that:

> '108. The guidelines set out the Re Atlantic Computers case are formulated for cases where proprietary rights, including security rights, such as those held by landlords, lessors or mortgagors, are sought to be exercised under the immediately preceding section 11(3)(c) of the IA (see page 542) . However, with appropriate modifications, these guidelines are clearly helpful in considering whether a creditor should be granted leave to enforce a trade debt under section 11(3)(d) of the IA.'

The relevant guidelines from the Court of Appeal in *Atlantic Computers* are:

(1) It is in every case for the person who seeks leave to make out a case for him to be given leave.

(2) The prohibition in section 11(3)(d) (now Sch B1, para 43) is intended to assist the company, under the management of the administrators, to achieve the purpose for which the administration order was made. If granting leave to a creditor to exercise his contractual or restitutionary rights and sue for the payment of his debt is unlikely to impede the achievement of that purpose, leave should normally be given.

(3) In other cases the court has to carry out a balancing (exercise, balancing the legitimate interests of the creditor and the legitimate interests of the other creditors of the company. This is to enable a balance to be struck between the statutory objective of enforcing the prohibition to assist the company to achieve the object for which the administration order was made and the statutory power to relax the prohibition where it would be inequitable for the prohibition to apply.

(4) Greater importance is given to those with proprietary interests than to those who are mere unsecured creditors. The underlying principle is that an administration for the benefit of unsecured creditors generally should not be conducted at their expense or at the expense of secured or preferential creditors save where this may be unavoidable and, even then, only to a limited extent.

(5) It will normally be a sufficient ground for the grant of leave if significant loss would be caused to the creditor by the refusal. However, that loss should not prevail if substantially greater loss would be caused to others by the grant of leave.

(6) In assessing these matters the court will have regard to matters such as: the financial position of the company, its ability to pay the debt, the administrators' proposals, the period for which the administration order has been in force and is expected to remain in force, the effect on the administration if leave were given, the effect on the applicant if leave were refused, the end result sought to be obtained by the administration, the prospects of that result being achieved, and the history of the administration so far.

(7) In considering these matters it will often be necessary to assess how proba-
     ble the suggested consequences are. Thus, if loss to the applicant is virtu-
     ally certain if leave is refused, and loss to others a remote possibility if
     leave is granted, that will be a powerful factor in favour of granting leave.

(8) The conduct of the parties may also be a material consideration.

(9) The court will not decide a dispute as to whether the debt in question is due
     unless it is a short point that must be decided.

1 [1992] Ch 505, CA.
2 [2003] EWHC 439; [2003] All ER (D) 201 (Jan); [2003] BPIR 890 at para [105] (Judge Anthony
   Thornton QC).

For example, in a claim for a protective award under TULRCA 1992, s 188
where the claim can only be determined by an employment tribunal and cannot
be determined in the liquidation, the judge will require to be satisfied that the
claim has some prima facie merit and prospect of success – see *Re Hartlebury
Printers Ltd[1]*, citing the Australian (NSW) case of *Capita Finance Group Ltd v
Rothmans Ltd[2]*.

In *Re Hartlebury Printers*, Morritt J had to deal with an application by trade
unions to bring claims for protective awards against a company in liquidation.
So the moratorium in s 130(2) was applicable. Morritt J commented (at page
477):

> 'The claims of the union and any derivative rights of the employees are only jus-
> tifiable before the industrial tribunal. Thus this is not a case where the rights
> sought to be enforced can be determined in the liquidation. In those circum-
> stances I should grant leave if I am satisfied that the claim the union wishes to
> advance has some prima facie merit and prospect of success. As Rogers CJ
> Comm D said in *Capita Finance Group Ltd v Rothwells Ltd* (1989) 15 ACLR 348
> at 349 in relation to a provision of the Companies (New South Wales) Code 1981
> in identical terms to s 130(2) of the Insolvency Act 1986:

> 'It is necessary to understand the rationale which buttresses the requirement for
> showing the existence of a prima facie case. The provisional liquidators and liq-
> uidator respectively are entitled to be protected from involvement in court pro-
> ceedings which may be perhaps only of a nuisance nature or which may be
> thought to be totally devoid of any substance. The resources of the company in
> liquidation should not be frittered away in defending baseless claims.'

1 [1983] 1 All ER 470 at 477 (Morritt J).
2 (1989) 15 ACLR 348 (Rogers CJ).

5.28 The 2008 case of *Sunberry Properties Ltd v Innovate Logistics Ltd (in
administration)[1]* involved an application for leave to bring proceedings against a
company in administration for breach of a lease. The Court of Appeal reviewed
the authorities and followed *Re Atlantic Computer Systems* in holding that the
burden was on the claimant to make out its case and to satisfy the court that it was
inequitable for it to be prevented from commencing the intended proceedings.

The court, in seeking to give effect to the statutory purpose of the administration,
had to conduct a balancing exercise of the legitimate interests of the lessor and the
legitimate interests of other creditors of the company. Accordingly, it was neces-

sary to compare the financial loss suffered by the landlord, if permission to commence proceedings was refused and he was temporarily denied the relief sought, with the loss suffered by the other creditors if permission to issue proceedings was granted. Account had to be taken of money paid by the administrators to compensate the landlord. See also the balancing exercise between an insolvent landlord and a tenant in *Somerfield Stores Limited v Spring (Sutton Coldfield) Limited*[2].

1 [2008] EWCA Civ 1261; [2009] 1 BCLC 145; [2008] All ER (D) 163 (Nov), CA.
2 [2009] EWHC 2384 (Ch); [2009] All ER (D) 68 (Oct) (Judge Purle QC sitting as a deputy judge of the High Court).

Employment tribunal claims

5.29   In *Carr v British International Helicopters Ltd*[1], the EAT held that proceedings (including those for a protective award) before the employment tribunal were within the prohibition in s 11(3).

There are quite short time limits for most claims before the Employment Tribunal. For example a claim for unfair dismissal must be brought within three months of the effective date of dismissal, or within such further period as the tribunal considers reasonable in a case 'where it is satisfied that it was not reasonably practicable for the complaint to be presented before the end of that period of three months' – ERA 1996, s 111(2).

Allowing a former employee to lodge his or her claim at the ET (but perhaps not proceed any further) would avoid the issue of the employee potentially being out of time for the ET claim. It may be that the fact that the employee could not bring the claim because of the insolvency moratorium would be a good reason for allowing a late claim in ET. But it seems to be silly to allow this to get in the way.

Note the comment in *Carr v British International Helicopters Ltd* at p 481 that the employee could apply to the ET for leave late on the basis that the moratorium meant that it was not reasonably practicable to apply earlier.

The EAT also commented that, in the case of claims for unfair dismissal or redundancy, leave should only rarely be refused. The EAT stated[2]:

> 'Further, it seems to us to be likely that it will only be in rare cases that it will be appropriate for consent to be refused to the bringing of proceedings for unfair dismissal, or in respect of redundancy. The guidelines set out by the Court of Appeal in *Re Atlantic Computer Systems plc (No 1)* [1991] BCLC 606, [1992] Ch 505 stress that the purpose of the prohibition in s 11 is to enable the company to achieve the object for which the order was made, and the purpose of the power to give leave is to enable the court to relax the prohibition where it would be inequitable for the prohibition to apply, and that the court has to balance the interests of the parties concerned. However, the employment protection legislation is designed, in the main, for the protection of employees. One of the principal objects of the legislation is to secure the speedy presentation and disposal of employees' claims, and it is very hard to see that, in the ordinary case, it is likely to be really prejudicial to the administration of the company that such matters should be so dealt with. That is perhaps particularly so in a case such as this, where the employee worked for the administrator for a substantial period after the administration order was made, and the administrator might well be regarded as having adopted his contract of employment.'

But it should be noted that this was a decision by the EAT, which is not the normal court or tribunal where the issue of leave will be decided. This will usually be the court with jurisdiction over the relevant insolvency process – see para 5.16 above.

1 [1994] 2 BCLC 474; [1994] ICR 18; [1994] IRLR 212; [1993] BCC 855, EAT.
2 [1994] 2 BCLC 474 at page 485.

5.30 In *Re Divine Solutions (UK) Ltd*[1] Hart J on the facts refused leave to an employee to continue a claim for unfair dismissal that seems to have already started before the company went into administration. Hart J held (at para [10]) that:

> 'It is for the applicant under s 11(3)(d) to establish why the leave should be granted and the function of the court is (it is agreed between counsel in their sub-missions to me) to perform a balancing act between the legitimate interests of the applicant creditor and those of the general body of creditors whose interests the administrators seek to protect by the discharge of their statutory functions.'

Hart J noted that the administration order against the company was limited in time to one year so that the inconvenience and prejudice to the employee would only apply for a limited period. The administration was likely to be succeeded by liquidation, and it would be for the liquidator at that stage to consider the employee's claim (this was a pre-September 2003 administration, so the administrator had only limited powers to deal with existing claims).

Hart J noted the applicant's claim that she would be adversely affected in her search for a new job by not being able to show that she was unfairly dismissed did not amount to a sufficient reason to give leave.

Hart J went on to note the administrators' contentions against the application that the administrators 'take the conventional view' that (at para [8], subdividing the paragraph):

> 'the administration order has been made for the purposes of either a voluntary arrangement, or a realisation of the assets',

> 'it is not part of the administrators' duties to agree, compromise, or otherwise to consider the claims of creditors, that being a matter to be dealt with either as part of the voluntary arrangement or by the liquidators in a liquidation and'

> 'if one were to make an exception for Mrs Powell (given the personal circum-stances which are urged to apply to her case) it would be difficult to resist making the same exception for all the other claimants and potential claimants in respect of their employment by the company in relation to which there have been a number of (as I understand it) claims intimated, and'

> 'even without those additional claims the need for the administrators to turn their attention to dealing with a matter outside the normal scope of their duties, namely the conduct of this unfair dismissal litigation, risk having such an impact on the administration as to render its essential purposes abortive and that they might therefore have to consider whether it was proper for the administration order to continue in force,'

Hart J held that it was not appropriate to grant leave, having regard to:

- the relatively limited period during which the stay under s 11 would continue to operate,

- the paucity of the evidence of prejudice filed on behalf of the applicant in this case, and

- the potential effect which granting leave would have on the discharge by the administrators of their functions during the period of the administration.

1 [2003] EWHC 1931; [2004] BCC 325; [2004] 1 BCLC 373 (Hart J).

5.31   In the case *In the matter of Angel Biotechnology Ltd (in administration) v Taylor*[1] Sir Andrew Morritt C held that the fact that the administrator had given an undertaking not to oppose an application to the employment tribunal to extend time to bring unfair dismissal proceedings (under s 111(2)(b) of ERA 1996) after the normal 3 month limit could not bind the employment tribunal, which would still have to be satisfied that it had not been reasonably practicable for the complaint relating to redundancy and unfair dismissal to be presented in time.

In those circumstances it had not been unreasonable for the registrar to permit (under para 43(6) of Sch B1 to IA 1986) previous employees of the company in administration to bring proceedings for unfair dismissal before the employment tribunal.

1 16 October 2007; [2007] All ER (D) 223 (Oct) Sir Andrew Morritt C. There seems not to be a full report of this decision, only a summary.

LEAVE FROM ADMINISTRATOR

5.32   In *Re Atlantic Computer Systems plc*[1] the Court of Appeal also gave guidance on the way administrators should exercise their discretion as to whether or not to give consent, holding[2]:

'An administrator is an officer of the court. He can be expected to make his decision speedily, so far as he can do so. He may be able at least to make an interim decision, such as agreeing to pay the current rents for the time being. The administrator should also make his decision responsibly. His power to give or withhold consent was not intended to be used as a bargaining counter in a negotiation in which the administrator has regard only to the interests of the unsecured creditors. When he refuses consent it would be helpful if, unless the reason is self-evident, he were to state succinctly why he has refused and also why he is not prepared to pay the rental arrears or at least the current rentals. A similar approach should be adopted by the administrator when secured creditors seek his consent to enforce their security. It should not be necessary, therefore, for the Companies Court to be swamped with applications under section 11, or for administrations to be subjected regularly to the expense and disruption of such applications. Should it become necessary for a lessor or owner of goods or the owner of a security to make an application to the court, the court has ample powers, by making orders as to costs and giving directions to the administrator, either as its own officer or as envisaged by section 17, to ensure that the applicant is not prejudiced by an unreasonable decision of an administrator.'

1 [1992] Ch 505, CA (see also *Bristol Airport plc v Powdrill* [1990] Ch 744; [1990] 2 All ER 493; [1990] BCLC 585, CA) .
2. At pages 529 and 530.

5.33   In Australia there are similar (but not identical) stays on proceedings if there is an administration or liquidation. The principles outlined by the courts in Australia are likely to be on the same lines as those in Great Britain.

It has been held that leave will only rarely be granted to sue a company in administration – see *Foxcroft v The Ink Group Pty Ltd*[1].

Foxcroft v The Ink Goup Pty Ltd[1] involved an application by an employee for leave to start proceedings in the Industrial Relations Court of Australia against his former employer (in administration). The employee argued that the court should examine the same factors that it would if it were considering an application for leave to proceed against a company in liquidation. Young J disagreed and dismissed the application saying:

> "There is…quite a big difference between a company in administration and a company in liquidation. A company in administration is seeking to continue to trade and is…seeking to maximise the chance of it remaining in business. A company in liquidation is one where the liquidator is seeking not to trade but to realise the company's assets as soon as possible for the best price, in order to be able to distribute the net available funds to the creditors and in some circumstance, the members."

Young J considered that to allow the employee to proceed with his action would not only take the administrator's attention from what he needs to do under the relevant legislation in a relatively short period of time, but it would also involve costs in running the legal action on behalf of the administrator, and perhaps give the employee some advantage over other creditors or potential creditors.

Young J commented, "it seems to me that an application [for leave] will rarely be granted". Young J added that where the liability the subject of the intended proceedings is insured, the administrator would normally consent or the court will give conditional leave, but that outside this field it was hard to see situations where it would be proper to grant leave, though doubtless there are such situations.

See the paper by Patrick Holmes and David Salter "Should I stay or should I go?"[2].

1 (1994) 12 ACLC 1063; (1994) 15 ACSR 203 (Young J). .
2 Given in Sydney on 2 March 2005 at the Corporate Insolvency & Restructuring forum. Available on the web at: www.aar.com.au/pubs/pdf/insol/pap12may05.pdf.

5.33   In *Buckingham v Pan Laboratories (Australia) Pty Limited (in liquidation)*[1], Jacobson J summarised the principles that should be followed if considering a grant of leave in a liquidation case:

> 'The principles which govern the exercise of the discretion to grant leave

65 In *Re Sydney Formworks Pty Ltd* [1965] NSWLR 646 at 649-650, McLelland, CJ in Eq, when dealing with a predecessor of the existing s 471B of the Act, said that the obvious intention of the section is:-

> "to ensure that the assets of the company in liquidation will be adminis-tered in accordance with the provisions of the Companies Act and that no person will get an advantage to which, under those provisions, he is not properly entitled, and to enable the Court effectively to supervise all claims brought against the company which is being wound up."

66 In *Re A J Benjamin (In Liq.) and The Companies Act* (1969) 90 WN (Pt 1) (NSW) 107 at 109-110, Street J said:-

> "Where a company is being wound up as an insolvent company it is recog-nized that the legislative policy contemplates the assets of the company being taken under the control of a liquidator and administered with due regard to the rights inter se of the creditors of the company. Independent actions by creditors are not encouraged in a winding up. Responsibility for satisfying the rights of creditors is placed upon the liquidator. ... Leave is not to be withheld simply and solely as a punishment: the primary consid-eration is the enabling of an orderly winding up. If no prejudice, procedural or substantive, will flow to those having interests in the winding up, an applicant has a strong case for gaining the leave he seeks."

67 In an often cited passage from the judgment of McPherson J in *Ogilvie-Grant v East* (1983) 7 ACLR 669 at 672, his Honour said that the preferable explanation for the requirement of leave is that a company in liquidation should not be subject to a multiplicity of actions which would be expensive and time consuming.

68 In *Vanguard Pty Ltd (in Liq) v Fielding* (1992-93) 10 ACSR 373 a Full Court (Wilcox, Burchett and Beazley JJ) reviewed the authorities on the question of the evidence which is required to support the grant of leave. Their Honours held at 380 that it is unnecessary to demonstrate a prima facie case against the company in the technical sense of that term. Their Honours said at 380 that the test to be applied is akin to that which is used for the grant of interlocutory relief. That is to say, the evidence must demonstrate that there is a serious question to be tried.

69 In *Nommack (No 100) Pty Ltd v FAI Insurances Ltd (in Liq)* (2003) 45 ACSR 215, Burchett J said at 221 that the authorities establish that the factors which determine whether it is appropriate to grant leave include: the amount and seri-ousness of the claim, the degree of complexity of the legal and factual issues involved and the stage to which proceedings, if already commenced, have pro-gressed.'

1 [2004] FCA 597 (Jacobson J).

5.34   In the Australian case *J F Keir Pty Ltd v Priority Management Systems Pty Ltd*)[1], Rein JA discussed (at paras [8] and [9]) the position in relation to whether or not to grant leave in an administration:

> '8 .... I have also found helpful the notes to s 440D in "Corporations Legislation 2007", J R Harris and R Baxt, Lawbook Co, in which the learned authors set out at [440D.30] the matters that will be taken into account namely:

1.   Whether the claim has a solid foundation and gives rise to a serious dispute.

2.   Whether the administrator would be unreasonably distracted from his or her statutory duties and be obliged unnecessarily to incur substantial legal costs.

3.   Whether the company is insured against the liability the subject of the claim.

4.   Who appointed the administrator.

5.   Whether the applicant will suffer any disadvantage if leave is not granted.

6.   Whether there are good reasons for allowing a creditor to depart from the general intention of Part 5.3A which is that a creditor ought not be able to take action against the company in such circumstances.

9 In *Auburn Council v Austin Australia Pty Ltd (in liq)* [2007] NSWSC 130 at [128] and *Complex Pty Ltd v Auslat Properties Macquarie Waters Pty Ltd* [2007] NSWSC 435 at [15], Einstein J approved the statement of general principles in "Ford's Principles of Corporations Law", Prof H A J Ford, Justice R P Austin and Prof I M Ramsay, LexisNexis, relevantly noting on the question of factors which the court might consider:

> 'x. there are many factors that the Court might consider, including the amount and seriousness of the claim, the degree of complexity of the legal and factual issues involved and importantly, the stage to which the proceedings, if already commenced, may have progressed [cf *Ogilvie-Grant v East* (1983) 7 ACLR 669 at 672]. [see generally *Oceanic Life Ltd v Insurance and Retirement Planning Services Pty Ltd (in liq)* (1993) 11 ACSR 516 at 522].'

1 [2007] NSWSC 748 (Rein AJ).

CHAPTER 6

Effect of insolvency proceedings on employees

6.1   The effect on contracts of employment of the entry of an employer into insolvency proceedings differs between the various types of proceedings.

LIQUIDATIONS

Court winding up

6.2   The effect of the making of a winding-up order by the court is that, from the date of its publication[1], the order has the effect of automatically dismissing all the employees of the company with immediate effect[2].

1 See *Re General Rolling Stock Co, Chapman's case* (1866) LR 1 Eq 346 (Lord Romilly MR).
2 See *Re General Rolling Stock Co* (1866) LR 1 Eq 346, *Re Oriental Bank Corpn, MacDowall's case* (1886) 32 ChD 366 (Chitty J) and *Commercial Finance Co Ltd v Ramsingh-Mahabir* [1994] 1 WLR 1297, PC.

6.3   The reason for this is unclear, but the principle seems too long-standing to be likely to be overturned now by a court. It has been suggested that the winding-up order constitutes notice to the employees that the company is unable to perform its part of the contract and the employees are deemed to accept this repudiation. Alternatively, it has been argued that the courts have desired to free employees from the obligations of continuing to serve a doomed employer. These arguments would however be equally applicable to a creditors' voluntary winding up (where automatic termination does not apply –see para 6.8 below).

The courts in Australia have refused to follow the similar principle in cases involving the appointment of a receiver by the court – see para 6.14 below.

It might be argued that the enactment of the transfer of undertakings legislation (from 1981) – see Chapters 19 to 24 below – could mean that the courts should revisit this automatic dismissal principle on the basis that the business of the company could be transferred (although any such argument is weakened by the fact that the insolvency provisions in TUPE 2006 mean that TUPE is unlikely to apply in a liquidation).

6.4   All employees will have their contracts terminated on a court winding up, including a managing director[1].

1 *Fowler v Commercial Timber Co Ltd* [1930] 2 KB 1, CA.

6.5   Dismissals which take effect on the making of a winding-up order by a court involve a breach of contract by the company for which the employee is entitled to claim damages, effectively by means of a proof of debt in the liquidation[1]. The employee's claim is subject to the usual contractual duty to mitigate[2]. It is not usually relevant that the employee has assisted the winding up (eg voted for any relevant resolution)[3].

1 See, for example, *Re RS Newman Ltd* [1916] 2 Ch 309, CA.
2 See *Re Gramophone Records Ltd* [1930] WN 42; 169 LT Jo 193; 69 L Jo 201. Note also that mitigation may not be required if there is a contractual payment in lieu of notice (PILON) provision – see paras 2.28 to 2.36 above.
3 *Fowler v Commercial Timber Co Ltd* [1930] 2 KB 1, CA.

6.6   If the liquidator continues the business of the company, then it seems that the liquidator and the employee can agree that there is no termination and employment with the company continues[1].

1 See *Re English Joint Stock Bank, ex p Harding* (1867) 3 Eq 341 (Wood V-C); *Re Oriental Bank Corp; MacDowall's case* (1886) 32 ChD 366 (Chitty J); *Reid v The Explosives Co Ltd* (1887) 19 QBD 265, CA; the Australian case of *Re Associated Dominions Assurance Society Pty Ltd* (1962) 109 CLR 512 (Taylor J); *Powdrill v Watson* [1995] 2 AC 394 at 440G, HL; and in Ireland, Hamilton J in *Donnelly v Gleeson* (1978).

6.7   The Enterprise Act 2002 introduced amendments into IA 1986 from September 2003 so that in some cases a winding-up can be converted into an administration[1]. If this occurs, the (now) administrator may want to keep employing the relevant employees and so avoid the redundancy and dismissal claims that otherwise would be triggered as a result of the court winding-up. This may involve a waiver of the dismissal and re-engagement of the employees (with their consent). The issues are discussed in the newsletter 'Dear IP' issued by the Insolvency Service in December 2003[2].

In Australia a similar issue (on redundancy in a receivership) arose in *McEvoy v Incat Tasmania Pty Ltd*[3]. In that case Finkelstein J held that employees who were retained and not made redundant at the start of the receivership had no preferential claim to a redundancy amount that would have been payable had they in fact then been made redundant.

1 See paras 37 and 38 of Sch B1, IA 1986.
2 See Article 4 of Chapter 11, available at the Insolvency Service website: www.insolvency.gov.uk/insolvencyprofessionandlegislation/dearip/dearipmill/chapter11.htm#16.
3 [2003] FCA 810, 21 ACLC 1463 (Finkelstein J). See also paras 8.47 and 12.35 below.

Voluntary winding up

6.8   Unlike the position in a court winding up (see para 6.2 above), generally the entry by an employer company into voluntary winding up (whether members' or creditors') by the passing of the appropriate resolution (see para 4.14 above) does not have the effect of automatically terminating the contracts of employment[1].

However, the liquidator in a voluntary winding up has only a limited power to continue to carry on the business of the company so far as it is necessary for the beneficial winding up of the company[2]. See *Re Wreck Recovery and Salvage Co*[3] and *Re Great Eastern Electric Co Ltd*[4] in relation to the limits on the power of liquidators to carry on business.

Accordingly, in practice, the effect of the passing of a resolution for the voluntary winding up of a company is that the company is likely to cease to carry on business after a short time at which point the employment of all employees will also cease[5].

1 See *Midland Counties District Bank Ltd v Attwood* [1905] 1 Ch 357 (Warrington J); *Gerard v Worth of Paris* [1936] 2 All ER 905, CA, the Australian case of *Re Matthew Bros Ltd* [1962] VR 262 and *Fox Bros (Clothes) Ltd v Bryant* [1979] ICR 64, EAT.
2 IA 1986, s 87 and Sch 4, para 5.
3 (1880) 25 ChD 353, CA.
4 [1941] Ch 241 (Simmonds J).
5 See *Reigate v Union Manufacturing Co (Ramsbottom) Ltd* [1918] 1 KB 592 at 606, CA.

RECEIVERS

Receivers appointed out of court

6.9   A receiver appointed out of court under a power given in a security document (usually a floating charge) is almost always constituted by the security document, as the agent of the company and not of his appointor (at least until the appointment of a liquidator)[1]. Accordingly, there is no change in the identity of the employer of relevant employees and usually no termination of their employment[2]. Lightman J commented at first instance in *Leyland DAF*[3] that insolvency may be a general anticipatory breach entitling an employee (or supplier) to treat the contract as discharged. He referred on this to *Re Phoenix Bessemer Steel Co*[4].

There will, however, be a dismissal if the company ceases to carry on business – see *Re Foster Clark Limited's Indenture Trusts*[5] or if there is a court liquidation, but note now the effect of TUPE (see Chapters 19 to 24 below) if there is a transfer of an undertaking.

1 IA 1986, s 44(1)(a) also provides that an administrative receiver is deemed to be the agent of the company, unless and until the company goes into liquidation.
2 See *Powdrill v Watson* [1995] 2 AC 394 at 440G, HL; *Re Mack Trucks (Britain) Ltd* [1967] 1 WLR 780 (Pennycuick J); *Deaway Trading Ltd v Calverley* [1973] 3 All ER 776 (NIRC); *Nicoll v Cutts* [1985] BCLC 322, CA and, in Australia, *James Millar Holdings Ltd v Graham* (1978) 3 ACLR 604.
3 [1995] 2 AC 394 at 407 (Lightman J).
4 (1876) 4 ChD 108, CA.
5 [1966] 1 All ER 43 (Plowman J).

6.10   The position may be different if the appointment of the receiver is inconsistent with the position of the employee. For example, it has been held that the appointment of a receiver will normally have the effect of automatically discharging and terminating the employment of a managing director, given that the receiver will take over control of the management of the company and that this will, in effect, mean that the managing director has no further duties[1]. This rule appears to apply both when the receiver is an administrative receiver and when the receiver is not an administrative receiver. It has been argued, however, that the appointment of a receiver in these circumstances should not automatically terminate employment, but should rather be treated as a repudiatory breach by the company entitling the employee to elect either to treat his contract as ended, or conversely entitling him to waive the breach and continue in employment.

1 See *Re Mack Trucks (Britain) Ltd* [1967] 1 WLR 780 (Pennycuick J) and *Griffiths v Secretary of State for Social Services* [1974] QB 468 (Lawson J).

6.11   Where a receiver has been appointed and a liquidator is subsequently appointed, this will terminate the receiver's authority to continue to carry on the business as agent of the company and will usually operate to terminate the employment of the employees (see para 6.2 above)[1].

1 See *Deaway Trading Ltd v Calverley* [1973] 3 All ER 776, NIRC.

Court-appointed receiver

6.12   The position differs in relation to a receiver appointed by order of the court. In this case the assets of the company pass under the control of the receiver. The court-appointed receiver is not the agent of the company, but is an officer of the court[1].

1 See *Burt, Bolton & Hayward v Bull* [1895] 1 QB 276, CA and *Moss Steamship Company Ltd v Whinney* [1912] AC 254, HL.

6.13   The English cases indicate that the effect of the appointment of the court receiver is to terminate all contracts of employment[1] in a similar way to that applying on the making of a winding-up order by the court (and subject to the same issues – see para 6.3 above).

1 See *Reid v The Explosives Company Ltd* (1887) 19 QBD 265, CA and comments in *Re Foster Clark Limited's Indenture Trusts* [1966] 1 WLR 125 (Plowman J) and *Nicoll v Cutts* [1985] BCLC 322, CA.

6.14   However, more recently, the Courts in Australia have refused to follow this approach. In *Sipad Holding DDPO v Popovic*[1] Lehane J described it as 'by no means self evidently right or convincing'. Instead he held that the issue of whether or not the appointment of a court receiver had effect to terminate contracts of employment should depend on the facts of each case (ie in effect the same treatment as for an out of court receiver). Lehane J preferred to follow Beech J in *International Harvester Export Co v International Harvester Australia Ltd*[2] and the more general rule in relation to contracts in *Parsons v Sovereign Bank of Canada*[3].

1 [1995] FCA 1737; (1996) 12 ACLC 307 at 309. Noted in (1996) 2 Receivers, Administrators & Liquidators Quarterly 267.
2 [1983] 1 VR 539 (Beech J).
3 [1913] AC 160, PC.

6.15   In *South Western of Venezuela (Barquisiment) Railway Co*[1] two directors were appointed as receivers and allowed remuneration by the court. The company's articles of association also contained provision for directors to be paid. Buckley J held that the two directors were entitled to the pay for being a director during the receivership period as well as the remuneration for being a receiver, but it is arguable that the decision is inconsistent with the termination of employment contracts envisaged in *Reid v The Explosives Co Ltd*[2].

1 [1902] 1 Ch 701 (Buckley J).
2 (1887) 19 QBD 264, CA.

ADMINISTRATORS

6.16   The effect on employees of the appointment of an administrator is similar to the effect on them of an appointment of a receiver out of court. The employment by the company is not terminated – see the decision of Lord Browne-Wilkinson in *Powdrill v Watson*[1]. An administrator, like a receiver appointed out of court, is the agent of the company[2].

1 [1995] 2 AC 394 at 448F, HL. See Chapter 18 (Carrying on business – adopted employment contracts) below.
2 IA 1986, s 14(5) (pre-15 September 2003 administrations) and Sch B1, para 69 (post-14 September 2003 administrations).

6.17   IA 1986, Sch B1, para 99 (IA 1986, s 19 for pre-2003 administrations) contains provisions which deal with adoption of employment contracts (these provisions give a similar statutory position to that of an administrative receiver – see Chapter 18 (Carrying on business – adopted employment contracts) below. This is consistent with the fact that often the primary purpose of the appointment of the administrator is to preserve (or give the chance of preserving) the continuation of the business of the company.

6.18   In *Re Atlantic Computer Systems plc*[1], the Court of Appeal preferred to analyse the position of an administrator in relation to unsecured claims as being closer in most respects to that of a liquidator than to that of a receiver (see para 17.47 below). However, in relation to employees the effect of the appointment of an administrator is more like the effect of the appointment of an administrative receiver. Existing employment contracts are not thereby automatically terminated, unless perhaps the specific employment contract is inconsistent with the administration (by analogy with the receivership case of *Re Mack Trucks (Britain) Ltd*[2] – see para 6.10 above).

1 [1992] Ch 505, CA.
2 [1967] 1 WLR 780 (Pennycuick J).

DECISION TO TERMINATE

6.19   In those situations where the appointment of the relevant insolvency practitioner does not automatically result in termination of contracts of employment, it may still, of course, be the case that the insolvency practitioner (acting as controller of the company) decides that contracts of employment should be terminated. In such a situation, the issue for the employee (and the insolvency practitioner) is the nature of the rights of the employee both as against the company and, potentially, as against the insolvency practitioner himself.

6.20   Obviously, where the company is insolvent in the sense of being unable to pay its debts, the employee will be in a better position if:

●   the employee's claim is given priority over other unsecured claims; or

●   some party other than the company (eg the government or the insolvency practitioner) is placed in a position of liability as well as the company.

6.21   The position on termination of employment, the nature of claims against the company (in particular for preferential debts) and claims against the government (in particular the National Insurance Fund) are dealt with below (see Chapters 7 to 13 below).

6.22   However, the insolvency practitioner may decide (if he or she has the power) that it is in the interests of the insolvency to continue the business and for the company to continue to employ all or some of the employees. The rights of employees in this situation are also discussed below (see Chapter 15 (Carrying on business) below).

PAYMENTS PRIOR TO APPOINTMENT OF INSOLVENCY PRACTITIONER

6.23   In certain circumstances, in order to protect the position of creditors, provision is made in the Insolvency Act 1986 for the insolvency practitioner (in particular an administrator or a liquidator) to be able to reverse transactions and payments that have been made before his or her appointment.

6.24   There are two main sets of statutory provisions[1] dealing with this:

(a)   IA 1986, s 127 which provides that, in a court winding up, any dispositions of the company's property made after the commencement of the winding-up (which under s 129 will in most cases be the date of the presentation of a winding-up petition) and before the date of appointment of the liquidator are made void unless approved by the court (similarly IA 1986, s 10 and para 43 of Sch B1 in the case of an administration); and

(b)   IA 1986, ss 238 and 239 which are applicable to an administration or a liquidation (but not a receivership) and provide for the invalidation of a pre-insolvency transaction if it is at an undervalue (s 238) or constitutes an undue preference (s 239), providing certain conditions are fulfilled.

1 See generally *Vulnerable Transactions in Corporate Insolvency* (Hart Publishing, 2003, Eds John Armour and Howard Bennett).

6.25 There is no reason, in principle, why these provisions are not applicable to transactions with employees.

Insolvency Act 1986, s 127

6.26 There seems to be no automatic rule that payment of remuneration to employees will be validated for the purpose of s 127 (see, for example, *Re International Cable Co*[1]): the usual rules will apply. If the payments are necessary for the company's business to continue and such continuation of the business is in the interests of the general body of creditors then it seems that the court will usually validate the payments[2].

1 (1892) 8 TLR 307 (Stirling J).
2 See *Re Gray's Inn Construction* [1980] 1 WLR 711, CA; *Denney v John Hudson & Co Ltd* (1992) BCC 503, CA and the Australian cases of *Tellsa Furniture Pty Ltd (In Liq) v Glendare Nominees Pty Ltd* (1987) 9 NSWLR 254; *Adelaide Truss & Frame Pty Ltd v Bianco Hiring Services Pty Ltd* (1993) 11 ACLC 192, *Home v White* (1993) 11 ACLC 783 and *Prospect Electricity v Advanced Glass Technologies of Australia Pty Ltd* [1996] NSWSC 510; (1996) 14 ACLC 1721, NSWCA.

Insolvency Act 1986, ss 238 and 239

6.27 In relation to ss 238 and 239, in practice, payments of normal remuneration made to employees during the relevant periods before the formal insolvency in which transactions can be challenged (either two years in the case of 'connected persons' or six months in the case of other persons before insolvency) are unlikely to be challenged by the insolvency practitioner unless there is some unusual element (eg the payment is considered to be excessive) or the employee concerned is sufficiently senior to constitute, in effect, an 'insider', and thus a person who, in effect, the directors desired to prefer[1].

1 See *Re MC Bacon Ltd* [1990] BCLC 324 (Millett J), *Re Beacon Leisure Ltd* [1992] BCLC 585 (R Wright QC), *Re Fairway Magazines Ltd* (1992) BCC 924 (Mummery J) and *Re Ledingham-Smith* [1993] BCLC 635 (Morritt J).

National minimum wage

6.28 During the passage of the National Minimum Wage Act 1998 through Parliament, the Solicitor General (Lord Falconer) commented that employers could be expected to pay the minimum wage ahead of other civil debts (see para 9.44 below). The existence of the relevant penalties for failure to pay the NMW could be a factor for the courts in deciding whether to validate payments.

Employee as a connected person

6.29 It is generally easier for an insolvency practitioner to rely on ss 238 and 239 where the other party is a person 'connected' or 'associated' with the company within the meaning of IA 1986, ss 249 and 435[1].

1 See generally on the difficulties with these sections, Chapter 41 below.

National minimum wage

6.30   Employees are usually connected persons (IA 1986, ss 249, 435(4)) but are not treated as connected for the purpose of:

● the presumption as to undue preference – s 239(6), or

● establishing the relevant time of a transaction at an undervalue or the giving of an undue preference – see s 240(1)(a).

Perhaps rather oddly, the presumption in s 240(2) that, in the case of a connected person, the company is unable to pay its debts, applies to employees – there is no exclusion in s 240(2).

6.31   For an example of this see the decision of the Court of Appeal in *Katz v McNally*[1] where directors were forced to repay the amount that the company had paid to them in respect of various loan accounts because they could not rebut the presumption that the payments were an undue preference. Similarly, see the decision of Hazel Williamson QC (sitting as a deputy High Court judge) in *Re Brian D Pierson (Contractors) Ltd*[2].

1 [1999] BCC 291, CA, on appeal from *Re Exchange Travel (Holdings) Ltd (No 3)* [1996] 2 BCLC 524 (Rattee J).
2 [1999] BCC 26 (Hazel Williamson QC).

Pension trustee as connected person

6.32   In *Re Thirty-Eight Building Ltd (No 1)*[1] Hazel Williamson QC held that a pension scheme with five trustees was not connected with the company. Accordingly, the shorter (six-month) period to challenge payments to the scheme as a preference applied. Four of the five trustees were connected (two of them owned the company and the other two were their children) but the fifth was not (it was an independent trustee, presumably as then required by the Inland Revenue as part of its approval process for a small self-administered scheme).

1 [1999] 1 BCLC 416; [1999] OPLR 319 (Hazel Williamson QC).

6.33   The deputy judge held that the fact that one of the trustees was not connected meant that the trustees as a body were not connected, even though the first four trustees were the only beneficiaries under the scheme (IA 1986, s 435(5)(b) excludes pension trustees from the usual rule that trustees are deemed to be connected if a beneficiary under the trust is a connected person).

6.34   The deputy judge expressly reserved the position on the interpretation of s 435(5)(b) in a case where all the trustees are connected to the company.

6.35   The deputy judge, in a later judgment *Re Thirty-Eight Building Ltd (No 2)*[1] refused to review or vary her earlier decision. She held that it was immaterial that the trustees had to act by a majority (ie not unanimously) or that the company could remove the independent trustee.

1 [2000] 1 BCLC 201 (Hazel Williamson QC).

6.36 There may be a contrast to be drawn between the decision in *Re Thirty-Eight Building Ltd* with the decision of Neuberger J in *Re Torvale Group Ltd*[1]. He held that a transaction involving five trustees was invalid under s 322A(2) of the Companies Act 1985[2] for infringing a provision in the articles of association even though only one of the five trustees was a director. Neuberger J validated the transaction (acting under s 322A of the Companies Act 1985) in the circumstances of the case.

1 [1999] 2 BCLC 605 (Neuberger J).
2 Now CA 2006, s 41.

6.37 It would also be possible for an employee to be forced to repay amounts to the company if these had been paid in breach of the duties of the directors to the company and the employee was aware of this. See, for example, *Re Halt Garage (1964) Ltd*[1] where remuneration paid to a director who had ceased to have any active part in the business was held by Oliver J to be excessive and unreasonable and to be recoverable by the liquidator.

1 [1982] 3 All ER 1016 (Oliver J).

6.38 Overpayment of employees (eg payment of a redundancy payment in excess of their entitlements) can be a misfeasance for which a director can be liable – see, for example, *Re Brian D Pierson (Contractors) Ltd*[1].

1 [1999] BCC 26 (Hazel Williamson QC).

6.39 Payments authorised by an insolvency practitioner (eg a receiver) once in place to employees are unlikely to be challengeable (by a later liquidator or administrator) as being undue preferences (ie under ss 238 or 239) even though they may be made by the receiver as agent on behalf of the insolvent company. See the decision of the High Court in Australia in *Sheahan v Carrier Air Conditioning Pty Ltd*[1] but compare *G&M Aldridge Pty Ltd v Walsh*[2].

1 (1997) 147 ALR 1; (1997) 189 CLR 407, Australian High Court.
2 [2001] HCA 27; (2001) 203 CLR 662, [2002] BPIR 482, Australian High Court.

IMPACT ON SHARE SCHEMES

6.40 Many companies have established share schemes as incentives for their employees or employees of a subsidiary. If the company in which the shares are issued or to be issued enters into an insolvency process, it is likely that the value of the shares will be worthless.

There could still be value in the shares on the insolvency of the employer if either:

- the issuing company was not in fact insolvent and so there could be some value in the shares; or

- the employer is a subsidiary and the issuing company remains solvent.

6.41   Even if some value remains in the shares, the relevant scheme may provide that the scheme terminates on an insolvency (eg options can no longer be exercised). So the employee may not have any claim to shares not already owned by the employee.

6.42   If the employee has an SAYE option, there is a linked savings arrangement. The employee will be able to decide not to exercise the option and keep the savings.

6.43   If the shares are already held by the employee but are nil or only part paid, the employee will be liable to pay the balance of any amounts due on the shares. On a liquidation, shareholders are liable to contribute to the assets of the company the amount (if any) unpaid on the shares – see IA 1986, s 74(2)(d).

CHAPTER 7

Effect of termination of employment

7.1   This Chapter discusses the impact of insolvency on the rights of employees in relation to dismissal and also, where there are redundancies, for trade unions or employee representatives to be consulted under the Trade Union and Labour Relations (Consolidation) Act 1992 (TULRCA 1992), s 188 (see para 3.2 above).

TERMINATION

7.2   As explained in Chapter 5 above, the effect of the appointment of an insolvency practitioner may be automatically to terminate relevant contracts of employment. This is the case with the appointment of a court receiver or a court liquidator. In other cases, the insolvency practitioner may himself decide to arrange for the company to terminate the relevant contracts of employment.

BREACH OF CONTRACT

7.3   Even if the appointment of the relevant insolvency practitioner does not have the effect of automatically terminating a contract of employment (and the insolvency practitioner does not take action to arrange for the company to termi-nate an employment contract), if the company commits a breach of contract (eg non payment of wages) which is sufficiently serious[1] then this will entitle the employee to elect to terminate the contract and hence to treat himself as con-structively dismissed. The employee is then able to terminate his future obliga-tions under the contract and claim damages and/or dismissal remedies as a result.

1 See *Western Excavating (ECC) Ltd v Sharp* [1978] QB 761, CA and paras 2.27 and 2.38 above.

EMPLOYEE'S OBLIGATIONS

7.4   If the contract is terminated where the company is in fundamental breach of contract, the employee will be freed from any further obligations under the contract (eg to serve during any notice period), unless the obligation can be construed to survive even a breach of contract by the employer[1].

1 See eg the Court of Appeal in *Campbell v Frisbee* [2002] EWCA Civ 1374, [2003] ICR 141 at paras 16 to 22 holding that the issue of whether a continued confidentiality duty would survive termination of the employment contract was not suitable to be decided upon on an application for summary judgment.

7.5   In the case of a restrictive covenant on the employee (eg prohibiting competition against the employer for a period after termination of employment), where the contract states that the covenant still operates following a breach of contract by the employer, the covenant will be enforceable only if it satisfies the general public policy requirement of reasonableness. It seems that the courts will almost invariably hold that it is unreasonable for an employer to enforce a restrictive covenant where the employer is in breach of contract[1]. However, one of the judgments (Phillips LJ) in the Court of Appeal in *Rock Refrigeration* suggested that this principle (derived from the decision of the House of Lords in *General Billposting* in 1909) might not accord with current legal principles or the requirements of business efficacy. Arguably, some restrictions could survive and remain enforceable. However, Philips LJ considered it was not necessary to decide on the point.

   If there has been no breach by the employer (eg where there is an administration and employment continued), restrictive covenants may remain enforceable (see paras 7.40 to 7.42 below).

1 See *General Billposting Co Ltd v Atkinson* [1909] AC 118, HL; *Measures Bros Ltd v Measures* [1910] 2 Ch 24, CA; *Briggs v Oates* [1991] 1 All ER 407 (Scott J); *Living Design (Home Improvements) Ltd v Davidson* [1994] IRLR 69 (Ct of Sess) and *Rock Refrigeration Ltd v Jones* [1997] ICR 938, CA.

STATUTORY DISMISSAL CLAIMS OF EMPLOYEES

7.6   In addition to any contractual claims (eg for wrongful dismissal) the employee may also have the statutory right to claim for redundancy or unfair dismissal under ERA 1996 (see Chapter 2 above).

7.7   Termination of an employment contract by operation of law (eg on the making of a winding-up order) is, under ERA 1996, s 136(5), treated as a dismissal for the purposes of the statutory provisions relating to redundancy. However, there is no equivalent of s 136(5) for the purposes of the statutory provisions relating to unfair dismissal. It seems that there can be no liability for unfair dismissal where termination of employment takes effect by operation of law through a court winding up or court receivership (see paras 6.2 and 6.9 above) – see the EAT in *Barnes v Leavesley*[1].

1 [2001] ICR 38 at para 23, EAT.

7.8   However, given that such a termination clearly constitutes a breach of contract entitling the employee to bring a claim for wrongful dismissal (see

Chapter 5 above), there seems little logic in not treating such a termination as a dismissal for statutory unfair dismissal purposes as well.

7.9   In Canada, the Supreme Court in *Re Rizzo & Rizzo Shoes Ltd*[1] held that it was appropriate to interpret the Ontario Employment Standards Act giving entitlement to severance (redundancy) and holiday pay as applying on the bankruptcy of an employer, even though the termination of employment may not have been a voluntary act. The relevant statutory wording in Ontario differs from that in the ERA 1996, but the reasoning of the Canadian Supreme Court is equally applicable. It clearly extended the statutory protection for policy reasons based on the need to protect employees 'by requiring employers to comply with certain minimum standards' and to compensate long-serving employees for their years of service and investment in the employer's business. It would also produce absurd consequences if the statute did not apply on a bankruptcy. The court commented that the effect of this would be that:

> 'those employees "fortunate" enough to have been dismissed the day before a bankruptcy would be entitled to such payments but those terminated on the day the bankruptcy becomes final would not be entitled.'

(see paras 24 to 29 of the judgment).

   See also to like effect in Australia, Young CJ in *Re Beverage Packers (Australia) Pty Ltd*[2].

1 [1998] 1 SCR 27, Canadian Supreme Court.
2 [1990] VR 446 (Young CJ).

7.10   Conversely, in *Commercial Finance Co Ltd v Ramsingh-Mahabir*[1], the Privy Council held that a statute of Trinidad and Tobago providing for severance benefits following 'retrenchment' (defined as 'the termination of employment of a worker at the initiative of the employer') did not apply where the employees were automatically dismissed by operation of law on the making of a winding-up order. The Privy Council considered (at page 1301B) that:

> 'redundancy means the existence of surplus labour in an undertaking for whatever cause. It does not apply to the termination of employment simply because the business has ceased to exist.'

See also the comments of the EAT in *Barnes v Leavesley*[2].

1 [1994] 1 WLR 1297, PC.
2 [2001] ICR 38 at page 42, EAT.

7.11   In practice, if there is no dismissal by operation of law (eg in an out of court receivership or administration), any dismissal or termination of employment in an insolvency situation is most likely to be by reason of redundancy and hence for a potentially fair reason under ERA 1996, s 98(2). Accordingly, unless there is some other unfairness involved (eg unfair redundancy selection), no claim for unfair dismissal will arise.

7.12   In *Fox Brothers (Clothes) Ltd v Bryant*[1], a case involving a voluntary winding up, Kilner-Brown J doubted whether 'there can be an unfair dismissal in the case of a properly conducted entry into liquidation'.

1 [1978] IRLR 485 (Kilner-Brown J).

7.13   Conversely, there are comments in *Pambakian v Brentford Nylons Ltd*[1] that 'receivers and managers should be aware of the requirements of good industrial relations' with regard to consulting employees in relation to a hive down as much as employers.

1 [1978] ICR 665, EAT at page 674.

7.14   However Fox Brothers was decided before the decision of the House of Lords in *Polkey v AE Dayton Services Ltd*[1] to the effect that there could still be an unfair dismissal even if there was only a failure to follow proper procedures and dismissal would have occurred in any event. Accordingly, Kilner-Brown J's statement should be regarded as too wide, so that a potential for unfair dismissal findings remains in an insolvency.

1 [1988] AC 344; [1987] IRLR 503, HL.

7.15   *Polkey* also emphasised the need generally for employers to consult with employees before a dismissal. Failure to consult would render the dismissal unfair unless it would be 'utterly useless' (see page 355B) or 'in exceptional circumstances of the particular case, the procedural steps normally appropriate would have been futile, could not have altered the decision to dismiss and therefore could be dispensed with' (Lord Bridge at page 364G).

7.16   With effect from 1 October 2004 until 6 April 2009 (when it was repealed by the Employment Act 2008), section 34 of the Employment Act 2002 inserted a new s 98A(2) into ERA 1996 stating that:

> 'failure by an employer to follow a procedure in relation to the dismissal of an employee shall not be regarded for the purposes of section 98(4)(a) as by itself making the employer's action unreasonable if he shows that he would have decided to dismiss the employee if he had followed the procedure'.

7.17   This was effectively seen as a statutory reversal of the *Polkey* decision. The new provision is subject to s 98A(1), which makes a dismissal automatically unfair where:

(i)   one of the statutory dismissal and disciplinary procedures set out in Part 1 of Schedule 2 to the Employment Act 2002 applies in relation to the dismissal, and

(ii)   the employer fails to comply with the requirements of that procedure.

7.18   The EAT had been grappling with the extent of the statutory reversal. In *Alexander v Bridgen Enterprises Ltd*[1], the EAT held that 'a procedure' referred to any fair procedure that the employer would be expected to follow, including the ACAS Code. In *Mason v Governing Body of Ward End Primary School*[2] another division of the EAT held that the *Polkey* reversal in s 98A only applied to a breach of the employer's own internal procedures (whether contained in a policy, contract or merely custom and practice).

Most recently, in *Kelly-Madden v Manor*[3] and *YMCA Training v Stewart*[4], the EAT preferred the reasoning in *Alexander* to that in *Mason*.

1 [2006] IRLR 422, EAT.
2 [2006] IRLR 432, EAT.
3 [2007] IRLR 17, EAT.
4 UKEAT/0332/06/ZT, 6 December 2006.

7.19 With effect from 6 April 2009, the statutory dismissal procedure in s 98A was repealed by the Employment Act 2008 (subject to transitional provisions)1. This looks like a return to the previous position under *Polkey*, but in addition, Employment Tribunals are given power to increase or reduce awards by up to 25% where the employer or employee unreasonably fails to comply with a new Acas Code of Practice on Disciplinary and Grievance Procedures.

1 See further on the new provisions, the article by Astrid Sanders, 'Part One of the Employment Act 2008: 'Better' Dispute Resolution?' (2009) 38 ILJ 30.

7.20 The question of whether dismissal would have occurred anyway (despite any procedural unfairness) will be an issue for the employment tribunal to decide, but dire financial straits may, depending on the circumstances, be a matter the tribunal can take into account[1].

1 See Mummery LJ in *Warner v Adnet Ltd* [1998] IRLR 394, CA.

PROTECTIVE AWARDS/CONSULTATION BEFORE REDUNDANCY

7.21 Where dismissal is by reason of redundancy, the obligations to consult trade unions or employee representatives as to proposed redundancies and to notify the Secretary of State under the Trade Union and Labour Relations (Consolidation) Act 1992, ss 188 and 193 can arise (see Chapter 3 above). Failure to comply properly with the consultation obligation under s 188 can give rise to a claim for a protective award against the employer[1].

1 TULRCA 1992, ss 189, 190.

7.22 The protective award is a preferential debt if it relates to a period before insolvency started (see Chapter 9 (Preferential Debts) below) and is also guaranteed out of the National Insurance Fund (see Chapter 13 (National Insurance Fund) below). But it is a liability on the employer, not its officers or the insolvency practitioner (see Chapter 8 below). Nor does it achieve a super priority under the adoption provisions in IA 1986 – see Chapter 18 (Carrying on business – adopted employment contracts) below and *Re Huddersfield Fine Worsteds, Krasner v McMath*[1] and *Day v Haine*[2].

A protective award in relation to redundancies made before the "relevant date" for proving claims is a preferential debt – see para 9.21 below and Lord Hoffmann in *Mann v Secretary of State*[3], holding:

> 'On 13 May 1993 Swan Hunter Shipbuilding & Engineering Group Ltd. ("Swan Hunter") went into administrative receivership. The administrative receivers, acting as agents of the company, closed down the business and on 28 May 1993 dismissed 408 employees on the grounds of redundancy. They made no attempt to consult with the union. This is commonly the case when the business of a company in administrative receivership is closed down. The duty of the administrative receivers is to protect the interests of the debenture holder who appointed them. The protective award is a debt of the insolvent company. The debenture holder will have a charge that, subject to preferential claims, takes priority over the company's unsecured debts. Employees have preferential claims over property subject to a floating charge, but only in respect of remuneration accrued before the appointment of the administrative receivers: Insolvency Act 1986, Schedule 6, paragraph 9. So liability for a protective award cannot fall upon the debenture holder and there is normally no effective sanction against failure by the administrative receiver to consult.'

1 [2005] EWCA Civ 1072; [2005] 4 All ER 886; [2006] ICR 205, CA. See further para 12.180 below.
2 [2007] EWHC 2691 (Ch), [2008] ICR 452 (Sir Donald Rattee) at para [37]. This point not discussed in the Court of Appeal [2008] EWCA Civ 626, [2008] ICR 1102; [2008] 2 BCLC 517, CA – see para 7.23 below.
3 [1999] ICR 898 at 903C, HL.

7.23   In *Day v Huine*[1], the Court of Appeal (overturning Rattee J at first instance) held that a claim for a protective award relating to dismissals that took place before the appointment of an administrator were provable as debts in the later insolvency even though the relevant protective awards were made by the employment tribunal after the appointment of the administrator.

The Court of Appeal held that the protective awards were provable in the liquidation even though they had not been fixed (by a judgment in the employment tribunal) at that time. The Court of Appeal considered that the amount of the award was mandated by the relevant EU legislation and so the award had less of a contingent character (compared to, say an award of costs in litigation) and so was provable.

This leaves open the position in a different case where the relevant dismissals occurred after the "relevant date" for proving for claims in the insolvency – ie where the decision to make the dismissals was one by the insolvency practitioner or even had been made before the appointment of the IP, but not yet carried out at the time of the IP's appointment.

1 [2008] EWCA Civ 626; [2008] ICR 1102; [2008] 2 BCLC 517, CA.

7.24   Both the protective award and the award for failure to consult under TUPE (see para 3.9 above) are based on the seriousness of the employer's default (eg in failing to consult properly) and are not liable to be reduced from the relevant maximum merely because the redundancies (or transfer) would have happened in any event and consultation would not have made a difference.

The Court of Appeal held in *Susie Radin Ltd v GMB*[1] that where an employer had not engaged in any meaningful consultation before making redundancies, a tribunal could make a protective award for the maximum period (90 days) without regard to the fact that consultation would not have affected the outcome. The Court of Appeal held that s 189(2) ensures that consultation takes place in accordance with s 188 by providing a sanction against non-compliance, in the form of financial compensation paid by the employer. There is nothing in the statute to link the length of the protected period to any loss suffered by the employees. As the focus is on the severity of the employer's default, the tribunal is entitled to start with the maximum protected period and see if there are any mitigating factors justifying a reduction. In this case there were none.

1 [2004] EWCA Civ 180; [2004] 2 All ER 279, CA – see also para 21.3 below. Followed and applied in *Day v Haine* [2008] EWCA Civ 626; [2008] ICR 1102; [2008] 2 BCLC 517, CA.

7.25   A similar approach is likely to be taken in relation to the award (maximum 13 weeks) for failure to inform or consult under TUPE – see the decision of the Scottish EAT in *Sweetin v Coral Racing*[1].

1 [2006] IRLR 252, EAT.

7.26   In *Amicus v GBS Tooling Ltd (in administration)*[1], the decision in *Susie Radin* was applied, but the EAT held that in the case of a company in insolvency proceedings, some credit could be given for discussions with the unions about the company's financial circumstances before the redundancies had been decided. A decision of the employment tribunal to award a reduced protective award (70 days instead of the full 90) was upheld.

1 [2005] IRLR 683, EAT.

SPECIAL CIRCUMSTANCES

7.27   There is no specific exemption from the applicable UK consultation requirements applicable in a situation of insolvency. In particular, the obligation on the company under section 188 to consult with any recognised trade union at the 'earliest opportunity' or, after 1 March 1996, 'in good time' remains applicable – see *Re Hartlebury Printers Ltd*[1].

1 [1993] 1 All ER 470 (Morritt J).

7.28   The underlying Directive (98/59/EC[1]) allows member states to include a derogation where the redundancies arise 'from termination of the establishment's activities as a result of a judicial decision' (art 3.1). The UK has not taken advantage of this potential derogation. It will, in any event, be construed narrowly – see the decision of the ECJ in *Dansk Metalarbejderforbund (acting for Lauge) v Lonmodfagmes Garantiford*[2].

1 See para 3.13 above.
2 [1998] ECR 1-8737 (Case C-250/97), ECJ.

7.29   However, TULRCA 1992 does envisage that the minimum time limits for consultation under s 188 of 30 days (if 20 or more employees) or 90 days (if

100 or more employees) are subject to reduction if there are special circumstances which render it not reasonably practicable for the employer to comply, provided the employer takes all such steps towards compliance as are reasonably practical in the circumstances[1].

Normally this is a question of fact – see *E Green & Son (Castings) Limited v ASTMS*[2]; *Angus Jowett & Co v NUTGW*[3] and *Industrial Chemicals Ltd v Reeks*[4].

1 TULRCA 1992, ss 188(7), 193(7).
2 [1984] ICR 352, [1984] IRLR 135, para 20.
3 [1985] ICR 646, [1985] IRLR 326, para 26.
4 EAT/0076/04/RN, (2004) 7 July, EAT at para 11.

7.30   The onus is on the employer to show that there were special circumstances and that it had done all that was reasonably practicable to comply[1]. Insolvency can be, but does not necessarily amount to, a special circumstance. In *The Baker's Union v Clarks of Hove*[2], Geoffrey Lane LJ (as he then was) referred (at page 159) to the judgment of the Industrial Tribunal and held:

> 'What they said, in effect, was this, that insolvency is, on its own, neither here nor there. It may be a special circumstance, it may not be a special circumstance. It will depend entirely on the cause of the insolvency whether the circumstances can be described as special or not. If, for example, sudden disaster strikes a company, making it necessary to close the concern, then plainly that would be a matter which was capable of being a special circumstance; and that is so whether the disaster is physical or financial. If the insolvency, however, was merely due to a gradual run-down of the company, as it was in this case, then those are facts on which the industrial tribunal can come to the conclusion that the circumstances were not special. In other words, to be special the event must be something out of the ordinary, something uncommon; and that is the meaning of the word ''special'' in the context of this Act.'

1 TULRCA 1992, s 189(6).
2 [1979] 1 All ER 152, CA.

7.31   For an example of a full 90-day protective award where an administrator made employees redundant on the day after administration started, see *TGWU v Morgan Platts Ltd (in administration)*[1].

1 [2003] All ER (D) 9 (Jun), (2003) EAT/0646/02, EAT.

7.32   Cases on this point include:

- *Association of Pattern Makers and Allied Craftsmen v Kirvin Ltd*[1] – failure of business after trading in genuine and reasonable expectation that redundancies will be avoided can be special circumstances.

- *Hamish Armour v ASTMS*[2] – refusal by government of further loan can be a special circumstance.

- *Angus Jowett & Co v NUTGW*[3] – on the facts, financial circumstances leading to appointment of a receiver not sudden or unforeseen, therefore not a special circumstance.

- *USDAW v Leancut Bacon Ltd*[4] – sudden action of a bank in withdrawing credit facilities when proposed sale fell through could be a special circumstance.

- *Re Hartlebury Printers Ltd*[5] – administration is not, on its own, a special circumstance, but administrators who were seeking to avoid a winding up were not proposing the redundancies which occurred on the making of a winding-up order.

- *GMB v Rankin and Harrison*[6] – mere shedding of employees by a receiver in order to make the sale of a business more attractive is not a special circumstance, nor is the fact that the business could not be sold and there were no orders.

- *Iron and Steel Trades Confederation v ASW Holdings PLC (in administrative receivership)*[7] – likely futility of consultation not a special circumstance.

- *Smith v Cherry Lewis Ltd*[8] – fact of insolvency (and that company is unlikely to be able to pay any award) does not of itself impact on whether an award should be made or its amount.

- *Industrial Chemicals Ltd v Reeks*[9] – sudden loss of sole customer resulting in plant closure not enough to demonstrate not reasonably practical to consult.

- *Electrical and Engineering Staff Association v Ashwell Scott Ltd*[10] – not a special circumstance to bring forward the date of redundancies because the union had disclosed the proposals to the employees.

1 [1978] IRLR 318, EAT.
2 [1979] IRLR 24, EAT.
3 [1985] IRLR 326, CA.
4 [1981] IRLR 295, EAT.
5 [1992] 1 All ER 470 (Morritt J).
6 [1992] IRLR 514, EAT.
7 [2005] All ER (D) 174 (Oct); UKEAT/0694/04/DM, EAT.
8 [2005] IRLR 86, EAT.
9 EAT/0076/04/RN, (2004) 7 July; [2004] All ER (D) 102 (Jul), EAT.
10 [1976] IRLR 319, IT.

7.33   The subsequent making of a winding-up order is not in itself a factor which should be treated as bringing the protected period (ie the period of any protective award) to an end – see the decision of the EAT in *AEEU and GMB v Clydesdale Group plc*[1].

1 [1995] IRLR 527, EAT.

7.34   Mere ignorance of the statutory obligation is not a special circumstance (see *UCATT v H Rooke & Son Ltd*[1] and *Secretary of State for Employment v Helitron Ltd*[2]), nor (when this was a requirement) was failure to realise that a trade union is recognised (see *Joshua Wilson & Bros Ltd v USDAW*[3]).

1 [1978] ICR 818; [1978] IRLR 204, EAT.
2 [1980] ICR 523, EAT.
3 [1978] 3 All ER 4; [1978] IRLR 120, EAT.

7.35   An administrator or administrative receiver needs to decide, within 14 days of first appointment, whether or not to arrange for the insolvent company to continue to employ a particular employee[1]. If the employment does continue, the employment will be 'adopted', with consequences on the priority of claims of the employee (see Chapter 15 (Carrying on business) below). It may be arguable that the shortness of this period could mean that a dismissal by the company to avoid adoption is a special circumstance for the purposes of TULRCA 1992.

1 IA 1986, ss 19, 44(2), Sch B1, para 99(5)(a).

7.36   Section 34 of the Trade Union Reform and Employment Rights Act 1993 amended ss 188(7) and 193(7) so that the special circumstances defence no longer applies if the failure to consult (or, as the case may be, to notify the Secretary of State) arose because of a failure of the person controlling the employer (directly or indirectly) to provide information to the employer. This reflected the change to the original Collective Redundancies Directive made by Directive 92/56/EEC.

In *GMB and Amicus v Beloit Walmsley Ltd (in administration)*[1], the EAT held that the decision of the employer's American parent company to withdraw financial support did not constitute allow the 'special circumstances' defence to apply.

The reference in this provision to the "person controlling the employer" is likely to include an insolvent practitioner appointed over the employer.

TUPE 1981 did not include such a provision, but applying from 6 April 2006, TUPE 2006 changed the position and includes a similar provision – see reg 15(6) and para 21.7 below.

If it is not the employer, but instead an entity controlling the employer (eg an insolvency practitioner) that makes the decision to arrange for a transfer, this is unlikely to be a special circumstance[2]. Regulation 13(12) of TUPE 2006 states:

> '(12) The duties imposed on an employer by this regulation shall apply irrespective of whether the decision resulting in the relevant transfer is taken by the employer or a person controlling the employer.'

1 [2003] ICR 1396; [2004] IRLR 18, EAT
2 On this, see the comments in the draft report (September 2005) by T Mocroft for the MG Rover Task Force at page 9, commenting that the special circumstances defence was argued where a separate third party supplier had to close down suddenly because of the loss of orders from MG Rover (due to its collapse).
See http://www.advantagewm.co.uk/mg-rover-insolvency-report.pdf

7.37   Failing to inform and consult by reason of a desire to keep the proposals confidential is unlikely to amount to enough (at least on its own) to allow the special circumstances defence to be available. Such a desire for commercial confidentiality looks unlikely to qualify as being sufficiently 'special' – see the discussion in *Redundancy: the law and practice*[1].

1 (McMullen ed) (Sweet & Maxwell, 2nd edition, 2001), at pages 262 and 263.

NOTIFICATION OF SECRETARY OF STATE

7.38   Failure to notify the Secretary of State in accordance with s 193 of proposed redundancies is a criminal offence under TULRCA 1992, s 194, for which the insolvency practitioner may also be liable by virtue of s 194(3). Failure to consult with trade unions or employee representatives under s 188 is not a criminal offence.

7.39   In *Junk v Kuhnel*[1], the ECJ held that under the Collective Redundancies Directive, consultation (and notice to the Secretary of State) must take place before notice of any dismissal is given. In order to comply with this judgment, with effect on and from 1 October 2006, s 193 of TULRCA 1992 was amended[2] to require that notice must be given to the Secretary of State before any notice was given to terminate employment.

1 C-188/03, [2005] IRLR 310, ECJ.
2 See the Collective Redundancies (Amendment) Regulations 2006, SI 2006/2387.

ENFORCEMENT OF POST-TERMINATION COVENANTS

7.40   Employers sometimes look to restrict the ability of an employee to compete with the employer, either after employment has terminated (a restrictive covenant) or during a period of 'garden leave' when the employee, having given notice, is required to remain employed (and so is paid), but is not actively given any work. Such covenants may not be enforceable if the employer has already broken the employment contract (see paras 6.4 and 6.5 above).

7.41   Such restrictions are only enforceable by injunction if they can be shown to be no wider than is reasonably necessary to protect the employer's legitimate business interests. If the employer is in an insolvency process, then it may be less clear that it has a legitimate business interest to protect.

7.42   In *Sendo Holdings plc (in administration) v Brogan*[1], Dobbs J granted an injunction against an employee in relation to a period of garden leave, even though the employer was in administration. Dobbs J commented:

> '[21] Secondly, the Claimant [Sendo] submits that the court should give effect to the employer's decision to invoke the clause, as Sendo had a legitimate interest which is set out as follows. As the company is in administration, its role and interest is to maximise value for creditors. That is what the company seeks to do. The company and its work do not cease to exist because Sendo has sold certain assets to Motorola. Sendo had a legitimate interest in exercising the right to place Mr Brogan on garden leave, namely the interests of the company in administration. It was always the intention of the administrators to ask for Mr Brogan's assistance during the garden leave period. They have indicated they would like him to help, but since his repudiation of the contract on 9 July, they have not been able to progress matters in this regard. Sendo has a legitimate interest to protect, maintain and adhere to the obligations under the contract. These include taking steps to ensure that Mr Brogan was put on garden leave for the duration of his notice period, not to compete, and other similar clauses. To do other than deliver on the contractual promise will put Sendo at risk to claims from Motorola. The contract itself would have been worth substantially less to the company had the garden leave provision not been part of that contract. It was in the company's best interest to agree to such terms and to honour them.'

1 [2005] EWHC 2040; [2005] All ER (D) 50 (Aug), (Dobbs J).

CHAPTER 8

Personal liability of Insolvency Practitioners

LIABILITY OF INSOLVENCY PRACTITIONER

8.1   Generally, the statutory claims (unfair dismissal, redundancy, protective awards) under ERA 1996 and TULRCA 1992 are liabilities of the employer and no other person (see, for example, TULRCA 1992, s 188(8)). Similarly claims by an employee under the employment contract will usually only be possible against the employer (and not a third party such as a director or insolvency practitioner).

In a formal insolvency, even if the insolvency practitioner arranges for employment to continue, it is the insolvent company that remains the employer – see Chapter 15 (Carrying on Business) below.

The position of the insolvency practitioner is similar to that of a director[1].

1 See eg Ross Grantham 'The Limited Liability of Company Directors' [2007] LMCLQ 362 and Pinto & Evans *Corporate Criminal Liability* (2ⁿᵈ edn, 2008, Sweet & Maxwell).

8.2   In the absence of a statutory provision[1], the courts will generally only allow the separate corporate status to be pierced (ie the corporate veil to be lifted) (eg to allow a claim against another group company) in extremely limited circumstances. In *Ord v Belhaven Pubs Ltd*[2], the Court of Appeal reaffirmed that rule, overturning *Creasy v Breachwood Motors*[3] where a claim by an employee had been allowed to follow to another group company that had later succeeded to the business.

1 For example the powers of the Pensions Regulator under PA 2004 to make third parties liable for pension scheme funding in some circumstances by issuing contribution notices or financial support directions. See Chapter 37 (TPR: Moral Hazard powers) below.
2 [1998] 2 BCLC 447, CA.
3 [1992] BCC 638; [1993] BCLC 480 (Richard Southwell QC sitting as a Deputy Judge of the High Court).

8.3   Accordingly, any liability that arises on an employer company does not, in the absence of a specific provision, extend to a third party such as the insolvency practitioner, even if the insolvency practitioner has caused the breach of the relevant statutory provisions or has caused the redundancy or unfair dismissal claim to arise.

8.4   Thus, for example, there is no legally enforceable remedy for inducing an unfair dismissal – see the decision of Dyson J in *Wilson v Housing Corporation*[1]. This can be supported on the general principle that, where a statute prescribes a remedy, then it is the only remedy available (see, for example, *O'Laoire v Jackel International Ltd*[2] and *Scally v Southern Area Health Board*[3]).

1 [1998] ICR 151 (Dyson J).
2 [1990] ICR 197, CA.
3 [1992] 1 AC 294, HL.

INDUCING BREACH OF CONTRACT?

8.5   A third party to a contract:

- who induces one party to the contract to breach the contract can be liable in tort to the other contracting party – *Lumley v Gye*[1]; or

- who intentionally causes a person loss by unlawfully interfering with the liberty of others, can be liable to that person – *Allen v Flood*[2].

These two torts were recently analysed by the House of Lords in *OBG Ltd v Allan*[3]. Lord Hoffmann held:

> '5   But the important point to bear in mind about *Lumley v Gye* is that the person procuring the breach of contract was held liable as accessory to the liability of the contracting party. Liability depended upon the contracting party having committed an actionable wrong. Wightman J made this clear when he said, at p 238: "It was undoubtedly prima facie an unlawful act on the part of Miss Wagner to break her contract, and therefore a tortious act of the defendant maliciously to procure her to do so …
>
> *Causing loss by unlawful means*
>
> 6.   The tort of causing loss by unlawful means has a different history. It starts with cases like *Garret v Taylor* (1620) Cro Jac 567, in which the defendant was held liable because he drove away customers of Headington Quarry by threatening them with mayhem and vexatious suits. Likewise, in *Tarleton v M'Gawley* (1790) 1 Peake NPC 270 Lord Kenyon held the master of the Othello , anchored off the coast of West Africa, liable in tort for depriving a rival British ship of trade by the expedient of using his cannon to drive away a canoe which was approaching from the shore. In such cases, there is no other wrong for which the defendant is liable as accessory. Although the immediate cause of the loss is the decision of the potential customer or trader to submit to the threat and not buy stones or sell palm oil, he thereby commits no wrong. The defendant's liability is primary, for intentionally causing the plaintiff loss by unlawfully interfering with the liberty of others.'

1 (1853) 2 E & B 216.
2 [1898] AC 1, HL.
3 [2007] UKHL 21; [2008] 1 AC 1, HL. See J O'Sullivan 'Intentional Economic Torts in the House of Lords' [2007] CLJ 503 and P-W Lee 'Inducing Breach of Contract, Conversion and Contract as Property' (2009) 29 OJLS 511.

8.6   It seems inappropriate for the person running a company, whether a director or an insolvency practitioner, to be liable in tort to a third party if he causes the company to breach a contract with the third party, whether with an employee or anyone else.

The director or insolvency practitioner will probably know the terms of the contract and so will have the requisite knowledge for the tort to apply – see Lord Hoffmann at para 39 in *OBG Ltd v Allan*[1]. And it seems unlikely that the director or insolvency practitioner could claim that he or she did not intend to breach the contract (eg where it was decided that the company should terminate employment without notice in breach of contract. The desire to save money for the company (rather than to positively hurt the employee) would not be enough to mean that the tort would not apply – see Lord Hoffmann at para 42 in *OBG Ltd v Allan*[1]:

> 'If someone knowingly causes a breach of contract, it does not normally matter that it is the means by which he intends to achieve some further end or even that he would rather have been able to achieve that end without causing a breach. Mr Gye would very likely have preferred to be able to obtain Miss Wagner's services without her having to break her contract. But that did not matter. Again, people seldom knowingly cause loss by unlawful means out of simple disinterested malice. It is usually to achieve the further end of securing an economic advantage to themselves.'

1 [2007] UKHL 21; [2008] 1 AC 1, HL.

8.7   But despite this it is considered that it is inappropriate to impose a liability on an internal officer such as a director or insolvency practitioner in these circumstances. The decision (eg of the board) for the company to act in a way that may be a breach of contract is an internal decision. Otherwise the company could not act at all. Directors or insolvency practitioners will end up with a conflict of duty if they were potentially liable to the third party (eg an employee) in these circumstances. They presumably consider it to be in the best interest of the company to arrange for the breach, but may become reluctant to act in such a way if they then end up owing damages for a breach of a tort duty to the third party.

8.8   Lord Hoffmann and Lord Nicholls gave the two leading judgments in *OBG Ltd v Allan*[1]. They did not differ on the issue in relation to inducing breach of contract. The case did not concern a claim by a third party against a receiver or director, but instead one of the claims was by a company (OBG) against a receiver who had been wrongfully appointed. Lord Nicholls commented (at para 218):

> 'The receivers did not intend to "induce" OBG to breach of any of its contracts. The receivers honestly believed they were entitled to act on behalf of OBG in exercise of their powers as administrative receivers. So the tort of inducing a breach of contract does not avail OBG.'

1 [2007] UKHL 21; [2008] 1 AC 1, HL.

8.9   An insolvency practitioner is thought not to have any common law liability for inducing breach of contract (see the decision of the majority in *Welsh Development Agency v Export Finance Co Ltd*[1] in relation to receivers). Liquidators also have a statutory right to disclaim unprofitable contracts[2].

1 [1992] BCLC 148, CA.
2 IA 1986, s 178.

8.10   There are some judicial comments that the position of administrators may differ – see *Astor Chemicals Ltd v Synthetic Technology Ltd*[1] and *Re Sibec Developments Ltd*[2], but compare *Re P & C and R & T (Stockport) Ltd*[3]. But these seem inconsistent with the position of receivers and liquidators and incompatible with the role of administrators.

1 [1990] BCC 97 (Vinelott J).
2 [1993] 2 All ER 195, [1993] BCC 148 (Millett J).
3 [1991] BCLC 366 (Scott J).

8.11   An administrator owes no duties to unsecured creditors in absence of special relationship or assumption of individual responsibility – see *Lathia v Dronsfield Bros Ltd*[1] and *Kyrris v Oldham*[2] (drawing an analogy with directors and following the decision of the Court of Appeal in *Peskin v Anderson*[3]).

The Privy Council in *Hague v Nam Tai Electronics*[4] confirmed a similar lack of any duty owed by a liquidator to individual creditors (as opposed to all creditors as a class). The Privy Council referred to *Kyrris* and *Peskin*[3] and also to the Hong Kong decision of Barma J in *Grand Gain Investment Limited v Borrelli*[5].

1 [1987] BCLC 321 (Sir Neil Lawson).
2 [2004] 1 BCLC 305, CA.
3 [2001] 1 BCLC 372, CA. See also *Charalambous v B&C Associates* [2009] EWHC 2601 (Ch) (Michael Furness QC).
4 [2008] UKPC 13; [2008] BPIR 363, [2008] All ER (D) 319 (Feb), PC.
5 [2006] HKCU 872 (Barma J).

8.12   Similarly, in *Burgess v Auger*[1], Lightman J held that neither a debenture holder nor a receiver owed any duties of care to directors, shareholders or employees.

1 [1998] 2 BCLC 478 (Lightman J).

8.13   However, in *SCI Games Ltd v Argonaut Games plc*[1] the judge, David Young QC, refused to strike out a claim against administrators for unlawful interference with contractual relations.

1 [2005] All ER (D) 54 (Jul); [2005] EWHC 1403, ChD Patents court (David Young QC). Noted in (2005) IL&P 2005 no 4 page 140.

8.14   The position of an insolvency practitioner should not be worse than that of a director. In *Crystalens Ltd v White*[1] there is only a limited report, but it seems that Gloster J held that where an employee director was acting in good faith in the best interests of his company, and within the scope of his authority as an agent of the company, he could not be held liable for procuring the company to commit a breach of contract (absent additional features such as conspiracy and dishonesty), and had no duty of care to a counterparty to ensure that the company complied with its contractual obligations.

1 [2006] EWHC 2018 (Ch); 7 July 2006, QBD (Comm), Case No: 2005 Folio 990 (Gloster J).

8.15 Individual officers or employees of a company can be directly liable for some torts that they commit. If the elements of the tort can be established against the individual, it is no defence against personal liability for the individual to show that he was acting in the course of his employment.

8.16 But generally some direct tort or involvement seems to be needed – see *Standard Chartered Bank v Pakistan National Shipping Corp*[1] (deceit and fraudulent representation). A director may (depending on the tort alleged) not be liable, however, if he did no more than carry out his constitutional role in the governance of the company – see *MCA Records v Charly Records*[2]. See also *Koninklijke Philips Electronics NV v Princo Digital Disc GmbH*[3]. A director is not directly liable to a third party in negligence causing financial loss, absent a special relationship. Lord Rodger in *Standard Chartered Bank v Pakistan National Shipping Corp* cited Lord Steyn in *Williams v Natural Life Health Foods Ltd*[4] as follows:

> 'The issue in that case related to the personal liability of a director for a misleading projection, prepared in large part by him and issued by the company, as to the profits which the plaintiffs might earn by opening a health food ship under a franchise. Lord Steyn, with whom the other members of the House concurred, said, at p 835:
>
> "But in order to establish personal liability under the principle of Hedley Byrne, which requires the existence of a special relationship between plaintiff and tortfeasor, it is not sufficient that there should have been a special relationship with the principal.
>
> There must have been an assumption of responsibility such as to create a special relationship with the director or employee himself."
>
> Since the plaintiffs had failed to show a special relationship with the director himself, the House held that he was not liable. Lord Steyn was dealing with the tort of negligence where a claimant must establish that the defendant owed him a duty of care.'

See also the Australian High Court in *Houghton v Arms*[5] and the Court of Appeal in *Contex Drouzhba Ltd v Wiseman*[6].

1 [2003] 1 AC 959 at 973 to 974 and 968; [2003] 1 All ER 173, HL.
2 [2003] 1 BCLC 93, CA.
3 [2003] All ER (D) 51 (Sep); [2004] 2 BCLC 50 (Pumfrey J). See also *Società Esplosivi Industriali Spa v Ordnance Technologies (UK) Ltd* [2007] EWHC 2875 (Ch); [2008] 2 BCLC 428 (Lindsay J).
4 [1998] 1 WLR 830, 834-835, HL.
5 [2006] HCA 59 at para [40], High Court.
6 [2007] EWCA Civ 1201; [2008] 1 BCLC 631, CA.

8.17 The position of an insolvency practitioner is unlikely to differ from that of an employee or director in this regard.

It seems unlikely that employees could be considered to be in a special relationship with, and for there to have been an assumption of responsibility by, an insolvency practitioner (or director). Directors of companies acting as trustees have been held not to incur a direct tort duty in negligence to beneficiaries of the trust – see *HR v JAPT*[1] and *Gregson v HAE Trustees Ltd*[2].

1 [1997] OPLR 123 (Lindsay J). See Pollard 'Pension Schemes: Corporate Trustees' (2000) 14 Trust Law International 2.
2 [2008] EWHC 1006 (Ch); [2008] 2 BCLC 542; [2008] All ER (D) 105 (May); [2008] PLR 295; [2008] WTLR 1 (Robert Miles QC sitting as a Deputy Judge of the High Court). Noted in [2008] CLJ 472.

POTENTIAL LIABILITY

8.18   It does not follow from the foregoing general principles that an insolvency practitioner can ignore the statutory or common law obligations relating to employees imposed on the company. The insolvency practitioner will still be concerned that, so far as reasonably possible, the company does not incur liabilities or break any relevant duties for three principal reasons:

- In order not to breach the duty that the insolvency practitioner owes to the company to maximise recoveries for creditors (ie to minimise liabilities); and

- If there is a sale of the business in prospect, the transferee/purchaser will, under TUPE, take over employment liabilities incurred by the insolvent company. The sale proceeds received by the insolvent company are likely to be reduced to reflect any outstanding (but unpaid) liabilities; and

- In some cases a direct personal civil or criminal liability is imposed by statute on company officers or the insolvency practitioner.

DUTY TO THE COMPANY/MINIMISE LIABILITIES

8.19   First, if the company incurs liabilities which could have been avoided this reduces the amounts recoverable by the creditors (or the shareholders if the company is solvent). An insolvency practitioner is under a duty to seek to maximise the amounts recovered.

8.20   This duty can be enforced by action by the company (see, for example, *Re Home and Colonial Insurance Co Ltd*[1]) or in limited circumstances by guarantors or mortgagors[2].

A statutory duty is also owed to pay preferential creditors who will therefore have a claim if the amount paid to them is reduced as a result of a breach of duty – see *Westminster Corporation v Haste*[3] and *IRC v Goldblatt*[4].

1 [1930] 1 Ch 102 (Maugham J).
2 Eg *China & South Sea Bank v Tan Soon Gin* [1990] 1 AC 536, PC; *Standard Chartered Bank Ltd v Walker* [1982] 1 WLR 1410, CA and *American Express International Banking Corpn v Hurley* [1985] 3 All ER 564 (Mann J).
3 [1950] Ch 442 (Dankwerts J).
4 [1972] Ch 498 (Goff J).

8.21   Lord Sutherland commented in the Scottish case *Larsen v Henderson*[1] to the effect that a receiver owes a duty of care to employees of the company to act reasonably in taking decisions which affect them. But this is unsupported by the previous authority he cited. On this basis, the comments should not be followed. They are also inconsistent with the later decision of the Privy Council in *Downsview Nominees Ltd v First City Corpn Ltd*[2] on the duties receivers owe to third parties, and run against the general trend of decisions on duties owed to third parties – see eg *Caparo Industries plc v Dickman*[3] and *Welsh Development Agency v Export Finance Co Ltd*[4] and para 8.5 above.

1 [1990] IRLR 512, [1990] SLT 498 (Lord Sutherland).
2 [1993] AC 295, PC.
3 [1990] 2 AC 605, HL.
4 [1992] BCLC 148, CA.

TUPE LIABILITY

8.22   Second, an insolvency practitioner who is looking to arrange for the insolvent company to sell all or part of its business as a going concern (so that TUPE 2006 applies) will be concerned that any purchaser may look to reduce the price paid (or seek indemnities from the insolvency practitioner – but insolvency practitioners are reluctant to agree to them) if it is concerned about potential liabilities to employees incurred by the insolvent company.

8.23   The purchaser will take over all such liabilities in relation to the employees who transfer (and any who were dismissed by reason of the transfer unless an economic, technical or organisational reason entailing changes in the workforce can be shown), including liabilities that relate to actions before the transfer (see Chapter 23 below). Accordingly the insolvency practitioner will be concerned to reduce such liabilities so far as possible, even though the insolvency practitioner may not be personally liable for them.

DIRECT CIVIL OR CRIMINAL LIABILITY

8.24   Third, in some cases, legislation provides for direct civil or criminal liability to be imposed in an employment context on third parties who are not employers, such as insolvency practitioners. For example:

(a)   the IA 1986, s 44(1)(b) imposes liability on administrative receivers for some liabilities under adopted employment contracts (see Chapter 18 (Carrying on business) below). In the case of an administration, there is no personal liability on the administrator in relation to adopted contracts, but the relevant liabilities are given a priority claim on the assets as part of the expenses of the administration;

(b)   TULRCA 1992, s 194(3) can impose criminal liability for failure to notify the Secretary of State of impending redundancies (see para 8.25 below);

(c) ERA 1996, ss 180 and 190 and PSA 1993, ss 157, 169 may be held to impose criminal liabilities on insolvency practitioners (see para 8.25 below) for failure to comply with requests from the Secretary of State for information about claims on the National Insurance Fund – see Chapter 13 (National Insurance Fund) below;

(d) insolvency practitioners generally look to arrange for the insolvent company to deduct income tax and national insurance from amounts paid to employees and may have criminal liability if national insurance contributions are not paid – see Chapter 25 (PAYE and National Insurance) below;

(e) insolvency practitioners may incur direct liability for knowingly aiding unlawful (eg sex, race, disability or age) discrimination (see para 8.39 below);

(f) a person aiding, abetting, counselling or procuring harassment of an individual can render that person liable to criminal or civil liability under the Protection from Harassment Act 1997 – see s 7(3A). This could conceivably apply to an insolvency practitioner; and

(f) insolvency practitioners may incur criminal liability if they fail to ensure, under the National Minimum Wage Act 1998, that the employer pays at least the national minimum wage (£5.80 per hour from 1 October 2009) – see para 9.44 below.

CRIMINAL LIABILITY AND CIVIL PENALTIES

8.25 Various employment statutes impose criminal liabilities upon employers in certain circumstances. In order to take account of corporate employers, there is commonly[1] an extension to this criminal liability so that where the corporate employer has committed an offence and it is shown that this was committed

> 'with the consent or connivance of, or to be attributable to any neglect on the part of, any director, manager, secretary or other similar officer of the body corporate, or any person who was purporting to act in such capacity'

then that person is also guilty of that offence[2].

It follows that an insolvency practitioner may also be potentially liable. There are several elements before liability can be established:

● there must have been an offence committed by the company. So if there are any defences available to the company (eg that it was not reasonably practicable for the company to avoid the offence[3]), then the IP may rely on these too[4]. In practice the automatic stay on criminal proceedings against the insolvent company (if it is in administration or court liquidation) will mean that leave is needed for a criminal prosecution against the company in the first place – see Chapter 5 (insolvency Moratorium) above; and

- the insolvency practitioner must be within the class of being 'any director, manager, secretary or other similar officer of the body corporate'; and

- although the underlying offence by the company may be absolute, the ancillary liability section imposes additional requirements as to the state of mind of the IP in order to show his 'consent' or 'connivance' or 'neglect'.

In relation to the first element, the need for the company to have committed the relevant offence, there is no need for the company actually to have been convicted, but it is obviously more difficult for the prosecution to succeed in a prosecution of an officer if there has been no underlying conviction. The stay on proceedings on the company in court liquidation or administration applies to criminal proceedings against the company (see *In re Rhondda Waste Disposal Ltd*[5] and Chapter 5 above), but in some cases this may not matter – see the Court of Appeal in *R v Dickson*[6], where Leggatt LJ commented (at page 722G):

> "We however accept Mr Dagg's [counsel for the Crown] submission that the appellants could, even in the absence of the company, have been found guilty of the relevant offences upon proof that the company had committed the substantive offences. In many cases, if not most, that would be an undesirable course for the prosecution to adopt, because it would involve proof of the commission of an offence by what, on that footing, would be an absent party."

The second and third elements are discussed below.

1 See, for example: Trade Union and Labour Relations (Consolidation) Act 1992, s 194(3); Social Security Administration Act 1992, s 115; PSA 1993, ss 157, 168, 169; PA 1995, s 115; and ERA 1996, ss 180 and 190.
2 Similar provisions appear in other statutes such as the Fire Precautions Act 1971, s 23(1), the Health and Safety at Work etc Act 1974, s 37(1) and the Environmental Protection Act 1990, s 157(1). See, for example, the discussion by Bergman in (1999) New Law Journal 1436 and the article by Kirkham and Puttock 'Environmental risks and health and safety retribution – a short guide for practitioners' (2007) 23 Insolvency Law & Practice 189.
3 Eg the wording in the Health and Safety at Work etc Act 1974, ss 2 and 3.
4 See Lord Hope at para [32] in *R v Chargot Ltd (t/a Contract Services)* [2008] UKHL 73; [2009] 1 WLR 1; [2008] All ER (D) 106 (Dec), HL. See para 8.36 below and the note by Brenda Barrett [2009] 36 ILJ 215.
5 [2001] Ch 57, CA.
6 [1991] BCC 719, CA.

8.26 R3 commented in its newsletter in September 2005 in relation to the Health & Safety Executive that:

> 'We understand there have been several instances recently where the H&SE has taken a close and in some cases critical interest in the way IPs meet their legal commitments under the relevant legislation, where there may be differing views on an IP's personal liability which could lead to action being taken against an appointment holder. R3 would be interested to hear if any members have recently been involved in Health & Safety Executive inquiries, or if there are any general concerns regarding the role of the HSE.'

8.27   Subsequently in October 2007 the Health and Safety Commission (HSC) and Institute of Directors (IOD) issued a leaflet 'Leading Heath and Safety at Work'[1]. This includes, at page 7, a statement on legal liabilities.

> 'Legal liability of individual board members for health and safety failures
>
> If a health and safety offence is committed with the consent or connivance of, or is attributable to any neglect on the part of, any director, manager, secretary or other similar officer of the organisation, then that person (as well as the organisation) can be prosecuted under section 37 of the Health and Safety at Work etc Act 1974.
>
> Recent case law has confirmed that directors cannot avoid a charge of neglect under section 37 by arranging their organisation's business so as to leave them ignorant of circumstances which would trigger their obligation to address health and safety breaches.
>
> Those found guilty are liable for fines and, in some cases, imprisonment. In addition, the Company Directors Disqualification Act 1986, section 2(1), empowers the court to disqualify an individual convicted of an offence in connection with the management of a company. This includes health and safety offences.
>
> This power is exercised at the discretion of the court; it requires no additional investigation or evidence.
>
> Individual directors are also potentially liable for other related offences, such as the common law offence of gross negligence manslaughter. Under the common law, gross negligence manslaughter is proved when individual officers of a company (directors or business owners) by their own grossly negligent behaviour cause death. This offence is punishable by a maximum of life imprisonment.'

Note: equivalent legislation exists in Northern Ireland, ie article 34A of the Health and Safety at Work (Northern Ireland) Order 1978 and article 3(1) of the Company Directors Disqualification (Northern Ireland) Order 2002.

1 See www.hse.gov.uk/pubns/indg417.pdf

8.28   Similar wording in PA 1995, s 10(5) and (6) renders officers etc of a body corporate individually liable for any civil penalties levied under s 10 by the Pensions Regulator (formerly the Occupational Pensions Regulatory Authority or OPRA) on the body corporate for failure to comply with the relevant provisions of PA 2004, PA 1995, PSA 1993 and the relevant regulations.

IP as an officer etc

8.29   In *Re B Johnson & Co (Builders) Ltd*[1] the Court of Appeal held that a receiver was not a 'manager' or 'officer' for the purposes of various provisions in what is now the Companies Act 2006 (dealing with liability of a manager or officer for misfeasance). However in *Re Home Treat Ltd*[2] Harman J held that an administrator could be an officer (citing *Re X Co Ltd*[3] in relation to liquidators).

1 [1955] Ch 634, CA.
2 [1991] BCLC 705 (Harman J).
3 [1907] 2 Ch 92 (Parker J).

8.30   The intention of the criminal provisions mentioned above is clearly to impose criminal liability on the persons actually in charge of the running of the company. See, for example, the discussions in *R v Boal*[1] relating to the Fire Precautions Act 1971, s 23; in *Armour v Skeen*[2] relating to the Health and Safety at Work etc Act 1974, s 37(1) and in *Woodhouse v Walsall MBC*[3] in relation to the Control of Pollution Act 1974, s 87.

Halsbury's Laws[4] comments:

> ' "Manager" means, in every day language, a person who has the management of the whole affairs of the company[5]. It connotes a person holding, whether de jure or de facto, a position in or with the company of a nature charging him with the duty of managing the affairs of the company for the company benefit[6]. It does not include a local manager[7]'

1 [1992] QB 591, CA.
2 [1977] IRLR 311, Ct of Sess.
3 [1994] 1 BCLC 435; (1993) Env LR 30, DC.
4 4th edition, Volume 7(1), Companies at para 1072.
5 *Gibson v Barton* (1875) LR 10 QB 329, DC at 336 per Blackburn J. Halsbury also cites elsewhere on this: *Tesco Supermarkets Ltd v Nattrass* [1971] 1 QB 133, DC at page 142, per Fisher J (reversed without affecting this point [1972] AC 153, HL).
6 *Re B Johnson & Co (Builders) Ltd* [1955] Ch 634, CA at page 661, per Jenkins LJ.
7 *Registrar of Restrictive Trading Agreements v WH Smith & Son Ltd* [1969] 3 All ER 1065, CA at page 1069, per Lord Denning MR.

8.31   It therefore seems likely that an insolvency practitioner will be within the ambit of the provision, either as being a 'manager' or as being a person purporting to act as a director or manager.

In *Re Mineral Resources Ltd; Environment Agency v Stout*[1], Neuberger J (as he then was) seems to have assumed that a liquidator could fall within such a provision. He was dealing with potential liability in relation to a waste management licence held by a company which had entered liquidation. He commented (at page 763):

> 'It is also said that the functions of the liquidator would be very different from those which he normally has. Again, it seems to me that that must follow from the conclusion that the liquidator cannot disclaim a waste management licence. However, if the liquidator has not the necessary expertise to deal with such a licence, he can no doubt employ an appropriate person to deal with it; alternatively, he can step down as liquidator. It was also suggested that the liquidator might be liable, even criminally liable, for the company's failure to comply with the conditions of the licence. In this connection, s 157(1) of the 1990 Act provides:
>
> > "Where an offence under any provision of this Act committed by a body corporate is proved to have been committed with the consent or connivance of, or to have been attributable to any neglect on the part of, any director, manager, secretary or other similar officer of the body corporate

> ... he as well as the body corporate shall be guilty of that offence and shall be liable to be proceeded against and punished accordingly."

I do not consider this provision need concern a conscientious honest liquidator. If the company has run out of money, and is therefore incapable of complying with the conditions of a waste management licence, I cannot see how it could be said that, unless the liquidator has in some way behaved imprudently or worse, he could be liable under s157 of the 1990 Act because he has not come up with his own money to enable the company to comply with its obligations. Nor do I see how the liquidator could be held liable, whether criminally or otherwise, for the company having failed to comply with its obligations due to lack of funds, simply because some of the funds of the company had been used to pay the liquidator his reasonable fees, whether in connection with the licence or other reasonable matters in connection with the liquidation.'

1 [1999] 1 All ER 746; [1999] 2 BCLC 516; [1998] BPIR 576 (Neuberger J). Neuberger J's decision was later overturned (on a different point) by the Court of Appeal in *Re Celtic Extraction Ltd (in liquidation); Re Bluestone Chemicals Ltd (in liquidation)* [1999] 4 All ER 684.

8.32   There is further doubt as to whether a provision of the kind described above applies to insolvency practitioners because the provision refers to officers of the company whereas in some cases (eg administrators and liquidators in a court winding up) the insolvency practitioner is an officer of the court and not an officer of the company; but in *Re Hartlebury Printers Ltd*[1] Morritt J rejected this argument, albeit in another context entirely. Harman J in *Re Home Treat Ltd*[2] took the same position.

1 [1993] 1 All ER 470 (Morritt J).
2 [1991] BCC 165 (Harman J). See generally on this question the article by Anthony Hofler 'Elephants and officers: problems of definition' (1996) 17 Company Lawyer 258.

Consent, connivance or neglect

8.33   In deciding whether or not a person has consented to the commission of an offence, it is unclear whether knowledge of the relevant act that constitutes the offence is needed (compare *Re Caughey, ex p Ford*[1] and *Lamb v Wright & Co*[2] with *James & Son Ltd v Smee*[3] and *Mallon v Allon*[4]).

Separately to this, knowledge that the relevant facts constitute an offence is not needed – see para 8.37 below.

1 (1876) 1 ChD 521, CA.
2 [1924] 1 KB 857 (McCardie J).
3 [1955] 1 QB 78, DC.
4 [1964] 1 QB 385, DC.

8.34   Connivance is defined in the Oxford English Dictionary as 'The action of conniving; the action of winking at, overlooking or ignoring (an offence, fault, etc.); often implying secret sympathy or approval: tacit permission or sanction; encouragement by forbearing to condemn.'

In practice it means encouragement or consent. The House of Lords discussed connivance (in a matrimonial context) in *Godfrey v Godfrey*[1].

1 [1965] AC 444, HL. See also *Churchman v Churchman* [1945] P 44, CA, at page 51 'Connivance implies that the husband has been accessory to the very offence on which his petition is founded, or at the least has corruptly acquiesced in its commission'.

8.35   Neglect implies a failure to perform a duty. The person concerned must know (or ought to know) of the duty – see (in a different context) the discussion of 'neglect' in *Re Hughes, Rea v Black*[1], For examples of cases discussing offences attributable to a director's neglect see *Crickitt v Kusaal Casino Ltd (No 2)*[2] and contrast *Huckerby v Elliot*[3]. It may be that there is no duty to check the conduct of an experienced member of staff whom the officer should be able to expect to act in accordance with his instructions, unless there is something to prompt him to check[4].

1 [1943] Ch 296 (Simonds J). See also *R v R McMillan Aviation Ltd and McMillan* [1981] Crim LR 785.
2 [1968] 1 All ER 139, HL.
3 [1970] 1 All ER 189, DC.
4 *Lewin v Bland* [1985] RTR 171 (D), cited in Card, Cross and Jones *Criminal Law* (14th ed, 1998) at p 697.

8.36   Most recently, the House of Lords in *R v Chargot Ltd (t/a Contract Services)*[1] held that the test (in a health and safety context):

> 'in the end of the day, will always be whether the officer in question should have been put on inquiry so as to have taken steps to determine whether or not the appropriate safety procedures were in place.''

R v Chargot Ltd (t/a Contract Services)[1] was a case on s 37 of the Health and Safety at Work etc Act 1974. Lord Hope (with whom the other members of the House of Lords agreed) followed the recent Court of Appeal decision in *R v P*[2] and held:

> 'Liability of officers
>
> 32. The prosecution of a director, manager, secretary or other similar officer under section 37 requires it first to be established that a body corporate of which he is an officer has committed an offence under one of the other provisions in that Part of the Act. Where the offence that is alleged against it is a breach of section 2(1) or section 3(1) the considerations mentioned above will, of course, all apply. So he can say in his defence that there was no breach of that provision by the body corporate or, if there was, that it was not reasonably practicable for the body corporate to avoid it. It is only when it is proved that an offence under one of those provisions has been committed that the question can arise at to whether the breach was something for which the officer too can be held criminally responsible. Then there are some additional facts and circumstances that must be established. The offence which section 37 creates is not an absolute offence. The officer commits an offence under this section only if the body corporate committed it with his consent or connivance or its commission was attributable to any neglect on his part. These are things relating to his state of mind that must be proved against him.
>
> 33. Here too the circumstances will vary from case to case. So no fixed rule can be laid down as to what the prosecution must identify and prove in order to estab-

lish that the officer's state of mind was such as to amount to consent, connivance or neglect. In some cases, as where the officer's place of activity was remote from the work place or what was done there was not under his immediate direction and control, this may require the leading of quite detailed evidence of which fair notice may have to be given. In others, where the officer was in day to day contact with what was done there, very little more may be needed. In *Wotherspoon v HM Advocate* 1978 JC 74, 78 Lord Justice General Emslie said the section is concerned primarily to provide a penal sanction against those persons charged with functions of management who can be shown to have been responsible for the commission of the offence by a body corporate, and that the functions of the office which he holds will be a highly relevant consideration. In *R v P Ltd* [2008] ICR 96 Latham LJ endorsed the Lord Justice General's observation that the question, in the end of the day, will always be whether the officer in question should have been put on inquiry so as to have taken steps to determine whether or not the appropriate safety procedures were in place. I would too. The fact that the penalties that may be imposed for a breach of this section have been increased does not require any alteration in this test. On the contrary, it emphasises the importance that is attached, in the public interest, to the performance of the duty that section 37 imposes on the officer.

34. In *Attorney-General's Reference (No 1 of 1995)* [1996] 1 WLR 970 the questions were directed to the effect of section 96(1) of the Banking Act 1987 which is in identical terms to section 37 of the 1974 Act. Lord Taylor of Gosforth CJ said at p 980 that where "consent" is alleged against him, a defendant has to be proved to know the material facts which constitute the offence by the body corporate and to have agreed to its conduct of the business on the basis of those facts. I agree, although I would add that consent can be established by inference as well as by proof of an express agreement. The state of mind that the words "connivance" and "neglect" contemplate is one that may also be established by inference. The offences that are created by sections 2(1) and 3(1) are directed to the result that must be achieved by the body corporate. Where it is shown that the body corporate failed to achieve or prevent the result that those sections contemplate, it will be a relatively short step for the inference to be drawn that there was connivance or neglect on his part if the circumstances under which the risk arose were under the direction or control of the officer. The more remote his area of responsibility is from those circumstances, the harder it will be to draw that inference.'

1 [2008] UKHL 73; [2009] 1 WLR 1; [2008] All ER (D) 106 (Dec), HL. Discussed by Victoria Howes in 'Duties and Liabilities under the Health and Safety at Work Act 1974: A Step Forward?' (2009) 38 ILJ 306
2 [2007] EWCA Crim 1937, [2008] ICR 96, [2007] All ER (D) 173 (Jul), CA.

8.37   It is clear that an officer will be liable under these provisions if he or she consents or connives in a particular action, whether or not he or she was aware that the action was a breach of the relevant legislation. In effect ignorance of the law is not a defence here – see the decision of the Court of Appeal in *Attorney-General's Reference (No 1 of 1995)*[1] and similarly the House of Lords (in relation to a different offence) in *Grant v Borg*[2].

In *R v Chargot Ltd (t/a Contract Services)*[3], Lord Hope approved this point, commenting (at para [34]):

'34. In Attorney-General's Reference (No 1 of 1995) [1996] 1 WLR 970 the questions were directed to the effect of section 96(1) of the Banking Act 1987 which is in identical terms to section 37 of the 1974 Act. Lord Taylor of Gosforth CJ said at p 980 that where "consent" is alleged against him, a defendant has to be proved to know the material facts which constitute the offence by the body corporate and to have agreed to its conduct of the business on the basis of those facts. I agree, although I would add that consent can be established by inference as well as by proof of an express agreement. The state of mind that the words "connivance" and "neglect" contemplate is one that may also be established by inference.'

1 [1996] 1 WLR 970, CA, discussed by Joanna Gray in *The Corporate Dimension* (1998, ed B Rider).
2 [1982] 2 All ER 257, HL.
3 [2008] UKHL 73; [2009] 1 WLR 1; [2008] All ER (D) 106 (Dec), HL.

8.38   There is now a similar obligation on directors and other officers (with a similar definition to that discussed in para 8.29 above) in relation to unpaid national insurance contributions. From 1 April 1999 the relevant authority (now HMRC) has had power to serve a personal liability notice on a director or other officer where a body corporate has failed to pay NICs and this is 'attributable to fraud or neglect on the part of one or more individuals who, at the time of the fraud or neglect, were officers of the body corporate' (Social Security Administration Act 1992, s 121, inserted by the Social Security Act 1998). See further Chapter 33 (Contributions to pension schemes) below.

EMPLOYMENT DISCRIMINATION LEGISLATION

8.39   Unlike the bulk of statutory employment liabilities (which are imposed solely on the employer – see para 7.3 above), individual employees and officers can incur liability for unlawful discrimination (eg age, sex, race or disability discrimination).

The legislation renders discrimination against employees on a prohibited ground unlawful. It also prohibits victimisation or harassment on a prohibited ground (victimisation and harassment are widely defined and can include sending a letter to an employee purporting to warn him of the consequences of ongoing equal pay claim – see the House of Lords decision in *Derbyshire v St Helens Borough Council*[1].

1 [2007] UKHL 16; [2007] 3 All ER 81 (HL).

8.40   The relevant legislation provides that acts of employees and agents (which will include insolvency practitioners) will be treated as being carried out by the employer/principal[1]. The acts must be done 'in the course of his employment'[2] in the case of employees or within the authority of an agent. So the employer company will be liable for the discriminatory acts of its employees and agents.

1 Sex Discrimination Act 1975, s 41; Race Relations Act 1976, s 32; Disability Discrimination Act 1995, s 58; Employment Equality (Sexual Orientation) Regulations 2003 (SI 2003/1661), reg 22; Employment Equality (Religion or Belief) Regulations 2003 (SI 2003/1660), reg 22; and Employment Equality (Age) Regulations 2006 (SI 2006/1031), reg 25.

2 This is widely defined – see *Jones v Tower Boot Co Ltd* [1997] 2 All ER 406; [1977] IRLR 168, CA, *Chief Constable of Lincolnshire v Stubbs* [1999] IRLR 81, EAT and *Sidhu v Aerospace Composite Technology Ltd* [2000] IRLR 602, CA.

8.41   These provisions have effect to make the employer vicariously liable. This is subject to a defence:

• in the case of employees, if the employer can show that it took such steps 'as were reasonably practicable to prevent the employee from doing the act'; and

• in the case of agents if the agent did not act with the authority (express or implied and whether precedent or subsequent) of the employer.

Knowingly aiding discrimination

8.42   The legislation[1] goes on to provide that a third party (eg another employee or the insolvency practitioner) can also be liable if he or she knowingly aids unlawful discrimination. The legislation states (taking the example of s 42 of the Sex Discrimination Act 1975):

'(1)   A person who knowingly aids another person to do an act made unlawful by this Act shall be treated for the purpose of this Act as himself doing an unlawful act of the like description.

(2)   For the purposes of subsection (1) an employee or agent for whose act the employer or principal is liable under section 41 (or would be so liable but for section 41(3)[2]) shall be deemed to aid the doing of the act by the employer or principal.'

1 Sex Discrimination Act 1975, s 42; Race Relations Act 1976, s 33; Disability Discrimination Act 1995, s 57; Employment Equality (Sexual Orientation) Regulations 2003 (SI 2003/1661), reg 23; Employment Equality (Religion or Belief) Regulations 2003 (SI 2003/1660), reg 23; and Employment Equality (Age) Regulations 2006 (SI 2006/1031) reg 26.
2 The defence for an employer that it took reasonable steps to prevent the employee carrying out the discrimination.

8.43   If enacted, the Equality Bill[1] currently before Parliament will replace this provision with an equivalent prohibition:

106 Aiding contraventions

(1)   A person (A) must not knowingly help another (B) to do anything which contravenes Part 3, 4, 5, 6 or 7 or section 102(1) or (2) or 105 (a basic contravention).

(2)   It is not a contravention of subsection (1) if

(a)   A relies on a statement by B that the act for which the help is given does not contravene this Act, and

(b)   it is reasonable for A to do so.'

This clause uses the phrase 'knowingly help' instead of 'knowingly aids', but it seems unlikely that any change in effect is intended. The explanatory notes to the

Bill comment (at para 357) that 'This clause is designed to replicate the effect of similar provisions in current legislation'.

1 Clause 106, Equality Bill as published on 24 April 2009.

8.44   Accordingly, an employee complaining about (say) selection for redundancy on the basis that it was indirect sex discrimination could claim against the insolvency practitioner who decided on the redundancies as well as against the insolvent company.

8.45   In practice the insolvency practitioner would be acting as the agent of the company in making the decision, so he or she would be deemed to have aid the doing of the act by the company.

8.46   The employee would have to show that the aid given by the insolvency practitioner was given 'knowingly'.

8.47   For the leading cases on what kinds of aid can make a third party liable, see the decisions of the House of Lords in *Anyanwu v South Bank Student Union*[1] and *Hallam v Avery*[2] and of the Court of Appeal in *Gilbank v Miles*[3]. A more recent case (discrimination by a union) is *Shepherd v North Yorkshire County Council*[4].

It is unlikely that a solicitor giving advice to a client can be held to be "aiding" discrimination by the client. The decision is ultimately that of the client. In *Bird v Sylvester*[5], Laws LJ commented (at para [20]):

> 'Extreme situations may be envisaged in which the solicitor himself actively promotes, perhaps for a malign motive, oppressive actions, and actively carries them along. I would, however, suggest that it is very difficult to see how a solicitor who confines himself to giving objective legal advice in good faith as to the proper protection of his client's interests, and acts strictly upon his client's instructions, could be at risk of an adverse finding under s 33 of the Race Relations Act.'

There could be an analogy here with an insolvency practitioner appointed over an employer, although it is more likely that any involvement in unlawful discrimination by an insolvency practitioner would fall to be considered as being that of the directing mind of the employer.

1 [2001] UKHL 14; [2001] 2 All ER 353, HL.
2 [2001] UKHL 15; [2001] 1 WLR 655, HL
3 [2006] EWCA Civ 543; [2006] ICR 1297, CA.
4 [2006] IRLR 190, EAT.
5 [2007] EWCA Civ 1052; [2008] ICR 208; [2008] IRLR 232, CA.

8.48   It seems that a third party (such as an IP) can be liable under this 'knowingly aids' head in the legislation if the third party is aware of the intended acts (that are discriminatory), but the third party does not have to know that they are in fact illegal under the discrimination legislation.

8.49   In *Hallam v Avery*[1], the Court of Appeal found that two police officers were not liable as knowing aiders under the Race Discrimination Act where they had given (misleading) information to a council and the council then illegally discriminated.

Hale LJ held (at para [44]):

> '... it is clear that the unlawful act of discrimination must actually have been committed. While I agree that a mere suspicion that it might be committed should not be enough, it would be asking to much to insist that the aider must at the time when the aid is rendered know for certain that an unlawful act will take place. Accordingly, I agree with Judge LJ that it is enough for the person giving assistance to know that such an act is being contemplated by the principal. I also agree that he does not have to know that it is in fact unlawful.'

The decision of the Court of Appeal was upheld by the House of Lords, but on other grounds (as to whether or not what the police officers had done amounted to 'aid'). Lord Bingham held[2]:

> 'This conclusion makes it unnecessary to address the issue which most exercised the Court of Appeal and to which most of the argument in the House was directed: the extent of the knowledge which an aider must have so as to be liable under section 33(1). It is tempting to offer guidance on that question, and I would not wish to be understood as approving the Court of Appeal's guidance. But it does not appear, from the paucity of decided cases, that the problem is one which often arises in practice and it may be that in most cases (as in *Anyanwu v South Bank Student Union*), there will be little doubt that aid was given knowingly if it is found to have been given at all. Any observations that the House might make would, in the circumstances, be unauthoritative, and would further have the vulnerability of observations not rooted in the facts of a particular case. On balance I consider that this issue should be left to be decided when it arises.'

1 [2000] 1 WLR 966, CA.
2 *Hallam v Avery* [2001] UKHL 15; [2001] 1 WLR 655, HL at [11].

8.50   To similar effect in other fields:

- The decision of the Jersey Court of Appeal in *Midland Bank Trust Co (Jersey) Ltd* v *Federated Pension Services*[1], holding that trustees could be liable for a knowing breach of trust even if they did not realise that what they were doing was a breach; and

- The House of Lords in *Grant v Borg*[2], holding that an individual could be guilty of an offence under the Immigration Act of knowingly staying beyond the leave granted to enter the UK, even though the individual did not realise that it was an offence.

1 [1995] JLR 352, Jersey CA.
2 [1982] 2 All ER 257, HL and see *Attorney-General's Reference (No 1 of 1995)* [1996] 1 WLR 970, CA.

8.51   In *Sinclair Roche & Temperley v Heard (No 1)*[1], the EAT referred to the decisions of the Court of Appeal and House of Lords in *Hallam v Avery* and held (at [53]):

> '53.   In those circumstances the Court of Appeal decision remains binding on the Employment Appeal Tribunal and the Employment Tribunal, although,

as can be seen, it leaves a very wide ambit of fact-finding open to the tribunal. However two matters are clear:

53.1 The element of knowledge is on any basis additional to the element of aid. Whereas discrimination can be, and very often is, unconscious, aiding cannot be.

53.2 If there is the conclusion that this additional element exists, it is not satisfactory or sufficient for a tribunal simply to say that it does, without giving its reasons and making the relevant findings, none of which occurred in this case.'

1 [2004] IRLR 763, EAT.

8.52 In *Allaway v Reilly*[1], the EAT also discussed the meaning of "knowingly", in this case in the context of the Sex Discrimination Act. The decision concerned an application to strike out a claim against a fellow employee. Lady Smith referred to *Anyanwu* and *Hallam* and held (at para [15]):

'15. As ever, it is best to have resort to the words of the statute. Thus, if a fellow employee does an act in the course of his employment which has the effect of discriminating against the claimant employee on grounds of sex and that is a result which can be concluded to have been within his knowledge at the time he carried out the act in question, the requirements of the subsection are met. Discrimination does not have to be what he intended nor does it have to have been his motive. It is enough that, on the evidence, the conclusion can be drawn that discrimination as the probable outcome was within the scope of his knowledge at the time. It would not need to be in the forefront of his mind nor would he need to have specifically addressed his mind to it. It must be that it would be enough if , in all the circumstances , it can properly be concluded that it was within the knowledge that was possessed by the alleged discriminator Inevitably, whether or not it can be concluded that the alleged discriminator did an act "knowingly" is going to depend on the facts and circumstances of each particular case and care should be taken not exclude from proof any case in which it is arguable that, on the available material, that is something which can be established. As was commented by Lord Steyn in *Anyanwu*, at paragraph 24:

".... vagaries in discrimination jurisprudence underline the importance of not striking out such claims as an abuse of the process except in the most obvious and plainest cases. Discrimination cases are generally fact sensitive and their proper determination is always vital in our pluralistic society. In this field perhaps more than any other the bias in favour of a claim being examined on the merits or demerits of its particular facts is a matter of high public interest."'

Lady Smith went on to hold (at para [33]):

'33. Otherwise, the claimant's appeal amounted in essence to a plea that the claimant should not be pursuing the second respondent as an individual and I can appreciate the stress that his doing so must be causing. However, it is not correct to say, as Mr O'Carroll did, that the scheme of the legislation is that the primary liability rests with the employer; to do so is to ignore the use of the words "as well as", in section 41(1). Further, I agree that reliance cannot, in the circum-

115

stances, properly be placed on what was said on the matter in *Krishna*[2]. Rather, the fact is that the claimant is, in the circumstances, entitled to do as he is doing in including the second respondent as an individual so as to seek to call the person who he sees as the discriminator, to account.'

1 [2007] IRLR 864, EAT.
2 *Krishna v Argyll and Bute Council* (EAT/446/99). Lady Smith had earlier referred to counsel having argued based on the decision in Krishna:

'After that, reliance was placed on the case of *Krishna v Argyll and Bute Council & Anr* EAT/446/99 where an individual employee had been named as second respondent in a race discrimination case and Lord Johnston commented obiter, that:

"...we would offer the view that this should not happen where it is accepted, or albeit at least averred, that in a discrimination case the employer was the employer of the alleged discriminator in the sense that he or she was acting in the course of his employment when the alleged discrimination took place."'

8.53   The legislation generally includes an express defence for the third party if he or she acts in reliance on a statement from the other person that act being aided is not unlawful and it is reasonable to rely on that statement.

8.54   If there is a transfer of a business, generally all liabilities of the transferor connected with the transferring employees (or any former employees whose employment was terminated for a reason connected with the transfer) will transfer to the transferee – see *Allan v Stirling District Council*[1]. However, some claims (eg liabilities relating to pensions or consultation obligations) may now remain behind with the company and not transfer to the purchaser under TUPE 2006 (see Chapters 20 and 24 below).

1 [1995] ICR 1082; [1995] IRLR 301, Court of Session.

8.55   The transferor cannot remain liable under the discrimination legislation as an aider of any discrimination – see the Northern Ireland Court of Appeal in *Clarke v Mediguard Services Ltd*[1]. But this does not go so far as to exempt a third party (not the transferee/employee), such as an insolvency practitioner.

1 [2000] NI 73, NI CA.

8.56   In *Way v Crouch*[1], the EAT discussed whether an employment tribunal had power to decide that liability as between an aider and employer could be joint and several. The EAT held that it was clear from the statutory language in sections 65 and 66 of the Sex Discrimination Act 1975 (in particular s 65(1)(b)) that an employment tribunal in cases of sex discrimination was entitled as a matter of law to make an award on a joint and several basis. The EAT commented that:

'[20] In our judgment this statutory language make it quite clear that an Employment Tribunal in cases of sex discrimination is entitled as a matter of law to make an award on a joint and several basis. We note that there is similar language in s 56(1)(b) of the Race Relations Act 1975; s 8(6)(b); s 8(3) of the Disability Discrimination Act 1995; reg 30(1)(b) of the Employment Equality (Religion or Belief) Regulations 2003, SI 2003/1660 and reg 30(1)(b) of the Employment Equality (Sexual Orientation) Regulations 2003, SI 2003/1661.'

Regulation 38(1)(b) of the Employment Equality (Age) Regulations 2006 (SI 2006/714) is to the same effect.

1 [2005] ICR 1362; [2005] IRLR 603, EAT.

8.57   The EAT in *Way v Crouch*[1] went on to hold:

'[23] We are conscious that this is the first decision of the Employment Appeal Tribunal which has squarely held that a joint and several award of compensation can be made in a discrimination case. We therefore think it will be helpful for employment tribunals if we set out some of the factors they must have regard to when considering making such an award.

They are as follows:

(1)   The practice of Employment Tribunals since 1975 confirms that in almost every case it will be unnecessary to make a joint and several award of compensation in a discrimination case. The present practice of apportioning liability (where appropriate) between individual employees and employers works well in practice and does justice to the individual case.

(2)   If an Employment Tribunal considers it necessary to make a joint and several award of compensation then it should make clear its reasons for doing so.

(3)   If an Employment Tribunal considers it necessary to make a joint and several award of compensation it must have regard to the language of s 2(1) of the Civil Liability (Contribution) Act 1978 which provides that:

"(1)   Subject to sub-section (3) below in any proceedings for contribution under Section 1 above the amount of the contribution recoverable from any person shall be such as may be found by the Court to be just and equitable having regard to the extent of that person's responsibility for the damage in question."

In other words, it is not appropriate in almost any case for an Employment Tribunal to make a joint and several award which is 100% against each respondent. That is to do violence to the language of s 2(1) of the 1978 Act which specifically directs the attention of the Employment Tribunal "to the extent of that person's responsibility for the damage in question".

(4)   What s 2(1) of the 1978 Act makes clear is that it is not a permissible option for an Employment Tribunal to make a joint and several award of compensation because of the relative financial resources of the respondent. For example, an Employment Tribunal cannot make such an award because it believes that a company is more likely to be able to satisfy such an award or because a corporate respondent may be insolvent or in receivership or liquidation. That is to ignore the clear language of s 2(1) of the 1978 Act.

(5)   In providing guidance to an Employment Tribunal about the meaning of s 2(1) of the 1978 Act, we can do no better than refer to the discussion in *Clerk and Lindsell on Tort* (17th edn, 1995) at para 4 – 63 (pp 154 -155). The editors of that standard practitioners' work take the view that the word "responsibility" in s 2(1) of the 1978 Act refers both to the extent to which each tortfeasor caused the damage and to their relative culpability. There is

extensive reference to the relevant case law in the footnotes to that paragraph of *Clerk and Lindsell*.'

1 [2005] ICR 1362; [2005] IRLR 603 (EAT) at para [23].

8.58 The EAT's comments are highly relevant to insolvency cases. The relevant employee or ex-employee will be conscious that he or she may not be able to recover any award made against the insolvent company. So he or she will have an incentive to argue for the tribunal to apportion as much liability as possible on to a third party aider, such as the IP. The EAT's comments at point (4) above will mean that recoverability is not a valid ground for apportioning more liability onto the IP:

'For example, an Employment Tribunal cannot make such an award because it believes that a company is more likely to be able to satisfy such an award or because a corporate respondent may be insolvent or in receivership or liquidation. That is to ignore the clear language of s 2(1) of the 1978 Act.'

8.59 The EAT's judgment in *Way v Crouch* was followed by the EAT in *Rooproy v Rollins-Elliott*[1]. A decision of the employment tribunal was set aside on the grounds that it should have realised that it had power to apportion an award and that it was not appropriate for it to have taken into account that the employer company was by now in liquidation. The EAT referred to *Way v Crouch* and held:

'For the reasons given in that judgment, and which are incorporated into this judgment, we decided that an employment tribunal did, in exceptional cases, have the legal power to make such an award. What that judgment does point out is that the effect of section 2(1) of the Joint Tortfeasors (Liability) Act 1978[2] does not permit an employment tribunal to make an award of compensation in a discrimination case on a joint and several basis because one of the parties is insolvent. Section 2(1) of the 1978 Act focuses the attention of the employment tribunal on conduct and culpability of each tortfeasor. Financial ability to pay is an irrelevant consideration and if an employment tribunal took it into account that would amount to an error of law.'

1 UKEAT/0822/04/MAA; [2005] All ER (D) 27 (Jul) (EAT).
2 Presumably intended to be a reference to the Civil Liability (Contribution) Act 1978.

8.60 The Court of Appeal in *Gilbank v Miles*[1] upheld a decision of the ET and EAT that a sole director (and majority shareholder) was jointly and severally liable with the employer under the 'knowingly aids head. The relevant discrimination was not just by the director but involved other employees as well. The Court of Appeal upheld the joint and several award, noting that it had the effect of imposing the liability on the director, as the employer company had been dissolved – see Sedley LJ at para [49]:

'49. The present problem arises because the corporate employer has been dissolved and struck off the register and cannot pay compensation. In the light of the statutory scheme, the personal liability of the sole director and salon manager, Ms Miles, for her own discriminatory acts is not in dispute. What she disputes is her liability to compensate Ms Gilbank for the discriminatory conduct of other employees.'

The Court of Appeal did not refer to any culpability issue in relation to why a joint and several award was appropriate. The decisions of the EAT in *Way v Crouch* and *Rooproy v Rollins-Elliott* were not cited in the judgments of the Court of Appeal. *Way v Crouch* had been cited by the EAT[2], but the culpability point was not expressly mentioned.

1 [2006] EWCA Civ 543, [2006] ICR 1297, CA.
2 (2005) 14 September; UKEAT/0396/05/MAA, EAT.

IP INDEMNITY FROM COMPANY/ASSETS?

8.61 It is unclear if an IP would be entitled to claim an indemnity out of the assets of the company if he or she incurred a liability under the provisions mentioned above[1].

Rule 2.67 states:

'(1) The expenses of the administration are payable in the following order of priority—

(a) expenses properly incurred by the administrator in performing his functions in the administration of the company;'

There may well be an argument that such a liability was not 'properly' incurred and so should not be reimbursed. This is a difficult area.

1 In an administration see r 2.67(1)(a) of the Insolvency Rules 1986 (SI 1986/1925, as amended). In a liquidation see r 4.218(1)(a).

8.62 The term 'properly' also appears in s 31 of the Trustee Act 2000 in relation to the indemnity for trustees out of trust property:

'(1) A trustee—

(a) is entitled to be reimbursed from the trust funds, or

(b) may pay out of the trust funds,

expenses properly incurred by him when acting on behalf of the trust.'

In a trust context, the phrase 'properly incurred' has been construed as meaning 'reasonably as well as honestly incurred' (*Re Beddoe*[1]).

1 [1893] 1 Ch 547 at 562, CA.

8.63 In Australia, in *Re Just Juice Corporation Pty Ltd*[1], Gummow J considered, among other matters, whether debts incurred by a receiver were incurred as the result of improper conduct of the receivership and, therefore, not properly incurred in the course of the receivership. Gummow J held:

'47. I accept the submission by counsel for ABN that the determination of whether a debt was properly incurred by the receiver in the course of the receivership involves an examination of the duties imposed upon him by virtue of his acceptance of the office of receiver. Accordingly, the inquiry as to whether a debt was properly incurred within the meaning of cl 1 of the ABN Indemnity is not necessarily restricted to an examination, in isolation or as between the receiver and the trade creditor, of the transaction which created the liability for which the receiver seeks recoupment under a contract of indemnity with the secured creditor which appointed him as receiver.

48. In particular, the receiver, in exercising the powers given him by his appointment was obliged to meet certain standards of conduct. I have referred to the position at general law. As I have indicated, if the Debts were incurred in consequence of negligence default or breach of duty in improper performance of the applicant's duties as receiver, the Debts would not attract an obligation to indemnify the applicant. The Debts would not have been properly incurred.

49. Do the express terms of the ABN Indemnity produce a different result by use of the term `properly incurred' in a particular context?

50. Some assistance, by way of analogy, is provided by the rule that a trustee is entitled to reimbursement for moneys paid for expenses "properly incurred" in the execution of the trust. The phrase "properly incurred" has been construed as meaning "reasonably as well as honestly incurred" (*Re Beddoe* [1893] 1 Ch 547 at 562) and the inquiry may extend to an examination of the general performance by the trustee of the "duty to execute the trust with reasonable diligence and care": *RWG Management Ltd v Commr for Corporate Affairs* [1985] VR 348 at 396.'

But it may be that a wider view is taken in the UK and payments made or liabilities incurred by an IP in good faith are covered – see *Freakley v Centre Reinsurance International Co*[2] at para 16 and the discussion at para 18.142 below.

1 (1992) 8 ACSR 444 at p 455 (Gummow J).
2 [2006] UKHL 45; [2006] 1 WLR 2863, HL.

CHAPTER 9

Preferential debts

GENERAL

9.1   In practice, save for the special situations where the insolvency practitioner can become personally liable or a 'super priority' is imposed (see Chapters 15 to 18 (Carrying on business) below), claims of an employee in an insolvency will be claims against the (insolvent) employer company and not against the insolvency practitioner personally.

9.2   An employee (or former employee) may have a claim for unpaid wages, damages for breach of contract on termination of employment (see para 2.25 above), redundancy payments, or for other benefits such as medical cover and pensions rights. A legally enforceable claim is needed.

9.3   Such claims will generally be unsecured and the employee will, like any other creditor, be forced to seek recovery in the relevant insolvency proceedings. This will be by way of proof of debt in a liquidation or post-14 September 2003 administration or by a legal claim in a receivership.

9.4   There may be difficulties in evaluating the level at which a proof of debt from an employee can be admitted in relation to any claim for a contractual pension. There are three main alternatives:

(a)   an actuarial value; or

(b)   the cost of purchasing with an insurer an equivalent annuity policy for the employee; or

(c)   the value of the future income stream to the member. There may be issues as to whether in a liquidation this should be discounted – compare the decision of the House of Lords in *Re Park Air Services*[1] on proving for future rentals under a lease.

This is to be contrasted with the position of a potential claim by the trustees of a pension scheme (e.g. under PA 1995, s 75), where the amount of the claim is usually fixed by the scheme provisions or statute (see Chapters 33 and 34 below).

1 [2000] 2 AC 172; [1999] 1 All ER 673, HL, sub nom *Christopher Moran Holdings Ltd* v *Bairstow*.

9.5   In each case such a payment may (unless paid into a scheme registered with HMRC) trigger a tax charge on the employee (ITEPA 2003, s 394 (as amended), formerly ICTA 1988, s 595).

9.6   The relevant date for assessing the claim in a liquidation is the date of winding up – see Chapter 16 below and the decision of Geoghegan J in Ireland in *Turner v Hospitals Trust (1940) Ltd*[1] where pension claims were held provable. It was held that they were contractual despite the company's contention that they were discretionary.

1 28 July 1993, unreported (1987/7586P).

9.7   An employee will generally have no claim on the company if his employment has transferred (under TUPE) to a purchaser/transferee of an undertaking from the company (see Chapter 20 below) – see *Allan v Stirling District Council*[1] and *Clarke v Mediguard Services Ltd*[2].

In *Wight v Eckhardt Marine GmbH*[3] the Privy Council confirmed that a claim did not remain provable if it was later discharged (after the relevant proof date). This was not a case involving TUPE, but the principles stated would apply in a TUPE case.

However, some claims (eg liabilities relating to occupational pensions or from 6 April 2006 consultation obligations) may now remain behind with the company and not transfer to the purchaser under TUPE 2006. Under TUPE 2006, if there is a transfer in some insolvencies some debts (covered by the national insurance fund) do not transfer – see Chapter 20 below.

1 [1995] ICR 1082, [1995] IRLR 301, Court of Session.
2 [2000] NI 73, NI CA.
3 [2003] UKPC 37; [2004] 1 AC 147, PC.

9.8   Although employees' claims are usually unsecured, the position of employees is, to an extent, improved by statutory provision making certain claims by employee's preferential debts. This gives those claims an enhanced status in insolvency proceedings.

9.9   Preferential debts are payable, generally, before unsecured claims (but after insolvency expenses). They are generally payable after secured claims, save that preferential debts rank ahead of claims secured by a floating charge[1]. Claims for preferential debts are given special protection in administrations and voluntary arrangements (see, for example, in relation to a CVA, IA 1986, s 4(4)(a)).

If there is insufficient to meet all the preferential claims, they will rebate in equal proportions in a distribution – IA 1986, s 175(2)(a).

Preferential creditors and the prescribed part

9.10   The Enterprise Act 2002 amended the priority order applicable to the distribution of assets in an insolvency (liquidation, administration, administrative receivership, etc).

For insolvencies beginning on or after 15 September 2003:

(a) the category of preferential creditors was reduced (mainly by the exclusion of the Crown in respect of taxes, etc); and

(b) a new section, s 176A, was added into the Insolvency Act 1986. This provides that, where there is a floating charge created on or after 15 September 2003, a 'prescribed part' to be taken out of the property within the floating charge and instead made available to pay unsecured debts. This prescribed part is set out in the Insolvency Act 1986 (Prescribed Part) Order 2003[2] and cannot exceed £600,000. Broadly it is a percentage of the value of the company's property which is subject to the floating charge: 50% of the first £10,000, plus 20% of anything thereafter (subject to the £600,000 maximum).

1 IA 1986, ss 40, 175, CA 2006, s 754, CA 1985, s 196.
2 SI 2003/2097.

9.11   The usual priority order for distributions then becomes as follows:

1   Expenses

2   Fixed charges

3   Preferential debts

4   Floating charges and prescribed part

5   Unsecured creditors

9.12   This raises the question as to whether creditors who have preferential debts (ie mainly employees) are entitled to join in with other unsecured creditors when looking at any distribution out of the prescribed part.

9.13   Two cases in 2008 confirmed that both a fixed security holder and a floating charge holder are not able to participate (as regards any balance of their debt unpaid out of the fixed or floating security) as unsecured creditors in the distribution out of the 'prescribed part'. Both these cases held that such creditors still did not count as having 'unsecured debts'. This meant that s 176A(2) did not allow them to participate in any distribution out of the prescribed part.

9.14   In *Re Airbase (UK) Ltd: Thorniley v Revenue and Customs Commissioners*[1], Patten J. held that s 176A had this effect. He did this both by reference to the precise wording in section 176A with reference to the definition of 'secured creditor' and 'security' in IA 1986, s 248.

Paten J held that this was the correct interpretation of s 176A even though the normal rule is that a secured creditor is allowed to prove for the balance of his debt alongside unsecured creditors – Rule 2.83 of the Insolvency Rules 1986[2] enables a 'secured creditor' to prove for the balance of his debt, after deducting the amount realised or to prove for the whole debt 'as if it were unsecured' if he first surrenders his security. This scenario will, of course, only arise if there were other assets (outside the security) that could pass down the chain to the unsecured creditors.

Patten J. referred to an earlier case, *Re Permacell Finesse Limited (in liquidation)*[3] The reasoning of that case was apparently the same as that of Patten J. in *Re Airbase*.

1 [2008] EWHC 124 (Ch); [2008] 1 WLR 1516; [2008] 1 BCLC 437 (Patten J).
2 SI 1986/1925, as amended.
3 Unreported, 13 November 2007; [2007] EWHC 3233 (Ch), Judge Purle QC (sitting as High Court Judge).

How does this affect preferential creditors?

9.15   In practice, a preferential creditor cannot have a preferential part of his claim unsatisfied if there is to be a prescribed part. This is because the claims of a preferential creditor in relation to a preferential debt rank ahead of floating charges. So if it was not possible to satisfy the preferential debts, there would be no assets left to fall into the floating charge (and hence no prescribed part).

9.16   But a preferential creditor may have claims which exceed the preferential debt. For example, remuneration owed to an employee is generally preferential, but there is a cap of £800 on the preferential debt. So that if the employee has a greater amount outstanding than this, the first £800 will be preferential, but the balance will be non-preferential.

9.17   The effect of the decision of Patten J in *Re Airbase* is that if the employee's claim were secured (eg by a charge over assets), then the employee could not claim for the balance of his or her claim not satisfied by the security.
    Patten J did not deal with the position of preferential creditors in his judgment. In one sense they look the same as the position of fixed or floating charge holders, the balance of any debt is generally provable alongside general unsecured creditors. But it seems to me that, unlike holders of floating charges or fixed charges, preferential creditors are not secured creditors. They hold no 'security' within s 248, instead their claims are treated as having preferential status by operation of law.

9.18   Accordingly there seems to be no reason on the wording of s 176A to treat preferential creditors in the same way as secured creditors. So it is logical that preferential creditors should be able to claim on the prescribed part (in the same way as other unsecured creditors who are not preferential) to the extent of any excess claim which is non-preferential.

9.19   Presumably the same result occurs where a creditor whose two debts, one of which is secured and the other of which unsecured (eg holds a fixed charge securing a specific debt, but holds another unsecured debt as well). Presumably such a creditor would be treated as an 'unsecured creditor' for the second debt for the purposes of s 176A even though he is a secured creditor for the purposes of the first debt. There seems no good reason to treat the security as meaning that all claims are secured.

9.20   The Society of Practitioners of Insolvency (SPI) (now R3) issued a Statement of Practice (SIP 14) in June 1999 on 'A Receiver's Responsibility to Preferential Creditors (England & Wales)'. This gives guidance on:

(a)   relevant statutory provisions – ss 40, 386, 387(4) of, and Sch 6 to the Insolvency Act 1986, and Sch 4 to the Pension Schemes Act 1993;

(b)   categorisation of assets and the allocation of proceeds as between fixed and floating charges;

(c)   apportionment of costs incurred in the course of the receivership;

(d)   determination and payment of preferential debts; and

(e)   disclosure of information and responses to queries raised by creditors whose debts are preferential.

9.21   This Chapter focuses on the particular issues that arise in relation to employee claims.

For further discussion of the position of preferential claims by employees in Australia and New Zealand (similar but not identical to the UK) see the book by Christopher Symes *Statutory Priorities in Corporate Insolvency Law*[1] and the articles by Christopher Symes, 'Do not miss the employee as a statutory priority creditor in corporate insolvency'[2] and by Paul Heath, Preferential payments in bankruptcy and liquidations in New Zealand[3].

For a comparative study over 62 jurisdictions see Janis Sarra, 'Employee and Pension Claims during Company Insolvency'[4].

1 Ashgate Publishing, 2008.
2 (1998) 26 ABLR 450.
3 (1996) 4 Waikato Law Review 24.
4 Thomson Carswell, Toronto, 2008.

RELEVANT DATE

9.22   Generally, preferential claims are assessed as at the 'relevant date' as defined in IA 1986, s 387. This is usually:

●   the date of the appointment of the administrative receiver; or

●   the date the company enters administration (which, post 2003, depends on whether it is an out-of-court or court administration); or

●   the date of the relevant winding-up order or resolution,

●   depending on the relevant insolvency proceedings.

See also the discussion in Chapter 16 (Provable debts) below.

9.23   If there is a court winding up and the winding-up order follows on an earlier administration, the relevant date is the date on which the company enters administration (similarly if there is a company voluntary arrangement).

However, before the changes made by the Enterprise Act 2002, this did not apply if an administration was followed by a voluntary winding up.

9.24   In *Re Lune Metal Products Ltd (In administration)*[1], the Court of Appeal held that, in a pre-15 September 2003 administration (ie governed by IA 1986 before the Enterprise Act 2002 came into force), the court has no power to make directions under s 14(3) that a particular class of creditors could be paid.

The aim in previous cases had been to allow preferential creditors to be treated in the voluntary winding up as if it were a court winding up. *Re Mark One (Oxford Street) plc*[2] was reversed and *Re Powerstore (Trading) Ltd*[3] followed. See also Neuberger J in *Re Philip Alexander Securities and Futures Ltd*[4] and Arden J in *Re UCT (UK) Ltd*[5].

1 [2006] EWCA Civ 1720; [2007] 2 BCLC 746; [2006] All ER (D) 225 (Dec), CA.
2 [1999] 1 All ER 608; [1999] 1 WLR 1445 (Jacob J).
3 [1997] 1 WLR 1280 (Lightman J).
4 [1999] 1 BCLC 124 (Neuberger J).
5 [2001] 2 All ER 186 (Arden J).

9.25   Note that, unlike claims on the National Insurance Fund (see Chapter 13 below), it is not a requirement for employment to have been terminated for an employee's claim to be preferential.

9.26   In *Re MG Rover Espana SA*[1], Judge Norris QC allowed an administrator to make payments to overseas employees that would be outside the priority order under English law. He held that paragraph 66 of Sch B1 to IA 1986 permits an administrator to depart from the strict ranking of claims if he thinks it likely to assist achievement of the broader purpose of administration[2].

1 [2006] EWHC 3426; [2005] BPIR 1162; [2006] BCC 599 (Judge Norris QC). Noted in (2005) 21 Insolvency Law & Practice 91. See also Chapter 40 below.
2 Applying *Re Mount Banking plc* (25 January 1994, unreported), *Re WBSL Realisations 1992 Ltd* [1995] BCC 1118 and *Re TXU UK Ltd (In Administration)* [2002] EWHC 2784, [2003] 2 BCLC 341.

9.27   In *Re MT Realisations, Digital Equipment Co Ltd v Bower*[1], liquidators had been appointed after an earlier administration. The court had previously ordered the administrators to pay available funds into a trust account for the benefit of creditors who would have been preferential creditors of the company if a compulsory (court) winding-up order had been made. Laddie J held that the liquidators were not bound by this order and so could use later funds (received after the discharge of the administrators) for other creditors.

1 [2003] EWHC 2895 (Ch); [2004] 1 WLR 1678; [2004] 1 All ER 577 (Laddie J).

CATEGORIES OF PREFERENTIAL DEBTS

9.28   The categories of preferential debts are set out in IA 1986, Sch 6. Until the changes made by the Enterprise Act 2002 (for insolvencies starting on or after 15 September 2003 – see SI 2003/2093) they included, besides claims relevant to employees, certain taxes, mainly those which are collected by a company at source and which are payable to the government, such as amounts deducted under the PAYE system or in respect of national insurance and VAT.

9.29   The categories of preferential debt relevant to employees are:

(a)   remuneration – category 5 in Sch 6;

(b)   pensions contributions – category 4 in Sch 6; and

(c)   for insolvencies starting before 15 September 2003 (when the Enterprise Act 2002 came into force), PAYE and national insurance – categories 1 and 3 in Sch 6.

REMUNERATION

9.30   Two categories of remuneration are made preferential under category 5 in Sch 6:

(a)   remuneration owed in respect of the whole or any part of the four months prior to the relevant date, subject to a maximum claim of £800[1]. This limit has not changed since 1976;

(b)   amounts owed by way of accrued holiday remuneration (see Sch 6, para 14(2)) in respect of any period before the relevant date. There is no limit on the amount of accrued holiday remuneration which is preferential (see further para 9.35 below).

1 Insolvency Proceedings (Monetary Limits) Order 1986 (SI 1986/1996), art 4.

9.31   Only remuneration owed to an employee is preferential, not amounts owed to a self-employed contractor[1]. There is no definition of the term 'employee' in IA 1986. The test seems to be the same as that used to determine whether an individual is employed or self-employed in ERA 1996 (see paras 2.4 above and 11.2 below). Fees payable to self-employed persons or non-executive directors will not be covered.

1 See *Re Ashley & Smith Ltd* [1918] 2 Ch 378 (Sargant J), *Re General Radio Co Ltd* [1929] WN 172 (Clauson J) and *Re CW & AL Hughes Ltd* [1966] 2 All ER 702 (Plowman J).

Definition of remuneration

9.32   Remuneration is defined for this purpose by paras 13 to 15 of Sch 6 to mean:

(a)   wages or salary;

(b)   remuneration in respect of a period of absence from work through sickness or 'other good cause' (Sch 6, para 15(a)).

In practice this should include payment for time off as a pension trustee (ERA 1996, s 59), as an employee representative (ERA 1996, s 62) and contractual or statutory maternity pay (under the Social Security Contributions and Benefits Act 1992, s 164, formerly the Social Security Act 1986, s 46), even though this pay is not included in the various terms expressly listed in Sch 6, para 13(2).

Although the Court of Appeal in *Clark v Secretary of State for Employment*[1] and the EAT in Scotland in *Balbirnie v Secretary of State*[2] held that maternity pay was not covered by the statutory right (now in ERA 1996, s 89(3)) to be paid during the statutory minimum notice period (until amendments made in 1994 by the Trade Union Reform and Employment Rights Act 1993), the position in relation to preferential debts under Sch 6 can be distinguished. The words 'or other good cause' do not appear in the provisions dealing with the statutory notice period;

(c) guarantee payments, remuneration for suspension on medical or maternity grounds and payments for time off under various sections in ERA 1996 and TULRCA 1992 (eg for trade union duties, ante-natal care, looking for work or making arrangements for training when under notice of dismissal by reason of redundancy) (see para 2.55 above); and

(d) any protective award made under TULRCA 1992, s 189 (see paras 3.6 and 7.21 above). Remuneration payable after the relevant date is not preferential. Thus, a protective award payable following redundancies made after the relevant date by the company at the direction of the insolvency practitioner cannot be preferential (see Lord Hoffmann in *Mann v Secretary of State*[3]) and is not an expense of the insolvency (see the Court of Appeal in *Re Huddersfield Fine Worsteds, Krasner v McMath*[4]).

Conversely, if the redundancies take effect before the relevant date (ie the start of the insolvency process), claims for protective awards are provable (and hence presumably preferential) even if the awards are only made by an employment tribunal after the start of the insolvency process – see the Court of Appeal in *Haine v Day*[5].

1 [1996] IRLR 578, CA.
2 (1993) 3 June (EAT(S) 31/93), EAT.
3 [1999] ICR 898 at 903C, HL.
4 [2005] EWCA Civ 1072; [2005] 4 All ER 886; [2005] IRLR 995, CA. See Chapters 17 and 18 (Carrying on business) below.
5 [2008] EWCA Civ 626; [2008] ICR 1102; [2008] IRLR 642; [2008] 2 BCLC 517, CA, distinguishing other cases on provable contingent debts, in particular *Glenister v Rowe* [2000] Ch 76, [1999] 3 All ER 452 (costs award in court case) and *R (on the application of Steele) v Birmingham City Council* [2005] EWCA Civ 1824; [2007] 1 All ER 73; [2006] 1 WLR 2380; [2006] ICR 869 (repayment of overpaid jobseeker's allowance).

9.33   Remuneration given preferential status includes:

● contractual commission (see the definition of remuneration in para 13(1)(a) of Sch 6 and *Re Earle's Shipbuilding*[1]);

● overtime – see the Canadian case of *Northland Fisheries Ltd v Scott*[2]:

- bonuses, if contractual and not discretionary – see, for example, the Australian cases (by reference to different statutes) of *Walker & Sherman v Andrew*[3] on appeal from *Re Galaxy Media Pty Ltd (in liq)*[4]. The test here is probably the same as to whether the employee would have a contractual damages claim for the bonus. The implied duty of trust and confidence may mean that there is a damages claim even where a bonus is stated to be conditional or discretionary in some aspects –see para 2.28 above and *Clarke v BET plc*[5] and *Horkulak v Cantor Fitzgerald International*[6].

Living or other expenses where payment is a contractual obligation may also be remuneration (see the New Zealand case of *Re R McGaffin Ltd*[5]).

1 [1901] WN 78.
2 [1975] 56 DLR (3d) 319.
3 [2002] NSWCA 214; (2002) 20 ACLC 1476, NSW CA.
4 [2001] NSWSC 917; (2002) 20 ACLC 73 (Santow J).
5 [1997] IRLR 348 (Timothy Walker J).
6 [2004] EWCA Civ 1287; [2005] ICR 402; [2004] IRLR 942, CA.
7 [1938] NZLR 764.

9.34 Conversely, statutory redundancy payments, unfair dismissal awards, pay in lieu of notice (unless perhaps payable during garden leave – see *Delaney v Staples*[1]) or damages for breach of contract are not preferential even if the right arose prior to the relevant date[2].

1 [1992] 1 AC 687, HL.
2 See *Northland Fisheries Ltd v Scott* [1975] 56 DLR (3d) 319 and the Australian cases of *Re VIP Insurances Ltd* [1978] 2 NSWLR 297, *International Harvester Export Co v International Harvester Australia Ltd* [1983] 1 VR 539 and *Re Farmer Furniture Pty Ltd* (1998) 16 ACLC 1110. Compare *Delaney v Staples* [1992] 1 AC 687, HL a case concerning the Wages Act 1986 (now Part 2 of ERA 1996).

9.35 The Canadian Supreme Court concluded in *Wallace v United Grain Growers Ltd*[1] that the expression 'salary, wages or other remuneration' would include an award of damages for wrongful dismissal. However this was in another context (whether such a claim would remain with the employee or vest in his trustee in bankruptcy).

1 [1997] 3 SCR 701, Canadian Sup Ct.

9.36 In Australia, remuneration has been held not to include an amount paid in lieu of notice under an industrial award.

9.37 Wages will probably remain such even if paid (at the employer's direction) to an employment agency – see the decision of the Court of Appeal (in relation to a different statute) in *Cil v Owners of the Turiddu*[1].

1 [1999] 2 All ER (Comm) 161, CA.

9.38 It may be arguable that the reference to 'wages or salary' in para 13 could also include amounts owed by way of pension contributions

– see the discussions in *The Halcyon Skies*[1] and *Barber v Guardian Royal Exchange*[2].

1 [1977] QB 14 (Brandon J).
2 [1990] 2 All ER 660, ECJ.

9.39   However, given the existence of a separate category of preferential debts relating to pension contributions in category 4 of Sch 6, this may be an unlikely interpretation. See for example (but in a different statutory context) in Australia, Wilcox CJ in *Ardino v Count Financial Group Pty Ltd*[1] (a case on the statutory jurisdiction of a court, in which it was held that 'wages' do not include superannuation payments) and similarly Warren J in *Ansett Australia Ground Staff Superannuation Plan Pty Ltd v Ansett Australia Ltd*[2].

1 (1994) 126 ALR 49 (Wilcox CJ).
2 [2002] VSC 576 (Warren J)

9.40   Conversely, in *Re Cooperants Societe mutuelle d'assuance-vie*[1], the Cour superieure du Quebec held that 'wages' in the Winding-up Act included unpaid contributions to a pension plan.

1 (1995) 14 CCPB 118.

9.41   Most recently in the UK, the EAT commented in *Benson v Secretary of State*[1] that pension contributions are not covered by the national insurance fund guarantee relating to 'arrears of pay' in the Employment Rights Act 1996.

1 [2003] IRLR 748, EAT, at para 20.

9.42   In any event in practice the £800 cap on claims for wages under category 5 is likely to limit the prospect of claims being made for pension contributions.

9.43   Remuneration does not include benefits in kind as such benefits would not constitute 'wages or salary' (see Chapter 13 in relation to claims on the National Insurance Fund).

NATIONAL MINIMUM WAGE

9.44   The National Minimum Wage Act 1998 requires employers to pay at least the national minimum wage (£5.80 per hour from 1 October 2009 for workers aged 22 or over[1]). Refusal or wilful neglect by an employer to pay this:

(a)   is a criminal offence (s 31). Under s 32, directors and other officers can also commit a criminal offence if the employer company commits an offence and this is due to their consent, connivance or neglect (for further analysis of the criminal liability see para 7.18 above); and

(b)   can render the employer liable to a financial penalty if it fails to comply with an enforcement notice (s 21).

Previous rates for the national minimum wage were:

Effective date	Hourly rate
1 October 2009	£5.80
1 October 2008	£5.73
1 October 2007	£5.52
1 October 2006	£5.35
1 October 2005	£5.05
1 October 2004	£4.85
1 October 2003	£4.50
1 October 2002	£4.20
1 October 2001	£4.10
1 October 2000	£3.70
1 April 1999	£3.60

1 See the National Minimum Wage Regulations 1999 (SI 1999/584), reg 11, as amended by SI 2009/1902. The rate for workers aged less than 22 is lower – from 1 October 2008 a development rate of £4.77 per hour for workers aged 18 - 21 inclusive; and £3.53 per hour for all workers under the age of 18, who are no longer of compulsory school age.

9.45   There are no express exemptions in the National Minimum Wage Act 1998 or the 1999 Regulations covering failure to pay by reason of insolvency.

9.46   The directors of an insolvent company will be concerned to ensure that payment of the minimum wage is made for the period leading up to insolvency. However in practice the minimum wage should be covered by the preferential debt claim and/or by the payment of the last eight weeks' wages (subject to a limit of £380 per week from 1 October 2009) out of the National Insurance Fund under ERA 1996, s 184(1) – see Chapter 13 (National Insurance Fund) below.

9.47   The preferential claim (even if paid in full) may not be enough to meet the national minimum wage. £800 spread over four months is less than £47 per week. This is less than £1.17 per hour for a 40 hour week.

9.48   The claim on the National Insurance Fund is better (although it only covers the last eight weeks). The maximum of £380 per week works out at slightly more than £7.91 per hour for a 48 hour week. Only if the employee works over about 66 hours will this amount reduce to less than £5.73 per hour.

9.49   The Working Time Regulations 1998 (SI 1998/1833) limit working time to an average of 48 hours per week, subject to exceptions.

9.50   It seems unlikely that the insolvency practitioner could be held liable for failing to ensure that the insolvent company pays the national minimum wage for a period of pre-insolvency service. It could be argued that if (say) the practitioner is appointed in the middle of the week, and a failure to pay wages due at the end of the week is by reason of the consent, connivance or neglect of the insolvency practitioner (and not the directors), this potentially gives rise to criminal liability.

9.51   This seems a bizarre result. In the absence of clarifying regulations, it is to be hoped that a court would take the view that the 1998 Act cannot be intended to overturn the established position on insolvency.

9.52   In 1998 the then Solicitor General (Lord Falconer) commented[1] during the passage of the National Minimum Wage Bill that:

> 'it is highly unlikely that a genuinely insolvent company or bankrupt employer would be subject to criminal prosecution for failure to pay the minimum wage if he had first postponed other payment obligations not involving a criminal offence and was still unable to pay the minimum wage due to financial collapse. Where he does have sufficient money however, it seems only right that he should use that to pay the minimum wage rather than to discharge other civil debts.'

1 See Hansard, House of Lords, 20 July 1998, Col 678.

9.53   The insolvency practitioner will, of course, be at risk of a potential criminal liability if he or she fails to ensure that the national minimum wage is paid by the company for any service after his or her appointment (see further Chapter 8 (Personal liability of insolvency practitioners) above).

9.54   If the company has in fact paid less than the national minimum wage during the period before insolvency, it seems likely that any claim by the employee (and consequently any preferential debt) should be calculated as if the legal claim was for at least the national minimum wage. This applies even though the employee may not have received the national minimum wage in the past and may not have claimed in the past – see *Paggetti v Cobb*[1], a decision of the EAT on unfair dismissal compensation.

1 [2002] IRLR 861, EAT.

Limitations on remuneration claims

9.55   The limit of £800 on any claim for remuneration is probably a limitation on gross remuneration so that tax and national insurance should be deducted after the limit is applied. Although there is no judicial authority on this point, such a treatment would be in line with the impact of the limit on claims on the National Insurance Fund – see *Parsons v BNM Laboratories Ltd*[1] and para 13.52 below.

9.56   The Review Committee on Insolvency Law and Practice[2] chaired by Sir Kenneth Cork commented in 1982 on the predecessor of Sch 6 that[3]:

> '1444   It is also desirable that the opportunity should be taken to clarify the provisions of section 319(4) of the 1948 Act. The subsection was first enacted in 1929 before the introduction of PAYE, and difficulties have arisen in practice in accommodating its wording to the calculations necessary in a system under which statutory deductions from wages fall to be made. It would be helpful if a figured example of the calculations required were contained in a Schedule to the Insolvency Act.'

Despite this no clarification has been included in the legislation. This does not seem to have led to any reported litigation, but this may be because in practice the remuneration claim is largely covered by the separate guarantee from the National Insurance Fund.

1 [1964] 1 QB 95, CA.
2 Cmnd 8558.
3 Para 1444 at page 327.

HOLIDAY REMUNERATION

9.57   Holiday remuneration is deemed to have accrued to an employee in respect of any period of employment if, under the contract of employment or by virtue of an enactment, that remuneration would have accrued in respect of that period had the employment continued until the employee became entitled to take the holiday – IA 1986, Sch 6, para 14(2).

9.58   Thus, for example, where a contractual holiday entitlement is given in respect of each month but the employee is not entitled to take holiday until a qualifying period has been served, the qualifying period is ignored in calculating accrued holiday remuneration.

9.59   Difficulties in apportioning periods of holiday can arise if the employee continues in employment after the relevant date (eg in an administration or receivership). Here the employee may actually receive his or her holiday (based on the accrual before the relevant date) during the period of continued work. This may then cancel the preferential debt claim – for examples of the difficulties, see *Re Douai School (Re a Company No 005174 of 1999)*[1] and the Australian case of *McEvoy v Incat Tasmania Pty Ltd*[2].

1 [2000] 1 WLR 502 (Neuberger J) and see paras 16.48 and 18.61 below.
2 [2003] FCA 810 (Finkelstein J) and see para 6.7 above and para 15.35 below.

9.60   It seems likely that a claim for holiday pay can only be made if there is a contractual right to such pay. This right is not implied automatically – see the decision of the Court of Appeal in *Morley v Heritage plc*[1], but may be implied by custom and practice – see the decision of the EAT in *Janes Solicitors v Lamb-Simpson*[2] – or under the Working Time Regulations.

It seems that a claim for holiday pay can be made for holiday carried over from a previous year if the contract of employment allows this[3].

1 [1993] IRLR 400, CA.
2 (1995) 27 June (EAT 323/94).
3 See the House of Commons Research paper 08/87 'Small Business, Insolvency and Redundancy' at page 56 (22 November 2008).

9.61   A right to paid holiday (and pay in lieu on termination) is now implied under the Working Time Regulations 1998[1]. Before 2007 this was up to a statutory limit of four weeks per annum (from 28 November 1999). From 2007 additional statutory leave was granted and (for leave years from 1 April 2009) is now a maximum of 28 days[2].

9.62 Holiday pay under the Working Time Regulations can be paid in advance by instalments during the year[3] (if the contract is clear on this and subject to the national minimum wage). Annual leave can accrue during sick leave periods – *Schultz-Hoff v Deutsche Rentenversicherung Bund* (Case C-350/06) and *Stringer and others v HM Revenue and Customs* (Case C-520/06)[4].

1 SI 1998/1833, reg 13.
2 SI 1998/1833, reg 13A, added by SI 2007/2079.
3 *Robinson-Steele v RD Retail Services Ltd* (cases C-131 and 257/04) [2006] ICR 932, ECJ and *Lyddon v Englefield Brickwork Ltd* [2007] All ER (D) 198 (Nov), EAT.
4 [2009] All ER (D) 147 (Jan), ECJ.

9.63 Remuneration in respect of a period of holiday includes any sums which would be treated as earnings under the social security legislation (IA 1986, Sch 6, para 15(b)). It is difficult to see what this is capturing – see the comments of the Court of Appeal in *Re Huddersfield Fine Worsteds, Krasner v McMath*[1] (in relation to the similar words in para 99 of Sch B1 to IA 1986).

1 [2005] EWCA Civ 1072; [2005] 4 All ER 886; [2005] IRLR 995, CA. See Chapters 17 and 18 (Carrying on business) below.

9.64 Pay in respect of holiday already taken before the relevant date will count as remuneration (and be subject to the £800 limit) rather than accrued holiday remuneration (Sch 6, para 15). Compare also the definition in Sch 6, para 14(2) with the definition of holiday pay in ERA 1996, s 184(3) for the purposes of claims on the National Insurance Fund – see Chapter 13 (National Insurance Fund) below.

Interest payable

9.65 Interest is payable in a liquidation on amounts for which a proof of debt has been admitted (subject to certain conditions) both in respect of the period up to the date of the liquidation (ie the date of the winding-up order or resolution) and thereafter[1].

1 IA 1986, s 189; Insolvency Rules 1986, r 4.93.

9.66 A similar provision applies in an administration that started on or after 15 September 2003[1].

1 Insolvency Rules 1986, r 2.88.

9.67 Where interest is payable up to the date of the liquidation on a preferential debt, then it seems that the interest itself is preferential (up to the £800 limit in the case of remuneration) on the basis that rr 4.93(1) and 2.88(1) of the Insolvency Rules 1986 provide that such interest is 'provable as part of the debt'.

9.68 Conversely, ss 189(2) and (3) of the Insolvency Act 1986 make it clear that interest payable in respect of the period after the liquidation is payable only if there is a surplus remaining after all debts proved in the liquidation have been paid and that interest on preferential debts receives no preference. Rules 2.88(7) and (8) of the Insolvency Rules 1986 are to similar effect in an administration starting on or after 15 September 2003.

Pension contributions

9.69   Certain contributions owing by the employer company to occupational pension schemes and state scheme premiums are made preferential by category 4 of IA 1986, Sch 6 (see also PSA 1993, s 128, formerly SSPA 1975, s 58). Category 4 (as amended by PSA 1993) refers to amounts owing by the company which fall within PSA 1993, Sch 4 (formerly SSPA 1975, Sch 3).

9.70   Chapter 10 below contains a fuller discussion of pensions as a preferential debt. Broadly, Schedule 4 covers the following categories of contributions and premiums:

(a)   Contributions from the employee to an occupational pension scheme (not a personal pension scheme) that have been deducted by the employer from earnings paid to the employee during the four months preceding the relevant date (see para 9.22 above) but have not yet in fact been paid to the pension scheme. If (which was probably fairly unusual) such contributions are separately identifiable (eg have been placed in a separate bank account of the employer) it is likely that they will be considered to have been impressed with a trust (see, for example, *Re Chelsea Cloisters Ltd*[1]) and hence achieve a super 'preferential' status, in any event in relation to that separate fund (see paras 26.4 and 33.3 below). For the meaning of the term 'occupational pension scheme' see para 2.60 above.

(b)   Contributions due from the employer to a contracted-out scheme (ie an occupational pension scheme which is contracted-out of SERPS, the state earnings related pension scheme – see PSA 1993, s 7(3)), but only in respect of the 12-month period preceding the relevant date (see para 9.22 above) and only where they are attributable to the provision of guaranteed minimum pensions (see PSA 1993, s 8(2)) or protected rights (see PSA 1993, s 10) under the scheme (ie not any larger amount of employer contributions).

If the contributions attributable solely to the provision of guaranteed minimum pensions cannot be identified, the preferential amount is deemed, under PSA 1993, Sch 4, para 2(3), to be a particular percentage of 'total reckonable earnings' (as defined in PSA 1993, Sch 4, para 2(4)).

(c)   State scheme premiums (within the meaning of the PSA 1993, ss 55–68 and before that SSPA 1975, ss 42–47) payable by the company in relation to service in the 12 months prior to the date of fixing the amount of the premium. Such premiums are payable to the Crown and relate to reinstating employees into SERPS. From 6 April 1997 only contributions equivalent premiums can usually be paid (these reinstate scheme members back into

SERPS where they have no vested benefits in the pension scheme because they have less than two years' qualifying service).

1 (1981) 41 P & CR 98, CA.

9.71   The Pensions Act 1995 contained some minor changes to Sch 4 (see ss 137(6) and (7) and para 85 of Sch 5). However the basic principle remains that pension contributions owed by the employer are only preferential if payable in the year preceding insolvency and they relate to contracted-out service – eg s 9(2B) rights or guaranteed minimum pensions (GMPs) (if contracted-out on a salary related basis) or to minimum payments (if contracted-out on a money purchase basis).

9.72   Because guaranteed minimum pensions (unlike protected rights) ceased to accrue after 6 April 1997 (see PSA 1993, s 9(2A) as amended by PA 1995, s 136(3)), this meant that under the original amendments made by PA 1995 for pension contributions after that date there was no preferential debt arising for employer contributions to a salary related contracted-out-scheme (but the preferential status remained for minimum payments to contracted-out money purchase schemes).

9.73   This was an odd result (but the then Department of Social Security confirmed this interpretation). In practice it was likely mainly to affect the Secretary of State and the National Insurance Fund (which will often have to meet such claims under PSA 1993, ss 123 to 125 and will then take over the claim against the insolvent employer – see Chapter 13 (National Insurance Fund) below). From 25 April 2000[1], the Welfare Reform and Pensions Act 1999 made further amendments to (in effect) reinstate a preferential debt status for contracted-out rights on a salary-related basis[2].

1 See SI 2000/147.
2 Welfare Reform and Pensions Act 1999, Sch 2, para 8.

9.74   There is a statutory obligation on employers under s 75 of the Pensions Act 1995 which requires an employer in some circumstances (eg where the scheme winds up or the company goes into liquidation or since April 2005 into administrative receivership or administration) to make up deficiencies in its pension scheme (subject to exceptions). However, this debt is specifically provided not to be a preferential debt (see also Chapter 34 below).

9.75   The Pensions Regulator has powers under PA 2004 to make some third parties liable for scheme funding (see Chapter 37 below). Enforcement by the Pensions Regulator of a financial support direction (FSD) under PA 2004 is usually by way of imposing a contribution notice (CN) under PA 2004 (see eg s 47).

Amounts due to the Trustees under a CN are a debt due – PA 2004, s 40(3). The 2004 Act does not state specifically that such a debt is non-preferential (contrast s 75 debts – see s 75(8), PA 1995), but on general principles, if payable by a third party (not an employer) it is unlikely to be a preferential debt under

Schedule 6 to IA 1986. This is because the pensions preferential debts under Schedule 4 to PSA 1993 refers to amounts due 'on account of an employer's contributions to a salary related contracted-out scheme' – PSA 1993, Sch 4, para 2.

9.76 In practice amounts due to the trustees will be likely not to be due from an employer. Para 2 does refer to an amount 'on account of' an employer's contributions, so an argument could be raised that this could cover amounts payable by a non-employer, but this seems unlikely to succeed.

Pensions as a preferential debt are discussed further below in Chapter 10.

PAYE and NI contributions

9.77 The Enterprise Act 2002 came into force on 15 September 2003 and amended Sch 6 to the Insolvency Act 1986 to remove (for insolvencies starting on or after that date) the previous preferential status of NICs and PAYE deducted by the company before the relevant date. Until then, national insurance contributions (NICs) and income tax (PAYE) which have been, or should have been deducted by an employer at source from remuneration paid to an employee in the 12 months preceding the relevant date were made preferential debts payable to the Secretary of State under categories 1 and 3 of IA 1986, Sch 6. There are transitional provisions (see SI 2003/2093, art 4).

9.78 In practice, however, an employee is not usually concerned as to whether or not such sums are in fact recovered by the Secretary of State. Unless the employee was somehow culpable (eg has contributed to the failure by the employer company to pay the contributions), he or she will normally be credited with the tax deducted or with the benefits in the state social security system as though such contributions had been paid in full by the employer[1]. Such a credit is also required by arts 7 and 10(b) of EC Directive 80/987, the Employment Insolvency Directive (see also Chapter 13 (National Insurance Fund) below).

1 Social Security (Contributions) Regulations 2001 (SI 2001/1004), reg 60 and Income Tax (Pay As You Earn) Regulations 2003 (SI 2003/2682), reg 72, formerly reg 42(2) and (3) of the Income Tax (Employments) Regulations 1993 (SI 1993/744).

9.79 Detailed guidance on the calculation of these preferential debts is set out in INS 1125 and INS 10325 of the HMRC Insolvency Manual – see http://www.hmrc.gov.uk/manuals/insmanual/ins1125.htm

SUBROGATION OF THIRD PARTIES

9.80 The Insolvency Act 1986, Sch 6, para 11 extends the category of preferential claims to include sums advanced by third parties (eg a bank) for the purpose of paying unpaid wages or holiday pay and which were applied to pay an amount to an employee which would otherwise have been preferential as being unpaid wages or accrued holiday pay (see para 8.19 above). The sums must have been advanced for that purpose.

9.81 Thus, if a bank lends (say) £200 to the company for the purpose of paying wages and the company uses this money to pay the last week's wages of an employee (who has no other claims) by paying (say) £150 to the employee and £50 to HMRC (PAYE and national insurance), then the bank's claim on the company for £200 will be preferential.

9.82 For an example (in Scotland) of preferential status transferring (in this case relating to VAT) see Lord Penrose in *Villaswan Ltd (in receivership) v Sheraton Caltrust (Blythswood) Ltd*[1].

1 [2000] BCC 188 (Lord Penrose).

9.83 It seems that the preference may apply if the lender advances money direct to the employees In the New Zealand case of *Waikato Savings Bank v Andrews Furniture Ltd*[1], dealing with the equivalent New Zealand section requiring money to be 'advanced by some person for that purpose', Prichard J held that the word 'advance' did not require a loan to the employer company but could cover a payment other than a loan, following Stout CJ in *Treadwell v Hutchings*[2]: 'to advance money is to furnish money for a specified purpose'.

The advance must be 'for the purpose' of being applied to meet wages or accrued holiday pay, but an express agreement between the lender and the company is not needed, provided the purpose was contemplated by the parties – see *Re Primrose (Builders) Ltd*[3] and *Re Rampgill Mill Ltd*[4].

1 [1982] 2 NZLR 520 (Prichard J).
2 [1925] NZLR 519, 523.
3 [1950] Ch 561, [1950] 2 All ER 334 (Wynn-Parry J).
4 [1967] Ch 1138 (Plowman J).

9.84 Banks often open separate 'wages accounts' to seek to maximise the priority available (with any receipts from the company being credited against other indebtedness) – see *Re E J Morel (1934) Ltd*[1], *Re Yeovil Glove Co Ltd*[2] and *Re James Rutherford & Sons Ltd*[3]. This is not however a requirement (it makes it easier for the bank to show that the priority should be available).

1 [1961] 1 All ER 796 (Buckley J).
2 [1962] 3 All ER 400, CA.
3 [1964] 3 All ER 137 (Pennycuick J).

9.85 The 2005 edition of the DTI Guide Employees' Rights on Insolvency of Employer[1] stated:

> 'Whether a wage cheque drawn from an overdrawn account is regarded as pay depends on the way the account is kept. An overdrawn ordinary current account out of which wage cheques were regularly drawn does not constitute money advanced for the purposes of paying employees' remuneration (*Re Primrose (Builders) Ltd* [1950] 2 All ER 334). If a separate wages account were set up, drawings from this account would normally constitute an advance.'

This passage does not appear in the 2008 edition issued by BERR, which merely states:

> 'In some cases a bank or other third party may lend the employer money to pay employees wages and make a separate claim in the insolvency (Insolvency Act 1986, schedule 6, part 11).'

1 See para 98 of 'Redundancy and Insolvency – A guide for insolvency practitioners to employees' rights on the insolvency of their employer' 2005 (Eighth Edition, URN 05/589).

2 See para 48 of the BERR booklet (URN 08/550). On the web at: http://www.insolvency.gov.uk/ guidanceleaflets/redundancypayments/guideforips/guideforips.htm

9.86   Commonly advances seeking to take advantage of this preference will be made by the company's bankers. But there is no reason to limit the application of paragraph 11 to payments by bankers. A third party funder can be involved – see Prichard J in the New Zealand case of *Waikato Savings Bank v Andrews Furniture Ltd*[1]

1 [1982] 2 NZLR 520 (Prichard J) at page 522.

9.87   The position is similar in Australia. In *Capt'n Snooze Management Pty Ltd v McLellan*[1], Hansen J in the Supreme Court of Victoria had to consider the situation of a loan made by Capt'n Snooze Management (CSM) to Dream Haven, a franchise operator which was in financial difficulties. The loan was made under a loan agreement which required that the loan 'will be used solely for the Purpose', the 'Purpose' being the payment of employee entitlements. The loan amount was actually paid into a general account of the company. Payments were made in and out of that account during the relevant period – not all payments were for employee entitlements.

1 [2002] VSC 432; (2003) 21 ACLC 121 (Hansen J). See the author's case note in Insolvency Intelligence (Jan 2005).

9.88   The Australian provision required two elements to be satisfied for it to operate. First, the money must have been advanced for the 'purpose' of making a payment of the specified kind. Secondly, the payment must have been made 'out of' the money advanced. Hanson J held that CSM's purpose in making the loans satisfied the first test, but that because the moneys advanced had gone into a mixed bank account, the second test was not satisfied, because it was not possible to say that the wages payments were 'out of' the amounts advanced by CSM.

9.89   Paragraph 11 of Sch 6 to the Insolvency Act 1986 is similar (but not identical) to the Australian provision. It includes the same concept of a payment 'for the purpose'. It does not however require that the payment to the employees be 'out of' the money advanced (contrast the predecessor to para 11 in Companies Act 1985, Sch 19, para 13). Instead the money advanced must have been 'applied' in payment of the preferential debt. It seems likely that the same result would have been reached based on the UK wording[1].

1 In *Capt'n Snooze*, a claim that the advances were held on a purpose trust, of the type in *Barclays Bank Ltd v Quistclose Investments Ltd* [1970] AC 567, HL, also failed.

9.90   This means that those seeking to lend money to companies in difficulties with a view to paying employee claims (and hence potentially seeking to gain the preferential status envisaged by para 11) are safer in either paying funds into a separate account (not a general trading account used for other purposes) or (perhaps) reaching an agreement with the bank.

9.91   The decision in *Capt'n Snooze* was followed in New South Wales in *Lombe v Wagga Leagues Club Ltd*[1]. It was held that priority could not be given where the advance was after the wages had been paid. Nor could there be priority if the money provided was not an advance (ie loan) but a payment under a deed of company arrangement that was not intended to be repaid (see paras 26 and 27 of the judgment).

1 [2006] NSWSC 3 (31 January 2006) (Barrett J).

9.92   In Australia, the Corporations Amendment (Insolvency) Act 2007 changed the Australian legislation (s 560) to make subrogation easier. The explanatory notes to the Corporations Amendment (Insolvency) Bill 2007[1] stated:

> '*Clarification of the rights of subrogated creditors*
>
> *Overview*
>
> 4.54 A 'subrogated creditor' is a person who is entitled to be substituted for another creditor in a liquidation because they have advanced funds to meet a particular creditor's debt. As a general rule, a subrogated creditor is treated as a substitute for the original creditor, retaining all their rights.
>
> 4.55 An example is the right of the Commonwealth to stand in the shoes of employee creditors after the Commonwealth has paid out the entitlements of those employee creditors under GEERS[1]. Banks may also advance funds to enable the payment of particular debts.
>
> 4.56 Under section 560 of the Corporations Act, where the company has paid wages, salary, superannuation contributions, money due for the various types of leave or a retrenchment payments using money advanced for that purpose by some other person, that creditor is entitled to the same priority in respect of that money as the recipient would have been entitled to if the payment had not been made.
>
> *Background*
>
> 4.57 A number of issues have been identified in relation to the rights of subrogated creditors.
>
> 4.58 First, it is unclear whether section 560 of the Corporations Act can apply to advances made after the relevant date. This issue has been recently highlighted as a consequence of the Commonwealth advancing funds through GEERS after a winding up begins or is taken to have begun. External administrators in practice have accepted advances from the Commonwealth under GEERS after the relevant date as advances for the purpose of section 560.

4.59 Second, it is unclear whether a subrogated creditor in a receivership or a voluntary administration retains their rights as a creditor when that administration moves into liquidation. The effect of this is that whilst the subrogated creditor enjoys the same priority as the creditor to whom it has advanced funds, they may not have the standing of that creditor, or enjoy the same rights (subrogated creditors enjoy rights as an "interested person" in some cases). The rights of subrogated creditors should be consistent across the different forms of external administration. Subrogated creditors should retain the rights of the original creditors.

4.60 Third, as currently worded, section 560 of the Corporations Act may permit voting rights associated with a single debt to be split among two or more persons. This may allow the outcome of creditors meetings to be manipulated.

4.61 Fourth, it is necessary to clarify the rights of a subrogated creditor in a DOCA. The Bill will make it mandatory for a DOCA to preserve the priority available to eligible employee creditors in a winding up under section 556 of the Corporations Act unless eligible employee creditors agree to waive their priority. In relation to subrogated creditors, a Court has ruled that a DOCA that imports the section 556 system of ranking will not without more import the statutory right conferred by section 560 on persons who advance money for the payment of priority claimants.[2]

4.62 Finally, it is necessary to address an issue highlighted in the decision in *Capt'n Snooze Management Pty Ltd v McLellan* [2002] VSC 432 (Capt'n Snooze), in particular the inclusion of the words "out of" in section 560. In Capt'n Snooze , Hansen J interpreted the requirement that a payment must be made "out of" monies advanced such that where the account from which the payments are made is in debit, or where the amounts advanced are "mingled" with other monies, the operation of section 560 would not be attracted.

4.63 The decision in *Capt'n Snooze* may affect a subrogated creditor's right of repayment of advances under section 560 of the Corporations Act. One way to address this issue would be for liquidators to establish a separate account, and use that separate account for the receipt and distribution of section 560 advances. However, the opening of separate accounts, and their administration, imposes an expense on liquidators. To avoid this expense, an amendment to section 560 will overcome the problem that has arisen from the decision in *Capt'n Snooze*. Specifically, section 560 will be amended to avoid the need for making an advance into a separate bank account.

4.64 These various concerns have been highlighted in the context of the administration of GEERS, where the Commonwealth's right to "stand in the shoes" of employee creditors after those employees have had their entitlements paid out under the GEERS scheme is critical for the operation of the scheme.[3]'

1 Available on Austlii: www.austlii.edu.au
2 *Re ACN 050 541 047 Ltd* [2002] NSWSC 586.
3 GEERS is the General Employee Entitlements and Redundancy Scheme. This is a government protection system, similar to the National Insurance Fund in the UK. See the book by Christopher Symes *Statutory Priorities in Corporate Insolvency Law* (Ashgate, 2008) at pages 146 to 156.

9.93 Obviously, the third party lender's claim is preferential only to the extent that the amount advanced is actually applied towards a preferential claim of the employee. Thus, the £800 limit also applies in the case of advances to pay wages. It seems that the better view is that the lender's claim will be preferential in respect of statutory deductions (PAYE and national insurance) only if these are in fact paid by the company to HMRC.

9.94 It would also seem that the third party's claim can be preferential only to the extent that there is an unused balance of the employee's claim within the £800 limit.

Example

Thus, if:

- an employee had unpaid wages in the last four months of £1,000; and

- a bank had advanced £700 to the company for the purpose of paying wages and this was used to pay the employee (and the relevant deductions),

the result would be that:

- the employee would still be owed £300 by the company (ie within the £800 limit)[1]; and

- the bank's claim would be preferential only as to £500 (ie the £800 limit less the employee's remaining claim for £300), not the whole £700 (even though, standing alone, the £700 claim would be preferential as within the £800 limit).

1 In this example, the employee may be able to make a claim on the National Insurance Fund (see Chapter 13 below) for up to £300.

9.95 This is the view taken by the Insolvency Service[1], although commenting in the context of an advance by a bank that:

> 'There is no case law on the interaction between the employee's claim and the bank's claim or which one takes precedence'.

1 See para 48 of 'Redundancy and Insolvency – A guide for insolvency practitioners to employees' rights on the insolvency of their employer' (URN 08/550). On the web at: http://www.insolvency.gov.uk/guidanceleaflets /redundancypayments/guideforips/guideforips.htm

This repeats the same view in the 8th edition (2005).

9.96 This view is supported by the decision of Wallace J in New Zealand in *Re Symphonia of Auckland Foundation Inc*[1]. The equivalent legislation in New Zealand, section 308, was identical to Companies Act 1985, Sch 19, para 13, the predecessor to para 11. It then allowed for a preferential debt (with a monetary limit of $1,500):

> '(3) Where any payment has been made -
>
> (a) To any servant or worker in the employment of a company, on account of wages or salary; or

(b)   To any such servant or worker or, in the case of his death, to any other person in his right, on account of holiday pay,

out of money advanced by some person for that purpose, the person by whom the money was advanced shall in a winding up have a right of priority in respect of the money so advanced and paid up to the amount by which the sum in respect of which the servant or worker would have been entitled to priority in the winding up has been diminished by reason of the payment having been made.'

Wallace J commented (at page 766):

'The crucial words of subs (3) of s 308 leave open the question as to when and in what circumstances payments by a third party "diminish" a servant's entitlement to priority. It is clear that payment of all the wages diminishes the servant's priority, with the priority of the servant then becoming the priority of the person who has paid the wages. However, the effect of payment of part of the wages is not clear.

In my view, so long as $1500 remains owing to a servant in respect of services rendered during the relevant four month period specified by s 308(1)(a), payment by a third party cannot be said to have diminished the servant's priority. I reach that conclusion partly because of the wording of s 308(1)(a) which states that "all" wages or salary in respect of services rendered during the relevant four month period are to be preferential. It seems to me that in those circumstances the "sum in respect of which the servant . . . would have been entitled to priority" cannot be said to have been diminished until there is less than $1500 of wages or salary owing to him in respect of services rendered during the relevant four month period. As the section is worded, it appears to me that it must be the sum of $1500 (rather than the total sum owing to the servant) which is "the sum in respect of which the servant . . . would have been entitled to priority". Once, however, there is less than $1500 owing, the servant's priority is diminished, eg, if a servant is owed $2000 and a third party pays $1000, then the servant is entitled to priority for $1000 and the third party for $500.

The above conclusion appears to me to be the only one open on the wording of the section. It may not be markedly equitable, but nor is the conclusion that the third party should receive the whole of the $1500, for the third party has paid only part of the wages (and possibly induced the servant to keep working for longer than he or she would otherwise have done). Moreover, it could be said that the principal aim of the section is to protect the servant.

With a view to doing equity, I have considered whether there is any warrant in the section for apportioning the priority on a pro rata basis, eg, whether the third party, having paid 60% of the wages, could receive 60% of the priority payment and the servant 40%. I cannot, however, see that the section permits such an approach. Section 308(4) seems to be directed only to the situation where, once priorities have been established, there are insufficient funds to meet the priority claims (including those of a third party who has advanced wages).

Mr Dench submitted that if s 308 is interpreted in the way in which I consider it must be, this would act as a disincentive for third parties to step in and make payment of wages. I accept that could be so in some circumstances, eg, under the

> interpretation which I consider must be adopted, a third party who pays some wages, but less than the full amount which qualifies for priority, does not gain the benefit of the right of subrogation. Indeed, if in the present case the Arts Council had paid all the employees on a pro rata basis (and in each case at least $1500 less than they had earned), the Arts Council would not have been entitled to any priority. However, payments of wages by a third party are only rarely made on an altruistic basis. If a third party desires to make payments it will need to assess all the circumstances and determine whether by making the payments it will achieve the right of subrogation to the servant's priority.'

Clearly Wallace J was influenced by the precise wording of s 308(3) in New Zealand.

1 [1984] 2 NZLR 759 (Wallace J).

9.97   But in the UK, para 11of Sch 6 is different and does not require the preferential claim of the employee to have been 'diminished'. There is no indication that a substantive change in the law was envisaged by the change made in IA 1985 (and IA 1986) from Companies Act 1985, Sch 19, para 13.

9.98   Potentially it would seem open to a lender (through the employer company) to specify to the employee at the time of payment that the relevant payment was in discharge of the latest debt first, so reserving the preferential claim to the lender. In practice this would be difficult to monitor or arrange. Absent a specific agreement, the UK courts arc likely to follow the employee priority as specified in the example above (and in the Insolvency Service guidance).

9.99   Wallace J did consider a pro-rata approach, but decided that this was not allowed by the wording of New Zealand legislation. Such a pro-rata approach is applied in England where mandatory set-off applies – see *Re Unit 2 Windows Limited* and Chapter 14 (Set-off) below.

Despite this, the UK courts are likely to follow the employee priority as specified in the example above (and in the Insolvency Service guidance). Pro rata allocation is likely to give rise to computational difficulties. The employee is likely to argue that any payment made went to reduce his or her longest outstanding wages claim first and did left him or her with the balance still due as a preferential debt.

Payment out of National Insurance Fund

9.100   If the Secretary of State makes a payment then the National Insurance Fund subrogates to the extent of that payment as a preferential creditor to the extent to which the employee's claim was preferential (see para 13.71 below). The level of the preferential claim of a third party lender (ie the £500 in the example in paragraph 9.94 above) is unaffected.

This view is supported by the decision of Wallace J in New Zealand in *Re Symphonia of Auckland Foundation Inc*[1].

1 [1984] 2 NZLR 759 (Wallace J). See para 9.96 above.

9.101   In relation to a preferential claim, the employee's claim and the Secretary of State's claim must be added together for computing preferential amounts due – ERA 1996, s 189(3).

9.102   Section 189(4) of ERA 1996 used to give the Secretary of State the right to be paid in priority to any other unsatisfied claims of employees (the so-called 'super-preference' status), but, this section was repealed for cases where the date of insolvency is on or after 15 September 2003 – see Chapter 13 (National Insurance Fund) below.

9.103   From that date the Secretary of State has equal preference with the employee – see s 189(3). However, if the insolvency date falls before 15 September 2003, the Secretary of State retains super-preferential status over the claims of employees[1].

1 See para 39 of the Insolvency Service booklet, 'Redundancy and Insolvency – A guide for insolvency practitioners to employees' rights on the insolvency of their employer' (URN 08/550). On the web at: http://www.insolvency.gov.uk/guidanceleaflets/redundancypayments/guideforips/guideforips.htm

9.104   The DTI used to make the point that insolvency practitioners should take care to separate claims for wages and holiday pay when making preferential dividends, 'otherwise there is a danger that the RPO could be under/overpaid'[1]. This advice does not appear in the revised Insolvency Service booklet.

1 See para 87 of 'Redundancy and Insolvency – A guide for insolvency practitioners to employees' rights on the insolvency of their employer' 2005 (8th Edition, URN 05/589).

9.105   The Insolvency Service in its booklet[1] gives examples of the inter-action of the preferential debts regime with the payments by the Redundancy Payments Office (RPO) out of the National Insurance Fund (NIF):

---

40 Example of distribution for an employee who was made redundant in June 2002 and the insolvency date is before 15 September 2003
An employee's gross claim against his former employer is as follows:

4 weeks' wages @ £5,00 per week = £2,000 (£800 preferential; £1,200 non-preferential)

6 weeks' holiday pay @ £500 per week = £3,000 (all preferential)

Total preferential claims = £3,800

Payments to an employee from the NI Fund are limited by statute, and the RPO paid £2,500 of the employee's claim as follows:

4 weeks' wages @ £250 per week = £1,000 (£800 preferential and £200 non-preferential).

6 weeks' holiday pay @ £250 per week = £1,500 (all preferential)

The RPO takes over the employee's rights in the insolvency in respect of the amounts it has paid him or her out of the NI Fund. For each category of preferential

---

payments, the RPO must be paid in full before the employee receives any balance of the preferential amount due.

For preferential claims:

> The total claim is £3,800 made up of £800 for wages and £3,000 for holiday pay.

> The RPO paid £800 wages and £1,500 holiday pay.

> The employee's remaining unpaid preferential claim is £1,500 holiday pay.

If a dividend of 70p in the pound is payable for preferential debts, then the amounts available are £560 for wages and £2,100 for holiday pay. From this, the RPO receives all the £560 available for wages plus the £1,500 it has paid out in holiday pay. The employee would receive no wages but £600 in holiday pay (i.e. the £2,100 available less the £1,500 paid to the RPO).

---

41. Distributions where the insolvency date is on or after 15 September 2003
The RPO retains its preferential ranking but no longer has a super-preference status over the preferential claims of employees. The requirement for the RPO to be paid in full before the employee is paid was removed [Employment Rights Act 1996 s 189(4)]. However, the requirement to add together the RPO and employee's preferential claims and treat them as one debt for the purpose of computing the preferential dividend remains [Employment Rights Act 1996 s 189(3)]. The need for apportionment between the Secretary of State's and the employee's preferential claims for wages arises because of the legal requirement for the claims to be treated as one for calculation of preferential debt statutory and the statutory limit on the amount payable, which is £800 on the wages payable in the 4 months immediately before the insolvency date. Any debts that fall outside of the 4-month period are out of scope for preferential purposes and do not need to be added to the employees gross claim for calculation purposes. The RPO would expect an amount equivalent to the percentage of the employees gross claim paid from the NIF on behalf of the employer. For example, if the RPO has paid 25% of the debt then they can expect 25% of the dividend.

Originally it was thought that all claims would need to be apportioned but we discovered there was no need to do so in the following cases.

- Holiday pay claims. As there is no limit on the preferential amount that can be claimed for holiday pay, there is no need for apportionment – the RPO can claim the full amount as preferential as can the employee.

- Wages claims: Apportionment is required only where an employee has a residual claim for wages in the insolvency. Where the employee has no residual wages claim (RPO paid full debt from NIF) – the RPO can claim the full amount as preferential (subject to the £800 limit on wages).

- Where the employees gross wages debt (including the amount paid by the RPO) is £800 or less then apportionment will not be required as the ultimate distribution will be the same whether or not apportionment is applied.

- Any weeks of a protective award that fall after the insolvency date will be out of scope for preference, as they do not fall within the 4-month period prior to the insolvency date.

42. Example of Apportionment of wages

The employee' s gross claim against the employer is £2,000 (£4 weeks at @ £500 within the 4-month limit).

The RPO pays £1240 (4 weeks @ £310)

The employee's residual claim is £760 (£2,000 less £1240 paid by the RPO).

The RPO has paid 62% of the debt and would therefore expect 62% of the £800 that is available to share between the employee and the RPO (on full dividend), which is £496. The same principle applies to a part dividend also.

Protective awards (PA) are treated as wages under ERA 1996 and Insolvency Act 1986, Schedule 6. The £800 limit on wages will apply to any period of a protective award that falls within the 4-month period before the insolvency date. Only the gross wages for that period needs to be added to the employee's gross claim for the calculation of the preferential amount due to the RPO. Any period of the award that falls after the insolvency date is automatically non-preferential and should not be added to the gross claim to calculate preferential claims.

As a PA payment is made some considerable time after all the other payments, the apportionment of the original preferential wages claims on the RP 11 and RP12 may need amendment as well as the proof of debt form. However, if the whole of the award falls after the insolvency date then there is no need to re-apportion the claim.

43. Example 1 of additional PA payment (no re-apportionment)

Insolvency date 11/12/06.

Dismissal date 27/11/06.

PA for 90 days starting on 27/11/06.

8 weeks max on the number of weeks payable from NIF with 4 weeks already paid by RPO (as in above example).

4 more weeks @ £310 payable of which 2 weeks in scope for preference

The revised gross claim is £3,000 (6 weeks @ £500)

The RPO paid £1,860 (6 weeks @ £310) – the residual claim is £1,140.

The RPO percentage has not changed from 62% so no re-apportionment is required. A revised proof of debt updating the amounts is required.

44. Example 2 of additional PA payment (re-apportionment required):

Weekly rate of pay is £250 and statutory limit is £310

Insolvency date 11/12/06.

Dismissal date 11/12/06.

PA for 90 days starting on 27/11/06 of which 2 weeks in scope for preference and which also overlaps with wages already paid

8 weeks max on wages payable from NIF

4 weeks @ £250 already paid by RPO

4 more weeks @ £250 payable (non-preferential) and 2 weeks @ £60 (top up to limit for 2 overlapping weeks of PA and wages).

147

The employee's gross claim for wages was originally £1000 and no apportionment was necessary as the RPO paid 100% of debt and was claiming the full £800 as preferential

Because of the overlapping 2 weeks of the PA and wages the employee now has a residual claim for wages and apportionment is required (2 weeks at £500 – double pay, and the application of the statutory limit of £310 to those weeks).

The gross claim is £1500 (2 weeks @ £250 and 2 weeks @ £500, which is their ordinary wages plus the PA). The RPO paid £1,120 (2 weeks @ £250 and 2 weeks @ £310 or 4 weeks @ £250 and 2 weeks @ £60 if you prefer). The employee's residual claim is £380 (2 weeks @ £190). The RPO has now paid 74.67% of the debt and would expect 74.67% of the £800, which is £576. Apportionment is now required.

The gross claim is £1830 (2 weeks @ £305 and 2 weeks @ £610). The RPO paid £1200 (2 weeks @ £290 and 2 weeks @ £310 or 4 weeks @ £290 and 2 weeks @ £20 if you prefer). The employee's residual claim is £630. The RPO has now paid 65.57% of the debt and would expect that % of the £800, which is £524.56. Re-apportionment is now required to show the adjusted % of the claims.

---

1 See paras 40 to 43 of the Insolvency Service booklet, 'Redundancy and Insolvency – A guide for insolvency practitioners to employees' rights on the insolvency of their employer' (URN 08/550). On the web at: http://www.insolvency.gov.uk/guidanceleaflets/redundancypayments/guideforips/guideforips.htm

CHAPTER 10

Pensions as a preferential debt

10.1   In relation to pensions claims, the categories of preferential debts are set out in Schedule 4 to the Pension Schemes Act 1993 (PSA 1993), as applied by IA 1986, Sch 6, category 4. Broadly, two pensions debts are preferential:

● unpaid employee contributions deducted from pay by the employer; and

● a limited amount of unpaid employer contributions.

10.2   Pension debts will remain claims against the transferor employer (and so potentially preferential) even if there is a transfer of employment liabilities under TUPE. This is because most liabilities under or relating to an occupational pension scheme are exempt from the transfer provisions in TUPE (see TUPE 2006, reg 10) – see Chapter 24 below.

UNPAID EMPLOYEE CONTRIBUTIONS

10.3   Amounts owing by way of unpaid employee contributions deducted by the insolvent employer from pay in the last four months before the relevant date[1], but not yet paid to the pension scheme are preferential. This only applies to amounts owing to an occupational pension scheme[2] (and not to a personal pension scheme[3] or a stakeholder pension scheme[4]).

1 Usually the date of formal insolvency – see IA 1986, s 387 and para 9.22 above.
2 See para 10.25 below as to the meaning of this term.
3 See para 10.26 below.
4 Unless established as an occupational pension scheme – this is unusual.

10.4   There is no limit on the amount that can be preferential in this category. In practice, for relevant tax registered (formerly Inland Revenue approved) schemes, there are relatively tight rules under the pensions legislation specifying time limits for the employer to pay employee contributions to the pension scheme (see para 10.40 below). If not paid within the time limit, there are reporting obligations to the Pensions Regulator and the potential for civil penalties and criminal sanctions.

149

UNPAID EMPLOYER CONTRIBUTIONS

10.5   The preferential status in respect of unpaid employer contributions does not apply to all amounts of funding or of contributions that may be payable by an employer. Instead it is limited so that it only applies to amounts owing in the last 12 months before the relevant date to a contracted-out occupational pension scheme. A contracted-out scheme is one that is certified as such by the contracting-out agency under the Pension Schemes Act 1993. In relation to employees within the scope of the contracting-out certificate, lower national insurance contributions are payable by both the employer and the employee and in exchange the scheme provides benefits in substitution for part of the state pension (funded by national insurance contributions). See further para 10.27 below.

10.6   So no preferential status applies to amounts owing to personal pensions, nor to an occupational scheme that is not contracted-out.

10.7   The amount that is preferential is linked to the amount of the national insurance rebate that applies when employees are members of contracted-out occupational pension schemes. The preferential amount is limited to a percentage of relevant earnings (between the lower earnings limit (LEL) and the upper accrual point (UAP)[1] for national insurance purposes). For a scheme contracted-out on a salary related basis, the percentage also varies depending on whether or not the scheme requires contributions to be made by the employee as well as the employer. If contributions are required from the employee, the percentage is 3%. If not, it is 4.6%.

1 Before 6 April 2009, the higher end of this band was the upper earnings limit (UEL), but this was changed to the UAP by the National Insurance Contributions Act 2008, s 4(1), Sch 1, paras 7, 13(1), (2). The UEL remains the upper end of the band for NI contributions, but not (now) benefits.

10.8   For a scheme contracted-out on a salary related basis with no requirement for employee contributions, this results in a maximum preferential amount in tax year 2009/10 of approximately £1,685 per employee (and then only for an employee in a non-contributory contracted-out scheme who has earned over the UAP of £40,040pa).

10.9   In practice protection is given to employees by the guarantee offered by the National Insurance Fund (see Chapter 13 (National Insurance Fund) below). If the Crown pays the relevant amount, it then takes over the claim of the employee (or scheme trustees), including the preferential status of that claim.

Category 4: 'contributions to occupational pension schemes'

10.10   Category 4 in Sch 6 to the Insolvency Act 1986 deals with preferential debts relating to contributions to occupational pension schemes etc. It states that it applies to 'any sum which is owed by' the insolvent company, but only if Sch 4 to the Pension Schemes Act 1993 also applies.

10.11   The contributions specified in Sch 4 to the Pension Schemes Act 1993 (as amended[1]) are, broadly:

- Paragraph 1: Contributions deducted by the employer from the employee's pay but not yet paid to an occupational pension scheme. This is limited to the four months before the relevant date;

- Paragraph 2: Contributions due from the employer to an occupational pension scheme in the 12 months preceding the relevant date. But this is limited to amounts due to a contracted-out scheme and then to a specific percentage of earnings within a band.

- Paragraph 3: contributions equivalent premiums. These are paid to re-instate an employee into the state pension system if he or she becomes con-tracted-out of that system by reference to an occupational pension scheme, but does not serve long enough to be given vested rights (a deferred pension).

1 Welfare Reform and Pensions Act 1999, s 18.

OVERVIEW AND POLICY ISSUES

Further preference?

10.12   Schedule 4 does not contain a general priority for any pension under-funding there may be in an occupational pension scheme.

10.13   Preferential treatment is not given to a pension fund in respect of any outstanding contributions that the company would normally have made or to contributions in respect of the entire shortfall of the pension scheme. This has become more important in recent years when pension fund deficits have grown (by a combination of reduced asset values, increased longevity and the increased cost of securing pension benefits with insurers).

10.14   The government had said that it was considering whether or not to make such underfunding liability a preferential debt.

10.15   In its pensions Green Paper[1] issued in December 2002, the government said:

Amending the priority order of creditors

73. We might also consider moving pension schemes up the order of priority for payment. At present, certain sums that are due to pension schemes are included for payment with other unsecured creditors at the bottom of the list of creditors. This group lies below preferential creditors (which include unpaid wages and certain pension contributions) and secured creditors (which include banks, mortgage lenders and so on who had made secured loans).

Some argue that pension scheme members should be given the same priority as preferential or secured creditors.

74. This would increase the overall level of funds available to schemes. However, it could also have significant wider economic consequences. In particular, employers with defined benefit schemes could find it harder to obtain secured loans, or see the cost of those loans increasing. So this is very unattractive.

75. One way of addressing this problem might be to create a new category of creditor. Pension schemes could be given a higher priority than other unsecured creditors but still have lower priority than preferential and secured creditors. This would reduce the potentially adverse economic effects. However, other unsecured creditors – for instance trade suppliers, consumers and employees – would lose out. They might consider they have at least as much right as a pension scheme to a share of the insolvent employer's assets. As a result, some – such as trade creditors – might have to downsize or go into insolvency themselves.

76. We need to strike a careful balance between the potential impact on business and the need to provide adequate protection for members. We would welcome views on this balance.

1 'Simplicity, Security and Choice: Working and Saving for Retirement' (Cm 5677) issued on 17 December 2002.

10.16   But there was nothing about this in the government's later Action Plan[1] issued on 11 June 2003. There was nothing in the Pensions Bill introduced into Parliament in February 2004 to enact any preferential status. The Pensions Bill subsequently became the Pensions Act 2004 and did not include any change to the preferential debt provisions. In particular s 75(8) remained unchanged to the effect that a debt under s 75 of the Pensions Act 1995 (see below) is not preferential[2].

1 'Simplicity, security and choice: working and saving for retirement – Action on occupational pensions' (Cm 5835).
2 The Pensions Act 2004 made significant alterations to s 75, but not to this provision.

10.17   In March 2004, an attempt was made to change this in the committee stage in the House of Commons on the Pensions Bill. The government explained that it had received various views in favour of such a step. But the CBI was strongly opposed, saying:

'Employers with DB schemes will find it harder to obtain secured loans or see the cost of loans increase… it could hinder future overseas investment into the UK'.

'Other unsecured creditors would lose out and find themselves penalised through no fault of their own.'

10.18   Chris Pond MP (The Under-Secretary of State for Work and Pensions) then said that:

'With a difficult decision to make on the balance of those arguments, we decided that it was not sensible to move forward with the option for the reasons outlined in the CBI's response.'

1 Hansard, House of Commons, Standing Committee B, Column 304, 18 March 2004.

Limit to contracted-out rights

10.19   In relation to employer pension contributions, Sch 4 to PSA 1993 was originally limited to amounts relating to contracted-out benefits (guaranteed minimum pensions (GMPs) and protected rights – see paras 10.32 and 10.33 below). This was presumably part of the state's aim to seek to protect these contracted-out rights even if they are not in fact provided by the pension scheme, ie to reduce the risk that the employee will in fact be worse off as a result of the scheme being contracted-out. Clearly if he or she had not been contracted-out the relevant state benefits would still have been payable (and unaffected by the solvency of the employer or of the pension scheme).

10.20   This aim continues, but now by reference to the term 'appropriate amount'[1] (broadly calculated as the NI rebate amount).

1 PSA 1993, Sch 4, para 2(1) and (3).

10.21   The existence of the statutory guarantee by the national insurance fund (see Chapter 13 (National Insurance Fund) below) is probably the main reason why the categories of, and limits on, employee preferential debts have not been increased. In many cases it is the state that is bearing the risk of non-payment by the insolvent employer[1].

1 But some employees may be better off under the preferential debt regime. For example employees outside the UK who are not covered by the national insurance fund cover. On territorial ambit see the decisions of the ECJ in *Danmarks Active Handelsrejsende (acting for Mosbaek) v Lonmod-tagernes Garantifund* [1998] All ER (EC) 112, [1998] ICR 954 and *Everson and Barrass v Secretary of State for Trade and Industry and Bell Lines Ltd (in liquidation)* [1999] ECR I-8903; [2000] IRLR 202, discussed in Chapter 13 (National Insurance Fund) below.

10.22   This is presumably one reason why the statutory winding-up priority[1] on the winding-up of relevant occupational pension schemes (which are not money purchase schemes) used to include a priority for contracted-out rights[2]. But this priority order was changed as a result of regulations which came into force on 10 May 2004[3]. Those regulations changed the statutory priority order so that deferred pensions are given priority over increases to pensions in payment. This change also removed the priority previously given to contracted-out benefits ahead of other benefits.

1 Pensions Act 1995, s 73.
2 See the Occupational Pension Schemes (Winding Up) Regulations 1996 (SI 1996/3126), reg 3(5), as amended by SI 1997/786, SI 1999/3198, SI 2000/2691, SI 2002/380 and SI 2004/403), substituting a new paragraph (c) into s 73(3) of the Pensions Act 1995.
3 Pension Schemes (Winding-Up) (Amendment) Regulations 2004 (SI 2004/1140).

10.23 Subsequently, the statutory priority order under PA 1995, s 73 changed again (with effect from 6 April 2005). This change reflected the coming into force of the Pension Protection Fund (PPF) – see Chapter 27 below. The priority formerly given to contracted-out rights has gone completely.

Some terms

10.24 It is not possible to understand the priority given by Schedule 4 without further explanation of the terms it uses.

10.25 Occupational pension scheme: The term 'occupational pension scheme is defined in s 1 of the Pension Schemes Act 1993[1]. See para 2.60 above on this.

1 Amended by PA 2004. Formerly the Social Security Act 1973, s 51(3)(a), and the Social Security Pensions Act 1975, s 66(1).

10.26 This term is to be contrasted with the term 'personal pension scheme' also defined in s 1 (and which covers most stakeholder pension schemes as well[1]). There is no preferential status given to outstanding contributions due to personal pension schemes (even if the employer contributes to them too).

1 Stakeholder schemes can be set up as occupational pension schemes, but the vast majority are not. See further on this pages xiii to xvi on 'Preliminary legal issues' in the book by Ian Greenstreet '*Stakeholder Pensions: a Special Report*' (Sweet & Maxwell, 2001).

10.27 *Contracted-out scheme*
This is defined in s 7(3) of the Pension Schemes Act 1993 as an occupational pension scheme that is named in a contracting-out certificate (itself defined in s 7(1)).

10.28 It is to be noted that this term only applies to an occupational pension scheme. A personal pension scheme that is used for contracting-out purposes is called an 'appropriate scheme' and is named in an 'appropriate scheme certificate'[1].

1 Pension Schemes Act 1993, s 7(1), (4).

10.29 Broadly a contracted-out scheme is one that passes a test and should provide a certain minimum level of benefits. If it passes the relevant tests, a contracting-out certificate is issued. This authorises the employer to pay, and deduct from the employee's pay, national insurance contributions at a lower rate (the contracted-out rate). The employee ceases to qualify for the relevant level of state benefits (but instead gets credited with benefits under the pension scheme). The relevant state benefits forgone were, until 5 April 2002, the benefits under the State Earnings Pension Scheme (SERPS). On 6 April 2002 further SERPS benefits ceased to accrue. National insurance contributions paid after that date go to qualify employees for the new State Second Pension (S2P)[1].

1 See Social Security Contributions and Benefits Act 1992, s 44(6)(a), as amended by the Child Support, Pensions and Social Security Act 2000, s 30(2)(b).

10.30   Contracting-out can either be with benefits:

- on a defined contribution or money purchase basis (Contracted-out Money Purchase or COMP) or

- on a defined benefit or salary related basis (Contracted-out Salary Related or COSR).

10.31   A single scheme can combine both bases – some employees being contracted-out on a money purchase basis, the others on a salary related basis. In this case the scheme is known as a Contracted-out Mixed Benefit Scheme or a COMB.

10.32   COMP

A COMP provides money purchase benefits instead of the relevant state benefit. The employer must pay a minimum amount (these are called 'minimum payments'[1]) into the COMP. These minimum payments are broadly equivalent to the saving in reduced national insurance contributions (employer and employee). The minimum payments are credited to a separate account within the COMP, where they form 'protected rights' which can only be used to provide benefits in a limited form.

   Contracting-out of a money purchase basis will cease to be available from a future date (probably 6 April 2012)[2].

1 Pension Schemes Act 1993, s 8(2).
2 Pensions Act 2007.

10.33   COSR

In contrast, under a COSR, defined benefits are provided. For employment before 6 April 1997 these defined benefits were a guaranteed minimum pension[1] (or 'GMP'), which was broadly equivalent to the forgone SERPS benefit. After 6 April 1997, GMPs ceased to accrue (but remain in place for contracted-out pensionable service before that date). Instead benefits after 6 April 1997 need to be certified by an actuary as (broadly) meeting a reference test laid down in statute and an actuarial guidance note[2]. The post April 1997 benefits provided are called 'Section 9(2B) rights'[3].

1 Pension Schemes Act 1993, s 8(2).
2 See ss 9(2B) and 12A of the Pension Schemes Act 1993 and actuarial guidance note GN28 issued by the Board for Actuarial Standards (which took over responsibility from the Faculty and Institute of Actuaries).
3 After s 9(2B) of the Pension Schemes Act 1993 (as inserted by the Pensions Act 1995). The term is not used in the Act itself, but it does appear in the Occupational Pension Schemes (Contracting-out) Regulations 1996 (SI 1996/1172), as amended.

Paragraph 1: Employee contributions

10.34   This paragraph covers contributions from the employee to an occupational pension scheme that have been deducted by the employer from earnings paid to the employee during the four months preceding the relevant date but which have not yet been paid to the pension scheme.

10.35 There is no monetary limit on the amount that can be claimed under this paragraph.

10.36 Note that it does not cover employee contributions to a personal pension scheme.

10.37 In practice the risk of failure of an employer to pay across to a pension scheme contributions deducted from pay is limited by both the possibility that the contributions will have been paid into a separate trust and by the existence of specific time limits on such payments under the Pensions Act 1995.

Separate trust?

10.38 Any amounts which the employer has deducted from wages or salary paid to the employee by way of contribution to the pension arrangement, but which the employer has not yet in fact paid to the relevant pension arrangement will probably, if these amounts have been placed in a separate account or fund, be impressed with a trust – see eg *Re Chelsea Cloisters Ltd*[1] and the cases mentioned in para 33.3 below.

1 (1981) 41 P&CR 98, CA.

10.39 Trust assets fall outside the assets available to the insolvency practitioner – see eg *Re Kayford Ltd*[1] and *Heritable Reversionary Company Ltd v Millar*[2]. See further Chapter 26 (Pensions and other trusts) below.

1 [1975] 1 All ER 604 (Megarry J).
2 [1892] AC 598, HL.

Pensions Act regulation?

10.40 From 1997, the Pensions Act 1995 has included (s 49) specific provision on payment of deducted contributions to pension schemes. An employer is under a duty to pay to an occupational pension scheme contributions that have been deducted from members' pay before the 19th of the month following the month when they were deducted from pay.

10.41 From 6 April 1997 to 3 April 2000 the Pensions Act 1995 made it a criminal offence for an employer to fail, without reasonable excuse, to pay the amount of such deducted employee contributions to the trustees of an occupational pension scheme[1]. Directors, officers and others (potentially including an insolvency practitioner[2]) can also be criminally liable if the failure occurred as a result of their consent, connivance or neglect[3].

1 Pensions Act 1995, s 49(8) and reg 16 of the Occupational Pension Schemes (Scheme Administration) Regulations 1996 (SI 1996/1715, as amended by SI 1997/768).
2 See Chapter 8 above.
3 Pensions Act 1995, s 115 and see Chapter 8 above.

10.42 Since 3 April 2000[1] only fraudulent evasion has been criminal and not also a simple negligent failure. It is currently an offence, under s 49 of the Pensions Act 1995, for a person knowingly to be concerned in the fraudulent evasion of this duty by an employer. The Occupational Pensions Regulatory Authority (OPRA)[2] brought successful prosecutions against company directors for fraudulent evasion[3].

1 When the amendments made by s 10 of the Welfare Reform and Pensions Act 1999 came into force.
2 Since 6 April 2005, OPRA has been replaced by the Pensions Regulator (PA 2004).
3 Peter Lavender was fined on 4 September 2003 at Gloucester Crown Court. David Watson was convicted on 9 August 2004 at Leeds Crown Court. The criminal offence of fraudulent evasion is committed where there is fraudulent evasion of the employer's requirement to pay pension contributions deducted from employees' earnings to the pension provider. The offences that were committed were breaches of s 111A(12) of the Pensions Scheme Act 1993 and s 24A of the Theft Act 1968. Details of the legal action taken by OPRA against Mr Watson for non-payment of contributions can be found at the OPRA archive on the Pensions Regulator website: www.thepensionsregulator.gov.uk/opraArchive/

10.43 Where an employer fails to pay member contributions within the prescribed time, the employer may be subject to a civil penalty levied by the Pensions Regulator under s 10 of the Pensions Act 1995. The maximum civil penalty under s 10 is currently £5,000 for an individual and £50,000 for others.

Paragraph 2: Employer contributions

10.44 This paragraph covers the contributions from the employer to a contracted-out scheme payable in the 12-month period preceding the relevant date[1].

Paragraph 2 only applies to contributions payable to a 'contracted-out scheme'. This term is not defined in Sch 4, but is defined in s 7(3) of PSA 1993. It only includes an occupational pension scheme and not a personal pension scheme (see paras 10.25 and 10.26 above).

1 Ie broadly the date of the relevant insolvency event (eg appointment of an administrative receiver, administration order etc). See Sch 4, para 4, cross referring to CA 2006 s 754(3) (formerly CA 1985, s 196(3)), and IA 1986, s 387. See para 9.22 above.

Preferential amount

10.45 So the preferential status is limited to a fairly small percentage of the earnings of members who are contracted-out by reference to the scheme.

10.46 For a salary related contracted-out scheme (COSR) the appropriate amount is a percentage applied to the 'reckonable earnings' of the employee. The reckonable earnings are those paid or payable in the 12 month period between the lower earnings limit (currently[1] £95 per week[2]) (LEL) and upper accrual point[3] (currently[4] £770 per week) (UAP).

1 Ie in tax year 2009/2010.
2 This is the LEL under the social security legislation – see reg 10 of the Social Security (Contributions) Regulations 2001, as amended by reg 5 of the Social Security (Contributions)

(Amendment) Regulations 2003. This is different to the employee's earnings threshold for payment of national insurance contributions, which is currently £97pw. This is not the LEL, but instead the amount at which National Insurance starts to be payable (the two de-linked in 1999). The LEL is still the right figure for Sch 4.

3 Before 6 April 2009, the higher end of this band was the upper earnings limit (UEL), but this was changed to the UAP by the National Insurance Contributions Act 2008, s 4(1), Sch 1, paras 7, 13(1), (2). The UEL remains the upper end of the band for NI contributions, but not (now) benefits.

4 Ie in tax year 2009/2010.

10.47 For example, in relation to a COSR (contracted-out final salary scheme), the percentage is 3% or 4.8%[1] (depending on whether or not the members pay contributions). This gives, for a COSR scheme that does not require employee contributions, a maximum amount of £1,685 (approx) per contracted-out active member (ie 4.8% of the annual UAP of £40,040 less LEL of £4,940, ie 4.8% of £35,100).

1 The Social Security (Reduced Rates of Class 1 Contributions) (Salary Related Contracted-out Schemes) Order 1996 (SI 1996/1054). There does not seem to be any later change to reflect the increased NI rebate payable from tax year 2002/03.

'3 Consequential provision

In paragraph 2(3)(a) of Schedule 4 to the Pension Schemes Act 1993 (priority in bankruptcy: employer's contributions to an occupational pension scheme), so far as the percentage specified in that paragraph applies in relation to earnings paid or payable on or after 6th April 1997, the percentage specified for non-contributing earners in relation to a salary related contracted-out scheme shall be 4.6 per cent.'

10.48 This preferential debt arises if any amounts are due in relation to unpaid employer contributions ('any sum owed') – even if enough has been paid to meet the contracted-out amount. So if there are any unpaid amounts (eg under the schedule of contributions maintained under s 58 of the Pensions Act 1995 or s 227 of the Pensions Act 2004[1]) a part will be preferential. Amounts due under a schedule of contributions are enforceable as a debt[2].

1 See Chapter 33 (Contributions to pension schemes) below.
2 Pensions Act 1995, s 59(2), and Pensions Act 2004, s 228(3).

10.49 In relation to a contracted-out money purchase scheme (COMP) the preferential debt is equal to the minimum payments payable by the employer (see above) in the 12 months before the relevant date[1]. If the minimum payments cannot be identified from the terms of the scheme, the 'appropriate amount' applies instead (this is the higher amount applicable to a COSR)[2].

1 PSA 1993, Sch 4, para 2(2).
2 PSA 1993, Sch 4, para 2(3).

10.50 The minimum payments payable by an employer are limited to the appropriate flat rate percentage national insurance rebate as applied to earnings between the LEL and the UAP[1]. These are currently 1.4% for the employer and 1.6% for the employee[2].

1 Pension Schemes Act 1993, s 42A(2). The UAP was substituted for the UEL with effect from 6 April 2009.

2 Fixed for tax years 2007/08 to 2011/12 by the Social Security (Reduced Rates of Class 1 Contributions, Rebates and Minimum Contributions) Order 2006 (SI 2006/1009) made under s 42B of the Pension Schemes Act 1993. Previously fixed at 1% for the employer and 1.6% for the employee for tax years 2002/03 to 2006/07 by the Social Security (Reduced Rates of Class 1 Contributions, and Rebates) (Money Purchase Contracted-out Schemes) Order 2001 (SI 2001/1355).

10.51　　Age related rebates are payable into COMPs as well, but these are funded by the parties paying the remaining national insurance contributions to the state and then HMRC paying the appropriate amount to the scheme. So they do not feature in any preferential debt.

Section 75, Pensions Act 1995

10.52　　In certain circumstances (including on the liquidation of the employer), the employer in relation to a defined benefit occupational pension scheme (such as a COSR) may become liable, under s 75 of the Pensions Act 1995, to the trustees of the pension scheme for a debt in respect of any deficit in the scheme[1]. A debt under s 75 can also arise when a scheme winds-up or when an employer in a multi-employer scheme becomes insolvent or ceases to participate in a multi-employer scheme.

1 See generally Chapter 34 below. There are exclusions – eg money purchase schemes, schemes without HMRC registration or with less than two members.

10.53　　A debt 'due by virtue only of' s 75 of the Pensions Act 1995 is not to be regarded as a preferential debt – s 75(8) of the Pensions Act 1995. So this seems to mean that any amounts payable under s 75 only (eg on the company entering liquidation) cannot be a preferential debt (seemingly even if the s 75 debt would otherwise come within Sch 4).

10.54　　So in order for a funding debt to be preferential it will need to be payable under some obligation outside s 75 – eg under the terms of the trust deed governing the scheme or under the schedule of contributions maintained (for relevant pension schemes) under ss 56 to 61 (minimum funding requirement) of the Pensions Act 1995 or the Pensions Act 2004. Amounts due under a schedule of contributions are treated as a debt[1].

1 Pensions Act 1995, s 59(2), and Pensions Act 2004, s 228(3). See Chapter 33 below.

10.55　　The Pensions Regulator has powers under PA 2004 to make some third parties liable for scheme funding (see Chapter 37 below). Enforcement by the Pensions Regulator of a financial support direction (FSD) under PA 2004 is usually by way of imposing a contribution notice (CN) under PA 2004 (see eg s 47).

Amounts due to the trustees under a CN are a debt due – PA 2004, s 40(3). PA 2004 does not state specifically that such a debt is non-preferential (contrast s 75 debts – see PA 1995, s 75(8)), but on general principles, if payable by a third party (not an employer) it is unlikely to be a preferential debt under IA 1986, Sch 6. This is because the pensions preferential debts under PSA 1993, Sch 4 refers to amounts due 'on account of an employer's contributions to a salary related contracted-out scheme' – PSA 1993, Sch 4, para 2.

In practice amounts due to the trustees will be likely not to be due from an employer. Para 2 does refer to an amount 'on account of' an employer's contributions, so an argument could be raised that this could cover amounts payable by a non-employer, but this seems unlikely to succeed.

Paragraph 3: Contributions equivalent premiums

10.56 Contributions equivalent premiums (CEPs) are paid[1] to re-instate an employee back into the state pension (SERPS or S2P) where they have no vested benefits in the pension scheme (because they have less than two years' qualifying service[2]). The premium is in fact now payable by the trustees of the occupational pension scheme[3] and not by the employer.

1 Pension Schemes Act 1993, s 55(2).
2 This is the maximum period that a pension scheme can currently provide before a member becomes entitled to a short service benefit on leaving the scheme (Pension Schemes Act 1993, s 71).
3 Pension Schemes Act 1993, s 55(2) and reg 51(1) of the Occupational Pension Schemes (Contracting-out) Regulations 1996 (SI 1996/1172).

10.57 Contributions equivalent premiums were payable by the employer if the contracted-out employment terminated before 6 April 1987[1]. So this preferential debt status is probably retained in case there are any such debts potentially remaining.

1 See reg 18(1A) of the Occupational Pension Schemes (Contracting-out) Regulations 1984 (SI 1984/380, as amended).

10.58 These premiums are preferential debts if payable by the company in relation to service in the 12 months prior to the relevant date. Such premiums are payable to the contracting-out authority.

10.59 Before 6 April 1997, more state scheme premiums[1] could have been paid and had preferential status under Sch 4 as originally enacted (and its predecessors). But these premiums have now been abolished (by the Pensions Act 1995), save for the 'deemed buy-back' premiums mentioned in para 12.27 below (and which do not have a preferential debt status).

1 Within the meaning of ss 55–68 of the Pension Schemes Act 1993, and before that ss 42–47 of the Social Security Pensions Act 1975.

Third party advances?

10.60 Preferential status is not available for those who may advance money to the company for the purpose of paying pension debts that are preferential (see Chapter 9 (Preferential Debts) above). IA 1986, Sch 6, para 11 of gives such a preferential status if money is advanced for the purpose of paying wages or holiday remuneration (Sch 6, paras 9 and 10). But para 11 only refers to paras 9 and 10 of Sch 6 and so does not apply to para 8 of Sch 6 (dealing with pensions contributions).

Crown subrogation

10.61 If the state ends up paying an amount to an employee (or to pension trustees) out of the National Insurance Fund (under the Pension Schemes Act 1993 and the Employment Rights Act 1996), the Crown takes over the employee's claim against the company to the extent it has been paid[1]. This includes taking over any preferential status of the employee's claim. The Crown's preferential claim against the company must be paid in full before any preferential payment is made to the pension scheme[2].

1 See the Pension Schemes Act 1993, s 127(2) and the Employment Rights Act 1996, s 189(2).
2 Pension Schemes Act 1993, s 127(3).

10.62 Oddly this was not changed by the Enterprise Act 2002. The equivalent provision in Employment Rights Act 1996, s 189(4) giving priority to the Crown in relation to employee wage claims etc paid out of the national insurance fund was repealed for insolvencies starting on or after 15 September 2003 by the Enterprise Act 2002 (so that the Crown's claim now ranks equally with the employee's remaining preferential claim, if any) – see Chapter 9 (Preferential Debts) above. This may not comply with the underlying EU Directive – see the ECJ in *Barsotti v IPNS*[1].

1 Case C-19/01, [2004] ECR I-2005 (ECJ).

Pensions as a wages claim?

10.63 As discussed in Chapter 9 (Preferential Debts) above, it is sometimes argued the remuneration category of preferential debts (category 5 in Sch 6) could include pensions contributions as well. This would be on the basis that the reference to 'wages or salary' in para 13 of Sch 6 could also include amounts owed by way of pension contributions (see eg the discussions of pensions as deferred pay in *The Halcyon Skies*[1] and *Barber v Guardian Royal Exchange*[2]).

1 [1977] QB 14 (Brandon J).
2 [1990] 2 All ER 660, ECJ.

10.64 However, given the existence of a separate category of preferential debts relating to pension contributions in category 4 of Sch 6, this is an unlikely interpretation.

10.65 See for example (but in a different statutory context) in Australia, Wilcox CJ in *Ardino v Count Financial Group Pty Ltd*[1] (a case on the statutory jurisdiction of a court, in which it was held that 'wages' do not include superannuation payments) and similarly Warren J in *Ansett Australia Ground Staff Superannuation Plan Pty Ltd v Ansett Australia Ltd*[2].

1 (1994) 126 ALR 49 (Wilcox CJ).
2 [2002] VSC 576 (Warren J).

10.66   Conversely, in *Re Cooperants Societe mutuelle d'assuance-vie*[1], the Cour superieure du Quebec held that 'wages' in the Winding-up Act included unpaid contributions to a pension plan.

1 (1995) 14 CCPB 118.

10.67   Most recently in the UK, the EAT commented in *Benson v Secretary of State*[1] that pension contributions are not covered by the National Insurance Fund guarantee relating to 'arrears of pay' in the Employment Rights Act 1996.

1 [2003] IRLR 748 at para 20, EAT.

10.68   In any event in practice the £800 cap on claims for wages under category 5 is likely to limit the prospect of claims being made for pension contributions.

ASW claim?

10.69   The decision of the ECJ in the *ASW* case[1] (see Chapter 12 (EC Employment Insolvency Directive) below) may result in increasing pressure for pension debts to be given a greater priority in insolvency proceedings (to reduce the risk of a claim on the state).

Such pressure may also rise if the levies payable into the Pension Protection Fund increase and are considered to be too high. The PPF is funded by a levy on other defined benefit occupational pension schemes. So there may in the future be pressure from those schemes (and the underlying employers and members) for the risk of claims to be reduced by a greater statutory preferential status for pension liabilities[2].

1 *Robins and Burnett v Secretary of State for Work and Pensions* (C-278/05), [2007] IRLR 270, [2007] PLR 55, ECJ. See further Chapter 12 below.
2 See for example the call for a preferential status for pensions claims from a conservative MP in a Commons debate: Hansard 24 February 2004, Col 238.

CHAPTER 11

Directors and controlling shareholders as employees

WHO IS AN EMPLOYEE?

11.1 The statutory protections (preferential debts, national insurance fund etc) generally only apply to employees and not (say) a person who is an officer only and not an employee (eg a non-executive director) or a person who is an agency worker or self-employed. The position of shareholders and directors is discussed in this chapter.

11.2 Section 230 of the ERA contains the relevant definitions:

230. Employees, workers etc

(1) In this Act 'employee' means an individual who has entered into or works under (or, where the employment has ceased, worked under) a contract of employment.

(2) In this Act 'contract of employment' means a contract of service or apprenticeship, whether express or implied, and (if it is express) whether oral or in writing.

…

(4) In this Act 'employer', in relation to an employee or worker, means the person by whom the employee or worker is (or, where the employment has ceased, was) employed.

(5) In this Act 'employment' –

(a) in relation to an employee, means (except for the purposes of section 171) employment under a contract of employment, and

(b) in relation to a worker, means employment under his contract;

and 'employment' shall be construed accordingly."

11.3 See generally Chapter 2 above on the test of who is an employee. The question arises whether or not in any individual case a person who is also a director or a substantial shareholder is also an employee. If not, then he or she does not qualify for various protections which are limited to employees. For example:

- Claims under employment protection legislation for unfair dismissal or redundancy. Note that discrimination laws generally extend beyond employees to cover office holders and 'workers' as well.

- Some claims of employees are preferential debts.

- Employees can claim payment under the National Insurance Fund under ERA 1996.

DIRECTORS AND CONTROLLING SHAREHOLDERS

11.4   In 2009, the Court of Appeal in *Neufeld v Secretary of State for Business, Enterprise and Regulatory Reform*[1] comprehensively reviewed the position in the light of previous cases on this point. The case was concerned with the National Insurance Fund, but the analysis extends to other areas too (eg the decision in *Clark v Clark Construction*[2] mentioned below was in an unfair dismissal case).

In *Neufeld*, the Court of Appeal dealt with the following general questions (at para [25]):

'(i)   can a controlling shareholder and director of a trading company become an employee of that company under a contract of employment?

(ii)   if yes, are there any guidelines which may assist tribunals in deciding whether in any particular case such a shareholder/director has become an employee?

The first question is not a novel one and has been considered in many authorities. It comes before us afresh because of what is regarded as confusion as to the principles which are applicable in answering it.'

1 [2009] EWCA Civ 280; [2009] 3 All ER 790; [2009] IRLR 475, CA.
2 [2008] IRLR 364; [2008] ICR 635, EAT.

11.5   In some senses, if the person is a major shareholder and (say) the sole director, then it can be argued that he or she has control of their own fate. It may be that they are highly unlikely to be dismissed so do not really need to protections available for general employees. But that is a policy matter and would be better put into effect by way of an express provision in the relevant legislation (which is the line taken by other countries).

The position as a general matter seems to have been relatively clear in the UK since the decision of the Privy Council in *Lee v Lee's Air Farming Ltd*[1]. The Privy Council held that Mr Lee qualified as an employee of the company and so an insurance claim could arise on his death. This was even though his job was to work as a pilot for a company which he controlled as the sole director and owner of 2999 of the shares (the other one was held by a solicitor).

But, as discussed in *Neufeld*, in 1997 in the combined appeals of *Buchan v Secretary of State* and *Ivey v Secretary of State*[2], the EAT held that a controlling shareholder of a company was not an employee for the purposes of the EPCA 1978 (now ERA 1996). The EAT considered that it would be inconsistent with the purpose of the Act to extend protection to a person who could not be dismissed from his position without his agreement. Mr Buchan had a 50% shareholding and was dismissed by the receiver after eight days. Mr Ivey had a 90% shareholding and was dismissed on the appointment of the receiver. In both cases the Industrial Tribunal concluded that they were not employees. The EAT refused to overturn this decision.

The decision in *Buchan* was subsequently followed in later EAT decisions, including *Robinson v Secretary of State*[3] and *Hernsley v Secretary of State*[4].

1 [1961] AC 12, PC.
2 [1997] IRLR 80, EAT.
3 30 April 1997, unreported.
4 20 June 1997, unreported.

11.6   However, in 1997 in *Fleming v Secretary of State*[1], the Inner House of the Court of Session doubted that *Buchan* should be seen as laying down a rule of law that a controlling shareholder/director could never be an employee. Instead this was seen as one relevant factor. The decision is ultimately one of fact for the tribunal. The Court of Session was also uncertain as to how relevant the fact of a controlling shareholding was when the dismissal was in fact by the insolvency practitioner (in that case a liquidator).

1 [1997] IRLR 682 (Inner House, Ct of Sess).

11.7   The decision of the Court of Session was followed by the Court of Appeal in 1999 in *Secretary of State v Bottrill*[1], which considered the reasoning in *Buchan* to be unsound.

Lord Woolf MR, handing down the judgment of the Court held (page 603):

> 'We recognise the attractions of having in relation to the ERA a simple and clear test which will determine whether a shareholder or a director is an employee for the purposes of the Act or not. However, the Act does not provide such a test and it is far from obvious what Parliament would have intended the test to be. We do not find any justification for departing from the well-established position in the law of employment generally. That is whether or not an employer or employee relationship exists can only be decided by having regard to all the relevant facts. If an individual has a controlling shareholding, that is certainly a fact which is likely to be significant in all situations, and in some cases it may prove to be decisive. However, it is only one of the factors which are relevant and certainly is not to be taken as determinative without considering all the relevant circumstances.'

Later in his judgment Lord Woolf MR made various comments (not, he emphasised, rigid guidelines) which he suggested may be of assistance to parties in future cases (page 604):

> 'The first question which the tribunal is likely to wish to consider is whether there is or has been a genuine contract between the company and the shareholder. In this context, how and for what reasons the contract came into existence (for example whether the contract was made at a time when insolvency loomed) and what each party actually did pursuant to the contract are likely to be relevant considerations.

If the tribunal concludes that the contract is not a sham, it is likely to wish to consider next whether the contract, which may well have been labelled a contract of employment, actually gave rise to an employer/employee relationship. In this context, of the various factors usually regarded as relevant (see, for example, Chitty on Contracts 27th edn (1994) para. 37- 008), the degree of control exercised by the company over the shareholder employee is always important. This is not the same question as that relating to whether there is a controlling shareholding. The tribunal may think it appropriate to consider whether there are directors other than or in addition to the shareholder employee and whether the constitution of the company gives that shareholder rights such that he is in reality answerable only to himself and incapable of being dismissed. If he is a director, it may be relevant to consider whether he is able under the Articles of Association to vote on matters in which he is personally interested, such as the termination of his contract of employment. Again, the actual conduct of the parties pursuant to the terms of the contract is likely to be relevant. It is for the tribunal as an industrial jury to take all relevant factors into account in reaching its conclusion, giving such weight to them as it considers appropriate.'

1 [1999] ICR 592; [1999] IRLR 326, CA.

11.8   Later decisions have considered that the Court of Appeal in *Bottrill* meant that the issue was one of fact for the tribunal to determine – see eg *Farleigh v Secretary of State*[1] and *Sellars Arenascene Ltd v Connolly*[2].

1 (2000) EAT/1282/99, EAT.
2 [2001] EWCA Civ 184; [2001] ICR 760; [2001] IRLR 222, CA.

11.9   There is a discussion of the case law (after *Bottrill*) in SPI Technical Release No 6, 'Treatment of directors' claims as employees in insolvencies', issued in August 1999.

11.10   In *Venables v Hornby*[1] (a tax case), Lord Millett commented that 'The fact that the person claiming to be an employee is the controlling shareholder and ultimately has the power to prevent his own dismissal does not prevent the existence of a genuine contract of employment' and cited the *Bottrill* decision.

1 [2003] UKHL 65; [2004] 1 All ER 627; [2003] 1 WLR 3022, HL.

11.11   In *Gladwell v Secretary of State for Trade and Industry*[1] the EAT applied *Bottrill* and held that the fact that a director was also the 50% shareholder in a company did not necessarily mean that he could not also be an employee. The employment tribunal had stated that a person could not be both employer and employee. The EAT held that this statement suggested that the tribunal had treated the question of control as likely to be inconsistent with the status as an employee. That was inconsistent with the authorities. A majority shareholder would in practice act as the employer, making decisions on behalf of the company in which he had shares, but that did not prevent him being an employee.

The EAT also held that the tribunal had been entitled to take the view that it would give little weight to an undated and unsigned contract.

1 [2007] ICR 264, EAT.

11.12   In *Neufeld*, the Court of Appeal reviewed the caselaw and decided (at para 93) that the guidance given by the Court of Appeal in *Bottrill* was in fact resulting in confusion in this area. The Court of Appeal commented:

> '[93] We comment that it was part of Mr Tolley's submissions in his skeleton argument that we could safely endorse the *Fleming* and *Bottrill* guidance, including that tribunals could and should have regard to the putative employee's controlling shareholding, because tribunals "can be trusted to use their experience and expertise to determine these issues in a practical and common sense manner". The evidence of the two cases under appeal gives us no confidence in that regard. The *Bottrill* guidance led to what was, with respect, an irrational decision in Mr Neufeld's case; and it nearly did the same in Mr Howe's case. There was plainly a need for clarification of the guiding principles. We hope that our judgment may go some way towards providing it.'

11.13   The Court of Appeal in Neufeld aimed to clarify the position. In October 2008, the Insolvency Service had previously commented in its publication 'Dear IP'[1] on the position as follows:

> 'The circumstances in which a director and majority shareholder of a company may be regarded as an employee (as defined in section 230 of the Employment Rights Act 1996) has been the subject of Court of Appeal decisions in re *Secretary of State for Trade and Industry v Bottrill* [1999] ICR 592 and *re Connolly v Sellers Arenascene Ltd* [2001] ICR 760 as well as the judgment of the Inner House of the Court of Session in *re Fleming v Secretary of State for Trade and Industry* [1997] IRLR 682.
>
> However, there have been a number of recent Employment Appeal Tribunal (EAT) decisions in which the legal approach has diverged from that stated in *Bottrill* and *Fleming* in particular. The trend of the recent EAT decisions has been to limit both the nature of the inquiry which should be undertaken by the Employment Tribunals, and the evidence which is to be regarded as relevant. There are conflicts and a consequent lack of clarity within the authorities which is deeply unsatisfactory as Employment Tribunals cannot be clear as to which approach they ought to follow. Consequently there is undoubted potential for confusion and error, and in turn unnecessary appeals.
>
> In view of this the Court of Appeal has granted the Secretary of State leave to appeal against the EAT judgment in the case of *re Neufeld v Secretary of State for Business Enterprise and Regulatory Reform*. The hearing date is anticipated to be in December 2008. Hopefully this will resolve the current state of confusion. In the meantime Redundancy Payments Services will continue to assess the employee status of directors in line with the *Bottrill* guidelines.'

1 Issue   37,   October   2008.   http://www.insolvency.gov.uk/insolvencyprofessionandlegislation/
dearip/dearipmill/hardcopy.htm

COURT OF APPEAL GUIDELINES IN *NEUFELD*

11.14   In April 2009, the Court of Appeal gave its decision in *Neufeld v Secretary of State for Business, Enterprise and Regulatory Reform*[1].

As the Court of Appeal stated in *Neufeld*:

> '29. It is, however, too late in the development of our jurisprudence, at any rate at the level of this court, to regard that particular control issue as providing a threshold obstacle to the creation of a valid contract of employment between a company and the one man who wholly controls it. The decision in *Lee v Lee's Air Farming Ltd* [1961] AC 12 shows that it is not. Whilst, as a decision of the Privy Council, it is not strictly binding on us, its correctness as an authority has not, so far as we are aware, been challenged, nor did Mr Tolley challenge it. He recognised that this court regarded it as sound law in *Bottrill*.'

The Court of Appeal referred to the judgment in *Lee* and held:

> '33.   Lee's case therefore establishes two propositions of direct present relevance. First, that an individual who owns all the shares in, and is the sole director of, a company – and so has total dominion over it – can also be employed by that company under a contract of service. Secondly, that it is no answer to the claimed creation of such a contract that the "control" condition that is essential to it is not satisfied. The answer to that point, even in relation to a "one man company" case, is that the company and the one man are not the same person; and it is the company that exercises the relevant control. In Lee's case the employer was the company and the employee was Mr Lee. The control necessary for the purposes of the claimed contract of service was exercisable by the company and it made no difference that in practice, so long as Mr Lee remained the sole governing director, that control would be and was exercised by him as the company's agent. The close identity that in reality existed between the company and Mr Lee did not prevent a contract for service being created.'

1 [2009] EWCA Civ 280; [2009] 3 All ER 790; [2009] IRLR 475, CA.

11.15   The Court of Appeal held:

> '[80] There is no reason in principle why someone who is a shareholder and director of a company cannot also be an employee of the company under a contract of employment. There is also no reason in principle why someone whose shareholding in the company gives him control of it – even total control (as in Lee's case) – cannot be an employee. In short, a person whose economic interest in a company and its business means that he is in practice properly to be regarded as their "owner" can also be an employee of the company. It will, in particular, be no answer to his claim to be such an employee to argue that: (i) the extent of his control of the company means that the control condition of a contract of employment cannot be satisfied; or (ii) that the practical control he has over his own destiny – including that he cannot be dismissed from his employment except with his consent – has the effect in law that he cannot be an employee at all. Point (i) is answered by Lee's case, which decided that the relevant control is in the company; point (ii) is answered by this court's rejection in *Bottrill* of the reasoning in *Buchan*.
>
> [81] Whether or not such a shareholder/director is an employee of the company is a question of fact for the court or tribunal before which such issue arises. In any such case there may in theory be two such issues, although in practice the evidence relevant to their resolution will be likely to overlap. The

first, and logically preliminary one, will be whether the putative contract is a genuine contract or a sham. The second will be whether, assuming it is a genuine contract, it amounts to a contract of employment (it might, for example, instead amount to a contract for services). We make clear that we are not of course suggesting that cases raising the first issue are likely to be common, and we think it probable that they will be relatively exceptional. Despite the repeated references in the authorities to the theoretical possibility of a contract being a sham, no such case has been discovered in the principal authorities to which we have been referred. We make no attempt to give any prescriptive guidance as to the resolution of such issues, but we at least offer the following general observations.'

SHAMS

11.16   The first question raised by the Court of Appeal in *Neufeld* was for the tribunal to look to se if the arrangements were in fact a sham.

The Court of Appeal held:

'[75] We come finally to the decision of the Employment Appeal Tribunal in *Clark v Clark Construction Initiatives Ltd and another* [2008] IRLR 364, [2008] ICR 635. This was not a claim against the Secretary of State but, in circumstances we need not explain, the case raised the like question of whether the controlling shareholder of a company was also its employee. The employment tribunal approached the resolution of that question by purporting to apply the guidance of (inter alia) *Bottrill*. They said:

"[That guidance] would seem to establish that what we have to do is to look at the whole picture which we have done. We should balance out all the factors and make a reasoned conclusion. We do that balancing exercise. It seemed to us that during the first and middle phases the Claimant was in business on his own account and not employed."

[76] In his judgment on the appeal to the appeal tribunal, Elias J reviewed the authorities and cited the guidance given by this court in *Bottrill*. He referred to *Connolly* (as a case in which the employment tribunal "had been unduly swayed by the single feature of the controlling shareholding"), *Gladwell* and *Nesbitt*. Elias J then suggested three circumstances in which it may be legitimate for a tribunal or court not to recognise what is on its face a legitimate employment contract. First, the exceptional case in which the company is itself a sham (which we understand to mean the case in which it is regarded simply as the alter ego of the individual). Second, where the contract was entered into for an ulterior purpose, for example to secure some statutory payment from the Secretary of State. Third, where the parties do not conduct their relationship in accordance with the contract. This will either be because they never intended to and the purported contract was a sham in the sense of Diplock LJ's description in *Snook v London & West Riding Investments* [1967] 2 QB 786 at 801, [1967] 1 All ER 518, [1967] 2 WLR 1020; or because the relationship has ceased to reflect the contractual terms. The latter type of case is the one that the *Bottrill* guidance had in mind in twice emphasising the potential relevance of whether the conduct of the parties is consistent with the contract.

[77] We respectfully agree with Elias J's summary of the types of case in which the court or tribunal may find on the facts that the purported contract is not a genuine contract. But, as we have said, that type of issue does not arise under either appeal before us, we received no argument on it and we were not invited to attempt to provide general guidance on it. We propose, therefore, to say no more about Elias J's suggested categories save two things. First, we would not wish to be taken as saying that there may never be other factual circumstances in which a conclusion of sham might be made. Second, an investigation of how the parties have conducted themselves under the purported contract may prove different things. We explain what we here have in mind in our summary of the relevant principles that we set out below.'

And later:

'[82] In cases involving an alleged sham, there will, as we have said, almost invariably be what purports to be a formal written employment contract, or at least a board minute or a memorandum purporting to record or evidence the creation of such a contract. The task of the court or tribunal will be to decide whether any such document amounts to a sham in the sense of the Snook guidance (and see also *Protectacoat*[1], to which we referred in para 37). Any such inquiry will usually require not just an investigation into the circumstances of the creation of the document but also into the parties' purported conduct under it, which will be likely to shed light on the genuineness or otherwise of the claimed contract. The fact that the putative employee has control over the company and the board, and so was instrumental in the creation of the very contract that he is asserting, will obviously be a relevant matter in the court's consideration of whether the contract is or is not a sham. It will usually be the feature that prompted the inquiry in the first place.

[83] An inquiry into what the parties have done under the purported contract may show a variety of things:

(i)   that they did not act in accordance with the purported contract at all, which would support the conclusion that it was a sham; or

(ii) that they did act in accordance with it, which will support the opposite conclusion; or

(iii) that although they acted in a way consistent with a genuine service contract arrangement, what they have done suggests the making of a variation of the terms of the original purported contract; or

(iv) that there came a point when the parties ceased to conduct themselves in a way consistent with the purported contract or any variation of it, which may invite the conclusion that, although the contract was originally a genuine one, it has been impliedly discharged.

There may obviously also be different outcomes of any investigation into how the parties have conducted themselves under the purported contract. It will be a question of fact as to what conclusions are to be drawn from such investigation.'

1 Protectacoat Firthglow Ltd v Szilagyi [2009] EWCA Civ 98; [2009] IRLR 365; [2009] All ER (D) 208 (Feb), CA and see para 2.11 above. Discussed by ACL Davies in 'Sensible Thinking About Sham Transactions: *Protectacoat Firthglow Ltd v Szilagyi*' (2009) 38 ILJ 318.

FACTORS ABSENT A SHAM

11.17   The Court of Appeal in *Neufeld* held (in paras [84] to [87]) that absent a sham the following steps need to be considered:

1   Is the claimed contract a true contract of employment?

   (a)   what was the position at the insolvency date? – eg if the contract is 5 years old what has happened since?

   (b)   if the contract is not in writing or is only brief, how have the parties conducted themselves? – see also para [55].

2   Were the formalities for a contract met (eg board minutes etc)?

3   If a director of the company:

   (a)   more needs to be shown to establish an employment relationship.

   (b)   was a salary paid – or just directors' fees?

   This seems to mean that in practice, absent more, a non-executive director of a public company is likely *not* to be considered to be an employee.

4   Control of the company or the existence of guarantees etc are not relevant factors (see also the comments at paras [49] and [50]).

5   Not drawing salary can point against a contract of employment if remuneration had generally been irregular. But if previously paid regularly, non-payment in the last month could not retrospectively diminish his right – see para [51], commenting on *Fleming*.

6   Not taking all the contractual holiday is not a pointer against employment status (taking more may be a pointer that the contract is not genuine) – see para [91]

7   Payment of tax and NI on amounts received are not a factor – PAYE deductions apply to office holders (eg directors) as well as to employees – *Fleming* at para [10], cited by the CA in *Neufeld* at para [47].

11.18   The Court of Appeal in *Neufeld* held:

'[84] In a case in which no allegation of sham is raised, or in which the Claimant proves that no question of sham arises, the question (or further question) for the court or tribunal will be whether the claimed contract amounts to a true contract of employment. As we have indicated, given that the critical question in cases such as those under appeal is as to whether the putative employee was an employee at the time of the company's insolvency, it will or may be necessary to inquire into what has been done under the claimed contract: there will or may therefore need to be the like inquiry as in cases in which an allegation of sham is made. In order for the employee to make good his case, it may well be insufficient merely to place reliance on a written contract made, say, five years earlier. The tribunal will want to know that the claimed contract, perhaps as subsequently varied, was still in place at the time of the insolvency. In a case in which the alleged contract is not in writing, or is only in brief form, it is obvious that it will usually be necessary to inquire into how the parties have conducted themselves under it.

[85] In deciding whether a valid contract of employment was in existence, consideration will have to be given to the requisite conditions for the creation of such a contract and the court or tribunal will want to be satisfied that the contract meets them. In *Lee's case* the position was ostensibly clear on the documents, with the only contentious issue being in relation to the control condition of a contract of employment. In some cases there will be a formal service agreement. Failing that, there may be a minute of a board meeting or a memorandum dealing with the matter. But in many cases involving small companies, with their control being in the hands of perhaps just one or two director/shareholders, the handling of such matters may have been dealt with informally and it may be a difficult question as to whether or not the correct inference from the facts is that the putative employee was, as claimed, truly an employee. In particular, a director of a company is the holder of an office and will not, merely by virtue of such office, be an employee: the putative employee will have to prove more than his appointment as a director. It will be relevant to consider how he has been paid. Has he been paid a salary, which points towards employment? Or merely by way of director's fees, which points away from it? In considering what the putative employee was actually doing, it will also be relevant to consider whether he was acting merely in his capacity as a director of the company; or whether he was acting as an employee.

[86] We have referred in the previous paragraph to matters which will typically be directly relevant to the inquiry whether or not (there being no question of a sham) the claimed contract amounts to a contract of employment. What we have not included as a relevant consideration for the purposes of that inquiry is the fact that the putative employee's shareholding in the company gave him control of the company, even total control. The fact of his control will obviously form a part of the backdrop against which the assessment will be made of what has been done under the putative written or oral employment contract that is being asserted. But it will not ordinarily be of any special relevance in deciding whether or not he has a valid such contract. Nor will the fact that he will have share capital invested in the company; or that he may have made loans to it; or that he has personally guaranteed its obligations; or that his personal investment in the company will stand to prosper in line with the company's prosperity; or that he has done any of the other things that the "owner" of a business will commonly do on its behalf. These considerations are usual features of the sort of companies giving rise to the type of issue with which these appeals are concerned but they will ordinarily be irrelevant to whether or not a valid contract of employment has been created and so they can and should be ignored. They show an "owner" acting qua "owner", which is inevitable in such a company. However, they do not show that the "owner" cannot also be an employee.

[87] We have, however, twice – and deliberately – used the word "ordinarily" in the last paragraph. We have used the word not because we foresee other circumstances but because "never say never" is a wise judicial maxim.'

11.19 The Court of Appeal in *Neufeld*[1] adopted the factors used by Elias J in the EAT in *Clark*[2], but with some comments:

Elias J factors (from *Clark*)	CA comments (from *Neufeld*)
98 How should a tribunal approach the task of determining whether the contract of employment should be given effect or not? We would suggest that a consideration of the following factors, whilst not exhaustive, may be of assistance:	
(1) Where there is a contract ostensibly in place, the onus is on the party seeking to deny its effect to satisfy the court that it is not what it appears to be. This is particularly so where the individual has paid tax and national insurance as an employee: he has on the face of it earned the right to take advantage of the benefits which employees may derive from such payments.	[88] In cases where the putative employee is asserting the existence of an employment contract, it will be for him to prove it; and, as we have indicated, the mere production of what purports to be a written service agreement may by itself be insufficient to prove the case sought to be made. If the putative employee's assertion is challenged the court or tribunal will need to be satisfied that the document is a true reflection of the claimed employment relationship, for which purpose it will be relevant to know what the parties have done under it. The putative employee may, therefore, have to do rather more than simply produce the contract itself, or else a board minute or memorandum purporting to record his employment.
(2) The mere fact that the individual has a controlling shareholding does not of itself prevent a contract of employment arising. Nor does the fact that he is practice able to exercise real or sole control over what the company does (*Lee*).	
(3) Similarly, the fact that he is an entrepreneur, or has built the company up, or will profit from its success, will not be factors militating against a finding that there is a contract in place. Indeed, any controlling shareholder will inevitably benefit from the company's success, as will many employees with share option schemes ([*Connolly*]).	
(4) If the conduct of the parties is in accordance with the contract that would be a strong pointer towards the contract being valid and binding. For example, this would be so if the individual works the hours stipulated or does not take more than the stipulated holidays.	
(5) Conversely, if the conduct of the parties is either inconsistent with the contract (in the sense described in para 96) or in certain key areas where one might expect it to be governed by the contract is in fact not so governed, that would be a factor, and potentially a very important one, militating against a finding that the controlling shareholder is in reality an employee.	

Elias J factors (from *Clark*)	CA comments (from *Neufeld*)
	[89] We consider that Elias J's sixth factor may perhaps have put a little too high the potentially negative effect of the terms of the contract not having been reduced into writing. This will obviously be an important consideration but if the parties' conduct under the claimed contract points convincingly to the conclusion that there was a true contract of employment, we would not wish tribunals to seize too readily on the absence of a written agreement as justifying the rejection of the claim. In both cases under appeal there was no written service agreement, but the employment judges appear to have had no doubt that the parties' conduct proved a genuine employment relationship.
(6) In that context, the assertion that there is a genuine contract will be undermined if the terms have not been identified or reduced into writing (*Fleming*). This will be powerful evidence that the contract was not really intended to regulate the relationship in any way.	
(7) The fact that the individual takes loans from the company or guarantees its debts could exceptionally have some relevance in analysing the true nature of the relationship, but in most cases such factors are unlikely to carry any weight. There is nothing intrinsically inconsistent in a person who is an employee doing these things. Indeed, in many small companies it will be necessary for the controlling shareholder personally to give bank guarantees precisely because the company assets are small and no funding will be forthcoming without them. It would wholly undermine the *Lee* approach if this were to be sufficient to deny the controlling shareholder the right to enter into a contract of employment.	[90] As for Elias J's seventh and eighth factors, we say no more than that we regard them as saying essentially what we have said above in our "never say never" paragraph. *[87] We have, however, twice – and deliberately – used the word "ordinarily" in the last paragraph. We have used the word not because we foresee other circumstances but because "never say never" is a wise judicial maxim.*
(8) Although the courts have said that the fact of there being a controlling shareholding is always relevant and may be decisive, that does not mean that that fact alone will ever justify a tribunal in finding that there was no contract in place. That would be to apply the *Buchan* test which has been decisively rejected. The fact that there is a controlling shareholding is what may raise doubts as to whether that individual is truly an employee, but of itself that fact alone does not resolve these doubts one way or another."	[90] As for Elias J's seventh and eighth factors, we say no more than that we regard them as saying essentially what we have said above in our "never say never" paragraph. *[87] We have, however, twice – and deliberately – used the word "ordinarily" in the last paragraph. We have used the word not because we foresee other circumstances but because "never say never" is a wise judicial maxim.*

1 [2009] EWCA Civ 280, [2009] IRLR 475; [2009] All ER (D) 40 (Apr), CA

2 *Clark v Clark Construction Initiatives Ltd* [2008] IRLR 364, [2008] ICR 635. EAT.

CHAPTER 12

EC Employment Insolvency Directive

12.1 EC Directive 2008/94/EC (the Employment Insolvency Directive) provides for 'the protection of employees in the event of the insolvency of their
employer'. It is a codification of the original 1980 Directive 80/987/EEC, as
amended by Directives 87/164/EEC and 2002/74/EC.

It generally requires member states to set up guarantee mechanisms for certain
claims of employees arising on employer insolvency.

The Commission has succeeded in various claims against member states for
failure to comply with this Directive (see eg *Commission v Italian Republic*[1] and
Commission v Hellenic Republic[2]).

1 [1989] ECR 143, ECJ.
2 [1990] ECR I-3917, ECJ.

12.2 In *Sumuelsson v Svenska Staten*[1], the EFTA Court held that Article 10(a)
of the 1980 Directive[2] allowing member states to 'take the measures necessary to
avoid abuses' should not be construed broadly. Accordingly, a provision in the
relevant Swedish law excluding individuals who had brought a claim in the previous two years in mainly the same activity was held to be contrary to the
Directive.

1 [1995] 3 CMLR 813, EFTA Court.
2 Now Article 12(a) of the 2008 Employment Insolvency Directive.

12.3 In *Barsotti v IPNS*[1], the ECJ held that payments actually made by
employers in respect of the relevant guarantee period must not be deducted
from the amount covered by the guarantee institution. It may be arguable that
the UK legislation does not comply with this principle as it envisages that the
employee's claim against the employer is transferred to the National
Insurance Fund (which then subrogates to any relevant claim in the insolvency). But the payments in *Barsotti* seem to have been paid by the employer
before the insolvency started and this may be a valid distinction for the UK
subrogation issue.

1 Case C-19/01, [2004] ECR I-2005, ECJ.

TWO MEMBER STATES INVOLVED

12.4   In 1997, the ECJ ruled in *Danmarks Active Handelsrejsende (acting for Mosbaek) v Lonmodtagernes Garantifund*[1] on the application of the Directive dealing with protection of employees in the event of the employer's insolvency where two or more member states were involved.

1 [1997] ECR I-5017; [1998] IRLR 150; [1998] ICR 954, ECJ.

12.5   The case involved an employee of an English company. The employee was resident and worked solely in Denmark. The English company had no presence in Denmark other than the employee and had not arranged to pay any Danish taxes or social security etc. The English company entered receivership in England and the Danish employee brought proceedings in Denmark for recovery of unpaid wages against the Danish Garantifund.

12.6   The ECJ held that the purpose of the Employment Insolvency Directive was that only one member state would be responsible for relevant claims in these circumstances and that it would be the state in which the proceedings for collective satisfaction of creditors, claims were instituted (or where it had been established that the employer's undertaking or business has been closed down). In *Mosbaek*, this seemed to mean that the claim of the employee should be made against the UK National Insurance Fund and not against the Danish equivalent.

12.7   However, three years later in 2000 in *Everson and Barrass v Secretary of State for Trade and Industry and Bell Lines Ltd (in liquidation)*[1] the ECJ came to a more logical conclusion. It distinguished *Mosbaek*[2] and held that if the employer company has established a branch in another member state, the guarantee institution which must accept responsibility for employees' outstanding claims under the Employment Insolvency Directive is that of the other member state in which the workers are employed. This will be the state to which the employer paid, or ought to have paid, contributions to the financing of the guarantee institution.

1 [1999] ECR I-8903; [2000] IRLR 202 (Case C-198/98), ECJ.
2 [1997] ECR I-5017; [1998] IRLR 150; [1998] ICR 954, ECJ.

12.8   After *Everson*, the 1980 Employment Insolvency Directive was amended by Directive 2002/74/EC. The 2002 amendment inserted a new Article 8a into the 1980 Employment Insolvency Directive and this has become Article 9 in the 2008 codification. This provides that:

> 'If an undertaking with activities in the territories of at least two Member States is in a state of insolvency within the meaning of Article 2(1), the institution responsible for meeting employees' outstanding claims shall be that of the Member State in whose territory they work or habitually work.'

This largely codifies the decision in *Everson*. Article 10 requires the administrative authorities and guarantee institutions in the member states to share relevant information.

12.9   In *Svenska staten represented by Tillsynsmyndigheten i konkurser*[1] *v Anders Holmqvist*[3] the ECJ considered Article 8a of the 1980 Directive. It held that

> 'in order for an undertaking established in a Member State to be regarded as having activities in the territory of another Member State, that undertaking does not need to have a branch or fixed establishment in that other State. The undertaking must, however, have a stable economic presence in the latter State, featuring human resources which enable it to perform activities there.
>
> In the case of a transport undertaking established in a Member State, the mere fact that a worker employed by it in that State delivers goods between that State and another Member State cannot demonstrate that the undertaking has a stable economic presence in another Member State.'

It followed that an employee of an insolvent Swedish transport company who delivered goods between Sweden and Italy was entitled to the benefit of the Swedish wage guarantee scheme.

1 The Supervisory Authority for Insolvencies in Sweden.
2 [2009] ICR 675; [2008] IRLR 970; [2008] All ER (D) 265 (Oct) (C-310/07), ECJ.

12.10   The ECJ noted that the Employment Insolvency Directive refers to 'activities' in another member state and that this looks to be a lesser connection than would be required for an 'establishment'. The ECJ considered that something more than a mere presence in the other state (even if on instructions of the employer) was needed. There must be a stable economic presence, although given modern technology and work patterns a physical presence (such as an office) may not be necessary.

Implementation of Directive in the UK

12.11   In practice, the provisions of ERA 1996, s 182 (see paras 10.34 to 10.50 below) are considered to satisfy the obligations in Art 3 of the Employment Insolvency Directive to provide a guarantee of pay owed to an employee. The limits in section 186 seem to be consistent with Art 4 which provides that member states may impose limits on the amounts claimable from the guarantee institutions mentioned in Art 3 in respect of pay.

12.12   In *Secretary of State v Mann*[1] Mr Mann was made redundant two weeks after receivers were appointed. An industrial tribunal later made a protective award under TULRCA 1992, s 189. The award related to the 90 days from the date of dismissal[2]. This was not paid by the employer and a claim was made on the Secretary of State under EPCA 1978, s 122 (now ERA 1996, s 184). The Secretary of State sought to reduce the amount payable in relation to the protective award by:

(a)   setting off amounts already paid by the Secretary of State under EPCA 1978, s 122(3)(b) (now ERA 1996, s 184(1)(b)) in lieu of the statutory minimum notice periods and setting off the payment of wages for the day of dismissal. This was in accordance with TULRCA 1992, s 190(3) (since repealed with effect from 30 August 1993 by the Trade Union Reform and Employment Rights Act 1993);

(b) applying the ceiling on a week's pay (then £205). This limit does not apply under s 189 to the protective award itself (see para 3.8 above), but it does apply to claims on the Secretary of State – EPCA 1978, s 122(5) (now ERA 1996, s 186(1)); and

(c) limiting the amount payable to eight weeks under EPCA 1978, s 122(3)(a) (now ERA 1996, s 184(1)(a)).

1 [1996] ICR 197, EAT; [1997] ICR 209, CA; [1999] ICR 898, HL.
2 See s 188(4)(a), TULRCA 1992.

12.13 Mr Mann brought proceedings claiming that these limitations were in breach of:

● the Collective Redundancies Directive (75/129/EEC) (in relation to (a) above) and

● the 1980 Employment Insolvency Directive (80/987/EEC) (in relation to (a), (b) and (c) above).

12.14 The House of Lords dismissed this claim on the primary ground that the Employment Insolvency Directive does not apply to an administrative receivership. There is no 'state of insolvency' within the Directive as there is no request to an authority for the opening of proceedings to satisfy collectively the claims of creditors. Accordingly, in relation to a receivership, the UK statutory provisions cannot be in breach of the Directives. The comments made in the case are useful guides to the attitudes of the courts in cases where the Directive does apply.

12.15 Set-off: the EAT held that, although set-off of pay and pay in lieu of notice from protective awards was authorised at the relevant time by TULRCA 1992, s 190(3), it was contrary to the Collective Redundancies Directive (see the decision of the ECJ in *Commission v United Kingdom*[1]) and so should not be allowed by the Secretary of State.

The Court of Appeal reversed this finding, holding that the Secretary of State could still rely on s 190(3) and that in any event a guarantee of the protective award and notice pay were not required by the Employment Insolvency Directive because they both related to periods after the insolvency.

The House of Lords agreed with the Court of Appeal that the repeal of s 190(3)[2] was not retrospective. The other reasons given by the Court of Appeal were not considered.

1 [1994] ICR 664, ECJ; [1994] ECR I-2479, ECJ.
2 See para 3.16 above.

12.16 Ceiling on a week's pay: the EAT held that the ceiling on a week's pay is allowed by Article 4 of the Employment Insolvency Directive. That allows for a ceiling consistent with the social policy of the Directive. The EAT considered that the £205 limit (then applicable) could be 'justified as avoiding the payment of sums going beyond the protection aimed at by the directive'.

The Court of Appeal did not consider this point definitively in light of its finding on the set-off point that the guarantee of the protective award and notice pay were not required by the Employment Insolvency Directive. However the Court of Appeal referred to the EAT's judgment and stated (at page 227F) that it was 'not sure that this definition of the social policy of the Directive deals adequately with the arguments advanced on behalf of the employees'. But for the finding that the guarantee in this case was outside the Employment Insolvency Directive, the Court of Appeal stated that it might have thought that a reference to the ECJ on this point would be appropriate.

Lord Hoffmann in the House of Lords did not have to decide the point (in light of his decision that administrative receiverships are outside the Employment Insolvency Directive). He did comment (at page 907) that the point was 'not an easily justiciable question' but that the limit did not seem 'unreasonably low'.

Later challenges in other cases to the limits have been rejected by the EAT (see para 13.37 below).

12.17   Eight–week period: the EAT held that the eight week limitation fell within the option given to member states by Art 4(2) of the Employment Insolvency Directive. This point was not pursued by the Court of Appeal.

Lord Hoffmann in the House of Lords held (at page 908) that the Employment Insolvency Directive (and hence s 122(3)(a) of EPCA 1978) should be read as allowing the employee to choose the eight weeks for which the guarantee from the Secretary of State is payable. In other words the employee can choose the best eight weeks available out of those where pay is due. This is because the eight-week period is a derogation in the Directive and so must be construed restrictively in the employee's favour.

In addition, it seems that the Employment Insolvency Directive may require any payment actually made to the employee to be appropriated first to any wages etc outstanding prior to the relevant eight-week reference period – see the decision of the ECJ in the later case of *Regeling v Bestuur van de Bedrijfsvereneniging*[1].

1 Case C-125/97 [1999] IRLR 379, ECJ.

12.18   Both the Court of Appeal and the EAT held that any claim against the government for damages for failure properly to incorporate the 'directives into UK law (under *Francovich v Italian Republic*[1]) could not be brought in the industrial tribunal (now the employment tribunal). Instead such a claim should be brought in the High Court or the county court, with the Attorney General as the defendant.

1 [1995] ICR 722, [1992] IRLR 84, ECJ.

12.19   There may be some divergence between:

- the requirement in ERA 1996 that the employer may be regarded as insolvent only if there are insolvency proceedings (see s 183 discussed at para 13.15 below) and

- the provisions of Art 2(1)(b) of the Employment Insolvency Directive which deems insolvency to include a situation where insolvency proceedings have not commenced, namely the situation where the 'competent authority' has established that the undertaking or business 'has been definitely closed down' but that the available assets are insufficient to warrant the opening of insolvency proceedings.

12.20   In practice, there seems to be no equivalent to the 'competent authority' in the UK. It could perhaps be argued that the Directive requires the UK to set up such an authority or at least extend the protections from the National Insurance Fund to apply even where there has been no formal insolvency proceedings (eg provide for the Secretary of State to be the competent authority).

12.21   The employment tribunal cannot be such a 'competent authority' – see the decision of the EAT in *Secretary of State for Employment v McGlone*[1].

1 [1997] BCC 101, EAT.

12.22   The Registrar of Companies has the power to strike off companies under the Companies Act 2006, s 1000[1] or on the application of a majority of the directors of a company.

However in *Charlton v Charlton Thermosystems (Romsey) Ltd*[2] the EAT held that such a striking-off by the Registrar of Companies does not constitute insolvency proceedings for the purposes of applying Tupe in the light of the ECJ cases on insolvency (see Chapter 13 below).

1 Formerly CA 1985, ss 652 and 652A (as inserted by the Deregulation and Contracting Out Act 1994).
2 [1995] IRLR 79; [1995] ICR 56 at page 64E, EAT.

12.23   In *Secretary of State for Trade and Industry v Walden*[1] the EAT rejected a claim against the Secretary of State on the grounds that a formal insolvency within s 183 had not been proved. The EAT held that it was not enough that the company may have been dissolved, pointing out that this may have occurred outside the grounds in s183 through a striking off by the Registrar of Companies under s 652 or 652A of the Companies Act 1985 (now Companies Act 2006, s 1000).

1 [2000] IRLR 168, EAT.

PENSIONS

12.24   Article 8 of the 2008 Employment Insolvency Directive (unchanged from the 1980 Directive) contains an obligation on member states to 'ensure that the necessary measures are taken to protect the interests of employees' and ex-employees, under occupational pension schemes following insolvency of the employer. Before the *ASW case* (see below), various UK governments appeared to take the view that the provisions of PSA 1993, ss 123 to 127[1] (see paras 13.54 to 13.59 below), were sufficient, together with other protections for benefits of members (see para 12.26 below), to comply with Art 8.

However, it is notable that Art 8 does not (unlike Art 4) expressly allow a member state to impose any monetary limits on the 'necessary measures', whereas PSA 1993, s 124 contains specific limits (see para 10.96 below). The government appeared to have believed that the existence of a trust fund (at least for private sector HMRC registered (formerly Inland Revenue approved) pension schemes) also forms part of the 'necessary measures'.

1 Formerly EPCA 1978, s 123.

12.25 However, a similar argument was rejected by the European Court in *Commission v Italian Republic*[1]. The Advocate General stated (at para 48, page 161):

> 'Of primary importance in my view is that Article 8 clearly requires measures to protect vested rights or rights in the process of being acquired under supplementary pension schemes. Since in general such rights depend on the length of employment in the undertaking, protection which is confined to the inviolability of funds actually set up and is not concerned with the adequacy of payments into such funds is obviously insufficient.'

1 [1989] ECR 143, ECJ.

12.26 In the UK, before 6 April 2005 (when the Pensions Protection Fund (PPF) under the Pensions Act 2004 started[1]), the protections were limited to:

(a) a limited guarantee from the National Insurance Fund under PSA 1993, s 124 (see paras 13.54 to 13.59 below);

(b) the existence of a separate trust fund (at least for private sector HMRC registered schemes)[2];

(c) the statutory obligation on an employer to contribute to pension schemes both before a winding up under the minimum funding requirement provisions in PA 1995 (see Chapter 33 below) and on a winding-up under PA 1995, s 75 and its predecessors (see Chapter 34 below), combined with the fact that some employer contributions are preferential debts (see Chapter 10 above);

(d) the fact that the government in effect guarantees the payment of contracted-out benefits even if there is an insolvency in a pension scheme which was contracted-out of the State Earnings Related Pension Scheme (SERPS) under PSA 1993 (formerly SSPA 1975). This is a deemed buy-back facility (see below);

(e) For some schemes, the extra support available for the Financial Assistance Scheme (FAS) established from 1 September 2005 under PA 2004[3]. This scheme provides assistance to certain members of pension schemes where the employer is insolvent. It applies to occupational pension schemes in respect of which liquidation proceedings were initiated between 1 January 1997 and 5 April 2005. According to the ECJ in the ASW case: *Robins and Burnett v Secretary of State for Work and Pensions*[4] it supplements retirement pensions at a level of about 80% of the pension expected. Following the ASW decision, the government increased the level of benefits payable under FAS. It now pays 90% of pensions with a cap of £26,000 (and so is not much less than the benefits under the PPF).

1 See Chapter 27 below.
2 Since 23 September 2005, an obligation to have a separate trust arises under PA 2004, s 252(2).
3 PA 2004, s 286 and the Financial Assistance Scheme Regulations 2005 (SI 2005/1986).
4 [2007] 2 CMLR 269; [2007] ICR 779; [2007] IRLR 270, [2007] PLR 55 (C-278/05), ECJ, at para 50.

Deemed buy-back[1]

12.27 If a scheme winds up after 6 April 1997 in a situation where the employer is insolvent and the funds available to the pension scheme are less than those required to restore state scheme rights for a period of contracted-out employment, a deemed buy-back can operate. Details are set out in publication CA15 issued by the contracting-out agency. The statutory provisions are in Sch 2 to PSA 1993 and relevant regulations[2].

1 For further details on deemed buy back see the talk given by Francois Barker and Philip Sutton at the Association of Pension Lawyers (APL) annual conference in November 2003 (see www.apl.org.uk).
2 Regulation 49 of the Occupational Pension Schemes (Contracting-out) Regulations 1996 (SI 1996/1172), and the Occupational Pension Schemes (Contracting-out) (Amount Required for Restoring State Scheme Rights and Miscellaneous Amendment) Regulations 1998 (SI 1998/1397, as amended by SI 1999/3069).

12.28 Deemed buy-back became less important with the increased protections under the Financial Assistance Scheme (FAS) (see para 12.26 above) and the Pension Protection Fund (PPF) now in force (see Chapter 27 below).

From 17 July 2008 it is now no longer possible for FAS qualifying members to be offered the option to buy back into the State Scheme via deemed buyback. This is the result of amendments made by reg 21 of the Financial Assistance Scheme (Miscellaneous Amendment) Regulations (SI 2008/1903). There is an exception if the member someone has, before the commencement of the provisions, been offered the opportunity to be reinstated by his scheme. They will still be able to select this option if they follow the appropriate procedure of making a written application in accordance with the 1996 Regulations. There is a discussion of the technical implications of this change in the HMRC Pensions Industry Newsletter (National Insurance Services to Pensions Industry: September 2008 Issue 34).

ASW CASE

12.29 However, it was not clear that these protections were sufficient to constitute 'necessary measures' for the purposes of Art 8. The second edition of this book (2000) stated that it must be arguable that the UK is in breach of its obligations under Article 8.

12.30   In *Robins and Burnett v Secretary of State for Work and Pensions*[1], various former employees of Allied Steel & Wire (ASW) brought proceedings against the UK government for failure to implement Art 8. These claims were referred to the ECJ in July 2005 and judgment was given in January 2007.

1 [2007] 2 CMLR 269; [2007] ICR 779; [2007] IRLR 270, [2007] PLR 55 (C-278/05), ECJ.

12.31   The ECJ was asked whether Art 8 of the Employment Insolvency Directive (Directive 80/987/EEC on protection of employees in the event of insolvency of their employer), is to be interpreted as requiring Member States to ensure, by whatever means necessary, that employees' accrued rights under supplementary company or inter company final salary pension schemes are fully funded by Member States in the event that the employee's private employer becomes insolvent and the assets of their scheme are insufficient to fund those benefits.
   Further,

(1)   If the answer to the first question is no, whether the requirements of Art 8 are sufficiently implemented by other legislation in force in the United Kingdom (UK); and

(2)   If the UK fails to comply with Art 8, what test should be applied in determining whether the infringement of Community law should attract liability in damages? In particular, is the mere infringement enough to establish the existence of a breach or must there have also been disregard by the Member States for the limits on its rule making powers?

Article 8 remains unchanged in the 2008 Directive.

12.32   In January 2007, having considered the arguments raised above about the protections provided under UK laws, the ECJ held that:

'1.   On a proper construction of Article 8 of Council Directive 80/987/EEC of 20 October 1980 on the approximation of the laws of the Member States relating to the protection of employees in the event of the insolvency of their employer, where the employer is insolvent and the assets of the supplementary company or inter-company pension schemes are insufficient, accrued pension rights need not necessarily be funded by the Member States themselves or be funded in full.

2.   A system of protection such as that at issue in the main proceedings is incompatible with Article 8 of Directive 80/987.

3.   If Article 8 of Directive 80/987 has not been properly transposed into domestic law, the liability of the Member State concerned is contingent on a finding of manifest and grave disregard by that State for the limits set on its discretion.'

12.33   The ECJ noted (para 43) the lack of express limitation in Art 8 of the Employment Insolvency Directive on the level of protections to be provided by member states (in contrast to the express limits allowed on pay claims), but held that the requirement to 'ensure that the necessary measures are taken' does not oblige member states to fund the benefits in full (para 35) and allows members states some latitude as to the means to be adopted (para 36). A full guarantee of benefits is not required (para 42).

12.34 The ECJ went on to hold that the protections in place in the UK (for scheme insolvencies before 6 April 2005) were not compatible with Art 8. The ECJ noted (at paras 57 to 59):

> '57 Nevertheless, having regard to the express wish of the Community legislature, it must be held that provisions of domestic law that may, in certain cases, lead to a guarantee of benefits limited to 20 or 49% of the benefits to which an employee was entitled, that is to say, of less than half of that entitlement, cannot be considered to fall within the definition of the word 'protect' used in Article 8 of the Directive.
>
> 58 On that point, it may be noted that in 2004, according to unchallenged figures communicated to the Commission by the United Kingdom:
>
> – about 65 000 members of pension schemes suffered the loss of more than 20% of expected benefits;
>
> – some 35 000 of them, that is to say, nearly 54% of the total, suffered losses exceeding 50% of those benefits.
>
> 59 It must therefore be concluded that a system such as that established by the United Kingdom legislation does not ensure the protection provided for by the Directive and does not constitute proper implementation of Article 8 thereof.'

This conclusion was not altered by the setting up of the Financial Assistance Scheme (FAS) under the Pensions Act 2004. The ECJ noted that (at paras 60 and 61):

> '60 That conclusion is not shaken by the introduction from 1 September 2005 of a scheme such as the FAS, even though that scheme is applicable to winding-up procedures initiated between 1 January 1997 and 5 April 2005.
>
> 61 It is apparent from unchallenged information contained in the documents before the Court that the FAS:
>
> – does not cover members of the scheme who were more than three years away from retirement on 14 May 2004;
>
> – helps only about 11,000 of the non-pensioner members of the schemes concerned, that is to say, less than 13% of the total number of members.'

12.35 The ECJ went on to hold (para 69) that, given that Article 8 of the Employment Insolvency Directive has not been properly transposed into domestic law, the UK will be liable for damages suffered by individuals only if a court finds that:

● the rule of law infringed should be intended to confer rights on individuals;

● the breach should be sufficiently serious;

- there should be a direct causal link between the breach of the obligation incumbent on the State and the damage sustained by the injured parties.

This issue was referred back to the UK courts to decide. The ECJ did give some guidance on this issue, holding that the national court must take account of all the factors (para 76) and that the factors include (para 77):

- the clarity and precision of the rule infringed;

- the measure of discretion left by that rule to the national authorities;

- whether the infringement or the damage caused was intentional or involuntary,

- whether any error of law was excusable or inexcusable; and

- the fact that the position taken by a Community institution may have contributed towards the adoption or maintenance of national measures or practices contrary to Community law.

The ECJ noted (para 80) that none of the parties had 'been able to suggest with precision the minimum degree of protection that in their view is required by the Directive, if it should be considered that the latter does not impose a full guarantee.'

The ECJ also commented (at para 81) that:

> 'The national court may also take into consideration Commission report COM(95) 164 final of 15 June 1995 (not published in the Official Journal of the European Communities), concerning the transposition of the Directive by the Member States, which has been cited in observations submitted to the Court and in which the Commission had then concluded (p. 52): "The abovementioned rules [adopted by the United Kingdom] appear to meet the requirements of Article 8 [of the Directive]". As the Advocate General has observed in point 98 of her Opinion, that wording may, although careful, have reinforced the view of the Member State concerned with regard to the transposition of the Directive into domestic law.'

12.36   The decision of the European Court in *Francovich v Italian Republic*[1] was relied on by the ECJ as previous authority for the proposition that a member state can be liable to individuals in damages in some circumstances where the member state has failed properly to implement Directives (see also the House of Lords in Kirklees *MBC v Wickes*[2]). *Francovich* is in fact a decision involving a claim against Italy for failure properly to implement the Employment Insolvency Directive (see *Commission v Italian Republic*[3]).

1 [1992] IRLR 84, ECJ.
2 [1993] AC 227, HL.
3 [1989] ECR 143, ECJ.

12.37   Although not mentioned by the ECJ in *ASW/Robins*, claims cannot be brought against a member state where insolvency occurred before 23 October 1983, the last date by which the Employment Insolvency Directive should have been implemented – *Suffritti v Instituto Nazionale della Previdenza Sociale (INPS)*[4].

1 C-140/91; [1992] ECR I-6337; [1993] IRLR 289, ECJ.

12.38   If the government had lost the damages claim in *ASW/Robins* when it was heard by the UK courts, there may well have been increasing pressure for pension debts to be given a greater priority in insolvency proceedings.

12.39   From 6 April 2005, for eligible schemes of companies that enter insolvency after 5 April 2005, the Pension Protection Fund (PPF) under the Pensions Act 2004 will, in practice, provide protection for some (but not all) defined benefits under relevant occupational pension schemes (see Chapter 18 below).

The level of protection provided by the PPF was substantially greater than that under the FAS. Broadly all pensions (for those aged over the normal pension age) (but with limited future increases); and 90% of pensions for those below normal pension age, with a cap of roughly £25,000pa. Following the decision in *ASW/Robins*, the government increased the level of benefits payable under FAS. It now pays 90% of pensions with a cap of £26,000 (and so is not much less than the benefits under the PPF).

The existence of the cap will mean, for those with large pensions that only a proportion of their pension will be protected by the PPF. This may, in some cases be less than the 20% figure criticised by the ECJ in *Robins*. It remains to be seen if the PPF would survive a challenge before the ECJ based on Article 8, but my guess is that it would.

12.40   There could have been an argument that the obligation under Art 8 does not extend to contracted-out pension schemes, but only to those which are not contracted-out. This is on the basis that the Article refers to 'schemes outside the national statutory social security system' and it could be argued that a contracted-out scheme is in fact in substitution for part of the state social security system rather than fully supplemental to the state social security schemes'.

This was one of the arguments used in relation to the Acquired Rights Directive and Tupe in *Warrener v Walden Engineering*[1] in the industrial tribunal although a later industrial tribunal found to the contrary on this point in *Perry v Intec Colleges*[2] and the EAT in *Warrener*[3] agreed with this. It does not seem to have been raised in the ECJ case involving ASW, *Robins and Burnett v Secretary of State for Work and Pensions*[4].

1 [1992] OPLR 1, EAT.
2 [1993] IRLR 56, IT.
3 [1993] IRLR 420, EAT.
4 [2007] 2 CMLR 269; [2007] ICR 779, (C-278/05), ECJ.

CHAPTER 13

National Insurance Fund

STATE GUARANTEE

13.1   In addition to the advantage given to some claims of employees by granting them preferential status (see Chapter 6 above), certain claims of employees are, in effect, guaranteed by the State out of the National Insurance Fund under ERA 1996, ss 166–170 and Pt IX (ss 182–190) and PSA 1993, Ch II, Pt VII (ss 123–127).

For a comparative study over 62 jurisdictions see Janis Sarra, *Employee and Pension Claims during Company Insolvency*[1].

1 Thomson Carswell, Toronto, 2008.

13.2   The claim must be that of an employee and not (say) a person who is an officer (and not an employee)[1] or an agency worker or someone who is self-employed[2]. The position of shareholders and directors is discussed in Chapter 11 above.

1 See *Eaton v Robert Eaton Ltd* [1988] IRLR 83, EAT.
2 See para 2.3 above and *McLane v Secretary of State for Employment* (1992) 21 April. (1992), Industrial Relations Legal Information Bulletin (July) and *McMeechan v Secretary of State* [1997] ICR 549, CA.

WHEN DOES THE PERSON NEED TO BE AN EMPLOYEE?

13.3   The EAT and the Court of Appeal have held that the person has to be an 'employee' as at the date when the company became insolvent.

The EAT in *Neufeld*[1] held (at para 14):

> 'It seems to me that application of sections 182-183 of the Employment Rights Act yields the answer that the date when the question in section 230 is to be answered is the date of the insolvency i.e. was the Claimant an employee at the date of the insolvency?'

The EAT followed Mummery P in *Rajah v The Secretary of State for Employment*[2] (at page 6):

'There may well have been a change during the life of the company in Mr Rajah's relationship with it. The company started as a partnership company. Originally there were other shareholders. There were other directors. What we have to look at, however, is what the Industrial Tribunal had to look at was the position at the relevant date. The relevant date for the purpose of deciding whether the Secretary of State is liable to make payments out of the national insurance fund to employees of an insolvent company is the date at which the company became insolvent not the position as it was two years, five years or ten years previously.'

The EAT in *Neufeld* commented (at para 15) that:

'15. That proposition is supported by Lord Coulsfield's judgment in the Inner House in *Fleming v Secretary of State for Trade and Industry* [1997] IRLR 682 at paragraph 10. Both were cited to the Court of Appeal in *Bottrill* where neither account was disputed.'

This was approved by the Court of Appeal in *Neufeld v Secretary of State for Business, Enterprise and Regulatory Reform*[3] at para 6.

1 *Neufeld v A & N Communications In Print Ltd (in liq)* [2008] All ER (D) 156 (Apr), EAT.
2 Unreported EAT 7 July 1997 (available on Bailii).
3 [2009] EWCA Civ 280; [2009] 3 All ER 790; [2009] IRLR 475, CA.

13.4   This appears to be a bit of a simplification. Section 182(c), ERA 1996 includes a requirement that 'on the appropriate date' the employee was entitled to be paid the whole or part of a relevant debt. The term 'appropriate date' is defined in s 185 (but none of the cases noted above seem to have referred to the wording used in this section). The term is defined in s 185 as (broadly – see para 13.30 below):

- the date on which the employer became insolvent for pay and holiday pay – s 185(a); and

- if later, the later date of the termination of the employee's employment for other debts – s 185(b) and (c).

13.5   In the case of a claim based on an 'employment' that terminated before the onset of insolvency, there seems no reason to test the employment status on the insolvency date – instead the date of termination is most relevant.

13.6   If the termination is on or after the date of insolvency, the most appropriate date for carrying out the test looks to be the date of termination. In practice it is perhaps unlikely that the person's employment status will have changed since the date of the insolvency – see for example the comment by the Court of Appeal in *Neufeld* (at para [44]) on the position in *Buchan* that.

'[44] Mr Buchan was in fact dismissed by the company's administrative receivers, but the appeal tribunal held that as his 50% shareholding had previously enabled him to block any decision to dismiss him, he was never an employee of the company and his purported dismissal did not make him one. Mr Ivey was, a fortiori, similarly not an employee: the label on his purported service contract was not conclusive as to its substantive effect.'

13.7   Thus in *Rajah*[1], the employment tribunal held that Mr Rajah was not an employee at the date of the insolvency. This was upheld by the EAT, commenting:

> 'The position at the date of the insolvency of the company in June 1993 was that, on the findings of fact made by the Tribunal, Mr Rajah was the sole person oper-ating the company. For eight months or so he had not been receiving salary and there had been no payment of tax and National Insurance contributions. The posi-tion was that, unlike an ordinary employee, the payments which he received were not salary but out of the loan account standing to his credit. In our view, it is dif-ficult, in those circumstances, to question the decision the Tribunal that Mr Rajah was not an employee at the date when the company became in insolvent in June 1993. At that date he was operating the company on his own. He was not receiv-ing a salary and had not been for some time. Those are two important factors which would entitle the Tribunal to reach the conclusion that he had not satisfied them that he was an employee.'

1 Unreported EAT 7 July 1997 (available on Bailii).

CLAIMS ON THE NATIONAL INSURANCE FUND

13.8   An employee is able to look to the National Insurance Fund to pay a claim up to the limits imposed by the relevant sections in ERA 1996 and PSA 1993 (see para 10.1 above). Any claim of the employee in excess of these limits would need to be dealt with as a claim on the insolvent employer company in the usual way. The National Insurance Fund, having paid a claim to an employee, is subrogated to the rights of the employee in the sense that the Secretary of State then has a matching claim against the company. Where the claim of the employee is preferential, the claim by the National Insurance Fund will also be preferential, now ranking equally with the preferential element of the employee's remaining claim (see para 13.71 below).

The Insolvency Service says that it processes redundancy claims on the National Insurance Fund with three weeks of receipt of the relevant forms for 81.9% of claims and within six weeks for 94.8% of claims (see the Insolvency Service annual report for 2008/09[1]). This is likely in most cases to be faster than a distribution made by an insolvency practitioner in an insolvency.

1 See page 18. www.insolvency.gov.uk/pdfs/annual2008-09web.pdf

13.9   A summary of the operation of the National Insurance Fund in relation to employees' claims on insolvency is given in two booklets issued by BERR:

● *'Redundancy and Insolvency – A guide for insolvency practitioners to employees' rights on the insolvency of their employer'*[1]; and

● *'Insolvency of Employers: Safeguard of occupational pension scheme con-tributions'*.

1 URN 08/550. On the web at: http://www.insolvency.gov.uk/guidanceleaflets/redundancypayments/ guideforips/guideforips.htm This replaced the previous DTI booklet – Eighth Edition 2005 (URN 05/ 589).

13.10   Claims were formerly met out of the Redundancy Fund, but this was wound up and its assets and liabilities transferred to the National Insurance Fund with effect from 1 February 1991 under s 13 of the Employment Act 1990.

13.11   An employee will only have a claim on the National Insurance Fund if his or her employer has become insolvent within the meaning given by ERA 1996, s 183(1) and PSA 1993, s 123. There is a different rule for claims for redundancy pay – see para 10.56 below.

TUPE

13.12   The Redundancy Payments Service of BIS (formerly BERR) will check (see the questionnaire in form IP14) whether there has been a transfer of an undertaking from the insolvent company to a transferee/purchaser, so that the employee has automatically become an employee of the transferee/purchaser under the Transfer of Undertakings (Protection of Employment) Regulations 2006 (see Chapters 20 to 24 below).

13.13   If there has been such a transfer of employment (or liability), no liability will usually remain on the transferor/company and, accordingly, there will be no claim on the National Insurance Fund.

13.14   An employee will generally have no claim on the transferor company if his employment has transferred (under TUPE) to a purchaser/transferee of an undertaking from the company – see *Allan v Stirling District Council*[1] and *Clarke v Mediguard Services Ltd*[2]. However, some claims (eg liabilities relating to pensions or consultation obligations) may now remain behind with the company and not transfer to the purchaser/transferee under TUPE 2006 (see para 9.7 above and Chapter 19 below). There are also special rules on transfers in some insolvencies (see Chapter 20 below)

1 [1995] ICR 1082; [1995] IRLR 301, Court of Session.
2 [2000] NI 73, NI CA.

NATIONAL INSURANCE FUND: MEANING OF 'INSOLVENCY'

13.15   In order for claims to be made on the National Insurance Fund under ERA 1996, s 182 or PSA 1993, s 124 the employer must have become insolvent within the meaning given to the term by ERA 1996, s 183(1) (the test in PSA 1993, s 123 is identical).

13.16   In the case of claims for redundancy payments, either:

● the employer must either have become insolvent within the meaning given by ERA 1996, s 166(5) – this is identical to s 183(1), or

- the employee must show that he has taken all reasonable steps to recover the payment (see eg *Pollard v Teako (Swiss) Ltd*[1]).

1 (1967) 2 ITR 357, IT.

13.17 Sections 183(3) and 166(7) require that, in the case of a corporate employer:

(a) a winding-up order has been made or a resolution for voluntary winding up passed; or

(b) the company is in administration for the purposes of IA 1986; or

(c) a receiver or manager of its undertaking has been properly appointed (or possession taken by debenture holders of property of the company subject to a floating charge). Appointment under a fixed charge is not enough – see the decisions of the EAT in *Secretary of State for Employment v Stone*[1] and in *Parry v Secretary of State*[2]; or

(d) a voluntary arrangement under the IA 1986, Pt 1 has been approved.

Although not listed in ERA 1996, the various insolvency regimes under the Banking Act 2009 will also count as an insolvency for these purposes, so that relevant employees will be able to claim on the National Insurance Fund. This is because article 3 of the Banking Act 2009 (Parts 2 and 3 Consequential Amendments) Order 2009[3] deems references to winding-up or liquidation or administration to include bank liquidation or bank administration under the 2009 Act. This applies to the enactments listed in the Schedule, which include the Employment Rights Act 1996, the Pensions Act 1995, the Pensions Act 2004, the PPF Entry Rules Regulations 2005[4] and the Financial Assistance Scheme Regulations 2005[5].

The same applies to building societies – see the Building Societies (Insolvency and Special Administration) Order 2009[6].

1 [1994] ICR 761, EAT.
2 EAT/1301/98, 23 September 1999.
3 SI 2009/317.
4 SI 2005/590.
5 SI 2005/1996.
6 SI 2009/805 –adding a new s 90C into the Building Societies Act 1986 and see para 1 of Sch 2 applying the Banking Act 2009 (Parts 2 and 3 Consequential Amendments) Order 2009.

13.18 The list is exhaustive in relation to claims under s 182. The mere (factual) existence of insolvency is not enough—see the decisions of the EAT in *Secretary of State for Employment v McGlone*[1] and in *Secretary of State for Trade and Industry v Key*[2]. Nor is it enough if one partner in a partnership becomes bankrupt (but the others do not) – see the decision of the EAT in *Secretary of State v Forde*[3].

1 [1997] BCC 101, EAT.
2 [2003] All ER (D) 171 (Oct); [2004] BPIR 214, EAT.
3 [1997] ICR 231; [1997] IRLR 387, EAT.

13.19 Similarly, it is not enough that the company has been struck off by the Registrar of Companies under CA 2006, ss 1000 to 1003[1] – see para 12.22 above and the decision of the EAT in *Secretary of State v Walden*[2].

1 Formerly CA 1985, s 652 or 652A.
2 [2000] IRLR 168, EAT.

13.20 These provisions can extend to employers which are companies incorporated outside Great Britain. However, in order for a claim to be made, the company must, under s 183 (and s 166(5)), have entered insolvency proceedings within Great Britain (it seems that this requirement could contravene Art 2 of the Employment Insolvency Directive – see Chapter 12 above).

13.21 In practice, the requirements in ERA 1996 will mean that a British insolvency practitioner has been appointed in relation to the company.

There is clear jurisdiction for a foreign company to be wound up in the UK (see IA 1986, ss 220, 221, 225), but it was in the past more difficult for an administration order to be made (see *Re International Bulk Commodities Ltd*[1] and *Re Dallhold Estates (UK) Pty Ltd*[2]). A UK insolvency process can now be started under the EC Regulation on Insolvency Proceedings 2000 or the Cross-Border Insolvency Regulations 2006 (SI 2006/1030) – see Chapter 40 (Overseas employees and insolvencies) below.

1 [1993] Ch 77 (Mummery J).
2 [1992] BCC 394 (Chadwick J).

13.22 The fact that making a winding-up order in England and Wales will enable employees to make claims under these sections may be a ground on which a winding-up petition may be granted against a company incorporated outside Great Britain – see *Re Eloc Electro-Optieck and Communicatie BV*[1].

But a UK insolvency order may perhaps be resisted if this would be contrary to the general interest of an overseas insolvency proceeding – see the discussion in Chapter 40 (Overseas employees and insolvencies) below.

1 [1982] Ch 43 (Nourse J).

13.23 Express provision was in the past made in s 196(7)[1] of ERA 1996, to the effect that Pt XII of ERA 1996 would apply to employment where, under his contract of employment, the employee ordinarily works inside the territory of a member state of the European Union. (Similarly PSA 1993, s 165(8) in relation to claims under PSA 1993, ss 123–127).

1 Formerly EPCA 1978, s 141(2A).

13.24 This reflected the extension of s 141(2A) of EPCA 1978 (but not s 165(8) of PSA 1993) from 9 March 1995 to cover Austria, Finland, Iceland, Norway and Sweden by the Insolvency of Employer (Excluded Classes) Regulations 1995 (SI 1995/278). The extension was consistent with the decision of the ECJ in *Danmarks Active Handelsrejsende v Lonmodtagernes Garantifund*[1].

1 Case C-117/96 [1998] IRLR 150, ECJ. See para 12.4 above.

13.25 In practice, many of the claims within Pt XII of ERA 1996 were, before 25 October 1999, only applicable to employees who ordinarily work in Great Britain (eg claims for statutory notice under s 86 and for unfair dismissal were so restricted by ERA 1996, s 196).

13.26 However, ERA 1996, s 196 was deleted by ERA 1999, s 32 with effect from 25 October 1999[1]. For an analysis of the extra-territorial issues this raises in other employment claim areas, see the decision of the House of Lords on unfair dismissal in *Lawson v Serco Ltd*[2].

1 See SI 1999/2830, in particular the transitional provisions in para 7 of Sch 3.
2 [2006] UKHL 3, [2006] 1 All ER 823, HL.

13.27 Other claims within Pt XII were, and are, not so limited (eg claims for back wages and holiday pay).

13.28 Generally, the governing law of the employment relationship is irrelevant for the purposes of ERA 1996 (ERA 1996, s 204)). Similarly, employees of a company incorporated in England and Wales who work in another member state may be able in some cases to bring claims against the National Insurance Fund, subject to insolvency proceedings being commenced in Great Britain. The government may, perhaps, look to limit this, given the ability to claim against the insolvency funds of other member states (see paras 12.4 above).

CLAIMS FOR PAY

13.29 Under s 182, ERA 1996 the Secretary of State must make payment out of the National Insurance Fund if he is satisfied, following a written application, that:

(a) the employer has become insolvent (see para 13.15 above); and

(b) employment of the employee has been terminated[1] (unless the deemed termination provisions in reg 8(3) of TUPE 2006 apply – see Chapter 20 below); and

(c) on the appropriate date the employee was entitled to be paid a relevant debt.

1 Note that this differs from the position of preferential debts – there is no requirement of termination of employment for a debt to be preferential – see Chapter 8 (Preferential Debts) above.

Appropriate date

13.30 The appropriate date is defined in ERA 1996, s 185 and is generally the later of the date on which the employer became insolvent and the date of termination of employment.

In relation to a claim for arrears of pay or holiday pay, the appropriate date is the date the employer became insolvent.

In relation to a protective award or basic award in unfair dismissal cases, the appropriate date can be the later date on which the award was made.

See para 13.3 above for a discussion of the applicable date in the context of deciding when a person needs to be an employee.

Relevant claim

13.31   The relevant claims of employees in respect of which an entitlement to claim arises are defined or set out in s 184(1) and (2). They include:

(a)   arrears of pay for up to eight weeks;

(b)   amounts due for failure to give the statutory minimum period of notice required by ERA 1996, s 86 (see para 2.28(a) above);

(c)   any holiday pay (see the definition in ERA 1996, s 184(3) and para 10.83 below) entitlement for up to six weeks which accrued during the 12 months prior to the appropriate date;

(d)   any basic award of compensation for unfair dismissal (within the meaning of ERA 1996, s 118) but not any compensatory award – see paras 2.45 to 2.49 above; and

(e)   a reasonable sum by way of reimbursement of any fee or premium paid by an apprentice or articled clerk.

13.32   Under s 184(2), arrears of pay for the purposes of s 184 include:

•   guarantee payments,

•   remuneration on suspension on medical or maternity grounds under ERA 1996, ss 64, 68,

•   payments for time off under Pt VI of ERA 1996 (ss 50–63) and TULRCA 1992, s 169 (see paras 2.55 to 2.59 above), and

•   remuneration under a protective award under TULRCA 1992, s 189, (see para 3.6 above).

This is a similar list to that used for preferential payments (see para 9.32 above).

13.33   Pay does not include amounts of salary left outstanding by a director on a loan account—see the decision of the EAT in *Secretary of State v Forster*[1].

Nor does it include contractual guarantee payments (more generous than the statutory level) – see the EAT in *Benson v Secretary of State*[2].

1 7 July 1987 (EAT 220/87).
2 [2003] IRLR 748, EAT.

13.34   Pay does not include a compensatory award for unfair dismissal – see *Connor and Hine v Secretary of State*[1], where the EAT held that the compensatory award was clearly excluded by the UK legislation and that this was consistent with the Employment Insolvency Directive. The EAT considered:

'two parallel decisions of the European Court, namely *Caballero v Fogasa*[2] [2003] IRLR 115, (Fogasa being the Spanish guarantee institution) and *Valero v Fogasa*[3] C-520/03. In both of those cases, the European Court was addressing a situation in which, whereas under Spanish law, a particular kind of unpaid compensation was otherwise recoverable against an employer and guaranteed by Fogasa in the event of insolvency, there was a difference as between Fogasa's liability under the guarantee and the liability of a solvent employer by reference to the method by which such compensation arose. It was made, by Spanish legislation, a precondition of recoverability against Fogasa that the unpaid compensation had been found due by a Spanish Court or legal process, whereas if it had simply been the subject of agreement or compromise, it was not recoverable against Fogasa. That was found by the Employment Tribunal, to be an unjustified distinction; if there were any concern in Spain about possibly sham compensation agreements, then art 10(1) of the Directive would enable steps to be taken to avoid such abuse; but not by ruling out the entirety of any claims not covered by Spanish Court procedures.

[31] The passage in the judgment in *Caballero* is at paras 33 and 34 of the judgment of the court:

> "33. It is clear from both the grounds of the order for reference and the written observations of the Spanish Government that, under Spanish law, all workers who are unfairly dismissed are in the same situation in the sense that they are entitled to 'salarios de tramitación'. However, in the event of the employer's insolvency, Article 33(1) of the Workers' Statute treats dismissed workers differently to the extent that the right to payment by Fogasa of claims relating to 'salarios de tramitación' is acknowledged only in respect of those determined by judicial decision.

> 34. Such a difference in treatment can be accepted only if it is objectively justified."

A similar result was achieved by the disapproval of the European Court in *Valero*. It is quite plain that that is a wholly different situation. That is a case in which the definition of pay was, by the national law, the same in each case. The kind of compensation that is recoverable was identical in both circumstances. But an unjustifiable trammel was placed in the one case and not in the other. It is plain that the justification for the distinction in this case is simply one of limiting, or putting a ceiling upon, the quantum of compensation guaranteed by the government, whereas no such justification was put forward in the Spanish case. The only justification that was put forward, as appears from para 35 of the judgment in *Caballero* was the risk of abuses which the court found could, and should, have been dealt with in some other way, and did not justify the distinction.'

1 [2006] All ER (D) 61 (Feb); 20 December 2005; (UKEAT/0589/05/SM, UKEAT/0590/05/SM), EAT.
2 *Caballero v Fondo de Garantía Salarial* (C-442/00) [2002] ECR I-11915; [2003] IRLR 115: [2002] All ER (D) 166 (Dec), ECJ.
3 *Valero v Fondo de Garantia Salarial* (C-520/03) [2004] All ER (D) 278 (Dec), ECJ.

13.35 Pay probably includes a claim by an employee to have his pay made up to the national minimum wage under the National Minimum Wage Act 1998 (see the comments of the then Solicitor General, Lord Falconer, during the Act's passage through Parliament[1]).

1 Hansard, House of Lords, 20 July 1998, Col 679. See para 9.44 above for further background on the National Minimum Wage Act.

13.36 Under s 186(1), where the amount of a claim is referable to a period of time, the amount of the debt must not exceed the usual limit applicable to claims under ERA 1996. This figure is £350 per week where the relevant date (see para 10.36 above) falls on or after 1 February 2009[1]. This limit applies to the amounts under s 184 even where they are not usually limited (eg pay, holiday pay and pay in lieu of notice).

1 See arts 3 and 4(2) of the Employment Rights (Increase of Limits) Order 2008 (SI 2008/3055) and para 2.49 above.

13.37 The limit on a week's pay was approved by the EAT in *Secretary of State v Mann*[1]. But the Court of Appeal in *Mann*[2] was more doubtful and might have referred the issue to the ECJ, but for its finding on another point (see para 12.16 above). Later challenges to the limits were rejected by the EAT in *Titchener v Secretary of State*[3] and in *Connor and Hine v Secretary of State*[4].

1 [1996] ICR 197, EAT.
2 [1997] ICR 217, CA.
3 [2002] IRLR 195, EAT.
4 [2006] All ER (D) 61 (Feb); 20 December 2005 (UKEAT/0589/05 and UKEAT/0590/05).

13.38 For these purposes it is clear that where an employee claims for failure to give notice, the claim is for compensation for breach of contract (ie the claim is not a statutory claim independent of any contractual entitlement) and the employee is under a duty to mitigate any loss – see *Westwood v Secretary of State for Employment*[1], *Secretary of State v Cooper*[2], *Secretary of State v Thomson*[3] and *Secretary of State v Stewart*[4].

1 [1985] AC 20, HL.
2 [1977] ICR 766, EAT.
3 20 January 1995 (EAT 313/94).
4 [1996] IRLR 334, EAT.

13.39 Debts due to the employer from the employee must also be set-off and deducted (at least in a liquidation) – see *Secretary of State v Wilson and BCCI*[1] and Chapter 14 (Set-off) below.

Set-off of wages paid and pay in lieu of notice against a protective award was upheld by the Court of Appeal in *Secretary of State v Mann*[2] (see para 12.15 above), but is not now applied following the repeal of TULRCA 1992, s 190(3) in August 1993[3].

Set-off of claims for pay against a later payment (eg unemployment benefit or a job seekers allowance) is not allowed under the Employment Insolvency Directive – see the decision of the ECJ in *Maso v INPS*[4].

1 [1996] IRLR 330, EAT.
2 [1997] ICR 217, CA.
3 See *Secretary of State v Mann* [1997] ICR 209, CA at page 223E.
4 Case C-373/95; [1997] ECR 1-4051; [1997] 3 CMLR 1244, ECJ.

13.40   As for any other claim for breach of contract (see para 2.34 above), the Secretary of State is entitled to reduce the claim to reflect the fact that it is tax free (up to £30,000) in the employee's hands – see para 2.34(c) above. See the decisions of the EAT in *Secretary of State for Employment v Cooper*[1] and *Munday v Secretary of State for Employment*[2].

1 [1987] ICR 766, EAT.
2 6 November 1989 (EAT) (1991) Industrial Relations Legal Information Bulletin 422.

13.41   In practice this means that an employee cannot lodge a claim (on form IP2 – see further para 13.77 below) until after the end of the statutory notice period as he will not know until then how much to deduct by way of mitigation.

13.42   If the insolvency practitioner decides that the company should continue in business (see Chapters 15 to 18 (Carrying on business) below), continued employment by the company (or the insolvency practitioner) after the relevant date at which the claim is made (see para 13.30 above) will reduce any claim for pay in lieu of statutory notice (and will take effect before the £350 per week limit has been applied – see para 13.53 below).

13.43   It is arguable that it is not necessary in order for an employee to make a claim on the National Insurance Fund under ERA 1996, s 184 for accrued holiday pay that the employee show a contractual entitlement to accrued holiday pay on termination of employment. Section 184(3) of ERA 1996 defines holiday pay to include:

> 'any accrued holiday pay which under the employee's contract of employment would in the ordinary course have become payable to him in respect of the period of a holiday if his employment with the employer had continued until he became entitled to a holiday'.

13.44   This seems to imply that a claim can be made on the National Insurance Fund even if there is no contractual entitlement to accrued holiday pay on termination of employment. *Westwood v Secretary of State for Employment*[1] can be distinguished as that case related to claims for pay in lieu of statutory notice and was decided based on EPCA 1978, s 51 (now ERA 1996, s 91(5)) which refers to such a claim as being for 'breach of the contract'.

1 [1985] AC 20, HL – see para 13.38 above.

13.45   The existence of a contractual entitlement for accrued holiday pay on termination of employment should be mentioned in the statutory statement of terms given to the employee under ERA 1996, s 1.
    If there is no express contractual right to pay in lieu of accrued holiday entitlement, then it seems that the courts may be reluctant to imply a right – see the decision of the Court of Appeal in *Morley v Heritage plc*[1] – but depending on the facts a right may be implied by (say) custom and practice – see the decision of the EAT in *Janes Solicitors v Lamb-Simpson*[2].

1 [1993] IRLR 400, CA.
2 (1996) 541 IRLB 15 (EAT 323/94).

13.46 A right to paid holiday (and pay in lieu on termination) is implied from 1 October 1998 under regs 13 and 14 of the Working Time Regulations 1998[1] up to the statutory entitlement of 28 days per annum (this was originally 15 days and has risen to 28 days from 1 April 2009).

1 SI 1998/1833, as amended.

13.47 The liability of the Secretary of State under s 184(1)(b) (see para 13.31(b) above) in relation to a claim for failure to give the statutory minimum notice is narrower than the employer's general common law liability. In *Secretary of State for Employment v Haynes*[1] the EAT held that the Secretary of State's liability is limited to the loss of remuneration payable under ss 86–91 (minimum period of notice) and ss 220–229 (a week's pay) of ERA 1996 (formerly EPCA 1978, Schs 3 and 14).

1 [1980] ICR 371, EAT.

13.48 In *Haynes* it was held that holiday stamps did not constitute remuneration for the week in which they were purchased, but rather were remuneration for the week when the holiday was taken. In *S & U Stores v Wilkes*[1] the National Industrial Relations Court held that remuneration did not include benefits in kind.

1 [1974] ICR 645, NIRC.

13.49 The Department of Employment considered that, on the basis of these cases, certain benefits, such as luncheon vouchers, can be considered sufficiently close to pay to be treated as remuneration, but that employers' pension contributions (by analogy with holiday stamps) cannot.

13.50 The Department of Employment's view in relation to pension contributions is not shared by the Society of Practitioners of Insolvency (SPI), now R3. SPI Technical Release No 5 (August 1999) indicates that the *Haynes* case should not be treated as authority for excluding pension contributions from remuneration (see para 6 of Technical Release No 5).

The SPI view is to be preferred, at least in relation to contributions to a money purchase arrangement (eg a stakeholder plan). Part of the reasoning in *Haynes* was that the holiday stamps were remuneration only in the weeks in which the holiday was taken but this cannot be the case in relation to pension contributions which are clearly earned in respect of the relevant week worked (see, for example, *Hopkins v Norcros plc*[1] where the Court of Appeal held that pension payments were not available to be offset against a damages claim).

1 [1994] ICR 18, CA.

13.51 Section 182 extends to include the claim of a woman on maternity leave to pay in lieu of the statutory minimum notice. Paragraphs 2 and 3 of Sch 3 to EPCA 1978 were amended by the Trade Union Reform and Employment Rights Act 1993 to clarify this point (see now ERA 1996, ss 88, 89).

The Court of Appeal in *Clark v Secretary of State for Employment*[1] rejected a claim that this applied even before the amendments. This was on the basis that failure to allow such claims would not be unlawful sex discrimination contrary to art 141 of the EU Treaty (formerly article 119 of the Treaty of Rome).

1 [1996] IRLR 578, CA.

13.52   Deductions for tax are made from a claim under s 182 based on the statutory maximum for a week's pay after the statutory maximum is applied and not before – see *Parsons v BNM Laboratories Ltd*[1], *Morris v Secretary of State for Employment*[2] and *Titchener v Secretary of State*[3].

1 [1964] 1 QB 95, CA.
2 [1985] ICR 522, [1985] IRLR 27, EAT.
3 [2002] IRLR 195, EAT.

13.53   Thus, in respect of an employee with a claim for one week's pay outstanding and unpaid of (say) £400 would:

● first any deduction (other than tax) would be applied (eg as a result of the duty to mitigate);

● then his claim against the National Insurance Fund would be reduced to the statutory maximum week's pay (currently £350); and

● then any tax deductions applicable (eg income tax unpaid and national insurance) would be applied to the £350,

resulting in (say) a net claim of £200.

CLAIMS FOR PENSION CONTRIBUTIONS

13.54   Sections 123 to 125 of PSA 1993 (formerly EPCA 1978, s 123) provide that the Secretary of State shall, on application being made to him (see below), pay into the resources of a relevant occupational pension scheme or personal pension scheme (as defined in s 123 – see para 2.75 above) where he is satisfied that:

(a)   the employer has become insolvent (see para 13.15 above); and

(b)   at that time there remained unpaid relevant contributions falling to be paid by the employer to the scheme.

'Relevant contributions'

13.55   The term 'relevant contributions' is defined by s 124(2) to mean contributions either:

(a)   payable by an employer on its own account; or

(b)   payable on behalf of an employee, provided that it has actually been deducted by the employer from the pay of the employee.

Limitation on claim

13.56　In relation to contributions due from an employer on its own account (ie not contributions deducted from the pay of an employee), the amount claimable from the National Insurance Fund is limited by PSA 1993, s 124(3) and s 124(3A) (as inserted with effect from 2 October 1995 by PA 1995, s 90) to the least of:

(a)　the amount unpaid on the date the employer became insolvent which had been payable in the 12 months preceding that date;

(b)　in the case of a scheme which is not a money purchase scheme, the amount certified by an actuary to be necessary to meet the scheme liabilities on dissolution to or in respect of employees of the company; and

(c)　10 per cent of the total amount of remuneration paid or payable to employees in the 12 months preceding the date of insolvency (remuneration for this purpose includes statutory sick pay, maternity pay, etc – see PSA 1993, s 124(4)).

13.57　The amount of the claim in respect of unpaid contributions on behalf of an employee is limited, by PSA 1993, s 124(5), to amounts deducted from the pay of the employee during the 12 months preceding the date of insolvency.

13.58　The section covers payments owed to a money purchase scheme as well as a final salary pension scheme (see SPI technical bulletin, 14 November 1993 and now PSA 1993, s 124(3A), added by PA 1995, s 90). This amendment resolved any lingering doubts as to whether the limitation in PSA 1993, s 124(3)(b) meant that this provision could not apply to money purchase schemes (see the comments in Hansard, House of Commons, 13 June 1995, cols 548, 549).

13.59　PSA 1993, s 125 deals with the evidence required by the Secretary of State. A certificate is required from the relevant insolvency practitioner as to the amounts unpaid, unless the Secretary of State waives this requirement[1].

1 PSA 1993, s 125(5).

PROCEDURE FOR CLAIM

13.60　An application for payment of unpaid contributions by the Secretary of State must be made by the person competent to act on behalf of the pension scheme[1]. A member of the scheme is unlikely to be such a 'person competent to act' – see the EAT in *Campbell v Secretary of State*[2]. In practice, the person competent to act will be the trustees of the pension scheme, who will complete Form IP8 and Part 1 of Form IP7 and ask the insolvency practitioner to complete Part 2 of Form IP7. Where the claim relates to unpaid employer contributions, the actuary to the scheme must also certify amounts due under s 123(3)(b) by completing Form IP10. There may, in practice, be some interrelation with the employer debt obligation under PA 1995, s 75.[3]

13.61   Further information on the practical aspects of claims under what are now ss 123–127 of PSA 1993 (formerly s 123 of EPCA 1978) is given in a booklet (IL2) issued in 2002 by the DTI (and now published by BERR) called '*Insolvency of Employers: Safeguard of occupational pension scheme contributions*' (URN 02/594).

13.62   This booklet makes the point that a claim for pensions contributions cannot be made under s 124 against the National Insurance Fund in respect of remuneration that has not actually been paid – in other words 'where the employer has failed to pay part or all of the due salary or wages for a period of time'. This is presumably meant to be an application of the condition in s 124(2) that the pension sum must have been 'deducted from the pay of the employee'.

13.63   Some (limited) guidance was also given to the actuary by Guidance Note GN4, issued by the Institute and Faculty of Actuaries and later taken over by the Board of Actuarial Standards (BAS). This pointed out (para 3) that the legislation does not make it clear how benefits should be valued. The guidance leaves this to the actuary to decide, suggesting that either cash equivalents (ie statutory transfer values) or the cost of buying out in the insurance market could be used.

   GN4 ceased to apply from 30 November 2008. It was disapplied by the BAS on the basis that it merely gave an interpretation of the legislation and so was 'out of scope' (see page 22 of the BAS consultation paper issued in April 2008).

Claims for redundancy payments

13.64   ERA 1996, ss 166 and 167 contain provisions which apply to statutory redundancy payments and which provide a similar guarantee of payment to that provided by s 182.

13.65   Section 167(1) provides for the Secretary of State to make a payment out of the National Insurance Fund where he is satisfied:

(a)   that the employee is entitled to an 'employer's payment'; and

(b)   that either:

   (i)   the employee has taken all reasonable steps (other than legal proceedings) to recover the payment from the employer but the employer has refused or failed to pay. Note that it seems that it will usually be necessary to take proceedings before an employment tribunal, which are not regarded as legal proceedings within the meaning of ERA 1996, s 166(4), but this is not an invariable rule[1]; or

   (ii)   that the employer is insolvent (see para 13.15 above) and that the whole or part of the payment remains unpaid.

1 See *Jeffrey v Grey* (1967) 2 ITR 335, IT.

13.66   The tests in s 167 are alternative tests. Unlike claims under s 182 (see para 13.15 above), formal insolvency proceedings are not necessary – see eg the decision of the EAT in *Secretary of State for Employment v McGlone*[1].

1 [1997] BCC 101, EAT.

13.67   Relevant 'employer's payments' are defined in s 166(2) to include statutory redundancy payments payable under Pt XI of ERA 1996 (ie ss 135 to 181 dealing with redundancy payments – see paras 2.50 to 2.54 above) and payments due under an agreement covered by an order under ERA 1996, s 157, provided that the employee has at least two years' continuous service[1].

1 ERA 1996, s 167(2).

13.68   The amount of the payment out of the National Insurance Fund is then calculated in accordance with ERA 1996, s 168. This contains specific provisions dealing with cases where the payment is due under an agreement in respect of which an order is in force under ERA 1996, s 157 (ie an exemption order from the Secretary of State where there is an agreement between an employer and a trade union) and special cases where an industrial tribunal has determined that employers are liable to pay any part of redundancy payment.

13.69   The Secretary of State has power under s 169 to require information from the employer as to the level of claims (failure to provide information is an offence for which the insolvency practitioner could be liable – see ERA 1996, ss 169(2), 169(3), and 180 and Chapter 8 above). Provision is made in s 170 for references to the employment tribunal of claims relating to payments under s 167 (see para 13.78 below).

13.70   If there has been a previous payment by the Secretary of State (on the insolvency of a previous employer), this will break statutory continuity of employment for the purposes of a claim on the Secretary of State on the insolvency of the second employer, even if there later appears that there was a TUPE transfer to the second employer (and so no dismissal or liability to a redundancy payment on the first insolvency) – see the decision of the Court of Appeal in *Lassman v Secretary of State*[1].

1 [2000] IRLR 411, CA.

SUBROGATION OF THE SECRETARY OF STATE

13.71   Provision is made in ERA 1996, ss 167(3), (4) and 189 and PSA 1993, s 127 for the Secretary of State to become subrogated to the right of the employee (or the pension scheme) against the employer company where the Secretary of State has made a payment out of the National Insurance Fund under ERA 1996, ss 82, 167 or PSA 1993, s 124.

This means that it is clear that the payment by the National Insurance Fund does <u>not</u> have the effect of reducing the total amount payable by the insolvent company. The amount paid by the NI Fund does reduce the employee's claim, but the Secretary of State takes over that claim.

See to similar effect the decision of David Richards J in relation to the Financial Services Compensation Scheme (FSCS) in *Financial Services Compensation Scheme Ltd v Abbey National Treasury Services plc*[1]. In contrast (but dealing with a different structure) in Australia in *Re Leonard Thomas Hinde*[2] a trustee of a private trust fund was held to be able to take into account (when deciding how much to pay to employees) the fact that the Commonwealth of Australia had made payments under a separate scheme (GEERS[3]).

1 [2008] EWHC 1897 (Ch); [2008] All ER (D) 36 (Aug) (David Richards J).
2 [2007] NSWSC 640 (Rein AJ).
3 For a discussion of GEERS in Australia, see para 9.92 above.

13.72 The predecessors of these provisions (in EPCA 1978) were amended by the Employment Act 1989, s 19, Sch 6 to clarify the then priority of the Secretary of State in receivership cases, following the decision of Peter Gibson J in *Re Urethane Engineering Products Ltd*[1].

1 [1988] BCLC 128 (Peter Gibson J), subsequently upheld by the Court of Appeal [1991] BCLC 48, CA.

13.73 In cases where a claim falling within s 182 of ERA 1996 or s 124 of PSA 1993 is preferential (redundancy claims under s 166 are not preferential), the claim of the Secretary of State on the employer is also preferential – s 189(2) and (3) of ERA 1996.

13.74 The preferential claim of the Secretary of State used, under s 189(4) of ERA 1996, to have a 'super preference' status in that the Secretary of State's claim ranked ahead of any remaining preferential claim of the employee. Section 189(4) was repealed with effect from 15 September 2003 by the Enterprise Act 2002 (subject to savings – eg where an administration petition was presented before that date).

13.75 For insolvencies starting on or after 15 September 2003, the claims of the Secretary of State and any remaining claim of the employee rank equally as preferential debts.

13.76 The Insolvency Service (now part of BERR) outlines the impact of the inter-action of the preferential debts regime with the payments by the Redundancy Payments Office (RPO) out of the National Insurance Fund (NIF) in its guide '*Redundancy and Insolvency – A guide for insolvency practitioners to employees' rights on the insolvency of their employer*' at paras 40 to 44[1].

40 Example of distribution for an employee who was made redundant in June 2002 and the insolvency date is before 15 September 2003

An employee's gross claim against his former employer is as follows:

4 weeks' wages @ £500 per week = £2,000 (£800 preferential; £1,200 non-preferential)

6 weeks' holiday pay @ £500 per week = £3,000 (all preferential)

Total preferential claims = £3,800

Payments to an employee from the NI Fund are limited by statute, and the RPO paid £2,500 of the employee's claim as follows:

4 weeks' wages @ £250 per week = £1,000 (£800 preferential and £200 non-preferential).

6 weeks' holiday pay @ £250 per week = £1,500 (all preferential)

The RPO takes over the employee's rights in the insolvency in respect of the amounts it has paid him or her out of the NI Fund. For each category of preferential payments, the RPO must be paid in full before the employee receives any balance of the preferential amount due.

For preferential claims:

The total claim is £3,800 made up of £800 for wages and £3,000 for holiday pay.

The RPO paid £800 wages and £1,500 holiday pay.

The employee's remaining unpaid preferential claim is £1,500 holiday pay.

If a dividend of 70p in the pound is payable for preferential debts, then the amounts available are £560 for wages and £2,100 for holiday pay. From this, the RPO receives all the £560 available for wages plus the £1,500 it has paid out in holiday pay. The employee would receive no wages but £600 in holiday pay (i.e. the £2,100 available less the £1,500 paid to the RPO).

41. Distributions where the insolvency date is on or after 15 September 2003

The RPO retains its preferential ranking but no longer has a super-preference status over the preferential claims of employees. The requirement for the RPO to be paid in full before the employee is paid was removed [Employment Rights Act 1996 s 189(4)]. However, the requirement to add together the RPO and employee's preferential claims and treat them as one debt for the purpose of computing the preferential dividend remains [Employment Rights Act 1996 s 189(3)]. The need for apportionment between the Secretary of State's and the employee's preferential claims for wages arises because of the legal requirement for the claims to be treated as one for calculation of preferential debt statutory and the statutory limit on the amount payable, which is £800 on the wages payable in the 4 months immediately before the insolvency date. Any debts that fall outside of the 4-month period are out of scope for preferential purposes and do not need to be added to the employee's gross claim for calculation purposes. The RPO would expect an amount equivalent to the percentage of the employee's gross claim paid from the NIF on behalf of the employer. For example, if the RPO has paid 25% of the debt then they can expect 25% of the dividend.

Originally it was thought that all claims would need to be apportioned but we discovered there was no need to do so in the following cases.

- Holiday pay claims. As there is no limit on the preferential amount that can be claimed for holiday pay, there is no need for apportionment – the RPO can claim the full amount as preferential as can the employee.

- Wages claims: Apportionment is required only where an employee has a residual claim for wages in the insolvency. Where the employee has no residual wages claim (RPO paid full debt from NIF) – the RPO can claim the full amount as preferential (subject to the £800 limit on wages).

- Where the employees gross wages debt (including the amount paid by the RPO) is £800 or less then apportionment will not be required as the ultimate distribution will be the same whether or not apportionment is applied.

- Any weeks of a protective award that fall after the insolvency date will be out of scope for preference, as they do not fall within the 4-month period prior to the insolvency date.

42. Example of Apportionment of wages

The employee' s gross claim against the employer is £2,000 (£4 weeks at @ £500 within the 4-month limit).

The RPO pays £1240 (4 weeks @ £310)

The employee's residual claim is £760 (£2,000 less £1240 paid by the RPO).

The RPO has paid 62% of the debt and would therefore expect 62% of the £800 that is available to share between the employee and the RPO (on full dividend), which is £496. The same principle applies to a part dividend also.

Protective awards (PA) are treated as wages under ERA 1996 and Insolvency Act 1986, Schedule 6. The £800 limit on wages will apply to any period of a protective award that falls within the 4-month period before the insolvency date. Only the gross wages for that period needs to be added to the employee's gross claim for the calculation of the preferential amount due to the RPO. Any period of the award that falls after the insolvency date is automatically non-preferential and should not be added to the gross claim to calculate preferential claims.

As a PA payment is made some considerable time after all the other payments, the apportionment of the original preferential wages claims on the RP 11 and RP12 may need amendment as well as the proof of debt form. However, if the whole of the award falls after the insolvency date then there is no need to re-apportion the claim.

43. Example 1 of additional PA payment (no re-apportionment)

Insolvency date 11/12/06.

Dismissal date 27/11/06.

PA for 90 days starting on 27/11/06.

8 weeks max on the number of weeks payable from NIF with 4 weeks already paid by RPO (as in above example).

4 more weeks @ £310 payable of which 2 weeks in scope for preference

The revised gross claim is £3,000 (6 weeks @ £500)

The RPO paid £1,860 (6 weeks @ £310) – the residual claim is £1,140.

The RPO percentage has not changed from 62% so no re-apportionment is required. A revised proof of debt updating the amounts is required.

44. Example 2 of additional PA payment (re-apportionment required):

Weekly rate of pay is £250 and statutory limit is £310

Insolvency date 11/12/06.

Dismissal date 11/12/06.

PA for 90 days starting on 27/11/06 of which 2 weeks in scope for preference and which also overlaps with wages already paid

8 weeks max on wages payable from NIF

4 weeks @ £250 already paid by RPO

4 more weeks @ £250 payable (non-preferential) and 2 weeks @ £60 (top up to limit for 2 overlapping weeks of PA and wages).

The employee's gross claim for wages was originally £1000 and no apportionment was necessary as the RPO paid 100% of debt and was claiming the full £800 as preferential

Because of the overlapping 2 weeks of the PA and wages the employee now has a residual claim for wages and apportionment is required (2 weeks at £500 – double pay, and the application of the statutory limit of £310 to those weeks).

The gross claim is £1500 (2 weeks @ £250 and 2 weeks @ £500, which is their ordinary wages plus the PA). The RPO paid £1,120 (2 weeks @ £250 and 2 weeks @ £310 or 4 weeks @ £250 and 2 weeks @ £60 if you prefer). The employee's residual claim is £380 (2 weeks @ £190). The RPO has now paid 74.67% of the debt and would expect 74.67% of the £800, which is £576. Apportionment is now required.

The gross claim is £1830 (2 weeks @ £305 and 2 weeks @ £610). The RPO paid £1200 (2 weeks @ £290 and 2 weeks @ £310 or 4 weeks @ £290 and 2 weeks @ £20 if you prefer). The employee's residual claim is £630. The RPO has now paid 65.57% of the debt and would expect that % of the £800, which is £524.56. Re-apportionment is now required to show the adjusted % of the claims.

1 See paras 40 to 43 of the Insolvency Service booklet, 'Redundancy and Insolvency – A guide for insolvency practitioners to employees' rights on the insolvency of their employer' (URN 08/550). On the web at: http://www.insolvency.gov.uk/guidanceleaflets/redundancypayments/ guide-forips/guidcforips.htm

Procedure on claims from the Secretary of State

13.77 In practice, where an insolvency practitioner had been appointed, the Secretary of State used, before September 1997, to utilise the services of that insolvency practitioner as his agent (called the 'employer's representative') for the purposes of processing and then (having been put in funds by the Secretary of State) paying claims made under ERA 1996, s 182 and PSA 1993, s 124. However, the insolvency practitioner was not used in relation to claims under s 166 (redundancy payments) or to make payments compensating for lack of notice.

Claims are now handled by the Insolvency Service through the Redundancy Payments Office (RPO).

The Redundancy Payments Service (RPS) is moving towards a new claims handling system known as CHAMP.

The employee makes a relevant claim by filling out form RP1. The insolvency practitioner then verifies the claims by completing for RP14 and sending that to the Insolvency Service. The Insolvency Service requires the insolvency practitioner (and not an agent or employee) to sign the form (see the comments in para 28 of 'Dear IP – Issue 37 – October 2008' issued by the Insolvency Service), relying on the definition of relevant officer in ERA 1996, s 87(4).

13.78 If the National Insurance Fund rejects a claim or fails to pay, the employee (or trustees of the pension scheme, as appropriate) may apply within three months of the decision (or such further period as is reasonable) to an employment tribunal (see ERA 1996, s 170 and 188 and PSA 1993, s 126(2)).

13.79 Section 4(3) of the Employment Tribunals Act 1996 (ETA 1996) provides that proceedings in an Employment Tribunal under ERA 1996, s 188 and PSA 1993, s 126 are to be heard by the (legally qualified) Employment Judge (formerly called the chairman) of the tribunal alone, without the usual two lay members. Section 28 of ETA 1996 similarly provides for any appeal from such a case to the Employment Appeal Tribunal (EAT) to be heard by the presiding judge alone (unless the judge otherwise directs).

13.80 Section 4(3) of ETA 1996 did not originally extend to claims against the Secretary of State brought under ERA 1996, s 170 relating to redundancy payments. It was understood that section 170 claims were excluded because it was felt that they more often (when compared with claims under ERA 1996, s 188) dealt with questions of fact (eg has there been a redundancy?). However s 4(3) was widened, when s 3(3)(a) of the Employment Rights (Dispute Resolution) Act 1998 came into force, to include claims under ERA 1996, s 170.

13.81 In *Smith v Secretary of State*[1] the EAT gave leave to appeal to the Court of Appeal on 'the real and troubling question' of whether the Employment Tribunal (or indeed the EAT itself) constitutes 'an independent and impartial tribunal established by law' as will be required by article 6 of the European Convention on Human Rights as to be applied to the UK by the Human Rights Act 1998. The EAT's concerns arose because the members of the Employment Tribunal are appointed by the Secretary of State and hence arguably lack 'transparent objective independence' from the Secretary of State when deciding on these claims.

1 [2000] IRLR 6, EAT.

13.82   But in *Scanfuture UK Ltd v Secretary of State*[1] the EAT held that changes made in 1999 to the constitution of the EAT meant that such fears were now groundless.

1 [2001] ICR 1096, EAT.

13.83   An employee (or trustees of the pension scheme, if appropriate) bringing an action against the Secretary of State under ERA 1996, ss 170, 188 or 124 or PSA 1993, s 126 need not join the ex-employer as a party to the proceedings – see *Jones v Secretary of State for Employment*[1].

13.84   However the ex-employer should be joined in the proceedings (note that leave will be needed to do this if the employer is in administration or court liquidation – see paras 4.46 to 4.58 above) if information (eg as to the level of remuneration) is disputed between the employee and the Secretary of State – see *Bradley v Secretary of State for Employment*[2].

1 [1982] ICR 389, EAT.
2 [1989] ICR 69, EAT.

13.85   The position in relation to payment of interest by the Secretary of State on claims was discussed in the decision of the EAT in *Secretary of State for Employment v Reeves*[1]. The EAT held that the National Insurance Fund is not liable to pay any interest on a claim for a redundancy payment until 42 days after a decision against the Secretary of State in an employment tribunal.

This is the case even if interest is payable by the employer on the redundancy payment under art 3(1) of the Employment Tribunals (Interest) Order 1990[2], following an employment tribunal order against the employer.

1 [1993] ICR 508, EAT.
2 SI 1990/479. Originally called the Industrial Tribunals (Interest) Order 1990. The name was changed by Employment Rights (Dispute Resolution) Act 1998, s1(2)(b).

13.86   An employee loses his or her right to a statutory redundancy payment if he or she does not, in general, make a written claim within six months of the relevant date (ERA 1996, s 164). This will mean that the employee also loses the right to claim against the Secretary of State.

It makes no difference that the employee thought that he or she was not entitled to a redundancy payment because he (mistakenly) thought that there had been a transfer under TUPE – see the decision of the EAT in *Crawford v Secretary of State*[1].

In relation to claims reflecting an underlying EU Directive (ie those against the National Insurance Fund), the usual rules on time limits will apply. This means that they must not discriminate against the European claim and not make impossible in practice or excessively difficult the exercise of the rights recognised by Community law (principle of effectiveness) – see recently the ECJ in *Visciano v Istituto nazionale della previdenza sociale (INPS)*[2].

1 [1995] IRLR 523, EAT.
2 C-69/08, [2009] All ER (D) 210 (Aug), ECJ.

13.87   In some circumstances, loans can be made by insolvency practitioners to employees in advance of their claims on the National Insurance Fund being settled. Any such loan is made by the insolvency practitioner personally (not by the insolvent company) and is recovered out of the proceeds of the employee's claim on the National Insurance Fund[1].

1 A sample form of a loan agreement (and authority for the insolvency practitioner to deduct the loan from amounts received from the National Insurance Fund) used to be set out at the end of previous editions of booklet IL1, Employees' Rights on Insolvency of Employer, issued by the Department of Employment. See para 13.19 above. The current edition of IL1 comments that the 'IP loan scheme' ceased to operate on 1 April 2003.

STATUTORY MATERNITY, SICK, PATERNITY AND ADOPTION PAY

13.88   There are special provisions dealing with claims by employees for statutory sick pay and statutory maternity, paternity and adoption pay where the employer becomes insolvent.

In relation to statutory maternity pay, the liability under the Social Security Contributions and Benefits Act 1992, s 164[1] passes (in relation to periods after the employer becomes insolvent) from the insolvent employer[2] to the Commissioners for HMRC[3] under reg 7(3) of the Statutory Maternity Pay (General) Regulations 1986 (SI 1986/1960).

This applies even if the employee started maternity leave before the onset of insolvency and the relevant business closed during the maternity leave – see the EAT in *Secretary of State for Employment v Cox*[4].

1 Formerly the Social Security Act, s46.
2 The definition is similar to that in ERA 1996, s 183 – see paras 13.15 to 13.28 above.
3 This was transferred from the Secretary of State on 1 April 1999 under the Social Security Contributions (Transfer of Functions, etc) Act 1999.
4 [1984] ICR 867; [1984] IRLR 437, EAT.

13.89   Similarly, the liability under s 151 of the Social Security Contributions and Benefits Act 1992[1] to pay statutory sick pay passes to the Commissioners for HMRC when the employer becomes insolvent[2] by virtue of reg 9B of the Statutory Sick Pay (General) Regulations 1982[3].

This only applies where the employer becomes insolvent on or after 6 April 1987 – reg 9B(3).

The liability under Parts 12ZA and 12ZB of the Social Security Contributions and Benefits Act 1992 to pay statutory paternity or adoption pay passes, when the employer becomes insolvent[4], to the Commissioners for HMRC by virtue of regulation 43 of the Statutory Paternity Pay and Statutory Adoption Pay (General) Regulations 2002[5].

1 Formerly the Social Security and Housing Benefits Act 1982, s 1.
2 The definition is similar to that in ERA 1996, s 183 – see paras 13.15 to 13.28 above.
3 SI 1982/894, as amended.
4 The definition is similar to that in ERA 1996, s 183 – see paras 13.15 to 13.28 above.
5 SI 2002/2822.

13.90   Any liability of the employer company for a period prior to the onset of insolvency does not pass automatically to the Commissioners for HMRC, but remains a debt owed by the employer (which will be preferential as part of the employee's remuneration up to the £800 limit – see para 9.30 above).

13.91   However, the Commissioners for HMRC will assume liability for such claims if an adjudicating authority (eg an adjudication officer) has determined that the employer was liable to pay to the employee:

- statutory maternity pay (see reg 7(1) of the Statutory Maternity Pay (General) Regulations 1986); or

- statutory sick pay (see reg 9A of the Statutory Sick Pay (General) Regulations 1982, as amended); or

- statutory paternity pay or statutory adoption pay (see reg 43(1) of the Statutory Paternity Pay and Statutory Adoption Pay (General) Regulations 2002).

SUMMARY OF STATUS OF EMPLOYEES' CLAIMS

13.92   The following table sets out the varying status of employees' claims:

Claim on National Insurance Fund (NIF) under ERA 1996	*Preferential debt (Insolvency Act 1986, Sch 6)*
(1) Relevant date: employee must be entitled to be paid the relevant debt on the appropriate date – ERA 1996, s 182(c).	relevant date = date of winding-up order or, if earlier, date of appointment of provisional liquidators or administrator (IA 1986, s 387).
(2) Arrears of pay: Section 184(1)(a) – claim from NIF for up to a maximum eight weeks at up to £380* per week (ie £3040 max). To include: (i) guarantee payments; (ii) remuneration on suspension on medical or maternity grounds under ss 64 and 68; (iii) any payment for time off – ERA 1996, Pt VI; (iv) remuneration under a protective award made under TULRCA 1992, s 189. (appropriate date = date of formal insolvency except for protective award.)	Yes (Sch 6, para 9) – remuneration for maximum of four months before relevant date. Maximum amount £800. Remuneration to include (Sch 6, para 13): (i) a guarantee payment under ERA 1996, Pt III; (ii) a medical or maternity suspension payment under ERA 1996, ss 64, 68; (iii) a payment for time off under ERA 1996, ss 53, 56 or TULRCA 1992, s 169; (iv) remuneration under a protective award made by an industrial tribunal under TULRCA 1992, s 189; (v) pay for absence through sickness or other good cause (see Sch 6, para 15(a)).

Claim on National Insurance Fund (NIF) under ERA 1996	*Preferential debt (Insolvency Act 1986, Sch 6)*
(3) Holiday pay: Section 184(1)(c) – claim from NIF for up to a maximum of six weeks at up to £380* per week for holiday taken (but not paid) in 12 months before appropriate date (appropriate date = date of formal insolvency.)	Yes (Sch 6, para 10) – for accrued holiday remuneration relating to any period of employment before relevant date made for a person whose employment has been terminated whether before, on or after relevant date.
(4) Notice pay: Section 184(1)(b) – claim from NIF for statutory minimum notice period (s 86(1)(2)) at up to £380* per week. (appropriate date = later of date of formal insolvency and date of termination of employee's employment.)	No
(5) Statutory redundancy pay: Section 166 – claim from NIF not strictly dependent on insolvency of employer – can claim before insolvency provided employee has taken all reasonable steps to obtain payment; payment calculated on normal principles.	No
(6) Unfair dismissal: Section 184(1)(d) – claim from NIF for basic award – payment calculated on normal principles. (appropriate date = latest of date of formal insolvency and date on which the award was made.) Compensatory award not claimable.	No
(7) Statutory sick pay: Not covered in ERA 1996 but statutory sick pay after date of formal insolvency is a liability of Commissioners for HMRC – Statutory Sick Pay (General) Regulations 1982, reg 9B.	No, unless part of 'remuneration' – see (2) above

Claim on National Insurance Fund (NIF) under ERA 1996	*Preferential debt (Insolvency Act 1986, Sch 6)*
(8) Statutory maternity pay: Not covered in ERA 1996 but maternity pay as from the week in which formal insolvency occurs is a liability of the Commissioners for HMRC – Statutory Maternity Pay (General) Regulations 1986, reg 7(3).	No, unless part of 'remuneration' – see (2) above
(9) Statutory paternity and adoption pay: Not covered in ERA 1996 but maternity pay as from the week in which formal insolvency occurs is a liability of the Commissioners for HMRC – Statutory Paternity Pay and Statutory Adoption Pay (General) Regulations 2002, reg 43.	No, unless part of 'remuneration' – see (2) above
* Figure usually revised annually – see para 2.49 above.	

13.93   The following table sets out the varying status of pension claims on the NIF and as preferential claims:

Pension Contributions from	Claim on National Insurance Fund under PSA 1993, s 124	Preferential debt (PSA 1993, Sch 4)
Employer	12 months (limited to 10% of payroll) to OPS or PP	12 months (limited to contracted-out percentage) to OPS only (not PP).
Employee (if deducted from pay)	12 months to OPS or PP	4 months to OPS only (not PP).

CHAPTER 14

Set-off

14.1   In any insolvency it may not only be the case that the employee has a claim against the insolvent employer (eg unpaid wages, holiday pay, redundancy payments, etc) but also that the employee has liabilities to the employer (eg season ticket loans, mortgages, etc).

Difficult issues can arise as to the impact of these employee liabilities on the amounts claimable by employees both from the insolvent employer and from other sources such as the National Insurance Fund – see Chapter 10 (National Insurance Fund) above.

LIQUIDATION SET-OFF

14.2   Where the employer company is in liquidation, set-off is mandatory under rule 4.90[1] of the Insolvency Rules 1986[2]. This requires the compulsory set-off of cross claims where there are 'mutual credits, mutual debits or other mutual dealings'.

The Insolvency Rules 1986 generally only apply in England and Wales and do not apply to Scotland (see Rule 0.3). There are no equivalent mandatory set-off provisions applicable in Scotland under the Insolvency Act 1986 or the Insolvency (Scotland) Rules 1986[3].

1 Rule 4.90 was substituted by Rule 23 of the Insolvency (Amendment) Rules 2005 (SI 2005/527), subject to transitional provisions for insolvencies before 1 April 2005 (see rule 3).
2 SI 1986/1925.
3 SI 1986/1915.

14.3   Rule 4.90 is very wide. Where cross claims exist between an employee and employer, set-off under rule 4.90 will apply unless an exception to set-off is applicable, for example:

(a)   lack of mutuality (eg the employer's claim is as trustee for a third party). However, the Crown is one body so (for example) the Secretary of State can set off

   (i)   against an insolvent employer's claim for overpaid VAT,

(ii) the amount owed by the employer under ss 88 and 135 of the Employment Rights Act 1996 to the Secretary of State (in the guise of the National Insurance Fund) arising because the Fund has paid out to various employees

– see *Frid v Secretary of State*[1];

(b) the claim arises in respect of a new transaction entered into after, in effect, the employee had notice that the liquidation was commencing (or if the liquidation was preceded by an administration, the date the employee had notice of the administration). Such claims are not allowed for set-off (rule 4.90(2)). However, the claim can be contingent at the time of insolvency – *Frid v Secretary of State*[1];

(c) one of the cross claims is not for a money amount. For example, an employee who has possession of a company car cannot set-off the value of the car against any claim the employee may have against the company[2];

(d) one of the claims is a proprietary claim rather than a simple debt (see Browne-Wilkinson V-C at first instance in *Guinness plc v Saunders*[3]). For example, where the employer's claim arises from breach of fiduciary duty owed by the employee (eg because the employee has taken money from the company in breach of duty) set-off will not be allowed – see *Zemco Ltd v Jerrom-Pugh*[4] and *Manson v Smith*[5].

(e) in *Re a Company (No 1641 of 2003)*[6] Judge Norris QC held that a director could not set-off his claim for holiday pay and pay in lieu of notice against a loan from the company that was illegal under CA 1985, s 330 (now CA 2006, s 197), Judge Norris relied on Millett LJ in *Manson v Smith*, Hall V-C in *Re Anglo-French Co-operative Society, ex P Pelly*[7] and the House of Lords in *Smith (Administrator of Cosslett (Contractors) Ltd) v Bridgend BC*[8]. But it may be that the employer company can insist on set-off – see *Clark v Cutland*[9];

(f) set-off under rule 4.90 is not allowed if it would infringe the rule against double proof. For example, a director who has guaranteed a bank loan to the company may have a contingent claim on the company to indemnify him. However, that cannot be set off against other amounts he owes the company as his claim would infringe the rule against double proof (because it would be in respect of the same claim as made by the bank) – see Neuberger J in *Re Glen Express Ltd*[10].

(g) if the phoenix company provisions apply. *Archer Structures Ltd v Griffiths*[11] involved a director who was held to be jointly and severally liable with his insolvent company under the 'phoenix company' provisions in ss 216 and 217 of the Insolvency Act 1986. The company had a counter-claim against the third party. Judge Kirkham held that the director could not rely on the insolvent company's right of set-off under rule 4.90 to reduce the amount of a claim that the third party had against the director.

1 [2004] UKHL 24; [2004] 2 AC 506, HL.
2 See *Lord's Trustee v Great Eastern Railway Co* [1908] 2 KB 54, CA and *Rolls Razor Ltd v Cox* [1967] 1 QB 552, CA.

3 [1987] 3 BCC 520 at 527 (Browne-Wilkinson V-C).
4 [1993] BCC 275, CA.
5 [1997] 2 BCLC 161, CA.
6 [2003] EWHC 2652; [2004] 1 BCLC 210 (Judge Norris QC).
7 (1882) 21 Ch D 492 (Hall V-C).
8 [2001] UKHL 58 at [35]; [2002] 1 AC 336, HL.
9 [2003] EWCA Civ 810; [2003] 4 All ER 733; [2004] 1 WLR 783, CA.
10 19 October 1999, [2000] BPIR 456 (Neuberger J), applying *Re Fenton Ex p Fenton Textile Association Ltd* (No.1) [1931] 1 Ch 85, CA.

11 [2003] EWHC 957; [2004] 1 BCLC 201 (Judge Kirkham).

14.4   Rule 4.90 is mandatory and must be applied by the liquidators of the employer. It is self executing, so that no action is needed by the liquidator or creditor (see the decision of the House of Lords in *Stein v Blake*[1]). It also overrides any contractual stipulation to the contrary (see the House of Lords decisions in *National Westminster Bank v Halesowen Presswork*[2] and *British Eagle v Air France*[3]).

Walton J held in *Re Unit 2 Windows Ltd*[4] that liquidation set-off applies to those claims of an employee which are preferential (see para 14.21 below).

1 [1996] AC 243, HL.
2 [1972] AC 705, HL.
3 [1975] 2 All ER 390, HL.
4 [1985] 3 All ER 647 (Walton J).

Set-off in administrations (starting on or after 15 September 2003)

14.5   From 15 September 2003, the Insolvency Rules 1986 were substantially amended in relation to administrations starting on or after that date in the light of the changes made by the Enterprise Act 2002. These changes include the insertion of a new set-off rule, rule 2.85, applicable to administrations starting on or after 15 September 2003[1]. Rule 2.85 only applies where:

- the administrator is authorised to make a distribution to creditors (court approval is needed for a distribution to creditors who are not secured or preferential[2]); and

- the administrator has given notice to creditors under rule 2.95 of the proposed distributions (28 days notice is required).

Otherwise rule 2.85 broadly follows rule 4.90 and the same interpretations by the case law will apply.

The term "distribution" is not defined in either rule 2.85 or 2.95. This raises some doubts as to what will constitute a distribution triggering the set-off provision in rule 2.85.. For example does it catch a payment to a fixed charge or floating charge holder? The Financial Markets Law Committee (FMLC) discussed this issue in its 2007 paper, *Administration set-off and expenses*, reaching the view that rule 2.85 only starts to apply if a distribution is made to unsecured creditors (or secured creditors for any unsecured part of their claims) and that unsecured creditors include preferential creditors[3].

The Insolvency Rules 1986 generally only apply in England and Wales and do not apply to Scotland (see rule 0.3). There are no equivalent mandatory set-off provisions applicable in Scotland under the Insolvency Act 1986 or the Insolvency (Scotland) Rules 1986[4].

1 See rule 5 of the Insolvency (Amendment) Rules 2003 (SI 2003/1730). Rule 2.85 was substituted by rule 9 of the Insolvency (Amendment) Rules 2005 (SI 2005/527), subject to transitional provisions for insolvencies before 1 April 2005 (see rule 3).
2 Para 65 of Sch B1 to IA 1986.
3 Section 5, Issue 108, November 2007. Available at www.fmlc.org. Set-off uncertainties were also raised by the FMLC in its 18 August 2009 letter to the Insolvency Service (also on the FMLC website).
4 SI 1986/1915.

Set-off in receivership and other administrations

14.6   In:

- a receivership; or

- an administration starting before 15 September 2003 (see eg *Isovel Contracts Ltd v ABB Building Technologies Ltd*[1]); or

- an administration starting on or after 15 September 2003 where no notice of intention to make a distribution to creditors has been issued,

there is no provision corresponding to rules 2.85 and 4.90 providing for mandatory set-off. Whether set-off is available to either party (the employer or the employee) will depend on the usual rules relating to set-off, ie whether the cross claims are liquidated or whether they arise out of the same transaction[2].

In Australia it has been held that equitable set-off is not available in an employment context (outside insolvency):

- to reduce an amount payable under a statutory provision – *Walker v Secretary, Department of Social Security*[3]. This may then extend to statutory payments under employment legislation.

- To allow set-off where the payments are for different purposes eg a payment for a Christmas bonus against a debt for salary at the termination of employment – see *Pacific Publications Pty Ltd v Cantlon*[4] and *Logan v Otis Elevator Co Pty Ltd*[5].

If a non-insolvency set–off was to apply in a post 2003 administration before any notice of distribution was given, then it seems likely that the set-off needs to be exercised before the notice is given[6]. This is on the basis that the set-off rule overrides any other set-off provision (see para 14.4 above).

For further details of the rules relating to set-off see the looseleaf book *Tolley's Insolvency Law* and the book by S.Rory Derham, *The Law of Set-off*. For a discussion of the position in Australia, see the article by Jennifer Fisher and Michael Will "*Payback: using set-off to recover money from employees at time of termination*"[8].

1 [2002] 1 BCLC 390 (Simon Berry QC sitting as a deputy judge of the High Court).
2 See *Newfoundland Government v Newfoundland Railway Co* (1887) 13 App Cas 199, PC.
3 (1995) 56 FCR 354; 129 ALR 198 (Spender and Cooper JJ)
4 (1983) 4 IR 415, at p421.
5 [1999] IRCA 4; (1999) 94 IR 218 at p 227, Industrial Relations Court of Australia.
6 See para 3.4 of the paper issued by the Financial Markets Law Committee (FMLC) on Issue 108, *Administration set-off and expenses* (November 2007). Available at www.fmlc.org.
7 3rd edition, Oxford University Press, 2003.
8 (2008) 21 Australian Journal of Labour Law 101.

PROBLEMS WITH SET-OFF

14.7   The position as to whether set-off will be available in relation to cross claims between an employer and an employee, whether under the mandatory provisions in rule 2.85 or 4.90 or under the general law relating to set-off, is complicated by a number of factors:

(a)   the limits on set-off imposed by Part 2 of ERA 1996 (formerly the Wages Act 1986);

(b)   the application of set-off to different types of claims (eg preferential/non-preferential and secured/unsecured);

(c)   the tax/national insurance position relating to deductions from pay; and

(d)   the effect of set-off on the rights of an employee to claim from the National Insurance Fund.

The factors listed at (a) to (d) are discussed further below.

LIMITS ON SET-OFF IMPOSED BY PART II OF THE EMPLOYMENT RIGHTS ACT 1996

14.8   Part 2 of ERA 1996 (ss 13–27) consolidated the provisions on deductions from wages formerly contained in the Wages Act 1986. Section 13 of ERA 1996 generally prohibits an employer from making deductions from the 'wages' of any employee unless:

(a)   the deduction is required by a statutory provision or a relevant provision of the employee's contract; or

(b)   the employee has previously signified in writing his agreement or consent to the making of the deduction.

There are various further exceptions in s 14, including reimbursement of over-paid wages or expenses.

14.9   The term 'wages' is widely defined for this purpose in the ERA 1996, s 27 and will extend to include most claims of an employee arising on the insolvency of his or her employer.

217

14.10   However, s 27(2) excludes certain payments from the definition of 'wages', including, in particular, 'any payment referable to the worker's redundancy', and 'any payment by way of a pension, allowance or gratuity in connection with the worker's retirement or as compensation for loss of office'. Thus, claims of the employee for redundancy payments and/or unfair dismissal, etc will not be protected by Part 2 of ERA 1996, although it is noticeable that any sum payable (as part of an unfair dismissal claim) in pursuance of an order for reinstatement or re-engagement under ERA 1996, s 113 is expressly included within the meaning of the word 'wages'.

14.11   There is no provision within ERA 1996, expressly exempting insolvent employers from the obligations under Part 2 of ERA. Accordingly, in order for set-off to be applied by the employer, in relation to claims which relate to sums within the definition of 'wages', one of the exceptions within ERA 1996 must apply.

14.12   In the case of a liquidation (or an administration starting on or after 15 September 2003) it is clear that set-off under rules 2.85 and 4.90 of the Insolvency Rules 1986 is allowed by ERA 1996. Such a deduction by way of set-off under rules 2.85 and 4.90 is mandatory (see para 11.4 above) and hence it is 'required by a statutory provision' within the exception in ERA 1996, s 13(1)(a).

This is consistent with the decision of the EAT in relation to the application of liquidation set-off in relation to a claim by an employee against the National Insurance Fund in *Secretary of State for Employment v Wilson*[1], although the Wages Act point was not raised.

1 [1997] ICR 408; [1996] IRLR 330, EAT.

14.13   In cases of insolvency not involving liquidation or post September 2003 administration (eg receivership or pre 2003 administration) there is no such statutory set-off provision and hence set-off by the employer (acting through the relevant insolvency practitioner) will be permitted only if one of the other exceptions in Pt 2 of ERA 1996 (eg written consent of the worker) is available.

It could be argued that equitable set-off is a substantive defence and so if the defence is available it means that the employee is not in fact entitled to the wages (and so there is no deduction). This however seems unlikely to be upheld by a court given what seems to be the intention of Part 2 of ERA 1996. See the book by S Rory Derham, *The Law of Set-off*[1]. In Australia a similar view has been taken on set-off in relation to a similar statute – see *Conti Sheffield Real Estate v Brailey*[2] and *BGC (Australia) Pty Ltd v Phippard*[3].

1 3rd edition, OUP, 2003, at page 182.
2 (1992) 48 IR 1; (1992) 72 WAIG 1965.
3 [2002] WASCA 191 (18 July 2002), Western Australia Court of Appeal.

14.14   In *Re Douai School (Re a Company No 005174 of 1999)*[1] the administrators had arranged for the company to pay holiday pay to the relevant school teachers for the holiday prior to the appointment of the administrators. The administrators had (mistakenly) considered that this holiday pay was a 'qualifying liability' and so entitled to super priority under s 19(7) of the Insolvency Act 1986 (see paras 16.48 and 18.61 below).

On Neuberger J holding that this was not the case, the administrators sought to claim that the amount paid had been paid under a mistake of law and so was repayable (and hence could be set off against the later holiday pay which Neuberger J had found did constitute a qualifying liability).

Neuberger J rejected this claim, holding that it would contravene ss 13 and 15 of ERA 1996 protecting employees against unauthorised deductions (s 13) and having to make payments to employers (s 15). The easement (in ss 14(1)(a) and 16(1)(a)) allowing deductions 'in respect of an over-payment of wages' did not apply. The wages were due and payable by the company. Any payment had been made by the administrators as agent of the company.

1 [2000] 1 WLR 502 (Neuberger J).

14.15   It has been argued that, although the Truck Acts were repealed on 1 January 1987 by the Wages Act 1986, s 11, the contractual term (that wages are payable in coin and not otherwise) incorporated into the relevant contracts of employment by the Truck Act 1831, s 1 could still remain in pre-1987 contracts. Even if this is the case, any possible restriction on set-off will now be contractual only and hence overridden in the case of liquidation or post September 2003 administration by the mandatory set-off under rules 2.85 and 4.90. Any such implied term could still be relevant in cases of set-off in other cases (eg a receivership).

APPLICATION OF SET-OFF TO DIFFERENT TYPES OF CLAIMS

14.16   Where set-off applies and there are different types of claims it is necessary to allocate any relevant set-off between the different claims. Where an employee owes more to the employer than is owed by the employer to the employee, the effect of set-off will be to extinguish the employee's claims on the employer and to reduce the employer's claims against the employee by a corresponding amount. The following example indicates how this works.

Example

The employer owes the employee	£600 on current account £600 redundancy pay
The employee owes the employer	£2,000 season ticket loan £10,000 mortgage (secured)

(Note: for simplicity this example uses claims of the employee which are not subject to tax deductions.)

Set-off will apply to reduce the employee's total indebtedness to the employer by £1,200 from £12,000 to £10,800.

14.17 Set-off applies even where an amount owed by an employee to his employer is secured, as with the mortgage loan in the above example. See the Court of Appeal in *Re Deveze, ex p Barnett*[1]; Jonathan Parker J in *Re ILG Travel*[2] and the Australian High Court in *Hiley v Peoples Prudential Assurance Co Ltd*[3].

1 (1874) LR 9 Ch App 293, CA.
2 [1996] BCC 21 (Jonathan Parker J).
3 (1938) 60 CLR 468, High Court.

Allocation of set-off between debts

14.18 How is the £1,200 reduction in the example in para 14.16 to be applied between the two loan debts of the employee?

14.19 The employer may prefer to seek to reduce the season ticket loan first (say on the basis that it is unsecured or at a nil interest rate).

Conversely, the employee may want to reduce his mortgage first and leave the season ticket loan outstanding in full.

14.20 The usual rule is that, in the absence of a contractual obligation to pay and apply moneys to a particular obligation, where a debtor has more than one obligation to a creditor, it is open to the debtor, either before or at the time of making a payment, to appropriate it to a particular obligation. If no such appropriation is made, then the creditor may apply the payment to whichever obligation or obligations he or she wishes: see *The Mecca*[1].

1 [1897] AC 286, HL and Halsbury's Laws of England, 4th edn, vol 9 (Contract), paras 956 and 957.

14.21 There is authority that no such allocation by either the employer or the employee is possible when applying mandatory set-off in liquidation (and now in a post September 2003 administration). Walton J in *Re Unit 2 Windows Ltd*[1] held that the position in England and Wales was that liquidation set-off was mandatory and hence must be applied rateably between debts (ie no allocation or appropriation by the insolvent or the creditor was possible). Walton J was dealing with a situation where the creditor was owed more by the company than the creditor owed the company, but his judgment is equally applicable in the converse situation. Thus, he held (at pages 650 and 651) that:

> '... on examining the terms of s 31[2] it seems to me to be indisputable that (i) that section itself gives no guidance whatsoever as to the setting off of the company's claim against any particular debt or debts, or portions of debts or debts otherwise due from the company to the creditor, and (ii) that section itself gives no right, either to the company or the creditor, the debtor or the creditor, to appropriate the amount to be set off against any particular debt or debts, or portions of debt or debts otherwise due.

> On the other hand, it is quite clear that the provisions of s31 are not intended to confer any particular benefit on either debtor or creditor; they are intended merely to represent an accounting exercise ...

220

Accordingly I now turn to counsel for the Crown's alternative submission, namely that the amount to be set off should be set off rateably between all the Crown's claims against the company. It seems to me that this solution of the problem is not simply a solution faute de mieux. It is, if one comes to think about it, the only logical and sensible solution. Given that s 31 is not in any way intended to benefit debtor or creditor, but to be a mere accounting exercise, and that the right of either side to appropriate as he or it might wish is excluded, what other solution can there possibly be than to apply the rateable approach?'

Walton J refused to follow a dictum of Buckley J to the contrary in an earlier case: *Re E J Morel (1934) Ltd*[3].

The same view is taken in Australia – see *Central Brake Service (Newcastle) Pty Ltd v Central Brake Service (Sydney) Pty Ltd (In Liq)*[4].

1 [1985] 1 WLR 1383; [1985] 3 All ER 647; [1985] BCLC 31 (Walton J). See Derham *The Law of Set-off* at pages 316 to 318.
2 Section 31 of the Bankruptcy Act 1914, the predecessor of rule 4.90 of the Insolvency Rules 1986.
3 [1962] Ch 21 (Buckley J).
4 (1989) 7 ACLC 1199, 1202 (Needham AJ). The point was left open on appeal – *Central Brake Service (Sydney) Pty Ltd (In Liq) v Central Brake Service (Newcastle) Pty Ltd* (1992) 27 NSWLR 406 at page 411, (1989) 7 ACLC 1199 at page 1202, NSW CA.

14.22   The position seems to be different in Scotland. In *Turner v Lord Advocate*[1] Lord Kirkwood in the Court of Session distinguished *Re Unit 2 Windows* on the basis that the statutory set-off provision (s 31[2] in *Re Unit 2 Windows*) did not apply in Scotland[3].

He allowed the Inland Revenue to set off the total payment against its non-preferential debt. This case involved a receivership, where the receiver had argued that a VAT recovery payment due from the Crown should be set off pro-portionately between the non- preferential and preferential elements debts owing to the Crown, as was the position in England.

Lord Kirkwood held that in Scotland the law of compensation applies to set-off – ie there is no balancing of accounts, and a creditor (in this case the Revenue) can apply the set-off to whichever class of debts is most favourable to him or her.

1 [1993] BCLC 1463; [1993] BCC 299 (Lord Kirkwood).
2 Section 31 of the Bankruptcy Act 1914, the predecessor of rule 4.90 of the Insolvency Rules 1986.
3 The Insolvency Rules 1986 generally only apply in England and Wales and do not apply to Scotland (see rule 0.3). There are no equivalent mandatory set-off provisions applicable in Scotland under the Insolvency Act 1986 or the Insolvency (Scotland) Rules 1986 (SI 1986/1915).

14.23   BERR, in its guidance on the impact of insolvency[1] indicates that *Re Unit 2 Windows* and *Turner v Lord Advocate* are being followed on this issue.

1 See Appendix 8 of 'Redundancy and Insolvency – A guide for insolvency practitioners to employ-ees' rights on the insolvency of their employer' (URN 08/550). On the web at: http://www.insolvency.gov.uk/guidanceleaflets/redundancypayments/guideforips/guideforips.htm.

14.24   If *Re Unit 2 Windows* is followed, this has the effect in the example of spreading the £1,200 reduction rateably between the two loans, ie one-sixth to the season ticket loan and five-sixths to the mortgage, reducing these loans by 10 per cent each to £1,800 (season ticket loan) and to £9,000 (mortgage).

14.25 In the converse situation, where the employer owes more to the employee than the employee owes to the employer, similar rules of rateable reduction should, following *Re Unit 2 Windows*, apply. Note that set-off will not apply if the claim of the employee is secured by a mortgage or charge etc, granted by the employer unless the employee submits a proof of debt for the secured debt (see *Re Norman Holding Co Ltd*[1]). In practice it will be very unusual for employees to hold security.

1 [1990] 3 All ER 757 (Mervyn Davies J).

14.26 Where the mandatory set-off rules under the Insolvency Rules do not apply (eg a receivership or a pre 2003 administration or a post 2003 administration, but with no distribution made), it seems that apportionment between different debts may be possible.

In *Re William Hall (Contractors) Ltd*[1] Plowman J held that a bank, which was a secured creditor, was entitled to apply its security to its non-preferential debts and prove for its preferential debts in the liquidation of the company. Lord Kirkwood in *Turner v Lord Advocate* explained this as 'In a case where s 31 did not apply, there was no general equity which required rateable allocation'.

This point is discussed in the book by S Rory Derham, *The Law of Set-off*[2] at page 843.

1 [1967] 2 All ER 1150, [1967] 1 WLR 948 (Plowman J).
2 3rd edition, Oxford University Press, 2003.

TAXATION TREATMENT ON ANY SET-OFF

14.27 Insolvency practitioners generally do not in practice contest that they should arrange for income tax and national insurance contributions to be deducted under the PAYE system from payments the insolvent company makes to employees – see Chapter 25 (PAYE and national insurance) below.

14.28 The obligation to deduct income tax under the PAYE system applies 'on the making of a relevant payment to an employee" by an employer – Income Tax (Pay As You Earn) Regulations 2003, reg 21(1)[1]. Insolvency practitioners will therefore seek to ensure the deduction of PAYE and national insurance from any payments made to employees in respect of unpaid wages and holiday pay (and other termination damages payments to the extent they exceed £30,000[2]).

1 SI 2003/2682. See previously ICTA 1988, s 203 and the definition of emoluments in reg 2(1) of the Income Tax (Employments) Regulations 1993 (SI 1993/744).
2 See Chapter 25 (PAYE and national insurance)below.

14.29 Where there is set-off (eg because of employee loans) it is unclear whether there is a 'payment' within reg 21.

14.30   There seems to be no judicial authority as to whether it is the gross amount of the employee's pay or the net amount (ie after deduction of income tax and NICs) which is taken into account for the purposes of the set-off.

14.31   The BERR guide Employees' Rights on Insolvency of Employer[1] indicates (para 33) that deductions of income tax and national insurance must be made from the gross amounts owed to the employee:

> '33. Set off of debts between employee and employer
>
> Occasionally, an employee will owe money to his or her employer at the appropriate date. In such cases the employee's entitlement under the insolvency provisions will be the net amount owed after set-off, see the EAT case of Secretary of State for Employment v 1) Wilson & ors and 2) BCCI [1996] IRLR 330. (Income tax and ERNIC, however, are payable on the gross amount owed before set-off.) You must give the RPO full written details of the amount owed to the employer and the gross amounts owed to the employee and attach it to the RP14A. If there is a written agreement between the employer and employee on repayment, you should provide a copy. It is essential that the information be forwarded to the RPO immediately you become aware of it. Unless you give this information at the outset, the RPO will not be able to initiate the set-off. You will, therefore, have to pursue the individual for the money owed to the insolvent company.'

1 See Appendix 8 of 'Redundancy and Insolvency – A guide for insolvency practitioners to employees' rights on the insolvency of their employer' (URN 08/550). On the web at: http://www.insolvency.gov.uk/guidanceleaflets/redundancypayments/guideforips/guideforips.htm.

14.32   A previous version of this guide from the Department of Employment (1995) used to go on to state that the insolvency practitioner would then make a claim on the National Insurance Fund in respect of the deductions. The example it cited (at para 53) was as follows:

> 'An employee is owed £500 arrears of wages. The tax and [national insurance] due on this figure is, say, £170 leaving a balance of £330. The employee owes £350 to the employer. After set-off, the net amount paid to the employee is nil and the employer's representative claims £170 from the Department to be paid to the Inland Revenue'.

14.33   This example was a little difficult to understand. Presumably the employer's representative (ie the insolvency practitioner) could only claim the £170 from the Department of Trade and Industry if it was part of the employee's claim on the National Insurance Fund under ERA 1996? The company will, in effect, have paid (through the set-off) the £170 on behalf of the employee with the £170 and should therefore account to HMRC – see Chapter 25 (PAYE and national insurance) below. A claim on the Department (ie on the National Insurance Fund) should be relevant only if the company did not pay HMRC.

14.34   In practice, the insolvency practitioner will be prudent in allowing set-off against the net amount only. So, in the Department of Employment's example above, the insolvency practitioner would pay £170 to the Inland

Revenue, leaving a net amount of £330 owed to the employee and available for set-off. After set-off, a balance of £20 remains owing by the employee to the company.

This is on the basis that the Crown has a claim on the amount of income tax and national insurance deduction, with the effect that there is a third party interest in this part of the employee's claim. The existence of such an interest means there is no exact mutuality and hence set-off should not occur against that part of the employee's claim.

Alternatively, the same approach could be defended on the basis that, if payment were made the employee would in fact receive the net amount only after deduction of income tax and national insurance, so that set-off is appropriate only against the net amount.

As a practical matter this course has the effect of protecting the position of the insolvency practitioner; it maximises the employer's claims against the employee.

14.35 If notice pay is involved, the set-off should be applied to the net amount which the employer owed the employee after allowance for the duty on the employee to mitigate his losses. Note the impact of the decision of the Court of Appeal in *Abrahams v Performing Rights Society*[1], holding that there is no duty to mitigate if there is a clause in the contract providing for full pay in lieu of notice and this is triggered by the employer. This decision is discussed in *Gregory v Wallace*[2] (a case against administrators made following *Paramount*[3]) and in *Cerberus Software Ltd v Rowley*[4].

1 [1995] ICR 1028, CA.
2 [1998] IRLR 387, CA.
3 *Powdrill v Watson* [1995] 2 AC 394, HL. See Chapter 18 (Carrying on business) below.
4 [2001] EWCA Civ 78; [2001] IRLR 160 and see also *Zepbrook Ltd v Magnus* (2006) 18 October; UKEAT/0382/06/MAA; [2007] All ER (D) 188 (Jan), EAT.

CLAIMS ON THE NATIONAL INSURANCE FUND

14.36 As discussed in Chapter 13 (National Insurance Fund) above, s 166 and Pt XII of ERA 1996 provide that, if an employer becomes insolvent, certain debts are to be paid to employees by the Secretary of State from the National Insurance Fund. These debts include statutory redundancy payments (s 166) and arrears of pay, holiday pay and notice pay (Pt XII). The rights of the employees in respect of these debts then transfer to the Secretary of State.

14.37 The question of set-off is not expressly dealt with in s 166 or Pt XII. The provisions require that 'the employer is liable to pay' (s 166) or that the employee 'was entitled to be paid' (Pt XII) the relevant amount. Given that the effect of the mandatory set-off under rules 2.85 and 4.90 is that, after the set-off has been accounted for, no amount (or only the balance after set-off) may be due from the employer, it follows that in a relevant administration or liquidation only the amount (if any) net of set-off of the employee's loans and other indebtedness remains to be paid by the employer. On this basis, claims should be paid by the National Insurance Fund only after taking into account set-off. In some cases this may mean that an employee will have no claim on the National Insurance Fund (because he or she owed more to the employer than was owed by the employer).

14.38 The EAT held in *Secretary of State for Employment v Wilson*[1] that set-off applies first. The BERR Guide, Employees' Rights on Insolvency of Employer[2] follows this approach. Although set-off is not mentioned expressly, the decision of the House of Lords in *Mann v Secretary of State*[3] also supports this approach. The House of Lords held that the Secretary of State (and the National Insurance Fund) is only a guarantor, liable only for whatever the employer was liable to pay for the employee. There is a contrast here with the express set-off provision in other contexts of claims on government approved guarantees[4].

1 [1996] IRLR 330, EAT.
2 See para 33 of 'Redundancy and Insolvency – A guide for insolvency practitioners to employees' rights on the insolvency of their employer' (URN 08/550). On the web at: http://www.insolvency.gov.uk/guidanceleaflets/redundancypayments/guideforips/guideforips.htm.
3 [1999] ICR 898, HL.
4 Eg in the Financial Services Compensation Scheme established under s 213 of the Financial Services and Markets Act 2000 (see COMP 12.2.4R in the FSA manual) and, before its repeal, Banking Act 1987, s 60(7) dealing with set-off in relation to claims on the Deposit Protection Board.

14.39 If payment is made by the National Insurance Fund to employees in relation to their claims against the employer, it would seem that, in effect, such employees would have to that extent transferred their rights against the employer to the National Insurance Fund. In the case of the statutory 'assignment' to the National Insurance Fund, this would not affect any priority of the employee's claim as being preferential (see ERA 1996, s 189 in relation to claims under s 182; in relation to s 166 the point is not relevant as rights to redundancy payments are not preferential). Whether set-off should be applied by an insolvency practitioner to reduce this subrogated claim of the Secretary of State to reflect a debt owed by the employee will not be relevant if the position is that only net claims (ie after any set-off) are made against the National Insurance Fund.

14.40 Any other assignment of an employee's claim on the National Insurance Fund should mean that the claim is no longer that of an employee and hence ceases to be one due from the National Insurance Fund. This is a similar position to that reached in relation to claims on the former Deposit Protection Board under the Banking Act 1987 – see the decision of the House of Lords in *Deposit Protection Board v Dalia*[1].

1 [1994] 2 AC 367, HL.

14.41 Set-off applies to any claim that the Crown has in relation to the National Insurance Fund against any claim that the company may have against the Crown (eg for overpaid tax) – see *Frid v Secretary of State*[1].

Since 2008, there has been a statutory set-off provision in relation to amounts owing by and to HMRC – Finance Act 2008, s 130. The section has effect without prejudice to any other power of HMRC to set off amounts.

Section 130 does not apply in Scotland, but only in England, Wales and Northern Ireland – s 130(8). It also does not apply to allow HMRC to set-off a post insolvency credit (ie an amount due from HMRC relating to periods after or matters after the insolvency started) against a pre-insolvency debit (ie amount due by the insolvent company to HMRC) – s 131. An insolvency proceeding for this purpose includes liquidation, administration, administrative receivership or voluntary arrangement – s 131(5).

1 [2004] UKHL 24; [2004] 2 AC 506, HL.

CHAPTER 15

Carrying on business

15.1   The position commonly arises that, in the interests of the relevant insolvency proceedings, the insolvency practitioner wishes to arrange for the insolvent employer company to continue to carry on all or part of its business.

For this purpose the insolvency practitioner will wish the company to continue the employment of some (if not all) of the employees. The impact of such a decision on both the rights of the employees and on the nature of the claims of the employees is complex.

WHO IS THE EMPLOYER?

15.2   In most cases, the employer will continue to be the insolvent company and will not become the insolvency practitioner personally. This is because the insolvency practitioner acts as the agent of the company, whether he or she is:

●   a liquidator (see *Stead Hazel and Company v Cooper*[1] and the Court of Session in *Smith v Lord Advocate*[2]); or

●   an administrator (see para 69 of Sch B1 to IA 1986, formerly IA 1986, s 14(5)); or

●   an administrative receiver (see IA 1986, s 44).

1 [1933] 1 KB 840 (Lawrence J).
2 1978 SC 259, Inner House, Court of Session.

15.3   Conversely, a receiver appointed by the court acts as a principal and not as an agent (see para 4.8 above and note the comparison made with a liquidator in *Stead Hazel & Co v Cooper*[1]).

Professor Freedland has argued in his book *The Personal Employment Contract*[2] that the analysis that the employer remains the company if an administrator or administrative receiver is appointed over the company is:

> 'open to the objection that it strains the capacity for internal transformation of the employing entity beyond its logical breaking point, by treating the employing entity as retaining its sole identity although its management is wholly in the hands

of an external person, neither a director of the company nor a worker for the company.'[3]

Professor Freedland argues that instead the employment relationship should be regarded as:

> 'partially transformed by the addition of the receiver or administrator as the other of two employing entities, between them making up a joint multi-personal employing party.'

My view is that, in this case, Professor Freedland's analysis is unlikely to be followed. The employer remains the company, not the insolvency practitioner, albeit that there are then duties on the IP relating to the treatment of claims of the employees (eg adoption and expenses issues, addressed below in this Chapter). Professor Freedland's argument that the appointment of the IP has fundamentally changed the management structure of the company would also apply in other contexts (eg. a contested take-over), but this approach has not been argued. In addition it is difficult to see why employment contracts should be affected, but not other contracts[4].

Professor Freedland's analysis (elsewhere in his book) of other areas (for example the issues arising in relation to agency contracts or the Unfair Contract Terms Act 1977) has been adopted by the Court of Appeal – see *Dacas v Brook Street Bureau (UK) Ltd*[5] and *Commerzbank AG v Keen*[6].

1 [1933] 1 KB 840 at 843.
2 2nd edn, OUP, 2003.
3 Page 505.
4 See for example *Re Newdigate Colliery Ltd* [1912] Ch 468, CA and the cases cited at para 9 – 51 in Goode *Principles of Corporate Insolvency Law* (Sweet & Maxwell, 3rd edn, 2005).
5 [2004] EWCA Civ 217; [2004] ICR 1437; [2004] IRLR 358, CA.
6 [2006] EWCA Civ 1536; [2007] IRLR 132, CA at para [101].

Continuity of employment

15.4   If an insolvency practitioner, other than a court appointed receiver, does elect to continue the business of the company, and continued employment is accepted by the employee in cases where the employee would otherwise be automatically dismissed (ie on a court winding-up – see para 5.2 above), then there is no dismissal at that stage but the employee's contract of employment with the company continues.

The decision of the Industrial Tribunal to the contrary in *Golding and Howard v Fire, Auto and Marine Insurance Co Ltd*[1] must be regarded as wrong on this point and the decisions of the Scottish Industrial Tribunal in *McEwan v Upper Clyde Shipbuilders Ltd*[2] the Court of Session in *Smith v Lord Advocate*[3] and of the Australian High Court in *Re Associated Dominions Assurance Society Pty Ltd*[4] are to be preferred.

1 [1968] ITR 372, IT.
2 (1972) 7 ITR 296, IT.
3 1978 SC 259, Inner House, Court of Session.
4 (1962) 109 CLR 516, High Court.

15.5 In the case of an administrator or out of court receiver, it is clear that the company remains the employer – see *Powdrill v Watson*[1]. The decisions in *Re Mack Trucks (Britain) Ltd*[2] and the Australian case of *James Miller Holdings Ltd v Graham*[3] are also authority for there being continuity of employment with the company where the receiver arranges for it to continue to trade. The same applies to a receiver who is not an administrative receiver – see *Hughes v Secretary of State*[4].

1 [1995] 2 AC 394 at 448F, HL
2 [1967] 1 WLR 780 (Pennycuick J).
3 (1978) 3 ACLR 604 (McGarvie J).
4 (1995) 13 December (EAT/204/094), EAT.

INSOLVENCY PRACTITIONER AS EMPLOYER?

15.6 It is possible for the insolvency practitioner personally to employ continuing employees, but in practice insolvency practitioners are reluctant to accept the personal liability this involves. Although it is generally possible to include in a contract a limit on contractual claims (eg to assets controlled by the insolvency practitioner in the particular insolvency), any such limitation will be ineffective as regards statutory claims under ERA 1996. It is only possible in limited circumstances to contract out of or limit the relevant statutory rights – see generally ERA 1996, s 203.

15.7 If, perhaps unusually, an employee were to cease to be employed by the company but become employed by the insolvency practitioner personally, there is no express provision in ERA 1996 dealing with such a change in employment.

15.8 It may be that the insolvency practitioner could, in those circumstances, be regarded as taking over the business of the company so that the relevant continuity of employment exists by virtue of the general provisions in ERA 1996, s 218 or under the Transfer of Undertakings (Protection of Employment) Regulations 2006 (TUPE) which covers the situation where there has been a change of employer.

However, in *Deaway Trading Ltd v Calverly*[1] (decided before TUPE 1981 took effect) it seems to have been assumed that the predecessor of s 218 would not apply so that, technically, continuity appeared to have been broken. It was ultimately decided that, in view of the fact that there had been no change in the legal owner of the business, continuity in fact was preserved. It is likely that court would now hold that there was a TUPE transfer – see eg *Charlton v Charlton Thermosystems (Romsey) Ltd*[2].

The Court of Session has held that there is continuity of employment when a liquidator decides that the business of the company should carry on – see *Smith v Lord Advocate*[3].

1 [1973] 3 All ER 776, NIRC.
2 [1995] ICR 56; [1995] IRLR 79, EAT.
3 1978 SC 259, Court of Session.

15.9 In *Belhaven Brewery Co Ltd v Berekis*[1] the Employment Appeal Tribunal held that where a trustee in bankruptcy had been appointed and decided to carry on a business (so that, in a similar manner to a court receiver, the employees became employed by the trustee personally) continuity of employment was preserved for the employees both under ERA 1996, s 218 (then EPCA 1978, Sch 13, para 17(2)) and under TUPE 1981.

1 (1993) IDS Brief 494 (June 1993), EAT.

Status of benefits

15.10 Other difficulties, including the following, may arise. Many employee benefits will be covered by insurance, such as medical insurance, in the name of the company, not in the name of the insolvency practitioner. For example, pension benefits will, under the terms of the relevant pension scheme, be applied only for employees of participating employers. Unless the insolvency practitioner himself were able to (and did in fact) become a participating employer in the pension scheme, pension benefits would cease to accrue and the employee would be treated as having left pensionable service on the date that he ceased to be employed by the insolvent company (and became employed by the insolvency practitioner).

Status of other claims

15.11 One particular reason for the insolvency practitioner not becoming the employer might be to seek to make it clear that any liabilities owed to the employee up to the date of insolvency (eg termination, unpaid wages etc) did not become a responsibility of, or expense of, the insolvency practitioner, but rather remained as claims against the company. This would result in the insolvency practitioner assuming liability only for claims in respect of employment after the date of his appointment, but in practice this will be almost impossible to achieve without there being a TUPE transfer – see eg *Charlton v Charlton Thermosystems (Romsey) Ltd*[1] meaning that all liabilities would pass to the insolvency practitioner personally (thus defeating the objective).

1 [1995] ICR 56; [1995] IRLR 79, EAT.

CONTINUING TO TRADE – TREATMENT OF EMPLOYEES' REMUNERATION

15.12 In making the decision as to whether or not to continue to trade (and continue to arrange for the company to continue to employ all or some of its employees), the primary duty of the insolvency practitioners will usually be to the creditors of the company. The insolvency practitioners must balance:

- the potential increased recovery for the creditors if the company's business continues as a going concern (eg a sale of the business as a going concern may realise more than would the closure of the business and its liquidation on a non-trading basis);

against;

● the costs of continuing to trade.

15.13 One of the key issues for the insolvency practitioners will be to assess the costs of continuing to carry on the business. Obviously the insolvency practitioners will need, as a practical matter, to ensure that the company meets its ongoing expenses. It has been stated that the insolvency practitioners could run the risk of incurring liability under IA 1986, s 213 for fraudulent trading if they do not arrange this[1].

1 See the comments of Lightman J at first instance in *Re Leyland Daf* [1995] 2 AC 394 at 407. For arguments to the contrary see Segal and Moss 'The Expenses Doctrine in Liquidation. Administrations and Receiverships' [1997] Company Financial and Insolvency Law Review 1 at pages 19 and 20.

15.14 Thus the insolvency practitioners will need to ensure that (say) rent is paid on the premises, hire charges are paid for vital equipment (eg photocopiers etc) and services bills (eg water and electricity) are paid. Obviously if such ongoing costs are not paid, the other contracting party (landlord, service provider, utility company etc) are likely to terminate the arrangements thus defeating the object of continuing to trade.

15.15 This is all achieved without the need for any statutory priority or liability on insolvency practitioners. It merely relies on market forces. If the relevant third party has sufficient bargaining power (eg is a vital supplier) then it is open to that third party to insist on payment of all arrears of payments as a condition to allowing the services to continue – see *Leyland DAF Ltd v Automotive Products plc*[1] (and earlier cases).

1 [1994] 1 BCLC 245, CA.

15.16 This gave too great an advantage to the monopoly suppliers of utilities (water, gas, telephones and electricity) and they are now barred by statute from requiring payment of arrears before allowing continuing services (see IA 1986, s 233).

15.17 Although in *Re St Ives (Windings) Ltd*[1] it was held that an administrator did not have power to pay existing creditors of the company, in *Re John Slack*[2] Scott J (as he then was) distinguished this case and held that administrators had the power to pay pre-existing creditors if this was necessary to ensure the survival of the company.

1 (1987) 3 BCC 634 (Harman J).
2 (1990) [1995] BCC 1116 (Scott J).

15.18 The changes in the Enterprise Act 2002 now give administrators in an administration starting on or after 15 September 2003 a general power to pay creditors in some circumstances (IA 1986, Sch B1, para 65). See also *Re MG Rover Espana SA*[1] and *Re Collins & Aikman Europe SA*[2] discussing the power under para 66 of Schedule B1 – see Chapter 40 below.

1 [2006] EWHC 3426; [2005] BPIR 1162; [2006] BCC 599 (Judge Norris QC).
2 [2006] EWHC 1343; [2006] BCC 861 (Lindsay J).

15.19 All these considerations apply equally to employees of the insolvent company. In practice if the insolvency practitioners wish to arrange for the company to continue to trade, they will need to arrange for (at least) ongoing wages to be paid to the employees kept on. To do otherwise would be likely to result in the employees walking out and claiming damages for constructive dismissal.

15.20 Indeed the need to keep the employees on may result in the insolvency practitioners agreeing to arrange for the company to meet any unpaid wages, relating to periods prior to their appointment. In some cases a 'loyalty bonus' may be offered by insolvency practitioners to employees in an attempt to make sure that they do not voluntarily leave employment (see para 18.140 below).

NATIONAL MINIMUM WAGE

15.21 As mentioned above (see para 9.44), the National Minimum Wage Act 1998 requires employers to pay at least the national minimum wage (£5.80 per hour from 1 October 2009). Failure by an employer to pay this:

(a) is a criminal offence (NMWA 1998, s 31). Under s 32, directors and other officers can also commit a criminal offence if the employer company commits an offence and this is due to their consent, connivance or neglect (see para 8.18 above); and

(b) can render the employer liable to a financial penalty if it fails to comply with an enforcement notice (NMWA 1998, s 21).

15.22 The insolvency practitioner will, as an officer etc (see para 8.18 above) be at risk of a potential criminal liability if he or she fails to ensure that the national minimum wage is paid for any service after he or she takes charge of the company.

TERMINATION CLAIMS

15.23 The need to keep employees (and to pay at least the national minimum wage) will be pushing insolvency practitioners to ensure that employees are paid for the services they render after the start of formal insolvency. However, insolvency practitioners will be reluctant to ensure that the amounts paid to employees (or indeed other third parties) includes any costs arising only as a result of the ultimate termination of any employment (ie termination cost – category 3 in para 15.25 below).

15.24   Thus, if for example the insolvency practitioners' attempt to ensure that the company trades out of its difficulty fails, and this results in a cessation of trading (and dismissal of the relevant employees), the insolvency practitioners will not consider it appropriate to arrange for priority for payment to employees of amounts due to them on termination of their contract (eg damages for breach of contract without proper notice, unfair dismissal claims, protective awards etc).

15.25

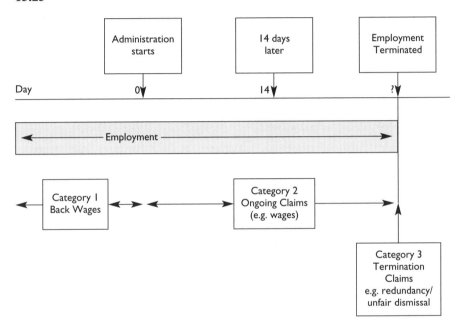

The claims of employees can perhaps be divided into three categories:

● **Category 1: Back wages**: Claims relating to a period of employment prior to the appointment of the insolvency practitioner. The obvious example is any payment of wages or other sums which have fallen due and payable by the company but which have not been paid. The due date for payment of some of these claims could be delayed so that, although they relate to a period of employment prior to the appointment of the insolvency practitioner, they in fact fall due and payable only after the insolvency practitioner has been appointed. Examples of this are bonus payments only due after the year in which they are earned and pension obligations.

● **Category 2: Ongoing claims**: Claims arising in respect of ongoing employment during the course of the insolvency proceedings. Obviously if the insolvency practitioner arranges for the company to continue the employment of the existing employees, then further amounts will fall to be payable by the company by way of remuneration for the services provided by the employee that ongoing employment such as wages, accrual of pension rights, benefits in kind (eg car, medical insurance).

- **Category 3: Termination claims**: If the employment by the company of an employee is terminated, then various sums may become legally due and payable by the company by way of termination costs (see generally Chapter 7 (Effect of termination of employment) above).

15.26 Termination claims can include damages for breach of contract (see para 2.25 above), statutory claims for unfair dismissal or redundancy (see para 2.37 above) and a protective award (see para 3.6 above).

15.27 A broad balance needs to be struck between the interests of the employees and those of the creditors generally. Generally, it seems fair for the relevant system to seek to ensure that:

(a) category 1 claims (back wages) are provable and recoverable in the proceedings in the same way as other claims (see para 15.28 below);

(b) category 2 claims (ongoing costs) are paid by the insolvency practitioner, or at least made a first charge on the available assets (see para 15.31 below); and

(c) category 3 claims (termination claims) are provable in the insolvency proceedings (see para 15.33 below) – although there is an issue here in that the relevant termination may not have occurred at the time fixed for proving debts.

Category 1 claims

15.28 Category 1 claims (back wages) will have some preferential status (see Chapter 9 above) and protection from the National Insurance Fund (see Chapter 13 above). Parliament has laid down the extent of the statutory protection and this should be respected.

15.29 In practice if there is a sale of the business of the insolvent company, category 1 claims of some (and possibly all) employees will pass to the (presumably solvent) purchaser under TUPE and so be paid in full (thereby achieving a super-preferential status – the amount paid by the purchaser will presumably be reduced as a result, leaving less for the other creditors). This is discussed further in Chapters 16 to 18 below.

15.30 As mentioned above (see para 15.20) vital employees may be able to use their bargaining power to force the insolvency practitioner to meet claims for back wages etc on the threat of otherwise leaving employment (and see para 18.140 below).

Category 2 claims

15.31 The balance of fairness seems to be that on going claims by employees (category 2 claims) – eg for wages while employed – should be met in relation to their continued employment by the insolvent company during the period of office of the insolvency practitioner. It should be relatively easy for the insolvency practitioner to assess the relevant costs (at least for cash wages – benefits in kind may be more difficult) and decide whether it is suitable for the purposes of the insolvency process – ie usually in the interests of creditors generally – for the employment to continue and the business to be carried on (see para 15.12 above).

15.32 If the decision to continue to trade is made it is only fair that the employees concerned be paid in respect of their continued services – presumably the insolvency practitioner has decided that their continued employment will benefit creditors. The employees will naturally be reluctant to continue to work unless they are paid.

Category 3 claims

15.33 In relation to category 3 claims (termination claims), often the employees have not suffered a termination immediately on the insolvency process starting, if they have continued to be employed and will have been paid for that period of employment. If the alternative was their dismissal on the appointment of the insolvency practitioners, then their claims would have ranked in the insolvency in the usual manner (ie preferential to a certain limited extent – see Chapter 9 – but otherwise usually unsecured and also guaranteed by the National Insurance Fund again to a certain limited extent – see Chapter 13).

15.34 Subject to any increase in the termination claim (eg as a result of having accrued extra service or as a result of salary or compensation limits having increased), it is difficult to see why, as a matter of fairness, the employees should have any legal right to an increased priority of some sort in respect of these termination claims.

15.35 One problem is that dismissal will not occur until after the appointment. So does this mean that such post-appointment claims are not provable in a liquidation or relevant post September 2003 administration (because they do not exist at the date of liquidation/administration)? – see Chapter 16 below and for example the comments of Gowans J in the Australian case, *Re Matthew Bros*[1]. This does not arise in pre-15 September 2003 administrations or receiverships where there is no formal mechanism for a proof of debt.

1 [1962] VR 262 (Gowans J). See also *McEvoy v Incat Tasmania Pty Ltd* [2003] FCA 810, 21 ACLC 1463 (Finkelstein J) and paras 6.7 and 9.59 above

15.36 In practice, before 1986, the position was that, commonly, receivers would arrange that the ongoing pay and remuneration of employees was met by the company. However, in 1985, the Court of Appeal in *Nicoll v Cutts*[1] held that there was no legal requirement for a receiver to pay an employee even for such ongoing salary incurred during the course of the receivership (category 2 under the categorisation in para 15.25 above).

1 [1985] BCLC 322, CA.

15.37 It must be queried whether the above decision was in fact right (see the comments in relation to the potential liability for fraudulent trading under IA 1986, s 213 by Lightman J in *Re Leyland Daf*[1]). The facts of *Nicoll v Cutts* are slightly unusual in that it appears that the employee who was bringing his claim had been ill throughout the period that the receiver had been in office, but had given some assistance (from his sick bed) to the receiver[2].

1 [1995] 2 AC 394 at 407 – see paras 15.13 above and 18.21 below.
2 See further the article by Roger Gregory in (1994) 1 Receivers, Administrators and Liquidators Quarterly 143. *Nicoll v Cutts* has been followed in Australia – see *Sipad Holding DDPO v Popovic* [1995] FCA 1737; (1995) 14 ACLC 307 (Lehane J) and *McEvoy v Incat Tasmania Pty Ltd* [2003] FCA 810; 21 ACLC 1463 (Finkelstein J).

15.38 The Insolvency Bill 1985 (subsequently enacted and consolidated in IA 1986) was passing through Parliament at the time of the decision in *Nicoll v Cutts*. Amendments were introduced providing for a statutory priority to be granted to certain claims of employees. These are discussed further below.

15.39 Given the need to balance the interests of the employees and those of the creditors generally, specific provision has been made by Parliament and by the courts. These include:

- **Preferential debts/NI Fund**: Schedule 6 to the IA 1986 makes some claims of employees as at the relevant date preferential up to a limit (see Chapter 9 above) and the Employment Rights Act 1996 guarantees payment of some claims (whether arising before or after the insolvency date) out of the National Insurance Fund (see Chapter 13 above).

- **Insolvency expenses**: control by the courts of liquidators and administrators (as officers of the court) to force them to pay some claims arising in the course of the insolvency. This is known as the doctrine of 'insolvency expenses' (or more particularly as 'liquidation expenses' or 'administration expenses') and is discussed in Chapter 17 on below. It seems that this control does not apply to receivers (but see para 17.63 below).

- **Adopted contracts**: Paragraph 99 of Schedule B1 to IA 1986[1] and ss 37 and 44 of IA 1986 (as amended by IA 1994) impose specific duties and liabilities on administrators and receivers (but not liquidators) in relation to 'adopted' employment contracts. These provisions are discussed in Chapter 18 below.

1 Inserted by the Enterprise Act 2002 and replacing (for administrations starting on or after 15 September 2003) similar (but not identical) provisions in s 19 of IA 1986.

Specific provisions

15.40 Generally, although the insolvency practitioner will usually act as the agent of the company concerned (and hence will not usually incur any personal liability towards those who have contracted with the company), the effect of the special rules can be either:

(a) personal liability: to impose personal liability on the insolvency practitioner (ie as, in effect, the guarantor that payments will be made); or

(b) charge on assets: to make the relevant claims of the employee rank as expenses of the relevant insolvency (similarly to other insolvency expenses, for example the fees of the insolvency practitioner) and hence payable out of the assets of the company in priority to practically all other claims.

The position of the insolvency practitioner obviously differs between the two types of liability.

In the first case the insolvency practitioner has a personal liability, regardless of the level of assets under his or her control.

15.41 However, in the second case the insolvency practitioner may be more willing to accept that the relevant claims of the employees are given a priority out of the assets of the company (perhaps even to the exclusion of the insolvency practitioner's fees and expenses) given that, should the assets prove to be insufficient, no further personal liability rests on the insolvency practitioner.

15.42 The next three chapters examine the issues in relation to employees in greater depth:

• The impact on proof of claims where business is continued by the insolvency practitioner (mainly in an administration – see Chapter 16 below

• The rules relating to insolvency expenses and when employee liabilities will have priority as a result – see Chapter 17 below

• The special statutory rules relating to 'adoption' of employment contracts and the priority that can follow – see Chapter 18 below.

Carrying on business – provable debts

PROVABLE DEBTS

16.1   If an insolvent company continues to trade, despite the entry into formal insolvency, then the question arises as to how any relevant claims of the employees who remain employed by the company, are affected as provable debts in the insolvency.

16.2   This situation is most likely to arise in an administration. In practice companies are unlikely to continue to trade after a liquidation (see para 4.18 above and IA 1986, s 87). Trading is more likely to continue in an administrative receivership, but the numbers of those will steadily reduce (given into the entry into force of the Enterprise Act 2002). In any event formal proof of debts is not applicable in a receivership.

16.3   The position has become more complicated in an administration with the changes (from September 2003) made by the Enterprise Act 2002. It is now possible for such administrations to include a distribution to creditors, together with a set-off in such a case (see Chapter 14 above). A need for a proof before a dividend can be paid in an administration only arises if a notice of a distribution to creditors is given by the administrator.

16.4   The Insolvency Rules 1986 dealing with proof of debt in an administration broadly mirror, in Part 2, the provisions dealing with proof of debt applicable in a liquidation (found in Part 4).

16.5   For an administration, the relevant time line may well then be as follows:

(i)   Company enters administration

(ii)   Employees remain employed after the entry into administration

(iii)   Employees are dismissed (or transferred to another company under TUPE)

(iv)   Company subsequently enters liquidation (or perhaps is dissolved without a form of liquidation).

A distribution could be made by the administrator out of the administration either before the relevant termination date for the employees or after.

What then is the position of the employees in seeking to prove any part of their claims in the administration?

16.6   The Insolvency Rules are tolerably clear in stating that the following applies to distributions by the administrator:

Claim	Administration	Subsequent liquidation
Proof date	Date of entry into administration rule 2.72(3)	Date of liquidation rule 4.75
Preferential debts ('relevant date'):	date of administration IA 1986, s 387(3A)	date of administration IA 1986, s 387(3)(a) to (ba)
Set-off (cut off date)	date of administration rule 2.85	date of administration rule 4.90(2)(b) and (c)

Note that in any liquidation following on from an administration, the date of the administration is the relevant date for both preferential debts and set-off. However the date for proofs of general claims in the liquidation moves to the date of the liquidation (and not the date of the administration).

16.7   As noted in Chapter 13 above, claims by employees on the National Insurance Fund do not register by reference to a proof date. Provided the company has in fact entered the relevant insolvency process and employment has been terminated (s 182, ERA 1996), the National Insurance Fund should pay the relevant protected debts. The Secretary of State then subrogates to the relevant claims of the employees. To the extent that those claims are preferential or provable etc then claims can be made in the administration or liquidation by the Secretary of State.

16.8   When looking at the amounts that can be made the subject of a proof by the employees (or by the Secretary of State if there was any subrogation) in an administration, it becomes necessary to analyse whether those claims are in fact provable at all.

16.9   The issue mainly arises in relation to termination claims of the employees (eg protective awards, unfair dismissal etc). These are the Category 3 claims specified in Chapter 15 (Carrying on business) above.

16.10   As at the proof date, ie the date of the administration, the contracts of employment have not been terminated by the insolvent company – instead they have been continued. So as at the date of the administration it is not in fact possible to say that any termination claim will actually fall due and be payable. Employees may resign or transfer under TUPE (see Chapter 20 below) and so not be dismissed or have any termination claim at all against the insolvent company.

16.11   How then are these contingent and future claims of the employees dealt with as part of the proof process?

16.12   There could potentially be a risk that relevant claims are not provable at all. Nor in some cases will they constitute administration expenses or claims covered by the adoption provisions – see Chapters 17 and 18 below. In this case there could be a risk they could fall into a 'black hole' and not be claimable against anyone. In *Re Allders Department Stores Ltd*[1], Lawrence Collins J noted that:

> 'there is nothing in my judgment in *Re Toshoku Finance* [2002] 3 All ER 961, [2002] 1 WLR 671 which requires a different conclusion. It is not the ratio of that case that any liability imposed on a company which is not provable as a debt is thereby rendered a 'necessary disbursement'. The context in which Lord Hoffmann referred to the fact that certain debts could not be proved shows that he was justifying the treatment of certain debts as expenses, and not offering a definition of what liabilities were disbursements. Even if that were the crucial test for winding up, there would be no reason to apply it to administration. Although the current regime envisages a distribution to secured and preferential creditors without a subsequent liquidation, in the normal case of an administration which does not succeed in rescuing the company, the company will go into liquidation and the statutory payment obligation will be a provable debt under r 13.12B.'

1 [2005] 2 All ER 122 (Lawrence Collins J).

16.13   In practice it is important to note two potential mitigations to this (at least as far as the employee is concerned):

(a) Some (not all) claims will be met by the National Insurance Fund – and so that fund will take any shortfall; and

(b) If the administration is followed by a liquidation, the termination claims of the employees will be provable in that liquidation (at least as against any remaining assets transferred by the administrator to the liquidator).

16.14   Rule 12.3 in the Insolvency Rules 1986 (as amended) provides that:

> 'subject as follows: in administration, winding up and bankruptcy, all claims by creditors are provable as debts against a company…, whether they are present or future, certain or contingent, ascertained or sounding only in damages.'

Rule 13.12 (as amended) goes on to state as follows:

> '13.12 "Debt", "liability" (winding up)
>
> (1)   "Debt", in relation to the winding up of a company, means (subject to the next paragraph) any of the following—
>
> > (a)   any debt or liability to which the company is subject at the date on which it goes into liquidation;
> >
> > (b)   any debt or liability to which the company may become subject after that date by reason of any obligation incurred before that date; and
> >
> > (c)   any interest provable as mentioned in Rule 4.93(1).

(2) [tort claims]

(3) For the purposes of references in any provision of the Act or the Rules about winding up to a debt or liability, it is immaterial whether the debt or liability is present or future, whether it is certain or contingent, or whether its amount is fixed or liquidated, or is capable of being ascertained by fixed rules or as a matter of opinion; and references in any such provision to owing a debt are to be read accordingly.

(4) In any provision of the Act or the Rules about winding up, except in so far as the context otherwise requires, "liability" means (subject to paragraph (3) above) a liability to pay money or money's worth, including any liability under an enactment, any liability for breach of trust, any liability in contract, tort or bailment, and any liability arising out of an obligation to make restitution.

(5) This Rule shall apply where a company is in administration and shall be read as if references to winding-up were a reference to administration.'

Note that this applies to administrations as well – see rule 13.12(5).

16.15 Rules 12.3 and 13.12 are very wide. Having said that, it is clear that in order to be provable the liability must exist in some form at the relevant date (i.e. the date of which the company entered administration or went into liquidation). Rules 4.75 (liquidation) and 2.72(3) (administrations) require a relevant proof of debt to include the total amount of the relevant claim 'as at the date on which the company went into liquidation/entered administration'.

16.16 Similarly Form 4.26 (Affidavit on debt) requires the creditor to declare on oath that the company 'was and still is justly and truly indebted to me' as at the date of which the company went into liquidation. These words were noted by Lord Hoffmann in the Privy Council in *Wight v Eckhardt Marine GmbH*[1] at paragraph [34]:

> '34 This view is supported by the statutory form of proof. The Companies Law (2002 rev) appears to be based upon the United Kingdom Companies Act 1948 and their Lordships will therefore refer to the form of proof prescribed by rule 94 and Form 59 of the Companies (Winding-up) Rules 1949 (SI 1949/330). In the United Kingdom these have been replaced by rule 4.77 and Form 4.26 of the Insolvency Rules 1986 (SI 1986/1925) but there is no material difference. In each case the creditor is required to swear that the company "on … the date when the company went into liquidation was *and still is* justly and truly indebted to me …" (Emphasis added.)'

1 [2003] UKPC 37; [2004] 1 AC 147, PC.

16.17 In order for a claim to exist in some form as at the relevant insolvency date (and so be potentially provable) it seems that there must have been an obligation at that time arising at the terms of an existing contract or statute.

16.18 The decision of the House of Lords in *Secretary of State for Trade and Industry v Frid*[1] was concerned with the availability of set-off under rule 4.90

(see Chapter 14 above). But the issue turned on whether the relevant debt was provable at the set-off cut off date.

Lord Hoffmann commented, at paragraph 9:

> '9 It is not however necessary for the purposes of rule 4.90(2) that the debt should have been due and payable before the insolvency date. It is sufficient that there should have been an obligation arising out of the terms of a contract or statute by which a debt sounding in money would become payable upon the occurrence of some future event or events. The principle has typically been applied to claims for breach of contract where the contract was made before the insolvency date but the breach occurred afterwards (*In re Asphaltic Wood Pavement Co* (1885) 30 ChD 216) or claims for indemnity by a guarantor where the guarantee was given before the insolvency date but the guarantor was called upon and paid afterwards: *Jones v Mossop* (1844) 3 Hare 568; *In re Moseley-Green Coal and Coke Co Ltd, Ex p Barrett* (1865) 12 LT (NS) 193.'

In *Day v Haine*[2] the Court of Appeal had followed the decision of Lord Hoffmann in *Frid* noting that the position in relation to set-off depended on only provable debts being able to be set-off.

1 [2004] UKHL 24; [2004] 2 AC 506, HL.
2 [2008] EWCA Civ 626, [2008] ICR 1102, CA, see para [34]. See paras 16.27 and 16.40 below.

16.19   Lord Hoffmann was dealing with a question about whether set-off could be available to a guarantor (in this case the National Insurance Fund) even though it had only paid under the underlying debt after the insolvency date. Lord Hoffmann held that this was allowed even though the claim of the guarantor (or national insurance fund) was contingent at the date of insolvency.

16.20   It is to be noted that the facts in *Frid* seemed to have involved claims made by employees who had been dismissed before the start of the insolvency (a creditors' winding-up or liquidation) (see the decision at first instance in *Frid*[1]). So the issue of set-off (or proving) for termination claims arising after the date of the insolvency did not arise in that case.

1 [2003] 2 BCLC 284 (David Mackie QC sitting as a Deputy Judge of the High Court).

16.21   There does not seem to be any decided case law authority dealing clearly with the status of termination claims as provable debts in these circumstances. Then position seems to depend on the linkage of the claim with an existing (pre insolvency) contract and whether the amount of any claim depends on a termination or on a court or tribunal discretion.

16.22   *Re T&N Ltd (No 2)*[1] was a case on whether or not tort claims were provable. David Richards J referred to the decision of the Court of Appeal in the bankruptcy case of *Glenister* (see below) and commented[2]:

> 'Likewise, there are a number of Australian decisions concerning statutory provisions whereby personal liability for the debts of an insolvent company can be imposed on a director, if he has been convicted of a relevant offence. In such a

case, the liability is imposed by the civil court in the exercise of its discretion. These provisions have been held not to create a contingent liability of the director at the time of his bankruptcy because any liability is dependent on a subsequent exercise of judicial discretion: see, for example, *Corporate Affairs Commission v Karounos* (1985) 3 ACLC 410.'

In South Australia in *Corporate Affairs Commission v Karounos*[3] Prior J held that a liability of a director to make payments following a liquidation of the company was not a provable debt in the director's bankruptcy. This was despite the fact that the facts giving rise to the claim related to actions by the director before his bankruptcy. However the relevant conviction and court order imposing liability would only be made after the bankruptcy started. So Prior J held that:

'An order made under sec. 374d certainly gives rise to a liability, but it is not a debt or liability to which the bankrupt was subject at the date of the bankruptcy. The offences occurred before the date of bankruptcy but the liability resulting from any order I make is contingent upon the conviction of 15 August 1984. My order and the conviction are both after the date of bankruptcy. Nor is the debt or liability to which he may become subject before his discharge ''by reason of an obligation incurred before the date of bankruptcy''. The obligation is not incurred until after conviction and the order now sought. Thus, even if these proceedings were proceedings by a creditor, they are not with respect to any provable debts. The order sought is not a debt provable in the current bankruptcy (cp. in *Re Pitchford* [1924] 2 Ch 260).'

1 [2005] EWHC 2870 (Ch); [2006] 2 BCLC 374; [2006] 3 All ER 697; [2006] 1 WLR 1728 (Lawrence Collins J).
2 [2006] 3 All ER 697 at page 719.
3 (1985) 3 ACLC 410 (Prior J).

16.23   In *Day v Haine*[1] Sir Donald Rattee, and then the Court of Appeal, had to consider the situation where employees had been dismissed before the insolvency date but their claims for protective awards for failure to consult under TULRCA 1992 were not in fact heard by the employment tribunal until after the insolvency date. The question was whether the protective awards (which were in fact payable by the National Insurance Fund) were provable debts in the liquidation.

1 [2008] EWCA Civ 626; [2008] ICR 1102; [2008] IRLR 642; [2008] 2 BCLC 517, CA on appeal from [2007] EWHC 2691 (Ch); [2008] ICR 452; [2007] All ER (D) 298 (Oct) (Sir Donald Rattee).

16.24   At first instance[1], Sir Donald Rattee held that they were not provable (and they were not expenses of the administration/liquidation either). This was because he felt that they did not have sufficient connection with the position as at the insolvency date, given that the amount of the protective award was within the discretion of the employment tribunal – such amount as it considers 'just and equitable' (s 189(4)(b), TULRCA 1992). Sir Donald Rattee felt that he was bound by two decisions of the Court of Appeal in bankruptcy matters: *Glenister* and *Steele*.

1 [2007] EWHC 2691 (Ch); [2008] ICR 452; [2007] All ER (D) 298 (Oct) (Sir Donald Rattee).

16.25   In *Glenister v Rowe*[1] the Court of Appeal had held that an award of costs made after the start of bankruptcy in legal proceedings was not provable as a debt in the bankruptcy (even though the proceedings had been started before then). This was because the relevant costs were discretionary in the court.

In 2007, the same result as in *Glenister* was reached by the High Court in Australia in *Foots v Southern Cross Mine Management Pty Ltd*.[2]

Some Australian cases seem to have drawn a distinction between costs orders after in bankruptcy (not provable in the bankruptcy – *Foots v Southern Cross Mine Management Pty Ltd*) and costs orders in a corporate liquidation, which may be provable – see *Environmental & Earth Sciences Pty Ltd v Vouris*[3] and *McDonald v Commissioner for Taxation*[4] . The latter two cases were decided before the High Court decision in *Foots*, but do not seem to have expressly overruled.

1 [2000] Ch 76; [1999] 3 All ER 452, CA. See also *In re British Goldfields of West Africa* [1899] 2 Ch 7, CA.
2 [2007] HCA 56, Kirby J dissenting.
3 [2006] FCA 679; (2006) 230 ALR 119; (2006) 57 ACSR 629 (Graham J).
4 [2005] NSWSC 2; (2005) 187 FLR 461 (Barrett J).

16.26   Similarly in *R (on the application of Steele) v Birmingham City Council*[1], the Court of Appeal had held that the claim by the Secretary of State to reclaim overpaid jobholders allowances did not arise until the Secretary of State had made a determination (as envisaged under the relevant Act). Accordingly there was no obligation to repay until that determination has been made and therefore the claim was not a provable debt in the bankruptcy.

It seems that there would be different result in relation to jobseekers allowance if the Secretary of State had made the relevant determination before bankruptcy – see *R (on the application of Balding) v Secretary of State for Work and Pensions*[2], distinguishing *Steele*.

In *R (on the application of Mohamed) v Southwark London Borough Council*[3] it was held that a claim for council tax for occupation of premises after date of bankruptcy was not provable.

In *Casson and Wales v The Law Society*[4] it was held that a compensatory award by the Solicitors Disciplinary Tribunal made after the date of a bankruptcy was a discretionary award and so not a provable debt in the bankruptcy.

1 [2005] EWCA Civ 1824; [2007] 1 All ER 73; [2006] 1 WLR 2380; [2006] ICR 869, CA.
2 [2007] EWCA Civ 1327; [2008] 3 All ER 217; [2008] 1 WLR 564, CA.
3 [2009] EWHC 311 (Admin); [2009] All ER (D) 233 (Feb) (Geraldine Andrews QC sitting as a deputy judge of the High Court).
4 [2009] EWHC 1943 (Admin) (Richards LJ and Maddison J).

16.27   The Court of Appeal on the appeal in *Day v Haine*[1] reversed the decision of Sir Donald Rattee and distinguished *Glenister* and *Steele*. The Court of Appeal noted that the effect of a claim not being provable is different in a bankruptcy compared to a company insolvency (although the wording of the relevant statutes on provable claims is the same). In a bankruptcy if a claim is not provable then it does not fall away as part of the bankruptcy but remains an enforceable claim on the bankrupt. Conversely if a claim is not provable in a corporate insolvency, then it may fall away altogether.

1 [2008] EWCA Civ 626; [2008] ICR 1102; [2008] IRLR 642; [2008] 2 BCLC 517, CA.

16.28   In *Day v Haine*, the Court of Appeal felt able to distinguish *Glenister* and *Steele*. This was on the basis that in fact although a discretion was given to an employment tribunal under TULCRA 1992, in practice because the obligation was part of a European obligation flowing from a directive, in practice the tribunal's discretion was limited (following the Court of Appeal in *Susie Radin Ltd v GMB*[1]). A full award (90 days) should be made unless there were reasons not to make such an award.

In *Day v Haine*, the Court of Appeal considered that this meant that the position of a protective award (relating to dismissals before the insolvency started) could be distinguished from the two bankruptcy cases and so the protective award was provable in the insolvency.

1 [2004] EWCA Civ 180; [2004] 2 All ER 279, CA – see para 21.3 below.

16.29   In practice, it would be better had the Court of Appeal felt able to distinguish the bankruptcy cases as not applying for this purpose in a company insolvency. In *Re T&N Ltd (No 2)*[1], David Richards J commented[2], having noted the decision in *Glenister*:

> 'I comment in passing that, while producing a just result on the facts of the case, the decision is likely to produce an unjust result when applied to the similar provisions governing proof in the winding up of a company.'

1 [2005] EWHC 2870 (Ch); [2006] 2 BCLC 374; [2006] 3 All ER 697; [2006] 1 WLR 1728 (David Richards J).
2 [2006] 3 All ER 697 at page 719.

16.30   Note that in *Day v Haine*, the relevant dismissals had occurred before the insolvency date. The position where the dismissals had only occurred after the insolvency date was not mentioned in the decision either at first instance or by the Court of Appeal.

The Court of Appeal held that realistically the employment tribunal 'did not have a discretion to refuse an award'. The Court of Appeal also considered that in fact the obligation to make the award had arisen before the date of liquidation in the sense that the obligation had been incurred before that date at which the company went into liquidation – see paragraph [55].

16.31   In the case of a claim by an employee for a termination amount where termination of employment did not occur before the insolvency date, that claim must be both contingent and future as at the insolvency date.

CONTINGENT AND FUTURE CLAIMS

16.32   Future claims are still provable, but a discount is applied – rule 2.89 (administration) of the Insolvency Rules 1986. A five per cent per annum discount rate applies – rule 2.105.

16.33   Where a claim is contingent, then the administrator has to estimate the value of the debt for which a proof can be submitted – rule 2.81. This estimate can be revised later. In practice this is similar to rule 4.86 applicable in a liquidation.

16.34   If the contingency later falls due or revised estimate as to the liability can be made, then the proof can be adjusted – For example in *Re Northern County of England Fire Insurance Co*[1], Jessel MR held that a policy holder could prove for the full amount of the fire claim even though the fire only occurred after the entry of the insurance company into insolvency.

This probably does not apply to claims by the pension scheme under section 75 of the Pensions Act 1995 where the amount is fixed at the insolvency date and is not subject to later variation to take account of (say) a lower rate of securing a buy-out – see *Gleave v Board of the Pension Protection Fund sub nom Re Federal-Mogul Aftermarket UK Ltd*[2] and para 34.28 below.

1 (1880) 17 Ch D 337 (Jessel MR).
2 [2008] EWHC 1099 (Ch); [2008] BPIR 846; [2008] All ER (D) 287 (May) (David Richards J) – see further Chapter 34 (Section 75) below. On *Gleave*, see Stuart Firth and Stephen Davies QC 'Clearing up the mess: applying the basic principles of insolvency law' (2009) 22 Insolvency Intelligence 117.

16.35   If a contingency happens after the relevant insolvency date but before the proof is lodged that is, at least, strong evidence of the value of the claim as at the date of insolvency – *Stein v Blake*[1].

In *Ellis and Company's Trustee v Dixon –Johnson*[2] PO Lawrence J held:

> 'The true rule as to proving contingent liabilities against a bankrupt's estate is, in my opinion, as follows: The claim must be stated as on the day of the receiving order: if, when the proof is lodged, the contingency has not happened, the amount of the claim must be estimated as accurately as possible; if the contingency happens before the proof is lodged, that fact is pro tanto evidence of the true value of the claim as at the date of the receiving order, and there will, as a rule, be no difficulty in arriving at the amount of the claim; if the contingency happens after the proof is lodged and it appears that the amount at which the damages have been estimated is below the true value, the creditor will be allowed to amend his proof or lodge a fresh proof at any time during the continuance of the bankruptcy, but not so as to disturb prior dividends.'

1 [1996] 1 AC 243, HL.
2 [1924] 1 Ch 342 at page 375 (PO Lawrence J).

16.36   A later adjustment to the proof cannot affect prior dividends.

If the amount of any proof is increased after a dividend has been paid, the prior dividend cannot be disturbed, but the increased proof is entitled to catch up out of later dividends before further amounts are payable to other creditors. The increased proof ranks in all later dividends –see rules 2.101 (administration) and 4.182(2) (liquidation) and 11.8(1) and (2).

If an amount of a proof is reduced or expunged after a dividend has been paid (eg if a contingency did not occur), the creditor becomes liable to repay any amount over paid – rule 11.8(3).

In *Stanhope Pension Trust Ltd v Registrar of Companies*[1] Hoffmann LJ (as he then was) commented:

> 'It is a general principle of insolvency law that although a creditor can prove (or increase the amount of his proof) at any time during the liquidation, distributions which have already been properly made cannot be disturbed.'

1 [1994] 1 BCLC 628, CA

16.37   Creditors who are dissatisfied with decisions about extent of proof etc can apply to court to review the decision – rules 2.78 (administration) and 4.83 (liquidation).

APPLICATION TO EMPLOYEE CLAIMS

16.38   Applying these principles to different sorts of potential employee termination claim, the following is suggested:

Nature of Claim	Provable if termination after insolvency date?
Protective award	No – too contingent
TUPE claim	No – too contingent
Unfair dismissal claim	No – too contingent
Statutory redundancy pay	No – too contingent
Contractual redundancy pay	No – too contingent
Wrongful dismissal claim	Yes - derives from employment contract
Holiday Pay	Preferential if in respect of any period of employment before the date of insolvency, but only if employment is terminated (before the date of insolvency) Paras 10 and 14(2), Sch 6, IA 1986[1]
s75 claim by pension trustees	Unlikely to be relevant. Section 75 claim is triggered by the insolvency, although is contingent on a failure notice. Debt is deemed to arise immediately before the insolvency s 75(4A), PA 1995 (and see Chapter 25 below).
CN or FSD by Pensions Regulator	No – too contingent. Depends on future exercise of discretion – similar to *Glenister* and *Steele*.

16.39   It is difficult to be definitive as to which claims are provable and which are not.

16.40   Protective awards: At one end of the scale in relation to termination claims are protective awards. Such claims arise if there is a relevant dismissal without proper consultation (see Chapter 3 above). So if the dismissal is after the insolvency date, this looks as though it is not provable at all.

There could be an argument that the obligation to consult may have arisen before dismissal (may even in some senses have arisen before the insolvency date), but this seems tenuous.

In *Day v Haine*[1], at para [88] of the judgment, the Court of Appeal referred to the obligation to consult under s 188 as being one which 'plainly arose before the liquidation of the company'. This may point to a need to consider the situation where the dismissals may have been made after insolvency, but arguably an obligation to consult arose before insolvency.

An obligation to consult under TULRCA can arise even if no dismissals ultimately take place.

1 [2008] EWCA Civ 626; [2008] ICR 1102; [2008] IRLR 642; [2008] 2 BCLC 517, CA.

16.41   **TUPE claims:** Various claims can arise against the insolvent company under TUPE if there is a relevant transfer after the insolvency date. Most relevant liabilities to and in respect of employees will transfer under TUPE to the relevant transferee and no liability would remain with the transferor (the insolvent company) – see para 19.5 below. But some liabilities will remain with the insolvent company – see para 19.7 below – eg liabilities for non-transferring employees or under the information and consultation obligations (TUPE 2006, reg 15(9)).

The obligation under TUPE to inform and consult representatives of employees applies 'long enough before' a relevant transfer takes place to allow consultation (see Chapter 3 above). It has been held that this means that the obligation to inform and consult can arise even though no transfer ultimately takes place – see the EAT in *Banking Insurance and Finance Union v Barclays Bank plc*[1] and in *South Durham Health Authority v UNISON*[2].

So depending on the relevant timing, it could be argued that this consultation obligation could have arisen before the insolvency date, even if no transfer actually ultimately took place.

Even if a transfer did take place, the transferor (the insolvent company) would remain liable for any breach (under TUPE 2006 this is a joint and several liability with the transferee – see reg 15(9) and para 21.15 below).

The amount of any award for failure to comply with the information and consultation obligation under reg 15 is such amount as the tribunal considers to be 'just and equitable, having regard to the seriousness of the failure of the employer to comply with his duty', subject to a maximum of 13 weeks' pay. This is similar to the position in relation to protective awards in giving a discretion to the tribunal. The principles stated by the Court of Appeal in *Day v Haine*[1] in relation to protective awards under TULRCA 1992 will also apply here, namely that TUPE enacts a European obligation and the TUPE award is meant to be penal and so should be for the full amount unless there are good reasons to the contrary (see para 16.28 above).

1 [1987] ICR 495, EAT.
2 [1995] ICR 495; [1995] IRLR 407, EAT.
3 [2008] EWCA Civ 626; [2008] ICR 1102; [2008] IRLR 642; [2008] 2 BCLC 517, CA.

16.42   **Unfair dismissals:** In relation to an unfair dismissal claim, this includes an element of discretion. The compensatory award is fixed as an amount as the employment tribunal considers to be just and equitable (ERA 1996, s 123).

Unlike protective awards, there is generally a qualification period for unfair dismissal claims – namely one year's prior service. However it still looks like a claim that only crystallises on a dismissal and not by reference to previous period of service. The amount of the basic award does relate to age and prior service (see Chapter 2 above).

16.43   In a case before an industrial tribunal, *MSF v Parkfield Castings*[1], the tribunal considered that claims by employees for unfair dismissal and protective awards against a company in administration, were not prohibited by the statutory moratorium on claims then under s 11(3)(d), IA 1986. The tribunal seems to have considered that the employees were not creditors of the company before any award had been made by a tribunal and, accordingly, fell outside the prohibition on proceedings in the section.

This decision is considered to be wrong in relation to the statutory moratorium (see Chapter 5 above) but could still be relevant in relation to a proof of debt issue.

In Australia, claims by employees for an award from the Industrial Relations Commission have been held not to be a provable debt, even where the circumstances giving rise to the claim occurred before the date on which the winding-up began – see *Silbermann v One.Tel Ltd*[2] applying comments in *Fisher v Madden*[3] and *Buckingham v Pan Laboratories (Australia) Pty Limited (in liquidation)*[4].

1 (1993) IDS Brief (February) (IT).
2 (2002) 20 ACLC 846 (Gzell J)
3 [2002] NSWCA 28; (2001-2002) 54 NSWLR 179, NSW CA.
4 [2004] FCA 597 (Jacobson J).

16.44   Statutory redundancy: Similarly in relation to statutory redundancy claims – again the amount is fixed by reference to a combination of age and prior service (see Chapter 2 above).

For an example in a discrimination context of it being held that (in effect) redundancy awards did not (broadly) accrue over past service – see the House of Lords in *Barry v Midland Bank plc*[1].

It could be argued that the tax case of *IRC v Cosmotron Manufacturing Co Ltd*[2] points the other way. The Privy Council held that payments of redundancy pay reflected obligations incurred during the course of the relevant business and so remained deductible even though only paid after the business had shut down.

1 [1999] 3 All ER 974; [1999] 1 WLR 1465; [1999] ICR 859; [1999] IRLR 581, HL.
2 [1997] 1 WLR 1288; [1997] STC 1134, PC.

16.45   Contractual redundancy: Similar principles should apply to as to statutory redundancy. True the obligation flows from an existing contract, but the claim is triggered by the termination.

16.46   Discrimination dismissals: If the relevant discrimination only occurred after the insolvency date then again it looks too contingent. There is no qualifying period here. But the insolvency practitioner may be personally liable if he or she has aided such discrimination – see Chapter 8 (Personal liability of Insolvency Practitioners) above.

16.47   **Wrongful dismissal claims:** These look like claims for breach of contract. They derive from the underlying contract and so therefore seem as though they should be provable. It could be arguable that the amount of the proof should be limited to the relevant claim that could have been made as at the insolvency date less any pay actually received since then – i.e. credit should be given for later (paid) service after the insolvency date. This should be given whether or not this notice was in fact given by the insolvency practitioner?

16.48   **Holiday pay:**
   Holiday pay can cause some issues. Accrued holiday pay as at the insolvency date will be a preferential debt if the employment is actually later terminated (see Sch 6, IA 1986). If the employee has accrued holiday entitlement as at the insolvency date and later actually takes the holiday (and is paid), then any claim will reduce. Apportioning holiday actually taken can be difficult – see *Re Douai School*[1].

   Payment of accrued holiday pay and long service leave entitlements has been an issue over the years in Australia. Generally see *Re Matthew Bros*[2] and *McEvoy v Incat Tasmania*[3]. It was held in those cases that even following the statutory changes in Australia, there was no requirement imposed on receivers to pay holiday pay or long service leave for employees who had not been dismissed by the receiver on his appointment.

   In *Incat,* Finkelstein J noted that the position of a liquidation (where employment and business would usually cease) and receivership (where is may continue) were fundamentally different. He commented:

> 'Yet there are many respects in which a receivership is unlike a liquidation. In most cases, once a company is placed into liquidation all employees will, in due course, be dismissed because a liquidation usually spells the death of a company. Receiverships are different. In the first place, they do not affect the existence of the company. Secondly, it is often in the interests of the chargee that the company continue its business. To that end, staff are kept on and are often unaffected by the receivership. In those cases, a construction which places employees of a company in receivership on the same footing as employees of a company which has been wound up will operate in a discriminatory fashion, as the former employees will both keep their jobs and be paid out as if they had lost them.'

1 [2000] 1 WLR 502 (Neuberger J) and paras 9.59 above and 18.61 below.
2 [1962] VR 262 (Gowans J).
3 [2003] FCA 810 (Finkelstein J).

CHAPTER 17

Carrying on business – insolvency expenses

INSOLVENCY EXPENSES: INTRODUCTION

17.1   The Insolvency Rules 1986[1] contain a list of expenses applicable in a liquidation and in an administration. The general rule is that insolvency expenses are payable by the insolvency practitioner out of the relevant assets of the company in priority to the other claims in the insolvency process.

Secured claims take the relevant secured property out of the assets within the insolvency and so are not subject to this priority – see *Buchler v Talbot*[2] and para 4.19 above.

Administrative receivership is an enforcement process under the relevant floating change and so is not generally governed by the Insolvency Rules.

1 SI 1986/1925, as amended.
2 [2004] UKHL 9; [2004] 2 AC 298, HL.

17.2   The relevant rules are in rules 4.218 to 4.218E (liquidations) and 2.67 (administrations) (as amended for those starting on or after 15 September 2003). Separate special provisions apply in relation to adopted employment contracts (see Chapter 18 below)

17.3   The Court of Appeal in *Re Atlantic Computer Systems plc*[1] dealt with the position of administrators in relation to liabilities incurred during the course of an administration. The court analysed the position by comparison with the position of liquidators on one hand and receivers on the other. Accordingly, the judgment contains a detailed review of the position in relation to liquidators, receivers and administrators[2].

1 [1992] Ch 505. CA.
2 For a detailed analysis (before the decisions in *Toshoku* and *Freakley* and the changes made by the Enterprise Act 2002), see Segal and Moss 'The Expenses Doctrine in Liquidation. Administrations and Receiverships' [1997] Company Financial and Insolvency Law Review 1 at pages 19 and 20

17.4   However this analysis (at least in relation to liquidators) was considered and, to an extent disagreed with by the House of Lords in *Re Toshoku Finance UK plc: Kahn v IRC*[1]. Subsequently it seems that the position have shifted back (at least for administrators in administrations starting before 15 September 2003) – see the decision of the House of Lords in *Freakley v Centre Reinsurance International Co*[2].

1 [2002] UKHL 6; [2002] 1 WLR 671, HL.
2 [2006] UKHL 45; [2006] 1 WLR 2863, HL.

INSOLVENCY EXPENSES: LIQUIDATORS

17.5 In *Re Atlantic Computer Systems plc*, Nicholls LJ (as he then was) gave the judgment of the court. In relation to liquidators he referred to the IA 1986, s 130(2). This provides that, following the making of a winding-up order by the court, no action or proceeding can be commenced or continued against the company or its property except by leave of the court (see Chapter 5 (Insolvency moratorium) above).

17.6 Nicholls LJ referred to the decision of Jessel MR in *Re Traders' North Staffordshire Carrying Co, ex p North Staffordshire Railway Co*[1] and commented that the attitude of the court in considering whether to grant leave to a person to seize the property of the company (as opposed to the property of the applicant, such as property under lease or mortgage) was to consider if the granting would be inconsistent with the purpose for which Parliament had imposed the prohibition on proceedings. The effect would be to give preference to the creditor whereas the intention of Parliament 'was to prevent any such preference being obtainable after commencement of the winding up'.

1 (1874) LR 19 Eq 60 (Jessel MR).

17.7 Nicholls LJ commented further (at page 522):

'However, the matter stands differently if the debt, in respect of which the creditor is seeking to exercise a remedy against the company's property, was a new debt incurred by the liquidator for the purposes of the liquidation. In such a case the grant of leave would not be inconsistent with the purpose of the legislation. In such a case it is just and equitable that the burden of debt should be borne by those for whose benefit the insolvent estate is being administered. The court should exercise its discretion accordingly. The creditor should be at liberty to enforce his rights against the company's property if his debt is not paid in full. Further, and by way of corollary, since the debt was incurred for the purposes of the liquidation, it is properly to be regarded as an expense of the liquidation and it ought to be paid as such. The court will direct the liquidator accordingly.

'This latter principle is not confined to new debts incurred by the liquidator. It applies also to continuing obligations under existing contracts such as leases which the liquidator chooses to continue for the benefit of the winding up. Thus, the principle is applicable in respect of rent accruing due while the liquidator retains the leasehold land for the purpose of the winding up. The lessor should be paid in full, or be allowed to distrain. The principle is equally applicable in the case of other liabilities incurred in the course of winding up; for example where rates become due in respect of land occupied by the liquidator for the purpose of the winding up: see *Re International Marine Hydropathic Co*[1].'

1 (1884) 28 Ch D 470, CA.

17.8 Further, Nicholls LJ continued (at page 523):

'It is important to keep in mind that this principle, relating to outgoings on property retained by a liquidator for the purposes of winding up, is no more than a principle applied by the court when exercising its discretion in a winding up. The principle, which it will be convenient to call the "liquidation expenses" principle, is a statement of how, in general, the court will exercise its discretion in a common form set of circumstances. The liquidator himself has power, in a suitable case, to pay the relevant outgoings. But the court retains an overriding discretion, to give leave under s 130(2) or to give directions to a liquidator that the relevant outgoings shall be paid by him as expense of the liquidation.'

17.9 However in *Re Toshoku Finance UK plc, Kahn v IRC*[1], the House of Lords held that whether or not debts should count as expenses of a liquidation is not a matter for the discretion of the court. The application of rule 4.218 of the Insolvency Rules 1986 (SI 1986/1925 – see para 17.32 below) is mandatory when determining what type of expense counts as a liquidation expense (see para 38 of the judgment).

However although the court has no discretion in deciding what types of expenses are entitled to priority, the categories set out in r 4.218 should be interpreted in the light of established legal principles.

1 [2002] UKHL 6; [2002] 1 WLR 671, HL.

17.10 Lord Hoffmann gave the only judgment. He drew a fundamental distinction between debts under pre-liquidation contracts and those arising post liquidation. He held (at para 25):

'Thus debts arising out of pre-liquidation contracts such as leases, whether they accrue before or after the liquidation, can and prima facie should be proved in the liquidation. In this respect they are crucially different from normal liquidation expenses, which are incurred after the liquidation date and cannot be proved for'.

17.11 So Lord Hoffmann considered that debts incurred after the commencement of the liquidation would automatically be liquidation expenses (within rule 4.218(a) of the Insolvency Rules 1986). He stated (at para 30):

'Expenses incurred after the liquidation date need no further equitable reason why they should be paid. Of course it will generally be true that such expenses will have been incurred by the liquidator for the purposes of the liquidation. It is not the business of the liquidator to incur expenses for any other purpose. But this is not at all the same thing as saying that the expenses will necessarily be for the benefit of estate. They may simply be liabilities which, as liquidator, he has to pay'.

17.12 But expenses under pre-liquidation contracts would normally only be provable in the liquidation. However, Lord Hoffmann accepted and approved the line of authority that allows certain amounts under such pre-liquidation contracts to be treated as liquidation expenses, following the decision of the Court of Appeal in *Lundy Granite Co*[1].

1 (1871) LR 6 Ch App 462, CA.

17.13   The *Lundy Granite Co* principle is one which permits, on equitable grounds, the concept of a liability incurred as an expense of the liquidation to be expanded to include liabilities incurred before the liquidation in respect of property afterwards retained by the liquidator for the benefit of the insolvent estate. Lord Hoffmann held that this principle was not a matter of general unfettered judicial discretion, but instead was a settled legal principle. He held (at para 38):

> 'The second point is the proposition that whether debts should count as expenses of the liquidation is a matter for the discretion of the court. In my opinion there is no such discretion. Rule 4.218 determines what counts as expenses, subject only to the limited discretion under s 156 of the 1986 Act to re-arrange the priorities of expenses inter se. The court will of course interpret r 4.218 to include debts which, under the *Lundy Granite Co* principle, are deemed to be expenses of the liquidation. Ordinarily this means that debts such as rents under a lease will be treated as coming within para (a) [of rule 4.218], but the principle may possibly enlarge the scope of other paragraphs as well. But the application of that principle does not involve an exercise of discretion any more than the application of any other legal principle to the particular facts of the case.'

17.14   Although IA 1986, s 130 is applicable only to a winding up by the court, it seems that similar principles in relation to 'liquidation expenses' will apply to a voluntary winding up, even in the absence of any statutory prohibition on proceedings – see *Re Levi & Co Ltd*[1]. The court has a discretion to give directions to the liquidator under the IA 1986, s 112 to pay relevant outgoings as expenses of the liquidation. This may allow it to direct the liquidator (under the *Lundy Granite Co* principle) to pay relevant outgoings as expenses of the liquidation. Rule 4.218 of the Insolvency Rules 1986 applies to a creditors' voluntary winding up and to a winding up by the court, but not to a members' voluntary winding up (see rule 4.1).

1 [1919] 1 Ch 416 at 423 (Astbury J).

17.15   Although there is little case law on the subject, it seems that the 'liquidation expenses' principle outlined by Nicholls LJ and Lord Hoffmann will apply also to outgoings in respect of employees where they are retained in the business at the instance of a liquidator.

17.16   Most of the relevant cases relate to liabilities of a company in relation to leases of land. It is clear from these cases that the liabilities in respect of rent accrued during the period up to the date of the appointment of the liquidator are merely provable in the liquidation and do not count as liquidation expenses.

17.17   Conversely, where the liquidator has retained the property for the purposes of the liquidation (and it seems some positive action is needed for this), the future rent may be a liquidation expense – see for example, *Re ABC Coupler and Engineering Co Ltd (No 3)*[1]. The Court of Appeal cited this with approval in 2006 in *Thomas v Ken Thomas Ltd*[2], holding:

> 'It strikes me that, at least normally, it would seem wrong in principle that a tenant should be able to trade under a CVA for the benefit of its past creditors, at the present and future expense of its landlord. If the tenant is to continue occupying the landlord's property for the purposes of trading under the CVA (and hopefully trading out of the CVA) he should normally, as it currently appears to me, expect to pay the full rent to which the landlord is contractually entitled – see by analogy, in the administration context, *Re Atlantic Computer Systems plc* [1992] Ch 505, 542(g) – 543(b) and, in a liquidation context, *Re ABC Coupler & Engineering Co Ltd (No 3)* [1970] 1 All ER 650.

1 [1970] 1 All ER 650 (Plowman J).
2 [2006] EWCA Civ 1504; [2006] All ER (D) 100 (Oct), at para 34.

17.18 For pre-liquidation contracts, it seems that the liquidator must have some control over the asset retained. However, it seems that this is not the case for post-liquidation claims arising by statute eg for tax or the community charge or rates – see *Re Toshoku Finance UK plc; Kahn v IRC*[1] overruling *Re Kentish Homes Ltd*[2] on this point (see also below).

1 [2002] UKHL 6; [2002] 1 WLR 671, HL.
2 [1993] BCC 212; [1993] 1 BCLC 1375 (Sir Donald Nicholls V-C).

Status of termination claims as insolvency expenses

17.19 The position of any claims of employees on the subsequent termination of their employment by the company (at the instigation of the liquidator) is more difficult; obviously such claims may relate to damages for breach of contract (eg failure to give notice), unfair dismissal claims, redundancy pay, protective awards, etc (see para 15.23 above). It is unclear whether such termination claims rank as liquidation expenses.

17.20 In principle, it would seem arguable that, to the extent that such termination claims would have arisen on termination of employment by the company at the date of appointment of the liquidator, such claims should be provable as a debt in the liquidation and should not rank as liquidation expenses. To argue otherwise would effectively give such termination claims a priority over other claims on the company. While it would seem in principle that this can be justified in relation to claims which relate to further work done as part of the winding up (and which presumably benefit the creditors), in principle it would seem wrong to extend this priority to claims which relate to earlier periods of employment. It may, of course, be the case that the effect of continuing employment has been to increase the termination claims (eg where the period of continuous employment of an employee gains a completed year whilst the employee is in continuing employment at the instigation of the liquidator, so that statutory claims for redundancy and notice periods, etc are increased).

257

17.21 There is (perhaps surprisingly) little case law on the topic of liquidation expenses. Astbury J in *Re Levi & Company Ltd*[1] held that sums (relating to dilapidations) payable on the termination of a lease entered into by the company prior to the appointment of the liquidator but where the liquidator had elected that the company should retain possession for some seven years (receiving sub-rents from a sub-tenant) were liquidation expenses. No attempt appears to have been made to apportion the dilapidation claims between periods before and after the commencement of the liquidation (this may have been difficult to do given the length of time for which the liquidator continued the occupation). Astbury J did state (at page 419) that:

> 'It is suggested that some portion of the dilapidations may have been caused before the commencement of the liquidation, but that consideration is of no importance in the present case, having regard to the covenant by the lessees to deliver up the premises in good repair at the expiration of the term.'

1 [1919] 1 Ch 416 (Astbury J).

17.22 The court's attitude may well have been influenced by the existence of the sub-lease; it may have seemed unfair for the liquidator to collect rent and, presumably, sums in respect of dilapidations from the sub-tenant but not pay the head landlord.

17.23 Similarly, in the Australian case of *Re Matthew Bros*[1] Gowans J held that a payment in lieu of long service leave to which the employee had become entitled by virtue of service both before and after commencement of the winding-up was a liquidation expense.

1 [1962] VR 262 (Gowans J).

17.24 Conversely, in *Re ABC Coupler and Engineering Co Ltd (No 3)*[1], Plowman J held that rent due under a lease was to be apportioned between the periods before and after the commencement of the liquidation.

1 [1970] 1 All ER 650 (Plowman J).

17.25 However, in the Paramount Airways case, *Powdrill v Watson*[1] the argument was raised that the position of an administrator or administrative receiver should be treated in a similar way to the position of a liquidator, as outlined above, so that it was argued that liability is limited to liabilities incurred in relation to services actually rendered (ie not category 3 termination claims). However, in the House of Lords, Lord Browne-Wilkinson referred (at page 450) to the 'salvage' cases applicable to liquidations. He held that:

> 'Although the authorities show that debts incurred before the liquidation do not obtain priority, they indicate that even on the salvage principle all liabilities under a contract incurred after the time of adoption of the contract by a liquidator are entitled to priority.'

1 [1995] 2 AC 394, HL.

17.26   Lord Browne-Wilkinson then referred to *Re S Davis and Co Ltd*[1] and *Re Levi & Company Ltd*[2] (*Re Matthew Bros* was cited in argument but not in Lord Browne-Wilkinson's opinion). He went on to state that:

> 'The salvage principle in liquidation indicates that if a liquidator adopts a contract for the purpose of the more beneficial conduct of a liquidation, all such liabilities under such contract after the date of adoption are entitled to priority.'

1 [1945] Ch 402 (Cohen J).
2 [1919] 1 Ch 416 (Astbury J) – see para 17.21 above.

17.27   These comments add to the uncertainty for liquidators. For example, it is not clear whether the 'salvage principle' extends only to contractual liabilities (as is the case for receivers and administrators under the statutory provisions relating to 'adopted employment contracts' – see para 18.72 below) or if it extends as well to statutory liabilities (eg for unfair dismissal).

17.28   Subsequently in Australia, the courts held that a court appointed receiver was not liable for claims of employees, even for services after the date of the appointment. In *Sipad Holding DDPO v Popovic*[1] Lehane J held that any such liability was incurred 'when the contracts of employment were entered into by the company before the receiver's appointment'. *Powdrill v Watson* was not cited.

1 [1995] FCA 1737; (1996) 14 ACLC 307 at 310 (Lehane J).

17.29   A 2005 case in the UK dealt with the status of employee claims in an administration. In *Re Allders Department Stores Ltd*[1] it was argued that the same rule on expenses should apply in an administration as in a liquidation so that statutory liabilities for unfair dismissal and redundancy awards should be treated as an insolvency expense following the House of Lords decision in *Re Toshoku Finance*.

1 [2005] EWHC 172 (Ch); [2005] 2 All ER 122 (Lawrence Collins J).

17.30   Lawrence Collins J gave a number of reasons for rejecting that claim:

> 'I do not consider that the statutory liabilities for redundancy payments or unfair dismissal claims would be 'necessary disbursements' for the purposes of r 2.67(1)(f).
>
> First, it would be inconsistent with the scheme of the legislation if the payments referred to in Sch 6 were to be treated as preferential, and yet all other employee-related payments are to be paid as an expense of the administration. That would be to give the Sch 6 payments (which include protective awards) a lesser priority than other types of payments, when the policy appears to have been to give them a greater priority.
>
> Second, there is nothing in my judgment in *Re Toshoku Finance* [2002] 3 All ER 961, [2002] 1 WLR 671 which requires a different conclusion. It is not the ratio of that case that any liability imposed on a company which is not provable as a debt is thereby rendered a 'necessary disbursement'. The context in which Lord Hoffmann referred to the fact that certain debts could not be proved shows that he

was justifying the treatment of certain debts as expenses, and not offering a definition of what liabilities were disbursements. Even if that were the crucial test for winding up, there would be no reason to apply it to administration. Although the current regime envisages a distribution to secured and preferential creditors without a subsequent liquidation, in the normal case of an administration which does not succeed in rescuing the company, the company will go into liquidation and the statutory payment obligation will be a provable debt under r 13.12B.

Finally, a construction of r 2.67(1)(f) which applied it to statutory redundancy payment liabilities and other statutory liabilities would have such adverse policy consequences on the administration regime that it is impossible to see that such a result could have been intended.'

The first and third reasons seem equally valid for a liquidation.

17.31   In *Exeter City Council v Bairstow, Re Trident Fashions*[1] David Richards J was concerned with the question of whether non-domestic rates on premises occupied by the company during the course of the administration were payable as an expense of the administration proceedings. Following the principles laid down by the House of Lords in *Re Toshoku Finance*, he held that that non-domestic rates were payable as a 'necessary disbursement' under rule 2.67(f) of the Insolvency Rules 1986. David Richards J held that the more flexible approach envisaged in pre 15 September 2003 administrations under *Re Atlantic Computers* and in *Re Freakley* did not apply in post-14 September 2003 administrations, given that the underlying insolvency rules had changed to a form similar to those applicable in a liquidation.

David Richards J referred to the decisions relating to liabilities to employees of the Court of Appeal in *Re Huddersfield Fine Worsteds Ltd*[2] and of Lawrence Collins J in *Re Allders Department Stores Ltd*[3]. He did not cast any doubt on the decisions, but distinguished *Re Allders Department Stores*, holding (at para 77):

'It appears to me that the principal basis of the decision was that because of the special treatment of certain categories of employment-related claims under paragraph 99 and under schedule 6, it would be inconsistent to treat further categories as expenses under rule 2.67. I concur with that analysis.'

The actual decision in *Re Trident Fashions* on non-domestic rates was reversed from 1 April 2008 by the Non-Domestic Rating (Unoccupied Property) (England) Regulations 2008[4]. Regulation 4(l) provides that companies in administration are not liable for rates in respect of empty properties for the whole period of the administration.

1 [2007] EWHC 400 (Ch); [2007] All ER (D) 45 (Mar) (David Richards J).
2 [2005] 4 All ER 886, CA. See para 17.59 below.
3 [2005] 2 All ER 122 (Lawrence Collins J).
4 SI 2008/386.

Priority of debts and liabilities: liquidations

17.32   Where the assets of the company are insufficient to meet all liquidation expenses, the priority by which the expenses are payable is set out in rule 4.218(3) of the Insolvency Rules 1986[1].

'(3) Subject as provided in Rules 4.218A to 4.218E, the expenses are payable in the following order of priority—

(a)   expenses which—

    (i)   are properly chargeable or incurred by the provisional liquidator in carrying out the functions conferred on him by the court;

    (ii)   are properly chargeable or incurred by the official receiver or the liquidator in preserving, realising or getting in any of the assets of the company or otherwise in the preparation or conduct of any legal proceedings, arbitration or other dispute resolution procedures, which he has power to bring in his own name or bring or defend in the name of the company or in the preparation or conduct of any negotiations intended to lead or leading to a settlement or compromise of any legal action or dispute to which the proceedings or procedures relate;

    (iii)   relate to the employment of a shorthand writer, if appointed by an order of the court made at the instance of the official receiver in connection with an examination; or

    (iv)   are incurred in holding an examination under Rule 4.214 (examinee unfit) where the application for it was made by the official receiver;]

(b)   any other expenses incurred or disbursements made by the official receiver or under his authority, including those incurred or made in carrying on the business of the company;

(c)   the fees payable under any order made under section 414 or section 415A, including those payable to the official receiver (other than the fee referred to in sub-paragraph (d)(i) below), and any remuneration payable to him under general regulations;

(d)

    (i)   the fee payable under any order made under section 414 for the performance by the official receiver of his general duties as official receiver;

    (ii)   any repayable deposit lodged under any such order as security for the fee mentioned in sub-paragraph (i);

(e)   the cost of any security provided by a provisional liquidator, liquidator or special manager in accordance with the Act or the Rules;

(f)   the remuneration of the provisional liquidator (if any);

(g)   any deposit lodged on an application for the appointment of a provisional liquidator;

(h)   the costs of the petitioner, and of any person appearing on the petition whose costs are allowed by the court;

(j)   the remuneration of the special manager (if any);

(k)   any amount payable to a person employed or authorised, under Chapter 6 of this Part of the Rules, to assist in the preparation of a statement of affairs or of accounts;

> (l) any allowance made, by order of the court, towards costs on an application for release from the obligation to submit a statement of affairs, or for an extension of time for submitting such a statement;
>
> (la) the costs of employing a shorthand writer in any case other than one appointed by an order of the court at the instance of the official receiver in connection with an examination;
>
> (m) any necessary disbursements by the liquidator in the course of his administration (including any expenses incurred by members of the liquidation committee or their representatives and allowed by the liquidator under Rule 4.169, but not including any payment of [corporation] tax in circumstances referred to in sub-paragraph (p) below);
>
> (n) the remuneration or emoluments of any person who has been employed by the liquidator to perform any services for the company, as required or authorised by or under the Act or the Rules;
>
> (o) the remuneration of the liquidator, up to any amount not exceeding that which is payable under Schedule 6
>
> (p) the amount of any corporation tax on chargeable gains accruing on the realisation of any asset of the company (without regard to whether the realisation is effected by the liquidator, a secured creditor, or a receiver or manager appointed to deal with a security);
>
> (q) the balance, after payment of any sums due under sub-paragraph (o) above, of any remuneration due to the liquidator;
>
> (r) any other expenses properly chargeable by the liquidator in carrying out his functions in the liquidation.'
>
> Rule 4.218(3), Insolvency Rules 1986

Normally, remuneration for employees will count as 'expenses properly chargeable or incurred by . . . the liquidator in preserving, realising or getting in any of the assets of the company' within rule 4.218(a)(ii) and thus have priority over all other liquidation expenses.

1 SI 1986/1925, as amended.

17.33   Alternatively, (but less likely) claims by employees may be considered to be 'remuneration or emoluments of any person who has been employed by the liquidator to perform any services for the company, as required or authorised by or under the Act or the Rules' within rule 4.218(3)(n) and thus rank just ahead of the remuneration of the liquidator under rule 4.218(3)(o).

But such an interpretation of the equivalent provisions in relation to administration in rule 2.67(1)(g) was rejected by Lawrence Collins J in *Re Allders Department Stores Ltd*[1] (see para 17.58 below). It seems that rule 4.218(3)(n) only applies to persons actually employed by the liquidator (and not by the company).

1 [2005] 2 All ER 122, [2005] EWHC 172 (Ch) at para 23.

17.34   This is subject to the limited discretion of the court under s 156 of the Insolvency Act 1986 to re-arrange the priorities of the liquidation expenses inter se (rule 4.220).

17.35   In practice, the effect of continuing to employ various employees may well be to reduce the claims of those employees in respect of any termination on the date of commencement of the liquidation. Any claim for damages for wrongful dismissal will need to be subject to reduction to reflect the fact that the employee has been able to mitigate his loss (even if he does not accept the offer from the liquidator) by accepting continued employment with the company (see, for example, *Reid v The Explosives Company Ltd*[1]).

1   (1887) 19 QBD 264, CA.

17.36   A claim for a redundancy payment will still arise at the date of termination of employment even if there is re-employment by the liquidator, on the basis that the offer of re-employment will be made after the date of appointment of the liquidator and will not fall within ERA 1996, s 138(1) because an offer would not have been made by the employer (or an associated employer) before the ending of the employment under the previous contract – see *Rowan v Machinery Installations (South Wales) Ltd*[1].

1   [1981] ICR 386, EAT.

17.37   Given the uncertainty as to whether or not termination claims would rank as liquidation expenses, it may be that a liquidator would seek to make it a term of a contract for employment which continues after the appointment of a liquidator that any such termination claims would not rank as liquidation expenses.

17.38   In practice, as a matter of insolvency law, the principle relating to liquidation expenses is one imposed by the courts for the sake of the proper conduct of the liquidation. There would seem to be no reason why the courts should seek to impose a rule that expenses would rank as liquidation expenses even where the party seeking to claim had expressly agreed in advance that his claim would not so rank. There is an analogy here with the courts allowing a contractual subordination to prevent a claim in an insolvency – see eg *Re SSSL Realisations (2002) Ltd*[1].

1   [2006] EWCA Civ 7; [2006] Ch 610; [2007] 1 BCLC 29, CA.

17.39   The argument that certain of the termination claims are statutory under ERA 1996 and it is not possible to contract out of such obligations (by virtue of ERA 1996, s 203), should not cause a difficulty here. The employer company is still liable in full, and the question is the extent of the liability of the insolvency practitioner or the extent to which the liability of the company can be met as an insolvency expense and hence given priority.

17.40   In practice, a liquidator in any event has only a limited power to continue to carry on the business of the company 'so far as may be necessary for its beneficial winding up' (see IA 1986, Sch 4, para 5 and para 4.18 above).

INSOLVENCY EXPENSES: ADMINISTRATORS

17.41   It is quite common for administrators to continue the business of the company during the administration. Indeed the purpose of the appointment of an administrator is commonly to seek to provide for:

- the survival of the company as a going concern[1]; or

- a better result for the company's creditors as a whole than would be likely if the company were wound-up[2].

1 See IA 1986, Sch B1, para 3(1)(a), replacing IA 1986, s 8(3)(a).
2 See IA 1986, Sch B1, para 3(1)(b), replacing IA 1986, s 8(3)(d).

17.42   An administrator is deemed to act as the agent of the company[1]. In addition, following the appointment of an administrator, no legal process or steps to enforce security can be commenced or continued against the company except with the leave of the court or the administrator[2].

1 IA 1986, Sch B1, para 69, replacing IA 1986, s 14(5).
2 IA 1986, Sch B1, para 43, replacing IA 1986, s 11(3)(d) – see Chapter 5 (Insolvency moratorium) above).

17.43   Unlike an administrative receiver, an administrator does not have a statutory indemnity out of the assets of the company for liabilities incurred by him or her. However, IA 1986, Sch B1, para 99 (replacing IA 1986, s 19) does deal with the position of an administrator in relation to such liabilities on termination of the administration.

Priority of debts and liabilities: administrations

17.44   IA 1986, Sch B1, para 99(3) (replacing IA 1986, s 19(4)) provides that the administrator's remuneration and any expenses properly incurred are to be charged on and paid out of any property of the company which is in the custody and control of the administrator in priority to any security within para 70 (ie any security which, as created, was a floating charge). It seems implicit that the priority in para 99(3) applies even if there is no actual floating charge.

17.45   As originally enacted (and before its amendment by the Insolvency Act 1994), IA 1986, s 19(5):

- gave priority to debts or liabilities incurred by an administrator 'under contracts entered into or contracts of employment adopted by him . . . in the carrying out of his . . . functions' and

- stated that relevant sums are to be charged on and paid out of any property of the company which is in the custody and control of the administrator in priority to any charge arising under s 19(4).

17.46   Section 19(5) went on to state that the administrator is not to be taken to have adopted a contract of employment by reason of anything done or omitted to be done within 14 days after his appointment (for further discussion of this provision see para 18.132 below).

Rule 2.67 of the Insolvency Rules 1986 now states:

'2.67

(1) The expenses of the administration are payable in the following order of priority—

    (a) expenses properly incurred by the administrator in performing his functions in the administration of the company; (b) the cost of any security provided by the administrator in accordance with the Act or the Rules;

    (c) where an administration order was made, the costs of the applicant and any person appearing on the hearing of the application and where the administrator was appointed otherwise than by order of the court, any costs and expenses of the appointor in connection with the making of the appointment and the costs and expenses incurred by any other person in giving notice of intention to appoint an administrator;

    (d) any amount payable to a person employed or authorised, under Chapter 5 of this Part of the Rules, to assist in the preparation of a statement of affairs or statement of concurrence;

    (e) any allowance made, by order of the court, towards costs on an application for release from the obligation to submit a statement of affairs or statement of concurrence;

    (f) any necessary disbursements by the administrator in the course of the administration (including any expenses incurred by members of the creditors' committee or their representatives and allowed for by the administrator under Rule 2.63, but not including any payment of corporation tax in circumstances referred to in sub-paragraph (j) below);

    (g) the remuneration or emoluments of any person who has been employed by the administrator to perform any services for the company, as required or authorised under the Act or the Rules;

    (h) the remuneration of the administrator agreed under Chapter 11 of this Part of the Rules;

    (j) the amount of any corporation tax on chargeable gains accruing on the realisation of any asset of the company (without regard to whether the realisation is effected by the administrator, a secured creditor, or a receiver or manager appointed to deal with a security).'

17.47 It was against this statutory background that the Court of Appeal in *Re Atlantic Computer Systems plc*[1] decided that the position of an administrator was more properly considered to be treated in the same way as a liquidator (given the similar statutory prohibition on legal proceedings – see para 4.50 above) rather than as an administrative receiver.

1 [1992] Ch 505, CA.

17.48 The Court of Appeal decided that a flexible approach should be adopted in relation to administration expenses, Nicholls LJ (as he then was) stating (at page 528):

'If this flexible approach is right, there is no room in administrations for the application of a rigid principle that, if land or goods in the company's possession under an existing lease or hire-purchase agreement are used for the purposes of an administration, the continuing rent or hire charges will rank automatically as expenses of the administration and as such be payable by the administrator ahead (so it would seem) of the pre-administration creditors. Nor, even, for a principle that leave to take proceedings will be granted as of course. Such rigid principles would be inconsistent with the flexibility that, by giving the court a wide discretion, Parliament must have intended should apply.

This conclusion is consistent with s 19(5). If an administrator adopts an existing contract of employment, the liabilities arising under that contract are automatically payable as provided in that subsection. As to other existing contracts 'adopted' by an administrator, creditors have no automatic preference or priority.'

17.49   Nicholls LJ had earlier referred to the freeze on actions contained in s 11(3) (now para 43 of Sch B1) and commented that it was a like prohibition to that which exists when a winding-up order is made. He went on to state (at page 527):

'We regard this feature as of cardinal importance, distinguishing an administration from an administrative receivership in a respect vital to the matter now under consideration. This feature, coupled with the further feature that the court has power to give directions to the administrator on the conduct of an administration, leads inexorably to the conclusion that much of the reasoning which caused the courts to adopt what we have referred to as the ''liquidation expenses'' principle in the case of liquidations is also applicable in administrations but subject, in our view, to a very important qualification. In liquidations the principles on which the court will exercise its discretion have hardened into a set practice, both in relation to ''possession'' cases and in the application of the ''liquidation expenses'' principle. In ''possession'' cases leave is granted as of course. And in the circumstances in which the ''liquidation expenses'' principle is applicable, entitlement to have the outgoings paid as an expense of the liquidation seems to have become more or less automatic. In our view there is no place for comparable hard-and-fast principles in the case of administrations. The reason for this difference is that the objectives of winding up orders and administration orders are different and, hence, the approach that should be adopted by the court when exercising its discretion under the two regimes is different. In the case of winding up the company has reached the end of its life . . . In contrast, an administration is intended to be only an interim and temporary regime.'

17.50   Although the Court of Appeal went on to give some general guidance as to the principles which should be kept in mind by the administrator and the court in deciding whether or not to agree to particular actions (see pages 501 and 502 of the judgment), this guidance was expressly confined to the position where leave was sought to exercise existing proprietary rights, including security rights, against a company in administration. No guidance was given as to the position for contractual claims for 'administration expenses' and the position therefore remains unclear.

17.51   As mentioned in para 17.50 above, the analysis by Nicholls LJ in *Re Atlantic Computer Systems plc* of the position in relation to liquidations was overturned by the House of Lords in *Re Toshoku Finance UK plc; Kahn v IRC*[1], Lord Hoffmann giving the only reasoned decision.

1 [2002] UKHL 6; [2002] 3 All ER 961; [2002] 1 WLR 671, HL.

17.52   However, there is no hint in the speech of Lord Hoffmann that the principles laid down by Nicholls LJ should not continue to be followed in relation to administrations. Given the fundamental differences between liquidation and administration, it would seem likely that those principles would survive in relation to administrations, but this remained to be seen.

17.53   In Australia (by reference to a different set of statutory provisions), Warren J held in *Ansett Australia Ground Staff Superannuation Plan Pty Ltd v Ansett Australia Ltd*[1] referred to the English case law and held that pension claims did not rank as insolvency expenses.

1 [2002] VSC 576 (Warren J).

17.54   In *Freakley v Centre Reinsurance International Co*[1] the House of Lords dealt with a claim by insurers who had the right (under an insurance contract entered into before the administration started) that expenses incurred by the insurers (on behalf of the company) should be treated as expenses of the administration and so given priority under s 19(4) or (5) of IA 1986 (this was a pre September 2003 administration). The House of Lords held that they were not entitled to such a priority. The administrators had not authorised the expenses. But the House of Lords seems to have re-stated a more flexible approach compared to *Toshoku*. Lord Hoffmann again gave the only judgment. He did not refer to *Toshoku* at all (although it was cited to the court). He referred to *Atlantic Computers* with approval holding:

> '16 There seems to me no reason of policy why such obligations (which may or may not be in the interests of the administration) should be given priority over the company's other debts. As I have said, the purpose of administration under the 1986 Act was simply to impose a moratorium to allow time to find a way of saving the business or realising it to better advantage than in a liquidation. It was not intended to alter substantive rights or priorities more than was necessary to enable this objective to be achieved. The provisions of section 19(4) and (5) entrust to the administrator (subject to the supervision of the court) the power to decide what expenditure is necessary for the purposes of the administration and should therefore receive priority. But there is no reason to extend that priority to expenditure which neither the administrator nor the court has specifically approved.

> 17 The Court of Appeal in *re Atlantic Computer Systems plc* [1992] Ch 505 said that the court, exercising its supervisory powers over an administration, has a broad discretion to authorise or direct the administrator to make payments or enter into contracts for the purposes of the administration. In the exercise of this power, the court can in my opinion direct the administrator to authorise or ratify particular claims-handling expenditure by the insurers, with the result that their

right to reimbursement would have priority under section 19(5). It would however be unusual for the court to make such a decision, involving questions of business judgment, contrary to the opinion of the administrator that such expenditure, while no doubt in the interests of the insurers, was not necessary for the very limited purposes of the administration. It would also require much more evidence of the particular expenditure than is available to your Lordships.

1 Sub nom *Centre Reinsurance International Co v Curzon Insurance Ltd* [2006] UKHL 45; [2006] 1 WLR 2863, HL.

17.55 In relation to employee claims in an administration (starting pre-15 September 2003), Lawrence Collins J distinguished *Toshoku* in *Re Allders Department Stores Ltd*[1] (see para 17.57 below).

1 [2005] EWHC 172, (Ch); [2005] 2 All ER 122 (Lawrence Collins J).

17.56 The second edition of this book commented that in practice, employees did not seem to raise the issue of administration expenses as a claim against administrators independent of the statutory 'adoption' priority in IA 1986, s 19 (see Chapter 18 below). The second edition of this book went on to make the point that it would be arguable that the insolvency expenses principle should not produce any greater priority (if it did, the argument would arise that this is inconsistent with the intentions of Parliament in s 19 and now in para 99).

17.57 As mentioned above (see para 17.29 above), in *Re Allders Department Stores Ltd*[1] it was argued that the same rule on expenses should apply in an administration as in a liquidation so that statutory liabilities for unfair dismissal and redundancy awards should be treated as an insolvency expense following the House of Lords decision in *Re Toshoku Finance*[2].

1 [2005] EWHC 172 (Ch); [2005] 2 All ER 122 (Lawrence Collins J).
2 [2002] UKHL 6; [2002] 3 All ER 961; [2002] 1 WLR 671.

17.58 Lawrence Collins J gave a number of reasons for rejecting that claim, holding (at para 24):

'I do not consider that the statutory liabilities for redundancy payments or unfair dismissal claims would be 'necessary disbursements' for the purposes of r2.67(1)(f).

First, it would be inconsistent with the scheme of the legislation if the payments referred to in Sch 6 were to be treated as preferential, and yet all other employee-related payments are to be paid as an expense of the administration. That would be to give the Sch 6 payments (which include protective awards) a lesser priority than other types of payments, when the policy appears to have been to give them a greater priority.

Second, there is nothing in my judgment in *Re Toshoku Finance* [2002] 3 All ER 961, [2002] 1 WLR 671 which requires a different conclusion. It is not the ratio of that case that any liability imposed on a company which is not provable as a debt is thereby rendered a 'necessary disbursement'. The context in which Lord Hoffmann referred to the fact that certain debts could not be proved shows that he was justifying the treatment of certain debts as expenses, and not offering a definition of what liabilities were disbursements. Even if that were the crucial test for winding up, there would be no reason to apply it to administration. Although the current regime envisages a distribution to secured and preferential creditors without a subsequent liquidation, in the normal case of an administration which does not succeed in rescuing the company, the company will go into liquidation and the statutory payment obligation will be a provable debt under r 13.12B.

Finally, a construction of r 2.67(1)(f) which applied it to statutory redundancy payment liabilities and other statutory liabilities would have such adverse policy consequences on the administration regime that it is impossible to see that such a result could have been intended.'

17.59   In *Re Huddersfield Fine Worsteds Ltd*[1], the Court of Appeal did not consider the administration expenses issue or refer to rule 2.67 (*Re Allders* is mentioned as having been included in the skeleton arguments, but is not cited in the Court of Appeal judgment. Having said that, Neuberger LJ reinforced his decision that a protective award is not an adoption expense by stating that to afford such a liability priority would represent a change in the law which 'significantly weakened' the rescue culture underlying the administration regime. It would increase the costs of administrations where contracts were adopted and so make it more difficult for administrators to adopt employment contracts.

1 [2005] EWCA Civ 1072; [2005] 4 All ER 886, CA. See also Chapter 18 (para 18.79 below).

17.60   In *Day v Haine*[1] Sir Donald Rattee at first instance held that liabilities for protective awards did not constitute either a provable debt (see para 16.23 above) or could be considered to be an insolvency expense. But his judgment on this latter point is short:

'[37] Finally, counsel for the representative employee submitted that alternatively the company's liability under the protective award made after the commencement of the liquidation is a necessary disbursement by the liquidator in the course of his administration within Insolvency Rule 4.218(1)(m) and therefore payable out of the company's assets in priority to the company's debts, by virtue of r 4.218. In my judgment, this argument is misconceived. Rule 4.218 deals with the order of priority for "expenses of liquidation" (see the opening words of r 4.218(1)). I fail to see how liability for protective awards can possibly be said to be an expense of the liquidation. I find nothing in *Re Toshoku Finance UK plc* [2002] UKHL 6, [2002] 3 All ER 961, [2002] 1 WLR 671, on which counsel for the employee relied, to give any support for his argument on this point.

[38] In my judgment, the liquidator's submissions are correct. The protective awards are not provable as debts of the company in the liquidation and are not payable as expenses of the liquidation. I appreciate this seems to produce a harsh result for the employees concerned, but in my judgment it is a conclusion I am compelled to reach on the present state of the law. The harshness of the result is no doubt remediable by Parliament for the future, if it thinks fit.'

1 [2007] EWHC 2691 (Ch); [2008] ICR 452 (Sir Donald Rattee) at para [37]. This point not discussed in the Court of Appeal [2008] EWCA Civ 626, [2008] ICR 1102; [2008] 2 BCLC 517, CA – see para 6.23 above and Chapter 16 above.

17.61   As mentioned above (see para 17.31 above), in *Exeter City Council v Bairstow, Re Trident Fashions*[1] David Richards J was concerned with the question of whether non-domestic rates on premises occupied by the company during the course of the administration were payable as an expense of the administration proceedings. Following the principles laid down by the House of Lords in *Re Toshoku Finance*, he held that that non-domestic rates were payable as a 'necessary disbursement' under rule 2.67(1)(f) of the Insolvency Rules 1986.

David Richards J held that the more flexible approach envisaged in pre September 2003 administrations under *Re Atlantic Computers* and in *Re Freakley* did not apply in post-2003 administrations, given that the underlying insolvency rules had changed to a form similar to those applicable in a liquidation (see also to the same effect Briggs J in *Lomas v RAB Market Cycles (Master) Fund Limited*[2]).

David Richards J referred to the decisions relating to liabilities to employees of the Court of Appeal in *Re Huddersfield Fine Worsteds Ltd*[3] and of Lawrence Collins J in *Re Allders Department Stores Ltd*. He did not cast any doubt on the decisions, but distinguished *Re Allders Department Stores*, holding (at para 77):

> 'It appears to me that the principal basis of the decision was that because of the special treatment of certain categories of employment-related claims under paragraph 99 and under schedule 6, it would be inconsistent to treat further categories as expenses under rule 2.67. I concur with that analysis.'

1 [2007] EWHC 400 (Ch); [2007] All ER (D) 45 (Mar), (David Richards J).
2 [2009] EWHC 2545 Ch at para [100] (Briggs J).
3 [2005] 4 All ER 886, CA. See also Chapter 18 (para 18.79 below).

17.62   In *Re Leeds United Association Football Club Ltd; Fleming v Healy*[1], Pumfrey J followed Lawrence Collins J in *Re Allders Department Stores* and held that damages for wrongful dismissal did not count as an expense in administration.

In the *Leeds United* case, the football club had entered administration. The administrators did not wish to terminate the players' contracts since they would lose the club's most valuable assets – the players could move to another club without any compensation or transfer fee being paid. However, if the contracts were adopted, the club might subsequently incur substantial liabilities if the players were not paid. Accordingly, the administrators sought to defer all or part of the remuneration payable to the players until they could be sure that they could pay all or part of the deferred remuneration – either as an expense of the administration or by a purchaser under TUPE which would apply on a sale of the club's business to another company.

The administrators applied to court for a declaration as to whether or not compensation for any future wrongful dismissal claims would have the super priority afforded by the adoption provisions in IA 1986, Sch B1, para 99 (see Chapter 18 below) or, if not, would count as necessary disbursements for the purpose of rule 2.67(1)(f) of the Insolvency Rules 1986.

In relation to the insolvency expenses issue under rule 2.67, counsel suggested on behalf of the players that liabilities for wrongful dismissal would count as 'necessary disbursements' for the purpose of rule 2.67(1)(f) so as to have priority as administration expenses (but not the super priority afforded by paragraph 99).

Pumfrey J held that, in respect of the liabilities for wrongful dismissal claims, he should follow the decision of Lawrence Collins J in *Re Allders* and noted that David Richards J had in *Re Trident Fashions: Exeter City Council v Bairstow* earlier in the year agreed with the decision of Lawrence Collins J.

Accordingly, Pumfrey J held that payments in respect of damages for wrongful dismissal were not 'necessary disbursements' under rule 2.67(1)(f).

1 [2007] EWHC 1761 (Ch); [2007] ICR 1688; [2007] All ER (D) 385 (Jul) (Pumfrey J)

INSOLVENCY EXPENSES: RECEIVERS?

17.63 Most receivers (ie those not appointed by the court – see para 4.23 above) are not officers of the court. A company in receivership has no statutory protection from legal actions (see para 4.49 above). Accordingly it seems that the insolvency expenses principle does not apply to receivers; they will not be ordered by the court to make payment of such expenses – see the decisions of the Court of Appeal in *Nicoll v Cutts*[1] and *Re Atlantic Computer Systems plc*[2].

1 [1985] BCLC 322, CA.
2 [1992] Ch 505, CA.

17.64 It has been argued[1] that this is inconsistent with earlier case law but this position seems to have been accepted by the House of Lords in *Powdrill v Watson*[2].

1 See the article by Roger Gregory in (1994) 1 Receivers, Administrators and Liquidators Quarterly 143.
2 [1995] 2 AC 394 at 441D.

17.65 The position seems to be the same in Scotland. Section 60(1)(c) of IA 1986 (which has no equivalent in England and Wales) provides for there to be a priority in a receivership for 'creditors in respect of all liabilities, charges and expenses incurred by or on behalf of the receiver'. The section was not amended by the IA 1994.

In *Lindop v Stuart Noble & Sons Ltd*[1] an employee was retained by the receivers and later dismissed. He claimed for his pay in lieu of notice under s 60(1)(c). Lord MacFadyen in the Court of Session held that this section did not have the effect of giving such a priority to the employee's claim. He held that this would have been a bizarre result following the Insolvency Act 1994 and would give a greater preference in Scotland than would be the case in England. On appeal, this view was upheld by the Inner House of the Court of Session[2].

1 [1999] BCC 616; 1998 SCLR 648 (Lord MacFadyen).
2 [2000] BCC 747; 1999 SCLR 889, Inner House, Ct of Sess.

NEW CONTRACTS – RECEIVERS

17.66 IA 1986 s 44(1)(b) imposes a personal liability on administrative receivers 'on any contract entered into by him in the carrying out of his functions (except in so far as the contract otherwise provides)'. Section 37(1)(a) is the same for other receivers.

These sections were derived from s 492(3) CA 1985 and before that s369(2), CA 1948. This obligation applies to all contracts, not just employment contracts. Some protection is given to the other contracting party by the notice provisions in s39, IA 1986 (formerly s 370, CA 1948), that the receiver must put details of the receivership on orders, invoices etc.[1]

1 There is also a notification obligation in IA 1986, s 46 (formerly CA 1985, s 493).

17.67   For example, in *Re Mack Trucks (Britain) Limited*[1], Pennycuik J held that where a receiver had arranged for a new employment contract between the company and an employee, the receiver was then personally liable for damages on dismissal of the employee without full notice.

1 [1967] 1 WLR 780 (Pennycuik J).

17.68   Generally, the receiver arranging for existing contracts to continue will not amount to an entry into a new contract for the purposes of ss 44 or 37 – see para 15.4 above and *Nicoll v Cutts*[1] and, in Australia, *Sipad Holding v Popovic*[2] and *McEvoy v Incat Tasmania Pty Ltd*[3].

1 [1985] BCLC 322, CA – see also para18.2 below.
2 [1995] FCA 1737; (1996) 14 ACLC 307 (Lehane J).
3 [2003] FCA 810, 21 ACLC 1463 (Finkelstein J).

17.69   It may be unclear whether a new contract has been entered into at the instance of the receiver. It can often be a difficult question to decide if an existing contract has been varied or replaced.

The relevant test would be likely to be whether the effect of the new agreement is that the existing contract is rescinded or whether it is merely varied. A rescission will take effect to replace the original contract (so that the receiver will have personal liability – unless excluded), whereas in the case of a variation, the original contract will continue to exist in an altered form.

17.70   If this is the appropriate test, then guidance can be taken from various decisions which outline the difference between a variation and a rescission, which have arisen particularly in the case of oral variations or rescissions of contracts which are required to be in writing. A general analysis of the contractual position is contained in *Chitty on Contracts* (29th edn, 2004) at para 22–028.

17.71   Generally the decision on this point will depend on the intention of the parties to be gathered from an examination of the terms of the subsequent agreement and from all the surrounding circumstances[1].

1 See *United Dominions Trust (Jamaica) Ltd v Shoucair* [1969] 1 AC 340, PC; *Compagnie Noga d'Importation et d'Exportation SA v Abacha (No 4)* [2003] EWCA Civ 1100; [2003] 2 All E.R. (Comm) 915, CA and *Sookraj v Samaroo* [2004] UKPC 50; [2004] All ER (D) 133 (Oct), PC.

17.72   Rescission will be presumed when the parties enter into a new agreement which is entirely inconsistent with the old, or, if not entirely inconsistent with it, inconsistent with it to an extent that goes to the very root of it. The change must be fundamental and:

> 'the question is whether the common intention of the parties was to 'abrogate', 'rescind', 'supersede' or 'extinguish' the old contract by a 'substitution' of a 'completely new' or 'self subsisting' agreement' – see *British & Beningtons Ltd v N.W. Cachar Co. Ltd*[4].

1 [1923] AC 48 at 62 and 67.

17.73 Similarly, in *Morris v Baron & Co*[1], Lord Dunedin commented:

> 'The difference between variation and rescission is a real one, and is tested, to my thinking, by this: In the first case there are no such executory clauses in the second arrangement as would enable you to sue upon that alone if the first did not exist; in the second you could sue on the second arrangement alone, and the first contract is got rid of either by express words to that effect, or because, the second dealing with the same subject-matter as the first but in a different way, it is impossible that the two should be both performed.'

See also *Chitty on Contracts* paras 22-029 and 22-034.

1 [1918] AC 1 at 25, HL.

17.74 Employment tribunals have to decide in other contexts whether the terms of employment amount to a different contract from that under which the employee was previously employed (see eg *Hogg v Dover College*[1]).

In *British Broadcasting Corporation v Kelly-Phillips*[2], Evans LJ commented (at p 858):

> 'There is a clear distinction in law between an agreement which varies an existing contract and one which replaces an existing contract, which ceases to have effect. In employment law terms, 'renewal' is distinguished from 're-engagement', and the concept is the same. Whilst it is sometimes clear into which category a particular agreement falls, the distinction can be notoriously difficult to draw. That was demonstrated by old authorities such as *Morris v Baron* [1918] AC 1 and it has reappeared in more modern decisions on the statutory provisions with which we are concerned, and their predecessors since 1965.'

See also the EAT in *Potter v North Cumbria Acute Hospitals NHS Trust*[3].

1 [1990] ICR 39, EAT.
2 [1998] 2 All ER 845, CA.
3 [2009] All ER (D) 24 (May), EAT.

TABLE OF EMPLOYEE CLAIMS IN ADMINISTRATION – EXPENSES OR ADOPTED

17.75 The table below attempts to give some broad outlines of the position of administrators and after the IA 1994. See also the chart at the end of Chapter 18 in relation to adoption priority before and after the changes made by IA 1994 on 15 March 1994.

Type of claim	Administration expense?	Priority on adoption on or after 15 March 1994?
Cash wages or salary	No – adoption expense	YES, subject to having been incurred while in office
Contractual bonus	No – adoption expense	Same as wages or salary (can be difficult question as to when incurred AND whether is in respect of services after the adoption – eg when payable or over the period in relation to which it is calculated?)
Contractual benefits in kind	No – if excluded as adoption expense, then no reason to include as insolvency expense – *Re Allders* and *Leeds United*	NO (not a 'liability to pay a sum')
Discretionary benefits (eg discretionary bonus)	NO	NO
Pay in lieu of notice/ damages for breach of contract	No – if excluded as adoption expense, then no reason to include as insolvency expense – *Re Allders* and *Leeds United*	NO - not wages or salary unless express term – *Delaney v Staples, Huddersfield* and *Leeds United*
Holiday pay (contractual)	No – adoption expense	YES for holiday taken while business continued, YES for pay in lieu at termination if it relates to service after adoption (see *Re Douai School*)
Maternity/sickness pay	No – adoption expense	Arguably NO (not a liability in respect of services rendered after the adoption?) – difficult time apportionment under IA 1986, s44(2C)(a) and Schedule B1, para 99(6)(b)
Health and safety claims	No – adoption expense	Probably YES (implied contractual duty)

Type of claim	Administration expense?	Priority on adoption on or after 15 March 1994?
Redundancy claims	No – if excluded as adoption expense, then no reason to include as insolvency expense – *Re Allders* and *Leeds United*	NO (not a liability in respect of services rendered after the adoption)
Unfair dismissal claims	No – if excluded as adoption expense, then no reason to include as insolvency expense – *Re Allders* and *Leeds United*	NO – statutory only, not a liability 'under' contract
Protective awards	No – *Day v Haine* (Sir Donald Rattee)	NO – statutory only, neither a liability 'under' contract - nor 'wages or salary' - *Huddersfield*
Pension contributions	No	YES if contractual and a money purchase occupational scheme, probably NO if a personal pension scheme or if a final salary scheme – see below
Deficit claims by pension trustees (Pensions Act 1995, s 75)	No	NO – statutory only, not a liability 'under' contract, also liability is to trustees, not employees

275

CHAPTER 18

Carrying on business – adopted employment contracts

'ADOPTED' EMPLOYMENT CONTRACTS

18.1 The IA 1986 introduced special statutory rules relating to 'adoption' of employment contracts by administrators or administrative receivers or receivers (not liquidators) and the super priority for some employee liabilities that can follow.

The provisions were not clear and a series of court cases followed (culminating in the decision of the House of Lords in 1995 in the *Paramount* case). Parliament reacted to the difficulties by enacting changes by IA 1994, amending the relevant provisions for employment contracts adopted on or after 15 March 1994. The provisions remain obscurely drafted (this is proving not to be an easy area for Parliament and the relevant draftsman).

The provisions were further amended by the Enterprise Act 2002 for administrations starting on or after 15 September 2003. It is likely that no substantive change was intended (but the fact that there are changes at all raises issues). The provisions continue to cause difficulties – The Court of Appeal in *Krasner* castigated the new drafting as being 'on any view … unsatisfactory' and a 'thoroughly unsatisfactory piece of drafting'.

This Chapter looks at the case law and the later legislative changes.

BACKGROUND

18.2 As mentioned above (see para 15.36) the practice of receivers before 1986 had generally been to ensure that the salaries of employees were met in relation to work performed during the receivership (ie category 2 claims) if they continued to work for the insolvent company during the receivership.

However in 1985 doubt was thrown on whether this was legally required by the decision of the Court of Appeal in *Nicoll v Cutts*[1]. The Insolvency Bill 1985 (subsequently enacted and consolidated in the IA 1986) was passing through Parliament at the time of this decision. Amendments were introduced providing for a statutory priority to be granted to certain claims of employees in both a receivership and the new administration procedure introduced by IA 1986.

1 [1985] BCLC 322, CA.

18.3 Sections 37 and 44 of IA 1986 impose personal liability on receivers and administrative receivers and s 19(5) imposed a first priority on claims on the assets of a company in administration for certain claims of employees. These provisions caused difficulty and ss 19 and 44 were amended by IA 1994.

Subsequently, s 19 was repealed and replaced for administrations starting on or after 15 September 2003 by new provisions inserted by the Enterprise Act 2002 (see para 18.53 below). These are discussed further below.

18.4 The meaning of these 'adoption' provisions as originally enacted in IA 1986was (to put it mildly) less than clear. In particular it seemed that:

- they could give priority to termination claims (category 3 in the categories set out in para 15.25 above) in an administration or receivership and,

- in addition, could give priority in a receivership to back wages (category 1 above).

The priority only arises in respect of 'adopted' contracts of employment. A 14-day window is given when nothing that the insolvency practitioner does is to be construed as adopting a contract of employment.

18.5 Accordingly, after 1986, receivers and administrators had an almost invariable practice of giving all employees a notice stating that they were not adopting the contracts of employment. This practice seemed to be supported by a decision in 1987 of Harman J in *Re Specialised Mouldings* (unreported). However in that case, no reasons were given and a final judgment was never delivered.

18.6 The position was dramatically changed by the Court of Appeal's decision in *Re Paramount Airways Ltd (No 3)* (reported as *Powdrill v Watson*[1]) which, because of its implications for administrators and receivers, led to amending legislation (IA 1994) being rushed through Parliament in March 1994. The amending legislation was not retrospective and only applied to employment contracts adopted on or after 15 March 1994.

1 [1994] 2 All ER 513, CA.

18.7 The *Paramount* case (on the position under the original unamended legislation) continued and in March 1995, the House of Lords in *Powdrill v Watson*[1] gave judgment in the combined appeals in three cases, *Paramount Airways*, *Leyland Daf* and *Ferranti*.

1 [1995] 2 AC 394, HL.

18.8 The decision of the Court of Appeal in holding that a mere notice of non-adoption was not effective to prevent adoption under IA 1986 was upheld, but the House of Lords ruled that the effect of adoption was that the 'super priority' applicable under ss 19 and 44 only extended, as a matter of interpretation, to contractual liabilities incurred during the relevant administration or receivership.

Lord Browne-Wilkinson gave the leading speech (with which the other four Law Lords agreed), setting out a number of principles applicable to the three cases.

This Chapter does on to deal with the three cases, the House of Lords' judgment and the amending legislation.

Paramount Airways to the Court of Appeal

18.9   In *Paramount Airways, Powdrill v Watson* administrators had been appointed. As was then almost universal, they had arranged to serve each of the employees with a letter stating that the administrators should not be taken to have 'adopted' the employment contracts of the employees. However, the letter confirmed that the administrators would ensure that the company continued to pay the employees during the period they were in actual employment. A 'loyalty bonus' was also promised.

18.10   These payments were made, but when the administrators discovered they could not sell the business as a going concern, they arranged for the company to dismiss all the remaining employees without notice. One of the employees, Captain Watson, claimed that he was entitled to various amounts consequent upon his dismissal, in particular damages for breach of contract and also various statutory claims, including unfair dismissal. He claimed that these liabilities were given a 'super priority' by virtue of what was then IA 1986, s 19(5) on the basis that his contract of employment had been 'adopted' by the administrators.

18.11   The administrators sought directions from the High Court as to the priority of the employees' claims. The employees were successful at first instance before Evans-Lombe J[1] and also before the Court of Appeal. In effect, these courts held that the unilateral notice served by the administrators was ineffective. The administrators must be taken to have 'adopted' the contracts of employment if they had arranged for the company to continue to employ the individuals concerned.

1 [1993] BCC 662 (Evans-Lombe J).

18.12   The lower courts also held that the consequence of adoption was that a liability under an adopted contract of employment is given the priority under s 19(5) if it was 'liability incurred while the administrator was in office'.

18.13   This liability would clearly exclude back wages (category 1 – see para 15.25 above) relating to the period prior to adoption of the employment contract, but would include ongoing claims (category 2 liabilities) eg wages and salary and, most crucially, the courts seem to have assumed that it would also include any contractual termination liabilities (category 3 liabilities) eg the contractual termination claims of the employees where they have been dismissed by the administrators (ie damages for breach of contract for the unexpired notice period and contractual redundancy claims).

18.14   Subsequently in Australia, the courts held that a court appointed receiver was not liable for claims of employees even for services after the date of the appointment. In *Sipad Holding DDPO v Popovic*[1] Lehane J held that any such liability was incurred 'when the contracts of employment were entered into by the company before the receiver's appointment'. *Paramount Airways* was not cited.

1 [1995] FCA 1737; (1996) 14 ACLC 307 (Lehane J) at page 310.

18.15   The House of Lords subsequently impliedly confirmed (see below) that the various statutory termination claims (eg unfair dismissal and protective awards) do not qualify for the statutory priority. They are not claims 'under' the employment contract.

Insolvency Act 1994

18.16   Following the decision of the Court of Appeal in *Paramount Airways*, Parliament responded quickly to claims by insolvency practitioners that the decision, in effect, forced administrators and receivers to a crucial choice within the first 14 days after their appointment.

18.17   Subject to this statutory grace period, the interpretation of the Court of Appeal meant that receivers and administrators were in effect being required to weigh:

(a)   on the one hand the prospect of a greater recovery for creditors (and probably also the preservation of jobs) if the business of the insolvent company could be continued and perhaps sold as a going concern (the 'rescue culture'); and

(b)   on the other hand the fact that, if such a rescue failed, any dismissal liabilities of the employees concerned (in particular damages for breach of contract) would in effect be given a 'super priority', ranking ahead of other claims on the assets of the company (ie in effect to the detriment of the other creditors).

18.18   In effect, unless the insolvency practitioners could be reasonably certain that a sale as a going concern would necessarily succeed, the likelihood seemed that they would not arrange for the company to continue to trade, but instead dismiss all the employees within the first 14 days after their appointment[1].

1 See the comments to similar effect in relation to the uncertainties under the new post-2003 administration provisions in Sch B1 to IA 1986 made to the Court of Appeal in *Re Huddersfield Fine Worsteds Ltd* [2005] 4 All ER 886 at para 4.

18.19   Parliament accordingly reacted by passing the IA 1994. In relation to contracts of employment adopted on or after 15 March 1994, this amended the provisions of IA 1986, ss 19 and 44 dealing with the position of administrators and administrative receivers (but not, illogically, s 37 dealing with the position of receivers who are not administrative receivers).

18.20 The 1994 Act limited the 'super priority' under ss 19 (administrators) and 44 (administrative receivers) to 'qualifying liabilities'. These were defined as liabilities under the employment contract to make payments of wages, salary and contributions to occupational pension schemes in respect of services rendered after the adoption of the contract of employment. The amended sections still refer to 'adopted' employment contracts (without attempting to define this term). However the 1994 Act only applies to contracts of employment adopted on or after 15 March 1994. In effect Parliament headed off the continuing problem in relation to future insolvencies, leaving the position of past insolvencies until the meaning of the 1986 Act had been confirmed by the House of Lords.

Leyland Daf and Ferranti

18.21 Subsequently, a test case was taken to the High Court in the receiverships of Leyland Daf and Ferranti. Lightman J in *Leyland Daf*[1] confirmed that the principles outlined in the Court of Appeal in *Paramount Airways* were applicable to receiverships as well, so that the unilateral notices served by the receivers were ineffective.

1 [1995] 2 AC 394 (Lightman J).

18.22 Lightman J also considered the difference in wording between s 44, dealing with administrative receivers, and s 19, dealing with administrators. He held that the lack of an express temporal limitation in s 44 (unlike s 19) meant that if contracts of employment were adopted, then a receiver was personally liable on the contracts of employment for all the company's liabilities no matter when incurred (eg even if before the receiver's appointment or after his discharge).

18.23 Thus, Lightman J held that the position of receivers differed from that of administrators in that:

(a) the liability of receivers is personal (ie is not merely a priority claim over assets); and

(b) the liability of receivers was not expressly limited and seemed (on a literal approach) to extend to claims arising prior to their appointment and after they ceased to be in office.

In both cases, only contractual claims are covered (the same for administrators as for receivers).

18.24 Lightman J gave leave for an accelerated appeal to the House of Lords. The appeals in these two cases were heard (together with the appeal from the Court of Appeal in *Paramount Airways*) by the House of Lords in December 1994.

House of Lords

18.25   The decision of the House of Lords was given in March 1995[1]. Lord Browne-Wilkinson gave the only speech.

1 *Powdrill v Watson* [1995] 2 AC 394, HL.

18.26   The insolvency practitioners argued strongly that the decisions of the lower courts were wrong. They pointed to the mischief that was intended to be remedied by ss 19 and 44, arguing that they are only intended to amount to a statutory reversal of the decision of the Court of Appeal in *Nicoll v Cutts*[1]. In effect, it was argued that the sections are only intended to reverse the decision in that case in so far as it held that receivers were not liable even to pay wages to employees for their services during the period after the appointment of a receiver until his appointment terminated. The insolvency practitioners also argued that the word 'adopt' used in ss 19 and 44 should be given a restricted meaning.

1 [1985] BCLC 322, CA.

18.27   The second line of attack by the insolvency practitioners was to point to the absurdity of the result if the decision of Lightman J were upheld in relation to receivers. Receivers would be personally liable for contractual liabilities to employees if their employment contracts were adopted even in respect of liabilities incurred prior to the receivership and in relation to liabilities incurred after the receivership had terminated. An example would be if the company managed to trade out of its receivership so that the receiver ceased to act, but the company continued to trade. On the literal wording of s 44 (as found by Lightman J) the receiver would continue to be liable on the contract of employment without any time limit.

18.28   Lord Browne-Wilkinson (with whom the rest of the House of Lords agreed) held in favour of the insolvency practitioners on the second point. Lord Browne-Wilkinson considered that a plain reading of s 44 (ie without any temporal limitation) gave rise to such an absurd result that it was legitimate to construe the section in a way that gave a more reasonable meaning. In effect, Lord Browne-Wilkinson considered that there was no reason for distinguishing between the position of receivers and administrators and, accordingly, s 44 should be construed in exactly the same way as s 19, ie the only liabilities in relation to adopted employees which are made the personal liability of receivers are those incurred while the receiver is in office.

18.29   However, on the primary argument of the insolvency practitioners (see para 18.26 above), Lord Browne-Wilkinson felt that the meaning of the plain words of the statute were insufficiently absurd to require the word 'adopt' in s 19 (and hence s 44) to be interpreted in such a way as to allow insolvency practitioners to exclude or modify the effect of the sections merely by a unilateral notice to employees. In the words of Lord Browne-Wilkinson (at page 450B):

> ' . . . the consequences of giving the word 'adoption' its all-or-nothing meaning, although unfortunate, are not absurd.'

18.30   Clearly Parliament had intended to reverse the decision of the Court of Appeal in *Nicoll v Cutts*. The fact that it had chosen such unclear words and, in effect, acted through such a blunt instrument, did not make the House of Lords feel that it could act so as to restrict the meaning of the statute nor seek to bring it into with the more limited provisions now in place under IA 1994 (but only in relation to contracts of employment adopted on or after 15 March 1994 – see para 18.19 above).

18.31   In effect, the House of Lords seems to have considered that although the literal meaning of s 44 was absurd (because there was no temporal limitation), the consequence of giving a literal meaning to s 19 (which already contains an express temporal limitation) was not so absurd to allow the section to be construed in a way that its language could not sustain.

18.32   The judgment of Lord Browne-Wilkinson is intriguing in many respects. Not least because he states during his judgment that, at the close of argument, he had felt persuaded by the argument of the insolvency practitioners as to the meaning of 'adopt' but had changed his mind during preparation of his judgment.

The retrospective effect of the decision in Paramount

18.33   Insolvency practitioners were then faced with the prospect of a series of claims by employees stretching back over the period since December 1986 (when IA 1986 came into force) up to the present day in relation to receiverships and administrations involving adoption of employment contracts before 15 March 1994 (the date fixed in IA 1994).

18.34   In practice, employees whose employment was terminated by receivers or administrators after the end of the 14-day grace period will potentially have a claim to the extent that they did not receive full contractual damages for any failure to give proper notice.

18.35   The position was slightly muddied by the fact that some of the claims of the employees would have been met by the National Insurance Fund under the statutory guarantee in what is now ERA 1996 (formerly EPCA 1978) (see Chapter 10 above). The government indicated that it would not seek to recover from insolvency practitioners where the National Insurance Fund has paid such claims of adopted employees.

18.36   Employees would also, when bringing claims, need to show that they have complied with the usual rules regarding mitigation and allowance for earnings received during the notice period etc (see Chapter 2 above). Accordingly, the beneficiaries of the decision of the House of Lords are likely to have been, in the main, those employees who earned over the statutory maximum applicable to claims under the National Insurance Fund or had longer notice periods than the statutory maximum.

18.37   The then government refused (in 1994) to introduce corrective retro-spective legislation (contrast the retrospective Truck Act 1940, following the decision of the House of Lords in *Pratt v Cook, Son & Co (St Paul's) Ltd*[1]), the position of insolvency practitioners remained somewhat difficult. The position of receivers and administrators is dealt with in turn below.

1 [1940] AC 437, HL.

ADOPTED CONTRACTS BEFORE 1994

Receivers

18.38   Receivers owe a personal liability to relevant employees by virtue of the statutory provisions. This, in effect, amounts to a form of 'guarantee' of the con-tractual obligations of the company. This applies regardless of whether the company ever had assets to meet the claim (and to indemnify the receiver).

18.39   Receivers were probably under no direct duty to seek out claims and can wait to see what claims arise. The lack of a general representation procedure under English law for this type of claim means that it is very much up to indi-viduals whether or not they bring claims.

18.40   Some claims will be statute barred. The normal six year limitation period under the Limitation Act 1980 applicable to simple contract claims should apply. There may be rare instances where the employment contract was entered into as a deed, where the limitation period will be 12 years instead. Jules Sher QC (sitting as a deputy High Court Judge) held in *Re Maxwell Fleet and Facilities Management Ltd*[1] that the normal limitation periods would apply (see also para 18.45 below).

1 [1999] 2 BCLC 721; [2000] 1 All ER 464 (Jules Sher QC, sitting as a deputy High Court Judge).

Administrators

18.41   The position of administrators is slightly more complex. Unlike receivers they do not incur a personal liability to pay a relevant claim, but instead under IA 1986, s 19 (pre 15 September 2003 administrations) or Sch B1, para 99 (post-14 September 2003 administrations) the amount of the relevant claims of the employees are given the 'super priority' status referred to above and are made a first charge over the assets of the company.

18.42   The administrator's duty is not to pay out such claims, but merely, in effect, to note that such a charge exists. In practice, in order to make the admin-istrator personally liable for some claim for breach of statutory duty (eg handing over the assets of the company without making provision for such a claim) an action would need to be brought.

18.43   Administrators may be under a duty to seek to inform employees of their potential claims. As an officer of the court[1], an administrator owes a duty to act fairly – see *Ex p James*[2].

1 An administrator is an officer of the court, whether appointed by the court or outside – IA 1986, Sch B1, para 5.
2 (1874) 9 Ch App Cas 609, CA.

18.44   There may be some prospect of seeking to have the administrator disgorge his own remuneration (which ranks in priority behind the claims of adopted employees). The position may be affected by the discharge under IA 1986, Sch B1, para 98 (formerly IA 1986, s 20) that is sought by administrators on termination of their administration (when they commonly hand over to a liquidator or supervisor of a voluntary arrangement).

18.45   Jules Sher QC (sitting as a deputy High Court judge) held in *Re Maxwell Fleet and Facilities Management Ltd*[1] that the normal limitation periods apply to administrations. Unlike a winding up, an implied stay of a limitation period could not be found. However, he also held that although the limitation period for an employee's 'Paramount' claim starts to run at the latest when the employees are dismissed, an administrator was obliged, by s 19(5) of IA 1986 (see now IA 1986, Sch B1, para 99(4) and (5)), to pay employees' claims even if they are outside the limitation period. Paragraph 99(4) states that the relevant sums 'shall be charged on and payable out of' property of the company under the custody or control of the administrator (the wording in s 19(5) was similar).

1 [1999] 2 BCLC 721 (Jules Sher QC, sitting as a deputy High Court Judge).

AFTER THE INSOLVENCY ACT 1994

18.46   Following IA 1994, the position has become a bit clearer, but questions still remain (this area of the law seems fated to be cursed with measures rushed through Parliament with little time for the drafting to be polished).

18.47   For administrators and administrative receivers (but not, strangely, for receivers who are not administrative receivers) the wording added by IA 1994 made it clear that for contracts adopted on or after 15 March 1994, super priority is only given for a 'qualifying liability' (IA 1996, ss 19(6) and 44(1)(b)).

18.48   The wording added by the 1994 Act unfortunately differed for administrators when compared to administrative receivers.

18.49   For administrations starting before 15 September 2003 the priority applied to 'sums payable in respect of debts or liabilities incurred . . . under contracts' (IA 1986, s 19(6)).

18.50   For administrations starting on or after 15 September 2003, the wording added by the Enterprise Act 2002 is slightly different: 'a sum payable in respect of a debt or liability arising out of a contract…' (Sch B1, para 99(4)).

18.51   For administrative receivers, the priority applies to 'any qualifying liability on any contract of employment…'(IA 1986, s 44(1)(b)), but later referring to a qualifying liability as being a 'liability under a contract of employment (s 44(2A)).

18.52   In *Inland Revenue Commissioners v Lawrence*[1], the Court of Appeal held that the wording in s 19 was wide enough to cover the company's liability to pay to HMRC the PAYE and primary NIC contributions that should be deducted from payment of wages (see Chapter 24 below). It is unclear whether the Court of Appeal thought that such a liability was given priority because of the width of the words 'in respect of' appearing in section 19 or whether they considered the PAYE and NIC deductions really to be payments to the employee and to form part of wages or salary. The point is important because:

(a)   the wording in s 44(1)(b) seems more restrictive in referring only to a liability 'on' any contract of employment – indeed Sedley LJ considered that 'sums payable on contracts' would have a different meaning (he did not refer to s 44, so it is unclear whether he was meaning to draw a distinction between administrators and administrative receivers); and

(b)   if the wide meaning of 'in respect of' is preferred, this may mean that the priority (at least as against administrators) extends to other amounts payable by the employer (eg pension contributions and other benefits) even though they are not covered by the employment contract.

1 [2001] 1 BCLC 145, CA.

ENTERPRISE ACT 2002: ADMINISTRATIONS STARTING ON OR AFTER 15 SEPTEMBER 2003

18.53   Section 19 of IA 1986 (dealing with administrators) was repealed (subject to savings) from 15 September 2003 by the Enterprise Act 2002. The repeal does not apply for administrations already started before 15 September 2003. Section 44 of IA 1986 (dealing with administrative receivers) was unaffected.

The provisions dealing with employees that were formerly in section 19 are now found in an amended form in IA 1986, Sch B1, para 99:

'Vacation of office: charges and liabilities

99

(1)   This paragraph applies where a person ceases to be the administrator of a company (whether because he vacates office by reason of resignation, death or otherwise, because he is removed from office or because his appointment ceases to have effect).

(2)   In this paragraph—

'the former administrator' means the person referred to in sub-paragraph (1), and

---

'cessation' means the time when he ceases to be the company's administrator.

(3)   The former administrator's remuneration and expenses shall be—

(a)   charged on and payable out of property of which he had custody or control immediately before cessation, and

(b)   payable in priority to any security to which paragraph 70 applies.

(4)   A sum payable in respect of a debt or liability arising out of a contract entered into by the former administrator or a predecessor before cessation shall be—

(a)   charged on and payable out of property of which the former administrator had custody or control immediately before cessation, and

(b)   payable in priority to any charge arising under sub-paragraph (3).

(5)   Sub-paragraph (4) shall apply to a liability arising under a contract of employment which was adopted by the former administrator or a predecessor before cessation; and for that purpose—

(a)   action taken within the period of 14 days after an administrator's appointment shall not be taken to amount or contribute to the adoption of a contract,

(b)   no account shall be taken of a liability which arises, or in so far as it arises, by reference to anything which is done or which occurs before the adoption of the contract of employment, and

(c)   no account shall be taken of a liability to make a payment other than wages or salary.

(6)   In sub-paragraph (5)(c) 'wages or salary' includes—

(a)   a sum payable in respect of a period of holiday (for which purpose the sum shall be treated as relating to the period by reference to which the entitlement to holiday accrued),

(b)   a sum payable in respect of a period of absence through illness or other good cause,

(c)   a sum payable in lieu of holiday,

(d)   in respect of a period, a sum which would be treated as earnings for that period for the purposes of an enactment about social security, and

(e)   a contribution to an occupational pension scheme.'

18.54   It is not clear that any change to the position in comparison with s 19 was intended – see *Re Huddersfield Fine Worsteds Ltd, Krasner v McMath*[1]. The wording has however changed and still differs (for no logical reason) from that applicable under s 45 to an administrative receiver.

1 [2005] EWCA Civ 1072; [2005] 4 All ER 886; [2005] IRLR 995, CA – see further para 18.79 below.

18.55   In *Re Huddersfield Fine Worsteds, Krasner v McMath*, Neuberger LJ in the Court of Appeal commented on the differences between s 19 and para 99 of Sch B1 to IA 1986:

> '[46] Of course, it would not be inherently surprising if the amendments effected to the 1986 Act by the 2002 Act resulted in some changes in the law. Indeed, it could be said to be surprising if amendments to a statute do not lead to any changes in the law. Having said that, it is clear that, before it was amended by the 2002 Act, the 1986 Act did not accord super-priority status to protective awards, and it would therefore be surprising if the amendments affected by the 2002 Act did result in such awards having super-priority, unless there was some justification for it. It would represent a change in the law which significantly weakened the rescue culture in many cases. It appears clear that it would be a change which was wholly unheralded by any actual or perceived abuse or unfairness in the administration regime before the 2002 Act came into force. There is no trace of any relevant recommendation or proposal, whether in a judgment, a textbook, a consultation paper, or an article in the relevant professional press.'

18.56   The term qualifying liability is defined from 15 March 1994 so that it is limited to a liability under the contract of employment satisfying the conditions below:

Term	Administrative Receiver	Administration (started before 15 September 2003)	Administration (started on or after 15 September 2003)
'under' or 'on' a contract of employment?	'on' and 'under' IA 1986, s 44(1) and (2A)	'under' IA 1986, s 19(6)	'under' Sch B1, para 99(5)
wages or salary or contribution to an occupational pension scheme	IA 1986, s 44(2A)(a)	IA 1986, s 19(7)(a)	Sch B1, para 99(6)
incurred while the IP is in office	IA 1986, s 44(2A)(b)	IA 1986, s 19(6)	Sch B1, para 99(5)(b) provides for exclusion of a liability which 'arises' or is 'done' or 'occurs' before adoption
which is in respect of services rendered wholly or partly after the adoption of the contract of employment	IA 1986, s 44(2A)(c)	IA 1986, s 19(7)(b) and (8)	Wording in Sch B1, para 99(5)(b) is different 'no account shall be taken of a liability which arises, or in so far as it arises, by reference to anything which is done or which occurs before the adoption of the contract of employment'

WAGES OR SALARY: HOLIDAY PAY

18.57   Wages or salary will include any bonuses payable (if contractual). See for example, the Australian case (by reference to different statutes), *Walker & Sherman v Andrew*[1].

1 [2002] NSWCA 214, NSW CA.

18.58   Holiday pay and pay during 'a period of absence from work through sickness or other good cause' is covered by s 19(9) (for an administration starting before 15 September 2003) and s 44(2C)(a) (for an administrative receiver). It is treated as wages or salary for the period in which the leave is taken. This seems to mean that it is a qualifying liability only if actually taken (this may have been an incentive to dismiss employees on holiday or sick).

18.59   Paragraph 99 in Schedule B1 (for an administration starting on or after 15 September 2003) deals with holiday pay differently. Paragraph 99(6)(a) treats a sum payable in respect of a period of holiday as wages or salary (and so with the potential super priority), stating that it is 'treated as relating to the period by reference to which the entitlement was earned.

18.60   Pay in lieu of holiday is treated as wages or salary in respect of the services rendered in the period by reference to which the holiday entitlement arose. This can give rise to difficult attribution issues.

18.61   In *Re Douai School (Re a Company No. 005174 of 1999)*[1] Neuberger J (as he then was) held that the terms of the contract of employment should be considered in deciding whether or not a liability is a qualifying liability. In that case he held that the relevant teachers' contracts envisaged that they would accrue holiday for the period after the relevant term worked. This meant that the holiday pay for the holiday after the term worked (and after the adoption of the employment contracts) was a qualifying liability and so entitled to super preferential status.

1 [2000] 1 WLR 502 (Neuberger J).

18.62   The changes introduced by the Insolvency Act 1994 were relatively clear (but confusion has now been introduced by the changes in wording under the Enterprise Act 2002 for administrators) in limiting the super priority to ongoing claims (category 2 in para 15.25 above) only.

18.63   Indeed, the changes seem to limit such priority to contractual claims and to cash payments only. Only cash payments will be:

- a liability to 'pay a sum by way of wages or salary or contribution to an occupational pension scheme' – s 44(2A)(a), IA 1986 (administrative receivers); or

- a sum payable – para 99(4) – and wages or salary – para 99(4)(c) (administrators in post 15 September 2003 administrations)

Although the Court of Appeal held in *Irving v Revenue and Customs Comrs*[1] that a transfer of assets in specie can be a 'liability to pay a sum' for tax purposes, it based this view very much on the tax framework. Rimer LJ commented at para [38]):

> 'In common with the Special Commissioners and Blackburne J, I am of the view that—subject always to a consideration of the particular context in which it is used—the more natural meaning of the phrase 'pays a sum' is 'pays a sum of money'.'

Sedley LJ agreed (see para [50]).

Accordingly, it seems unlikely that a non-cash obligation (eg to pay a benefit in kind) would be considered to be 'wages or salary' under IA 1986 and so have priority as an adopted liability.

Thus statutory claims (eg for unfair dismissal) and contractual non-cash claims (eg for benefits in kind) are excluded from the definition (see para 18.101 on below).

1 [2008] EWCA Civ 6; [2008] STC 597; [2008] All ER (D) 178 (Jan), CA.

18.64 Claims for back wages (category 1) and termination claims (category 3) were clearly excluded. They will not be 'in respect of services rendered wholly or partly after the adoption of the contract of employment'. Somewhat oddly, these words were not included in Sch B1, para 99 (as introduced by the Enterprise Act 2002). It may be that the intention was that the same effect would be achieved by the provision in Sch B1, para 99(5)(b) that:

> 'no account shall be taken of a liability which arises, or in so far as it arises, by reference to anything which is done or which occurs before the adoption of the contract of employment'

18.65 In practice there remain some unresolved issues, in particular those relating to pensions and for receivers who are not administrative receivers.

18.66 However, in practice it is understood that generally, administrators and administrative receivers are not seeking further to limit the super priority under IA 1986, as amended by the 1994 Act. It is thought that they are either accepting the priority under the Act or are still issuing unilateral notices of non-adoption (presumably in the latter case with little prospect of any legal effect, save perhaps for senior and experienced employees – see para 18.69 below).

UNRESOLVED ISSUES

18.67 Practitioner unaware of employee: There will be a few cases where receivers and administrators may claim that they have not in fact adopted employment contracts because they did not in fact know of (nor arranged for the payment of) the relevant employee. Such cases arose in the Employment Appeal

Tribunal in *Doegar v Herbert Mueller Ltd*[1] and before Laddie J in *Re Antal International Ltd*[2]. In both cases it was held that no adoption had occurred.

1 19 May 1994 (867/93) IDS Brief 529, EAT.
2 [2003] 2 BCLC 406 (Laddie J).

18.68 **Procedure for employees to follow**: It seems that in England and Wales the court can give directions (under IA 1986, s 35) setting out a procedure to be followed by employees bringing a claim against receivers following *Paramount*, but that directions cannot be given in Scotland (under IA 1986, s 63) – see the decision of the Inner House of the Court of Session in *Jamieson Petitioners*[1].

1 [1997] BCC 682, Ct of Sess.

18.69 **Contract out?**: Is it possible for the employee and employer expressly to agree to contract out of the statutory priority?

Such an agreement was argued before Lightman J in *Re Leyland Daf*[1], but he held that a unilateral notice was ineffective in this regard as not being an agreement. He relied on employment cases such as *Jones v Associated Tunnelling*[2] where it has been held that consent to a change is not to be implied by an employee just continuing to work after having received a notice from the employer if the change does not have an immediate practical impact on the employee.

1 [1995] AC 394 (Lightman J).
2 [1981] IRLR 477, EAT.

18.70 The point of whether an express agreement could be effective was not addressed by the House of Lords in *Powdrill v Watson*, which merely held that a unilateral notice was ineffective. Lightman J had held that an express agreement would be effective.

18.71 Note that even a unilateral notice may be effective in some cases – eg with a senior employee. In *Armstrong v Credit Suisse Asset Management*[1] the Court of Appeal distinguished *Jones* and *Powdrill v Watson* and granted an interlocutory injunction restraining employees of 'experience and sophistication' in relation to a restrictive provision contained in a handbook delivered to the employee but never expressly agreed to by the employee.

1 [1996] ICR 882, CA.

STATUTORY CLAIMS?

18.72 **Contractual or statutory?** The divide between contractual and statutory claims can be difficult to draw.

18.73 Claims for breach of the minimum notice periods implied by statute under ERA 1996 (and formerly under EPCA 1978) are contractual claims (see the decision of the EAT in *Secretary of State v Wilson*[1], approved by the House of Lords in *Secretary of State v Westwood*[2]).

1 [1978] 1 WLR 568, EAT.
2 [1985] AC 20, HL at 41G.

18.74 It is unclear whether the same applies to (say) claims for breach of health and safety rules or maternity and sickness pay (see for example the discussion of the contractual/statutory divide in another context by the Divisional Court in *Norweb plc v Dixon*[1]).

1 [1995] 3 All ER 952, DC.

18.75 In the context of comparing a statutory equal pay claim against a contractual pay claim for the purposes of the test of equivalence under European law in relation to time limits, the EAT commented in *Levez v T H Jennings (Harlow Pools) Ltd*[1] that many contractual terms are imposed by statute so that 'the judicial basis of the claim is the same whether or not the term sought to be enforced is express, implied or 'imposed'.'

1 [1999] IRLR 764, EAT.

18.76 Unfair dismissal: Unfair dismissal claims arise solely under ERA 1996 and so are not contractual. They are not covered by the super priority – see Evans-Lombe J in *Paramount Airways*[1] and the decision of the EAT in *Albion Automotive Ltd v Shaw*[2].

1 [1993] BCC 662 at 675 (Evans-Lombe J).
2 (1995) 4 October (EAT 523/94).

18.77 Statutory redundancy payments: Similarly the right to a statutory redundancy payment is not contractual and so not covered by the super priority – see the decision of the EAT in *Hughes v Secretary of State for Employment*[1].

1 (1995) 13 December (EAT/204/94). Cited in *Re Allders Department Stores* [2005] EWHC 172 (Ch); [2005] 2 All ER 122 (Lawrence Collins J) at para 18.

18.78 An additional factor indicating that neither right is contractual is that both of these rights are enforceable only in the employment tribunal (and not in the High Court).

Huddersfield case: protective awards/pay in lieu of notice

18.79 In *Re Huddersfield Fine Worsteds Ltd and Globe Worsted Co Ltd/Re Ferrotech Ltd/Re Granville Technology Group Ltd*[1], the Court of Appeal held that most payments in lieu of notice and protective award payments for the period of the adoption of a contract are not 'wages or salary' for the purposes of para 99 of Sch B1 to IA 1986. Accordingly, they are not payable as administration expenses in priority to an administrator's remuneration and expenses or preferential claims.

1 [2005] EWCA Civ 1072; [2005] 4 All ER 886; [2005] IRLR 995, CA.

18.80 The Court of Appeal in *Huddersfield* acted on an urgent basis. In the previous month, Peter Smith J had held in *Re Huddersfield Fine Worsteds Ltd/Re Globe Worsted Co Ltd*[1] that such liabilities did rank as administration expenses. However, a few days later, Etherton J in *Re Ferrotech Ltd and Re Granville Technology Group Ltd*[2] held that they did not.

1 [2005] EWHC 1682 (Ch); [2006] 2 BCLC 160; [2005] All ER (D) 387 (Jul) (Peter Smith J)
2 [2005] EWHC 1848 (Ch); [2006] 2 BCLC 160; [2005] All ER (D) 45 (Aug) (Etherton J).

18.81 The Court of Appeal judgment therefore clarifies the position after these conflicting first instance decisions. No application for leave to appeal the decision was made.

Background

18.82 As discussed above, Sch B1, para 99(5) provides that 'a liability arising under a contract of employment' which is adopted by the administrator shall have priority to the remuneration and expenses of the administrator. However, such priority extends, by virtue of sub-paragraph (c), only to a liability to make payment in respect of 'wages or salary' which is given an extended meaning by para 99(6).

18.83 The Court of Appeal considered whether:

- liabilities for protective employment awards under s 189 of the Trade Union and Labour Relations (Consolidation) Act 1992; and

- payments in lieu of notice

should be given the priority afforded by para 99.

Decision

18.84 Neuberger LJ (who gave judgment for the Court of Appeal) held that a liability must get through a 'double gateway' before an employee can contend that a sum due is within the ambit of para 99:

- Firstly, the sum must be a 'liability arising under a contract of employment'.

- Secondly, the sum concerned must be 'wages or salary', albeit that that expression is given an extended meaning by para 99(6).

18.85 Neuberger LJ held that a liability for a protective award, while arising 'because of' the existence of an employment contract, cannot be described as one 'arising under' a contract of employment. Even if such liability were 'wages or salary' for the purposes of para 99(6), it did not follow that it should therefore be treated as a liability arising under a contract of employment so as to get through the first gateway (see paras 38 to 40).

293

18.86　As to whether such awards were wages or salary, para 99(6)(d) provides that wages or salary includes 'in respect of a period, a sum which would be treated as earnings for that period for the purposes of an enactment about social security.' There were several different interpretations suggested as to the meaning of para 99(6)(d). Neuberger LJ stated that paragraph 99(6)(d) was a 'thoroughly unsatisfactory piece of drafting' (para 29), each interpretation of which raised difficulties. However, Neuberger LJ held that the least unsatisfactory construction was that adopted by Etherton J at first instance in *Re Ferrotech* and *Re Granville*. The reference to 'a period' in para 99(6)(d) should be to one or other of the periods referred to in para 99(6)(a) or (b) – ie a period of holiday or illness. Accordingly, Neuberger LJ held that a protective award payment did not fall within para 99(6)(d) and so was not 'wages or salary'.

18.87　Neuberger LJ accepted that such a construction gave an unnatural reading of 'a period' in paragraph 99(6)(d) and that it was difficult to see what it covered in practice. However, such a construction raised fewer problems than the other suggested interpretations. In fact, he stated that the same criticisms could have been made of para 99(6)(d)'s predecessor, namely s 19(10) of IA 1986 (as inserted by IA 1994).

18.88　Neuberger LJ reinforced his decision that a protective award is not an administration expense by stating that to afford such a liability priority would represent a change in the law which 'significantly weakened' the rescue culture underlying the administration regime. It would increase the costs of administrations where contracts were adopted and so make it more difficult for administrators to adopt employment contracts.

A similar view was reached by Sir Donald Rattee in *Day v Haine*[1] (but the judgment on this point is very short).

1 [2007] EWHC 2691 (Ch); [2008] ICR 452 (Sir Donald Rattee) at para [37]. This point not discussed in the Court of Appeal [2008] EWCA Civ 626; [2008] ICR 1102; [2008] 2 BCLC 517, CA – see para 7.23 above and Chapter 16.

18.89　Neuberger LJ also dismissed the argument that payments in lieu came within paragraph 99. The only exception was a payment in lieu claim that fell within Lord Browne-Wilkinson's 'category 1' claim in the Wages Act case of *Delaney v Staples*[1]. These are so-called 'garden leave' payments, where an employer gives proper notice of termination and rather than requiring the employee to work his notice, gives him the wages attributable to the notice period in a lump sum.

1 [1992] 1 AC 687, HL.

18.90　Conversely, Neuberger LJ held that pay in lieu claims within the three other categories outlined by Lord Browne-Wilkinson are not within the para 99 priority. These three other categories are:

'(2)　The contract of employment provides expressly that the employment may be terminated either by notice or, on payment of a sum in lieu of notice, summarily …

(3)   At the end of the employment, the employer and the employee agree that the employment is to terminate forthwith on payment of a sum in lieu of notice

(4)   Without the agreement of the employee, the employer summarily dismisses the employee and tenders a payment in lieu of proper notice.'

18.91   Accordingly, Neuberger LJ held that a protective award payment and most payment in lieu claims did not get through the first or second gateway and they were not administration expenses within paragraph 99.

18.92   This looks clearly to be the right answer from the Court of Appeal, although they had to struggle surprisingly hard to get there. The inability of Parliament (in practice the DTI and the Parliamentary draftsman) to provide simple guidelines for insolvency practitioners on the priority of on-going expenditure (particularly in relation to employee claims) is getting rather embarrassing.

18.93   Following on the Paramount Airways debacle over the original IA 1986 (and the meaning of when an employment contract is 'adopted'), we now seem to have problems both with the correcting IA 1994 and the changes made (inadvertently?) by the Enterprise Act 2002.

18.94   All of this would be rather easier to deal with if the legislation were clearer (it is not rocket science to look at the types of potential employee claims and decide which, if any of them has a priority) and if these recent cases at least referred to some of the other decisions in this area (eg *Lindop v Stuart Noble & Sons*[1] in the Inner House of the Court of Session on the expenses argument and *Inland Revenue Commissioners v Lawrence*[2] in the Court of Appeal on the extent of the super priority for payment of PAYE tax under the old s 19).

1   1999 SCLR 889; [2000] BCC 747, Inner House, Court of Session – see para 17.65 above.
2   [2005] EWCA Civ 1072; [2005] 4 All ER 886; [2005] IRLR 995; [2001] 1 BCLC 145, CA – see para 18.52 above.

18.95   R3 has discussed this with the DTI. The President of R3 wrote on 27 October 2005 to members about a meeting with Gerry Sutcliffe MP, Under-Secretary of State for Employment Relations and Consumer Affairs, to discuss matters of current concern to the insolvency profession. This letter included the following section:

'The second matter of concern was the recent spate of cases on employee costs and administrations. Although the Court of Appeal decision in Huddersfield Fine Worsteds, Ferrotech and Granville was helpful, there is no denying that the drafting of the legislation is defective and it is not impossible that in a future case the House of Lords might come to a different conclusion. The Under-Secretary agreed that the legislation needed to be corrected. Unfortunately the correction cannot be included in the Company Law Reform Bill, and will have to await a later legislative opportunity. In the meantime we will have to continue to take comfort from the Court of Appeal decision.'

LEEDS UNITED – WRONGFUL DISMISSAL

18.96 In *Re Leeds United Association Football Club Ltd; Fleming v Healy*[1], Pumfrey J followed the principles in Court of Appeal in *Re Huddersfield Fine Worsteds* and Lawrence Collins J in *Re Allders Department Stores* and held that damages for wrongful dismissal did not count as an 'wages or salary' having super priority under adopted contracts (nor was it an administration expense – see para 17.62 above).

1 [2007] EWHC 1761 (Ch); [2007] ICR 1688; [2007] All ER (D) 385 (Jul) (Pumfrey J)

18.97 In the *Leeds United* case, the football club had entered administration. The administrators did not wish to terminate the players' contracts since they would lose the club's most valuable assets – the players could move to another club without any compensation or transfer fee being paid. However, if the contracts were adopted, the club might subsequently incur substantial liabilities if the players were not paid. Accordingly, the administrators sought to defer all or part of the remuneration payable to the players until they could be sure that they could pay all or part of the deferred remuneration – either as an expense of the administration or by a purchaser under TUPE which would apply on a sale of the club's business to another company.

18.98 The administrators applied to court for a declaration as to whether or not compensation for any future wrongful dismissal claims would have the super priority afforded by the adoption provisions in para 99, Sch B1, IA 1986 or, if not, would count as necessary disbursements for the purpose of rule 2.67(1)(f) of the Insolvency Rules 1986.

18.99 Pumfrey J provided a useful summary of how paragraph 99 works. Paragraph 99(4) provides that a sum payable in respect of a debt or liability arising out of a contract entered into by the administrator has priority to the administrator's remuneration and expenses and to any floating charge holder – ie such amounts have 'super priority'. Paragraph 99(5) applies sub-paragraph (4) to any liability arising under an adopted employment contract. However, the effect of paragraph 99(5)(c) is to reduce the width of that provision to payments of 'wages or salary' alone. That term is broadened to include the matters listed in sub-paragraph (6), although that paragraph does not contain a definition of 'wages or salary'. The issue to be decided was whether, in addition to the matters specified in paragraph 99(6), the phrase 'wages or salary' included sums payable in respect of damages for wrongful dismissal. Pumfrey J held that it did not.

18.100 Pumfrey J determined that the words 'wages or salary' are to be given their normal meaning and cited the House of Lords decision in *Delaney v Staples*, dealing with the then Wages Act. This case held that for a payment to constitute 'wages' in its ordinary meaning it should be 'referable to an obligation on the employee under a subsisting contract of employment to render his services'. Lord Browne-Wilkinson then identified four types of wages in lieu of notice, the fourth of which was concerned with payments made in breach of contract. According to the House of Lords (approving a Court of Appeal case *Gothard v Mirror Group Newspapers Limited*[1]), such payments were designed by the employer to extinguish any claim for damages for breach of contract – i.e. wrongful dismissal – and during the period to which the money in lieu relates, a person is not employed by his employer. As such, they could not be wages.

Accordingly, Pumfrey J held that if the administrators were to adopt the players' contracts and subsequently dismissed them, any damages payable for wrongful dismissal would not be 'wages' within paragraph 99(5)(c). Further, Pumfrey J referred to the Court of Appeal decision *in Re Huddersfield Fine Worsteds Limited*[2] which considered the meaning of the word 'wages' in paragraph 99. Pumfrey J held that he was bound by that decision which had held that payments falling within Lord Browne-Wilkinson's fourth class of payments in lieu are not entitled to super priority.

1 [1988] ICR 729; [1988] IRLR 396, CA.
2 [2005] EWCA Civ 1072; [2005] 4 All ER 886, CA. See para 18.79 above.

Statutory obligation as breach of contract?

18.101 Can breach of a statutory obligation also be a breach of contract? No, stated the EAT in *Doherty v British Midland Airways*[1]. Maybe sometimes, suggested a different division of the EAT in *Greenhof v Barnsley Metropolitan Council*[2].

1 [2006] IRLR 90, EAT.
2 [2006] IRLR 98, EAT – and see IRLR comments at page 74.

18.102 In *Doherty*, the employee had claimed constructive dismissal based partly on an alleged failure by the employer to allow her various rights in relation to trade union activities. She claimed that the breach of the statutory protections in TULRCA 1992, ss 152 and 170, amounted to a breach of contract, entitling her to resign and claim constructive dismissal. The EAT held that conditions replicating statutory rights could not be implied into a contract of employment.

18.103 The EAT held:

> '25.   The first issue is the claim said by Counsel for the Claimant to be novel and without authority. Unabashed by that, Ms Rayner made the same point to us as she made to the Employment Tribunal, which is that there is, as a matter of contract, a right which corresponds in language to the three statutory rights protecting trade unionists when they carry out trade union activities. That right of action in contract is not arrived at by reason of any of the conventional tools, such as necessity, business efficacy, to make the contract workable, or to reflect the intentions of the parties. On the contrary, it is there because the statute provides such a right. In an engaging exchange with the bench, Ms Rayner said, "as a matter of logic, it must be right. There is no authority on this point." In an equally engaging exchange, Mr Bowers said it must be wrong.

26.Let us just paint a picture of how this would work if Ms Rayner were right. Today, across the road in the Strand, there would be sitting half a dozen courts, presided over by judges of the Queen's Bench, determining, for example, whether an employee of a London borough had been discriminated against on the grounds of his or her race. Some of these claims would be very old, because the time limit would not be three months but six years. The expertise in dealing with these matters, which is presently in the hands of employment tribunals, consisting, as they do, of persons with specialist knowledge of race relations, would be missing. So would the specialist judicial officer. So would the informal and user-friendly cost-free regime in which such claims are heard presently by employment tribunals. Any breach of the Race Relations Act 1976, on this thesis, would be actionable as a breach of contract. There would, of course, then be issues of costs. In a case where there had been racial harassment, one person missing from the drama would be the very perpetrator, since, whereas in an employment tribunal such person can be brought in as an aider and abetter, in a breach of contract this person would be absent.

27.That is just a brief snapshot as to why Ms Rayner's proposition is wholly misconceived in our judgment. It cannot be right that, as she put it, the range of rights set out in Professor Peter Wallington's estimable handbook, which takes pride of place on our bench, constitutes a contractual rulebook, actionable at the suit of an employee for every single breach that there is. The sole basis upon which her proposition was advanced was a passage in a book written by Mr Selwyn, in which he says that certain aspects of the statute may be the source of contractual terms. That of course is true of Equal Pay Act 1970, the National Minimum Wage Act 1998, the Working Time Regulations 1998, and other statutes which directly affect the contractual relationship. But in our judgment it does not provide a justification for the implication of a contractual term covering precisely the same territory as the statute. We reject this contention.'

18.104   Conversely, in *Greenhof*, the EAT held that a serious breach by an employer of its duty to make reasonable adjustments as required under the Disability Discrimination Act 1995, amounted to a breach of the implied duty of maintaining trust and confidence and consequently a repudiatory breach of contract entitling the employee to resign and claim constructive dismissal.

18.105   Although dealing with the issue of a claim for unfair dismissal (and not the adopted liabilities issue under IA 1986), these could be pointers to the adopted liabilities decision.

18.106   An analogy could perhaps be drawn with the decisions of the ECJ as to whether some benefits are 'pay'. In *Barber v Guardian Royal Exchange*[1] the ECJ had to decide whether pension benefits which replaced those provided by the state (contracted-out schemes) were pay within Art 119 (now Art 141 of the EU Treaty) or social security within Art 118 of the Treaty of Rome. The ECJ decided that the benefits had become pay. It did not matter that the minimum level was laid down by statute – minimum benefits such as sick pay and redundancy laid down by statute still became pay if they were payable by the employer.

1 [1990] ECR I-1889; [1990] 2 All ER 660; (C-262/88), ECJ.

18.107 In R *v Secretary of State, ex p Seymour Smith*[1], the House of Lords referred to the ECJ the question of whether or not awards for unfair dismissal are pay within Art119 of the Treaty of Rome. The ECJ ruled that such awards do constitute 'pay'.

1 [1999] ECR I-623; [1999] 2 AC 554, ECJ; [2000] 1 WLR 435, HL.

18.108 But these decisions are obviously construing a different provision.

It seems right to distinguish the decision of the Court of Appeal in *Hutchings v Islington Borough Council*[1] that the county court had jurisdiction to hear a claim based on a statutory pension right on the basis that this claim was 'founded on' a contract of employment.

1 [1998] ICR 1230; [1998] 3 All ER 445, CA.

18.109 Tortious liabilities: For example damages for personal injury caused by negligence. Such a claim is probably available both under tort and contract – see *Matthews v Kuwait Bechtel Corp*[1] and *Henderson v Merrett Syndicates*[2].

1 [1959] 2 QB 57, CA.
2 [1995] 2 AC 145, HL.

18.110 In any event it seems unlikely that a tort claim would not be considered as being 'under' the contract of employment – see the comments of Peter Gibson LJ in the TUPE case, *Bernadone v Pall Mall Services Group*[1].

1 [2000] IRLR 487, CA.

TABLE OF ADOPTED CLAIMS

18.111 The table below attempts to give some broad outlines of the position of administrators and administrative receivers both before and after the IA 1994. See also the chart at the end of Chapter 17 in relation to administration expenses

Type of claim	Priority on adoption before 15 March 1994?	Priority on adoption on or after 15 March 1994?
Cash wages or salary	YES, subject to having been incurred while in office (Paramount and Leyland DAF)	YES, subject to having been incurred while in office
Contractual bonus	Same as wages or salary (can be difficult question as to when incurred – eg when payable or over the period in relation to which it is calculated?)	Same as wages or salary (can be difficult question as to when incurred AND whether is in respect of services after the adoption – eg when payable or over the period in relation to which it is calculated?)

Type of claim	Priority on adoption before 15 March 1994?	Priority on adoption on or after 15 March 1994?
Contractual benefits in kind	YES, as above	NO (not a 'liability to pay a sum')
Discretionary benefits (eg discretionary bonus)	NO	NO
Pay in lieu of notice/ damages for breach of contract	YES	NO (not wages or salary unless express term – *Delaney v Staples, Huddersfield* and Leeds United)
Holiday pay (contractual)	YES	YES for holiday taken while business continued, YES for pay in lieu at termination if it relates to service after adoption (see *Re Douai School*)
Maternity/sickness pay	Probably YES (same as wages or salary) subject to argument that statutory and therefore not arising 'under' the contract	Arguably NO (not a liability in respect of services rendered after the adoption?) – difficult time apportionment under IA 1986, s 44(2C)(a) and Schedule B1, para 99(6)(b)
Health and safety claims	Probably YES (implied contractual duty)	Probably YES (implied contractual duty)
Redundancy claims	YES if contractual, NO if statutory only – Hughes	NO (not a liability in respect of services rendered after the adoption)
Unfair dismissal claims	NO – statutory only, not a liability 'under' contract – Paramount and *Albion Automotives v Shaw*	NO – statutory only, not a liability 'under' contract
Protective awards	NO – statutory only, neither a liability 'under' contract nor 'wages or salary' — Huddersfield	NO – statutory only, neither a liability 'under' contract – nor 'wages or salary' – Huddersfield

Type of claim	Priority on adoption before 15 March 1994?	Priority on adoption on or after 15 March 1994?
Pension contributions	YES if contractual, probably NO if a final salary scheme	YES if contractual and a money purchase occupational scheme, probably NO if a personal pension scheme or if a final salary scheme – see below
Deficit claims by pension trustees (Pension Act 1995, s 75)	NO – statutory only, not a liability 'under' contract, also liability is to trustees, not employees	NO – statutory only, not a liability 'under' contract, also liability is to trustees, not employees

PENSION CLAIMS

18.112 The position of the priority of claims in relation to pension schemes remains unhelpfully unclear. Money purchase occupational pension schemes (and in relation to employees whose contracts were adopted before 15 March 1994, personal pension schemes) would seem to be likely to be covered by the statutory priority on the basis that the liability to contribute is likely to be contractual and owed to each individual employee. The *Paramount Airways* case itself seems to have involved a money purchase scheme, with the contract of employment referring to a booklet which specified an employer contribution rate – see the comments of Evans-Lombe J at first instance[1].

1 [1993] BCC 662 at 666B (Evans-Lombe J).

18.113 Conversely, in relation to employment contracts adopted after 15 March 1994, the statutory provisions only refer to contributions to occupational pension schemes. The term 'occupational pension scheme' is not defined, but it seems likely that the definitions in section 1 of the Pension Schemes Act 1993 will be applied[1].

1 See para 2.60 above.

18.114 On this basis any liability to contribute to personal pension schemes will not be a qualifying liability with the 'super priority'. This is to be contrasted with the position in relation to the guarantee from the National Insurance Fund under PSA 1993 (see Chapter 13 above) which covers occupational schemes and personal pensions.

18.115 The position of final salary (defined benefit) pension schemes is much more obscure. In *Leyland Daf* and *Ferranti* cases, the relevant employees were given damages compensating them for the loss of benefits during the notice

301

period to which they were entitled but did not receive on termination of employment. Other pensions issues did not seem to be addressed and in this light the general comments by Lord Browne-Wilkinson in *Powdrill v Watson* to the effect that pension contributions are within the super priority must be regarded as not being definitive.

18.116   Thus where there are still adopted employees in the pension scheme, this may mean that claims are made by trustees (or by individual employees) that any deficit liabilities are also entitled to the super priority. It would seem clear that any such deficit claims which were raised merely under the relevant statute (eg the Pensions Act 1995 – eg the minimum funding requirement or employer debt provisions under PA 1995, s 75 or the Pensions Act 2004 – scheme specific funding – see Chapters 33 and 34 below) are statutory and so not covered by the statutory priority.

18.117   However, any claims that could be made by the trustees under the terms of the trust deed and rules governing the scheme could be categorised as contractual (see eg Lord Millett in *Air Jamaica v Charlton*[1]), but it is difficult to see that they are capable of enforcement by individual employees (as opposed to by trustees).

1 [1999] 1 WLR 1399, PC.

18.118   This makes it look unlikely to be a liability arising under the contract of employment – instead (like a protective award) it:

> 'no doubt arises because of the existence of a contract of employment'

(see the distinction made by Neuberger LJ in *Re Huddersfield Fine Worsetds*[1] at para 17).

1 [2005] EWCA Civ 1072; [2005] 4 All ER 886; [2005] IRLR 995, CA – see para 18.79 above.

18.119   There is some case law to indicate that there may be an obligation implied into the employment contract on an employer to fund a scheme.

18.120   Nourse LJ commented in *Mihlenstedt v Barclays Bank*[1] that:

> 'But it was a term of her contract of employment with the Bank that she should be entitled to membership of the pension scheme and to the benefits thereunder. From that it must follow, as a matter of necessary implication, that the Bank became contractually bound, so far as it lay within its power, to procure for the plaintiff the benefits to which she was entitled under the scheme.'

1 [1989] IRLR 522, CA at para 12.

18.121   In Australia, Warren J commented in *Ansett Australia Ground Staff Superannuation Plan Pty Ltd v Ansett Australia Ltd*[1] that:

> '245 The trustee and the fourth defendant submitted that a further basis exists for saying that the employer is liable to make such contributions as will ensure that

all defined benefits are paid to members of the Plan. The trustee and the representative defendants submitted that there was a contractual obligation imposed on Ansett to contribute an amount to the Plan that was sufficient to provide the benefits promised by the Plan including the retrenchment benefit under rule 1.13.

246 The trustee and the representative defendants relied upon two factors to support the assertion of the contractual obligation imposed on Ansett. First, the standard terms and conditions of Ansett that required all Ansett employees to be a member of one of the Ansett superannuation plans. Second, promises made by Ansett in the applicable Plan member booklets from time to time. The fact of the mandatory requirement of membership and the promises contained in the member booklets was not in issue. However, the approach to and application of those factors was challenged by the administrators. I have no difficulty that there was a contractual obligation imposed on Ansett. The question is, however, when the liability arising thereunder was incurred. On proper analysis, the obligation fell upon the administrators arising from two separate sources. First, under the trust deed and the superannuation legislative regime. Secondly, under the contracts of employment of the employees. I accept that the obligation of Ansett arises under both the trust deed and the SIS Legislation and also as an additional or commensurate obligation under the contract of employment. The liability that arises under either obligation is provable in the winding up pursuant to s. 553 of the Corporations Act. Indeed, the trustee submitted a proof of debt.'

1 [2002] VSC 576 (Warren J).

18.122 More recently in the UK, the EAT commented in *Benson v Secretary of State*[1] that pension contributions are not covered by the national insurance fund guarantee relating to 'arrears of pay' in the Employment Rights Act 1996

1 [2003] IRLR 748, at para 20, EAT.

18.123 Clearly, the definition of 'qualifying liability' is wide enough to cover contributions to a final salary occupational pension scheme. In the debate on the Insolvency Bill in the House of Lords on 22 March 1994, the relevant Minister of State (Lord Strathclyde) confirmed (at column 624 of Hansard) that the government intended that these words should cover payments to 'a pension scheme referable to a period of service, rather than in respect of services rendered'. The meaning is unclear but the Minister may have been trying to draw a distinction between a final salary scheme and a money purchase scheme.

18.124 Difficult problems would remain as regards apportionment of the claim (only that part of a claim relating to the period of adopted service should be claimable, unless it could be said that the whole claim is 'incurred' when it is demanded). It is difficult to see why an individual 'adopted' employee should, in effect, be entitled to raise the statutory priority to cover all members of the scheme, including pensioners and those who left service some time ago.

18.125 Conversely, failure to provide benefits under a final salary scheme (eg during a notice period) may well be contractual and (arguably) part of the individual employee's contract of employment. However, such a claim does not seem to be a 'contribution' within the IA 1994. In addition it may well not arise in respect of periods after the scheme has been wound-up (it is common for provision for the employer to be able to trigger a scheme winding up to be reserved in the scheme booklet and hence it is probably not a breach of contract). It may also be possible to offset against any pension claim any increased benefits that are granted under the pension scheme as part of the winding up (eg if the scheme is in surplus and the trustees resolve to increase benefits).

18.126 Even if the answer to all the above is that there is a liability under the IA 1994 on the administrator or administrative receiver to contribute and this liability constitutes a 'qualifying liability', how in fact is it to be calculated?

- Is the administrator or administrative receiver to be expected to contribute even if the scheme is in surplus?

- What if the scheme is in deficit?

- What do we mean by the terms 'surplus' and 'deficit' for this purpose?

18.127 It is currently quite easy for a scheme to be in surplus (using its own actuarial assumptions) but to be in deficit on a winding-up basis (assessed by reference to the cost of purchasing insurance company annuities – see Chapter 33 below). In addition, liabilities can be assessed on an ongoing basis (ie including provision for anticipated salary increases) or a termination basis (no such provision).

18.128 Is the administrator or administrative receiver meant to contribute an amount equal to any increase in liabilities occurring as a result of the continued employment (in pensionable service) of the relevant employees? If so, how is this liability to be calculated (by reference to the scheme's actuarial assumptions, by reference to statutory cash equivalents or by reference to insurance company buy-out costs?).

18.129 Even if the method of calculating the contribution rate can be fixed, the difficulties in dealing with a surplus or a deficit remain. Commonly, schemes and employers often used to establish a normal or regular funding cost (ie ignoring any surplus or deficit) and then adjusted this rate to reflect any perceived deficit or surplus (see eg the accounting standards FRS17 and IAS 19 for the requirement to follow this practice for accounting purposes). More common now is for deficits to be addressed by specific lump sum contribution provisions

18.130 In practice, the insolvency practitioner may well argue that:

(a) If there is a deficit, only the regular cost is payable. This is on the basis that the deficit must be attributable to the period of employment prior to the adoption of the contract. This is perhaps supported by the cryptic statement of Lord Strathclyde in the House of Lords, mentioned at para 18.123 above.

(b) If there is a surplus, the regular cost should be reduced to reflect this. This is on the basis that it represents the actual on-going cost and hence the liability attributable to the period of employment after adoption.

18.131 The position may have been affected by the introduction after 1997 (for relevant schemes) of the schedule of contributions under s 58 of the Pensions Act 1995 and now s 227 of the Pensions Act 2004. Amounts shown in the schedule are a statutory debt[1] – see further para 33.78 below.

1 See PA 1995, s 59(2) and PA 2004, s 228(3).

18.132 All of these liabilities in relation to a defined benefit pension scheme look unlikely to qualify as an adopted liability with the super priority. This is because:

- The funding liability is likely to be owed to the scheme trustees and not to the individual employee (see para 18.116 above).

- The liability will tend to be statutory and not contractual in many cases (*Huddersfield* again). Although there are pension schemes where there is a contractual funding provision under the scheme documents, it may be that this contractual provision is superseded by the statutory provisions on scheme specific funding in PA 2004 (see Chapter 33 below); and

- Any deficit or on-going contribution liability will relate to the period before the insolvency event and so not count. Such a liability will be excluded because:

- in relation to an administrative receiver, it does not count as being incurred while the IP is in office (IA 1986, ss 44(2A)(b)) or in relation to services rendered after the adoption of the employment contract (IA 1986, s 44(2A)(c)); or

- in relation to a post 2003 administration, it falls within para 99(5)(b) of Sch B1 which provides that 'no account shall be taken of a liability which arises, or in so far as it arises, by reference to anything which is done or which occurs before the adoption of the contract of employment'.

18.133 In relation to this third bullet, the liability will relate to the period before the formal insolvency event/adoption of the employment contract (usually after the 14 day period) because:

- Any s 75 deficit liability will (from 6 April 2005) relate to a period before the appointment of the insolvency practitioner (any s 75 debt is deemed for insolvency law purposes to arise immediately before the appointment (s 75(4A) and is contingent on either a scheme failure notice being issued or the scheme starting to wind-up (PA 1995, s 75(4C)) – see Chapter 34 below); and

- If the scheme is an eligible scheme to enter the Pension Protection Fund (PPF), the formal insolvency will (from 6 April 2005) usually trigger the start of an assessment period (see Chapter 28 below). During an assessment period, there is no further accrual of benefits (PA 2004, s133(5)) and no contributions can be paid to the scheme, save for any s 75 debt (PA 2004, s133(3), and PPF Entry Rules Regulations, reg 14) – see Chapter 28 below.

If there is a scheme rescue (or a non-segregation notice in a multi-employer scheme), the obligation revives (see para 33.85 below). If there is no scheme rescue etc, there can be no obligation to contribute to the scheme in relation to the assessment period (and hence no liability under an adopted employment contract).

TUPE TRANSFERS

18.134 Does the super priority remain if the administrator or receiver arranges for the business of the company to be sold and the Transfer of Undertakings (Protection of Employment) Regulations (TUPE) apply to transfer the employment of an employee whose contract of employment had previously been adopted by the administrator or receiver?

18.135 The insolvent transferor company generally ceases to be liable – see *Stirling District Council v Allan*[1] in relation to TUPE 1981. The position has not changed under TUPE 2006. The UK decided against including in the new TUPE (amended following amendments to the Acquired Rights Directive) to provide for joint and several liability for both the transferor and transferee generally following a TUPE transfer. Some liability can remain on the transferor – eg pensions (TUPE 2006, reg 10) and the new joint and several liability on the transferor and the transferee included in TUPE 2006 for failure to consult about a TUPE transfer – TUPE 2006, reg 15(9) (see Chapter 21 below).

1 [1995] IRLR 301, Court of Session, Inner House. See also *Clarke v Mediguard Services Ltd* [2000] NI 73, NI CA.

18.136 It is considered that the liability of a receiver must be viewed as a secondary liability (in a similar way to a guarantor) so that the receiver ceases to be liable if the company ceases to be liable. The same would then apply to the priority given in administrations. However, contrary views have been expressed.

FOURTEEN-DAY PERIOD FOLLOWING APPOINTMENT

18.137 Both s 44(2) (administrative receivers) and para 99 of Sch B1 (administrators) (replacing s 19) state that a contract of employment is not to be taken as adopted by reason of anything done or omitted to be done within 14 days after the appointment of the administrator or administrative receiver. Taken literally, this would seem to prevent an administrator or administrative receiver from making a final decision and positively acting to adopt an employment contract within the first 14 days.

18.138 Given that the clear intention of these provisions is to give a breathing space to the administrator or administrative receiver to decide whether or not employment contracts are going to be adopted, it seems an unnecessarily strict interpretation of these sections to preclude an employee from relying on a notification or decision of the administrator or administrative receiver made within the first 14 days but clearly intended to be final and to apply after the 14-day period has ended.

PAYE AND NATIONAL INSURANCE

18.139 Generally, insolvency practitioners have the practice of arranging for the insolvent company to deduct income tax and national insurance contributions from amounts paid by the insolvent company to employees – for a fuller discussion of the position in relation to liability to deduct these taxes see Chapter 25 below. The Court of Appeal in *Inland Revenue Commissioners v Lawrence*[1] held that such liabilities fall within the super-priority in relation to adopted employment contacts, but the rationale for this is unclear – see para 18.52 above.

1 [2001] 1 BCLC 145, CA.

VOLUNTARY PAYMENTS

18.140 Whatever the strict legal position as regards a liability to an employee, situations commonly arise where the continued employment and goodwill of certain employees is regarded by the insolvency practitioner as desirable in order to preserve the business and assets of the company and hence properly achieve the purpose of the insolvency proceedings (eg by maximising the value of the assets of the company for creditors).

18.141 In such circumstances, the insolvency practitioner may consider it appropriate to agree with the employees that payment should be made of amounts due to them, even where it is clear that those amounts would not otherwise rank as insolvency expenses or as a personal liability of the insolvency practitioner.

18.142 If such payments are made in good faith, they should be recoverable by the insolvency practitioner out of the assets of the insolvent company as expenses of the insolvency proceedings[1].

1 See *Nicoll v Cutts* [1985] BCLC 322, CA and *Freakley v Centre Reinsurance International Co* [2006] UKHL 45; [2006] 1 WLR 2863, HL at para 16.

18.143 Where there are certain crucial individuals necessary to the continued survival of the business, it may well be that such individuals can negotiate from the insolvency practitioner a premium (over and above their existing contractual rights) as the price of staying with the business. See for example the bonus agreement mentioned in the decision of the Court of Appeal in *Powdrill v Watson*[1] and the holiday pay arrangements of the administrator in *Re Douai School (Re a Company No 005174)*[2] noted by Neuberger J.

1 [1994] 2 All ER 513 at 515, CA.
2 [2000] 1 WLR 502 (Neuberger J).

18.144 Judge Norris QC also endorsed this in *Re MG Rover Espana SA*[1], holding that it was open to an administrator to make payments to employees outside the UK which would not be covered by the UK legislation.

1 [2006] BCC 599 (Judge Norris QC) – noted in (2005) 21 Insolvency Law & Practice 91. See also Chapter 40 below.

18.145 Where the insolvency practitioner does make a payment to the employee, he or she should be careful to make it clear that the payment relates to a liability which has the super-priority under the Insolvency Act and not in respect of some other debt (eg a liability relating to a period of employment before the appointment of the insolvency practitioner). See the decision of the Federal Court in Australia in *Krysh v Corrales Pty Ltd*[1] for an example of an implied appropriation. Contrast the decision (in relation to a warehouseman's lien) of the High Court of Australia in *Majeau Carrying Co Pty Ltd v Coastal Rutile Ltd*[2] where there was no express appropriation.

1 (1989) 7 ACLC 1006 (Marling, Pincus and Lee JJ).
2 (1973) 129 CLR 48 (Menzies, Gibbs and Stephens JJ).

18.146 If the insolvency practitioner mistakenly makes a payment, thinking the relevant liability has a super-priority, it will not ordinarily be possible to reclaim the payment (as being paid under a mistake of law) or seek to set the payment made off against another liability. See the decision of Neuberger J in *Re Douai School (Re a Company No 005174 of 1999)*[1].

1 [2000] 1 WLR 502 (Neuberger J) and see para 18.61 above.

CHAPTER 19

Transfer of undertakings: introduction and impact of Europe

TRANSFER OF BUSINESS

19.1 It will commonly be the case that an insolvency practitioner will decide that it is in the interests of the insolvency proceedings for the existing business of the insolvent employer company (or part of that business) to be transferred as a going concern.

19.2 Such a transfer can either be by way of a disposal of the business (or part) to an unconnected third party or, alternatively, by way of a hive-down of the business (or part) from the insolvent employer company to a subsidiary company newly formed for this purpose.

19.3 Such hive-downs were more frequent in the past (when there was the possibility of preserving tax losses), but have become less common following the change in the tax position made by the Finance Act 1986. However, such a hive-down may still be thought suitable, for example where the company is in liquidation and the liquidator considers that the power to continue the business given to the liquidator is insufficient.

Application of TUPE

19.4 The transfer of a business (particularly on an on going basis, rather than through an asset sale), whether to a third party or by way of a hive-down, will usually constitute a transfer of an undertaking within the meaning of the Transfer of Undertakings (Protection of Employment) Regulations 2006[1] (TUPE 2006). With effect for transfers on and after 6 April 2006, the 2006 Regulations replaced the Transfer of Undertakings (Protection of Employment) Regulations 1981[2] (TUPE 1981).

1 SI 2006/246.
2 SI 1981/1794 as amended.

19.5 If TUPE applies, the general legal principles relevant to such a transfer of business are that almost all liabilities owed by the insolvent company to or in respect of the employees employed in ('assigned' to) the relevant business will automatically transfer to the purchaser (TUPE 2006, reg 4). There are some limited exceptions.

19.6 Any liability for claims relating to protective awards under TULRCA 1992 (see para 3.6 above) for redundancies made by the transferor/company pass to the transferee/purchaser. In 1985 the EAT held in *Angus Jowett v NUTGW*[1] that a liability in relation to a protective award did not transfer under TUPE 1981. However, changes made to TULRCA 1992 in 1995 gave extended individual rights to employees. In *Kerry Foods Ltd v Creber*[2] the EAT held that a liability for a protective award will under TUPE transfer. Kerry Foods was followed by the EAT in *Alamo Group (Europe) Ltd v Tucker*[3] and in *Ladies' Health & Fitness Club Ltd v Eastmond*[4], in preference to the EAT's decision in *TGWU v James McKinnon Jr (Haulage)*[5] which had held to the contrary.

The liability for a compensatory award for failure to inform and consult under TUPE itself should also have transferred under TUPE 1981 (the liability is now joint and several under TUPE 2006, reg 15(9)).

1 [1985] ICR 646, EAT.
2 [2000] IRLR 10, EAT.
3 [2003] IRLR 266, EAT.
4 (2004) 21 January (UKEAT/0094/03/RN), EAT.
5 [2001] IRLR 597, EAT.

19.7 The insolvent company as transferor will retain no rights or liabilities to the transferring employees or under TUPE save:

(a) under TUPE 2006 (unlike TUPE 1981), the transferor retains joint and several liability with the transferee/ purchaser for any failure to comply with the information and consultation obligations under TUPE – TUPE 2006, reg 15(9),

(b) criminal liabilities are retained – reg 4(6);

(c) rights and liabilities in relation to an occupational pension scheme do not generally transfer – see eg *Hagen v ICI*[1] and further Chapter 24 below;

(d) if any affected employees of the insolvent transferor are not assigned to the transferring business, but are affected by the transfer, a consultation obligation may arise under TUPE 2006. If so, any liability for failure to comply would remain with the insolvent company;

(e) the insolvent company will remain liable for any failure to provide the transferor with the relevant details about the transferring employees under regulation 11 of TUPE 2006 – see para 13.144 below

(f) if the employee exercises his or her right to object to the transfer and terminate the contract of employment where the transfer involves a significant change which is to the employee's detriment – reg 4(9) and the decision in *University of Oxford v Humphries*[2];

(g) rights and liabilities in relation to an employee who exercises his right under regulation 4(8) of TUPE 2006 (TUPE 1981, reg 5(4A)) to object to the transfer, in circumstances where the employee had a right to terminate his contract under reg 4(9) of TUPE 2006 (TUPE 1981, reg 5(5)) on the basis of a substantial change in working conditions to his detriment, will remain with the transferor/company – see the decision of the Court of Appeal in *University of Oxford v Humphries*[2],

(f) TUPE 2006 contains special new rules applicable in some insolvencies, whereby some liabilities are retained – see further Chapter 20 below.

1 [2002] IRLR 31 (Elias J)
2 [2000] ICR 405, CA.

19.8 It has been argued that the company (or insolvency practitioner) retains its statutory liabilities to employees even after a TUPE transfer – for example, if the employees are preferential creditors of the company under Sch 6 to the IA 1986 in relation to outstanding remuneration (see Chapter 9 above) or if the insolvency practitioners owe *Paramount* liabilities to employees (see Chapter 18 above). It is thought that this is mistaken.

19.9 Generally, the transferor company will cease to have any liability to the transferred employees following a TUPE transfer – see the decision of the Inner House of the Court of Session in *Stirling District Council v Allan*[1] and the Northern Ireland Court of Appeal in *Clarke v Mediguard Services Ltd*[2]. So there can be no preferential debt remaining (there is no debt) and there is no place for a secondary liability to remain. Under TUPE 2006, this is subject to the new special rules applicable in some insolvencies and to the joint and several liability for failure to inform and consult.

1 [1995] IRLR 301, Inner House, Court of Session.
2 [2000] NI 73, NI CA.

19.10 It is clear that a transfer of an undertaking can be made by a company in insolvency (see *Teesside Times Ltd v Drury*[1] and *Thomsons Soft Drinks Ltd v Quaife*[2], cases on continuity of employment under EPCA 1978 (now consolidated into ERA 1996), and the cases in the European Court cited in para 19.29 below). However, there are three particular issues that arise in relation to transfers by insolvent companies:

(a) judicial interpretation of the underlying Acquired Rights Directive and TUPE indicated that the legislation may not apply in all insolvency situations. Special provision was made in the new Directive and is now incorporated in TUPE 2006 dealing with insolvencies;

(b) a special provision was made in TUPE 1981 in relation to hive-downs in insolvency; and

(c) the position where there are dismissals before or after the relevant transfer has been the subject of much judicial scrutiny (see Chapter 23 below).

1 [1980] ICR 338, CA.
2 8 June 1981, EAT.

Insolvency and TUPE

19.11   So far as an employee is concerned, TUPE operates as a matter of law to allocate liabilities and responsibilities relating to the employee between the transferor/seller and the transferee/purchaser of a business. Generally it is open to the transferor/seller and transferee/purchaser to agree how they will bear the economic cost of the operation of TUPE (eg a purchaser may seek indemnities from the seller for liabilities that arose before the transfer date or (which is more common in an insolvency situation) adjust the purchase price). It may be that an exception to this is that separate indemnities cannot cover the seller's liability to provide information to the purchaser – see TUPE 2006, reg 11 and para 21.21 below.

19.12   From the employee's perspective, assuming that both entities are solvent it may not matter particularly which of the two entities is in fact responsible.

However if the transferor/seller has (or is likely to) become insolvent, then it will be a matter of much more concern for the employees to seek to ensure that any rights and obligations have transferred to an acquirer of all or part of the relevant business of the insolvent entity. This is because the transferee/purchaser is much more likely to be solvent and, if it is, will be in a position to ensure that all obligations, including those which relate to service before any transfer, are in fact met in full.

19.13   TUPE 1981 did not expressly exclude transfers made by a business which is in insolvency proceedings (liquidation, administration or receivership). But special provision was made by TUPE 1981 to deal with hive downs in insolvency. New TUPE 2006 has expanded this special treatment where the transferor/seller is in insolvency proceedings (see Chapter 20 below).

19.14   TUPE does not fit well with the general laws on insolvency regarding priority of claims. A simple example shows this.

(a)   Say that a company enters insolvent liquidation. It has assets in the form of a business which is worth £1m. It has creditors totalling £2m of which £100,000 represents unpaid wages to employees. Let us assume that the claims of the employees are not preferential in liquidation, so rank equally with all the other creditors.

(b)   So if there is no sale of the business as a going concern, the position under the insolvency laws will be that all the creditors will receive 50p in the pound. This will include the employees to the extent of the liability to pay them their past wages.

(c)   Of course it could be open to the employees (depending on how they are essential they are to the business) to negotiate that their past wages are paid in full by any successor of the business. But absent this, the loss would fall on the employees.

(d)   However, if TUPE applies that when the business is transferred as a going concern, the purchaser will assume liability for the £100,000 in back wages.

In practice this means that the purchaser should take account of this liability when fixing the price it pays to the liquidator of the company for the business.

(e)   So the purchaser will pay only £900,000 for the business. The employees will be paid their back wage claim in full (the purchaser being solvent). The liability remaining with the insolvent company is now only £1.9m, but only £900,000 in assets have been received. So the remaining creditors, instead of receiving 50p in the pound, now receive only a bit above 47p in the pound.

(f)   In effect, because the claims of the employees are attached to the business assets, their claims of being given a super priority as a result of the TUPE transfer. In effect TUPE would have overwritten the general insolvency priority rules.

19.15   It may be argued that the insolvency practitioner (IP) now running the insolvent company needs to balance the benefits for the transferring employees of any super priority under TUPE against the potential adverse impact for the other creditors. It is unusual to give the IP a power to change to order of payment of claims outside the priority rules in the insolvency legislation, but this is not unknown (eg power to the IP to agree to pay one creditor where necessary to continue the business[1]). Professor Davies has pointed out in his article 'Employee claims in insolvency: Corporate rescues and preferential claims'[2], that an administrator (unlike an administrative receiver) is meant to be looking after the company/business a whole and not primarily the interests of one creditor.

1   See the section on 'voluntary payments' at the end of Chapter 18 above. And see Chapter 40 below.
2   (1994) 23 ILJ 141.

19.16   The 1977 Acquired Rights Directive (ARD) and TUPE 1981 made no express provision for such an insolvency situation. However, the European Court of Justice (ECJ) ruled in 1985 in *Abels*[1] that the ARD does not apply to transfers where the transferor/seller has been adjudged insolvent and the undertaking or business formed part of the assets of the insolvent transferor. In effect the ECJ read a limited insolvency exception into the ARD – an interesting example of judicial law writing. This is discussed in more depth below, but in summary:

(a)   It seems clear that the insolvency limitation to the old ARD only applied to insolvent liquidations. The old ARD probably applied to a solvent liquidation – see *Jules Dethier*[2] and *Europieces SA v Sanders*[3].

(b)   In addition the insolvency limitation probably did not apply to an administration (*Jules Dethier*) nor a receivership.

(c)   The UK enactment of the ARD is TUPE. TUPE 1981 did not contain an express exclusion of liquidations from its ambit. But the EAT held that old TUPE does not apply to a transfer from a company in liquidation. In *Perth & Kinross Council v Donaldson*[4], the EAT in Scotland held that TUPE 1981 did not apply to transfers taking place in the context of a liquidation.

This was because ARD did not apply to a liquidation. So TUPE 1981 should be seen as not applying as well.

(d)   The English Court of Appeal subsequently doubted the reasoning of the EAT in Donaldson. In *Oakley Inc v Animal Ltd*⁵, the Court of Appeal considered the reasoning of the EAT in *Donaldson* to be wrong, but did not give a very coherent reason why. It is unclear where this left the status of TUPE 1981 on this point (the Court of Appeal was concerned with a different set of regulations).

1   [1985] ECR 469, ECJ.
2   [1998] ECR I-1061, ECJ.
3   [1998] ECR I-6965; [1999] All ER (EC) 831, ECJ.
4   [2004] IRLR 121, EAT.
5   [2005] EWCA Civ 1191; [2006] Ch 337, CA.

ACQUIRED RIGHTS DIRECTIVE 1977

Applicability on insolvency

19.17   TUPE 1981 was enacted to implement EC Directive 77/187 (the 'Acquired Rights Directive' or 'ARD') 'on the approximation of the laws of the Member States relating to the safeguarding of employees' rights in the event of transfers of undertakings, businesses or parts of businesses'.

19.18   There was no express exception in the 1977 Directive for the case where the transferring business has become insolvent or entered into insolvency proceedings.

19.19   However, in 1985 in *Abels v Administrative Board of the Bedrijfsvereniging voor de Metaalindustrie en de Electrotechnische Industrie*¹, the European Court of Justice ruled that the ARD did not apply to transfers 'where the transferor has been adjudged insolvent and the undertaking or business in question forms part of the assets of the insolvent transferor'.

1   [1985] ECR 469; [1987] 2 CMLR 406, ECJ.

19.20   In Ireland, Hamilton J in the High Court held on 25 March 1985 in *Re Castle Brand Ltd*¹ that the Irish Regulations, SI 1980/306, enacting the Acquired Rights Directive could not, in the light of the relevant decisions of the European Court (presumably Abels), apply in a court liquidation. However, the Irish Regulations are worded differently to TUPE 1981 (in particular, reg 2(2) provided that expressions used in the Irish Regulations have the same meaning as in the Acquired Rights Directive).

1   Unreported. See the paper by Hugh Cooney, the liquidator of Castle Brand Limited, given to a conference at the Irish Centre for European Law in November 1988.

Applicability of TUPE 1981 on insolvency

19.21   However, TUPE 1981 did not expressly provide for the exclusion of the transfers made by insolvent companies. Regulation 4 of TUPE 1981 dealing with hive-downs (see para 20.55 below) was an indication that TUPE 1981 was intended to apply to insolvent companies. It would seem that this was permitted by virtue of Art 7 of the 1977 Acquired Rights Directive which stated that the Directive does not affect the right of Member States to introduce laws which are more favourable to employees – see, for example, *P Bork International A/S v Foreningen af Arbejdsledere i Danmark*[1].

1 [1985] ECR 469; [1987] 2 CMLR 406, ECJ.

19.22   There was nevertheless some doubt as to whether TUPE 1981 was in fact validly enacted to achieve this extended effect. TUPE 1981 was passed as a statutory instrument under the special procedure under s 2 of the European Communities Act 1972 relating to enactment of EC Directives (rather than by a formal Act of Parliament).

19.23   Accordingly, it was possible to argue that TUPE 1981 was ineffective in situations which are outside the Directive (following *Abels*), and therefore did not apply to transfers where the transferor has been 'adjudged insolvent'. The latter term may be limited to situations where there has actually been a court liquidation order (ie a court winding up).

19.24   The above argument was less easily sustainable following the enactment of the Trade Union Reform and Employment Rights Act 1993. Section 33 of the 1993 Act contained specific amendments to TUPE 1981 and may, by implication, have confirmed the statutory authority of all the provisions of TUPE 1981, including reg 4. TUPE 2006 was made under the new statutory power in s 38 of the Employment Relations Act 1999 so that this issue no longer arises.

19.25   The Divisional Court in *R v Secretary of State for Trade and Industry, ex p UNISON*[1] (in the context of challenging regulations amending the consultation obligations in relation to collective redundancies under TULRCA 1992) gave a wide interpretation to the powers given under s 2 of the European Communities Act 1972. However, in *Addison v Denholm Ship Management (UK) Ltd*[2], the EAT in Scotland expressed considerable concern with this approach.

1 [1996] ICR 1003, DC.
2 [1997] ICR 770, EAT, at 785C.

19.26   In 1993 in *Belhaven Brewery Co Ltd v Berekis*[1], the EAT held that it was not appropriate to refer to the Acquired Rights Directive as interpreted by the European Court in *Abels* to restrict the clear meaning of TUPE. Accordingly, the EAT held that TUPE 1981 did apply in an insolvency (the appointment of a trustee in bankruptcy).

1 UKEAT/724/92; (1993) IDS Brief 494, EAT.

19.27   In *Perth & Kinross Council v Donaldson*[1], the EAT in Scotland considered these arguments and held that because the ARD 1977 did not apply to transfers taking place in the context of liquidation proceedings, neither did TUPE

1981. A contractor, who was awarded contracts for maintaining the Council's housing stock, subsequently got into financial trouble. A liquidator was appointed who accepted an informal arrangement to continue the work for the council on an ad hoc basis. This was on the same terms as before, apart from the Council's new right to terminate the arrangement without notice. When the Council ended the ad hoc arrangement and took the work back in-house, the tribunal found that there had been a relevant TUPE transfer. The EAT overturned this because it would be outside the powers under s 2 (ultra vires) to apply the ARD to such an insolvency situation.

1 [2004] IRLR 121, EAT.

19.28   The English Court of Appeal subsequently doubted the reasoning of the EAT in *Donaldson*. In *Oakley Inc v Animal Ltd*[1], the Court of Appeal was considering the width of the regulation making power in s 2 of the European Communities Act 1972 (under which TUPE 1981 had been made). The Court of Appeal considered the reasoning of the EAT in *Donaldson* to be wrong, but did not give a very coherent reason why. It is unclear where this left the status of TUPE 1981 on this point (the Court of Appeal was concerned with a different set of regulations).

In *Transport & General Workers Union v Swissport (UK) Ltd (in administration)*[2], the EAT decided to follow the obiter comments in *Oakley v Animal* in preference to *Donaldson*.

1 [2005] EWCA Civ 1191; [2006] Ch 337, CA.
2 [2007] ICR 1593; [2007] All ER (D) 329 (Jun), EAT.

ECJ CASES ON ARD 1977

19.29   It is clear that ARD 1977 did not apply in a court liquidation involving an insolvency – *Abels*. It seems unlikely that the ARD 1977 would have applied where the transferor is in a creditors' voluntary winding up, even in the absence of a court order. Although the transferor company has not been 'adjudged insolvent', the company is insolvent and the lack of a judicial determination to that effect would seem irrelevant (see the comments by the European Court at paras 25 and 26 of the judgment in *D'Urso v Ercole Marelli Elettromeccanica Generale SpA*[1]).

1 [1991] ECR I-4105; [1992] IRLR 136 (ECJ).

19.30   Conversely, it would seem clear that the 1977 Directive (and therefore TUPE 1981) will have applied where the transferor is in a members' voluntary winding up. In such a case, the company is solvent and the reasons for not applying the Directive do not apply. This seems to follow from the ECJ decision in *Jules Dethier Equipment SA v Jules Dassy*[2], holding that the Acquired Rights Directive remained applicable in relation to a Belgian company being wound up by the court in circumstances where the company continued to trade and was not subject to 'insolvency proceedings'. This was later followed by the ECJ in

Europièces SA v Sanders[3] dealing with a Belgian voluntary liquidation voted by shareholders.

1 [1998] IRLR 266; [1998] ECR I-1061, ECJ.
2 C399/96, [1998] ECR 6965, [1999] All ER (EC) 831, ECJ.

19.31 Similarly, a receivership (whether administrative or not, and whether pursuant to a court order or not) does not necessarily involve a determination that the company is insolvent. The 1977 Acquired Rights Directive was likely to have been applicable – see the decision of Barrington J in the Irish High Court to that effect in *Mythen v Employment Appeals Tribunal*[1].

The House of Lords in *Secretary of State v Mann*[2] held that an administrative receivership did not fall within the 1980 Employment Insolvency Directive as there are no collective proceedings opened – see para 12.14 above. This analysis could also apply to TUPE, although the state of insolvency specified as necessary to trigger the 1980 Directive is more narrowly cast.

1 [1990] 1 IR 98 (Barrington J).
2 [1999] ICR 898, HL, at page 902.

19.32 An administration involves a court process (order or filing) but does not necessarily involve a liquidation. It is perhaps similar to the Dutch 'surseance von betaling' (or judicial leave to suspend payment of debts), which the European Court in *Abels* held did not exempt a transfer from the 1977 Directive. Following the ECJ decisions in *D'Urso, Spano v Fiat Geotech SpA*[1] and *Jules Dethier Equipement SA v Jules Dassy*[2] it seems that an administration whose purposes include:

- before 15 September 2003[3], the seeking of the survival of a business (ie for a purpose within the IA 1986, s 9(1)(a), (b) or (c)); or

- on or after 15 September 2003, of 'rescuing the company as a going concern' (ie the purpose specified in para 3(1)(a) of Schedule B1 to IA 1986)

are likely to have been within the 1977 ARD Directive.

1 [1995] ECR I-4321, ECJ.
2 [1998] IRLR 266; [1998] ECR I-1061, ECJ.
3 When the changes made to IA 1986 by the Enterprise Act 2002 came into force.

19.33 Conversely, an administration for the sole purpose of:

- the more advantageous realisation of the company's assets than would be effected on a winding up (ie within the IA 1986, s 9(1)(d)); or

- 'achieving a better result for the company's creditors as a whole than would be likely if the company were wound up (without first being in administration)', or 'realising property in order to make a distribution to one or more secured or preferential creditors' (ie the respective purposes specified in para 3(1)(b) and (c) of Sch B1 to the Insolvency Act 1986),

could have been argued to have been outside the 1977 ARD Directive.

19.34   The decision in *Re Hartlebury (Printers) Ltd*[1] does not assist on this point. Although Morritt J considered that administrations do not constitute a termination of an establishment's activities as a result of a judicial decision within the terms of the Collective Redundancies Directive (EC 75/129), the wording of this Directive differs from that of the Acquired Rights Directive[2].

1 [1993] 1 All ER 470 (Morritt J).
2 See comments of Sir Gordon Slynn as Advocate-General in *Abels* at 411.

19.35   In *Re Maxwell Fleet and Facilities Management Ltd (No 2)*[1], the argument was raised that regulation 4 of TUPE 1981 (dealing with hive-downs – see further para 13.105 below) was outside the ARD. David Mackie QC (sitting as a Deputy Judge of the High Court) commented:

> 'I also accept that, as the European cases show, some judicial insolvencies, those of a terminal kind, may be outside the directive. This is not a reason to adopt a different approach to construction. Furthermore, this particular administration is a procedure to which the directive unquestionably applies.'

1 [2000] 2 All ER 860 (David Mackie QC, sitting as a Deputy Judge of the High Court).

AMENDMENTS TO THE ACQUIRED RIGHTS DIRECTIVE

19.36   In June 1998 the EU council adopted a Directive, 98/50/EC, amending the original Acquired Rights Directive 1977. Member states were given three years to incorporate the changes into national law. The 1977 Directive and 1998 Directive were consolidated into the ARD 2001 (2001/23/EC).

19.37   The 2001 ARD Directive contains special provisions applicable in an insolvency so that:

(a)   the transfer provisions do not have to apply in some insolvency proceedings (eg liquidation); and

(b)   if the transfer provisions apply (whether in a liquidation or otherwise) then pre-insolvency or transfer debts do not have to transfer and/or representatives of the employees may agree changes in terms of employment.

19.38   Unless member states provide otherwise, the transfer provisions in ARD 2001 do not apply:

> 'where the transferor is the subject of bankruptcy proceedings (or any analogous insolvency proceedings) which have been instituted with a view to the liquidation of the assets of the transferor and are under the supervision of a competent public authority (which may be an insolvency practitioner authorised by a competent public authority)' [Article 5.1].

19.39   This is very similar to the wording used by the ECJ in its various judgments on the ARD 1977. It seems likely that the ECJ case law on the 1977

Directive is meant to continue to apply. Note that it differs from the 1980 Employment Insolvency Directive (which refers to "collective" proceedings).

ECJ cases

19.40 To summarise these cases:

Abels v Administrative Board of the Bedrijfsvereniging voor de Metaalindustrie en de Electrotechnische Industrie [1985] ECR 469, [1987] 2 CMLR 406

The ARD does not apply:

> 'in the context of insolvency proceedings instituted with a view to the liquidation of the assets of the transferor under the supervision of the competent judicial authority' (para 23).

19.41 However the ARD does apply in the case of a 'surseance van betaling' (judicial leave to suspend payment of debts). The ECJ held (at paras 28 and 29):

> '28 It is to be noted that proceedings such as those relating to a 'surseance van betaling' have certain features in common with liquidation proceedings, in particular inasmuch as the proceedings are, in both cases, of a judicial nature. They are, however, different from liquidation proceedings in so far as the supervision exercised by the court over the commencement and the course of such proceedings is more limited. Moreover, the object of such proceedings is primarily to safeguard the assets of the insolvent undertaking and, where possible, to continue the business of the undertaking by means of a collective suspension of the payment of debts with a view to reaching a settlement which will ensure that the undertaking is able to continue operating in the future. If no such settlement is reached, proceedings of this kind may, as in the present case, lead to the debtor's being put into liquidation.
>
> 29 It follows that the reasons for not applying the directive to transfers of undertakings taking place in liquidation proceedings are not applicable to proceedings of this kind taking place at an earlier stage.'

19.42 *D'Urso v Ercole Marelli Elettromeccanica Generale SpA* [1991] ECR I-4105, [1992] IRLR 136

The ECJ held that ARD 1977 applied to an Italian company in 'critical difficulties'.

19.43 The ECJ summarised *Abels*:

> '21 It is apparent from the tenor and grounds of the order for reference that, by this question, the Pretore di Milano seeks to ascertain whether the Directive is applicable to, in the words of Article 1(1) thereof, "the transfer of an undertaking, business or part of a business to another employer as a result of a legal transfer or merger", when the undertaking concerned is governed by provisions of the kind laid down in Decree-Law No 26 of 30 January 1979 on urgent measures for the special administration of large undertakings in critical difficulties (GURI No 36 of 6 February 1979) converted, with amendments, into Law No 95 of 3 April 1979 (GURI No 94 of 4 April 1979).

22 In order to answer that question it is necessary to recall the distinctions made by the Court, in particular in its judgment in Case 135/83 *H.B.M. Abels v Bedrijfsvereniging voor de Metaalindusrie en de Electrotechnische Industrie* [1985] ECR 469, which are also summarized by the Pretore di Milano.

23 The Court held that the Directive did not apply to transfers effected in bankruptcy proceedings designed to liquidate the transferor's assets under the supervision of the competent judicial authority. It based that conclusion on the fact that the Directive contains no express provision dealing with such liquidation proceedings (paragraph 17), on the purpose of the Directive, which was to prevent the restructuring of undertakings within the Common Market from adversely affecting the workers in the undertakings concerned (paragraph 18) and on the existence of a serious risk of a general deterioration in working and living conditions, contrary to the social objectives of the Treaty (paragraph 23) if the Directive were to apply to transfers effected in such liquidation proceedings.

24 In the same judgment, the Court held, however, that the Directive was applicable to a procedure like a "surséance van betaling" (suspension of payments), although that procedure did have some features in common with liquidation proceedings. The Court considered that the reasons which justified not applying the Directive in the case of liquidation proceedings were not valid when the procedure in question involved court supervision more limited than in liquidation proceedings and when its purpose was primarily to safeguard the assets and, where possible, to continue the business of the undertaking by means of a collective suspension of the payment of debts with a view to reaching a settlement which would ensure that the undertaking was able to continue operating in the future (paragraph 28).

25 Although in paragraph 28 of its judgment in the *Abels* case the Court mentions the extent of court supervision of the procedure, that reference, which is explained by the difficulty, mentioned in paragraph 12 of that judgment, of defining the concept of contractual transfer used in Article 1(1) of the Directive in view of the differences between the legal systems of the Member States, does not enable the scope of the Directive to be ascertained solely on the basis of a textual interpretation of the concept of contractual transfer, as paragraph 13 of the judgment indicates, or, consequently, its scope to be determined according to the kind of supervision exercised by the administrative or judicial authority over transfers of undertakings in the course of a specific creditors' arrangement procedure.

26 Given all the considerations set out in the judgment in the *Abels* case, the decisive test is therefore the purpose of the procedure in question.'

19.44   ECJ then went on to consider the Italian laws:

'27 The Italian Law of 3 April 1979 provides for the application by decree of the special administration procedure to undertakings which it defines. Under that Law, the decree has, or may have, two kinds of effects.

28 On the one hand, for the application "in all its effects" of the Law on Insolvency, it must be assimilated to the decree ordering compulsory administrative liquidation as provided for by Article 195 et seq. and Article 237 of the Law on Insolvency. It is apparent from those latter provisions taken together that, save for the particular features specific to it, compulsory administrative liquidation has effects which in substance are identical to those of bankruptcy proceedings.

29 Secondly, the decree ordering the special administration procedure to be applied may also authorize the undertaking to continue trading under the supervision of an auditor for a period to be determined according to the detailed provisions of the Law. According to Article 2 of the Law of 3 April 1979, the powers of that auditor include the power to draw up a programme whose implementation must be authorized by the supervisory authority and which must comprise, as far as is possible and taking account of creditors' interests, "a restructuring plan compatible with the trends of industrial policy, and specify the plants to be brought back into operation and those to be expanded as well as the plants or business units to be transferred".

30 It is apparent from the foregoing that legislation like the Italian Law on the special administration of large undertakings in critical difficulties has different characteristics depending on whether or not the decree ordering compulsory administrative liquidation authorizes the undertaking to continue trading.

31 If no decision is taken on that last matter or if the period of validity of a decision authorizing the undertaking to continue trading has expired, the aim, consequences and risks of a procedure such as the compulsory administrative liquidation procedure are comparable to those which led this Court to conclude, in its judgment in the Abels case, that Article 1(1) of the Directive did not apply to transfers of an undertaking, business or part of a business in a situation in which the transferor had been adjudged insolvent. Like insolvency proceedings, that procedure is designed to liquidate the debtor' s assets in order to satisfy the body of creditors, and transfers effected under this legal framework are consequently excluded from the scope of the Directive. As the Court pointed out in its judgment in Abels, without that exclusion, a serious risk of a general deterioration in the living and working conditions of workers, contrary to the social objectives of the Treaty, could not be ruled out.

32 On the other hand, it is apparent from the provisions of the Italian Law that when the decree ordering the application of the special administration procedure also authorizes the undertaking to continue trading under the supervision of an auditor, the primary purpose of that procedure is to give the undertaking some stability allowing its future activity to be safeguarded. The social and economic objectives thus pursued cannot explain nor justify the circumstance that, when all or part of the undertaking concerned is transferred, its employees lose the rights which the Directive confers on them under the conditions which it lays down.

33 In this regard, the national court points out in particular in its order for reference that the report on Decree-Law No 26/1979 states that the purpose of the procedure is to rescue the parts of an undertaking which are basically sound, that an undertaking under special administration may, for the purpose of resuming operations and supplementing plant, land and industrial equipment, obtain loans whose repayment is guaranteed by the State and, finally, that under the special administration procedure the protection of creditors' interests is less extensive than in other liquidation procedures and that, in particular, creditors are not involved in decisions concerning the continued operation of the undertaking.

34 The answer to the second question must therefore be that Article 1(1) of Council Directive 77/187/EEC of 14 February 1977 does not apply to transfers of undertakings made as part of a creditors' arrangement procedure of the kind provided for in the Italian legislation on compulsory administrative liquidation to which the Law of 3 April 1979 on special administration for large undertakings

in critical difficulties refers. However, that provision of that directive does apply when, in accordance with a body of legislation such as that governing special administration for large undertakings in critical difficulties, it has been decided that the undertaking is to continue trading for as long as that decision remains in effect.'

19.45   *Spano v Fiat Geotech SpA* [1995] ECR I-4321, C-472/93

The ECJ held that ARD 1977 applied to a company within the Italian process of being declared to be in 'critical difficulties'.

> '25 As the Commission and the plaintiffs in the main proceedings maintain, it is clear from the case-law of the Court that the Directive does not apply to transfers taking place in proceedings for the liquidation of the transferor' s assets, such as insolvency proceedings (see the judgment in *Abels*, cited above) or compulsory administrative liquidation under Italian Law (see the judgment in *D'Urso*), but it does apply to the transfer of an undertaking subject to a procedure aimed at ensuring the continuation of its business, such as the "surséance van betaling" procedure under Netherlands Law (judgment in Abels) or the special administration procedure under Italian Law in respect of large undertakings in critical difficulties, where it has been decided that the undertaking is to continue trading for so long as that decision remains in effect (see the judgment in *D'Urso*).'

19.46   *Jules Dethier Equipement SA v Jules Dassy* [1998] ECR I-1061, [1998] IRLR 266

The ECJ held that ARD 1977 applied to an undertaking being wound up by the court if the undertaking continues to trade during that procedure.

> '25 It follows from that case-law that, in deciding whether the Directive applies to the transfer of an undertaking subject to an administrative or judicial procedure, the determining factor to be taken into consideration is the purpose of the procedure in question (D'Urso and Others, paragraph 26, and *Spano and Others*, paragraph 24). However, as the Advocate General has stated in points 31, 41 and 45 of his Opinion, account should also be taken of the form of the procedure in question, in particular in so far as it means that the undertaking continues or ceases trading, and also of the Directive's objectives.
>
> 26 In this case, it is apparent from the information provided by the Cour du Travail that the objective of the Belgian procedure under which a company is wound up by the court is liquidation by realising the company's assets for the benefit of the company itself and, subsidiarily, of any creditors. It is not a condition for putting a company into liquidation that its liabilities must exceed its assets. Although liquidation may be a stage which precedes insolvency, it can also occur, as the Belgian Government states, when the members no longer wish to cooperate.
>
> 27 It follows that, although the objectives of a winding up by the court may sometimes be similar to those of insolvency proceedings, this is not necessarily the case, since liquidation proceedings may be used whenever it is wished to bring a company's activities to an end and whatever the reasons for that course.
>
> 28 Since the criterion relating to the purpose of the procedure for winding up by the court appears not to be conclusive, it is necessary to consider that procedure in detail.

29 According to the reference by the national court, in the case of a liquidation the liquidator, although appointed by the court, is an organ of the company who sells the assets under the supervision of the general meeting; there is no special procedure for establishing liabilities under the supervision of the court; and a creditor may as a rule enforce his debt against the company and obtain judgment against it. By contrast, in the case of an insolvency, the administrator, inasmuch as he represents the creditors, is a third party vis-à-vis the company and realises the assets under the supervision of the court; the liabilities of the company are established in accordance with a special procedure and individual enforcement actions are prohibited.

30 It is thus apparent that the situation of an undertaking being wound up by the court presents considerable differences from that of an undertaking subject to insolvency proceedings and that the reasons which have led the Court to rule out application of the Directive in the latter situation may be absent in the case of an undertaking being wound up by the court.

31 That is the case where, as in the main proceedings, the undertaking continues to trade while it is being wound up by the court. In such circumstances continuity of the business is assured when the undertaking is transferred. There is accordingly no justification for depriving the employees of the rights which the Directive guarantees them on the conditions it lays down.

32 The answer to the first question submitted for a preliminary ruling must therefore be that, on a proper construction of Article 1(1) of the Directive, the Directive applies in the event of the transfer of an undertaking which is being wound up by the court if the undertaking continues to trade.'

19.47   *Europièces SA v Sanders* [1998] ECR 6965, Case C-399/96 [1999] All ER (EC) 831

The ECJ held that the ARD applies to a voluntary winding-up:

'32 The Court therefore found in *Dethier Equipement* that the Directive applies in the event of the transfer of an undertaking which is being wound up by the court if the undertaking continues to trade. In particular, it observed at paragraph 31 that where the undertaking continues to trade while it is being wound up by the court, continuity of the business is assured when the undertaking is transferred. There is accordingly no justification for depriving the employees of the rights which the Directive guarantees them on the conditions it lays down.

33 So far as this case is concerned, it must be borne in mind that voluntary liquidation is essentially similar to winding up by the court, save for the fact that it falls to the shareholders in general meeting, and not to the court, to take the decision to wind up the company, appoint the liquidators and determine their powers. Only where a majority of the shareholders cannot be assembled must the company apply to the court for a declaration putting it into liquidation. The court then designates the liquidators in accordance with the company's articles of association or pursuant to the decision of the shareholders in general meeting, unless it is clear that disagreement between the shareholders will prevent them from taking a decision in general meeting, in which case the court itself appoints a liquidator.

34 Thus it would seem that, at least in some procedural respects, voluntary liquidation has even less in common with insolvency than winding up by the court.

35 In the light of the foregoing, it should be noted that the reasons which led the Court to hold in *Dethier Equipement* that the Directive can apply to transfers that occur while an undertaking is being wound up by the court are all the more pertinent where the undertaking transferred is being wound up voluntarily.

36 The answer to the first part of the question, as recast above, is therefore that Article 1(1) of the Directive is to be interpreted as meaning that the Directive applies where a company in voluntary liquidation transfers all or part of its assets to another company from which the worker then takes his orders which the company in liquidation states are to be carried out.'

19.48 *Commission of the European Communities v Italian Republic* (Case C-145/01)

Opinion of Advocate-General Leger (10 April 2003) that the ARD 1977 should not apply to 'an approved composition procedure consisting in the disposal of assets'. This looks to be similar to the UK company voluntary arrangement (CVA) under the Insolvency Act 1986 (see para 4.38 above). (The ECJ dismissed the case on 5 June 2003 without considering the ARD/insolvency issues):

19.49 The UK government indicated concern in its consultation paper of December 1997 about trying to distinguish between the different sorts of insolvency proceedings. The UK Government decided, in the drafting of TUPE 2006 in the UK to limit the insolvency exclusion by using the same words as in the ARD 2001 (a 'copy-out' approach).

19.50 In TUPE 2006, the exclusion in reg 8(7) only applies to the transfer and dismissal provisions (in regs 4 and 7). The obligation on the employer company to inform and (where appropriate) consult about a transfer will remain – see Chapters 20 and 42 below.

No transfer of debts due and payable/ability to change contracts

19.51 The UK government indicated in its consultation paper of December 1997 that it would support the insolvency changes allowed by ARD 2001.

19.52 Under ARD 2001, the option to exclude debts of the transferor employer would only apply to debts payable before the transfer or the opening of the insolvency proceedings. It could also only apply provided the proceedings give rise to protections at least equivalent to those provided under the Employment Insolvency Directive (80/987/EEC) – see Chapter 12 above.

19.53 If a general exclusion had been included in TUPE 2006, this could have raised the doubts as to whether the provisions in ERA 1996 fully comply with the 1980 Directive (eg the ceiling on a week's pay – see *Secretary of State v Mann*[1], discussed in para 12.12 above). There would then have been an incentive for employees to argue that failure to comply with the 1980 Employment Insolvency Directive means that any relevant UK legislation providing that existing debts do not transfer would have been invalid.

1 [1997] ICR 209 (CA); [1999] ICR 898, HL.

19.54   But TUPE 2006 includes only a limited non-transferablity provision, in practice limited to debts covered by the National Insurance Fund (see Chapter 20 below). So this issue does not arise.

19.55   Under ARD 2001, the power to allow appropriate representatives of the employees to agree changes to terms and conditions would only apply 'so far as current law or practice permits' and then only to changes 'designed to safeguard employment opportunities by ensuring the survival of the undertaking, business or part of the business'.

TUPE 2006: Terminal and non-terminal insolvencies

TUPE 2006

20.1   TUPE 2006 made four specific insolvency related changes[1]:

- The hive down provision in TUPE 1981 reg 4 (see para 20.55 below) was repealed[2];

- In terminal proceedings (reg 8(7)) – ie insolvency proceedings with a view to the liquidation of assets of the transferor (eg a court liquidation), the transfer and dismissal provisions in Regulations 4 and 7 do not apply.

- In non–terminal insolvency proceedings (reg 8(6)) proceedings not with a view to the liquidation of assets (eg a trading administration):

    (i)   liabilities covered by the 'relevant statutory schemes' – ie by the national insurance fund – do not transfer to a purchaser/transferor; and

    (ii)   changes in employment terms can be agreed with appropriate representatives of the employees.

1 ARD Article 6.1 gave member states the option to allow an insolvency practitioner to decide on employee representation issues. This was not taken up in TUPE 2006 – see the annex to the explanatory memorandum to TUPE 2006.
2 See page 32 of the March 2005 Consultation document – http://www.dti.gov.uk/er/TUPE_consult.htm

20.2   TUPE 2006 is remarkably unclear in its application to insolvencies. In particular:

- the decision whether or not a particular insolvency is terminal or non-terminal – ie falls within regulation 8(6) or 8(7) (or neither); and

- the impact of regulation 8(6) on payment of some debts by the NI Fund.

20.3   A motion to revoke TUPE 2006 was heard by the House of Lords on 3 May 2006 and narrowly defeated (79 votes to 77). R3 subsequently wrote to the relevant minister, Lord Sainsbury of Turville commenting on the issues and some of the points made in the debate (a copy is set out in (2006) 22 Insolvency Law & Practice 190).

R3 published its 'Response to Government about TUPE' following the defeat of this motion, arguing that the use of generic wording resulted in uncertainty about the types of insolvency procedures covered by the regulations and that interpretation of regulation 8(7) to exclude administration was flawed since:

- While the purpose of administration is set out in the form of a hierarchy, with the first objective being rescue of the company as a going concern, this objective can rarely be achieved. In most cases the purpose of the administration will be achieved through the second objective of achieving a better result for the creditors as a whole than would be likely on a winding up. This will usually be effected through the sale of the whole or part of the business (the business being an asset of the company) or the sale of assets on a piecemeal basis. Such activity should be characterised as a realisation, ie liquidation, of assets.

- It was wrong to state that administration is not instituted 'with a view to' liquidation of the assets on the ground that the first objective is to rescue the company and that the other objectives only come into play once that objective proves impossible. It may be apparent at the very beginning of the process that it will not be possible to save the company.

R3's concerns were vindicated by the decision in 2009 of the EAT in the *Oakland* case (see para 20.18 and Chapter 42 below)

TERMINAL INSOLVENCIES: PROCEEDINGS FOR LIQUIDATION OF ASSETS – REGULATION 8(7)

20.4   Regulation 8(7) of TUPE 2006 states:

> '(7) Regulations 4 and 7 do not apply to any relevant transfer where the transferor is the subject of bankruptcy proceedings or any analogous insolvency proceedings which have been instituted with a view to the liquidation of the assets of the transferor and are under the supervision of an insolvency practitioner.'

Under new reg 8(7) of TUPE 2006, the transfer and dismissal provisions in regs 4 and 7 of TUPE 2006 do not apply to any relevant transfer where:

> '(a)   the transferor is the subject of bankruptcy proceedings or any analogous insolvency proceedings which have been instituted with a view to the liquidation of the assets of the transferor', and
>
> (b)   the proceedings 'are under the supervision of an insolvency practitioner[1]'.

In order for reg 8(7) (or indeed reg 8(6)) to apply insolvency proceedings must have opened before the relevant TUPE transfer is made. It not enough if a practitioner has given advice, but is only formally appointed as the insolvency practitioner after the transfer has taken place – see the decision of the EAT in *Secretary of State for Trade and Industry v Slater*[2].

1 The term 'insolvency practitioner' has the same meaning as in the Insolvency Act 1986 – see TUPE 2006, reg 2(1).
2 [2008] ICR 54, EAT.

20.5 The wording in (a) above has been copied direct from article 5.1 of the 2001 ARD, which in turn reflects the ECJ case law on the directive, particularly in *Abels*[1]. This was a deliberate choice by the government. In the consultation document on proposed new TUPE issued in March 2005[2] the government stated (at page 28):

> '58. The effect of draft Regulation 8(1) is that if a transferor is in one of the types of insolvency proceedings specified in draft Regulation 8(6) – i.e. those types of proceedings encompassed by Article 5.2 of the Directive – draft Regulations 8(2) to 8(6) apply. Procedures that fall within Article 5.2 in the UK include in particular administration, company and individual voluntary arrangements and creditors' voluntary winding-up, but not administrative or any other receivership or members' voluntary winding up. However, draft Regulation 8(6) does not attempt to list all these different types of procedures individually; rather, it takes the alternative approach of 'copying out' the generic description in Article 5.2. The main reasons for this are that:
>
> (a) it makes for a much simpler provision – given that there are different (albeit largely equivalent) procedures in England and Wales, Scotland and Northern Ireland, which would make for a very lengthy list;
>
> (b) it 'future proofs' this provision against any changes in insolvency procedures that might be made at a later date; and
>
> (c) it ensures beyond doubt that the UK has not extended the coverage of this provision more widely than the Directive allows.'

1 See footnote on page 30 of the March 2005 consultation document.
2 Now at http://www.berr.gov.uk/consultations/page16387. Below called the 'DTI Condoc'.

20.6 There was no change in what became TUPE 2006 – see the DTI response to the consultation on TUPE (issued in February 2006)[1].

1 See www.dti.gov.uk/er/TUPE_govtresponse_feb06.pdf. Now at http://www.berr.gov.uk/consultations/page16387

20.7 This wording mirrors the existing ECJ case law on ARD 1977 (see above). It is likely that courts and tribunals will look to the previous ECJ decisions when deciding how to interpret the new provisions.

20.8 In practice in a UK context the 'liquidation' head in reg 8(7) seems likely to cover insolvent liquidations (voluntary and court). It is likely that it does not apply in the case of a solvent voluntary liquidation (eg a members' voluntary liquidation), because this is seen as not being an 'insolvency proceeding'. Given the ECJ case law, there may still be some doubt how the line will be drawn in the case of a court winding-up. See eg the decision of the ECJ in *Jules Dethier* (noted above).

20.9 In relation to a creditors' voluntary winding-up (CVL), the March 2005 consultation document notes (at page 30) that:

'8 The Government considers it possible that creditors' voluntary winding-up falls within the description in Article 5.1 as well as within the description in Article 5.2. If that is so – which is unclear on the basis of existing case law – then Regulation [8(7)][1] would apply in such cases, rather than Regulation 8(1)-(5).'

1 The note actually refers to reg 8(4) here, but presumably this is a cross referencing error.

20.10   The guidance notes issued on new TUPE in February 2006 by the DTI (see below) are more emphatic:

'The Department considers that "relevant insolvency proceedings" does not cover winding-up by either creditors or members where there is no such transfer.'

20.11   Conceivably reg 8(7) could also apply to those administrations where liquidation of assets is the reason for the administration, but it is unclear how this would be shown.

20.12   The test under regs 8(6) and 8(7) of TUPE 2006 seems to envisage that the purpose is fixed at the date the insolvency proceedings are started. In the case of administrations, para 3 of Sch B1 to the Insolvency Act 1986 deals (from 15 September 2003) with the purpose of an administration as follows:

'3(1)   The administrator of a company must perform his functions with the objective of—

(a)   rescuing the company as a going concern, or

(b)   achieving a better result for the company's creditors as a whole than would be likely if the company were wound up (without first being in administration), or

(c)   realising property in order to make a distribution to one or more secured or preferential creditors.'

20.13   Conceivably the underlying purpose of liquidating assets could fall within objectives (b) or (c). But it is unclear who is to have the 'view' referred to in reg 8(7) of TUPE 2006. It will not be clear from the filed documents (for example):

- the Notice of Appointment statutory declaration (Form 2.6B – this just includes a confirmation that 'the appointment is in accordance with Sch B1 to the Insolvency Act 1986') or

- the Statement of Proposed Administration (Form 2.2B, filed under para 18 of Sch B1) that must be filed (this just refers to 'the purpose of the administration' without specifying this any further).

20.14   The statement of proposals from the administrator under r 2.33(2)(m) of the Insolvency Rules 1986 does envisage that the administration can end by a creditor's voluntary liquidation – ie by a liquidation of assets. But arguably this may be too late to make the administration into a terminal proceeding for the purpose of TUPE. The insolvency process must have been 'instituted' with a view to the liquidation of assets – implying that the test involves looking at what happened when the process started.

In *Oakland v Wellswood (Yorkshire) Ltd*[1], the EAT relied on this statement from the joint administrators in their report (note that it was produced after the relevant transfer had been made).

1 UKEAT/0395/08; [2009] IRLR 250, EAT – see further para 20.18 below.

20.15 In practice the main qualifying insolvency is likely to be an insolvent court liquidation. But here it is likely to be unusual for the company to continue to trade (or for any employees to remain in place), so the prospect of a TUPE transfer may be small (a point made in the 2005 DTI Condoc – see page 30).

20.16 But there may be some cases where the insolvent employer is a service provider, so that the insolvency results in a further contracting-out (or a contracting-in) within TUPE see for example, the decision of the ECJ in *Güney-Görres v Securicor Aviation*[1].

1 C-232/04; [2005] ECR I-11237, [2006] IRLR 305, ECJ.

20.17 The previous (3rd) edition of this book commented that in these cases it must be arguable that continuity of employment of the employees would be preserved, on the basis that the continuity provisions in ERA 1996 merely refer to a 'transfer of undertaking' and are not excluded by reg 8(7) of TUPE 2006.

Oakland v Wellswood

20.18 In 2009, in *Oakland v Wellswood (Yorkshire) Ltd*[1] Judge Peter Clark in the EAT decided that a pre-pack administration business sale did not result in the employees automatically transferring under reg 4 of TUPE.

Contrary to previous government guidance, the EAT considered the report from the joint administrators and held that the transferor employer, in administration, was in a form of 'terminal insolvency' as being subject to 'bankruptcy proceedings or… analogous insolvency proceedings... instituted with a view to the liquidation of the assets of the transferor'.

Therefore regulation 8(7) of TUPE applied and the transferor's employees did not automatically transfer.

1 UKEAT/0395/08; [2009] IRLR 250, EAT.

The facts

20.19 Wellswood Limited (Oldco) traded as a wholesaler in fruit and vegetables. The claimant was an employee, co-director and 50% shareholder of Oldco. By mid-2006 Oldco was in financial difficulties. These culminated in an 'out of court' appointment of administrators over Oldco.

Prior to that appointment, one of Oldco's major suppliers had effectively agreed to buy Oldco's assets out of the administration as a pre-pack sale. To do so, the supplier set up a wholly owned subsidiary, Wellswood (Yorkshire) Limited (Newco). As well as the assets, Newco also took on some (but not all) of Oldco's employees. These included the claimant, but with a much reduced annual salary, down from £39,000 to £20,000 (later rising to £24,000). All of the employees of Oldco received statutory redundancy payments from the National Insurance Fund.

In a report dated January 2007 (ie after the pre-pack sale had taken place) the joint administrators set out the three statutory objectives of administration:

(a)   rescuing the company as a going concern;

(b)   achieving a better result for the creditors as a whole than would be likely on a winding up of the company; or

(c)   realising any property in order to make a distribution to one or more secured or preferential creditors.

They concluded that the first objective was not achievable for Oldco. In considering the second, they observed that any further period of trading to allow the marketing of the business and assets for sale would be likely to result in further losses and so reduce the funds available to creditors. They therefore anticipated that the company would move from administration to a creditors' voluntary liquidation.

Less than a year after the transfer, Newco dismissed the claimant who brought a claim for unfair dismissal against Newco. The claim was dismissed at first instance by the Employment Tribunal on the ground that the claimant had less than one year's service with Newco and he was precluded from relying on the transfer provision of TUPE because Oldco was 'the subject of bankruptcy proceedings or any analogous insolvency proceedings…instituted with a view to the liquidation of the assets of [Oldco]'. The claimant appealed.

The EAT judgment

20.20   Judge Peter Clark in the EAT upheld the Employment Tribunal and dismissed the appeal.

He accepted that 'where administrators continue to trade the business with a view to its sale as a going concern any relevant transfer will attract TUPE protection for those employees under regulation 4'. He distinguished that situation, though, from the facts of this case where it soon became apparent to the joint administrators that it was not possible for them to continue to trade the business. Instead, immediately on appointment they took steps to sell the assets to Newco.

Judge Clark held that the employment judge at first instance was entitled to conclude that the appointment of the joint administrators was with a view to the eventual liquidation of the assets of Oldco by way of a creditors' voluntary liquidation.

He held (at para [19]):

> 'The issue arises in this case because Parliament has declined to specify which particular insolvency proceedings are to be characterized as having been instituted with a view to the liquidation of the transferor company's assets. Nor do I derive any assistance from the BERR Guidance to the 2006 TUPE Regulations (issued March 2007) to which I have been referred. In these circumstances I reject Ms Toman's [counsel for the claimant's] submission that the answer to the question now posed is purely one of domestic insolvency law; rather, it is in my view a question of fact for the Employment Tribunal. I accept that where joint administrators continue to trade the business with a view to its sale as a going concern any relevant transfer in those circumstances will attract TUPE protection for employees under reg 4. However, that is not what happened in the present case on the

facts found by Judge Sneath. Having first been consulted by the Claimant on behalf of Oldco on 23 November 2006 it is clear from Mr Hull's report that it soon became apparent that due to its weak financial position it was not possible for the administrators to continue trading the business. Instead, immediately following their appointment on 6 December 2007 they took immediate steps to sell the assets to Newco, who took on the lease of Oldco's premises whilst retaining the book debts in Oldco. This was seen as the best course for realizing the optimum return for creditors in the final liquidation of Oldco. In my judgment the Judge was entitled to conclude that the appointment of Joint Administrators was with a view to the eventual liquidation of the assets of Oldco, by way of a CVL.'

He concluded (at para [20]):

'it seems to me that this construction accords with the policy behind art 5(1) and in turn reg 8(7); namely the 'rescue culture', whereby a purchaser, here Newco, is not put off by the effects of TUPE protection. The outcome, as demonstrated by this case, was that some jobs were preserved and the creditors benefited from the best available option'.

20.21   Administrators should, however, be cautious in relying on this case: the judge appeared to be heavily influenced by joint administrators' report and the fact that the company did not trade at all while the joint administrators were in office. Naturally each case will turn on its own facts in determining whether the administration was 'instituted with a view to the liquidation of the assets of the transferor'. The administrator report or other evidence of intention may well prove important in this respect.

20.22   Despite the comment in the 3rd edition of this book (see para 20.17 above), it does not seem to have been argued in the ET or the EAT that the claimant could look to his previous service with Oldco to establish the necessary period of continuous service with Newco even though there was not a TUPE transfer by reason of reg 8(7). Section 218(2) of the Employment Rights Act 1996 provides for there to be continuity of employment where there is a transfer of a business. This section does not refer to TUPE and should mean that continuity is preserved even if TUPE does not apply.

It is clear that a transfer of an undertaking can be made by a company in insolvency – see *Teesside Times Ltd v Drury*[1], and *Thomsons Soft Drinks Ltd v Quaife*[2], cases on continuity of employment under EPCA 1978 (now consolidated into ERA 1996).

The Court of Appeal gave judgment in an appeal in the *Oakland* case at the end of July 2009[3], but it refused to deal with the reg 8(7) point. Instead it decided the case on the basis that the continuity of employment provisions in ERA 1996, s 218(2) applied. Moses LJ in the Court of Appeal stated that:

'10. This court was thus furnished with full written submissions from the Secretary of State on the point and also a full skeleton on the point from Ms Toman [counsel for Mr Oakland]. Supplied with that, it was not surprising perhaps that Mummery LJ gave leave, and for my part I would wish to emphasise that there are strong grounds for thinking that both the Employment Tribunal and the Employment Appeal Tribunal took the wrong approach to their construction both to the Article 5 of the Directive and to Regulation 8.'

And later:

> '17 In those circumstances, adopting the wisdom of Rix LJ, it would seem to me most unwise for us to give a binding pronouncement on the correctness or otherwise of the contention that administration necessarily excludes the application of regulation 8(7). I would only, for my part, wish to emphasise that that is a strongly arguable point, and the only reason I agree that it should not be resolved today is that the Secretary of State is not here and, since the Wellswood (Yorkshire) Limited Administration, Newco, is in the process of being liquidated almost as we speak, and therefore has no representation here today, it would be unwise to reach and pronounce upon any definitive conclusion. Expressing regret that that cannot be done today, I would allow this appeal.'

In *Marra v Express Gifts Ltd*[4] in January 2009, the ET considered the EAT decision in *Oakland* and held that on the facts reg 8(7) did not apply where there was a transfer out of an administration. This case involved a transfer of some only of the insolvent company's assets and was made some 22 days after the insolvent company had entered administration. The insolvent company also seems to have carried on some business after the transfer.

For a further discussion of the issues on a 'pre-pack' insolvency – see Chapter 42 below.

1 [1980] ICR 338, CA.
2 8 June 1981, EAT.
3 [2009] EWCA Civ 1094, 31 July 2009, CA.
4 [2009] BPIR 508; ET case 2401065/08, ET.

Non-terminal proceedings – reg 8(6)

20.23   Regulation 8(6) of TUPE 2006 states:

> '(6) In this regulation 'relevant insolvency proceedings' means insolvency proceedings which have been opened in relation to the transferor not with a view to the liquidation of the assets of the transferor and which are under the supervision of an insolvency practitioner[1].'

1 The term 'insolvency practitioner' has the same meaning as in the Insolvency Act 1986 – see TUPE 2006, reg 2(1).

20.24   The term 'relevant insolvency proceedings' as used in reg 8(6) is likely to exclude liquidations, but should include most-administrations or administrative receiverships, unless there is an immediate sale/liquidation (eg a pre-pack sale).

20.25   The Government stated (at page 28) in its original guidance to TUPE 2006[1] that:

> 'Q. What types of insolvency proceedings are covered by these aspects of the Regulations?
>
> A. These provisions are found in Regulations 8 and 9. Those two Regulations apply where the transferor is subject to 'relevant insolvency proceedings' which are insolvency proceedings commenced in relation to him but not with a view to the liquidation of his assets. The Regulations do not attempt to list all these different types of procedures individually. It is the Department's view that "relevant

insolvency proceedings" mean any collective insolvency proceedings in which the whole or part of the business or undertaking is transferred to another entity as a going concern. That is to say, it covers an insolvency proceeding in which all creditors of the debtor may participate, and in relation to which the insolvency officeholder owes a duty to all creditors. The Department considers that 'relevant insolvency proceedings' does not cover winding-up by either creditors or members where there is no such transfer.

1 See www.dti.gov.uk/er/individual/tupeguide2006regs.pdf.
  Now on the BERR website at http://www.berr.gov.uk/files/file20761.pdf, URN07/758Y.

20.26   This is unclear. There is no reference to the term 'collective insolvency proceedings' in either the ARD or new TUPE. Nor is there any reference to any requirement that such a proceeding must be one 'in which all creditors of the debtor may participate, and in relation to which the insolvency officeholder owes a duty to all creditors'.

Note that the term 'collective proceedings' does appear in the Employment Insolvency Directive (see *Secretary of State v Mann*[1] and para 12.14 above).

1 [1999] ICR 898, HL.

20.27   The DTI issued further guidance in June 2006[1]. An extract is in the box below. The guidance makes the point that it cannot be authoritative and that only the courts and tribunals can provide this. But it is likely that in the meantime the National Insurance Fund will follow what is set out.

1 See the document 'Redundancy and Insolvency Payments' (URN 06/1368) issued on 9 June 2006, available on the DTI website: www.dti.gov.uk/files/file30031.pdf?pubpdfdload= 06%2F1368
  Now on the BERR website at http://www.berr.gov.uk/files/file30031.pdf

20.28

APPLICATION OF THE 2006 TUPE REGULATIONS TO SPECIFIC TYPES OF INSOLVENCY PROCEEDINGS (URN 06/1368)

5 The position regarding specific types of insolvency proceedings is as follows:

Bankruptcy
[not relevant]

Compulsory liquidation
Where a company is wound up by an order of the court on grounds that it is unable to pay its debts, regulations 4 and 7 of the 2006 TUPE Regulations do not apply as such proceedings are liquidation proceedings under the supervision of an insolvency practitioner that are analogous to bankruptcy proceedings. The position under case law was that on the

---

making of a winding-up order this operates to terminate the contracts of employment of any employees as at the date of the making of the order. Employees will be entitled to insolvency and redundancy payments out of the National Insurance Fund in accordance with the provisions of the Employment Rights Act 1996.

Creditors' voluntary liquidation

Where a liquidator sells a business run by a company that is in creditors' voluntary liquidation regulation 4 and regulation 7 will not apply. These provisions are disapplied by regulation 8(7) by virtue of the fact that creditors' voluntary liquidations are liquidation proceedings under the supervision of an insolvency practitioner that are analogous to bankruptcy proceedings. Accordingly a transfer of a business by the liquidator in a creditors' voluntary liquidation would cause the dismissal of those employees who immediately prior to the transfer were employed by the company unless prior to the transfer there is an agreement between the parties (including the employees) that the transferee is to be substituted as their employer. In the absence of any agreement substituting the transferee as their employer, employees whose contracts of employment with the transferee are terminated will be entitled to be paid redundancy payments and arrears of wages etc. from the National Insurance Fund in accordance with the provisions of the 1996 Act.

Members' voluntary liquidation

Members' voluntary liquidation is not an insolvency proceeding. It is by definition a solvent winding up. Therefore regulations 4 and 7 apply if there is a relevant transfer and regulation 8 is not applicable at all.

Administration

The Secretary of State takes the view that regulations 4 and 7 will always apply in relation to a relevant transfer that is made in the context of an administration. He takes the view that such proceedings do not fall within regulation 8(7). For this exception to apply the proceedings must be analogous to bankruptcy proceedings and involve the liquidation of the assets under the supervision of an insolvency practitioner. Administration is not in the view of the Secretary of State analogous to bankruptcy proceedings. The correct approach is to look at the main or sole purpose of the procedure rather than its outcome in a specific instance. The main purpose of bankruptcy proceedings is to realise the free assets of an insolvent debtor and share the proceeds after deduction of costs and expenses amongst all the debtor's creditors. This is not the main purpose of administration. It follows that Regulation 8(7) will not apply to administration. It is also the view of the Secretary of State that regulations 8(2) to (6) will apply to administration so that liabilities owed to transferring employees at the transfer date of the kinds described in Part XII of the Employment Rights

Act 1996 would fall to be paid out of the National Insurance Fund by the Secretary of State and not by the transferee.

Voluntary arrangements
A transfer in the context of a voluntary arrangement is subject to regulations 4 and 7 for the same reasons referred to in relation to administration. In a voluntary arrangement the debtor is left in control of the assets and the function of the insolvency practitioner is merely to supervise the arrangement. Regulations 8(2) to (6) will apply in relation to a relevant transfer where the transferor is subject to a voluntary arrangement. Liabilities owed to transferring employees at the transfer date of the kinds described in Part XII of the Employment Rights Act 1996 do not transfer to the transferee and would fall to be paid by the Secretary of State out of the National Insurance Fund.

Administrative receivership
Regulations 4 and 7 will apply to administrative receiverships. They are not analogous to bankruptcy proceedings since they are not collective proceedings and the exception in regulation 8(7) will accordingly not apply. Where there is a relevant transfer regulations 8(2) to (6) will apply so that liabilities owed at the transfer date to transferring employees of the kinds described in Part XII of the Employment Rights Act 1996 do not transfer to the transferee and would fall to be paid by the Secretary of State out of the National Insurance Fund.

Other types of receivership
Other types of receivership are not insolvency proceedings and so the provisions of regulation 8 do not apply to them. A relevant transfer by a receiver will therefore be subject to regulations 4 and 7.

Proceedings in other jurisdictions where a relevant transfer occurs in Great Britain
In this case it is necessary to consider whether the foreign proceedings are analogous to bankruptcy proceedings. If they are then the exception in regulation 8(7) will apply.

URN 06/1368

To summarise:

Does a TUPE Insolvency exemption apply?

20.29

Process	*Terminal – 8(7) or Non-terminal – 8(6)?*	*Comment*
Court liquidation (compulsory)	8(7)	A solvent liquidation may not be within 8(7) if company continues to trade – *Jules Dethier* In practice unusual for business to continue after order made (see eg DTI Condoc of March 2005, page 30) DTI Guidance in June 2006 (URN 06/1368) considers always within 8(7)
Creditors' voluntary liquidation (CVL)	8(7)	Govt thought possible could be within 8(6) as well as 8(7). But thinks 8(7) probably overrides (March 2005 Condoc, page 30, footnote 8) DTI notes on TUPE (Feb 2006) – more emphatic that CVL not within 8(6) DTI URN 06/1368 considers always within 8(7)
Members' voluntary liquidation (MVL)	Neither	Not an insolvency. Govt thought not in 8(6) (March 2005 DTI Condoc, page 28) DTI URN 06/1368 considers always outside 8(6) and 8(7)
Administration	8(6)	Could be in 8(7) in some circumstances? See *Oakland v Wellswood*, but consider *Abels* and *Jules Dethier* DTI URN 06/1368 considers always outside 8(7) but within 8(6)

Process	Terminal – 8(7) or Non-terminal – 8(6)?	Comment
Administrative Receivership	8(6)	DTI URN 06/1368 considers: always outside 8(7) as not collective proceedings and so not analogous to bankruptcy proceedings. within 8(6) Govt previously thought outside 8(6) as well – see p28 of March 2005 Condoc. Not a court 'proceeding'? (but neither is a CVL). Not a collective arrangement so outside? (Feb 2006 DTI guidance). But no 'collective' requirement is specified in 8(6).
CVA	8(6)	DTI URN 06/1368 considers same as administration, so always outside 8(7) but within 8(6) Govt Condoc p28. Consider A-G opinion in *Govt of Italy* case.
Receivership (not administrative)	Neither	DTI URN 06/1368 considers always outside 8(6) and 8(7) as not 'insolvency proceedings'. Would also be an issue in meeting the test that the proceedings are under the control of an 'insolvency practitioner'.
Striking off of company by Registrar of Companies under CA 2006, s 1000	Neither	Probably not insolvency proceedings – see *Charlton v Charlton Thermosystems (Romsey) Ltd* [1995] ICR 56 at page 64E and para 12.22 above
Non-UK proceedings	Depends	Need to consider if analogous to bankruptcy proceedings or not. May be an issue in meeting the test that the proceedings are under the control of an 'insolvency practitioner'.

NON-TERMINAL INSOLVENCIES – REGULATION 8(6)

What transfers?

20.30   ARD 2001, article 6 allows member states to choose that all debts do not transfer. The UK has adopted this in part in TUPE 2006. Regulation 8 of TUPE 2006 applies so that any liability which is covered by the National Insurance Fund under the statutory provisions in the Employment Rights Act 1996[1] broadly does not pass to the purchaser/transferor – reg 8(5).

1 The 'relevant statutory schemes' are (a) Chapter VI of Part XI of ERA 1996; and (b) Part XII of ERA 1996. These cover (broadly) statutory redundancy pay and some employment claims (eg holiday pay and up to eight weeks pay arrears, subject to the usual limits on weekly earnings) – see Chapter 13 above.

20.31   Instead the relevant employees (including any dismissed before the transfer) retain their claims against the insolvent transferor (and the National Insurance Fund). This applies even though in many cases otherwise they would not be able to claim because TUPE means they have not been dismissed by the transferor – reg 8(3).

20.32   Liabilities in excess of the statutory claims will pass to the transferee. It seems that this will probably mean that service before the transfer date will not count towards a later statutory redundancy payment if the employee is later made redundant by the purchaser/transferee[1].

But this is a complex area – see eg *Secretary of State v Lassman*[2], *Senior Heat Treatment v Bell*[3], and the discussion in *Harvey on Industrial Relations and Employment Law* at paras E299 to E326. The government seem to have intended a reset to zero – see page 24 of the Government's response to the public consultation on TUPE (February 2006)[4].

Any non-statutory liability (eg a contractual top-up right) will transfer (see eg para 7.16 in the explanatory memorandum to TUPE 2006[5]).

1 See, ERA 1996, s 214.
2 [2000] IRLR 411, CA.
3 [1997] IRLR 614, EAT.
4 See http://www.dti.gov.uk/er/TUPE_govtresponse_feb06.pdf and para 20.6 above
5 See the OPSI website: http://www.opsi.gov.uk/si/em2006/uksiem_20060246_en.pdf

20.33   The relevant statutory claims covered by the NI fund are:

NI Fund claims

The relevant claims of employees in respect of which an entitlement to claim arises on the NI fund are defined or set out in s 167 and 184 of ERA 1996. They include:

(i)   statutory redundancy pay,

(ii)   arrears of pay for up to eight weeks;

(iii) amounts due for failure to give the statutory minimum period of notice required by s 86 ERA 1996;

(iv) any holiday pay (see definition in s 184(3) ERA 1996) entitlement for up to six weeks which accrued during the 12 months prior to the appropriate date;

(v) any basic award of compensation for unfair dismissal (within the meaning of s 118 ERA 1996) but not any compensatory award; and

(vi) a reasonable sum by way of reimbursement of any fee or premium paid by an apprentice or articled clerk.

Under s 184(2), arrears of pay for the purposes of section 184 include guarantee payments, remuneration on suspension on medical or maternity grounds under ss 64 and 68 of ERA 1996, payments for time off under Pt VI of ERA 1996 and s 169 of TULRCA 1992 and remuneration under a protective award under s 189 of TULRCA 1992.

Under s 186(1), where the amount of a claim is referable to a period of time, the amount of the debt must not exceed the usual limit applicable under ERA 1996 to claims (ie £380 per week where the relevant date fell on or after 1 October 2009 – see para 2.49 above)

20.34 The Insolvency Service issued a statement of its intended practice in this area in a letter to insolvency practitioners on 3 April 2006 (just before TUPE 2006 came into force). It seems that it is taking the view that not all NIF claims are retained by the transferor.

20.35 The relevant extract from this letter is below:

Extract from letter from Insolvency Service to IPs – 3 April 2006

What the employees will be entitled to claim will depend on the following circumstances:

(1) Whether they transfer to the new owner.

If the employer *is insolvent on the transfer date*, to assist the rescue of all, or part, of an insolvent business, the Secretary of State will pay wages and holidays taken prior to the insolvency date but unpaid up to the statutory limits to employees who transfer to the new owner. No redundancy pay, accrued holiday entitlement or notice pay will be paid are there is no dismissal – the contract continues with the new employer. The transferee will pay the residual contractual debt. The Secretary of State's debt will stay with the insolvent company – it cannot be recovered from the transferee.

(2) Whether they are unfairly dismissed because of the transfer.

Employees who are unfairly dismissed because of the transfer will also be paid wages and holiday pay (as for those who transfer). RP and notice pay will not be paid, as they were not dismissed by reason of redundancy. Employees may make a claim to ET for an unfair dismissal award and breach of contract (notice). It will be for the ET to determine on the joint and several liabilities between the transferor and transferee.

(3) Whether the dismissal is for ETO reason.

There is no change to the payment procedure where the employee's dismissal is transfer related but is for ETO reasons entailing changes in the workforce. They are considered to be redundant and the RPO will pay redundancy, wages, holiday pay (including accrued entitlement) and notice pay as usual.

(4) Whether the employees have refused to transfer.

There is no change to the procedure for those who refuse to transfer. Wages and holidays will be paid. RP and CNP will be rejected as there is no redundancy and they are treated as having left employment of their own accord.

In cases where the transfer date is prior to the insolvency date, no payments for wages and holiday pay will be made by the RPO to employees who transfer, or those who are unfairly dismissed. It will be treated as a transfer under the solvent TUPE provisions. Employees dismissed for ETO reasons will be considered in the usual way and if the liability rests with the insolvent transferor, payment may be made to employees.

20.36   This letter raises a number of queries. The impact is outlined in the chart below (with comments in footnotes).

	Insolvency Service comments in letter of 3 April 2006 *When will the NI fund pay claims if the transferor employer in insolvency proceedings (within TUPE reg 8(6)) at date of transfer?*			
Statutory claims	*Employees transfer*	*Employees are unfairly dismissed because of the transfer*	*Is dismissal for an ETO reason?*	*Employees who refuse to transfer[1]*
1. Redundancy pay (RP)	Not payable – no dismissal[2]	Not payable – not dismissed by reason of redundancy	Will be paid by NI fund – considered to be made redundant[3]	Not payable – no dismissal

	Insolvency Service comments in letter of 3 April 2006 When will the NI fund pay claims if the transferor employer in insolvency proceedings (within TUPE reg 8(6)) at date of transfer?			
Statutory claims	*Employees transfer*	*Employees are unfairly dismissed because of the transfer*	*Is dismissal for an ETO reason?*	*Employees who refuse to transfer*[1]
2. Arrears of pay (up to 8 weeks) (including pay for holidays already taken)	Will be paid by NI fund	Will be paid by NI fund	Will be paid by NI fund – considered to be made redundant	Will be paid by NI fund
3. Accrued (but untaken) holiday pay (up to 6 weeks)	Not payable – no dismissal[4]	Not mentioned by Insolvency Service	Will be paid by NI fund – considered to be made redundant	Not payable – no dismissal[5]
4. Notice pay (CNP)(up to 13 weeks)	Not payable – no dismissal	Not payable – not dismissed by reason of redundancy[6] Employees may claim before an ET – up to ET to fix joint and several liabilities between transferor and transferee[7]	Will be paid by NI fund – considered to be made redundant	Not payable – no dismissal
5. Basic award on unfair dismissal	Not mentioned by Insolvency Service but presumably not payable as no dismissal	Employees may claim before an ET – up to ET to fix joint and several liabilities between transferor and transferee[8]	Not mentioned by Insolvency Service[9]	Not mentioned by Insolvency Service but presumably not payable as no dismissal

1 This is presumably meant to deal with the case where an employee refuses to transfer (under reg 4(7) of TUPE 2006) without any cause. Ie this section does not apply if the employee refuses to transfer by reason of a substantial change in working conditions to the material detriment of the employee (within reg 4(9) of TUPE). Note that in the reg 4(9) case, damages for failure to give notice are not payable – reg 4(10) (unless there has been a repudiatory breach of contract – reg 4(11)).

2 See also the comment at para 3 of URN 06/1368 issued by the DTI in June 2006.

3 In practice most ETO reasons will be the same as redundancy. TUPE 2006, reg 7(3)(b) allows an ETO reason dismissal still to qualify as a redundancy.

4 Not clear how the Insolvency Service reaches this view. TUPE, reg 8(3) deems there to be a termination of the employment and a termination (not dismissal) is all that is required under s 182, ERA 1996.

5 Not clear how the Insolvency Service reaches this view. TUPE, reg 8(3) deems there to be a termination of the employment and a termination (not dismissal) is all that is required under ERA 1996, s 182.

6 Not clear why redundancy is relevant here.

7 Not clear what this is talking about. An ET has no power under TUPE to allocate liability as between the transferor and the transferee. There is joint and several liability for failure to inform and consult about the transfer – reg 15(9) (but even here it is difficult to see how the ET has the ability to apportion liability). The Civil Liability (Contribution) Act 1978 will presumably apply.

8 See previous note.

9 May not be relevant. Unlikely to get redundancy payment *and* basic award – see ERA 1996, s 122(4).

20.37 If transfer takes place before the insolvency date, the Insolvency Service says it will only meet claims if any liability remains with the insolvent transferor (eg any employees dismissed for an ETO reason).

Looking at the four separate situations for employees in turn

(1) Employees transfer

20.38 In this situation, the relevant employees and the liabilities will transfer to the transferee/purchaser under reg 4 of TUPE 2006. But reg 8(3) will deem a termination of the employment contract for the purposes of reg 8(4)(b), the reference to the general NI fund provisions (but not reg 8(4)(a), the reference to the redundancy pay provision).

20.39 In relation to redundancy pay, a deemed termination looks not to be enough to trigger a liability. There must be a dismissal by reason of redundancy (ERA 1996, s 135(1)(a)). So it seems that the Insolvency Service is taking the view that no redundancy pay can be claimed from the NI fund under reg 8(4), if the employment actually continues and transfers to the purchaser/transferee.

20.40 R3 point out in its technical bulletin No 77 (November 2006) that

'3 It should be noted that although the Regulations appear to restrict the payment of redundancy pay out of the NI Fund to employees who have been dismissed before the transfer, and this appears to be the view of the Redundancy Payments Directorate in its latest guidance (see Appendix[1]), information given in the DTI's guide to the Regulations[2] and its response to the earlier consultation on the draft

Regulations[3] conveys a different view, suggesting that redundancy pay is also payable to employees who transfer.

The guide says (at page 29): 'the Regulations ensure that some of the transferor's pre-existing debts to the employees do not pass to the transferee. Those debts concern any obligations to pay the employees statutory redundancy pay or sums representing various debts to them, such as arrears of pay, payment in lieu of notice, holiday pay or a basic award of compensation for unfair dismissal. In effect, payment of statutory redundancy pay and the other debts will be met by the Secretary of State through the National Insurance Fund.' It adds in a footnote: 'The Regulations also provide for the payment of these sums on the date of the transfer even though they may not have actually been dismissed by the transferor on or before that date, as would normally be a requirement for such payments.'

The response to the consultation says (paragraph 5.7): 'Where statutory redundancy payments are made under this provision, the effect is to ensure that the transferred workers have to build up their future entitlement to redundancy payments with the new employer from zero.'

This is one example of the uncertainty which currently surrounds the interpretation of the Regulations.'

So it looks as if the intention behind these provisions in TUPE 2006 may have been defectively carried out. But there is no sign of any amendment.

1 This is a reference to the guidance issued by the DTI on 9 June 2006 in URN 06/1368. It was also attached to a letter to IPs sent by the Insolvency Service on 8 June 2006.
2 The DTI guide to TUPE 2006 (August 2006) see www.dti.gov.uk/files/file20761.pdf
3 The DTI response to the consultation on TUPE – see www.dti.gov.uk/er/ TUPE_govtresponse_feb06.pdf

20.41

Statutory claims	Insolvency Service comments in letter of 3 April 2006 When will the NI fund pay claims if the transferor employer in insolvency proceedings (within TUPE reg 8(6)) at date of transfer?	Comments
1. Redundancy pay (RP)	Not payable – no dismissal	See also the comment to the same effect at para 3 of URN 06/1368 issued by the DTI in June 2006
2. Arrears of pay (up to 8 weeks) (including pay for holidays already taken)	Will be paid by NI fund	

Statutory claims	*Insolvency Service comments in letter of 3 April 2006* *When will the NI fund pay claims if the transferor employer in insolvency proceedings (within TUPE reg 8(6)) at date of transfer?*	*Comments*
3. Accrued (but untaken) holiday pay (up to 6 weeks)	Not payable – no dismissal	Not clear how the Insolvency Service reaches this view. reg 8(3) of TUPE deems there to be a termination of the employment and a termination (not dismissal) is all that is required under s 182, ERA 1996. Presumably the argument is that the employment continues with transferee who will presumably allow the holidays in due course? But the same would apply
4. Notice pay (CNP) (up to 13 weeks)	Not payable – no dismissal	Not clear how the Insolvency Service reaches this view. Same issue as for holiday pay (see 3 above) – arguably no dismissal, so no liability for notice has arisen (within ERA 1996, s 184(1)(b).
5. Basic award on unfair dismissal	Not mentioned by Insolvency Service	Presumably not payable as no dismissal.

(2)   Employees are unfairly dismissed because of the transfer

20.42   Presumably the issue here is most liability relating to such employees will still transfer to the transferee/purchaser under reg 4(3) of TUPE 2006 as relating to a person who would have been employed immediately before the transfer 'if he had not been dismissed in the circumstances described in regulation 7(1)' – ie by reason of the transfer (or for a reason connected with the transfer) and not for an ETO reason – see Chapter 14 below. The category used in the Insolvency Service seems to envisage the term 'unfair dismissal' to cover this.

20.43   But unlike the situation where there is a transfer of employment (A above), here there is actually a dismissal. It is only the liability owed to the ex-employee that transfers, not the employment itself.

Statutory claims	Insolvency Service comments in letter of 3 April 2006 When will the NI fund pay claims if the transferor employer in insolvency proceedings (within TUPE reg 8(6)) at date of transfer?	Comments
1. Redundancy pay (RP)	Not payable – not dismissed by reason of redundancy	This may well often be right – although redundancy dismissals can still be unfair.
2. Arrears of pay (up to 8 weeks) (including pay for holidays already taken)	Will be paid by NI fund	Not clear how the Insolvency Service reaches this view. Same issue as for holiday pay (see 3 above) – arguably no dismissal, so no liability for notice has arisen (within ERA 1996, s 184(1)(b).
3. Accrued (but untaken) holiday entitlement (up to 6 weeks)	Not mentioned by Insolvency Service	Presumably payable by the NI fund. There seems no reason to distinguish holiday pay from arrears of pay
4. Notice pay (CNP) (up to 13 weeks)	Not payable – not dismissed by reason of redundancy. Employees may claim before an ET – up to ET to fix joint and several liabilities between transferor and transferee	Not clear why redundancy is relevant here Not clear what this is talking about. An ET has no power under TUPE to allocate liability as between the transferor and the transferee. There is joint and several liability for failure to inform and consult about the transfer – reg 15(9) (but even here it is difficult to see how the ET has the ability to apportion liability). The Civil Liability (Contribution) Act 1978 will presumably apply.
5. Basic award on unfair dismissal	Employees may claim before an ET – up to ET to fix joint and several liabilities between transferor and transferee	See comments on notice pay (4 above)

(3) Is dismissal for an ETO reason?

20.44   Presumably the issue here is that, unlike B above, liability relating to such employees will not transfer to the transferee/purchaser under reg 4(3) of TUPE 2006, because reg 7(2) will apply.

20.45   Presumably the intention is to refer to dismissals before the transfer date where liability does not transfer to the transferee/purchaser – ie those unconnected with the business transfer or connected with it, but for 'an economic, technical or organisation reason entailing changes in the workforce' – see Chapter 23 (TUPE: Impact on dismissals instigated by IP) below.

20.46   Given that all liability here remains with the transferor in any event (regardless of reg 8) and so the NI fund will be liable in the usual way, the Insolvency Service guidance seems just to be clarifying that it accepts this.

Statutory claims	*Insolvency Service comments in letter of 3 April 2006* *When will the NI fund pay claims if the transferor employer in insolvency proceedings (within TUPE reg 8(6)) at date of transfer?*	*Comments*
1. Redundancy pay (RP)	Will be paid by NI fund – considered to be made redundant.	In practice most ETO reasons will be the same as redundancy. Regulation 7(3)(b) of TUPE 2006 allows an ETO reason dismissal still to qualify as a redundancy.
2. Arrears of pay (up to 8 weeks) (including pay for holidays already taken)	Will be paid by NI fund – considered to be made redundant	Not clear why redundancy is relevant here
3. Accrued (but untaken) holiday pay (up to 6 weeks)	Will be paid by NI fund – considered to be made redundant	Not clear why redundancy is relevant here
4. Notice pay (CNP) (up to 13 weeks)	Will be paid by NI fund – considered to be made redundant	Not clear why redundancy is relevant here
5. Basic award on unfair dismissal	Not mentioned by Insolvency Service	May not be relevant. Unlikely to get redundancy payment and basic award – see ERA 1996, s 122(4)

(4)   Employees who refuse to transfer

20.47   This category seems to be meant to deal with the case where an employee refuses to transfer (under reg 4(7) of TUPE 2006) without any cause (in which case the employee's contract is terminated, but there is no dismissal – reg 4(8)).

20.48   I.e. this category does not apply if the employee refuses to transfer by reason of a substantial change in working conditions to the material detriment of the employee (within TUPE, reg 4(9)). Note that in the reg 4(9) case, damages for failure to give notice are not payable – reg 4(10) (unless there has been a repudiatory breach of contract – reg 4(11)).

Statutory claims	*Insolvency Service comments in letter of 3 April 2006* *When will the NI fund pay claims if the transferor employer in insolvency proceedings (within TUPE reg 8(6)) at date of transfer?*	*Comments*
1. Redundancy pay (RP)	Not payable – no dismissal.	
2. Arrears of pay (up to 8 weeks) (including pay for holidays already taken)	Will be paid by NI fund.	
3. Accrued (but untaken) holiday pay (up to 6 weeks)	Not payable – no dismissal.	Not clear how the Insolvency Service reaches this view. Reg 8(3) of TUPE deems there to be a termination of the employment and a termination (not dismissal) is all that is required under ERA 1996, s 182
4. Notice pay (CNP)(up to 13 weeks)	Not payable – no dismissal.	Not clear how the Insolvency Service reaches this view. Reg 8(3) of TUPE deems there to be a termination of the employment and a termination (not dismissal) is all that is required under ERA 1996, s 182
5. Basic award on unfair dismissal	Not mentioned by Insolvency Service.	Presumably not payable as no dismissal

Ability to agree contract changes

20.49   Also in 'relevant insolvency proceedings' (ie non-terminal insolvencies within reg 8(6)), reg 9 of TUPE 2006 removes the usual prohibition on changes to employment terms as a result of a TUPE transfer[1]. It removes any prohibition under TUPE that prevents 'the transferor or transferee (or an insolvency practitioner) and appropriate representatives of assigned employees agreeing to permitted variations'.

1 See *Wilson v St Helens Borough Council* [1999] 2 AC 52, HL and *Martin v South Bank University* [2004] IRLR 74, ECJ.

20.50   A 'permitted variation' is a variation to the contract of employment of an assigned employee where:

'(a) the sole or principal reason for it is the transfer itself or a reason connected with the transfer that is not an economic, technical or organisational reason entailing changes in the workforce; and

(b) it is designed to safeguard employment opportunities by ensuring the survival of the undertaking, business or part of the undertaking or business that is the subject of the relevant transfer.'

20.51   The DTI in its guidance on TUPE 2006 made the point that any variation must still comply with other statutory provisions – for example the minimum wage laws.

20.52   In suitable cases these provisions could be used to obtain employee agreement that any early retirement pension rights do not transfer under TUPE following the ECJ's decisions in *Beckmann*[1] and *Martin*[2] (see para 24.21 below).

1 *Beckmann v Dynamo Whicheloe Macfarlane* [2002] IRLR 578, ECJ.
2 *Martin v South Bank University* [2004] IRLR 74, ECJ.

20.53   'Appropriate representatives' are either an independent recognised trade union or individuals elected by the assigned employees.
Where assigned employees are represented by non-trade union representatives (reg 9(5)):

(a)   the agreement recording a permitted variation must be in writing and signed by each of the representatives who have made it or, where that is not reasonably practicable, by a duly authorised agent of that representative; and

(b)   the employer must, before the agreement is made available for signature, provide all employees to whom it is intended to apply on the date on which it is to come into effect with copies of the text of the agreement and such guidance as those employees might reasonably require in order to understand it fully.

20.54   Subject to this it seems that variations agreed by the relevant representatives will bind and apply to all transferring employees (even though they may not have otherwise authorised the representatives to agree contract terms on their behalf – see reg 9(6)).

Hive-down (old reg 4)

20.55   TUPE 1981 used to make specific provision (in reg 4) for hive-downs by insolvency practitioners, but this has not been carried forward into TUPE 2006. The special provision used to apply only to transfers by a receiver (whether an administrative receiver or not), an administrator and a liquidator appointed in a creditors' voluntary winding up.

20.56   Regulation 4 of TUPE 1981 was not expressed to apply to a liquidator appointed in a members' voluntary winding up or a liquidator appointed in a court winding up. Presumably the reason for this exclusion was that:

(a)   in the case of a members' voluntary winding up the company is presumed to be solvent and hence special provision is not needed; and

(b)   in the case of a court winding up the view was presumably taken that there is an automatic dismissal of all employees when the order is made (see para 5.2 above) and hence no transfer of business can include employees (this seems to ignore the possibility of the liquidator agreeing with an employee to continue the employment).

Time of transfer

20.57   Regulation 4 of TUPE 1981 used to provide that where a relevant transfer is made by an insolvency practitioner (presumably this meant transfers by the company at the instigation of the insolvency practitioner) to a wholly-owned subsidiary of the insolvent company, the statutory 'novation' of employment liabilities under reg 5 from the insolvent company to the wholly-owned subsidiary did not take place on the transfer, but rather was delayed until immediately before either the wholly-owned subsidiary ceased to be a wholly-owned subsidiary of the insolvent company or the relevant undertaking was transferred by the wholly-owned subsidiary to another person.

20.58   The reason for this delay was presumably to ensure that, if the wholly-owned subsidiary (or its business) is not ultimately sold by the insolvency practitioner, the employees remained as creditors of the insolvent company. If they had become creditors of the (presumably solvent) wholly-owned subsidiary their claims would, in effect, have been preferred because they would be payable out of the assets of the solvent company instead of being claims on the insolvent parent company. This is confirmed by the comments of David Waddington MP, the Under-Secretary of State for Employment, in the House of Commons when TUPE 1981 was introduced[1].

1 See Hansard HC, 7 December 1981, col 678.

20.59   In *Re Maxwell Fleet and Facilities Management Ltd (No 2)*[1], David Mackie QC (sitting as a Deputy Judge of the High Court) confirmed this.

> 'The regulations require that where there is a relevant transfer those employee liabilities will be assumed by the transferee provided the other conditions are satisfied. Regulation 4, although not specifically envisaged by the directive, enables the purpose of the directive to be achieved while permitting a business to be hived down to a subsidiary as is so frequently the case in English insolvencies. The purpose of the hiving down is achieved and the relevant transfer postponed (not cancelled) to meet the objective of the directive in passing responsibility for these employee liabilities to the ultimate transferee. There would otherwise be risks including that of the intermediary subsidiary created by the administrators being left with responsibilities which the directive intended should rest with the transferee, not the assetless intermediary.'

1 [2000] 2 All ER 860 (David Mackie QC, sitting as a Deputy Judge of the High Court).

20.60   The special provision may also have been intended to give the insolvency practitioner more time to arrange for dismissal of employees before the ultimate onwards sale to a third party took place, so that any liabilities to such employees would remain as liabilities of the insolvent company rather than pass to the purchaser (see the Industrial Tribunal decision in *Harris v Fiesana Ltd*[1]).

1 14 October 1983 (COIT 1474/167), IT.

20.61   If this was the intention, it cut against the interpretation of TUPE 1981 (and the ARD) as decided in the *Litster* decision[1] – see para 23.46 below. In *Re Maxwell Fleet and Facilities Management Ltd (No 2)*[2], David Mackie QC (sitting as a Deputy Judge of the High Court) held that an attempt to use reg 4 of TUPE 1981 to achieve such a result was not an orthodox hive-down, but instead an attempt to avoid employee liability transferring altogether. As such it failed. He held:

> 'The transaction on 9 April was not part of an orthodox hive down by which the viable parts of a business are segregated from the remainder and placed by the administrator in the position where they may continue to flourish and/or be sold. This transaction introduced an intermediary Dancequote for one purpose only, achieving the mutual wish of the contracting parties to transfer the business to FDML stripped of the liability to employees.' (para 36)

> 'In this case the agreement between the parties sought to achieve a purpose quite different from that of reg 4.' (para 37)

> 'It was the sale of a business on one day complicated by a mutual desire to avoid what would otherwise be the effect of the regulations. In substance it was a single transfer and I have no hesitation in finding, fortified by the authorities to which I have referred and by the sense of the final words in reg 4, that it should be construed to defeat an ingenious device designed to deprive employees of protection which would otherwise be available to them. Mr Altaras' alternative submissions, on the assumption that Litster's case applies, are ingenious but beset by the same artificiality of approach which that case invalidates.' (para 39)

1 *Litster v Forth Dry Dock and Engineering Co Ltd* [1989] 1 All ER 1134; [1990] 1 AC 546 (HL).
2 [2000] 2 All ER 860 (David Mackie QC, sitting as a Deputy Judge of the High Court).

20.62   There were some doubts as to whether reg 4 was in accordance with the requirements of the Acquired Rights Directive (see para 19.17 above). There is (and was) no express provision in the Acquired Rights Directive authorising a provision such as reg 4. Although transfers from certain insolvent companies have been held to be outside the Directive (see *Abels* and *D'Urso* discussed in para 19.29 above), this exemption probably did not apply to the same categories of insolvent employer as were listed in reg 4.

20.63   In *Re Maxwell Fleet and Facilities Management Ltd (No 2)*[1], David Mackie QC discussed these points, but held that 'reg 4, although not specifically envisaged by the directive, enables the purpose of the directive to be achieved while permitting a business to be hived down to a subsidiary as is so frequently the case in English insolvencies' (at para 37). In any event the insolvency in that case was an administration and 'this particular administration is a procedure to which the directive unquestionably applies' (para 38).

1 [2000] 2 All ER 860 (David Mackie QC, sitting as a Deputy Judge of the High Court).

20.64   For transfers after 5 April 2006, the point goes away because of the entry into force of TUPE 2006 (without any equivalent to old reg 4).

20.65   Extract from BIS guide to the new TUPE regulations: *Employment rights on the transfer of an undertaking: a guide to the 2006 TUPE regulations for employees, employers and representatives* (June 2009 version)[1].

'PART 6 – THE POSITION OF INSOLVENT BUSINESSES

To assist the rescue of failing businesses, the Regulations make special provision where the transferor employer is subject to insolvency proceedings.

First, the Regulations ensure that some of the transferor's pre-existing debts to the employees do not pass to the new employer. Those debts concern any obligations to pay the employees statutory redundancy pay or sums representing various debts to them, such as arrears of pay, payment in lieu of notice, holiday pay or a basic award of compensation for unfair dismissal (12). In effect, payment of statutory redundancy pay and the other debts will be met by the Secretary of State through the National Insurance Fund. However, any debts over and above those that can be met in this way will pass across to the new employer.

Second, the Regulations provide greater scope in insolvency situations for the new employer to vary terms and conditions after the transfer takes place. As was discussed in Part 3, the Regulations place significant restrictions on new employers when varying contracts because of the transfer or a reason connected with the transfer. These restrictions are in effect waived, allowing the transferor, the new employer or the insolvency practitioner in the exceptional situation of insolvency to reduce pay and establish other inferior terms and conditions after the transfer. However, in their place, the Regulations impose other conditions on the new employer when varying contracts:

- the transferor, new employer or insolvency practitioner must agree the "permitted variation" with representatives of the employees. Those representatives are determined in much the same way as the representatives who should be consulted in advance of relevant transfers (see Part 5 for more details);

- the representatives must be union representatives where an independent trade union is recognised for collective bargaining purposes by the employer in respect of any of the affected employees. Those union representatives and the transferor, new employer or insolvency practitioner are then free to agree variations to contracts, though the speed of their negotiations may be faster than usual in view of pressing circumstances associated with insolvency;

- in other cases, non-union representatives are empowered to agree permitted variations with the transferor, new employer or insolvency practitioner. However, where agreements are reached by non-union representatives, two other requirements must be met. First, the agreement which records the permitted variation must be in writing and signed by each of the non-union representatives (or by an authorised person on a representative's behalf where it is not reasonably practicable for that representative to sign). Second, before the agreement is signed, the employer must provide all the affected employees with a copy of the agreement and any guidance which the employees would reasonably need in order to understand it;

- the new terms and conditions agreed in a 'permitted variation' must not breach other statutory entitlements. For example, any agreed pay rates must not be set below the national minimum wage; and

- a 'permitted variation' must be made with the intention of safeguarding employment opportunities by ensuring the survival of the undertaking or business or part of the undertaking or business (13).

Q. What types of insolvency proceedings are covered by these aspects of the Regulations?

A. These provisions are found in Regulations 8 and 9. Those two Regulations apply where the transferor is subject to 'relevant insolvency proceedings' which are insolvency proceedings commenced in relation to him but not with a view to the liquidation of his assets. The Regulations do not attempt to list all these different types of procedures individually. It is the Department's view that 'relevant insolvency proceedings' mean any collective insolvency proceedings in which the whole or part of the business or undertaking is transferred to another entity as a going concern. That is to say, it covers an insolvency proceeding in which all creditors of the debtor may participate, and in relation to which the insolvency office holder owes a duty to all creditors. The Department considers that 'relevant insolvency proceedings' does not cover winding-up by either creditors or members where there is no such transfer.

(12) The Regulations also provide for the payment of these sums on the date of the transfer even though they may not have actually been dismissed by the transferor on or before that date, as would normally be a requirement for such payments.

(13) In addition, the sole or principal reason for the permitted variation must be the transfer itself or a reason connected with the transfer which is not an economic, technical or organisational reason.'

1 See link from the BIS website replacing previous versions issued by the DTI and then BERR: http://www.berr.gov.uk/files/file20761.pdf

CHAPTER 21

TUPE 2006: Information and consultation

INFORMATION AND CONSULTATION

21.1   There are no provisions in TUPE – or the equivalent consultation obligations, an collective redundancies in the Trade Union and Labour Relations (Consolidation) Act 1992 (TULRCA) – that automatically disapply the information and consultation obligations contained in that legislation in the case of potential or actual insolvency. See generally Chapter 7 above.

21.2   The employer must begin the information and consultation process in good time (TULRCA 1992, s 188(1A) and Art 7 of Council Directive 2001/23/EC (ARD)). The ARD and TUPE do not provide specific time periods, unlike the minimum periods for consultation for collective redundancies under ss 188(1A)(a) and (b) of TULRCA 1992.

21.3   The Court of Appeal held in *Susie Radin Ltd v GMB*[1] that where an employer had not engaged in any meaningful consultation before making redundancies, a tribunal could make a protective award for the maximum period (90 days) without regard to the fact that consultation would not have affected the outcome. The Court of Appeal upheld the tribunal's decision to make a protective award for the maximum amount under s 189(2) of TULRCA 1992 against Susie Radin Ltd for breach of the obligation to consult.

1 [2004] EWCA Civ 180; [2004] 2 All ER 279, CA.

21.4   The Court of Appeal held that s 189(2) ensures that consultation takes place in accordance with s 188 by providing a sanction against non-compliance, in the form of financial compensation paid by the employer. There is nothing in the statute to link the length of the protected period to any loss suffered by the employees. As the focus is on the severity of the employer's default, the tribunal is entitled to start with the maximum protected period and see if there are any mitigating factors justifying a reduction. In this case there were none. The appeal was dismissed.

21.5 A similar approach is likely to be taken in relation to the award (maximum 13 weeks) for failure to inform or consult under TUPE – see the decision of the Scottish EAT in *Sweetin v Coral Racing*[1].

1 [2006] IRLR 252, EAT.

21.6 However, (like TULRCA, s 188(7) and TUPE 1981, reg 11(2)) TUPE 2006, reg 15(2) states that if there are special circumstances which render it not reasonably practicable for the employer to comply with the relevant requirements the employer shall take all such steps towards compliance with the relevant requirements as are reasonably practicable in those circumstances.

The onus is on the employer to show that there were special circumstances and that it took all such reasonably practicable steps (TULRCA, s 189(6), TUPE 1981, reg 11(2) and TUPE 2006, reg 15(2)).

21.7 If it is not the employer, but instead an entity controlling the employer (eg an insolvency practitioner), that makes the decision to arrange for a transfer, this is unlikely to be a special circumstance[1]. Regulation 13(12) of TUPE 2006 states:

'(12) The duties imposed on an employer by this regulation shall apply irrespective of whether the decision resulting in the relevant transfer is taken by the employer or a person controlling the employer.'

1 On this, see the comments in the draft report (September 2005) by T Mocroft for the MG Rover Task Force at page 9, commenting that the special circumstances defence was argued where a separate third party supplier had to close down suddenly because of the loss of orders from MG Rover (due to its collapse). See http://www.advantagewm.co.uk/mg-rover-insolvency-report.pdf

21.8 Insolvency can be, but does not necessarily amount to, a special circumstance. In *The Baker's Union v Clarks of Hove*[1], Geoffrey Lane LJ (as he then was) referred to the decision of the Tribunal and held:

'What they said, in effect, was this, that insolvency is, on its own, neither here nor there. It may be a special circumstance, it may not be a special circumstance. It will depend entirely on the cause of the insolvency whether the circumstances can be described as special or not. If, for example, sudden disaster strikes a company, making it necessary to close the concern, then plainly that would be a matter which is capable of being a special circumstance; and that is so whether the disaster is physical or financial. If the insolvency, however, was merely due to a gradual run-down of the company, as it was in this case, then those are facts on which the tribunal can come to the conclusion that the circumstances were not special. In other words, to be special the event must be something out of the ordinary, something uncommon; and that is the meaning of the word 'special' in the context of this Act.'

1 [1979] 1 All ER 152, CA.

21.9 Other insolvency related circumstances that have been held not to be special circumstances include (see also para 7.32 above):

(a) financial circumstances that led to the appointment of a receiver that were neither sudden nor unforeseen – *Angus Jowett & Co v NUTGW*[1]; and

(b) the shedding of employees in order to make the sale of the business more attractive – *GMB v Rankin and Harrison*[2].

1 [1985] IRLR 326, CA.
2 [1992] IRLR 514, EAT.

21.10 Insolvency related circumstances that have been held to be special circumstances include:

(a) the failure of a business after trading in a genuine and reasonable expectation that redundancies could be avoided – *Association of Pattern Makers and Allied Craftsmen v. Kirvin Ltd*;

(b) the refusal by the government of a further loan – *Hamish Armour . ASTMS*; and

(c) the sudden action of a bank in withdrawing credit facilities when a proposed sale fell through – *USDAW v Leancut Bacon Ltd*[3].

See also para 7.32 above.

1 [1978] IRLR 318, EAT.
2 [1979] IRLR 24, EAT.
3 [1981] IRLR 295, EAT.

21.11 Historically, insolvency practitioners often ignored the information and consultation obligations imposed on employers under TULRCA and TUPE on the basis that the maximum liability was relatively small and, probably, only a small part of it was recoverable as a preferential debt (remuneration under a protective award for failure to inform and consult under TULRCA, s 189) and, if there was a TUPE transfer, it was sometimes thought that the liability would not transfer to the transferee. So the purchaser/transferee would not deduct the amount of any potential liability from the amount paid.

21.12 This has changed:

(a) the maximum liability is now significantly greater (90 days' pay under TULRCA and 13 weeks' pay under TUPE).

(b) The purchaser/transferee is likely to be concerned that liability for failure to consult will pass to it. TUPE 2006 expressly provides that liability for failure to consult is joint and several on the transferor and transferee – reg 15(9).

Even under TUPE 1981, it was probably the case that the liability will transfer under TUPE – see the decision of the EAT in *Alamo v Tucker*[1]. This decision confirmed the EAT's earlier decision in *Kerry Ltd v Creber*[2], that information and consultation liability (in Kerry it was TUPE related information and consultation liability) transferred under TUPE. The EAT disagreed with the Scottish EAT decision in *TGWU v McKinnon*[3], but it seems likely that it will be followed in future – see the later EAT decision in *Blue Diamond Services Ltd v McNeish*[4].

357

1 [2003] IRLR 266 EAT.
2 [2000] ICR 556, EAT.
3 [2001] ICR 1281, EAT.
4 [2003] All ER (D) 20, EAT.

21.13   The information and consultation process can be relatively quick and straightforward, especially if existing staff carry out the administrative functions and use standard form election (if necessary) and notification documentation.

21.14   The transfer to transferees of liability for protective awards (under TULRCA) and compensation (under TUPE) arising out of a failure to inform and consult can significantly devalue the business to be transferred. Allowing such a liability to arise where it could relatively easily be avoided may be inconsistent with the insolvency practitioner's objective to exercise his powers in the best interests of the insolvent company's creditors.

21.15   Under TUPE 2006, liability for failure to inform and consult is now joint and several on the transferor and the transferee – TUPE 2006, reg 15(9).

21.16   Liability for failure to inform and consult is imposed by the relevant legislation on the transferor. The legislation does not expressly impose liability on the underlying officers or on an insolvency practitioner. But some employment claims can be given priority as insolvency expenses (see Chapter 17 above) or 'super priority' under the Insolvency Act 1986 in relation to an administrator (or administrative receiver) if arising after the 'adoption' of the contract by the insolvency practitioner (see Chapter 18 above).

21.17   In *Re Huddersfield Fine Worsteds Ltd and Globe Worsted Company Ltd*; *Krasner v McMath/Re Ferrotech Ltd/Re Granville Technology Group Ltd*[1], the Court of Appeal held that most payments in lieu of notice and protective award payments for the period of the adoption of an employment contract are not 'wages or salary' for the purposes of para 99 of Sch B1 to the Insolvency Act 1986. Accordingly, they are not payable as administration expenses in priority to an administrator's remuneration and expenses or preferential claims.
    In practice this will mean that any employee is likely to bring a claim for failure to inform or consult etc against the (presumably solvent) purchaser/transferee in preference to a claim against the insolvent seller/transferor.

1 [2005] EWCA Civ 1072; [2005] 4 All ER 886; [2005] IRLR 995, CA – see para 18.79 above.

21.18   The same analysis should apply equally to claims under TUPE for breach of the information and consultation obligations under TUPE.

21.19   Potentially the purchaser may try to recover any amounts paid from the insolvent transferor (eg by proof in any liquidation). The reference in TUPE 2006 to the liability being joint and several (reg 15(9)), may mean that the purchaser is able to claim under the Civil Liability (Contribution) Act 1978. A court can allow a contribution if liability is joint (s 1(1)). The amount of contribution is assessed by the court based on what it finds to be 'just and equitable having regard to the extent of that person's responsibility for the damage in question' (s 2(1)).

21.20   It seems that any action for a contribution from the transferor/seller must be before a court, not in the employment tribunal (which does not seem to have jurisdiction to determine such claims).

There may be some issues as to whether such a claim is provable in the insolvency or may be too contingent – see eg *Glenister v Rowe*[1] and *Day v Haine* (see Chapter 16 (Carrying on business – provable debts) above).

The value of any such claim against the insolvent seller/transferor is likely to be limited in any event, given the limited recoveries likely to be available.

1 [2000] Ch 76, CA.
2 [2008] EWCA Civ 626; [2008] ICR 1102; [2008] IRLR 642, [2008] 2 BCLC 517, CA.

21.21   Given that the joint and several obligation is imposed by TUPE itself, it may be that any contractual arrangements between the transfer (insolvent company) and the transferee (purchaser) are invalid as contravening the prohibition on contracting out of TUPE in reg 18 (see para 22.19 below).

CHAPTER 22

TUPE 2006: Other changes

WHEN WILL TUPE APPLY?

22.1   The protections offered by TUPE obviously apply in the context of a transfer of an undertaking. The new TUPE regulations contain two changes to the way in which what amounts to a transfer of an undertaking is defined.

22.2   The first brings the definition of a transfer into line with the amended Acquired Rights Directive and subsequent case law. The new definition states that a relevant transfer involves the transfer of an economic entity that retains its identity. The definition of 'economic entity' also reflects that used in the Acquired Rights Directive, being 'an organised grouping of resources which has the objective of pursuing an economic activity, whether or not that activity is central or ancillary'. Although this may not on the face of it clarify what a business transfer is, in practice this is the test that has been adopted by courts and tribunals in recent years. The formal adoption of the new definition is unlikely to be of major significance.

22.3   While the use of this test has not given rise to many difficulties in a typical business sale situation, the same has unfortunately not been true in the outsourcing context. There has been a great deal of debate, as well as conflicting court decisions, about whether employees in an outsourcing situation are protected by TUPE. To date the answer has been a resounding 'maybe'.

22.4   The second, and more significant, change to the definition of transfer is the introduction of provisions that mean that TUPE will generally apply in an outsourcing situation. Any 'service provision change' (basically any first or second generation outsourcing or where an activity is brought in house) will amount to a transfer if:

- there is an 'organised grouping' of employees;

- the 'principal purpose' of which is to carry out activities on behalf of the client; and

- the activities continue after the transfer and are not in connection with a single specific event, or task, of short-term duration.

22.5   These conditions should ensure that the regulations operate wherever an organised grouping of employees provides a service to a particular client, for example provision of a staff canteen for a particular organisation. Situations where a customer is serviced by a variety of employees on an ad hoc basis, or where a dedicated team provides services to a number of different clients, are not caught.

22.6   The impact of this change is that customers and contractors can again operate on the basis that TUPE applies in the outsourcing context. This should reduce uncertainty, particularly in relation to outsourcing in labour intensive industries.

What is the impact on employees?

22.7   If an employee works in a business that is being transferred, and is employed by the transferor, his contract of employment is transferred to a transferee on its existing terms, along with all the transferor's rights, powers, duties and liabilities in connection with the contract. The new regulations clarify which employees will transfer and when it will be possible to change terms and conditions following a transfer.

SPLIT SERVICE EMPLOYEES

22.8   Until now it has not always been clear how a transfer affects an employee who provides services to a number of different business areas, only one of which is being transferred. For example, an HR manager may provide advice to two different business areas, only one of which is being transferred. The new regulations make it clear that such employees will only transfer with the business if they are 'assigned' to the transferring business on a permanent basis. This reflects the position that has been developed in case law and does not represent a major change for employers. Whether employees are actually assigned will continue to depend on factors such as the amount of time spent working for each element of the business and any contractual arrangements in place.

22.9   One area where there will continue to be uncertainty is what will happen where an employee is assigned to a transferring business, but is not employed by the transferor. Such a situation is common where an associated company is the employing entity. A strict reading of the regulations indicates that such an employee will not transfer, although in practice tribunals are sometimes willing to look at the reality of the situation rather than the strict legal position. This is likely to be an area where problems continue to arise.

DUE DILIGENCE

22.10   TUPE 2006 has imposed for the first time a statutory obligation on the transferor to make certain information about transferring employees available to the purchaser/transferee. The new duty applies to transfers taking place after 19 April 2006. The transferee/purchaser cannot agree with the transferor/seller to 'contract out' of the obligation (reg 18 and see further para 42.23 below).

- the identity and age of the employees concerned;

- their statutory particulars of employment (ERA 1996, s 1);

- details of any disciplinary procedure taken by an employer or any grievance procedure taken by an employee in the last two years;

- details of any court or tribunal proceedings brought by the employee against the employer in the past two years;

- information of any reasonable grounds that the employer has to believe that an employee may bring court or tribunal proceedings arising out of his employment; and

- information relating to any collective agreements that apply to those employees and that will have effect after the transfer.

22.11   Again, the obligation is likely to be significant in a relatively small number of cases, because this sort of information would typically be disclosed in any event. However, the obligation may be of assistance to the incoming contractor in a second generation outsourcing.

22.12   There is no exclusion based on a lack of knowledge. So it does not seem to be a defence to a claim against the insolvent company if the IP fails to arrange for disclosure of appropriate information because he or she is unaware of the facts.

Process

22.13   The information has to be provided at least 14 days before the completion of the transfer, unless it is not reasonably practicable to do so. The BIS guidance on TUPE[1] envisages that it would not be reasonably practicable to provide information in time where the identity of the transferee was not known until shortly before the transfer.

1 Q&A on page 21. See http://www.berr.gov.uk/files/file20761.pdf: 'Employment rights on the transfer of an undertaking: a guide to the 2006 TUPE regulations for employees, employers and representatives' (June 2009).

22.14   This may prove to be a defence for claims against a company in insolvency where the IP is newly appointed (eg on a 'pre-pack' administration – see Chapter 42 below) and so does not have the relevant information.

22.15   It is not necessary for the information to be in written form, provided it is in some other 'readily accessible form' such as computer files, and can be provided in instalments. Any changes to the information, once notified, must be given in writing.

22.16   The information may also be provided via a third party, for example the customer in an outsourcing situation where there is no relationship between incoming and outgoing contractors. The transferor remains liable if the third party fails to pass the information on to the transferee.

Enforcement

22.17 Under reg 12 of TUPE 2006, if a purchaser/transferee successfully complains about a failure to provide information, the employment tribunal will award it 'just and equitable' compensation having regard to any loss attributable to the matters complained of. For example, if the transferor had failed to disclose the existence of a discrimination claim, and compensation was awarded to the employee, the transferee would presumably be able to recover the sum payable from the transferor as part of its compensation. It is not at this stage clear how compensation will be decided in relation to a more open-ended liability, such as the failure to disclose a benefit or bonus scheme for example.

22.18 The terms of any contract between the transferor and transferee will also be relevant to the tribunal's determination of what compensation is just and equitable. However, to ensure that there is an incentive on the transferor to provide the information, the tribunal must award minimum compensation of £500 per employee in respect of whom information has not been provided unless it is just and equitable to award a lesser sum. DTI guidance indicates that the minimum penalty would probably not be awarded if the failure to disclose were trivial or inadvertent. There is no upper limit on compensation.

22.19 It is not possible for the agreement between the transferor/seller company with the purchaser/transferee to provide that the purchaser will not seek to claim under this regulation. This would be an attempt to contract-out of TUPE and so is invalidated by reg 18.
The BIS Guidance on TUPE[1] states:

> 'Q. Can the transferor and the new employer agree between themselves that this information should not be provided by contracting-out of the requirement?
>
> A. No. There is no entitlement to contract-out of the duty to supply employee liability information because that would disadvantage the employees involved.'

But if commercially feasible there seems to be no reason legally why the purchaser (or its parent etc) could not enter into a collateral contract with a third party (eg the IP) to pay to that third party any benefits received as a result of a claim under regs 11 or 12. Commercially that would have effect to deter any claim by the purchaser/transferee. See further Chapter 42 ('Pre-pack' administrations) below.

1 Q&A on page 21. See http://www.berr.gov.uk/files/file20761.pdf: 'Employment rights on the transfer of an undertaking: a guide to the 2006 TUPE regulations for employees, employers and representatives' (June 2009).

22.20 Liability for failure to inform is imposed by the relevant legislation on the transferor. The legislation does not expressly impose liability on the underlying officers or on an insolvency practitioner. But some employment claims can be given 'super priority' under the Insolvency Act 1986 in relation to an administrator (or administrative receiver) if arising after the 'adoption' of the employment contract by the insolvency practitioner – see generally Chapters 17 and 18 above.

22.21 In *Re Huddersfield Fine Worsteds Ltd and Globe Worsted Company Ltd, Krasner v McMath /Re Ferrotech Ltd/Re Granville Technology Group Ltd*[1], the Court of Appeal held that most payments in lieu of notice and protective award payments for the period of the adoption of an employment contract are not 'wages or salary' for the purposes of para 99 of Sch B1 to the Insolvency Act 1986. Accordingly, they are not payable as administration expenses in priority to an administrator's remuneration and expenses or preferential claims.

1 [2005] EWCA Civ 1072, [2005] 4 All ER 886, [2005] IRLR 995, CA – see Chapter 18 (Carrying on business – adopted employment contracts) above.

22.22 As stated in para 21.18 above, the same analysis should apply equally to claims under TUPE for breach of the information and consultation obligations under TUPE. This is a similar analysis to that for liability for failure to inform and consult with employees – see above. It is probably even clearer in relation to the information obligation to the purchaser/transferee as the liability for breach is owed to the purchaser, not the employees.

CHAPTER 23

TUPE: Impact on dismissals instigated by IP

DISMISSALS BY INSOLVENCY PRACTITIONER

23.1   On the sale or transfer of a business in circumstances where TUPE applies, it is clear that the effect of the TUPE regulations is to pass most liabilities in respect of employees employed in the business to the purchaser.

23.2   The liabilities which pass to the purchaser/transferee include both liabilities incurred prior to the transfer and those incurred after the transfer—see *Abels*[1] discussed at para 19.17 above.

1 *Abels v Administrative Board of the Bedrijfsvereniging voor de Metaalindustrie en de Electrotechnische Industrie* [1985] ECR 469; [1987] 2 CMLR 406, ECJ.

23.3   Thus, in a situation where an employee has a claim against the insolvent company (eg for unpaid wages) the effect of TUPE is that liability to meet the claim passes to the purchaser, along with the assets of the business. In practice, the purchaser of the business will reduce the price paid for the business to reflect the fact that he will have to discharge any existing liabilities. In effect, this means that the claims of employees, even those relating to a period prior to the commencement of insolvency proceedings, are given a preference because they will be paid in full, effectively out of the assets of the company. The amount realised by the insolvency practitioner (and available for other creditors) will be reduced by the amount of such claims of employees because the assets transferred have fetched a reduced price to take account of those claims – see para 19.14 above. This was the danger recognised by the European Court of Justice in *Abels* (see para 19.17 above).

23.4   However there seemed to be a way to avoid this. In cases where it was possible for a purchaser to arrange for the insolvency practitioner to dismiss the employees prior to the transfer, in circumstances where those employees did not automatically transfer under TUPE to the purchaser, the employees were left with their claims against the insolvent company.

23.5   Accordingly, before 1990 the practice grew of purchasers requesting, as part of the acquisition negotiations, that the insolvency practitioner arrange for the insolvent company to dismiss 'surplus' employees prior to the transfer, so that any claims of such employees remained as claims against the insolvent company rather than being transferred.

23.6   Some purchasers also took this to extremes, not merely requesting the insolvency practitioner to arrange for dismissal of 'surplus' employees but seeking the dismissal of all employees, and then rehiring those the purchaser wanted, free and clear of accrued rights such as length of continuous service, redundancy payments etc.

Meaning of 'immediately before the transfer'

23.7   This practice depended on a strict interpretation of reg 5(3) of TUPE 1981 which limited the statutory novation under TUPE to employees employed in the business by the transferor 'immediately before the transfer'.

23.8   The House of Lords in *Litster v Forth Dry Dock & Engineering Co Ltd (in receivership)*[1] gave a purposive interpretation to the phrase 'immediately before the transfer' as used in reg 5(3). The House of Lords held that TUPE must be construed to give effect to the Acquired Rights Directive so that in reg 5(3) of TUPE 1981, after the words 'immediately before the transfer' the words 'or would have been so employed if he had not been unfairly dismissed in the circumstances described by reg 8(1)', must be implied.

1 [1990] 1 AC 546, HL.

23.9   This view of the Acquired Rights Directive was confirmed by the ECJ in *Jules Dethier Equipement SA v Jules Dassy*[1].

1 [1998] IRLR 266, ECJ.

23.10   TUPE 2006 follows the *Litster* decision by including the following words in the main transfer reg 4(3):

> 'Any reference in paragraph (1) to a person employed by the transferor and assigned to the organised grouping of resources or employees that is subject to a relevant transfer, is a reference to a person so employed immediately before the transfer, or who would have been so employed if he had not been dismissed in the circumstances described in regulation 7(1)....'

23.11   This express wording in TUPE 2006 effectively follows the *Litster* judgment. So case law before 2006 on TUPE 1981 following *Litster* is likely to be followed when interpreting TUPE 2006. One specific difference is that TUPE 2006 just refers to someone who is 'dismissed' within reg 7(1), whereas the wording implied under *Litster* referred to 'unfairly dismissed'. It is unlikely that this could make any difference, given that both regulations are concerned with automatic unfair dismissal.

23.12 Since the *Litster* case there has been a significant amount of case law as to when dismissals by an insolvent company are to be regarded as being by reason of a subsequent transfer.

23.13 It is clear that dismissals made by the insolvent company at the request of a proposed purchaser will meet this nexus test.

23.14 It is less clear whether dismissals by the insolvency practitioner for operational reasons (because he takes the view that the insolvent company cannot afford to keep all the workforce on), but with a view to an ultimate sale of the business would also meet this factual test.

23.15 There has been less case law on whether, if the dismissals were by reason of the transfer, the purchaser would be able to reject liability by reason of showing that the dismissals were for an ETO reason (see para 14.68 below) in any event. Intrinsically if the employees had not in fact been taken on by the purchaser, it must in many cases be possible for the purchaser to show that it did not need those relevant employees (or at least has not gone out and hired others in their place).

23.16 The test in reg 4(3) means that employees who are dismissed before a transfer by the insolvent company (acting through the insolvency practitioner) by reason of the transfer, but unfairly (ie not for an economic, technical or organisational reason within reg 7) will still not become employees of the purchaser/transferee (see the decision of the House of Lords in *Wilson v St Helens Borough Council*[1]). The dismissal will still be effective.

1 [1999] 2 AC 52, HL.

23.17 However, any claims such former employees have against their employer in connection with their employment will transfer automatically to the purchaser.

23.18 Conversely, liability to an employee who was dismissed before the transfer, fairly or unfairly, for a reason unconnected with the transfer, will not transfer to the purchaser. The House of Lords in *Litster* expressly did not overrule the decision of the Court of Appeal in *Secretary of State for Employment v Spence*[1].

1 [1987] QB 179, CA and see paras 23.29 and 23.44 below.

23.19 Thus, where an insolvency practitioner, on being appointed, arranges for the insolvent company to dismiss some or all employees and some time later arranges for the insolvent company to sell the business, liability for such employees will only transfer to the transferee/purchaser, if the employee can show that he or she was dismissed by reason of the transfer.

23.20 For example in *Tsangacos v Amalgamated Chemicals Ltd*[1] the EAT held that a purchaser/transferee did not take over the liability of the vendor/transferor to an employee who had been dismissed four months before the transfer for a reason not connected with the transfer. He was not a person employed by the employer immediately before the transfer and so liability did not transfer.

1 [1997] ICR 154, EAT.

23.21 The question of whether an employee has been dismissed by the insolvent company, and liability for him or her thereby transfers to the transferee/purchaser notwithstanding such dismissal, is also relevant to BERR in deciding whether or not there has been a redundancy within the meaning of ERA 1996, s 139 which may be the subject of a claim on the National Insurance Fund under ERA 1996, s 166 (see Chapter 13 above).

23.22 This is a difficult area on which there has been a number of cases after *Litster*, but from which it is difficult to draw firm conclusions.

23.23 Clearly, given that the transferor is an insolvent company, it will usually be in the interests of the employee to seek to show that there has been a relevant transfer within TUPE, so that the (presumably solvent) purchaser/transferee has succeeded to all relevant liabilities owed to the employee (whether incurred before or after the transfer).

23.24 However, unusually, in *Ibex Trading v Walton*[1] the purchaser/transferee entered into liquidation on the third day of the tribunal hearing. It transpired that the transferor (in administration) held more assets than the transferee, so that it would be better for the employees if the liability remained with the transferor. Accordingly, the employees argued (successfully) that they should not be treated as transferred.

1 [1994] IRLR 564, EAT.

23.25 Clearly, if any dismissals are made after the transfer by the purchaser/transferee (or perhaps only take place at the same time as the transfer – see para 23.95 below), liability in relation to the employees will pass to the purchaser/transferee. The position is more difficult where the dismissals occur some time before the actual instant of transfer.

23.26 In order for liability to or in relation to employees dismissed before the transfer to pass to the purchaser:

(a) the employee must show that reg 7(1) applies, ie:

    'the sole or principal reason for his dismissal is the transfer itself or a reason connected with it'; and

(b) the employer must be unable to show that the sole or principal reason for the dismissal was 'an economic, technical or organisational reason entailing changes in the workforce of either the transferee or the transferor' (an ETO reason) – ie that reg 7(2) applies.

23.27 These are separate tests (see the Court of Appeal in *Warner v Adnet Ltd*[1]). In *Michael Peters v Farnfield*[2] the EAT held that under TUPE 1981 it was for the employee to show both (a) and (b) above. Conversely, in *Gateway Hotels v Stewart*[3] the EAT held that the onus was on the employer to establish an ETO reason.

1 [1998] IRLR 394, CA.
2 [1995] IRLR 190, EAT.
3 [1988] IRLR 287, EAT.

IS THE REASON FOR THE DISMISSAL TRANSFER-CONNECTED?

23.28 Various times can be identified as the time before a subsequent transfer at which dismissals can occur. These are listed below (in ascending order of probability of connection with an ultimate transfer):

(a) dismissals with no transfer in mind;

(b) dismissals to make the business more efficient with a view to trading out of insolvency or possible sale;

(c) dismissals to make the business more efficient and attractive to a potential purchaser — no specific purchaser identified;

(d) dismissal to make the business more attractive for an identified potential purchaser; and

(e) dismissal at the request of a potential purchaser.

23.29 If the insolvency practitioner decides that a sale of a business of the company is not likely and, accordingly, decides for business reasons to dismiss an employee, this is unlikely to be a dismissal connected with a subsequent transfer that may occur (see *Secretary of State for Employment v Spence*[1]).

1 [1987] QB 179, CA.

23.30 At the other extreme, if an insolvency practitioner arranges for the company to dismiss an employee at the request of a potential purchaser or in order to make the business more attractive for a specific identified purchaser, then such a collusive dismissal will almost inevitably be considered to be connected with the subsequent transfer – for example *Litster* itself, *Harrison Bowden v Bowden*[1]; *Ibex Trading v Walton*[2] and the decision of the Northern Ireland Court of Appeal in *Willis v McLaughlin & Harvey plc*[3].

1 [1994] ICR 186 at 191F, EAT.
2 [1994] IRLR 564 at 567, EAT.
3 [1998] EuLR 22, NI CA.

23.31 But contrast *Longden and Paisley v Ferrari Ltd*[1], where the EAT held that giving the receiver a list of employees to be retained did not amount to a request from the purchaser/transferee to dismiss the others.

1 [1994] IRLR 157, EAT.

23.32   In *Warner v Adnet Ltd*[1] the EAT refused to overrule a majority decision by the tribunal below that a potential transfer was the principal reason for the relevant dismissals.

1 (1996) 16 October (EAT 1041/95).

23.33   Similarly, in *Ward v Beresford & Hicks Furniture Ltd*[1] the EAT refused to overturn the finding of the industrial tribunal that employees (who had been dismissed about two weeks before a sale of the business) were dismissed to minimise the company's expenditure and not for a reason connected with the transfer.

1 (1996) 16 December (EAT 860/95).

23.34   In *Parmar v Ferranti International plc*[1], Mr Parmar was dismissed in December 1993 shortly after receivers were appointed. In October 1994 (over ten months later) there was a transfer of the relevant business. The EAT dismissed Mr Parmar's claim against the purchaser/transferee as almost bound to fail. The time gap was inconsistent with the transfer being the reason for the dismissal.

1 (1997) 13 March (EAT 710/96).

23.35   The position between these two extremes is more problematic. An insolvency practitioner will commonly decide that the best course of action in the insolvency is likely to be that he will seek at some stage to sell the company's business as a going concern. The insolvency practitioner may well decide that the business would prove more attractive to a purchaser with a slimmed down workforce and, accordingly, arrange for the company to make various dismissals at this early preparatory stage. This may occur well in advance of any advertising of the business or any approaches to potential purchasers.

23.36   A later stage would be dismissals in advance of any discussions or negotiations with potential purchasers. In all of these cases the dismissals will have occurred at a time when an ultimate transfer of the business was at least contemplated, if not a likelihood.

23.37   It could be argued that a dismissal at this stage is not one which is connected with the ultimate transfer (and so does not fall within reg 7(1) of TUPE 2006) for two reasons:

(a)   the sole or principal reason for the dismissal is likely not to be the prospect of a transfer, but rather will form part of a general restructuring by the insolvency practitioner for a number of other reasons not linked to an ultimate transfer (eg reducing ongoing costs to a minimum, seeking to trade out of the insolvency); and

(b)   the dismissal is not connected with an identified purchaser, because the identity of none of the potential purchasers is yet known. In effect the dismissal may be connected with a possible transfer, but it is not connected with 'the' ultimate transfer.

23.38   These two arguments may not succeed. The first, (a), raises questions of fact in each case, given the wording of TUPE which requires that the transfer (or a reason connected with it) be the only or principal reason for the dismissal.

23.39   For example, in *Honeycombe 78 Ltd v Cummins*[1], the EAT held that liability for employees dismissed 15 days before a TUPE transfer did not pass to the purchaser. This was because it was clear that there had been no collusion and that the administrator had dismissed them because the company had no assets and irrespective of any potential sale. The EAT held that the economic reason was paramount.

1 [2000] UKEAT 4 (10 December 1999).

23.40   The second argument, (b), was rejected by the EAT in *Harrison Bowden Ltd v Bowden*[1] but was accepted by a later EAT in *Ibex Trading v Walton*[2] (see the discussion below).

1 [1994] ICR 186, EAT.
2 [1994] IRLR 564, EAT.

23.41   This second argument (that any dismissal needs to be associated with an identified purchaser) suffers from the drawback that art 4(1) of the Acquired Rights Directive 2001[1] is clearer than reg 7 of TUPE 2006 in providing that:

> 'The transfer of the undertaking, business or part of a business shall not in itself constitute grounds for dismissal by the transferor or the transferee'.

1 Article 4(1) of ARD 1977 was similar.

23.42   This wording in the ARD seems to be clearer in providing that the dismissal can be connected with any transfer, not just a specific identified transfer. However, in *Swinnock v Grosvenor of Chester (Automotives) Ltd*[1] the EAT held that a dismissal while there were several possible purchasers could not fall within reg 8(1) of TUPE 1981 (now reg 7(1) of TUPE 2006).

1 (1994) 19 July (EAT 189/93).

23.43   The cases give some guidance, but a consistent set of guidelines is difficult to see.

The cases

23.44   In *Secretary of State for Employment v Spence*[1], the transferor company entered receivership and started to negotiate a business transfer under threat from the company's major customer to withdraw its work unless a transfer was agreed. The deadline imposed by the major customer expired and the receivers decided to dismiss the employees. In fact their negotiations were successful and the business was sold later that day. The transferee took on all the employees.

1 [1987] QB 179, CA.

23.45   The Industrial Tribunal held that there had been no collusion between the receivers and the transferee, but that the reason for the dismissals was the independent action by the receivers in deciding that, until a contract could be negotiated with the company's principal customer, there was no prospect of any work for the business. The decision that the purchaser was not liable under TUPE in relation to the dismissed employees was upheld by the Court of Appeal.

23.46   In *Litster v Forth Dry Dock & Engineering*[1], the House of Lords considered that *Spence* was rightly decided on those grounds. Lord Oliver (at page 575) considered that, in the context of the findings of fact by the Industrial Tribunal, the terminations in *Spence* were for a reason unconnected with the transfer.

1 [1990] 1 AC 546, HL. See para 14.8 above.

23.47   In *P Bork International A/S v Foreningen af Arbejdsledere i Danmark*[1] which was relied upon by the House of Lords in reaching its decision in *Litster*, the ECJ held that:

> 'In order to determine whether the employees were dismissed solely as a result of the transfer, contrary to article 4(1), it is necessary to take into consideration the objective circumstances in which the dismissal took place and, in particular, in a case such as this, the fact that it took effect on a date close to that of the transfer and that the employees were taken on again by the transferee'.

1 [1988] ECR 3057, [1990] 3 CMLR 701, [1989] IRLR 41, ECJ.

23.48   In *Ring & Brymer Ltd v Cryer*[1] the employer company went into receivership. Dismissals occurred about seven days before a transfer (and perhaps while negotiations for a sale were under way). The Industrial Tribunal refused to adjourn to allow the receiver to be summoned to give evidence and held that the dismissals were connected with the transfer so that liability passed to the transferee. The EAT overruled the Industrial Tribunal and remitted the case to be heard by a different tribunal on the grounds that the evidence of the receiver was of vital importance in this matter.

1 (1993) 28 January (EAT/670/92).

23.49   In *Harrison Bowden Ltd v Bowden*[1] Mr Bowden was dismissed by the receiver on a Thursday (31 January), but was re-employed on the following Monday (4 February) in preparation for the transfer which took place on the Friday (8 February). Mr Bowden was dismissed by the transferee shortly after and the question arose as to his statutory length of continuous service. The Industrial Tribunal held that the dismissal by the receiver, Mr Gibson, was connected with the transfer having stated:

> 'We really have to ask ourselves these questions. What was in the mind of Mr Gibson, what motivated him on 31 January 1991 when he dismissed this applicant? Was he dismissing to make the company more able to be transferred and more easily and/or at a better price? Was the dismissal therefore in direct connection with the transfer of the business to a proposed or possible buyer? Was it something totally independent whereby the receiver had come to the conclusion that he simply could not afford to have the staff and then at some later date an

approach was made to buy the business but it was long after the dismissal had taken place so the two were not connected, the one to the other?'

1 [1994] ICR 186, EAT.

23.50 The EAT dismissed an appeal by the transferee/purchaser. The EAT rejected three arguments raised by the transferee:

(a) that no specific transferee had been identified by the receiver—this is in effect the second argument above. The EAT felt that this argument would open a loophole in the legislation and that in any event the decision of the ECJ in *Bork* indicated that it was right to look back in time if a transfer occurred to see what had happened. There seems not to have been a prospective transferee identified in *Bork* at the time of the dismissals;

(b) that *Litster* only applies where there is collusion between the transferor and the transferee—The EAT studied *Litster* and came to the conclusion that, in effect, collusion was sufficient to make a dismissal connected with a transfer, but was not necessary;

(c) that the tribunal misdirected itself in considering that a dismissal would be connected with a transfer unless it took place long before the ultimate transfer—the EAT referred to *Bork* and considered that the tribunal had properly directed themselves. The matter was entirely within the fact finding province of the industrial jury.

23.51 In *Longden and Paisley v Ferrari Ltd*[1] the EAT refused to overrule the decision of the Industrial Tribunal that various employees were dismissed because of pressure on the receivers by the bank and not because of the proposed transfer. This was despite the fact that the purchasers had given the receivers a list of essential staff.

1 [1994] IRLR 157, EAT.

23.52 The Industrial Tribunal did not accept that that request necessarily carried with it a request that the other employees should be dismissed.

23.53 In *Ibex Trading Co Ltd v Walton*[1] the timing was as follows:

8 August 1991	Company (Ibex) enters administration.
August to October	Discussions about reducing workforce and wages of those remaining.
16 October	Letters of dismissal sent to 40 employees.
4 November	Dismissals took effect.
11 November	Offer made to purchase the business.
13 February 1992	Contract signed.
11 May 1993	IT hearing started.
13 May 1993	Purchaser/transferee enters liquidation.

1 [1994] IRLR 564, EAT.

23.54   As mentioned above, somewhat unusually, by the time this case reached the EAT, the employees had decided that the original company (Ibex) had more assets than the purchaser/transferee. Accordingly, they were arguing that liability had NOT passed to the purchaser/transferee. Conversely, the administrators were arguing that liability had passed. The EAT upheld the decision of the Tribunal that the transferor remained liable because the dismissals were not for a reason connected with the transfer. The EAT held (at page 567):

> '1. Contrary to what was said in the *Harrison Bowden* case, we attach significance to the definite article in regulation 8(1) "that employee shall be treated . . . as unfairly dismissed if the transfer or a reason connected with it is the reason or the principal reason for the dismissal". The link, in terms of time, between the dismissals and the transfers will vary considerably. In Litster the time difference was one hour; often it will be more. A transfer is not just a single event: it extends over a period of time culminating in a completion. However, here, the employees were dismissed before any offer had been made for the business. Whilst it could properly be said that they were dismissed for a reason connected with a possible transfer of the business, on the facts here we are not satisfied that they were dismissed by reason of the transfer or for a reason connected with the transfer. A transfer was, at the stage of the dismissal, a mere twinkle in the eye and might well never have occurred. We do not say that in every case it is necessary for the prospective transferee to be identified; because sometimes one purchaser drops out at the last minute and another purchaser replaces him.
>
> 2. In any event, it seems to us, on the facts, to be difficult to say, by reason of the timing of the dismissal and the sale of the business, that the employees would have been employed at the date of completion but for their dismissal.'

23.55   Conversely, the EAT disagreed with the Tribunal in its view that the decision in *Litster* only extended to collusive dismissals or dismissals at a time close to the transfer (and not months away).

23.56   *Ibex Trading* seems inconsistent with *Harrison Bowden*. However a different EAT held in the later case of *Michael Peters Ltd v Farnfield*[1] that the two cases are compatible. The EAT held (obiter) that:

> '3. Was the respondent dismissed by reason of the transfer? In our opinion he clearly was. The Tribunal were correct in finding that the probable reason for his dismissal was connected with the transfer because in order to achieve the transfer it was deemed necessary to reduce the number of staff employed by the group.
>
> Much attention has been focused on the use of the definite article in the later part of regulation 8(1). We see no significance in this. It is no more than a reference back to the words "relevant transfer" in the earlier part of the regulation. It has been held by the EAT in *Harrison Bowden Ltd v Bowden* [1994] ICR 186 that it is not necessary for the actual transferee to have been identified at or before the actual moment of dismissal, and Mr Elias concedes that it is not necessary for an actual contract to be in place—it can be projected. In our opinion, the later decision in *Ibex Trading Co Ltd v Walton* [1994] IRLR 564 is not inconsistent with *Bowden*.'

1 [1995] IRLR 190, EAT.

23.57   In *Parmar v Ferranti International plc*[1] (see also para 14.34 above) the EAT followed *Ibex* (as being the later decision). *Ibex* was also followed by the EAT in *Sidney Smith Castings Ltd v Hill*[2].

Some cases in the EAT have preferred to follow *Harrison Bowden* and not *Ibex*.

1 (1997) 13 March (EAT 710/96).
2 (1998) 17 February (EAT 242/97).

23.58   In *Morris v John Grose Group Ltd*[1] Mr Morris was employed by Mereside Motor Company Ltd until he was dismissed by reason of redundancy on 30 September 1996. The decision to make him redundant was made on 27 September 1996, the same day as receivers were called in. The reason he and other employees were made redundant was primarily to slim down the workforce so that the company could continue trading and to make it more attractive as a going concern in due course. On 5 November 1996 the business was transferred to John Grose Group Limited and on 24 December 1996 Mr Morris brought a claim against John Grose for unfair dismissal.

1 [1998] ICR 655, EAT.

23.59   The Industrial Tribunal considered whether John Grose were liable for his unfair dismissal by operation of regs 5 and 8(1) of TUPE 1981[1]. Following *Ibex*, the tribunal attached a great deal of significance to the words 'the transfer' and because at the date of his dismissal the receivers had not definitely decided to transfer the business to John Grose (although they had in mind the possibility of doing so) he could not be deemed to have been dismissed by reason of 'the transfer' ie the transferor only had 'a' transfer in mind.

1 See now regs 4 and 7(1) of TUPE 2006, to the same effect.

23.60   The EAT found that the words 'the transfer' as used in reg 8(1) could perfectly well mean 'transfer' or 'a transfer' and that the tribunal had erred in law in attaching significance to the definite article. The Tribunal should have asked itself whether a transfer to any transferee who might appear or a reason connected with such a transfer was the reason or principal reason for Mr Morris's dismissal. Accordingly, the EAT allowed Mr Morris's appeal and remitted the case to a fresh Industrial Tribunal.

23.61   In 2008 in *CAB Automotive Ltd v Blake*, the EAT followed *Morris* and approved the comment in *Morris* that the proper test for a tribunal is to decide:

> 'whether a transfer to any transferee who might appear, or a reason connected with such a transfer, was the reason or principal reason for the dismissal.'

The EAT went on to say that the proper approach was:

- 'The [employer] will seek to persuade the Tribunal that, on the proper approach to regulation 8(1), on the facts of this case, where at the time of the dismissal no offer was made to buy the assets of the transferor company and the transferee was not on the scene or identified, and had not even been formed, the transfer or a reason connected with it is not the reason or principal reason for the dismissals or that even if it is, regulation 8(2) applies in any event.

- The employees will be seeking to persuade the Tribunal not only that [the administrator] considered transfer was a realistic possibility but that he made the dismissals in order to encourage transfer.'

1 (2008) 12 February (UKEAT 0298/07); [2008] All ER (D) 155 (Feb).

23.62 In *Haulbridge Ltd v Rayner*[1] the EAT held that it was open to a Tribunal (having considered *Ibex*) to hold that dismissals were connected with the transfer within reg 8 of TUPE 1981 where the receiver knew that the potential purchaser was willing to rehire the employees.

1 (1998) 12 February (EAT 477/97).

23.63 It makes no difference that the insolvency practitioner was not aware that TUPE would apply later on the 'transfer' of a business. Dismissals can still fall within reg 7 of TUPE 2006 (formerly reg 8 of TUPE 1981) so that liability passes to the purchaser/transferee—see the decisions of the Court of Appeal in *Duratube Ltd v Bhatti*[1] and of the EAT in *Haulbridge Ltd v Rayner*[2].

1 (1997) 4 June, CA.
2 (1998) 12 February (EAT 477/97).

23.64 The position remains unclear for insolvency practitioners. It seems that dismissals even before negotiations have started with any potential purchasers will still be connected with the transfer unless the principal reason was not to make the business more attractive for a purchaser, but instead because the practitioner could not afford to keep the staff on. In practice this is a difficult question of fact, which will probably require an analysis of the state of mind of the insolvency practitioner at the time.

23.65 It is likely that the insolvency practitioner will have both reasons in mind at the time—it will not be a simple question of one reason or the other. In this case it is the question of fact (for the tribunal) to decide which is the principal reason. This is the critical issue—see the decision of the Court of Appeal in *Duratube Ltd v Bhatti*[1].

Where the employer has entered insolvency (eg administration), the relevant state of mind is that of the insolvency practitioner (and not any director even if he may have arranged for the insolvency practitioner to be appointed and 'stage managed' the process and the subsequent transfer – see the Court of Appeal in *Dynamex Friction Ltd v Amicus*[1].

1 (1997) 4 June, CA.
2 [2008] EWCA Civ 381; [2009] ICR 511; [2008] IRLR 515, CA.

23.66 Purchasers of a business from an insolvent company will not be in a position to be certain as to the state of mind of the insolvency practitioner. They will seek indemnities or (more usually) reduce the price paid (to the detriment of the creditors in the insolvency).

23.67 The question of timing of dismissals is still likely to be important. The desire to reduce the risk of a connection with any subsequent transfer may well mean that insolvency practitioners tend to make dismissals at an earlier stage than they would otherwise. It is ironic that, if this occurs, the effect of the protective provisions in TUPE will have been to reduce job security.

23.68 The position of a purchaser is more difficult if it seeks (as in *Ring & Brymer* and *Harrison Bowden*) to re-hire some of the dismissed workers (or others in their place) In practice, dismissals by an insolvency practitioner of 'surplus' employees to put the company's business in better shape for a possible ultimate sale are more likely to be dismissals for an 'economic, technical or organisational' reason within reg 7(2) of TUPE 2006 (old reg 8(2) of TUPE 1981). In such a case the remaining employees would still transfer and the mischief mentioned above of a purchaser seeking to take employees free and clear of accrued rights would have been stopped.

IS THERE AN ETO REASON?

23.69 Regulation 7(2) of TUPE 2006 (old reg 8(2) of TUPE 1981) provides an exception to the provisions of reg 7(1) dealing with automatic unfair dismissal where a dismissal is connected with the transfer. Regulation 7(3) provides that reg 7(1) does not apply where reg 7(2) applies ie if the sole or principal reason for the dismissal was:

> 'an economic, technical or organisational reason entailing changes in the workforce'

This is called below an 'ETO reason'.

23.70 The decision of the House of Lords in *Litster* operated to extend the impact of reg 8 of TUPE 1981. Not only did it regulate whether or nor a dismissal will be automatically unfair, it also applied to govern whether the transferee or the transferor is liable for any pre-transfer dismissals. It was implicit from this that liability for a pre-transfer dismissal would only pass to the purchaser/transferee if the exclusion in reg 8(2) did not apply. Even if the dismissal was for a reason connected with the transfer (and hence within reg 8(1) of TUPE 1981), the purchaser/transferee would not assume the liability if the reason (or principal reason) for the dismissal was an ETO reason.

This has now been expressly recognised in the wording of reg 7 of TUPE 2006.

23.71 This view of TUPE 1981 seemed to be accepted by the Department of Employment (prior to its absorption into the Department of Trade and Industry). The guidance of the Department, issued to insolvency practitioners in April 1991 by the Society of Practitioners of Insolvency (now R3), included the statement that claims would be accepted by the Department on the National Insurance Fund (ie accepting that there is still a liability of the transferor) where pre-transfer dismissals were for an ETO reason and which were connected with the transfer of a business.

23.72   Judicial authority for this was relatively sparse. In *Jules Dethier Equipement SA v Jules Dassy*[1] the ECJ did not address this issue directly, but confirmed that both the transferor and the transferee may, under Art 4(1) of the Acquired Rights Directive, lawfully dismiss employees for an ETO reason and that liability for employees wrongfully dismissed (contrary to Art 4(1)) passes to the transferee. The clear inference from this judgment is that liability for employees lawfully dismissed by the transferor (ie for an ETO reason within Art 4(1) of the Acquired Rights Directive) does not pass to the transferee.

1 [1988] ECR 1-1061;[1998] IRLR 266, ECJ.

23.73   Earlier, in *Michael Peters Ltd v Farnfield*[1], the EAT had stated that:

'In our opinion Mr Elias [counsel for the appellants ie the purchaser/transferee] is correct in submitting that in order to succeed in establishing that the appellants are liable for his dismissal, the respondent [ie the employee] has to prove the following matters:

. . .

3   That he was dismissed by reason of the transfer.

4   That he was not dismissed for any economic, technical or organisational reason.'

1 [1995] IRLR 190, EAT.

23.74   Similarly in *Honeycombe 78 Ltd v Cummins*[1], the EAT allowed an appeal holding that liability for pre-transfer dismissals did not pass to the business purchaser where the administrator had made the dismissal for an economic reason.

1 [2000] UKEAT 4 (10 December 1999), EAT.

23.75   Conversely, the EAT in *UK Security Services (Midlands) Ltd v Gibbons*[1] held that a purchaser/transferee was liable for a pre-transfer dismissal even if it could be shown that reg 8(2) applied. However, no reasons were given for this (and the transferee/purchaser was not legally represented). The decision must be regarded as wrong on this point.

1 (1991) 23 July (EAT 104/90), IDS Brief 472 (July 1992), EAT.

23.76   In the later case of *Parmar v Ferranti International plc*[1], the EAT held that an appeal by the employee should not be allowed, saying:

'It is plain on his case that there was an economic, technical or organisational reason for his dismissal, in that immediate redundancies were necessary if the receivers were to preserve any part of the Ferranti business. Accordingly this case does not fall within the extension to regulation 5(3) to TUPE articulated by Lord Oliver in *Litster*.'

1 (1997) 13 March (EAT 710/96), EAT.

23.77   In *Harris v Bulmas Plastics Ltd*[1] the EAT held that a purchaser of a business had no liability for the unfair dismissal of an employee made before the transfer by the transferor/seller, even though the dismissal was connected with the transfer, because an ETO reason was established.

1 (1996) 5 February (EAT 418/95), EAT.

23.78   Similarly the EAT in *Thompson v SCS Consulting Ltd*[1] held that where the dismissal is for an ETO reason and so reg 8(2) of TUPE 1981 applied, reg 8(1) was excluded and the extended construction of reg 5(3) in *Litster* did not apply.

1 [2001] IRLR 801, EAT, at para 37.

23.79   In order for reg 7(2) of TUPE 2006 to apply[1], any dismissal must not only be for an economic, technical or organisational reason, but it must also be one entailing changes in the workforce. Thus a dismissal merely because the employee will not accept new terms and conditions will not be an ETO reason— see the decision of the Court of Appeal in *Delabole Slate Ltd v Berriman*[2].

1 TUPE 1981, reg 8(2) of was identical on this.
2 [1985] IRLR 305, CA. See also *Crawford v Swinton Insurance Brokers* [1990] ICR 85 (EAT); *Porter and Nanayakkara v Queen's Medical Centre* [1993] IRLR 486 (Sir Godfray le Quesne, sitting as a deputy judge) and *London Metropolitan University v Sackur* UKEAT/0286/06/ZT, 17 August 2006, EAT.

23.80   Clearly redundancies will normally be an ETO reason (see the decisions of the EAT in *Meikle v McPhail (Charleston Arms)*[1] and *Gorictree Ltd v Jenkinson*[2]. However there may be a change in the workforce within reg 7(2) of TUPE 2006 (old reg 8(2) of TUPE 1981) even if the numbers employed do not reduce, but instead the nature of the individual jobs changes sufficiently – see *Porter v Queens Medical Centre*[3], *Trafford v Sharpe & Fisher (Building Supplies) Ltd*[4] and the Court of Appeal in *Wilson v St Helen's Borough Council*[5].

1 [1983] IRLR 351, EAT.
2 [1984] IRLR 391, EAT.
3 [1993] IRLR 486 (Sir Godfray le Quesne, sitting as a deputy judge).
4 [1994] IRLR 325, EAT.
5 [1997] IRLR 505, CA.

23.81   In the case of an insolvency, pre-transfer dismissals are likely to occur because the business will be shrinking. Although the insolvency practitioner is likely to be considering a sale of the business if this is possible, pre-transfer redundancies related to the running of the business should, it would have been thought, often be found to be for an ETO reason (at least where the employees concerned are not subsequently re-hired by the purchaser/transferee), so that liability does not pass to the purchaser/transferee – ie leaving the dismissal liability with the insolvent transferor (and the National Insurance Fund).

23.82 However, in many of the reported cases since *Litster*, the defences raised by the purchaser/transferee have not raised the ETO defence, but instead focused mainly on seeking to establish that any pre-transfer dismissals were not in fact connected with the transfer. This, as discussed above, is a difficult area and can depend on the state of mind of the insolvency practitioner. This seems odd, because on the analysis above, the ETO defence will be available to the purchaser/transferee even if the pre-transfer dismissals are connected with the transfer.

23.83 The position has been confused by the question of whether pre-transfer dismissals would be for an ETO reason if they were made at the request of a potential purchaser of the business. This will, of course be a common occurrence. The insolvency practitioner will probably be reluctant (all other things being equal) to dismiss employees too early (and increase the level of claims on the insolvent company) if there is a possibility that a purchaser would want those employees in the business.

23.84 In *Anderson v Dalkeith Engineering Ltd*[1], the EAT held that pre-transfer dismissals made at the request of the prospective purchaser were for an economic reason and hence within reg 8(2) of TUPE 1981 (now reg 7(2) of TUPE 2006).

1 [1994] IRLR 429, EAT.

23.85 However, subsequent decisions of the EAT have refused to follow *Anderson*, considering that the scope of the 'economic' limb of reg 8(2) in TUPE 1981 must be restricted to something relating to the conduct of the underlying business. A desire to achieve a sale or an enhanced price is not enough[1]. This line has also been taken by the Northern Ireland Court of Appeal in *Willis v McLaughlin & Harvey plc*[2]. These decisions would continue to apply in relation to reg 7(2) of TUPE 2006.

1 See *Wheeler v Patel and J Golding Group of Companies* [1987] IRLR 211 (EAT), *Gateway Hotels Ltd v Stewart* [1988] IRLR 287, EAT, and *Ibex Trading v Walton* [1994] IRLR 564, EAT.
2 [1998] EuLR 22, NI CA.

23.86 This seems fair. However, it seems perverse to argue that a pre-transfer dismissal will never be for an ETO reason if it is carried out at the request of (or with the consent of) the purchaser/transferee. Clearly, it will be difficult (if not impossible) to establish an ETO reason in circumstances where the purchaser/transferee subsequently re-employs the dismissed employees in the same job as before (such as occurred in *Litster* itself) or hires new employees or redirects its existing employees into the business.

23.87 However, if the business genuinely needs fewer employees, so that the dismissals are genuine redundancies when looked at by reference to the business itself, it is difficult to see why this should not be a valid ETO reason. Ultimately, in these circumstances, it is clear that had the purchaser/transferee taken on the employees concerned and then dismissed them, there would still be the possibility of an ETO defence for the purchaser (however the purchaser (presumably solvent) would, of course, have taken over all the liabilities owed to the employee in these circumstances). Thus, in *Willis v McLaughlin & Harvey plc*[1] Kerr J, in the Northern Ireland Court of Appeal considered that the decision of the EAT in *Wheeler v Patel*[2] did not rule out a dismissal at the request of a purchaser being for an economic reason:

> 'if it can be shown that the prospective purchaser would not proceed unless the employee was dismissed. In those circumstances it may be said that the employee is dismissed to enhance the prospects of the sale of the undertaking, but since this is necessary for the sale to proceed and the business could not otherwise survive, it is an economic reason which entails (ie requires) a change in the workforce.'

1 [1998] EuLR 22, NI CA.
2 [1987] IRLR 211, EAT.

23.88   For example in *Whitehouse v Blatchford & Sons Ltd*[1] a new contractor for hospital services took over the existing employees under TUPE, but then had to make one redundant because the hospital stipulated that fewer numbers of technicians were needed. The Court of Appeal held that this was an ETO reason.

1 [1999] IRLR 492, CA.

23.89   The cases confirm that the transferor/seller may lawfully dismiss for an ETO reason (ie in effect the transferor can rely on an ETO reason of the transferee). This follows from the decisions of the ECJ in *Jules Dethier Equipement SA v Jules Dassy*[1] and of the Court of Appeal in *Warner v Adnet Ltd*[2].

1 [1998] ECR 1-1061;[1998] IRLR 266, ECJ.
2 [1998] IRLR 394, CA.

23.90   See also supporting this the decisions of the EAT in *BSG Property Services v Tuck*[1] and *Kerry Foods Ltd v Creber*[2].

1 [1996] IRLR 134, EAT.
2 [2000] IRLR 10, EAT.

23.91   Regulation 7(2) of TUPE 2006 is the same as reg 8(2) of TUPE 1981 in allowing this. It refers to 'changes in the workforce of either the transferor or transferee before or after a relevant transfer.'

23.92   In one case on TUPE 1981, the EAT had been reluctant to allow this argument however. In *Michael Peters Ltd v Farnfield*[1], the EAT answered the question 'Was the respondent dismissed for an economic, technical or organisational reason within reg 8(2)?' by stating that:

> 'The Industrial Tribunal, having been referred to *Wheeler v Patel and J Golding Group of Companies* [1987] IRLR 211, found that he was not. They stated that they had no evidence that satisfied them that the respondent's dismissal was

related to the conduct of the business: 'His dismissal came about in order to achieve the transfer that took place for that reason and no other.'

In our opinion, the Industrial Tribunal were entirely correct in coming to this conclusion. We are not attracted by Mr. Elias's submission that the dismissal fell outside the Wheeler test because it went beyond the bare need to realise money, but was inextricably linked with the need to save the business itself, and that must relate to the conduct of the business.'

This statement was obiter. The EAT had already held that the respondent did not in fact transfer because he did not work in the business transferred.

1 [1995] IRLR 190, EAT.

23.93   In 2007 in Scotland in *Hynd v Armstrong*[1], the Inner House of the Court of Session dealt with a case where the existing employer (a firm of solicitors) dismissed an employee before (and in anticipation of) a split in the firm. This was in circumstances where the relevant successor firm did not want to carry on the business area in relation to the particular employee. Clearly the dismissal was by reason of the transfer, but was it for an ETO reason within reg 8(2) of TUPE 1981?

Rather bizarrely (and with reasoning that is difficult to follow), the Inner House held that it was not possible for the transferor to rely on a potential ETO reason of the transferee. So the individual in that case was able to claim unfair dismissal under reg 8(1) of TUPE 1981 even though the dismissal would have potentially been fair had it been carried out by the new firm (the transferee) after the transfer. The decision may have been set off on the wrong track by the finding of fact in the employment tribunal that the dismissal by the old firm (the transferor) was not a redundancy. Given that, but for the operation of TUPE, the old firm was ceasing carrying on all its business, it is difficult to see how that finding could stand and then be used to support the argument that the transferor did not have an ETO reason for dismissal (see para [31] of the judgment).

The Inner House did comment that allowing the transferor to rely on an ETO reason of the transferor would allow a transferee not to succeed to employment liabilities in an insolvency situation (para [32]) and that this would be inconsistent with the purpose of the ARD 'to provide for the protection of employees'. But in practice a line has to be drawn somewhere.

It may be that this decision (not strictly binding in England and Wales[2]) is given a narrow interpretation.

1 [2007] CSIH 16; [2007] IRLR 338; 2007 SC 409, Inner House, Ct of Sess.
2 See *Marshalls Clay Products Ltd v Caulfield* [2004] EWCA Civ 422; [2004] ICR 436, CA for a discussion of the status of a decision of the Inner House in England and Wales.

23.94   In 2001 in *Thompson v SCS Consulting Ltd*[1] the EAT usefully summarised the position:

'In our judgment the following principles are to be derived from the authorities and which apply for the purposes of this appeal:

(1)   Whether the correct approach to the interrelationship between Regs. 8(1) and 8(2) in a case such as this is to consider the facts on the basis of a pre-

liminary conclusion that the reason or principal reason for the dismissal is the transfer which may be displaced by a finding that the reason or principal reason is an ETO reason or on the basis that the two reasons are mutually exclusive, if where an ETO reason is raised, the tribunal concludes that the reason or principal reason for the dismissal was such a reason, Reg.8(2) applies; Reg. 8(1) is excluded; and the extended construction of Reg.5(3) in *Litster* does not apply. If, on the other hand, the tribunal concludes that the reason or principal reason was the transfer, Reg.8(2) does not apply, the *Litster* principle does or may apply; and the dismissals are automatically unfair. See *Litster, Whitehouse, Honeycombe 78 Ltd* and *Kerry Foods*.

(2) In deciding whether an ETO reason was or was not the reason or principal reason for the dismissal, the tribunal is making a factual decision. See *Whitehouse* and *Kerry Foods*.

(3) In making the factual decision in the tribunal must consider whether the reason was connected with the future conduct of the business as a going concern. See *Wheeler* and *Whitehouse*.

(4) The tribunal is entitled to take into account as relevant factual material whether there was any collusion between transferor and transferee and whether the transferor or those acting on its behalf had any funds to carry on the business or any business at the time of the decisions to dismiss. See *Spence, Litster, Honeycombe 78 Ltd.*

(5) An appellate tribunal should only interfere with such a factual decision if the tribunal erred in law by applying the wrong test, by considering an irrelevant factor, by failing to consider a relevant factor or by reaching a perverse decision.'

1 [2001] IRLR 801, EAT.

23.95 It seems likely that the purchaser/transferee will not succeed to any liability to employees who are dismissed by the transferor on or immediately before the transfer (ie on the same day as the transfer) for an ETO reason.

23.96 In *Wilson v St Helens Borough Council*[1] Lord Slynn seemed to support the view that the purchaser/transferee does not take over the liabilities in this case. He stated that:

'If the transferee does not take the employee because the latter has already been dismissed by the transferor, or because he himself dismisses the employee on the transfer, then he must meet all of the transferor's contractual and statutory obligations unless (a) the employee objects to being employed by the transferor or (b) the or the principal reason for dismissal is an economic, technical or organisational reason entailing changes in the workforce when the employee is not to be treated as unfairly dismissed and when for the purposes of the 1978 Act and the 1976 Order the employee is to be regarded as having been dismissed for a substantial reason justifying the dismissal as fair.'

1 [1999] 2 AC 52 at page 85, HL.

23.97 However, in *Kerry Foods Ltd v Creber*[1] the EAT seems to have held that the purchaser could succeed to the relevant liabilities in this situation. The comments of Lord Slynn are not mentioned in the EAT's judgment, which is generally confusing on this issue.

1 [2000] IRLR 10, EAT.

23.98 It is worth repeating again the statement made above (see para 23.26 above) in relation to the need for a dismissal to be connected with the transfer. In practice, the EAT decisions on ETO reasons will also increase the desire of insolvency practitioners to reduce the risk of a connection with any subsequent transfer, leading, as mentioned (at para 23.35 above), to earlier dismissals by insolvency practitioners and (ironically) reduced job security.

An 'economic, technical or organisational' reason

23.99 It does not seem to have been argued in the cases on TUPE 1981 that the insolvency of the insolvent transferring company could of itself constitute an 'economic, technical or organisational' reason (an 'ETO reason') within reg 8 of TUPE 1981 so that dismissals arising from it would not be automatically unfair, and so that liability for dismissed employees would not transfer to the purchaser. Regulation 8 of TUPE 1981 and reg 7 of TUPE 2006 both refer to an ETO reason as being one 'which entails changes in the workforce of either the transferor or the transferee'.

23.100 Given the reasoning of the European Court of Justice in *Abels* and *D'Urso* (see Chapter 19 above) it seems arguable that if the transferor is in insolvency proceedings for the purpose of an insolvent winding up (see para 19.16 above) then it is possible that this could be an ETO reason for any dismissals. Conversely, in situations where there is no insolvent winding-up (eg receiverships, members' voluntary winding-up and many administrations), the insolvency proceedings may not of themselves constitute an ETO reason.

23.101 The Department of Employment (later, as mentioned above, absorbed into the Department of Trade and Industry) previously indicated that not all dismissals by an insolvent company will constitute general redundancies (see the guidance of the Department, issued to insolvency practitioners in April 1991 by the Society of Practitioners of Insolvency (now R3)).

23.102 In effect, if reg 8(2) of TUPE 1981 dealing with 'economic, technical or organisational reasons entailing changes in the work force' does not apply, then the Department considered there will not be a redundancy. Presumably it took the view that the employees will transfer to the purchaser.

23.103 An example given by the Department was if there were a clause in the transfer agreement requiring an insolvent company to dismiss its employees before completion of the transfer. The Department considered that this would not necessarily fall within reg 8(2) of TUPE 1981 (reg 7(2) of TUPE 2006 is not materially different) because it would not be a reason which related to the conduct of the business and cited *Wheeler v Patel and J Golding Group of Companies*[1] and *Gateway Hotels Ltd v Stewart*[2] in support of this view.

1 [1987] ICR 631, EAT.
2 [1988] IRLR 287, EAT.

23.104 Further guidance was issued by the Department of Employment to the Society of Practitioners of Insolvency (now R3) – see SPI Technical Bulletin No 3 issued in April 1991 and Appendix 3 of Booklet IL1 (5th edition, 1995).

23.105 This is a difficult area. Contrast the decision in *UK Security Services (Midlands) Ltd v Jones*[1] where the EAT seems to have held that redundancy liability passes to the purchaser, even if the dismissal could be considered as being for an 'economic, technical or organisational' reason. This looks wrong as being inconsistent with *Litster* (see para 23.75 above).

1 IDS Brief 472 (July 1992) (104/90), EAT.

23.106 More recently, in 2000 the EAT in *Kerry Foods Ltd v Creber*[1] held that liability for an employee dismissed before the transfer but for an ETO reason will not transfer to the purchaser (even if the dismissal was unfair on general grounds).

1 [2000] IRLR 10, EAT.

23.107 It was initially unclear under TUPE 1981 whether liability would pass to the purchaser/transferee for pre-transfer dismissals even if the employee would not otherwise have qualified for an unfair dismissal remedy (eg because he or she did not have one year's[1] continuous service – see para 2.40 above).

1 Or two years before 1 June 1999.

23.108 Regulation 8(5) was added to TUPE 1981 by the Collective Redundancies and Transfer of Undertakings (Protection of Employment) (Amendment) Regulations 1995, (SI 1995/2587) to clarify that a transfer related dismissal does not automatically give rise to a remedy for unfair dismissal if such a right is excluded by what is now ERA 1996 (eg because the employee did not (then) have two years' continuous service). This reversed the decision of the EAT in *Milligan v Securicor Cleaning Ltd*[1] where the EAT held that the effect of TUPE was that the UK had not exercised the option in the Acquired Rights Directive to exclude from the ambit of the regulations those employees who did not have unfair dismissal rights. The decision of the EAT was in any event itself later overturned by the Court of Appeal in *MRS Environmental Services Ltd v Marsh*[2].

Regulation 7(6) of TUPE 2006 preserves this position.

1 [1995] IRLR 288, EAT.
2 [1997] ICR 995, CA.

CHAPTER 24

TUPE: Pension liabilities

EXCLUSION OF RIGHTS UNDER OR RELATING TO OCCUPATIONAL PENSION SCHEMES

24.1   Although reg 4 of TUPE 2006 (like reg 5 of TUPE 1981) generally provides for all the rights, powers, duties and liabilities of the transferor employer to be automatically assumed by the transferee, reg 10 of TUPE 2006 provides an exclusion for rights under or relating to occupational pension schemes (mirroring reg 7 of TUPE 1981).

24.2   Regulation 10 is a fairly wide exclusion which can have the effect of reducing the expectations of an employee in such circumstances. The employee would be left with his preserved rights under the company's scheme but with no corresponding pension rights as regards future service or as regards any shortfall resulting from being treated as an early leaver in the transferor company's scheme in relation to past service.

24.3   The exclusion under regulation 10 does not extend to liabilities relating to personal pension schemes.

OLD AGE INVALIDITY AND SURVIVORS: *BECKMANN*

24.4   As noted in para 10.6 above, TUPE 1981 and TUPE 2006 were both enacted in order to bring into force the Acquired Rights Directive. Article 3(3) of ARD 1977 and art 3(4) of ARD 2001 both provide an exclusion for pension schemes, stating that the general obligation of the transfer of employment rights does not apply to:

> 'employees' right to old-age, invalidity or survivors' benefits under supplementary company or inter-company pension schemes outside the statutory social security schemes in member states'.

24.5   Section 33 of the Trade Union Reform and Employment Rights Act 1993 amended reg 7 of TUPE 1981 (for transfers after 30 August 1993) so as to make it clear that any provisions in an occupational pension scheme that do not relate to benefits for old age, invalidity or survivors (eg a redundancy benefit found in certain public sector schemes) are treated as not being part of the scheme (so that liability for those other benefits will pass to the transferee).

24.6   The ECJ held in *Beckmann v Dynamo Whicheloe Macfarlane*[1] and *Martin v South Bank University*[2] that the exclusion of occupational pension schemes by the Acquired Rights Directive (and hence TUPE) should be construed narrowly. A bridging pension (payable up to the normal retirement age) triggered on (say) redundancy is probably not an 'old age' benefit and so not within the exemption now in reg 10(2) of TUPE 2006 and so the obligation may transfer. But both these cases involved public sector pension schemes with a bridging pension payable to NRD. This concept does not look to as readily apply to private sector pension schemes, where in contrast to those in the public sector:

(a)   there is usually a separate trust; and

(b)   there is usually not an express contractual obligation to provide a pension; and

(c)   any early retirement or redundancy pension is likely to be payable for life (and not just as a bridging pension to normal retirement age).

1 [2002] ECR I-4893, [2002] 2 CMLR 1152, [2003] ICR 50, [2002] IRLR 578 (C-164/00), ECJ.
2 [2003] ECR I-12859, [2004] 1 CMLR 472, [2004] ICR 1234 [2004] IRLR 74 (C-4/01), ECJ.

24.7   Subject to this, it is clear that the exclusion in reg 10 of TUPE 2006 is wide. It refers to liabilities 'under or in connection' with the employment contract. The same words in reg 7 of TUPE 1981 were given a wide meaning by the EAT in *Warrener v Walden Engineering Co Ltd*[1].

1 [1993] IRLR 420, EAT.

24.8   In *Hagen v ICI Chemicals*[1], Elias J held that the exclusion of pension liabilities from the transfer provisions in TUPE was wide enough to mean that liability for a negligent mis-statement made by the transferor in relation to the arrangements for occupational pensions did not transfer.

1 [2002] IRLR 31 (Elias J).

24.9   Various challenges to the width of reg 7 of TUPE 1981 were made. However in *Adams v Lancashire County Council*[1], the Court of Appeal confirmed that reg 7 was effective and a proper transposition of the Acquired Rights Directive. Regulation 10 of TUPE 2006 follows the same wording and the decisions should be followed. There is no obligation under the ARD on a transferee/purchaser to provide any occupational pension benefits following a TUPE transfer. The Court of Appeal followed the decision of the EFTA Court in *Eidesund v Stavanger Catering A/S*[2].

1 [1997] ICR 834, CA.
2 [1996] IRLR 684, EFTA Court.

PENSIONS ACT 2004

24.10 Under ss 257 and 258 of the Pensions Act 2004 and the Transfer of Employment (Pension Protection) Regulations 2005 (SI 2005/649)[1], from 5 April 2005, transferee employers are now obliged to provide pension benefits for transferring employees where the following conditions are satisfied:

- there is a TUPE transfer resulting in the transfer of employment of the employee from the transferor employer to the transferee employer; and

- immediately before the employee becomes employed by the transferee there is an occupational pension scheme in relation to which the transferor is the employer and the employee is:

  - an active member of the scheme; or

  - eligible to be such a member; or

  - in a waiting period to become eligible to be a member.

1 For a fuller discussion of these provisions see Pollard 'Pensions and TUPE' [2005] ILJ 127.

What is the protection?

24.11 Where the employee qualifies for protection, it is up to the transferee employer to choose what type of pension provision to make: either a defined benefit (DB) scheme of a specified standard or a money purchase occupational scheme (including stakeholder) to which the employer contributes at a specified rate.

Future money purchase benefits

24.12 The transferee company must secure that the employee is (or is eligible to be) an active member of an occupational money purchase pension scheme or a stakeholder scheme into which the transferee employer makes (or, in the case of a stakeholder scheme, offers to make) 'relevant contributions'.

24.13 The Transfer of Employment (Pension Protection) Regulations 2005 provide that these must be matching contributions of up to 6 per cent of the employee's basic pay.

Future DB scheme

24.14 The transferee employer must secure that the employee is or is eligible to be an active member of an occupational DB pension scheme which satisfies either:

- the statutory reference scheme test (for contracting-out purposes); or

- such other test as may be prescribed in regulations.

24.15   The Transfer of Employment (Pension Protection) Regulations 2005 provide that the second option will be complied with if either:

- the value of the benefits provided under the transferee's scheme is at least 6 per cent of pensionable pay (as defined by the scheme rules) for each year of employment together with the total amount of the employee's contributions and employees are not required to contribute (if at all) at a rate exceeding 6 per cent of pensionable pay; or

- the transferee employer must make 'relevant contributions' ie matching contributions of up to 6 per cent of the employee's basic (not pensionable) pay.

Timing

24.16   The transferee employer must provide the employee with the applicable pension provision with effect from either: (a) the date of the TUPE transfer; or (b) the end of the applicable waiting period, as appropriate.

Opting out

24.17   PA 2004 does allow the employee and the transferee employer to agree to contract out of these obligations and agree alternative arrangements. They can do this at any time after the employee becomes employed by the transferee – PA 2004, s 258(6).

Anti-avoidance provisions

24.18   PA 2004 contains anti-avoidance protection. The condition that immediately before the TUPE transfer there is a scheme in respect of which the employee is an active member/eligible to be one/in a waiting period will be regarded as being satisfied in any case where it would have been satisfied but for any action taken by the transferor by reason of the transfer – PA 2004, s 257(5).

Public sector and TUPE 2006

24.19   Notwithstanding the provisions of the Pensions Act 2004, the government policy of giving a 'broadly comparable' guarantee to public sector employees who transfer to the private sector will continue.

NO DISMISSAL CLAIM

24.20   Regulation 10(3) of TUPE 2006 is new. It is intended to confirm that in future a transferor will not be liable if the transferee fails to provide the transferred employees with the required level of pension benefits following the transfer (to the extent that there is such a liability previously, which was unclear).

Transfer of early retirement benefits

24.21   Neither the changes made by the Pensions Act 2004 nor the changes in TUPE 2006 affect the ECJ's decisions in the cases of *Beckmann*[1] and *Martin*[2] (see para 24.6 above) that benefits that were payable on redundancy or before normal retirement age are not benefits for 'old age' within what is now reg 10(2) of TUPE 2006 and so can transfer. In the case of TUPE 2006, the government stated when consulting on the draft regulations that it has intentionally not addressed this issue.

In suitable cases the change provisions in reg 9 of TUPE 2006 (see paras 20.49 to 20.54 above) could be used to obtain employee agreement that any of these early retirement pension rights do not transfer.

1 *Beckmann v Dynamo Whicheloe Macfarlane* [2002] IRLR 578, ECJ.
2 *Martin v South Bank University* [2004] IRLR 74, ECJ.

CHAPTER 25

PAYE and national insurance

OBLIGATION TO DEDUCT INCOME TAX AND NATIONAL INSURANCE

25.1   Insolvency practitioners generally arrange for the insolvent company to deduct income tax under the PAYE system and national insurance contributions from payments they arrange for the insolvent company to make to employees. This applies both to payments made in relation to employment before the appointment of the insolvency practitioner (eg by way of a dividend in a liquidation) and in respect of employment after the appointment (eg where an administrator or receiver arranges for the company to carry on the business).

Deductions by an employer are required under statute (see ITEPA 2003, s 684). A withholding from pay for such amounts as required by statute is allowed by Part 2 (Protection of Wages) of ERA 1996 – see s 13(1)(a) and if a determination has been received from HMRC (even if this is not a formal determination under reg 80 of the 2003 PAYE Regulations[1] – see ERA 1996, s 14(4) and the EAT in *Patel v Marquette Partners (UK) Limited*[2].

1 The Income Tax (Pay As You Earn) Regulations 2003 (SI 2003/2682).
2 UKEAT/190/08; [2009] ICR 569; [2009] IRLR 425, EAT.

25.2   This excludes any liability that the insolvent company may have to HMRC to pay amounts (eg PAYE or NICs) deducted from payments made to employees before the insolvency event – ie before the IP was appointed. Here the claims of HMRC are claims in the insolvency and provable in the normal way. For claims arising in an insolvency starting before 15 September 2003, such claims were preferential (see the Enterprise Act 2002 and Chapter 9 above).

Basis of obligation

25.3   The HMRC Insolvency Manual states[1]:

'An IP who engages or retains (or makes payments to former) employees is responsible as employer for

• operating and accounting for deductions of PAYE/NIC/SC (for former employees tax is deducted at the basic rate

- paying any interest due

- submitting the related returns.

If an IP disputes responsibility or refuses to pay over deductions or submit returns, immediately tell the IP that you are seeking advice from your Head Office and telephone DMB Process & Strategy (at Worthing (This text has been withheld because of exemptions in the Freedom of Information Act 2000)) or in Scotland submit a full report together with the relevant papers to EIS Edinburgh.'

1 See INS2205 – Employer cases at http://www.hmrc.gov.uk/manuals/insmanual/INS2205.htm

25.4   This personal obligation on IPs is presumably considered by HMRC to arise under the Income Tax (Pay As You Earn) Regulations 2003 (SI 2003/2682) (the '2003 PAYE Regulations').

25.5   The 2003 PAYE Regulations replaced the Income Tax (Employments) Regulations 1993 (SI 1993/744) (the 'PAYE Regulations 1993').

25.6   In relation to the PAYE Regulations 1993, the Revenue's view was apparently on the basis that either:

(a)   the insolvency practitioner was the person 'paying emoluments' and thus fell within the definition of employer in reg 2(1) of the PAYE Regulations 1993; or

(b)   the insolvency practitioner was the person with the general control and management of the employees and is thus deemed to be the employer by reg 4 of the PAYE Regulations 1993.

See eg INS3227 – Company Administration in the HMRC Insolvency manual[1].

1 Previously see para 2.408 in the Inland Revenue Insolvency Manual and the Inland Revenue response at para 7 of the technical release TR 799, issued in June 1990 by the Institute of Chartered Accountants in England and Wales, a copy of which is set out in Anthony Davis, *Taxation in Corporate Insolvency and Rescue* (6th edition, Bloomsbury Professional 2009).

25.7   The 2003 PAYE Regulations do not contain such a wide definition of 'employer'. Instead it is defined using the normal definition, including employment under a contract of service etc (see reg 2(1), cross referring to ITEPA 2003, s 4).

25.8   A policy decision[1] was taken to use the separate term 'other payer' in the 2003 PAYE Regulations, when dealing with payers who are not employers.

1 See para 39 of the Tax Law Rewrite commentary on the 2003 PAYE Regulations. Available next to the 2003 PAYE Regulations on the statutory instrument section of the Office of Public Sector Information Website, www.opsi.gov.uk.

25.9   The term 'other payer' is defined in reg 2(1) as meaning:

'a person making relevant payments in a capacity other than employer, agency or pension payer.'

25.10   Regulation 12 applies the 2003 PAYE Regulations to 'other payers' on the basis that they are 'treated as employers', with some exceptions. The basic obligation on an employer to deduct tax on making a relevant payment is contained in reg 21 (which applies to 'other payers').

25.11   In the PAYE Regulations 1993, the obligation to make deductions on payment made after employment has ceased was expressly extended by reg 24(1)(b) to a payment by:

> 'a trustee in bankruptcy, a receiver, a liquidator or any other person making such a payment in respect of an obligation of a former employer'

This list did not, for some reason, expressly include an administrator.

Regulation 24 has been replaced by reg 37 in the PAYE Regulations 2003. The express references to IPs have not however been repeated. The Tax Law Rewrite commentary states that the references to IPs were omitted as being 'unnecessary' (see para 312).

25.12   Regulations 2 and 12 of the PAYE Regulations 2003 were considered by the Court of Appeal in *R (on the application of Oriel Support Ltd) v Revenue and Customs Comrs*[1]. This was not an insolvency case, but involved payment of workers and employees not by the employer, but by a third party, Oriel, who provided services to the employer/labour provider. This service included payment of the relevant employees. Oriel was then reimbursed by the employer. Oriel sought to use its own PAYE code for the deductions (this would then allow it to offset some tax against other payments). The Revenue challenged this, arguing that the employer's PAYE code should be used.

The Revenue's view was upheld in the Court of Appeal. The payments made by Oriel were not on its own account and were payments on behalf of the employer.

Moses LJ held (at paras 17 and 18):

> 'Regulation 12 as interpreted in the lexicon in Regulation 2, requires the Revenue to look at the capacity in which the payment is received. It is plain beyond all argument that the worker receives those payments in his capacity as employee and not in his capacity other than employee. He receives those payments under his contract of employment: see the definition of employment in Regulation 2(1). It would be otherwise, as was canvassed by the judge in paragraph 37 of his judgment, if some other person made a payment (for example a bonus), otherwise than under a contract of employment. The example given by the Revenue is of a bonus paid by a manufacturer of a particular type of motor car to an employee working within a dealership. Such a payment is not received under the contract of employment but clearly it is taxable since its source is employment. Hence the need for references to "other payer" and "other payee" in Regulation 2.
>
> 18. No such difficulty arises here. When Oriel pays the labour providers' workers it discharges the labour provider's obligation to pay its workers whose personal services are provided to the end users under the worker's contract of employment with the labour provider. It is, as the judge pointed out, as simple as that.'

This analysis of course applies with equal force to an insolvency practitioner. The insolvent company remains the employer (see Chapter 15 above) and any payments made to employees are clearly made on behalf of the insolvent company (see eg the comments by Neuberger J about holiday pay in *Re Douai School*[2]).

1 [2009] EWCA Civ 401; [2009] All ER (D) 139 (May), CA.
2 [2000] 1 WLR 502 (Neuberger J) – see para 18.61 above.

25.13 The HMRC view seems to be that the obligations as to PAYE and national insurance contributions are independent of whether the insolvency practitioners have adopted the employment contracts (see Chapter 18 above) or have any personal liability under the relevant employment contracts.

25.14 It was argued[1] that the Inland Revenue's view as to the obligation of insolvency practitioners in relation to PAYE could be wrong. This was on the basis that old s 203 of ICTA 1988 only authorised regulations enabling the Inland Revenue to assess 'any person making any payment' of emoluments. This contrasted with ICTA 1988, s 349 which refers to persons 'by or through whom the payment is made'.

1 See Anthony Davis *Taxation in Corporate Insolvency and Rescue* (6th edition, Bloomsbury Professional, 2009) at paras 3.25, 5.29 and 5.60 (and see also the 5th edn (2003) at para 5.24).

25.15 But s 203, ICTA 1988 has now been replaced by s 684 of ITEPA 2003. Section 684 seems wider in including a general authorisation for regulations to deal with deduction of tax, with a specific list of areas that may be covered. The specific list includes reference to 'persons making payments'.

25.16 In any event, a wide interpretation of what became reg 4 of the PAYE Regulations 1993 was given by Hobhouse J in *Booth v Mirror Group Newspapers plc*[1]. This case involved payment by a related company and it was held that what became reg 4 of the PAYE Regulations 1993 applied and the paying company was required to deduct tax under the PAYE system.

1 [1992] STC 615 (Hobhouse J).

25.17 However, this case can be distinguished from the position of an insolvency practitioner. In *Booth*, the payment was actually being made by the related company on its own behalf rather than as an agent for any other person.

25.18 The 2003 PAYE Regulations were rewritten to clarify various anomalies in the law on PAYE. It was acknowledged in the commentary by the Tax Law Rewrite project that the new definitions may involve a change in the law[1]. The commentary discussed the decision in *Booth* and noted that the spectrum of potential payers includes:

> 'receivers making payments to former employees (for whom there are some special provisions – see regulation 37)'[2]

1 See para 112 of the Tax Law Rewrite commentary on the 2003 PAYE Regulations. Available next to the 2003 PAYE Regulations on the statutory instrument section of the Office of Public Sector Information Website, www.opsi.gov.uk.
2 See para 129. The special provision in reg 37 relates to payments after employment has ceased (and not to receivers).

25.19   Given that generally an insolvency practitioner is the agent of the company (see para 15.2 above), HMRC's view that the insolvency practitioner is always personally liable seems wrong in principle. HMRC do not argue that other agents (eg directors) are automatically personally liable.

25.20   In practice, insolvency practitioners will not take the point, but will try to arrange for tax to be deducted from relevant payments made to employees (or former employees) in order to reduce any liability on the part of the insolvent company.

25.21   It is also possible that the public policy principle found by the Court of Appeal in *Sargent v Customs and Excise Commissioners*[1] to oblige the payment of VAT by a receiver could apply here by analogy.

1 [1995] 1 WLR 821; [1995] STC 398, CA.

25.22   In *Re Grey Marlin Ltd*[1] it was held that tax liabilities (including PAYE and NIC liabilities) incurred by a company which continued to trade were held to be expenses of a winding up and so payable by a liquidator.

1 [1999] 4 All ER 429 (David Donaldson QC sitting as a deputy judge)

25.23   Similarly in *Re Toshoku Finance UK plc, Kahn v IRC*[1] the Court of Appeal held that corporation tax arising on interest deemed received was a liquidation expense. The liability was upheld by the House of Lords on appeal[2], but on a different basis. See Chapter 17 above.

1 [1999] STC 922, CA. Also reported as *Re Toshoku Finance UK plc* [1999] 2 BCLC 777.
2 [2002] UKHL 6; [2002] 1 WLR 671; [2002] 3 All ER 961, HL.

National insurance contributions (NICs)

25.24   Where insolvency practitioners have a liability to deduct tax under the PAYE system, they will also have a liability to deduct earnings-related national insurance contributions – see reg 67 of the Social Security (Contributions) Regulations 2001 (SI 2001/1004).

25.25   A person (eg the employing company) who is knowingly concerned in the fraudulent evasion of any national insurance contributions commits an offence under the Social Security Administration Act 1992, s 114 (as substituted by the Social Security Act 1998, s 61). If the company has committed an offence and it is shown that this was due to the consent or connivance of, or attributable to any neglect on the part of, the insolvency practitioner, then the insolvency practitioner may have committed an offence – see the Social Security Administration Act 1992, s 115 and Chapter 8 above.

25.26 In addition, liability for unpaid national insurance contributions owed by a body corporate can be imposed on individual officers of the body corporate if the failure to pay was, in the opinion of the Inland Revenue, attributable to the fraud or neglect of the individual culpable officers[1]. For a discussion of this provision, see the article by Richard Wilson *'Company Director – You're Nicked!'* in (1998) Taxation 1 October.

For an example of the use of the section against a director see *Inzani v Revenue and Customs Comrs*[2].

HMRC's tax bulletin 54[3] (August 2001) says that HMRC will only issue a personal liability notice under s 121C in "the most serious cases".

1 Social Security Administration Act 1992, s 121C(1), as inserted from 1 April 1999 by Social Security Act 1998, s 64.
2 SpC 529; [2006] STC (SCD) 279, [2006] SWTI 1354 (Special Commissioner Nicholas Aleksander). Discussed by Andy Taylor in (2009) 22 Insolvency Intelligence 79.
3 See www.hmrc.gov.uk/bulletins/tb54.htm.

25.27 The term 'officer' for this purpose could possibly include an insolvency practitioner as a person purporting to act as a 'director, manager, secretary or other similar officer of the body corporate'[1]. This wording is similar to the general provisions in many statutes imposing criminal liability (see Chapter 8 above).

1 Social Security Administration Act 1992, s 121C(9), as inserted by Social Security Act 1998, s 64.

25.28 However, s 121C(9) does differ slightly in referring to a 'person purporting to Act as such' rather than 'purporting to Act in such capacity'. Arguably this difference means that civil liability does not extend under s 121C to an insolvency practitioner on the basis that he or she is not purporting to Act as a director etc, even though it may be more probable that he or she is purporting to Act in such capacity.

HMRC tax bulletin 54 (August 2001) includes the comment that:

> 'Generally a Personal Liability Notice will only be issued to a person who is not a director or secretary of the company where that person substantially manages the affairs of the company or is a person in accordance with whose direction or instructions the directors of the company are accustomed to act.'

Calculating the deductible amount

25.29 The normal cumulative basis for calculating the amount to be deducted under the PAYE system does not apply to any payments made to the employee after employment has terminated where such payments have not been included in the certificate (P45) issued under reg 36 of the 2003 PAYE Regulations.

25.30 Where such payments are made, the deduction obligation is limited to the basic rate of income tax in force for the year in which the payment is made (2003 PAYE Regulations, reg 37).

LIABILITY IF CONTRACTS 'ADOPTED'

25.31 Administrators (and administrative receivers) may have a responsibility to pay PAYE and NICs on amounts of wages paid by them on adopted employment contracts. See the discussion in Chapter 18 above of the decision of the Court of Appeal in *Inland Revenue Commissioners v Lawrence*[1]. This case is cited as authority for this in para 1[2] of Chapter 8 of Dear IP issued by the Insolvency Service.

In their book *Corporate Administrations and Rescue Procedures*[3], Ian Fletcher, John Higham and William Trower argue (at para 20.13) that employee NICs (primary) are sums payable in respect of an employment contract and were so accordingly payable under the priority rules in IA 1986, s 19 for adopted employment contracts. They state that it was argued that employer NICs (secondary) were a different liability and not part of salary, as they were due to a different person under different legal requirements outside of the employment contract. Accordingly it says the view was taken that there was no obligation for an administrator to account for employer NICs.

However it goes on to say that, subsequent to the Enterprise Act 2002, it is now considered likely that all PAYE NIC liabilities (both primary and secondary) will be considered to be 'necessary disbursements' and so payable under rule 2.67(1)(f) of the Insolvency Rules 1986 (as amended). Accordingly it considers that these will need to pay in full in priority to the administrators' expenses. It considers this reverses the implications *of IRC v Lawrence*[1].

But to the contrary, see Davis *Taxation in Corporate Insolvency and Rescue* (6th edn, Bloomsbury Professional, 2009) at para 5.60 referring to Dear IP, para 12 to the effect that *IRC v Lawrence* continues to apply.

1 [2001] 1 BCLC 145, CA.
2 See www.insolvency.gov.uk/insolvencyprofessionandlegislation/dearip/dearipmill/chapter8.htm
3 2nd edn (Tottel Publishing, 2004).

IMPACT ON EMPLOYEE

25.32 In practice, an employee is not usually concerned as to whether or not the PAYE (or NIC) amount deducted is in fact recovered by the Secretary of State. Unless the employee was somehow culpable (eg has contributed to the failure by the employer company to pay the contributions), he or she will normally be credited with the tax deducted or with the benefits in the state social security system as though such contributions had been paid in full by the employer[1] (see para 9.78 above).

1 See Social Security (Contributions) Regulations 2001 (SI 2001/1004), reg 60 and Income Tax (Pay As You Earn) Regulations 2003 (SI 2003/2682), reg 72, formerly regulations 42(2) and (3) of the Income Tax (Employments) Regulations 1993 (SI 1993/744).

25.33 Such a credit is also required by arts 7 and 10(b) of EC Directive 80/987, the Employment Insolvency Directive (see Chapter 12 above).

SUMMARY OF PAYMENTS LIABLE TO INCOME TAX AND NATIONAL INSURANCE

25.34   The obligation to deduct income tax under the PAYE system will apply only to those payments made to employees which are taxable earnings or taxable specific earnings of the employee[1].

1 ITEPA 2003, ss 683 and 684, (formerly ICTA 1988, s 203).

25.35   In relation to termination payments, taxable under Chapter 3 of Part 6 of ITEPA 2003, the PAYE deduction obligation only extends to income which counts under that Chapter as employment income (ITEPA 2003, s 10(3)). This means that only the excess over the £30,000 exemption under ITEPA 2003, s 403, is subject to the PAYE deduction obligation (s 403 states that a termination payment only counts as employment income 'if and to the extent that it exceeds the £30,000 threshold').

25.36   Applying this rule to the list of likely termination claims of employees the position can be summarised as follows.

25.37

Claim	Income tax under Schedule E	NICs
(1) Unpaid wages	yes	yes
(2) Holiday pay	yes	yes
(3) Pay in lieu of notice	no (unless provided in contract or over £30,000)**	no
(4) Redundancy payments	no*	no
(5) Other statutory claims (eg unfair dismissal)	no**	no

*   Exempt from income tax as employment income by virtue of ITEPA 2003, s 309 (formerly ICTA 1988, s 579), subject to the qualification that payments so exempted may be taken into account under Chapter 3 of Part 6 of ITEPA 2003 (formerly ICTA 1988, s 148) – see note** below.

**   Taxable as employment income by virtue of Chapter 3 (ss 402 to 416) of Part 6 of ITEPA 2003 (formerly ICTA 1988, s 148) as termination payments, but subject to a £30,000 exemption under ITEPA 2003, s 403 (formerly ICTA 1988, s 188). The £30,000 figure was increased from £25,000 by FA 1988, s 74 with effect from 6 April 1988, but has not increased since.

CHAPTER 26

Pensions and other trusts

PENSION OBLIGATIONS – GENERAL

26.1   Where the insolvent employer company has operated a scheme (for example a pension scheme or other employee trust) for its employees, the position and liabilities of the company under or in relation to the scheme will depend on whether or not a trust is involved.

CONTRACTUAL OBLIGATIONS

26.2   Where the pension scheme is a simple contractual obligation of the company (eg a promise to pay a pension at a later date or a promise to contribute to a personal pension scheme), the employee will be left with the same remedies as are available for any other unsecured obligation.

26.3   However, some pension related obligations are given a special status, for example:

(a)   some claims in respect of guaranteed minimum pensions and employee contributions are preferential debts (see Chapter 10 above);

(b)   some amounts due to occupational or personal pension schemes are guaranteed by the National Insurance Fund (see Chapter 13 above);

(c)   the Pensions Act 1995, s 75 provides a statutory debt obligation in some circumstances – for example if a scheme winds up or if an employer goes into formal insolvency (eg liquidation, administrative receivership or administration) to pay to the scheme any shortfall in the funding of the scheme. This debt is specifically stated not to be preferential (see para 10.53 above). See further Chapter 34 below.

TRUSTS

26.4   Where the scheme involves a trust (all HMRC registered[1] private sector occupational pension schemes involve trusts[2]), the assets of the trust will not (even if the company is the sole trustee) be assets of the insolvent company and will not fall within the property of the company to be dealt with by the insolvency practitioner and used to pay general creditors under the insolvency regime – see eg *Re Kayford Ltd*[3] and *Heritable Reversionary Company Ltd v Millar*[4]. A similar analysis underpins the decision of the House of Lords in *Buchler v Talbot*[5], although that was a case looking at assets held under a floating charge.

If the insolvency company is a trustee, the insolvency practitioner may well take control of the actions of the company in how it acts as trustee (see below). But the assets in the trust will remain subject to the trust and not the insolvency distribution regime. For example, dispositions by the company out of the trust are not invalidated under IA 1986, s 127 (see para 6.24 above) if the trustee company is in a court winding-up – see the Australian case of *All Benefit Pty Ltd v Registrar-General*[6].

1 Registration with HMRC replaced the former approval by HMRC (or the Inland Revenue) from 6 April 2006, under the Finance Act 2004.
2 See PA 2004, s 252, (UK-based scheme to be trust with effective rules).
3 [1975] 1 All ER 604 (Megarry J).
4 [1892] AC 598, HL.
5 [2004] UKHL 9; [2004] 2 AC 298; [2004] 1 All ER 1289, HL.
6 (1993) 11 ACSR 578 (Master Burley), cited in 'Vulnerable Transactions in Corporate Insolvency' (2003, Eds John Armour and Howard Bennett) at para 8.20.

Fiduciary or beneficial powers and discretions

26.5   The powers and discretions of the insolvent company in relation to a pension trust (or indeed any other trust) can be divided between:

(a)   those which are fiduciary (ie held by the company in a fiduciary capacity so that the company owes a fiduciary duty to the trust beneficiaries as to how and when to exercise the power); and

(b)   those which are beneficial (ie held by the company in a beneficial capacity so that it may exercise them in its own interest and for its own benefit, perhaps binding itself with a contractual obligation in relation to the power). There may be an implied constraint based on the implied duty of mutual trust and confidence (see para 26.12 below).

26.6   Most powers and discretions of a company in relation to a pension trust are beneficial. Thus, a power to agree with the trustee to augmentations of benefits or to amendments to a scheme will almost always be a beneficial power – see *Imperial Group Pensions Trust Ltd v Imperial Tobacco Ltd*[1], *Mettoy Pension Trustees Ltd v Evans*[2] and *Re Courage Group's Pension Schemes*[3].

Similarly in Australia – see *Lock v Westpac Banking Corpn*[4] and *Ansett Australia Ground Staff Superannuation Plan Pty Ltd v Ansett Australia Ltd*[5].

1 [1991] 2 All ER 597 at 604 (Browne-Wilkinson V-C).
2 [1991] 2 All ER 513 at 551 (Warner J).
3 [1987] 1 All ER 528 at 544 (Millett J).
4 (1991) 25 NSWLR 593, [1991] PLR 167 (Waddell CJ in Eq).
5 [2002] VSC 576 (Warren J) – see paras 8.28; 9.65; 12.97 and 12.217 above.

26.7   Similarly, the power of an employer to appoint a new principal employer under a pension scheme was held in Scotland in *Independent Pension Trustee Ltd v LAW Construction Co Ltd*[1] not to be a fiduciary power. Lord Hamilton held (at page 268A) that 'It is a power which could legitimately be exercised by an employer to secure an advantage to himself'. It may be subject to a requirement only to be exercised for a proper purpose – see Millett J in *Re Courage Group's Pension Schemes*[2].

1 [1996] OPLR 259 (Lord Hamilton).
2 [1987] 1 All ER 528 (Millett J).

26.8   However, exceptionally employer powers may be fiduciary, depending on the circumstances. In 1991 in *Mettoy Pension Trustees Ltd v Evans*[1] for example, a power of the company to consent to augmentations in a winding-up was held by Warner J to be fiduciary. However this was in the unusual circumstances that the previous provisions had vested this augmentation power in the trustees and there was no evidence that the trustees had considered the implications of the change when agreeing to amend the scheme.

In 1997 in *National Grid v Laws*[2] Robert Walker J (who had been one of the counsel involved in *Mettoy*) commented (at page 177) that:

> 'Had *Imperial Tobacco*[3] been decided earlier and been cited in *Mettoy*, Warner J might possibly have come to a different conclusion as to whether the employer's power should be classified as fiduciary.'

See further the discussion of *Mettoy* at para 30.82 below.

1 [1991] 2 All ER 513 (Warner J).
2 [1997] PLR 157; [1997] OPLR 161 (Robert Walker J).
3 See *Imperial Group Pensions Trust Ltd v Imperial Tobacco Ltd* [1991] 2 All ER 597 (Browne-Wilkinson V-C).

26.9   In 2008 in *Bridge Trustees Ltd v Noel Penny (Turbines) Ltd*[1] Judge Purle QC (sitting as an additional Judge of the High Court) followed *Mettoy* and held that a power to distribute surplus given to the employer was a fiduciary power. This meant that the court could appoint a new trustee to exercise the power (the company had ceased to be in receivership, so the obligation under the Pensions Act 1995 to have an independent trustee – see Chapter 30 (Independent trustee obligations) below – had ended).

Judge Purle considered (at para [15]) that:

> 'It is evident that the statutory policy is to remove from an insolvent company the power to determine the destination of a pension surplus, once an insolvency practitioner has been appointed.'

The company did not appear in the relevant hearing and it does not seem that the judge was pointed to the cases (eg *National Grid*) doubting the decision in *Mettoy* on this point. Accordingly the decision in *Bridge Trustees* must be regarded as wrong on this point.

In *Scully v Coley*[2] the Privy Council dealt with an appeal from the courts in

Jamaica concerning the destination of a surplus on the winding-up of a pension scheme that had been established by Gillette. The main thrust of the decision concerns the meaning of who is a member of the scheme, but the Privy Council also briefly commented on the nature of employer's powers. Lord Collins gave the judgment and commented (at para [47]):

> '47 The final question is whether the provision that the allocation by the Administrator under Rule 12(c) is "subject to the approval of [Gillette]" gives Gillette a fiduciary power to withhold approval, with the consequence (say the respondents) that the trustees could make no allocation, which would then be left to the court: *McPhail v Doulton* [1971] AC 424 at 457.
>
> 48 This question was raised in argument before Brooks J and the Court of Appeal, but was not the subject of decision. On this point the Board is satisfied that the appellants are right. The argument between the parties was centred on the question whether the power was a fiduciary power, and their Lordships were referred to several cases on the distinction between a power in relation to which the duty of the employer was limited to a duty of good faith and a power in respect of which the employer was a fiduciary and which was to be exercised solely in the interests of the objects of the power: *Icarus (Hertford) Ltd v Driscoll* [1990] PLR 1; *Mettoy Pension Trustees Ltd v. Evans* [1990] 1 WLR 1587; *Imperial Group Pension Trust Ltd. v. Imperial Tobacco Ltd.* [1991] 1 WLR 589; *Re William Makin & Son Ltd* [1992] PLR 177; *British Coal Corp v British Coal Staff Superannuation Scheme Trustees* [1994] ICR 537 (overruled on other grounds in *National Grid Co plc v Mayes* [2001] UKHL 20, [2001] 1 WLR 864 (HL)).
>
> 49 The question is not primarily whether the power is a fiduciary power (as the respondents say) or an administrative power (as the appellants say), since there is no necessary contrast between the two. In *Weinberger v Inglis* [1919] AC 606 (a decision which it would now be impossible to justify on the facts: the General Purposes Committee of the Stock Exchange was held entitled to exclude British naturalised subjects of German origin from membership) the power to admit persons to membership was held (at 640) to be both an administrative power and a fiduciary power. The real question is what is the purpose for which the power was granted. It is not necessary to decide in what circumstances Gillette could withhold approval of allocation under Rule 12(c). The reason is that their Lordships are satisfied that the power to withhold approval could not be used to alter the allocation to the "then Members" and thereby to vary the Rules. There is already an express power in Rule 12(a) to change, modify or discontinue the Plan at any time. Gillette has not done so, and their Lordships consider it difficult (as the Board did in *Air Jamaica Ltd v Charlton* [1999] 1 WLR 1399, at 1411) to see how the Plan could lawfully be amended once it had been discontinued. Gillette has been kept informed at all times of the intentions of the Administrator and of the trustees, and is a party to these proceedings. Gillette's failure to withhold approval cannot be regarded as a refusal to exercise a trust power so as to give the court the power to vary the provisions for allocation.'

Unfortunately, the decision of the Privy Council does not give much guidance as to the reason why the employer in that case (Gillette) could not withhold its consent to the use of the surplus to increase benefits for members.

1 [2008] EWHC 2054 (Ch) (22 August 2008) (Judge Purle QC sitting as an additional judge of the High Court).
2 [2009] UKPC 29

26.10   Some powers and discretions will always be fiduciary, for example:

(a)   powers vested in the company in its capacity as trustee of the scheme – see *Icarus (Hertford) Ltd v Driscoll*[1] and *Re William Makin & Sons Ltd*[2],

(b)   the power to appoint or remove a trustee has been held to be a fiduciary power in relation to a private non-commercial trust in some old cases – see *Re Skeats' Settlement*[3] and *Re Shortridge*[4]. However this is an odd result. The better view is that these cases should not be followed in relation to commercial trusts such as pension schemes. Although there have been comments to the effect that the power will be fiduciary in *IRC v Schroder*[5] and *Mettoy Pension Trustees Ltd v Evans*[6] (see further the author's article in (1991) British Pension Lawyer no 37). The view that the power of appointment and removal of pension scheme trustees is not fiduciary is now given support by the decision of Judge O'Donoghue, (sitting as a deputy High Court judge) in *Simpson Curtis Pension Trustees Ltd v Readson Ltd*[7],

(c)   it is sometimes argued that a unilateral power of amendment in a pension scheme given to the company (rather than one which requires the consent of the trustees to its exercise) runs a risk of being held to be a fiduciary power.

The argument would be that a court could construe such a power as being fiduciary, because of its width (perhaps on the basis that a non-fiduciary power would be inconsistent with an irrevocable trust).

However, in *British Coal Corpn v British Coal Staff Superannuation Scheme Trustees*[8], Vinelott J held that a unilateral amendment power (with express restrictions on its ambit) was not a fiduciary power. Similarly the House of Lords in *National Grid v Laws*[9], construed a unilateral employer power as being subject to an implied limitation based on good faith but not that this would prevent the employer from acting in its own interests.

1 [1989] PLR 1 (Aldous J).
2 [1993] OPLR 171 (Vinelott J).
3 (1889) 42 ChD 522 (Kay J).
4 [1895] 1 Ch 278, CA.
5 [1983] STC 480 at 500 (Vinelott J).
6 [1991] 2 All ER 513 at 551 (Warner J).
7 [1994] OPLR 231 (Judge O'Donoghue, sitting as a deputy High Court judge). See the author's casenote in (1994) 8 Trust Law International 84.
8 [1995] 1 All ER 912 (Vinelott J).
9 [2001] UKHL 20, [2001] 2 All ER 417, HL at para 16.

Clarification by trust instrument

26.11   There is no reason why the trust instrument cannot clarify whether or not a power is fiduciary; unless perhaps in a situation where a non-fiduciary power would be inconsistent with there being a trust at all. Slade LJ held in *Bishop v Bonham*[1] that it was possible in the relevant document (in this case a mortgage) to exclude obligations otherwise implied by law.

1 [1988] 1 WLR 742 at page 752, CA.

Implied duty of mutual trust and confidence

26.12 Even where a power or discretion held by the company is beneficial, it may still be subject to an implied duty that it must be exercised in good faith. In other words it must not be exercised arbitrarily or capriciously or in a way so as to destroy or seriously damage the relationship of trust and confidence between the company and its employees and former employees – see *Milhenstedt v Barclays Bank International Ltd*[1], the Australian case *Lock v Westpac Banking Corpn*[2] and *Stannard v Fisons*[3].

1 [1989] IRLR 522, CA.
2 (1991) 25 NSWLR 593; [1991] PLR 167 (Waddell CJ in Eq).
3 [1992] IRLR 27, CA.

26.13 This duty of good faith may perhaps be enforced by the trustees as well as by employees or ex-employees – see *Imperial Group Pensions Trust Ltd v Imperial Tobacco Ltd*[1].

1 [1991] 2 All ER 597 (Browne-Wilkinson V-C).

26.14 For further analysis of the implied duty of trust and confidence in a pensions context, see the author's article 'Employers' powers in pension schemes: the implied duty of trust and confidence' (1997) 11 Trust Law International 93.

Importance of distinction

26.15 The distinction between a fiduciary power and a beneficial power can be crucial when the company becomes insolvent in the following situations:

(a) The insolvency practitioner (receiver, liquidator or administrator) taking control of the company may perhaps not have control a fiduciary power (see paras 17.16 to 17.44 below) but will control the exercise by the company of a beneficial power.

(b) In relation to pension schemes within independent trustee provisions in the Pensions Act 1995 (PA 1995), s 22 (see Chapter 21 below), if an independent trustee is appointed by the Pensions Regulator, fiduciary powers conferred on the employer pass, under s 25(2)(b), to the independent trustee (see Chapter 21 below). This does not apply to beneficial powers.

(c) Even where the insolvency practitioner would otherwise take control of a fiduciary power, there may be a conflict of interest which prevents the company (acting through the insolvency practitioner) from acting (see paras 17.45 to 17.57 below).

INSOLVENCY PRACTITIONERS AND FIDUCIARY POWERS

26.16   Where a fiduciary power, discretion or duty is vested in the insolvent company, the question as to whether the insolvency practitioner acting in relation to the company can control the exercise of that power is somewhat uncertain. The position varies depending on the type of insolvency practitioner.

LIQUIDATORS

26.17   A liquidator is given powers:

(a)   to manage the business of the company so far as may be necessary for its beneficial winding up[1];

(b)   to 'do all acts and execute, in the name and on behalf of the company, all deeds, receipts and other documents'[2]; and

(c)   'to do all such other things as may be necessary for winding up the company's affairs and distributing its assets'[3].

These powers are conferred by statute on liquidators in both a court winding up and a voluntary winding up[4].

1 IA 1986, Sch 4, para 5.
2 IA 1986, Sch 4, para 7.
3 IA 1986, Sch 4, para 13.
4 IA 1986, ss 165, 167.

Case law

26.18   There are several reported cases where it has clearly been accepted that a liquidator may control the exercise of fiduciary powers and duties held by the company, for example where the company is a trustee holding clients' assets – see *Re Berkeley Applegate (Investment Consultants) Ltd (No 2)*[1], *Re Eastern Capital Futures Ltd*[2], *Re Stetzel Thomson & Co Ltd*[3], *Re Biddencare Ltd*[4], *Re Telesure Ltd*[5] and *Tom Wise Ltd v Fillimore*[6].

See also the article '*The role of private law in protecting client assets*' by Nick Segal in (2009) 22 Insolvency Intelligence 88.

1 [1989] Ch 32 (Edward Nugee QC).
2 [1989] BCLC 371, (1989) 5 BCC 224 (Morritt J).
3 (1988) BCC 74.
4 [1994] 2 BCLC 160 (Mary Arden QC).
5 [1997] BCC 580 (Jacob J) – noted in (1997) 13 Insolvency Law & Practice 110.
6 [1999] BCC 129 (Rattee J).

26.19   There is clear authority in Australia (based on identical statutory provisions) that a liquidator should control the exercise of fiduciary functions by the insolvent company. In a judgment reviewing Canadian and English cases, Needham J in *Re Crest Realty Pty Ltd*[1] held (at page 672) that:

'part of a liquidator's duty in "winding up the affairs of the company" is to exercise the powers of the directors in the administration of trusts by the company, subject, of course, to the desirability of making application to the court either for directions or for the appointment of a new trustee where that is expedient.'

26.20   These principles have subsequently been followed in Australia – see *Grime Carter & Co Pty Ltd v Whytes Furniture (Dubbo) Pty Ltd*[2], *Re Indopal Pty Ltd*[3], *Re GB Nathan & Co Pty Ltd*[4], *13 Coromandel Place Pty Ltd v C L Custodians Pty Ltd (in liq)*[5]; *Re French Caledonia Travel*[6] and *Wells v Wily*[7].

1 [1977] 1 NSWLR 664 (Needham J).
2 (1983) ACLR 540; [1983] 1 NSWLR 158 (McLelland J).
3 (1987) 12 ACLR 54; (1987) 5 ACLC 278 (McLelland J).
4 (1991) 24 NSWLR 674; (1991) 9 ACLC 1291 (McLelland J).
5 [1999] FCA 144 (Finkelstein J).
6 [2003] NSWSC 1008; (2003) 48 ACSR 97 (Campbell J).
7 [2004] NSWSC 607 (Austin J).

26.21   As a matter of policy it would be preferable for the decision of Needham J to be followed in England. The 'affairs' of the company would seem clearly to include management of any trusts where the company is trustee so that the implied powers under the Insolvency Act 1986 (IA 1986); Sch 4, para 13 should extend to allow a liquidator to exercise fiduciary powers held by the company in relation to a trust (subject, in the case of pension trusts, to PA 1995, s 22 – see Chapter 30 below – and, in other cases, to a conflict of interest – see paras 26.45 to 26.57 below). The alternative would require either the directors of the company to act as part of their residual duties, the appointment of a new trustee or an application to court.

26.22   However, the position in England in relation to pension trusts is currently not clear cut. Aldous J, in *Icarus (Hertford) Ltd v Driscoll*[1], held that a liquidator could control powers held by the company as trustee of a pension scheme. But in *Mettoy Pension Trustees Ltd v Evans*[2], Warner J commented (at page 548) that he had doubts as to whether what is now para 13 of Sch 4 to IA 1986 was wide enough to give power to the liquidator to control the exercise of a fiduciary power.

1 [1989] PLR 1 (Aldous J).
2 [1991] 2 All ER 513 (Warner J).

26.23   *Mettoy* was subsequently followed by Vinelott J in *Re William Makin & Son Ltd*[1] where he stated (at page 177):

'Mr Moss QC submitted that the observations of Warner J in *Mettoy* that the exercise of a fiduciary power vested in the company cannot be necessary for distributing its assets is too widely stated and that the doubt he expressed "whether it may be necessary for winding up the affairs of the company" are not well founded. It may be that in a case where the surplus not applied to the benefit of the beneficiaries of a pension scheme is not caught by or needed to satisfy a floating charge which has already crystallised the exercise of the power to the extent of determining the proportion that should be so applied is a step that is necessary in order to determine what are the assets of the company available for distribution by the liquidator and the claims provable in the liquidation (including any claim by the debenture holder if in so far as not satisfied by assets caught by the floating charge). But, of course, in such circumstances the power cannot be exercised because of the liquidator's conflicting duties. It may also be that in the circumstances I have envisaged (that the whole surplus is caught by the floating charge and that there are no other assets not so caught in respect of which the debenture holders would be entitled to prove for any deficiency) the liquidator owes no conflicting duty. But then if that were the case it would not be necessary either for distributing the assets of the company or for winding up its affairs to determine what part of the surplus should be applied for the benefit of the beneficiaries under the scheme. In this case there is the further difficulty that the liquidator has already expressed his clear intention, if and so far as the power is vested in him, not to exercise it in favour of any beneficiary under the pension scheme.'

Vinelott J refused to follow the conflicting decision of Aldous J in *Icarus (Hertford) Ltd v Driscoll*[2].

1 [1993] OPLR 171 (Vinelott J).
2 [1989] PLR 1 (Aldous J).

26.24   I consider the decision of Vinelott J to be wrong on this issue (although Vinelott J subsequently commented obiter, to the same effect in *British Coal Corp v British Coal Staff Superannuation Fund Scheme Trustees*[1]). The other English and Australian cases referred to above are not mentioned in the judgment (and presumably were not cited).

1 [1995] 1 All ER 912 (Vinelott J).

26.25   It is clearly part of the liquidator's function to wind up the affairs of the company and it seems unduly restrictive to say that this does not include a fiduciary power or duty or that the liquidator cannot take control of these functions, subject to any conflict of interest issues. The practical effect of Vinelott J's decision (if followed) would be that none of the fiduciary powers of the company can be controlled by the liquidator. This would mean that several costly applications to the court for directions or for the appointment of a new trustee would be required[1]. Alternatively, the control of the company for this purpose would remain with the directors. Neither of these results seems desirable.

1 If a new trustee were needed for an occupational pension scheme, a (cheaper) alternative to an application to court is (now) a request to the Pensions Regulator – see further para 26.60 below.

26.26   In addition, Vinelott J's decision is inconsistent with the later decision of Jacob J in *Denny v Yeldon*[1] (see para 26.31 below) to the effect that an administrator could act for the company in exercising all of its powers relating to the pension scheme, based on the power of administrators under IA 1986, s 14(1)(a) to 'do all such things as may be necessary for the management of the affairs, business and property of the company'. It is difficult to see that this power differs materially from the powers given to liquidators under Sch 4 to IA 1986 (see para 26.21 above).

1 [1995] 3 All ER 624 (Jacob J).

26.27   However it should be noted that in *Denny v Yeldon*, Jacob J did not refer to Vinelott J's decisions in *Re William Makin* and *British Coal* and that his decision in relation to administrators is also partly based on the power of administrators to appoint and remove the directors of the insolvent company (a power which is not given to liquidators).

26.28   Michael Furness QC (sitting as a Deputy High Court judge) commented in *Chirkinian v Larcom Trustees*[1] on the appointment of a trustee (of an employee benefit trust) by a company acting through its liquidator. The comments were obiter. He seems to have accepted that a liquidator could make the appointment, but stated that any appointment of a trustee by a liquidator needed to be solely for the benefit of the relevant beneficiaries. He commented:

> '18 Finally, I wish to mention the question of the validity of the appointment of the Respondent as trustee. In the course of argument I asked Mr Arnfield if he was challenging the validity of that appointment, and he told me that on the evidence available he did not feel able to do so. For that reason I have disregarded this issue in deciding on the merits of this appeal. It is, however, an aspect of this case which has troubled me, for two reasons. The first is that the authorities show that a liquidator can only appoint a trustee if it is in furtherance of his statutory powers to do so. On this point see *Mettoy Pension Trustees Ltd v Evans* [1990] 1 WLR 1587 at 1616 and, more pertinently, *Simpson Curtis Pension Trustees Ltd v Readson Ltd* [1994] PLR 289. Secondly, even if the liquidator did have the power to make the appointment in this case, it appears from the Simpson Curtis case that, at least in English law, the power must be exercised solely for the benefit of the beneficiaries. In the absence of evidence I accept that it is possible that the appointment of the Appellant was made by the liquidator for entirely altruistic reasons. However, if the reason for the appointment of a UK resident trustee in place of the original offshore trustee was to facilitate a claim to recover the assets the appointment would arguably be invalid.'

1 [2006] EWHC 1917; [2006] All ER (D) 403 (Jul), [2006] BPIR 1363; [2006] WTLR 1523 (Michael Furness QC, sitting as a Deputy High Court judge).

26.29   In New Zealand, in *MacIntosh v Fortex Group Ltd*[1], the Court of Appeal referred to a conflict of interest where an employer also acted as trustee of its pension scheme. It held that this situation is far from uncommon and cannot affect the nature of claims by the members for unpaid contributions.

1 *Fortex Group Ltd (In Receivership and Liquidation) v MacIntosh* [1998] 3 NZLR 171, NZ CA.

ADMINISTRATORS

26.30   Administrators are given general powers to:

(a)   'do anything necessary or expedient for the management of the affairs, business and property of the company'[1]; and

(b)   to appoint and remove directors of the insolvent company[2].

1 IA 1986, Sch B1, para 59(1). For pre-15 September 2003 administrations, see IA 1986, s14(1)(a).
2 IA 1986, Sch B1, para 61. For pre-15 September 2003 administrations, see IA 1986, s 14(2).

26.31   In *Denny v Yeldon*[1], Jacob J held that these 'very wide' powers meant that an administrator could properly Act for the company in exercising its powers in relation to the pension scheme (including in that case agreeing to an amendment to the pension scheme). Jacob J held that this followed because both:

(a)   the 'company's pension scheme seems to me to be an intimate part of the company's affairs' so that the power in s 14(1)(a) (now para 59(1) of Sch B1) applied; and

(b)   'Suppose the opposite view, that the power were only in the directors of the company. Under the express power given by s 14(2)[2] the administrators could simply dismiss directors who would not amend the pension trust deed, or appoint enough of their own extra directors to achieve the same result. I think that leads to the conclusion that any power of the directors before an administration order is made is within the powers of the administrators after the order is made. Any other conclusion would be pointless'[3].

1 [1995] 3 All ER 624 (Jacob J).
2 Now para 61 of Sch B1 for administrations starting on or after 15 September 2003.
3 [1995] 3 All ER 624 at page 628j.

26.32   Jacob J also considered that the position of an administrator should be in line with that of an administrative receiver, citing *Re Edgar*[1] and *Simpson Curtis Pension Trustees Ltd v Readson Ltd*[2] – see paras 26.39 to 26.41 below). The problems regarding conflict applicable to liquidators (see para 26.45 below) may apply if the company is a trustee.

1 (1972) ACLC 27, 492 (Street CJ).
2 [1994] OPLR 231 (Judge O'Donoghue, sitting as a deputy High Court judge).

26.33   In *Polly Peck International plc v Henry*[1], Buckley J refused to authorise a change in the trustees of a money purchase scheme away from the company (now in administration) to a new independent trustee. The independent trustee would seek to be able to charge for its services (to be paid out of the assets of the scheme). The insolvent company could not charge the scheme for its role as trustee. Buckley J considered that the role of acting as trustee fell within the 'affairs' of the company (following Jacob J in *Denny v Yeldon*) and that the administrators (as partners in a leading city firm of accountants) were competent to carry out the required role, without any charge to the scheme.

1 [1999] PLR 135, [1999] 1 BCLC 407 (Buckley J).

Receivers and administrative receivers

26.34   Out of court receivers are appointed under a provision in a security document (see para 3.20 above) and their powers extend only to assets of the company charged by the security document. Assets held on trust are not assets of the company (see para 17.4 above) and will not fall within the security (unless perhaps the company carries on the business of being a professional trustee).

26.35 Accordingly, it seems that control of the limited category of any fiduciary powers and duties owed by the company (see para 26.10 above) will not usually pass to an out of court receiver – see *Mettoy Pension Trustees Ltd v Evans*[1], *Re William Makin & Son Ltd*[2] and *Buckley v Hudson Forge Ltd*[3].

1 [1991] 2 All ER 513 (Warner J).
2 [1993] OPLR 171 (Vinelott J).
3 [1999] PLR 151 at 167 (Lloyd J).

26.36 Such powers will presumably remain exercisable by the directors as part of their area of residual control following the appointment of a receiver – see *Newhart Developments Ltd v Co-operative Commercial Bank Ltd*[1], applied in *Watts v Midland Bank plc*[2] and *Tudor Grange Holdings Ltd v Citibank NA*[3]. In Scotland see *Shanks v Central Regional Council*[4] and *Independent Pension Trustee Ltd v LAW Construction Co Ltd*[5].

See also the article by Margaret Hemsworth 'Directors' Powers during an Administrative Receivership' (1999) Insolvency Lawyer 92.

1 [1978] QB 814, CA.
2 [1986] BCLC 15 (Peter Gibson J).
3 [1992] Ch 53 (Browne-Wilkinson V-C).
4 1987 SLT 410 (Outer House, Court of Session).
5 [1996] OPLR 259; 1997 SLT 1105 (Lord Hamilton).

26.37 Conversely, there seems no reason why a receiver (whether administrative or not) who has been given management powers should not exercise beneficial powers of the company under a pension scheme. For example in *Davis v Richards & Wallington Industries Ltd*[1] approval of a definitive trust deed by receivers on behalf of a company was noted by Scott J without comment.

1 [1990] 1 WLR 1511 at 1524 (Scott J).

26.38 This issue often gets caught up in the question of whether the power given to an employer to appoint and remove trustees of the pension scheme is fiduciary (ie must be exercised in the interests of the scheme beneficiaries and not in the employer's own interests). The better view is that this power is not fiduciary – see para 26.10 above.

26.39 In the Australian case of *Re Edgar*[1], Street CJ held that a charge giving the receiver power to run the business of the company was wide enough to allow a receiver to control the exercise of a power of appointment and removal of a trustee by the company. However, the report is relatively short and it does not seem that the issues mentioned above were raised.

1 (1972) ACLC 27, 492 (Street CJ).

26.40 *Re Edgar* was followed in Australia by McGarvie J in *James Millar Holdings Ltd v Graham*[2], to allow a receiver to control the exercise of powers apparently vested in the company as trustee. However, no reasons were given on this point, other than to follow *Re Edgar*.

1 (1978) 3 ACLR 604 (McGarvie J).

26.41   In *Simpson Curtis Pension Trustees Ltd v Readson Ltd*[1], Judge O'Donoghue, sitting as a deputy High Court judge, followed *Re Edgar* and held that receivers could exercise powers of appointment and removal of pension trustees, even if the power is fiduciary.

1 [1994] OPLR 231 (Judge O'Donoghue, sitting as a deputy High Court judge). This case is noted by the author in (1994) 8 Trust Law International 84.

26.42   The reasoning in *Re Edgar* and in *Simpson Curtis Pension Trustees Ltd v Readson Ltd* was subsequently followed in Scotland by Lord Hamilton in *Independent Pension Trustee Ltd v LAW Construction Co Ltd*[1].

1 [1996] OPLR 259 (Lord Hamilton).

26.43   An administrative receiver has implied powers under the IA 1986, s 42 and Sch 1 which include a power to carry on the business of the company[1] and to execute deeds etc[2] but not a power to manage the affairs of the company, unlike a liquidator or administrator – see paras 26.17 and 26.30 above.

1 IA 1986, Sch 14, para 1.
2 IA 1986, Sch 9, para 1.

26.44   By contrast, a court receiver (or provisional liquidator) is appointed by order of the court and his powers will be delineated by the order. There seems to be no reason why the order should not extend to give the court receiver (or provisional liquidator) power to control the exercise of fiduciary powers by the company.

CONFLICTS OF INTEREST

26.45   It is a general rule applicable to a fiduciary that he should not put himself in a position where his duty and interest (or duty and another duty) may conflict – see eg *Phipps v Boardman*[1].

1 [1967] 2 AC 46, HL.

26.46   However, there must be more than the remote possibility of a conflict of interest – see the discussion in *Re Wallace Smith & Co Ltd*[1] by Edward Nugee QC (sitting as a Deputy High Court judge) of *Re Esal (Commodities) Ltd*[2] and *Re Arrows Ltd*[3]

1 [1992] BCLC 970 at 987 (Edward Nugee QC sitting as a Deputy High Court judge).
2 [1989] BCLC 59, CA.
3 [1992] BCC 121 (Hoffmann J).

26.47   It is possible to exclude or modify the usual equitable rule on conflicts of interest:

● by an express provision in the trust instrument (see, for example, *Bray v Ford*[1] and *Kelly v Cooper*[2]), or

- by implication, for example, if the trust is established with an initial trustee who has a conflict of interest (see *Sargeant v National Westminster Bank plc*[3]), or

- if such a conflict is implicit – eg in the division between employer and member nominated trustees (see Scott V-C in *Edge v Pensions Ombudsman*[4] subsequently upheld by the Court of Appeal[5]).

1 [1896] AC 44, HL.
2 [1993] AC 205, PC.
3 (1990) P & CR 518, CA.
4 [1998] Ch 512 (Scott V-C).
5 [2000] Ch 602, CA.

26.48   If an insolvency practitioner is able to control the exercise of a fiduciary power by the insolvent company (eg possibly a liquidator in relation to a pension scheme where there is no independent trustee appointed under PA 1995, s 23 so the vesting of trustee powers in the independent trustee under s 25(2) does not apply – see Chapter 30 below), then a conflict of duties may arise between:

(a)   the insolvency practitioner's general duty (eg for a liquidator to maximise recoveries for creditors); and

(b)   the fiduciary duty owed by the company to the beneficiaries of the trust (ie including the members).

26.49   There may not always be a conflict, if, for example, the provisions of the pension scheme do not provide for any surplus funds to return to the company or if any surplus funds returned would be caught by a floating charge and not come under the control of a liquidator (as was the case in *Re William Makin & Son Ltd*[1] and see para 26.23 above). Similarly in the case of a money purchase scheme (conflict issues do not seem to have arisen in *Polly Peck International plc v Henry*[2]).

1 [1993] OPLR 171 (Vinelott J).
2 [1999] PLR 135, [1999] 1 BCLC 407 (Buckley J) and see para 26.33 above.

26.50   If there is a real conflict (eg if the company is trustee and the trustee has a discretion to augment benefits with any sums remaining falling to the company – see para 38.74 below), then it seems that this may disqualify the company (through its insolvency practitioner and perhaps anyone else) from exercising the fiduciary powers.

Case law

26.51   In *Icarus (Hertford) Ltd v Driscoll*[1], Aldous J allowed a liquidator to control the exercise of a fiduciary discretion by the company (acting as trustee). Conversely, in *Mettoy Pension Trustees Ltd v Evans*[2] (decided at the same time as *Icarus*), Warner J considered that the potential conflict prevented the liquidator from controlling a fiduciary power and decided that the court should exercise the power.

1 [1989] PLR 1 (Aldous J).
2 [1991] 2 All ER 513 (Warner J).

26.52   In *Re William Makin & Son Ltd*[1], Vinelott J decided to follow *Mettoy* in preference to *Icarus* and rejected an argument that any conflict of interest was impliedly authorised by the fact that the company had been appointed the initial trustee of the pension scheme. Vinelott J held that the insolvency of the company and the appointment of the liquidator created a new situation 'because the duty owed by the liquidator to the creditors precluded the exercise of the power in favour of the beneficiaries under the scheme'.

1 [1993] OPLR 171 (Vinelott J).

26.53   Similarly, in the New Zealand case of *Ibell v UEB Industries Ltd*[1], Gault J refused an application by a receiver for him to be appointed as a trustee of a pension scheme on the basis that the receiver had a conflict of interest.

1 (1990) 1 NZSC 40, 227 (Gault J).

26.54   The legal position is left regrettably uncertain. Conflicts of interest is a difficult area in relation to trusts, even without the intervention of insolvency. The courts have lamentably failed to give clear guidance as to the circumstances in which a sufficiently real conflict arises, particularly in a pensions (or employee trust) context.

26.55   Vinelott J's judgment in *Re William Makin & Son Ltd* is also the subject of criticism in other areas but was followed by Vinelott J in the later case of *British Coal Corpn v British Coal Trustees*[1] and (obiter) by Lloyd J in *Buckley v Hudson Forge Ltd*[2].

1 [1995] 1 All ER 912 (Vinelott J).
2 [1999] PLR 151 at 167 (Lloyd J).

26.56   In the conflicts area it fails to indicate why the onset of insolvency should operate to change the situation. The directors of the company would have owed duties (through the company) to shareholders and creditors. If the impact of a liquidation changes the situation it can only be because the business of the company will (in practice) cease (see paras 4.18 and 6.2 above). This is the reason for the change in the conflict situation envisaged by Warner J in *Mettoy*[1]. Different considerations may therefore arise in the case of an administration or a receivership.

1 [1991] 2 All ER 513 at 548 (Warner J).

26.57   In addition, if the cessation of the company's business (or its entry into insolvency proceedings) is a major change in the position of trustees as regards conflicts of interest, does this also affect the position of individual trustees who may also be members of the scheme (or directors or creditors of the company)? Should they also cease to act?

COMPANY AS PENSION TRUSTEE – REGULATOR POWERS

26.58   If the insolvent company is itself a trustee of an occupational pension scheme the Pensions Regulator (tPR) has (from 6 April 2005) taken over the powers of the old Occupational Pensions Regulatory Authority (Opra) under PA 1995 to act if it goes into liquidation or is the subject of a winding-up petition.

26.59   tPR may make an order suspending the company from acting as a trustee if a winding-up petition is presented[1]. Opra used to have power to disqualify the company from being the trustee of any occupational pension scheme if it has entered liquidation as defined in IA 1986, s 247(2) – ie voluntary or court[2].

But this power was deleted by the Pensions Act 2004 (presumably on the basis that the general power under the new s 3 of PA 1995, as amended by PA 2004, to make prohibition orders is now wide enough).

1 PA 1995, s 4(1)(d).
2 PA 1995, s 29(4)(b).

26.60   tPR also has a general power[1] to appoint a trustee in place of one removed under PA 1995, s 3 (prohibition orders) or otherwise disqualified (eg under PA 1995, s 29). tPR's powers under PA 1995, s 7 include a more general one to appoint a trustee if it is satisfied this is necessary (broadly) to ensure a scheme is properly run.

1 PA 1995, s 7.

CHAPTER 27

PPF: Pension Protection Fund

27.1　The Pensions Act 2004 established the Pension Protection Fund (PPF) with effect on and from 6 April 2005.

27.2　Broadly, the PPF is designed to provide a safety net for eligible occupational pension schemes. If a scheme is eligible (see Chapter 31 below) and a qualifying insolvency event occurs (ie the employer enters formal insolvency in Great Britain after 5 April 2005), an 'assessment period' will start.

27.3　During the assessment period (see Chapter 28 below) the PPF will look at the scheme to see if it has sufficient funds to meet the protected level of benefits provided by the PPF.

27.4　If the scheme does not, and the insolvency practitioner states that a scheme rescue is not possible, the scheme will enter the PPF (the first schemes entered in December 2006).

27.5　On entering the PPF, all the assets and liabilities (other than defined benefit liabilities to and in respect of members) of the scheme are transferred (under the Pensions Act 2004) to the PPF[1], which will:

- take over responsibility for the transferred external liabilities; and

- take over responsibility for any money purchase benefits[2]; and

- provide a protected level[3] of benefits to the members who were entitled to defined benefits.

1 PA 2004, s 161.
2 Money purchase (defined contribution) benefits are included in the obligations transferred to the PPF – see PA 2004, s 161(3)(a).
3 PA 2004, s 162 and Sch 7.

INSOLVENCY EVENT

27.6　An insolvency event is defined in s 121 of PA 2004 and reg 5 of the PPF Entry Rules Regulations[1]. The definition is important as it is used for much of

PA 2004 and for the amended employer debt provisions in s 75 of PA 1995 – see s 75(6C)(a).

1 The Pension Protection Fund (Entry Rules) Regulations 2005 (SI 2005/590), (the PPF Entry Rules Regulations).

27.7   An insolvency event (in relation to a company) is:

- a nominee submitting a report for a voluntary arrangement under Pt 1 of IA 1986 – s 75(3)(a);

- the directors of a company filing or lodging with the court documents and statements under para 7(1) of Sch A1 to IA 1986 dealing with the moratorium on directors proposing a voluntary arrangement – s 75(3)(b);

- an administrative receiver within IA 1986, s 251 being appointed – s 75(3)(ac;

- the company entering administration within the meaning of para 1(2)(b) of Sch B1, IA 1986 – s 75(3)(d);

- a resolution being passed for the voluntary winding-up of the company without a declaration of solvency under IA 1986, s 89 – s 75(3)(e);

- a creditors' meeting being held under IA 1986, s 95 to convert an MVL into a CVL – s 75(3)(f);

- an order for the winding-up of the company being made by the court under Pt 4 or 5 of IA 1986 – s 75(3)(g);

- an administration order being made by the court in respect of the company by virtue of any enactment which applies Pt 2 of IA 1986 (administration orders) (with or without modification) – reg 5(1)(a);

- a notice from an administrator under para 83(3) of Sch B1 to IA 1986 (moving from administration to creditors' voluntary liquidation) in relation to the company being registered by the registrar of companies – reg 5(1)(b);

- the company moving from administration to winding up pursuant to an order of the court under r 2.132 of the Insolvency Rules 1986 (conversion of administration to winding up – power of court) – reg 5(1)(c); or

- an administrator or liquidator of the company, being the nominee in relation to a proposal for a voluntary arrangement under Pt 1 of IA 1986 (company voluntary arrangements), summoning meetings of the company and of its creditors to consider the proposal, in accordance with IA 1986, s 3(2) of (summoning of meetings – reg 5(1)(d).

27.8   The definition of 'insolvency event' includes any winding-up by the court. Such a winding-up could occur in relation to a solvent employer.

The statutory list in ss 121(2) to (4) and in any regulations under s 121(5) is definitive – see PA 2004, s 121(6).

Although not listed in PA 2004 or the PPF Entry Rules Regulations, the various insolvency regimes under the Banking Act 2009 will also count as an insolvency event for these purposes. This is because article 3 of the Banking Act 2009 (Parts 2 and 3 Consequential Amendments) Order 2009[1] deems references to winding-up or liquidation or administration to include bank liquidation or bank administration under the 2009 Act. This applies to the enactments listed in the Schedule, which include ERA 1996, PA 1995, PA 2004, the PPF Entry Rules Regulations 2005[2] and the Financial Assistance Scheme Regulations 2005[3].

The same applies to building societies – see the Building Societies (Insolvency and Special Administration) Order 2009[4].

1 SI 2009/317.
2 SI 2005/590.
3 SI 2005/1996.
4 SI 2009/805 –adding a new s 90C into the Building Societies Act 1986 applying the Banking Act 2009 and see para 1 of Schedule 2 applying the Banking Act 2009 (Parts 2 and 3 Consequential Amendments) Order 2009.

27.9 Note that the following are *not* an insolvency event under s 121:

● a resolution being passed for a voluntary winding-up with a declaration of solvency (ie a members' voluntary liquidation);

● appointment of a provisional liquidator;

● appointment of a receiver who is not an administrative receiver – eg an LPA receiver (see paras 4.23 to 4.31 above);

● entry of the company into a non-UK insolvency proceeding.

Note that a members' voluntary liquidation (MVL) involves a declaration of solvency being given by the directors and so (in principle) the company is not insolvent. MVLs are generally outside the new definition of an 'insolvency event' in the Pensions Act 2004, (see PA 2004, s 121(2)), but an MVL triggers a s 75 debt (see para 34.22 below) and are within the independent trustee obligations in ss 22 to 26 of PA 1995 (see Chapter 30 below).

27.10 The definition of an 'insolvency event' relates only to insolvency proceedings under the Insolvency Act 1986 and so will not apply to an insolvency proceeding outside the UK even if applying to a UK company, eg under the Cross-Border Insolvency Regulations 2006 (SI 2006/1030) – see Chapter 40 (Overseas employees and insolvencies) below.

Generally a scheme can only enter an assessment period (or ultimately the PPF) if the employer (or for a multi-employer scheme all the employers – see Chapter 36 below) have a qualifying insolvency event occur in relation to them – see para 27.7 above for the relevant list.

QUALIFYING INSOLVENCY EVENT

27.11 A qualifying insolvency event in relation to an employer of an eligible scheme is an insolvency event that occurs on or after 6 April 2005[1]. This is irrespective of any previous insolvency event prior to this date.

In addition, in order to be an eligible scheme for entry into the PPF, the scheme must not have commenced wind up before 6 April 2005[2].

The guidance on the PPF website summarises the position[3].

Where there is a multi-employer scheme, the definition of 'qualifying insolvency event' in s 127(3) can be modified – see Chapter 36 below and the Pension Protection Fund (Multi-Employer Schemes) (Modification) Regulations 2005, (SI 2005/441, as amended).

1 See PA 2004, s 127(3), and the Pension Protection Fund (Eligible Schemes) Appointed Day Order 2005 (SI 2005/599).
2 PA 2004, s 126(2).
3. See www.pensionprotectionfund.org.uk/insolvency_guidance.pdf

ENTERING THE PPF OUTSIDE INSOLVENCY – s 129

27.12 But there is an alternative route available in some (limited) cases. Sections 128 and 129 of PA 2004 allow the trustees of a scheme to apply to the PPF if they become aware that the employer in relation to the scheme is unlikely to continue as a going concern. This does not require a formal insolvency of the employer in the UK, but is only available[1] where the prescribed circumstances in reg 7 of the PPF Entry Rules[2] apply. These are limited to public bodies, charities and trade unions in relation to which it is not possible for an insolvency event (as defined in s 121, PA 2004) to occur.

27.13 For a corporate employer the requirements are that the employer is either:

(a) a public body[3]:

   (i)   in relation to which it is not possible for an insolvency event as defined in or under s 121 of PA 2004 to occur; and

   (ii) which is not the employer in relation to an occupational pension scheme in respect of which a relevant public authority has either:

      (aa) given a guarantee in relation to any part of the scheme, any benefits payable under the scheme or any member of the scheme, or

      (bb) made any other arrangements for the purposes of securing that the assets of the scheme are sufficient to meet any part of its liabilities; or

(b) a trade union within the meaning of s 1 of TULRCA 1992 (meaning of trade union) in relation to which it is not possible for an insolvency event as defined in or under s 121 of PA 2004 to occur.

27.14 The PPF guidance[4] summarises the position:

'2.8 The Pension Protection Fund can also assess certain eligible occupational pension schemes where the employer cannot enter formal insolvency proceedings, for example some public bodies and unincorporated charities, in circumstances where that employer is unlikely to be able to continue as a going concern.

2.9 In these circumstances, as no insolvency event is available to the employer it will be for either trustees of the pension scheme or the Pensions Regulator to inform the Pension Protection Fund and request that the Pension Protection Fund assumes responsibility for the pension scheme. The assessment period will begin on the date of receipt by the Pension Protection Fund of the notification or application. Further information can be found in sections 128 & 129 and Regulations 7 & 8 of the Pension Protection Fund (Entry Rules) Regulations 2005.

2.10 It should be noted that this is not an alternative entry route for pension schemes. It is only for those pension schemes whose sponsoring employer cannot have a normal insolvency event.'

27.15   This list was extended from 1 April 2009 by the Pension Protection Fund (Miscellaneous Amendments) Regulations 2009[5] to include an 'EEA Credit Institution' and an 'EEA Insurer' (broadly such institutions established in the EEA, but outside the UK). The explanatory notes to the amending statutory instrument clarify that this change was made because such institutions cannot enter a UK insolvency proceeding:

'Any institution which is an overseas company but is also an European Economic Area ("EEA") credit institution (or a UK branch of one) or EEA insurer is currently unable to apply to the UK courts under section 221 of the Insolvency Act 1986. This means that an EEA credit institution and insurer can only be wound-up under the laws of the country where its head office is located. Because of this, the pension schemes of European Economic Area ("EEA") credit institutions and insurers cannot be taken over by the PPF. Regulation 2(2), (3) and (4) of these Regulations therefore makes provision, by amending the Entry Rules Regulations, so that such schemes may make an application to the Board of the PPF.'

27.16   The Government expanded on this in its comments on the consultation on the draft 2009 regulations[6]:

'12. Where an eligible scheme's sponsoring employer is based outside the UK and suffers an insolvency event (which is not a qualifying insolvency event for the purposes of Part 2 of the Pensions Act 2004) the employer can nevertheless generally apply for a winding up order from the court under section 221 of the Insolvency Act 1986 ("the 1986 Act") or Article 185 of the Insolvency (Northern Ireland) Order 1989 (S.I. 1989/2405). The eligible scheme would then be able to commence a PPF assessment period by virtue of section 121(3)(g) of the Pensions Act 2004.

13. The reasons that additional steps are needed to be taken in respect of EEA Credit Institutions and EEA Insurers are set out below in paragraphs 14 through 16.

14. Regulation 3(1) of the Credit Institutions (Reorganisation and Winding Up) Regulations 2004 (S.I. 2004/1045) provides that: "On or after the relevant date [5

May 2004] a court in the United Kingdom may not, in relation to an EEA credit institution or any branch of an EEA credit institution–

(a)   make a winding up order pursuant to section 221 of the 1986 Act or Article 185 of the 1989 Order [N. Ireland];

(b)   appoint a provisional liquidator;

(c)   make an administration order."

15. The equivalent provision for EEA Insurers is in regulation 4(1) of the Insurers (Reorganisation and Winding Up) Regs 2004 No. 353.

16. Any institution which is an overseas company but is also an EEA credit institution (or a UK branch of one) or EEA insurer is therefore currently unable to apply to the UK courts under section 221 of the 1986 Act. This means that an EEA credit institution and insurer can only be wound-up under the laws of the country where its head office is located. A winding-up in another jurisdiction would not satisfy the definition of "insolvency event" within section 121 of the Pensions Act 2004. Also, article 1(2) of the EC Regulation on Insolvency Proceedings 2000 does not apply to insolvency proceedings concerning "credit institutions".

17. Furthermore, the provisions within sections 127 to 129 of the Pensions Act 2004 do not apply to EEA Credit Institutions and EEA Insurers. Section 127 applies when an insolvency event has occurred with which EEA Credit Institutions and Insurers are unable to comply. The bodies to whom sections 128 and 129 apply are those listed under regulation 7 of the Entry Rules (public bodies, charities and trade unions).

18. The Government has decided not to extend the Regulations further at this stage. However, the Government would welcome views on whether the Entry Rules continue to work as intended, and in particular, whether there are other employers that should be treated along the same lines as those listed in regulation 7 of the Entry Rules. The Government will consider submissions for a future set of amendment regulations.'

1 See s 129(1)(b) and (4)(b).
2 Regulations 7 and 7A of the Pension Protection Fund (Entry Rules) Regulations 2005 (SI 2005/590, as amended).
3 A 'public body' is defined as 'a government department or any non-departmental public body established by an Act of Parliament or by a statutory instrument made under an Act of Parliament to perform functions conferred on it under or by virtue of that Act or instrument or any other Act or instrument.' – reg 1(3) of the PPF Entry Rules Regulations.
4. See www.pensionprotectionfund.org.uk/insolvency_guidance.pdf.
5 SI 2009/451.
6. See http://www.dwp.gov.uk/consultations/2007/ppf-2009-response.pdf

PPF PROTECTED BENEFITS

27.17   The PPF protected benefits[1] are summarised on its website as set out in the table below:

Compensation

Broadly speaking the Pension Protection Fund will provide two levels of compensation:

1. For individuals that have reached their scheme's normal pension age or, irrespective of age, are either already in receipt of survivors' pension or a pension on the grounds of ill health, the Pension Protection Fund will pay 100% level of compensation.

   In broad terms and in normal circumstances, this means a starting level of compensation that equates to 100% of the pension in payment immediately before the assessment date (subject to a review of the rules of the scheme by the Pension Protection Fund).

   The part of this compensation that is derived from pensionable service on or after 6 April 1997 will be increased each year in line with the Retail Prices Index capped at 2.5%. This could, potentially, result in a lower rate of increase than the scheme would have provided.

2. For the majority of people below their scheme's normal pension age the Pension Protection Fund will pay 90% level of compensation.

   In broad terms and in normal circumstances, this means 90% of the pension an individual had accrued immediately before the assessment date (subject to a review of the rules of the scheme by the Pension Protection Fund) plus revaluation in line with the increase in the Retail Prices Index between the assessment date and the commencement of compensation payments (subject to a maximum increase for the whole period calculated by assuming RPI rose by 5% each year). This compensation is subject to an overall cap, which equates to £26,050[2] at age 65 (the cap will be adjusted according to the age at which compensation comes into payment).

   Once compensation is in payment, the part that derives from pensionable service on or after 6 April 1997 will be increased each year in line with the Retail Prices Index capped at 2.5%. Again, this could result in a lower rate of increase than the scheme would have provided.

In addition there will also be compensation for certain survivors.

The Pension Protection Fund has the ability to alter the levy to meet its liabilities. However, in extreme circumstances compensation could be reduced.

- Revaluation and indexation could be reduced by the Pension Protection Fund if circumstances required it[3].

- Levels of compensation could be reduced by the Secretary of State on the recommendation of the Pension Protection Fund[4].

Source: PPF website http://www.pensionprotectionfund.org.uk/index/main-functions/compensation.htm

1 PA 2004, s 162 and Sch 7.
2 The compensation cap is fixed under para 26(7) and 27 of Sch 7. From 1 April 2006 it is £28,944.45 – see the Pension Protection Fund (Pension Compensation Cap) Order 2006 (SI 2006/347). 90% of this gives the £26,050 figure mentioned by the PPF.
3 PA 2004, Sch 7, para 29.
4 PA 2004, Sch 7, para 30.

SUMMARY OF PPF ROLE

27.18 The PPF summarises its role in its guidance to scheme trustees as follows:

The Assessment Period

If a qualifying insolvency event occurs in relation to an employer of an eligible scheme, this will trigger the beginning of an assessment period. During this period the Pension Protection Fund will assess whether or not it must assume responsibility for the scheme.

What happens during an assessment period?

During the assessment period the Pension Protection Fund looks to determine whether a scheme is eligible for entry. During this period the scheme continues to be administered by its trustees, subject to various restrictions and controls.

During the assessment period the Pension Protection Fund will look to establish the answer to two main questions:

1. Can the scheme be rescued? (For example, can the original employer continue as a going concern, or is another employer going to take the original employer over and assume responsibility for the scheme); and

2. Can the scheme afford to secure benefits which are at least equal to the compensation that the Pension Protection Fund would pay if it assumed responsibility for the scheme?

If the answer to either of these questions is 'yes' then the Pension Protection Fund will cease to be involved with the scheme once the relevant processes and procedures have been completed.

However, if the answer to both the questions is 'no', and the relevant process and procedures have been completed, then the Pension Protection Fund will assume responsibility for the scheme and compensation will then become payable.

A Pension Protection Fund assessment period is likely to last a minimum of one year and could be longer, depending on the complexity of the financial situation of both the employer and the scheme, and the possibility of a scheme rescue.

The role of trustees

During an assessment period, the trustees of the scheme retain responsibility for the administration of the scheme and for communicating with and making pension payments to scheme members. The trustees must continue to Act in the interests of all the scheme members.

However, during an assessment period, various restrictions and controls will apply in relation to the scheme. In particular, pensions will be restricted to Pension Protection Fund compensation levels [see compensation for more details].

The role of the Pensions Regulator

Once a scheme enters an assessment period, the Pension Protection Fund will work closely with the Regulator, keeping it informed of any relevant developments relating to the scheme. The Regulator may use its powers when problems arise on individual schemes.

For further information on the Pensions Regulator, visit its website at www.thepensionsregulator.gov.uk.

The role of the Pension Protection Fund

During an assessment period, the Pension Protection Fund will undertake a monitoring role in relation to the trustees of the scheme. This is to ensure that the trustees maintain the scheme in an appropriate manner for potential entry to the Pension Protection Fund. In certain circumstances, the Pension Protection Fund can issue directions to trustees in relation to areas such as the investment of the scheme's assets, the incurring of expenditure and the bringing or conduct of legal proceedings.

The Pension Protection Fund will also monitor the progress of the insolvency proceedings, liaising closely with the insolvency practitioner.

Where the Pension Protection Fund ultimately assumes responsibility for a scheme, arrangements will then be made to pay compensation to the scheme members.

Source: PPF website

27.19   At the end of the assessment period:

- If the valuation shows that the scheme assets are sufficient to pay at least protected liabilities, the PPF has no further involvement with the scheme and the scheme is required to wind-up outside of the PPF.

- If the valuation shows that the scheme assets are insufficient to pay protected liabilities the scheme enters the PPF. The property, rights and liabilities transfer to the Board of the PPF and the trustees or managers are discharged of their responsibilities towards the scheme and the scheme is treated as if it were wound up.

27.20

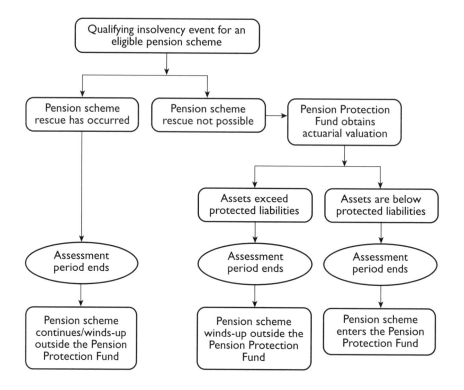

Source: PPF guidance for trustees:
*www.pensionprotectionfund.org.uk/index/trustee_guidance/detailed_trustee_*
guidance/tg_overview.htm

PENSIONS AND ADMINISTRATION – AN OVERVIEW

27.21   The position can get quite complex depending on how many participating employers are in the scheme and what the scheme rules say.

Assuming that a company is the only employer and it enters administration, the following happens in relation to the pension scheme:

1.   The scheme enters an 'assessment period'. The scheme is frozen during this period meaning that there is no further accrual of benefits, no contributions that were not already due are payable (save for any s 75 debt – see 5 below) and benefits are only payable out of the scheme at the PPF protected level. In practice this means that the administrator will stop deducting contributions from pay. The PPF protected level of benefits is (broadly) 100% of pension (for those aged over the NRA) and 90% of benefits, subject to a cap (of about £27,000pa) for those aged under NRA (even those who have retired early). There are special rules on ill health pensions and on pension increases.

428

2.   The administrator has to notify the trustees, the Pension Protection Fund (PPF) and the Pensions Regulator of his appointment and which schemes are in place. The Regulator may (but does not have to) appoint an independent trustee.

3.   The trustees stay in place but are subject to direction by the PPF. Any payments due have to be to the PPF.

4.   The administrator needs to decide in due course whether or not a scheme rescue will be possible. If it is he serves a 'scheme rescue notice'. A scheme rescue would be if the company exited administration in a solvent form or if someone came in and took over the scheme. If a scheme rescue is not possible, the administrator serves a 'scheme failure notice'.

5.   Entry into administration triggers a debt payable by the company under s 75, Pensions Act 1995 (this is unsecured and non-preferential). The debt is fixed by regulations (and quantified by the scheme actuary) as being the amount needed to fund the scheme up to full buy-out level. This debt does not become payable until certified and then only if a scheme failure notice has been issued (see 4).

6.   A full valuation of the scheme is carried out (a s143 valuation) to check if the scheme has sufficient assets (taking account of any s 75 debt recovery) to fund the PPF protected level of benefits. This can take some time (usually at least a year). If it does have sufficient assets, then the scheme will usually wind-up outside the PPF and provide what level of benefits it can. If it cannot then the PPF will take over the scheme and its assets and provide the PPF protected level of benefits itself. Either way the assessment period will then end.

For further details see the guidance on the PPF website:

http://www.pensionprotectionfund.org.uk/index/trustee_guidance/detailed_trustee_guidance.htm

For the impact on scheme specific funding obligations see para 33.102 below.

CHAPTER 28

PPF: notice obligations on IPs/ assessment period

INTRODUCTION

28.1   This Chapter looks at the position of insolvency practitioners (IPs) in relation to occupational pension schemes operated by the corporate body over which the IP has been appointed. This Chapter deals in particular with the inter-relation between the Pension protection Fund (PPF) and an IP under the Pensions Act 2004.

There must have been an insolvency event as defined in s 121 of PA 1994 and reg 5 of the PPF Entry Rules Regulations (see para 18.6 above).

28.2   There is a good introductory summary to PA 2004 in Technical Bulletin 70[1] issued by R3 in June 2005 and revised in May 2006. Guidance for insolvency practitioners has also been issued by the PPF[2].

1 See www.r3.org.uk
2. See www.pensionprotectionfund.org.uk/insolvency_guidance.pdf

What is an IP under the 2004 Act?

28.3   IPs are defined as a person acting as an insolvency practitioner in accordance with s 388 of the Insolvency Act 1986– see PA 2004, s 121(9)(a). There is also power to add other persons by regulations – see PA 2004, s 121(9)(b).

The definition in s 388 covers (in relation to a company) a person acting:

(a)   as its liquidator, provisional liquidator, administrator or administrative receiver, or

(b)   where a voluntary arrangement in relation to the company is proposed or approved under Part I of the Insolvency Act 1986, as nominee or supervisor.

28.4   An insolvency practitioner appointed outside the UK (eg in proceedings in another EU state) will not be an IP for the purposes of the Pensions Act 2004. This is the case, even if the practitioner is appointed in relation to a company incorporated in the UK – see Chapter 40 (Overseas employees and insolvencies) below.

Overview

28.5   The PPF summarises the process in the table in its guidance to IPs:

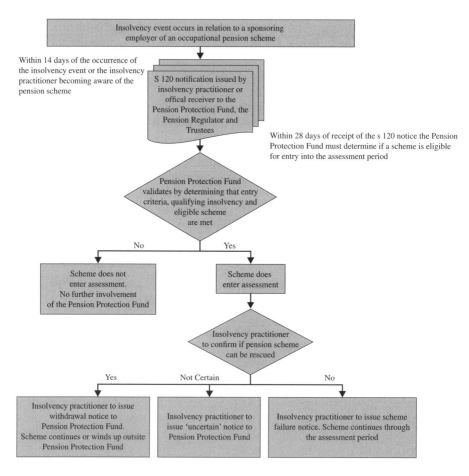

Source: PPF Guidance to IPs on the PPF Website
http://www.pensionprotectionfund.org.uk

NOTICE OBLIGATIONS ON INSOLVENCY PRACTITIONERS

28.6   There are now two separate notification obligations on IPs if they are appointed in relation to an employer of an occupational pension scheme:

(a)   The independent trustee provisions in the Pensions Act 1995 have been amended so that from 6 April 2005 the IP is no longer obliged to ensure that one of the trustees is independent. Instead the IP is obliged to notify the Pensions Regulator (tPR), the PPF and the trustees of his or her appointment. This is discussed further in Chapter 21 below.

(b) Part 2 of PA 2004 deals with the PPF. It includes, in Chapter 2, specific sections dealing with 'Information relating to employer's insolvency etc.'. These apply where an IP starts to act in relation to a person who is an employer in relation to an occupational pension scheme.

- Section 120 imposes a duty on an IP to serve a notice on tPR, the PPF Board and the trustees on becoming aware of the existence of an occupational pension scheme.

- Section 122 imposes a duty on the IP to serve another notice saying whether or not a 'scheme rescue' is possible.

28.7 Both of these obligations apply in relation to any 'occupational pension scheme' – not just defined benefit or HMRC registered (approved before April 2006).

28.8 Useful guidance is given by the PPF in their publication 'Guidance for insolvency practitioners and official receivers', available on the PPF website[1]

1 www.pensionprotectionfund.org.uk

Notice of insolvency event – s 120

28.9 As noted above, s 120 imposes an obligation on an IP acting in relation to an employer to give a notice to the PPF Board, tPR and to the trustees of an occupational pension scheme of the employer.

28.10 An 'employer' for this purpose (and s 122) includes a company which was an employer of active members in a scheme in the past if the company has continued to be treated as an employer for s 75 purposes – ie have a potential liability under s 75 to the scheme (see Chapter 32 and 34 below).

28.11 This is the view taken by the PPF – see the reference to a 'past employer' at page 3 of the PPF Guidance for Insolvency Practitioners (June 2006). This flows from reg 1(4) and (5)[1] of the PPF Entry Rules Regulations which expand the definition of employer in the same way as applies under s 75 (see Chapter 32 below).

1 Note that although reg 1(4) states that it applies for the purposes of Pt 2 of PA 2004, reg 1(5) states that it only applies for the purposes of the PPF Entry Rules regulations. It is not clear why there is a distinction or if, in practice, it matters.

28.12 This notice must be given within the 'notification period'. Under reg 4(1) of the Pension Protection Fund (Entry Rules) Regulations 2005 (SI 2005/590), (the PPF Entry Rules Regulations), this is the 14-day period beginning with the later of:

- the date of the relevant insolvency event – see s 121; and

- the date the insolvency practitioner becomes aware of the existence of the scheme.

28.13   The notice must be in 'such form and contain such information as may be prescribed' by regulations – s 120(4). The relevant information is set out in reg 4(2) of the PPF Entry Rules Regulations:

(a)   the name or type of the notice issued;

(b)   the date on which the notice is issued;

(c)   the name, address and pension scheme registration number of the scheme in respect of which the notice is issued;

(d)   the name of the employer in relation to the scheme in respect of which the notice is issued;

(e)   the nature of the insolvency event which has occurred and the date of the occurrence of that event;

(f)   the name of the insolvency practitioner in relation to the employer in relation to the scheme;

(g)   the date on which the insolvency practitioner acting over the employer in relation to the scheme was appointed to act or consented to act in relation to that employer or, in any case where the insolvency practitioner is the official receiver, the date on which the official receiver began to act in relation to that employer;

(h)   the address for communications at which the insolvency practitioner may be contacted by the PPF Board in connection with the issue of the notice; and

(i)   whether the notice issued contains any commercially sensitive information.

A form of notice is set out on the PPF Board's website[1].

Since April 2009, the PPF has provided an online service for IPs and s120 notices.

The PPF guidance for IPs (April 2009)[2] states:

> '2.4 In order to assist Insolvency Practitioners to comply with their statutory obligation under section 120, we have provided an online service, which is available on the Pension Protection Fund website at http://www.pensionprotectionfund.org.uk/index/forms/insolvency_practitioners.htm
>
> This facility enables the Insolvency Practitioner to enter the employer's name (the company name in which it last meaningfully traded), the individual IP registration number and the date and type of insolvency event on the site. If there is an occupational pension scheme in existence, the website will cause the necessary notice to be sent to the PPF, the Pensions Regulator and the trustees. Insolvency Practitioners will receive a reply advising them that the notice has been sent or that there is no scheme. In some limited circumstances, our databases will not be able to provide the information necessary for the facility to work. However, if that is the case, the Insolvency Practitioner will instead be advised to submit a s120 notice in the way described above.'

The Dear IP newsletter[3] from the Insolvency Service commented:

56) Pensions Act 2004 – new online section 120 notice service

Insolvency practitioners will soon be able to submit section 120 notices – which inform the Pension Protection Fund (PPF) about a company insolvency – through a new online service on the PPF website.

Under the relevant provisions, insolvency practitioners must send section 120 notices when any company which has an occupational pension scheme becomes insolvent. From 3 April 2009, insolvency practitioners should, for the first time, be able to submit these notices online.

The new service:

- makes use of a number of databases held by the PPF and will save insolvency practitioners considerable time, cost and effort

- enables insolvency practitioners to enter the employer's name, their individual IP registration number, the date they were appointed to act for that employer and the type and date of the insolvency event directly onto the web-based form rather than send a paper section 120 return. Insolvency practitioners should use the last name used by the company for meaningful trading, as any last minute name changes may not have filtered through to the PPF

- automatically sends a notice to the PPF, the Pensions Regulator and the scheme trustees if an occupational pension scheme exists, and

- sends a reply to insolvency practitioners confirming that a notice has been sent, and to whom – or that there is no eligible scheme.

But, there may be instances where the PPF does not hold the necessary information. If that is the case, it will tell practitioners to meet their statutory obligations by sending a paper section 120 notice, as they do now.

The new service can be found on the PPF website at http://www.ppf-forms.org.uk. Further information about section 120 obligations can also be found on the website at www.pensionprotectionfund.org.uk.

1 See www.pensionprotectionfund.org.uk/420308_s120notice.pdf
2 www.pensionprotectionfund.org.uk
3 Article 56 in Chapter 17 (Legislation). See the March 2009 update and www.insolvency.gov.uk/insolvencyprofessionandlegislation/dearip/dearipmill/hardcopy.htm

Insolvency event

28.14   An insolvency event is defined in PA 2004, s 121 – see Chapter 27 above.

A duty to notify can arise even if the insolvency event follows a previous insolvency event (which may already have been notified).

Notice of scheme status – s 122

28.15   Having notified the relevant persons that a relevant insolvency event has occurred (and an insolvency practitioner has been appointed), the IP comes under a further duty to issue notices confirming the status of the pension scheme (PA 2004, s 122).

28.16   This obligation only applies where a relevant insolvency event has occurred in relation to an employer (or a past employer – see above) in relation to an occupational pension scheme (not a personal pension scheme).

28.17   If the IP is able to confirm either:

● that a 'scheme rescue' is not possible (a scheme failure notice); or

● that a 'scheme rescue' has occurred (a withdrawal notice),

he or she must issue a notice to that effect – PA 2004, s 122(2). This notice must be copied to the PPF Board, tPR and the trustees of the pension scheme – PA 2004, s 122(6).

28.18   Again specimen forms are available on the PPF Board's website[1]. This notice must be issued as soon as reasonably practicable – s 122(7).

1 See www.pensionprotectionfund.org.uk/index/forms/insolvency_practitioners.htm

28.19   In addition, if, in prescribed circumstances, insolvency proceedings in relation to the employer are stayed or come to an end or a prescribed event occurs, then the person who is acting as an IP in relation to the employer immediately before that event must (if he has not been able already to give a notice about scheme rescue not being possible or having occurred), issue a notice to that effect – PA 2004, s 122(3) and (4). Again, this notice must be issued to the PPF Board, tPR and the trustees of the scheme as soon as reasonably practicable.

28.20   It is not clear to whom the original notice under s 122(2) or (4) must actually be issued – s 122(6) envisages that it is only copied to the PPF Board, tPR and Trustees. This is probably just inelegant drafting.

Again, this obligation applies in relation to any occupational pension scheme.

28.21   If the IP (or a former IP) fails to issue a notice that was required under s 122, the PPF Board may issue the notice instead – s 124. The PPF Board must copy the notice to tPR, the trustees of the relevant occupational pension scheme and to the IP (or if there is no IP, to the employer) – PA 2004, s 124(4).

Scheme rescue

28.22   Clearly key to these obligations are the questions of what is a 'scheme rescue' and whether or not it has occurred or is not possible. These are issues that are dealt with in relevant regulations – see PA 2004, s 122(5).

28.23   The term 'scheme rescue' is defined in reg 9 of the PPF Entry Rules Regulations[1]. In relation to a corporate employer a scheme rescue has occurred if (reg 9(1)):

(i) the company has been rescued as a going concern and the employer:

(a) retains responsibility for meeting the pension liabilities under the scheme, and

(b) has not entered into a binding agreement with the PPF to reduce the amount of the s 75 debt; or

(ii) another person or other persons has or have assumed responsibility for meeting the employer's pension liabilities under the scheme.

1 The Pension Protection Fund (Entry Rules) Regulations 2005, SI 2005/590, (the PPF Entry Rules Regulations).

28.24 In relation to a corporate employer, a scheme rescue is not possible if (reg 9(2)):

(i) the company has entered into an agreement after the assessment period began with the board of the PPF to reduce the amount of the s 75 debt (within reg 2(3)(c) – see below); or

(ii) the company is not continuing as a going concern and:

(a) no other person or persons has or have assumed responsibility for meeting the employer's pension liabilities under the scheme, and

(b) the insolvency practitioner is of the opinion that the employer's pension liabilities under the scheme will not be assumed by another person.

SANCTIONS FOR FAILURE TO GIVE NOTICES

28.25 There is no specific sanction in PA 2004 on an IP for failure to issue these notices under ss 120 and 122.

28.26 However, broadly these notices are designed to provide information to the PPF Board in relation to the potential for it to take over a relevant occupational pension scheme. The PPF will report IPs to their relevant Recognised Professional Bodies (RPBs) if they come across failures by IPs to give the relevant notices. The RPBs regulate the conduct of insolvency practitioners.

R3 commented on this in its bulletin to members in June 2008:

'Pensions & Members' obligations under the Pensions Act 2004

In the October 2007 edition of this bulletin, we drew your attention to members' failings in relation to Sections 120, 122 & 137 of this Act as the Pension Protection Fund "PPF" advised that there were serious delays in the notification of eligible schemes. We also advised you that the PPF were granting our members an amnesty to get their houses in order up which would expire on 1 January 2008.

Despite this warning, the position has not improved and our Training Director, David White, was advised by the PPF last month that currently, there were 208 notifications that were received more than 28 days after the date of which the officeholder first became aware of the pension scheme(s). David was also advised that in one sample batch of late notifications, the days late varied between 331 and 987 days late. Needless to say, all the miscreants have been reported to their RPBs.

The PPF have advised that they are now reporting all late notifications to the license holders' RPBs without exception. From the enquiries the PPF have made, it seems that simple checks such as examining the annual accounts or reviewing the payroll for deductions are not being done.'

The Insolvency Service in its Annual Review of Insolvency Practitioner Regulation (published in July 2009) included data on complaints made to the various RPBs.

The review includes (at page 19) the statistic that the PPF made over 27% of all complaints received by the RPBs (229 out of 828). The review reports that the PPF's complaints were 'in respect of possible failures of insolvency practitioners to notify the PPF that the employer of an occupational pension scheme was subject to a formal insolvency procedure'.

1 www.insolvency.gov.uk/insolvencyprofessionandlegislation/iparea/INS_Practitioners.pdf

ASSESSMENT PERIODS

28.27 If a 'qualifying insolvency event' (as defined in PA 2004, s127(3)) occurs in relation to an eligible scheme, then the 'assessment period' begins – see s 132.

28.28 A qualifying insolvency event is an insolvency event (see s 121 and Chapter 18 above) which does not fall within an existing assessment period. There are special rules for multi-employer schemes (see Chapter 36 below).

28.29 An 'eligible scheme' is (PA 2004, s 126) a scheme which:

- is not a money purchase scheme (ie a scheme providing only money purchase benefits – see PSA 1993, s 181(1), as applied by PA 2004, s 318(1) – see Chapter 29 below); and

- is not excluded by regulations – s 126(1)(b); and

- is not being wound-up immediately before 6 April 2005 – s 126(2).

28.30 Regulation 2 of the PPF Entry Rules Regulations defines an eligible scheme to exclude various schemes. These are discussed in the chart in Chapter 31 below.

28.31 The PPF website summarises the effect of reg 2 as follows:

However, some schemes will be exempt from the Pension Protection Fund. Regulations set out those schemes which are exempt from the Pension Protection Fund. This list is not exhaustive, however it is likely that the following pension schemes would be exempt:

- unfunded public service schemes;

- public sector schemes providing pensions to local government employees;

- schemes to which a minister of the Crown has given a guarantee;

- schemes which are not tax approved (or tax registered from April 2006) nor relevant statutory schemes under the tax rules for pension schemes;

- schemes with fewer than two members;

- schemes providing death in service benefits only;

- schemes which are relevant lump sum retirement benefit schemes;

- Chatsworth Estate Settlement Pension Scheme;

- schemes with fewer than 12 members where all members are trustees of the scheme;

- cross border schemes where the pension scheme in question is not UK registered;

- a superannuation fund as is mentioned in s 615(6) of the Income and Corporation Taxes Act 1988.

Schemes with a Crown guarantee will be exempt from the Pension Protection Fund. Schemes with a partial Crown guarantee will only be liable to pay the Pension Protection Fund levies for that part of the scheme that does not have a Crown guarantee.

Schemes which began to wind up or were completely wound up prior to 6 April 2005 are exempt from the Pension Protection Fund.

In addition, except in certain circumstances, schemes where a compromise agreement has been reached between the scheme trustees and the employer concerning a debt under s 75 of the Pensions Act 1995, will also be exempt from the Pension Protection Fund.

Source: PPF Website www.pensionprotectionfund.org.uk

28.32 The last paragraph in the PPF summary in the box above is a reference to reg 2(2) of the PPF Entry Rules Regulations and deals with agreements that have the effect of reducing an employer debt under PA 1995,s 75. This is discussed further in Chapter 35 below.

Assessment period

28.33   An assessment period starts when a qualifying insolvency event occurs – s 132. This may well be before the trustees receive the notice from the IP. The PPF will only confirm that it considers the scheme to be eligible after it receives the s 120 notice from the IP (its guidance indicates that it will try to do this within 28 days of receipt of the notice and relevant information, but this is not a period fixed in the legislation). The effect will be to confirm that the assessment period started when the relevant insolvency started.

28.34   During the assessment period:

- the PPF Board considers whether or not it needs to take over the pension scheme;

- Accrual of benefits and the powers of the trustees are limited during this period (see ss 132 to 142):

    - No new members can be admitted (s 133(2)).

    - No further contributions can be paid to the scheme – s 133(3) – save as prescribed in regulations (or which fell due and payable before the assessment period). Regulation 14 of the PPF Entry Rules Regulations allows an employer to pay further contributions where those contributions relate to:

        (a)   all or any part of that employer's liability for any debt due from him to the scheme under s 75 of PA 1995 which has not yet been discharged; and

        (b)   the value of an asset of the scheme arising from a debt or obligation referred to in s 143(5)(a) to (d) of the Act (Board's obligation to obtain valuation of assets and protected liabilities). Section 143(5) relates to statutory obligations on an employer under various provisions, including s 75 PA 1995 and under contribution notices, financial support directions or restoration orders issued by the Pensions Regulator under PA 2004.

    - No benefits can accrue (PA 2004, s 133(5)), save for an increase which would otherwise accrue in accordance with the scheme or an enactment (s 133(6)) This seems to envisage that there will be no additional pensionable service. Benefits payable are also subject to the limits in s138. Money purchase benefits can also accrue – s 133(8).

    - The board of the PPF can give directions to the trustees (or employer or scheme administrator) regarding exercise of his powers in relation to investment of scheme assets, expenditure, conduct of legal proceedings and amendments to the scheme[1] – s 134;

    - Schemes cannot start to wind-up unless this is ordered by the Pensions Regulator – s 135(2) and (3);

- Transfers out of the scheme can only be made in prescribed circumstances – s 135(4) and (5);

- Contribution refunds (for members whose pensionable service terminates with less than two years qualifying service) – s 135(6) and (7)

- Payment of scheme benefits is limited to the amounts that would be protected by the PPF (s 138).

- The Board of PPF is able to validate actions that would otherwise be prohibited (and so void) under s 135 (winding-up, discharge of liabilities etc) – s 136. This power does not extend to the prohibitions under s 134 (admission of new members, contributions etc).

- The PPF takes control of all rights of the pension scheme trustees as creditors (s 137). All relevant documents about creditor status (eg notices of creditor meetings and proof of debt forms) should be sent to the PPF (and not the trustees).

- All payments from the employer should go to the PPF (s 137).

1 Power to give directions in relation to scheme amendments added with effect from 21 July 2009 by the Pension Protection Fund (Entry Rules) (Amendment) Regulations 2009 (SI 2009/1552).

28.35   Contact details for the PPF are set out in the 'Guidance for insolvency practitioners and official receivers' on the PPF Board's website[1].

1 See www.pensionprotectionfund.org.uk/insolvency_guidance.pdf.

28.36   The trustees remain responsible for the administration of the scheme. So the R3 technical bulletin points out that enquiries from employees or pensioners should be passed to the trustees (and not the PPF).

28.37   A valuation of the scheme is prepared under PA 2004, s 143 to check if the funding level of the scheme is greater or lower than the amount needed to secure the PPF protected level of benefits.

Section 143 of the Pensions Act 2004 envisages that the PPF must, as soon as reasonably practical, obtain an actuarial valuation of the scheme as at the 'relevant time'. This ties in with s 127(2)(a) dealing with the duty of the PPF to assume responsibility of schemes following an insolvency event. The 'relevant time' is the time immediately before the qualifying insolvency event occurs – s 127(4)(b).

Section 143 allows for regulations to prescribe how assets and liabilities etc are to be determined, calculated and verified, and for certain various liabilities to be included or excluded. Section 143(6) also allows the PPF to issue guidance for the purposes of the actuarial valuation.

Sections 144 and 145 then deal with approval of valuations and when they become binding.

The relevant regulations are the Pension Protection Fund (Valuation) Regulations 2005 (SI 2005/672 as amended).

The regulations exclude from s 143 valuations amounts treated as a debt due to the trustees which are unlikely to be recouped without disproportionate costs or unlikely to recovered within a reasonable time – reg 3(a). The reference to 'amounts treated as a debt' is slightly odd here, but may be intended to cover s 75 liabilities.

Amounts due under the schedule of contributions, s 75 and employer-related investments etc are also excluded specifically for s 179 valuations (PPF levy) but not for s 143 valuations.

There are special rules for insurance policies etc.

Amounts due under contribution notices, financial support directions and restoration orders are included as an asset of the scheme if the relevant notice, direction or order was issued by the Regulator before the date the valuation is approved – reg 4.

Assets are to be valued by adopting 'the value of the assets of the scheme stated in the relevant accounts' – reg 5. The 'relevant accounts' are audited accounts for the scheme prepared in respect of the period ending with the 'relevant time' of the valuation.

The term 'relevant time' is defined in the regulations, but only for the purposes of s 179 (PPF levy calculations). It seems that for the purposes of s 143, the same definition of 'relevant time' should be used as in s 143 – that used in s 127(4)(b) i.e. the time immediately before the qualifying insolvency event.

This points to relevant accounts needing to be prepared and audited up to the date of the insolvency event.

The level of protected liabilities used in the valuation is fixed under reg 6. For a s 143 valuation, this is the cost of securing the relevant protected benefits (see Sch 7 to the Pensions Act 2004) to the member 'by means of an annuity purchased at the market rate at the relevant time' – reg 6(1)(a).

This is to be contrasted with the liability cost for a s 179 valuation, where guidance issued by the PPF under s 179(4) needs to be followed.

The net effect of this seems to be that market rates at the relevant time for annuity purchases need to be used for s 143 valuations (but not necessarily for s 179 valuations, where a prescribed set of market rates can be imposed by the PPF).

28.38   The PPF Board ceases to be involved with the scheme (and the assessment period ends) if a withdrawal event occurs – s 149. A withdrawal event includes the issuing by an IP of a withdrawal notice under s 122(2)(b) confirming that a scheme rescue has occurred – s 149(2)(a).

A withdrawal notice under s 122(2)(b) requires the IP to confirm that a scheme rescue has occurred (see above).

28.39   An assessment period ends when:

- The PPF assumes responsibility for the scheme; or

- A withdrawal notice becomes effective (eg that a scheme rescue has occurred).

28.40 According to the PPF guidance for Trustees:

The assessment period will conclude with the Board of the Pension Protection Fund assuming responsibility for a scheme when the following conditions have been met:

- A pension scheme rescue is not possible and a scheme failure notice is binding.

- A s 143 valuation shows that the pension scheme's assets are not sufficient to secure the Pension Protection Fund protected liabilities.

- The Board of the Pension Protection Fund's approval of the s 143 valuation is binding.

Within two months of the s 143 valuation becoming binding the Pension Protection Fund is required to issue a transfer notice.

On receipt of the notice the trustees are discharged of their responsibilities for administering the scheme and the assets and prescribed liabilities are transferred to the Board of the Pension Protection Fund.

The pension scheme is then treated as having wound up.

Source: PPF Guidance for Trustees

CHAPTER 29

tPR/PPF: Notifications and power to gather information

PPF

29.1   Sections 190 to 194 of PA 2004 give powers to the PPF Board to gather relevant information. Section 191(3)(d) expressly includes an insolvency practitioner (IP) in relation to an employer within the list of persons who can be required to provide information to the PPF following a written notice from the PPF.

TPR

29.2   There is a similar information provision power given to tPR – see PA 2004, s 72. Unlike s 191, this does not expressly state that it applies to IPs, but it does apply to professional advisers and employers and 'any other person appearing to the Regulator to be a person who holds, or is likely to hold, information relevant to the exercise of the Regulator's functions'. It seems likely that IPs are within this provision.

29.3   Failure to provide information is an offence (ss 77 and 193) (on indictment, fine and/or imprisonment of up to two years). Providing false or misleading information to the PPF Board or tPR is also an offence if done knowingly or recklessly – PA 2004, ss 80 and 195.

20.4   If a corporate employer commits an offence under PA 2004, then any relevant director, manager, secretary 'or other similar officer' can also be guilty of an offence if the offence of the company was committed with the 'consent or connivance of, or is attributable to any neglect on the part of' that person – PA 2004, s 309. It seems likely that this will extend to an IP who has control over a body corporate (see Chapter 8 (personal liability of insolvency practitioners) above).

NOTIFIABLE EVENTS – S 69

29.5   There is an obligation on employers in relation to eligible schemes to notify tPR of various events (PA 2004, s 69). The events are specified in the Pensions Regulator (Notifiable Events) Regulations 2005[1].

'Eligible schemes' are those eligible to be covered by the PPF, ie all schemes that are not money purchase schemes, prescribed schemes (eg schemes without Inland Revenue approval or registration) and schemes being wound up immediately before 6 April 2005 – see the chart at Chapter 31 below.

The notifiable events were amended with effect from 6 April 2009[2]. The two notifiable events (applicable to an employer) relating to a change in credit rating or a change in key employer posts were deleted. Such changes are no longer automatically notifiable.

1 SI 2005/900.
2 Occupational Pension Schemes (Miscellaneous Amendments) Regulations 2009 (SI 2005/2113).

29.6   The obligation does not apply if the Pensions Regulator otherwise directs – s 69(1). General directions were issued by tPR on 6 April 2005[1].

1 www.thepensionsregulator.gov.uk/pdf/Directions.pdf. See the chart at the end of this chapter.

29.7   A chart detailing the employer-related events (there are also trustee related events that the trustees are obliged to notify) is set out at the end of this chapter.

29.8   The list of notifiable events includes several that may well be relevant for an IP acting in relation to an employer:

- Any decision by an employer to compromise a debt owed to a scheme;

- A decision by the employer to cease to carry on business in the UK,

- Receipt of advice by the employer that it is trading wrongfully (within IA 1986, s 214),

- Breach of a banking covenant;

- Decision to relinquish control of an employer company.

The notifiable event in relation to debts is potentially quite wide. The term debt includes a contingent debt – see reg 1(2) of the Pensions Regulator (Notifiable Events) Regulations 2005.

See para 35.8 below for a discussion of this provision in relation to a potential s 75 debt and entry into a scheme apportionment arrangement (SAA) under the Employer Debt Regulations.

29.9   The obligation is to notify tPR as soon as reasonably practicable after the person becomes aware of the notifiable event (this can be before the actual action concerned, where regulations so require – eg the event that is a decision to make a transfer payment must be notified before the actual transfer is made).

29.10   The tPR Code of Practice[1] indicates that the obligation implies urgency[1]:

> 'For example, where a trustee is made aware of a notifiable event on a Sunday, the Regulator should be notified on Monday.'

1 Regulatory Code of Practice 02 on 'Notifiable Events'. See the tPR website: www.thepensionsregulator.gov.uk/pdf/codeNotifiableFinal.pdf
2 Para 16.

29.11   The tPR code of practice suggests that a procedure for making notifications should be put in place[1]. It envisages that there will not be a need for specialist advice, or to hold a trustee or board meeting, about the notification[2].

1 Regulatory Code of Practice 02, Para 17.
2 Para 18.

29.12   The notice to tPR must be in writing[1]; email and fax are acceptable[2].

A   standard   form   is   available   on   the   tPR   website   –   see www.thepensionsregulator.gov.uk.

1 PA 2004, s69(4)(a).
2 Regulatory Code of Practice 02, Para 21.

29.13   A trustee, actuary or other person under a duty to report breaches in the law to tPR under PA 2004, s 70, (see below) will be obliged to make a report if it becomes aware of a failure by the trustees or employer to notify under s 69.

Penalties

29.14   Failure to notify without reasonable excuse renders the company liable to a civil penalty under s 10 of PA 1995 (civil penalties). The maximum civil penalty is £50,000 for companies and £5,000 for individuals. Again, this penalty can extend to officers etc (and can catch IPs) – see PA 1995, s 10, and Chapter 8 above.

29.15   tPR has indicated in the code of practice that it will seek an explanation about any failure to notify. It has a range of actions it can take, including training or other assistance. tPR will also have regard to any failure to notify a relevant event when deciding whether or not to issue a contribution notice (under the moral hazard powers given to tPR by PA 2004 – see Chapter 37 below).

29.16   If a financial support direction has been made (or before April 2008 an approved withdrawal arrangement agreed under s 75 and the Employer Debt Regulations), the persons subject to the direction will also be obliged to notify various matters to tPR. These are likely also to include the s 69 events.

BREACHES OF LAW – S 70

29.17   Similarly, there is an obligation on employers and others involved with eligible pension schemes to notify tPR of relevant breaches of law (defined as a breach of legislation or a rule of law relating to the administration of the scheme and material to tPR) – see s 70. Again, there is a civil penalty under PA 1995, s 10, for failure without reasonable excuse to comply. As in relation to notifiable events under s 69, this civil penalty could attach to an IP.

The duty

29.18   Each of these persons must give a written report of the matter to tPR as soon as reasonably practicable where the person has reasonable cause to believe that:

- a duty relevant to the administration of the scheme has not been or is not being complied with; and

- that duty is 'imposed by or by virtue of an enactment or rule of law'; and

- the failure to comply is likely to be of material significance to tPR in the exercise of any of its functions.

Reasonable cause to believe

29.19   This looks like an objective test. So it would not be enough for a person under a duty to say that he or she did not realise there was a breach of duty.

29.20   Presumably building on this, the code of practice issued by tPR states that it considers those under a reporting duty should set up a formal internal procedure for ensuring that potential reporting events are recognised and considered. Even if not reported initially (because the breach is minor and so not material), tPR argues that it should be recorded internally in case a pattern emerges (which then could be material and so reportable).

29.21   The guidance also envisages that those under a reporting duty should investigate the position (eg ask questions of the trustees) if they have doubts about something and that they should take professional advice if they have doubts about whether there has been a breach of a relevant law.

What duties count

29.22   It is not very clear what duties are relevant for this purpose. It must be a breach of a duty relevant to the administration of the scheme. Clearly not all breaches of legislation trigger the duty to report to tPR. The breach must be 'relevant to the administration of the scheme'. It is not very clear what this is trying to specify. The code of practice issued by tPR states that it interprets this widely to include 'anything which could potentially affect members' benefits or the ability of members and others to access information to which they are entitled'.

29.23   This is pretty wide and will, in practice, catch practically all breaches by the trustees in relation to the scheme (eg of pensions legislation) and other breaches that could be relevant (eg a criminal offence involving dishonesty under some other statute).

29.24   The reporting obligation is not limited to breaches of duty by the trustees of a scheme. So it will cover breaches by third parties (eg the employer, an adviser, an administrator). Here the limitation that it must relate to the administration of the scheme is more relevant. A breach of some duty not relevant to the scheme is not reportable.

It must be imposed by an enactment or rule of law

Enactment

29.25   This is clearly any duty laid down in acts of parliament and statutory instruments (eg the disclosure regulations) (see definition of 'enactment' in PA 2004, s 318). The obligation is not limited to pensions legislation. So it includes other legislation (eg the Data Protection Act, the Trustee Acts, employment legislation, the discrimination legislation – possibly even the Human Rights Act).

Rule of law

29.26   The term 'rule of law' is more vague. Presumably it will include fiduciary duties imposed by law on trustees. It is not clear if contractual duties are to be included. This seems more unlikely (is it a rule of law that a contracting party must comply with its obligations?). General tort duties may fit in more readily. The question of whether the implied duty of mutual trust and confidence is to be included is also unclear.

Material significance to tPR in the exercise of any of its functions

29.27   The breach of duty must be 'likely' to be material to tPR. tPR has some fairly general functions (eg to wind up schemes, make court applications, collect information relevant to the PPF, prohibit trustees if they are not 'fit and proper'). So the ambit of this duty may be pretty wide.

29.28   tPR has issued a code of practice about what it wants under this section. This makes it clear that not all breaches are reportable. It states that material significance will depend on: the cause of the breach; the effect of the breach; the reaction to the breach; and the wider implications of the breach.

29.29   So, for example, tPR regards anything involving dishonesty or a breach that has a criminal penalty (eg making an employer-related loan) as always being material. However, an isolated breach of a less material duty which is promptly addressed by the trustees is probably not material.

29.30   A report to tPR must be:

- in writing; and

- given as soon as reasonably practicable after the person has reasonable cause to believe there is a reportable breach.

CONFLICTING DUTIES

29.31   Any duty owed by a person is not breached merely by making a report under ss 69 or 70 (PA 2004, ss 69(6) and 70(3)). Communications between a professional legal adviser and his client in connection with giving legal advice are protected (PA 2004, s 311). In the absence of legal proceedings being contemplated, this does not cover communications with third parties eg other advisers.

PENALTIES

29.32   Section 10 of the Pensions Act 1995 (civil penalties) applies for non-compliance without reasonable excuse. The maximum civil penalty is £50,000 for companies and £5,000 for individuals.

29.33   If a penalty falls on a company, any director or officer who consented to or connived in the act or omission or to whose neglect the act or omission was attributable may also be liable for a civil penalty. This is likely to extend to an IP – see Chapter 8 (personal liability of insolvency practitioners) above.

29.34   tPR has issued guidance and codes of practice on these provisions[1].

1 See http://www.thepensionsregulator.gov.uk/codesAndGuidance.

EMPLOYERS: EMPLOYER-RELATED NOTIFIABLE EVENTS

29.35

Employers (employer-related) reg 2(2)	*Exemption Conditions*	*Comment*
Debt recovery: (a) any decision by the employer to take action which will, or is intended to, result in a debt which is or may become due to the scheme not being paid in full.	None	Relates to any debt (not just ones from employer). Applies at decision stage. Wording is fairly wide – eg could apply to a release of a guarantee or change in employer.
Cease to carry on UK business: (b) a decision by the employer to cease to carry on business in the United Kingdom, or where the employer ceases to carry on business in the United Kingdom without such a decision having been taken, the cessation of business in the United Kingdom by that employer.	None	Applies at decision stage.

Employers (employer-related) *reg 2(2)*	*Exemption Conditions*	*Comment*
Wrongful trading advice etc: (c) receipt by the employer of advice that it is trading wrongfully within the meaning of s 214 of the Insolvency Act 1986 (wrongful trading), or circumstances being reached in which a director or former director of the company knows that there is no reasonable prospect that the company will avoid going into insolvent liquidation within the meaning of that section	None	Section 214(4) ...the facts which a director of a company ought to know or ascertain, the conclusions which he ought to reach and the steps which he ought to take are those which would be known or ascertained, or reached or taken, by a reasonably diligent person having both: (i) the general knowledge, skill and experience that may reasonably be expected of a person carrying out the same functions as are carried out by that director in relation to the company, and (ii) the general knowledge, skill and experience that that director has.
Breach of banking covenant: (d) any breach by the employer of a covenant in an agreement between the employer and a bank or other institution providing banking services, other than where the bank or other institution agrees with the employer not to enforce the covenant	A and B	Bank waiver means no notification obligation (but waiver would need to be before breach occurred)
Credit rating change before 6 April 2009: (e) any change in the employer's credit rating, or the employer ceasing to have a credit rating;	A, B and D	From 6 April 2009, this event was removed from the legislation Applied to any change (even if an improvement). Only applied to employer – not to (say) parent.
Decision to relinquish control: (f) a decision by a controlling company to relinquish control of an employer company, or where the controlling company relinquishes such control without a decision to do so having been taken, the relinquishing of control of the employer company by that controlling company	A and B	Covers the sale of any participating employer. Covers some group restructurings and probably decision to place participating employer in insolvency process. Applies at parent co decision stage.

Employers (employer-related) reg 2(2)	*Exemption Conditions*	*Comment*
Changes in key employer posts before 6 April 2009: (g) two or more changes in the holders of any key employer posts within the previous 12 months	A and B	From 6 April 2009, this event was removed from the legislation Included chief executive and any director or partner responsible in whole or part for financial affairs. Cumulative for each.
Conviction of a director: (h) the conviction of an individual, in any jurisdiction, for an offence involving dishonesty, if the offence was committed while the individual was a director or partner of the employer.	None	

29.36   Condition A is that the scheme is fully funded for the purposes of a 'section 179 valuation' (likely to be PPF buy-out) (MFR applies where no s 179 valuation has yet been carried out).

29.37   Condition B is that the trustees or managers have not incurred a duty to make a report (to tPR or Opra) in the previous 12 months under s 228(2) of the Pensions Act 2004 or s 59(1) of the Pensions Act 1995 of a materially significant failure by the employer to make a payment to the scheme in accordance with the schedule of contributions (see para 33.74 below).

29.38   Condition D was that the change in credit rating was not from investment to sub-investment grade where the credit rating was provided by a recognised credit rating agency (Standard and Poor's, Moody's or Fitch).

CHAPTER 30

Independent trustee obligations

SUMMARY

30.1 From 1990 to 2005, insolvency practitioners (IPs) appointed in relation to an employer were required to ensure that one of the trustees of a relevant occupational pension scheme is an independent person. These provisions were in ss 22 to 26B of the Pensions Act 1995.

30.2 With effect from 6 April 2005, this changed. The Pensions Act 2004 amended the independent trustee provisions in the Pensions Act 1995. There is now no requirement for there to be an independent person appointed. Any appointment of an independent trustee (IT) will be by the new Pensions Regulator (tPR), instead of by the insolvency practitioner.

The provisions do not apply to personal pension schemes[1].

1 But note the changes (from September 2005) to the definitions of the terms 'occupational pension scheme' and 'personal pension scheme' in s 1 of the Pension Schemes Act 1993, by s 239 of the Pensions Act 2004. See para 2.60 above.

POSITION BEFORE 6 APRIL 2005

30.3 When the employer in relation to a relevant occupational pension scheme had an insolvency practitioner (liquidator, administrator, administrative receiver) appointed to act, that IP had a duty to ensure that one of the trustees is an independent person. If not, the IP had to appoint an independent trustee (PA 1995, ss 22 and 23).

30.4 All the discretionary powers of the trustees (and powers vested in the employer in a trustee capacity) pass to the independent trustee (PA 1995, s 25(2)).

30.5 There were various exemptions from ss 22 to 26 (eg unapproved schemes, money purchase schemes) and amplifications (eg who is 'independent') in the 1997 Independent Trustee Regulations[1]. The 1997 Regulations also contained special provisions for multi-employer schemes.

For a detailed explanation of these provisions, see the second edition of this book.

1 Occupational Pension Schemes (Independent Trustee) Regulations 1997 (SI 1997/252 as amended by SI 1997/3038).

NEW RULES FROM 6 APRIL 2005

30.6   Section 36 of the Pensions Act 2004 amended ss 22 to 25 of the Pensions Act 1995 with effect on and from 6 April 2005. In insolvencies from that date, the Pensions Regulator (tPR) has taken over from the IP the responsibility for appointing an independent trustee.

30.7   Appointment of an independent trustee has ceased to be a requirement. Instead tPR has a discretion about whether or not to appoint an independent trustee.

As before, all the discretionary powers of the trustees (and powers vested in the employer in a trustee capacity) pass to the independent trustee if one is appointed by tPR under s 23 – see s 25(2).

30.8   Appointment of an independent person (within s 23) who is also on the register maintained by the Pensions Regulator under s 23(4) can, even prior to the onset of employer insolvency, also mean that a small occupational scheme is exempt form various provisions (even if all decisions do not need unanimity among member trustees). If there is such an independent trustee, the small scheme (less than 12 members who are all trustees) can still be exempt from:

● eligibility for entry into the Pension Protection Fund (and so does not have to pay the PPF levy) – see regs 2(1)(l) and 2(1)(m) of the Pension Protection Fund (Entry Rules) Regulations 2005 (SI 2005/590, as amended);

● the scheme specific funding provisions in PA 2004 – see regs 17(10(h) and (i) of the Occupational Pension Schemes (Scheme Funding) Regulations 2005 (SI 2005/3377, as amended); and

● the employer debt provisions in s 75, PA 1995 – see regs 4(1)(i) and (j) of the Occupational Pension Schemes (Employer Debt) Regulations 2005 (SI 2005/678, as amended).

See also the chart in Chapter 31 (Scope of the main pensions legislation) below.

Multi-employer schemes

30.9   In relation to a multi-employer scheme, the obligations under ss 22 to 26 of PA 1995 apply separately in relation to each employer[1]. The net effect is that each IP is under the relevant notification and other obligations.

1. Occupational Pension Schemes (Independent Trustee) Regulations 2005 (SI 2005/703), reg 10.

IP OBLIGATION TO NOTIFY TPR AND PPF

30.10   From 6 April 2005, the IP has ceased to have a role in the appointment of an IT under the statute. Instead the IP is required to notify (in writing) the Pensions Regulator, the trustees and the board of the Pension Protection Fund (PPF) of his or her appointment as soon as reasonably practicable (PA 1995, s 22(2B)). The IP must also give notice of ceasing to act (if after the cessation, s 22 will no longer apply to the scheme).

An IP for this purpose is a person who begins to act as an insolvency practitioner (as defined in the Insolvency Act 1986, s388) in relation to an employer in relation to the scheme – see Pensions Act 1995, ss 22(1)(a) and (3). The definition in s 388 covers (in relation to a company) a person acting:

(a)   as its liquidator, provisional liquidator, administrator or administrative receiver, or

(b)   where a voluntary arrangement in relation to the company is proposed or approved under Part I of the Insolvency Act 1986, as nominee or supervisor.

Note that the s22 obligation extends to a liquidator in a members' voluntary liquidation (MVL). MVLs are generally outside the new definition of an 'insolvency event' in the Pensions Act 2004, (see PA 2004, s 121(2)), but this does not apply for the purposes of the independent trustee obligations in ss 22 to 26 of the 1995 Act – PA 1995, s 22(3), was not amended by PA 2004.

30.11   This applies in relation to all occupational pension schemes (ie there is no exemption for, say, unregistered schemes or money purchase schemes).

30.12   This notification obligation rests alongside the separate obligation on IPs to notify the PPF, tPR and trustees under ss 120 and 122 of the PA 2004 (see Chapter 19 above).

30.13   The information to be provided by the IP is set out in reg 8 of the Occupational Pension Schemes (Independent Trustee) Regulations 2005[1]. This information is included within the information that also needs to be provided by an IP under s 120(2)[2] for PPF purposes, so the two notices can usefully be sent at the same time (arguably the notices need to be separate however – they must each specify that they are being given under the relevant section of PA 2004).

Note that this notification obligation under PA 2004, s 120 also applies to all occupational pension schemes, not just those eligible to enter the PPF.

1 SI 2005/703
2 See para 28.9 above and reg 4(2) of the Pension Protection Fund (Entry Rules) Regulations 2005 (SI 2005/590).

WHEN DO THE RULES UNDER PA 2004 APPLY?

30.14   The new rules apply in cases of formal insolvency of an employer (as previously[1]). They will also apply in addition if the scheme:

(1)   enters an assessment period in relation to the PPF under PA 2004, s 132. Often this will only be after an insolvency event anyway – PA 2004, s 132(2), but it could be after a relevant application – PA 2004, s 132(4); or

(2)   becomes authorised to continue as a closed scheme under s 153 of the 2004 Act (scheme thought to have enough assets to meet protected liabilities, but unable to obtain a full buy-out quotation)[2].

1 It seems that this will continue to apply even in the case of a member's voluntary liquidation (*MVL*). MVLs are generally outside the new definition of an 'insolvency event' in the Pensions Act 2004, (see PA 2004, s 121(2)), but this does not apply for the purposes of the independent trustee obligations in ss 22 to 26 of the 1995 Act – PA 1995, s 22(3), was not amended by PA 2004.
2 PA 1995, s 22(2A), inserted by PA 2004, s 36(2)(c).

30.15   Obviously the obligation on an IP to notify the Pensions Regulator etc only applies if an IP has been appointed.

30.16   The new rules on notification by an IP etc apply if any of the employers (see Chapter 32) in a multi-employer scheme enters a formal insolvency[1] (not just the principal employer as previously).
There are special provisions for where a partnership is the employer[2].

1 2005 IT Regulations, reg 10.
2 2005 IT Regulations, reg 11.

30.17   The new rules are also expressly stated to apply even if the company over which the IP is appointed had in fact ceased to have any relevant employees in the scheme immediately before the IP was appointed[1]. This would cover (say) the appointment of a liquidator by the court. The liquidator will be covered by the section even though all the employees of the company may have ceased to have been employed on the making of the winding-up order – see para 6.2 above – (and so before the IP was appointed).

1 2005 Regulations, reg 12.

EXISTING INSOLVENCIES UNDER WAY ON 6 APRIL 2005

30.18   There are no specific transitional provisions in PA 2004 or the relevant regulations or commencement orders. It seems that any powers and duties on IPs under the old legislation has ceased from 6 April 2005. Existing appointments of independent trustees presumably remained in place[1].

1 The explanatory memorandum issued with the Occupational Pension Schemes (Independent Trustee) Regulations 2005, SI 2005/703, includes a government comment to this effect.

TPR NOT OBLIGED TO APPOINT AN INDEPENDENT TRUSTEE

30.19   The IP was, before 6 April 2005, obliged to appoint an independent person if there was not one in place already (unless the scheme was excluded).

30.20 Under the new rules, tPR is not obliged to appoint an independent trustee. New s 23(1) merely says that the Regulator 'may' appoint an independent person. So tPR has a discretion not to appoint if it does not consider this appropriate.

30.21 The Pensions Regulator may issue guidance on how it will use its discretion. Presumably it will balance the cost of an independent trustee against the need to protect members.

30.22 It will be possible for the Pensions Regulator to decide not to appoint under s 23, but instead to make an appointment under its more general power in PA 1995, s 7[1]. Section 23 is without prejudice to the tPR powers under s 7 (PA 1995, s 23(7)).

1 See eg comments in the explanatory memorandum to the 2005 IT Regulations, stating that the s 7 power would be used 'very occasionally' with the vast majority of appointments being under s 23 and so being required to be of a person on the register of independent persons. See also the comments on the tPR website: http://www.thepensionsregulator.gov.uk/trustees/ trusteeRegister/register.aspx

IT APPOINTMENT EVEN IF ONE OF THE TRUSTEES IS AN INDEPENDENT PERSON

30.23 The tPR power under s 23 to appoint an IT does not fall away if there is already an independent person on the trustee board.

30.24 This contrasts with the power previously given (before 6 April 2005) to the IP, which only applied if the IP was satisfied that none of the trustees was independent.

WHO CAN BE APPOINTED AS AN INDEPENDENT TRUSTEE?

30.25 The statutory test in s 23(3) of whether or not a person is independent has not changed. As previously, the person must:

(a)   have no interest in the assets of the employer or the scheme (otherwise than as trustee),

(b)   be neither connected with, nor an associate of, the employer or the IP.

30.26 Under the 1997 Regulations, additional requirements for independence were imposed (person not to: (a) have provided services to the trustees or the employer in relation to the scheme in the last three years; or (b) be an associate of such a person; or (c) be an associate of a person who has an interest in the assets of the employer or the scheme otherwise than as trustee). These additional requirements have not been repeated in the 2005 IT Regulations and so no longer apply.

30.27   A new additional requirement is imposed by new s 23(1)(b) (inserted by PA 2004). The person must also be named on a register of independent persons maintained by tPR. The 2005 IT Regulations require tPR to maintain such a register.

Meaning of interest in the assets of the employer or the scheme

30.28   The expression 'interest in the assets of the employer or of the scheme' used in s 23(3)(a) is not defined further in PA 1995. As Lord Wilberforce pointed out in *Leedale v Lewis*[1]:

> 'The word "interest" is one of uncertain meaning and it remains to be decided on the terms of the applicable statute which, or possibly what other, meaning the word may bear.'

1 [1982] 3 All ER 808 at 816, HL.

30.29   The Court of Appeal in *Armitage v Nurse*[1] also considered the meaning of the word 'interest' when used in a statute (in this case the Limitation Act). Millett LJ cited Lord Wilberforce and held (at page 261) that:

> 'The meaning of the word must, therefore, be derived from the context in which it appears . . . The question thus depends upon identifying the legislative purpose which [the relevant section] is intended to achieve.'

1 [1998] Ch 241, CA.

30.30   It seems clear that a member of the scheme (ie an employee or ex-employee with rights under the scheme) will fall within the section, as will a spouse (or civil partner) of a member where the scheme provides for a spouse's (or civil partner's) pension as of right. A member (or spouse etc) seems clearly to be a person with an interest in the assets of the scheme.

30.31   In *Invensys Australia Superannuation Fund Pty Ltd v Austrac Investments Ltd*[1], Byrne J commented that:

> 'A member has no proprietary interest in the assets of his or her superannuation fund; the fund represents security for the payment in due course of the members' entitlements',

citing the two Privy Council pensions cases of *Air Jamaica Ltd v Charlton*[2] and *Wrightson Ltd v Fletcher Challenge Nominees Ltd*[3]. But that was in the context at looking at an interest in a surplus. In this context, a member seems to be a person with an interest in the scheme assets for the purposes of the IT provisions.

1 [2006] VSC 112 (Byrne J).
2 [1999] 1 WLR 1399 at 1409, PC.
3 [2001] UKPC 23; [2001] OPLR 249; [2001] PLR 207, PC.

30.32   A person with only a possible discretionary interest (eg a dependant where the pension is dependent on the exercise of a discretion, or a person who is possibly the nominated beneficiary under a discretionary death benefit) is less obviously caught – compare the tax cases *Gartside v IRC*[1] *Vestey v IRC*[2] and *Pearson v IRC*[3].

See also, in New Zealand, the decision of Nicholson J in *Capral Fiduciary Ltd v Ladd*[4] considering that such potential discretionary beneficiaries did not have an interest in a scheme (so that their consent to a scheme amendment was not needed).

Conversely, discretionary beneficiaries have been held by the Privy Council in *Schmidt v Rosewood Trust*[5] to have sufficient interest to be able to require trustees to pass information.

1 [1968] AC 553, HL.
2 [1980] AC 1148, HL.
3 [1981] AC 753, HL.
4 (1999) 1 NZSC 40, 455 (Nicholson J).
5 [2003] UKPC 26, [2003] 2 AC 709, PC.

30.33 It is also unclear what would constitute an 'interest in the assets of the employer' within s 23(3). It would seem likely that a creditor of the employer (at least in a liquidation) will have an interest in the assets. Similarly, a shareholder will have an interest in the assets (unless perhaps the company were so hopelessly insolvent that there was no possibility of any dividend).

30.34 How far an 'interest' would extend is unclear. No guidance is given by PA 1995 as to when an interest becomes too remote. Presumably a minor shareholder of a bank which has lent money to the employer would not be considered to have an interest, even though the value of the shareholding in the bank could perhaps increase if the bank made a larger recovery from the employer. Conversely, a major shareholder (eg the holding company) of the bank in these circumstances would seem more obviously to have an interest.

30.35 In practice, the courts will probably follow a common sense test based on the degree of interest and involvement of the person concerned in the assets.

APPLYING FOR AN IT

30.36 Before 6 April 2005, the scheme members could apply to court to enforce the duty on the IP to appoint an Independent Trustee (PA 1995, s 24). This statutory power to apply to court has been repealed.

30.37 Instead members will be able to apply to the Pensions Regulator in the normal way. Deciding whether or not to appoint an independent trustee under s 23 of PA 1995 is one of the regulatory functions of the tPR listed in PA 2004, s 93(2). tPR must issue guidance on how it will exercise these functions (PA 2004, ss 93(1) and 94).

30.38 The tPR will be able to review any decision it has already reached (PA 2004, s 101). So if it had decided not to appoint an IT, it could later change its mind. If it had decided that it would appoint an IT, it seems that it can change its mind, but nothing in the statute or the 2005 IT Regulations indicates that the IT's appointment will cease (it may be the terms of the appointment made by the tPR in an individual case indicate that the appointment can terminate in relevant circumstances).

HOW WILL THE TPR DECIDE?

30.39   Usually the power to appoint an IT will fall within the standard procedure of the tPR[1]. The general rule that a relevant function cannot be exercised until the potential for an appeal to the Pensions Regulator Tribunal has been exercised[2]. But this does not apply to the power to appoint an IT under s 23[2].

1 PA 2004, s 96.
2 PA 2004, s 96(5).
3 See PA 2004, s 96(6)(o).

30.40   Such an appointment could also count as an exercise of the special procedure under s 97 (see PA 2004, s 97(5)(p)).

The power to appoint an IT under PA 1995, s 23 is not one which is reserved to the Determinations Panel of the tPR (see PA 2004, s 10 and Sch 2).

30.41   The PPF, tPR issued a joint statement in June 2008 on 'The regulation of schemes in wind-up and in a Pension Protection Fund assessment period – A statement by the Pensions Regulator, the Pension Protection Fund, and the Financial Assistance Scheme (as part of the Department for Work and Pensions)'

This includes in the Appendix:

> 'Examples of when the regulator may use its powers
>
> Appointing trustees
>
> (i) Appointing an independent trustee at the request of scheme trustees
>
> The employer of a contracted-out money purchase scheme became insolvent and its business was closed. The two individuals acting as trustees at the time the employer ceased trading felt unable to co-ordinate the winding-up of the scheme. Members were complaining that their requests for transfer value quotations were being ignored, scheme accounts were overdue and scheme expenses were unpaid.
>
> At the request of the trustees the regulator considered the circumstances and appointed an independent trustee on the grounds that the existing trustees lacked the necessary level of skill and knowledge to wind up the scheme and to secure the proper use of the scheme's assets.
>
> (ii) Appointing an independent trustee at the request of the PPF
>
> The PPF made a request to the regulator for the appointment of an independent trustee because the trustees were not responding to the PPF's requests.

The regulator issued a warning notice and received an objection from the trustees who wished to deal with assessment and possible winding-up themselves.

After investigating the circumstances of the scheme the regulator decided to use its discretion to appoint an independent trustee with exclusive powers.

(iii) Appointing an independent trustee following a whistle-blowing report

A final salary pension scheme began winding up when employment ceased owing to the insolvency of the employer. It was not eligible for entry into the PPF.

The scheme actuary reported that the one remaining trustee had transferred part of the assets to an offshore fund which the actuary considered to be inappropriate.

The trustee did not respond to our enquiries.

The regulator appointed an independent trustee with exclusive powers.'

See the tPR website: http://www.thepensionsregulator.gov.uk/pdf/windingupjointstatement.pdf

CHALLENGING THE DECISION OF TPR

30.42 An appeal against a decision of tPR lies to the new Pensions Regulatory Tribunal (PRT). The PRT can give directions to the tPR – eg it can cancel the decision of the tPR and substitute its own decision (PA 2004, s 103).

IT AND DISCRETIONS OF THE TRUSTEES

30.43 An IT appointed by tPR under PA 1995, s 23 will continue to take over all discretions from the other trustees (and from the employer if exercisable as a trustee) (PA 1995, s 25(2), as amended). If the employer is the sole trustee, it will (as previously) cease to be a trustee on the IT being appointed (PA 1995, s 25(1)).

30.44 The new wording is clearer that the existing trustees can continue to act until an IT is appointed under s 23[1].

1 Before 6 April 2005, the better view was that the existing trustees lost their discretionary powers once old s 22 started to apply to the scheme (eg once an IP was appointed) even though no IT has yet been appointed. New s 23(2) is clearer in only removing the existing trustees' discretionary powers once an IT has been appointed by the tPR under s 23.

30.45 This does not necessarily apply if a trustee is appointed by tPR under PA 1995, s 7 instead. In this case the appointed trustee has the same power as the other trustees, unless tPR provides otherwise in its appointment order (PA 1995, s 7(3) and (4)).

PAYMENT OF THE IT'S FEES

30.46 Before 6 April 2005, the fees of the IT were payable out of the scheme assets (in priority to any other claims). The new provisions provide for tPR to have a discretion on this point. The IT is only entitled under the statute to its fees if this is provided for in the appointment order from tPR under PA 1995, s 23. tPR will be able to order that the IT's fees are payable either out of the scheme or by the employer (or both) (new PA 1995, s 25(6)). This is a new provision.

30.47 Any amounts payable by the employer under the tPR appointment are a debt due from the employer (new PA 1995, s 25(7)). Similar provisions apply to appointment by tPR under PA 1995, s 7[1].

1 See new s 8(1) and (2) of PA 1995, as substituted by PA 2004.

30.48 Given that in practice the employer may well be insolvent, the IT will be concerned to check that the relevant IP accepts that any sums payable are priority claims in the insolvency proceedings (eg as relevant insolvency expenses). This has not been clarified in the relevant regulations (or by an amendment to the Insolvency Rules).

30.49 In practice presumably the IP and the IT will assume that the expenses are to be treated as an expense of the insolvency under the relevant insolvency rules.

30.50 In *Re Toshoku Finance*[1], Lord Hoffmann commented that statutory liabilities will usually be a necessary expense of an insolvency proceeding (in that case a liquidation) and so hence have a priority under the relevant Insolvency Rules. He held:

> '[30] ... Expenses incurred after the liquidation date need no further equitable reason why they should be paid. Of course it will generally be true that such expenses will have been incurred by the liquidator for the purposes of the liquidation. It is not the business of the liquidator to incur expenses for any other purpose. But this is not at all the same thing as saying that the expenses will necessarily be for the benefit of estate. They may simply be liabilities which, as liquidator, he has to pay. For example, there will be the fees payable to fund the Insolvency Service, ranking as para (c) in R4.218(1), where the benefit to the estate may seem somewhat remote. There would be little point in a statute which specifically imposed liabilities upon a company in liquidation if they were payable only in the rare case in which it emerged with all other creditors having been paid ...

1 [2002] 3 All ER 961, HL – see Chapter 17 above.

30.51 But in *Re Allders Department Stores Ltd*[1], Lawrence Collins J refused to follow *Re Toshoku* in relation to employee redundancy claims, considering that they could be distinguished on the grounds that the Insolvency Act 1986 contains a specific regime for such claims.

1 [2005] 2 All ER 122 (Lawrence Collins J) – see also Chapter 17 above.

30.52 This is the case also for some claims in relation to a pension scheme (eg para 8 of Sch 6 to the Insolvency Act 1986 dealing with some contributions to occupational pension schemes being preferential debts and para 99(6) of Sch B1 to the 1986 Act dealing with liabilities in relation to adopted employment contracts including 'a contribution to an occupational pension scheme'). So it may be possible that the statutory claim under new PA 1995, s 25(6) and (7) is not in fact an insolvency expense, but instead (presumably) a provable debt.

See further the later decisions on the issue of expenses in *Freakley v Centre Reinsurance International Co*[1], *Re Huddersfield Fine Worsteds, Krasner v McMath*[2] and *Exeter City Council v Bairstow, Re Trident Fashions*[3] (discussed in Chapter 17 above).

1 [2002] UKHL 6; [2002] 1 WLR 671, HL.
2 [2005] EWCA Civ 1072; [2005] 4 All ER 886; [2005] IRLR 995, CA.
3 [2007] EWHC 400 (Ch); [2007] All ER (D) 45 (Mar) (David Richards J).

30.53 It is worth contrasting PA 1995, s 25(7) – which just states that the fees are payable as a debt by the employer – with s 26(3) – which provides that expenses incurred by an IP in providing information to trustees is an expense of the insolvency. Why does the later section deal with expenses, but the new s 25(7) does not? Is this an indication that they are not expenses of the insolvency?

30.54 Conversely, it seems odd for Parliament to provide for a payment to be a simple debt in the case of an employer who (by definition) is in an insolvency process. In most cases this will mean that the payment obligation will not be met in full unless it is made a relevant expense of the insolvency.

30.55 In practice a prospective IT is likely to seek clarification of the fees position before accepting any appointment. It is possible that the tPR may look for an indication of likely fees at the time of putting ITs onto the new register.

CONTROLS OVER THE IT'S FEES

30.56 The 2005 IT Regulations provide that any applicant to join the register maintained by the tPR must agree to 'have his fees and costs scrutinised by an independent adjudicator and to be bound by that adjudicator's final adjudication as to his fees and costs' (reg 3(e)(i)).

30.57 In addition an IT (and any trustee appointed by the Pensions Regulator under its general power in PA 1995, s 7) must provide, within a reasonable period following a request by a scheme member or relevant trade union, details of:

● the scale of fees that will be chargeable by the appointed trustee and payable by the scheme; and

● details of each of the amounts charged to the scheme by the appointed trustee in the past 12 months.

See reg 13 of the Occupational Pension Schemes (Independent Trustee) Regulations 2005 (SI 2005/703).

REMOVAL OF THE IT?

30.58 As previously, the IT cannot be removed under a provision of the Scheme (PA 1995, s 25(3)). But he or she could presumably be removed by the tPR under PA 1995, s 3[1] if tPR considered that the IT was not a 'fit and proper person' to act.

The IT may be able to resign if the scheme rules allow this.

1 As substituted by PA 2004, s 33.

30.59 The IT will cease to be a trustee if he or she ceases to be independent (PA 1995, s 25(4)) – unless the IT is the only trustee, in which case he or she stays in office until a new trustee is appointed (PA 1995, s 25(5)). The IT is under a duty to notify tPR 'as soon as reasonably practicable' if he or she ceases to be an independent person. The IT will be liable for a civil penalty if he or she fails without reasonable excuse to notify tPR (PA 1995, s 25(5A)).

30.60 The 2005 IT Regulations clarify that removal of the IT from the register of ITs maintained by tPR will not remove him or her from any current appointments[1] (but it will prevent the IT from any future appointments). It may be that the terms of the appointment made by the tPR in an individual case indicate that the appointment can terminate in relevant circumstances.

1 Regulation 7.

NOTICES

30.61 When appointed, an IP must give written notice to the tPR, the board of the Pension Protection Fund (PPF) and the trustees of the occupational pension scheme. This notice must be given 'as soon as reasonably practicable'[1] (PA 1995, s 23(2B)).

1 The Regulator is obliged to issue a general code of practice on what it considers to be a 'reasonable time' for such provisions – PA 2004, s 90(2)(a).

30.62 This notice must be given even in relation to what was previously an excluded scheme from the IT provisions in PA 1995 (eg a money purchase scheme).

30.63 The IP must notify the tPR, PPF and trustees if he or she ceases to Act as an IP, but only if immediately after this s 22 ceases to apply to the scheme. So this notification obligation does not apply if, for instance, an administration converts to a liquidation or one administrator ceases to act, but another is appointed.

30.64   This obligation arises in addition to the notification obligations on IPs under the PPF provisions – these oblige an IP to notify the PPF on appointment (PA 2004, s 120) and whether or not he or she considers a 'scheme rescue' to be possible (or not) – PA 2004, s 122.

30.65   Notices given under s 23 by an IP to the tPR etc must be in writing and contain prescribed information (PA 1995, s 23(2F)). The information to be provided by the IP is set out in reg 8 of the Occupational Pension Schemes (Independent Trustee) Regulations 2005.

30.66   The information to be provided by the IP is specified in Regulation 8, Occupational Pension Schemes (Independent Trustee) Regulations 2005:

(a)   that the notice is a notice given under s 22(2B) of the Pensions Act 1995;

(b)   the date of the notice;

(c)   the name and address of the scheme;

(d)   the pension scheme registration number;

(e)   the names and addresses of all trustees of the scheme;

(f)   the name of the employer or employers to which the circumstances set out in PA 1995, s 22(1) apply;

(g)   the name and address of the responsible person giving the notice; and

(h)   the date of the responsible person's appointment, or the date on which that appointment is to end.

30.67   The notification requirements introduced into PA 1995 by the Child Support, Pensions and Social Security Act 2000 (as new ss 26A to 26C) were repealed on 6 April 2005. They required trustees to notify Opra if (say) an IT appointment was not made.

INFORMATION TO MEMBERS

30.68   The IP still has to provide information to the trustees on request. Section 26 of PA 1995 remains in force. This requires an IP to provide information to the trustees of a scheme as soon as reasonably practicable after the receipt of a request. The information must be reasonably required by the trustees for the purposes of the scheme.

30.69   This obligation (as previously) is subject to the IP being satisfied that his expenses of providing information will be recoverable, either as an expense of the insolvency – PA 1995, s 26(2), or if there are not enough assets in the insolvency, met by the trustees – PA 1995, s 26(3).

30.70   The s 26 obligation applies whether or not an IT has been appointed. From 6 April 2005 it applies to all occupational pension schemes. The exemptions in the 1997 IT Regulations (for money purchase schemes, unapproved schemes etc[1]) no longer apply.

1 See reg 5 of the Occupational Pension Schemes (Independent Trustee) Regulations 1997 (SI 1997/252), which specified that ss 22 to 26 of PA 1995 did not apply to these exempted classes of scheme.

THE REGISTER OF POTENTIAL INDEPENDENT TRUSTEES

30.71   The conditions for inclusion in the register to be maintained by the Pensions Regulator are set out in reg 3 of the Occupational Pension Schemes (Independent Trustee) Regulations 2005 (see the annex to this chapter).

30.72   From October 2006, pension trustees are generally under an obligation as to the level of knowledge and understanding both of pensions law generally and of their own scheme (PA 2004, s 247). Generally new trustees (or directors of a corporate trustee) will be given a six month period of grace following their appointment before this obligation applies. But the regulations provide that this grace period will not apply to independent trustees under the insolvency provisions – see regs 3(a) and 4(a) of the Occupational Pension Schemes (Trustees' Knowledge and Understanding) Regulations 2006 (SI 2006/686).

IT IF ONE OF THE TRUSTEES IS AN INDEPENDENT PERSON ALREADY?

30.73   tPR's discretionary power to appoint an IT (with the specific powers given to an IT under the legislation) applies even if one or more of the existing trustees is an independent person (eg an independent trustee appointed under the scheme rules).

30.74   There is now no point in employers appointing their own independent trustee before the insolvency starts. The power given to the Pensions Regulator to appoint an IT will remain (although the fact that there is an existing independent person in place may perhaps influence tPR in deciding whether or not to appoint).

30.75   It seems likely that tPR will not be able to appoint an IT if the IP has previously appointed an IT before 6 April 2005 – new PA 1995, s 22(2) states that 'no more than one trustee may be appointed an independent trustee under subsection(1)'. The argument would be that an appointment by the IP before 6 April 2005 would have been under subsection (1), albeit the old version of subsection (1) before its substitution by PA 2004.

CESSATION OF OBLIGATIONS

30.76   Section 22(2) of PA 1995 provides that if s 22 applies by virtue of ss 22(1) (ie on an insolvency), s 22 (and, in effect, also ss 23–26 other than perhaps s 25(6)) ceases to apply in relation to a scheme if:

(a) some person other than the insolvent company becomes the employer (ie the employer of the persons in the description of employment to which the scheme relates[1]); or

(b) the insolvency practitioner ceases to act in relation to the employer[2].

1 PA 1995, s 22(2)(a).
2 PA 1995, s 22(2)(b). The IP must notify tPR, the PPF and the trustees of this – s 22(2C).

30.77 This means that s 22 continues to apply to a scheme while it is in an assessment period (under PA 2004, s 132) or authorised to continue as a closed scheme after an assessment period (under PA 2004, s 153).

30.78 Section 22(2)(a) is clearly designed to deal with the position where the company ceases to be a participating employer and all its employees transfer to a new (solvent) employer (eg as part of a TUPE business sale) who also takes over the scheme for example by deed of novation where the rights of the company are effectively taken over by the new employer.

30.79 The use of the present tense in s 22(2)(a) in the requirement for a new employer to become the employer, ie the employer of persons in the description or category to which the scheme relates, seems clearly to require the new employer not only to take over the employment, but also to become a participating employer in the pension scheme concerned. In other words, it is not enough that a new employer has taken over employment of the members (this would, of course, occur if the employees were dismissed and found new employment).

POWERS OF INDEPENDENT TRUSTEE

30.80 Powers vested in the trustees or managers of the scheme generally become exercisable only by the independent trustee[1]. Similarly, powers conferred on the employer (otherwise than as trustee or manager of the scheme) and which are exercisable by the employer at its discretion, but only as trustee of the power, are exercisable only by the independent trustee[2].

1 PA 1995, s 25(2)(a).
2 PA 1995, s 25(2)(b).

30.81 There was provision in PA 1995, s 25(2) that if there is more than one independent trustee the power remains exercisable by the person who could otherwise exercise it, but there was an overriding requirement for the consent of at least half of the independent trustees. This provision has been repealed from 5 April 2005 by PA 2004.

30.82 It may well be a difficult question of legal analysis as to whether or not a power exercisable by the employer is held by it 'as trustee of the power' within s 25(2)(b). Presumably this is designed to catch fiduciary powers such as those found by Warner J as a matter of interpretation in *Mettoy Pension Trustees Ltd v Evans*[1] see para 26.8 above. In particular, given that in the context of private trusts the power to appoint new trustees has been considered to be a fiduciary power (see para 26.10 above), it has been argued (in my view wrongly) that the right to appoint and remove the other trustees vests in the independent trustee.

In *Mitre Pensions Ltd v Pensions Ombudsman*[2] a dispute had arisen between the independent trustee and the two other trustees about their benefits as members. Eventually this went to the Pensions Ombudsman who criticised the independent trustee. On appeal by the independent trustee, the Inner House of the Court of Session commented (at para [16]):

> 'While the Ombudsman had suggested, in paragraph 41, that the appellants should have investigated taking steps to have EAF and JAF removed as trustees, the appellants had no power to remove them. Removal of trustees is dealt with in the Trust Deed and only the principal employer can remove trustees. Reference was made to *Mettoy Pension Trustees Limited v Evans* [1990] 1 PLR 9 at page 43[3]. However, the appellants could not reasonably have concluded that they had, without doubt, the power to remove the other two trustees simpliciter. Section 121(2) of the Act[4] was so obscure that the appellants could not have been confident of their right to remove the other trustees without being challenged in court. In any event, all that the Ombudsman said was that the appellants should have investigated the possibility.'

1 [1991] 2 All ER 513 (Warner J).
2 [2000] OPLR 349; 2000 GWD 22- 868 (Inner House, Ct of Sess).
3 This section of the judgment in *Mettoy* discussed whether or not a power held by an employer is a fiduciary power.
4 PSA 1993, s121(2) dealt with powers exercisable by the independent trustee and was replaced (in the same terms) by PA 1995, s25(2).

30.83 In the Scottish case of *Independent Pension Trustee Ltd v LAW Construction Co Ltd*[1] Lord Hamilton held (at 267H) that what is now s 25(2)(b)[2] only applies:

> 'to a class of power vested in the employer as such but which he may not exercise otherwise than exclusively in the interests of the members of the scheme'.

Accordingly, Lord Hamilton held that, what is now s 25(2)(b) will not extend to powers of the employer which are subject only to the implied duty of mutual trust and confidence or duties not to Act capriciously – see Imperial Group *Pension Trust Ltd v Imperial Tobacco Ltd*[3]. These will remain exercisable by the employer, acting through the insolvency practitioner – see Chapter 26 above.

1 [1996] OPLR 259 (Lord Hamilton).
2 Then SSPA 1975, s 57D(5).
3 [1991] 2 All ER 597 (Browne-Wilkinson V-C).

30.84 The powers of the independent trustee under PA 1995, s 25(2) override s 32 of PA 1995, dealing with decisions of trustees to be made by agreement of a majority of trustees, notices of meetings etc[1].

1 PA 1995, s 32(4).

30.85 It seems likely that the powers of the independent trustee under PA 1995, s 25(2) can themselves be overridden by an order (under PA 1995, s 8(4)) of the Pensions Regulator (formerly Opra) in relation to an appointment of a trustee by tPR under PA 1995, s 7, although the inter-relationship of the two sections is not absolutely clear. Section 8(4) allows tPR to give trustees appointed by it under s 7 of PA 1995 powers and duties exercisable by the trustee so appointed to the exclusion of the other trustees[1].

1 See the discussion of this point in (1999) 82 British Pension Lawyer 11.

30.86   Pension scheme trustees will often have delegated certain of their functions prior to the onset of insolvency. Benefit payments, for example, are commonly channelled through the employer's payroll and investment management is commonly delegated to a professional investment manager in order to avoid the requirement (imposed by the financial services legislation if this is not done) for the trustees to become authorised under the Financial Services and Markets Act 2000.

30.87   Although PA 1995, s 25(2)(a), provides that any discretionary powers exercisable by the trustees are to be exercisable only by the independent trustee, it is considered likely that a court would construe this section as continuing to allow the independent trustee to delegate relevant functions, rather than requiring him to exercise all discretions. (This view was shared by the Department of Social Security, although it should be noted that their view has no special status.)

MNT requirements

30.88   In relation to member-nominated trustees (or directors), the relevant provisions in PA 2004 provide that the relevant arrangements must not exclude member-nominated trustees (or directors) from the exercise of functions exercisable by the other trustees (or directors) merely because they are member-nominated[1].

1 PA 2004, ss 241(7) and 242(7). Previously PA 1995, s 16(7).

30.89   This could be seen as conflicting with the IT provisions. Before PA 2004, the legislation catered for this by an express exemption for the IT powers. PA 2004 deals with this differently. The member-nominated trustee/director provisions cease to apply if the relevant scheme becomes one 'to which section 22 of the 1995 Act ... applies'[1]. Section 22 applies to a scheme when an IP begins to act in relation to any of the employers (not just when an IT is appointed by tPR).

1 Occupational Pension Schemes (Member-nominated Trustees and Directors) Regulations 2006 (SI 2006/714), regs 2(b) and 3(b).

30.90   The net effect is that both the member-nominated trustee and member-nominated director provisions in ss 241 to 243 of PA 2004 cease to apply once an IP has been appointed in relation to the employer. In relation to a multi-employer schemes, this seems to apply while there is an IP acting in relation to any of the employers[1].

1 Occupational Pension Schemes (Independent Trustee) Regulations 2005 (SI 2005/703), reg 10.

ANNEX

30.91

Regulation 3 of the 2005 Regulations
Conditions for registration

(a) the applicant must not, at the time he is making the application or at any time while he is registered in the trustee register, be any of the following –

    (i) the subject of a prohibition order made under s 3 of the 1995 Act (prohibition orders),

    (ii) the subject of a suspension order made under s 4 of the 1995 Act (suspension orders), or

    (iii) disqualified for being a trustee of any trust scheme on any of the grounds set out in subsection (1) of s 29 of the 1995 Act (persons disqualified for being trustees), or by virtue of being the subject of an order made under subsection (3) or (4) of that section;

(b) the Regulator is satisfied that –

    (i) the applicant has sufficient relevant experience of occupational pension schemes,

    (ii) the applicant is a fit and proper person to Act as a trustee of an occupational pension scheme,

    (iii) the applicant operates sound administrative and accounting procedures, and

    (iv) the applicant has adequate indemnity insurance cover;

(c) where the applicant is not an individual –

    (i) each officer of the applicant must satisfy the conditions specified in paragraphs (a) and (b)(ii) above, and

    (ii) each key person must satisfy the conditions specified in paragraphs (a) and (b)(i) and (ii) above;

(d) the applicant has premises in the United Kingdom from which he conducts his business as a trustee of an occupational pension scheme, and he discloses the address of those premises to the Regulator;

(e) the applicant agrees –

    (i) to have his fees and costs scrutinised by an independent adjudicator and to be bound by that adjudicator's final adjudication as to his fees and costs,

    (ii) to the Regulator disclosing his name, business address and the areas of trustee work in which he specialises on the version of the trustee register which is to be publicly available,

---

(iii) to comply with reasonable requests of the Regulator to provide information to the Regulator, and

(iv) to inform the Regulator as soon as is reasonably practicable if he becomes disqualified under s 29 of the 1995 Act -

    (aa) for one of the reasons set out in subsection (1) of that section, or

    (bb) by virtue of being the subject of an order made under sub-section (3)(b) of that section.

CHAPTER 31

Scope of the main pensions legislation

STATUTORY PROVISION

31.1   The pensions legislation contains specific obligations on employers to fund occupational pension schemes. The Pensions Act 2004 (PA 2004) updated and strengthened the provisions in the Pensions Act 1995 (PA 1995). The key provisions of PA 2004 cover the following:

(a)   Scheme specific funding (SSF): This replaced the minimum funding requirement (MFR) under PA 1995 with new funding provisions. Broadly a schedule of contributions is now fixed by agreement between the trustees and the employers (or fixed by the Pensions Regulator if agreement cannot be reached). There are savings for schemes where the trustees have a unilateral right to fix contributions. SSF replaced the minimum funding requirement (MFR) and applied from the first formal actuarial valuation with an effective date on or after 22 September 2005[1] – see Chapter 33 (Contributions to pension schemes);

(b)   Employer debt: The statutory debt provisions in s 75 of the Pensions Act 1995 have been strengthened. In particular s 75 operates on a relevant trigger (eg a scheme winding-up or employer insolvency) to impose a non-preferential debt obligation on an employer by reference to the amount considered to be necessary to secure the scheme benefits on a buy-out with an insurer – see Chapter 34 (Section 75) below;

(c)   PPF: The Pension Protection Fund applies in some cases following employer insolvency to take over eligible schemes and provide a protected level of benefits – see Chapter 27 (Pension Protection Fund) above. The PPF is funded by the assets of schemes that enter the PPF, together with levies payable by eligible schemes – see para 31.13 below; and

(d)   The Pensions Regulator (tPR) was given powers in some circumstances to make third parties (persons associated or connected with an employer) liable for pension scheme funding – see Chapter 37 (tPR: Moral hazard powers) below.

1 See the transitional provisions in Sch 4 to the Occupational Pension Schemes (Scheme Funding) Regulations 2005 (SI 2005/3377).

31.2   From 1997 (and before PA 2004 came into force) provision had been made in the Pensions Act 1995 to impose a debt obligation on the employer to provide a minimum level of funding for revenue approved occupational pension schemes:

- minimum funding requirement: PA 1995, ss 56–61 imposed an obligation on employers (broadly) to maintain the funding of ongoing schemes at a minimum level set out in regulations and an actuarial guidance note. This was called the 'minimum funding requirement' (MFR);

- debt on the employer: PA 1995, s 75 imposed a debt obligation on employers when (broadly) the pension scheme wound-up or the employer entered liquidation or ceased to participate in the scheme.

31.3   These statutory obligations generally do not apply to money purchase pension schemes (ie those where all the benefits are money purchase). Separate provision is made for these schemes – see Chapter 38 (Money Purchase Schemes) below.

The obligations only apply in relation to occupational pension schemes, as defined in s 1 of PSA 1993 (see Chapter 2 above). The obligations do not apply in relation to personal pension schemes.

EXCLUSIONS FROM THE PPF/SSF/DEBT ON EMPLOYER PROVISIONS

31.4   The chart below summarises the occupational pension schemes excluded from the PPF, from scheme specific funding and from the debt on the employer provisions.

31.5   These exclusions are contained in:

(a)   the **'PPF Entry Rules Regulations'**: The Pension Protection Fund (Entry Rules) Regulations 2005, reg 2 (SI 2005/590, as amended);

(b)   the **'Scheme Funding Regulations'**: The Occupational Pension Schemes (Scheme Funding) Regulations 2005, reg 17 (SI 2005/3377, as amended); and

(c)   the **'Employer Debt Regulations'**: The Occupational Pension Schemes (Employer Debt) Regulations 2005, reg 4 (SI 2005/678, as amended).

31.6

Type of excluded scheme	*Not PPF eligible* *PPF Entry Rules Regs*	*Outside scheme specific funding* *Scheme Funding Regs*	*Outside s 75* *Employer Debt Regs*
Money purchase scheme	PA 2004, s 126(1)(a)	PA 2004, s 221(1)(a)	PA 2004, s 75(1)(a)
Unfunded schemes	Reg 2(1)(a), if public service	Reg 17(1)(b)	Reg 4(1)(a), if public service

Type of excluded scheme	Not PPF eligible PPF Entry Rules Regs	Outside scheme specific funding Scheme Funding Regs	Outside s 75 Employer Debt Regs
Public sector schemes providing pensions to local government employees	Reg 2(1)(b)	Reg 17(1)(a), if established under an enactment and guaranteed by a local authority	Reg 4(1)(b)
Schemes to which a Minister of the Crown etc has given a guarantee	Reg 2(1)(d)	Reg 17(1)(a), if established under an enactment	Reg 4(1)(d)
Schemes which are not tax approved (or tax registered from April 2006) nor relevant statutory schemes	Reg 2(1)(f) and (fa)	Reg 17(1)(e), if less than 100 members	Reg 4(1)(e)
Schemes with fewer than two members	Reg 2(1)(k)	Reg 17(1)(g)	Reg 4(1)(h)
Schemes providing death in service benefits only	Reg 2(1)(h)	Reg 17(1)(j), if death benefits secured by insurance policies	
Schemes which are relevant lump sum retirement benefit schemes	Reg 2(1)(g)		Reg 4(1)(f)
Chatsworth Settlement Estate Pension Scheme	Reg 2(1)(n)	Reg 17(1)(m)	Reg 4(1)(k)
Schemes with fewer than 12 members where all members are trustees of the scheme (and trustee decisions are unanimous or involve an independent trustee)	Reg 2(1)(l) and (m)	Reg 17(1)(h) and (i)	Reg 4(1)(i) and (j)
Schemes applying to members outside the EU/EEA		Reg 17(1)(d)(i), for members outside the EEA	
Schemes with main administration outside the UK	Reg 2(1)(j)	Reg 17(1)(d)(ii), for members outside the UK	

Type of excluded scheme	Not PPF eligible PPF Entry Rules Regs	Outside scheme specific funding Scheme Funding Regs	Outside s 75 Employer Debt Regs
Section 615 schemes	Reg 2(1)(i)	Reg 17(1)(f), if less than 100 members	Reg 4(1)(g), if not authorised or approved in relation to EU employers
Scheme is subject to a scheme failure notice		Reg 17(1)(k)	
Scheme (or section of a scheme) is being wound-up		Reg 17(1)(l), subject to yearly receipt of actuarial estimate of solvency (reg 18)	
Trustees have entered into a legally binding agreement which has effect to reduce any s 75 debt	Reg 2(2), subject to exceptions		
Schemes which have no employer after 6 April 2005 and have not been authorised under s 153, PA 2004 to continue as a closed scheme	Reg 2(1)(p)		

31.7 **Unregistered/ unapproved scheme**: This is an occupational pension scheme which provides relevant benefits (as defined in ICTA 1988, s 612(1)), but is neither registered with HMRC under the Finance Act 2004 (or before 6 April 2006 approved by HMRC under ICTA 1988) nor a relevant statutory scheme (as defined in ICTA 1988, s 611A).

31.8 Schemes not registered with HMRC that have 100 or more members are within the scheme specific funding provisions in Part 3 of PA 2004 (but not eligible for the PPF or within s 75). This flows from the requirement in the Directive on Institutions for Occupational Retirement Provision (the 'IORP Directive', 2003/41/EC) that funding is dealt with. The IORP Directive, article 5 allows schemes with less than 100 members to be excluded. Scheme specific funding is the UK enactment of the funding requirements of the IORP Directive.

31.9 **Section 615 scheme**: This is a superannuation fund only for employees outside the UK within ICTA 1988, s 615(6).

Schemes within s 615 that have 100 or more members are within the scheme specific funding provisions in Part 3 of PA 2004 (but not eligible for the PPF or within s 75). This flows from article 5 of the IORP Directive, which allows schemes with less than 100 members to be excluded. Scheme specific funding is the UK enactment of the funding requirements of the IORP Directive.

31.10   Less than two members: This is a scheme with less than two members. The term 'member' is defined in the PA 1995, s 124 as being either: an active member, a deferred member or a pensioner member. Generally, this will only include persons who are (or formerly were) employed members of the scheme – ie it will not include beneficiaries such as spouses or dependants (even if they are being paid benefits). It is unclear whether persons only covered under a scheme for lump sum benefits payable on death in service are members of that scheme for the purposes of the PA 1995 (the better view is that they are not).

31.11   Death benefit only schemes: Such schemes have specific exemptions, but it may well be the case that they do not count as occupational pension schemes in any event (and so are not within the legislation). See s 255 of PA 2004 and the discussion at para 2.69 above

31.12   Industry-wide lump sum scheme: This is a 'relevant lump sum retirement benefits scheme'. This is a scheme:

(i)   which has been categorised by HMRC for the purposes of its approval as a centralised scheme for non-associated employers;

(ii)   which is not contracted-out (ie contracted-out of SERPS and S2P – see PSA 1993, s 7(3) and para 10.27 above); and

(iii)   under the provisions of which the only benefits which may be provided on or after retirement (other than money purchase benefits derived from the payment of additional contributions by any person) are lump sum benefits which are not calculated by reference to a member's salary.

LIABILITY FOR PPF LEVY

31.13   The main levy payable to fund the PPF is the pension protection levy. This levy is payable under s 175(1) of the Pensions Act 2004 (and relevant determinations of the PPF Board). It is only payable by 'eligible schemes'. Under s 126, an 'eligible scheme' is an occupational pension scheme which:

(a)   is not a money purchase scheme, and

(b)   is not a prescribed scheme or a scheme of a prescribed description.

An occupational pension scheme which is not an eligible scheme is defined in reg 2 of the Pension Protection Fund (Entry Rules) Regulations 2005. Regulation 3 deems a scheme to continue to be an eligible scheme if eligibility would otherwise be lost in the following circumstances:

- the scheme ceased to be tax registered; or

- there is a death of a member which causes the scheme to become ineligible (e.g. because fewer than 12 members remain); or

- the employer in relation to the scheme, or the last remaining employer in relation to a multi-employer scheme, is dissolved.

However, the PPF will not assume responsibility for a scheme if it was not eligible for at least the duration of three years before the assessment period began or the duration of the scheme's existence (if less than three years) – PA 2004, s 146(1) and regs 3 and 21 of the PPF Entry Rules Regulations.

CHAPTER 32

Who is an employer under the pensions legislation?

EMPLOYER

32.1   The pensions legislation generally applies to impose duties and obligations (and some rights) on an employer in relation to an occupational pension scheme[1].

The general thrust of PA 2004 is that statutory funding obligations are imposed on the employer in relation to an occupational pension scheme.

In addition, the Pension Regulator's 'moral hazard' powers[2] under PA 2004 allow it, in some circumstances, to make third parties (ie non-employers) liable for pension funding, but only if they are associated or connected[3] with an employer.

This means that the meaning of who is an employer in relation to an occupational pension scheme is a crucial question. Often this will be obvious, but the underlying statutory definition (in PA 1995 and PA 2004) is not without its difficulties.

1 Examples of statutory rights (as compared to obligations), are:
   to be consulted about the statement of investment principles – Occupational Pension Schemes (Investment) Regulations 2005, reg 2(2)(a),
   to receive copies of actuarial valuations – PA 2004, s 224(7); and
   to agree scheme specific funding issues – PA 2004, s 229.
2 See Chapter 37 (tPR Moral hazard powers) below.
3 See Chapter 41 (Who is connected or associated?) below.

32.2   The term 'employer' is defined in PA 1995 as:

'the employer of persons in the description [or category] of employment to which the scheme relates'[1].

The words 'or category' that appear after 'description' are to be deleted by PA 2004, Sch 13, Part 1 at a date that is still to be appointed (it is not clear why this has not already happened).

1 PA 1995, s 124.

32.3   The PA 2004[1] uses the same definition for 'employer' as under PA 1995 except for the PA 2004 definition does not contain the words 'or category'.

Both the PA 1995 and PA 2004 sections allow for regulations to provide for an extended meaning[2].

1 PA 2004, s 318(1).
2 PA 2004, s 318(4), and PA 1995, s 125(3).

32.4   This seemingly simple expression is in fact quite difficult to construe. The use of the present tense, 'to which the scheme relates', seems to indicate that the company must still have employees who must be (in effect) active members.

32.5   The term 'active member' is defined in PA 1995, s 124(1), as a person who is in pensionable service under a scheme[1].

The term 'pensionable service' is defined (in the same section) as 'service in any description of employment to which the scheme relates which qualifies the member (on the assumption that it continues for the appropriate period) for pension or other benefits under the scheme'.

1 The definition in PA 1995, s 124 also applies for the purposes of PA 2004 – see PA 2004, s 318.

32.6   Clearly in order to fall within this definition, a company must have current employees (but see para 32.9 below for the potential impact of the statutory extensions to cover former employers).

If a company has current employees, are they 'persons in the description of employment to which the scheme relates'? Consider the alternatives set out below.

(a)   The company participates in the pension scheme and its employees are active members in pensionable service (ie currently accruing benefits).

  ●   Clearly the test is satisfied. The company is an employer.

(b)   The company formerly participated in the pension scheme and its current employees were formerly in pensionable service but are not currently (eg because the scheme has started to wind up, or the company has ceased to participate or each employee has 'opted out' of pensionable service). The employees have retained preserved pensions in the pension scheme and so are still members, but not active members. Other employers continue to participate.

  ●   It seems the better interpretation that the test (on its own) is not satisfied. The company is not an employer.

  ●   The use of the present tense, 'employment to which the scheme relates', means that the test is not satisfied because there is no-one currently in pensionable service (ie accruing extra benefits) as opposed to merely being in employment. This is also consistent with the effect of the extension provisions in the relevant regulations dealing with former employers (see para 32.9 below). The contrary argument is that the company is still an employer because the scheme still relates to the past employment of its current employees even though active membership and accrual of additional pensionable service has ceased.

(c) The scheme has been closed to future accrual, so that no members are currently accruing additional pensionable service, but the benefits have not been frozen on a leaving service basis. Instead benefits are based on the ultimate final salary – ie the varying salary payable while the members continue in service with the company.

- It looks to be arguable here that the members are still active members of this scheme and so the company is still an employer in relation to it.

(d) The company has ceased to have any current employees, but it has not formally stopped participating in the scheme and the scheme remains open (so that if a new employee were hired, he or she could become an active member).

- The use of the present tense, 'employment to which the scheme relates', points to the test not being satisfied because there is no-one currently in pensionable service (ie accruing extra benefits) as opposed to merely being in employment.

32.7 In *Hearn v Dobson*[1] Morgan J considered (in effect) the issues raised in (b) and (d) above in relation to the operation of the Scheme Funding Regulations[2]. He held that:

- On (b) the question was difficult to answer (and in the event he did not have to because he held that a separate definition in the Scheme Funding Regulations applied so that the company there was not an employer).

- On (d) he agreed that there must be a current contract of employment. In effect he confirmed that a company with no current employees could not be an employer under the definition in s 124.

1 [2008] EWHC 1620 (Ch); [2008] All ER (D) 233 (Jul) (Morgan J).
2 See also the talk by Katie Banks on '*Who is the employer?*' to be given at the APL Conference in November 2009 (forthcoming).

32.8 Morgan J held on these points (paras 69 to 72):

'69. In relation to the definition of "employer" in section 124, Mr Newman accepts that there must be a current contract of employment between the employer and the person who is said to be in the description of employment to which the Scheme in question relates. He says that the six non-members have current contracts of employment so the question becomes whether those six non-members are in the description of employment to which the Scheme in question relates. He submits that this Scheme does not distinguish between different descriptions of employment under an employer, for example, it does not distinguish between senior management and other staff. He submits that the scheme relates to all employees of, amongst others, CECA. On his submission, what matters is whether the non-member is eligible under the Rules of the Scheme to become a member. That submission was initially made in Mr Newman's skeleton argument without regard to the deed of amendment of 24th December 2002. That deed closed the Scheme to new members with effect from 1st January 2003. Accordingly, even on Mr Newman's submissions, it is difficult to see how the six non-members could assert that they are eligible to become members of the

Scheme and therefore they are in employment to which the Scheme relates. Mr Newman seeks to meet this difficulty by relying upon Rule B1.2 introduced by the deed of 24th December 2002. That provides that any employee of an Employer may be eligible for membership if the Trustees, CC and the specific Employer agree. Such a person's membership may be subject to such conditions as the Trustees think fit. One obvious difficulty with that submission is that CECA gave notice with effect from 27th February 2006 to terminate its liability to contribute to the Scheme and it is not conceivable that the Trustees, CC and CECA would agree to treat an employee of CECA as eligible for membership to the Scheme unless CECA committed itself again to make contributions under the Scheme. In this state of affairs, in my judgment, it is not possible to say that the six non-members, employed by CECA, are in a description of employment to which the Scheme in question currently relates and so CECA is not an employer under section 124 as a result of its employment of those six persons. Further, on this point, I will explain in the next few paragraphs (when I consider Mr Newman's submission as to the two deferred members) why I reach the conclusion that a person is only an employer during such time as it employs active members of the Scheme. As the six non-members cannot be said to be active members of the Scheme, CECA cannot be said to be an employer by reason of employing them.

70. I turn therefore to Mr Newman's argument that CECA is an employer because it currently employs two persons who are deferred members of the scheme. Mr Newman submits that those two persons are current employees of CECA and the Scheme in question relates to the description of employment in question, because they have rights as deferred members under the Scheme. The contrary argument is that their rights under the Scheme have nothing to do with their current employment but all derive from former employment; the Scheme did relate to their former period of employment but does not currently relate to their continuing employment. Mr Newman submits that if the draftsman of section 124 had wanted to restrict the definition of employer to a person who employs persons in pensionable service or employs active members (these terms being interchangeable) then the draftsman could, and would, have said so. There is some force in this point given that section 124(1) itself defines active members and refers to a person in pensionable service under the Scheme.

71. If the issue in this case turned on the meaning of "employer" in section 124, then whilst I have considerable doubts about Mr Newman's submission I would find the question more difficult to answer than it actually is. In my judgment, the answer in the present case does not turn on the meaning of "employer" in section 124 but instead turns on the meaning of "employer" in paragraph 1 of schedule 2 to the Scheme Funding Regulations. The definition of "employer" in section 124 is relevant to, but not decisive of, the meaning of "employer" in paragraph 1 of schedule 2. By virtue of section 11 of the Interpretation Act 1978, the definition of employer in section 124 is taken to be the definition of "employer" in schedule 2 to the Scheme Funding Regulations "unless the contrary intention appears". At this point, one needs to give attention to paragraph 3 of schedule 2. This deals with a case where one has an employer of active members, who then ceases to employ active members and who would then cease to be an employer, but for the operation of paragraph 3(1). The draftsman of the Scheme Funding Regulations plainly thought that one ceased to be an employer when one ceased to have active members. Mr Newman submitted that the above does not correctly describe the

operation of paragraph 3(1). He submits that paragraph 3(1) should be understood as referring to one special case where earlier statutory provisions had been enacted which had treated persons as deferred members even though they were not so treated under the rules of a particular scheme.

72. In my judgment, the provisions of paragraph 3(1) of schedule 2 are a clear statement that when an employer ceases to employ active members he ceases to be an employer. Paragraph 3 provides a context for the interpretation of "employer" in paragraph 1 of schedule 2. If I had been minded to give a different meaning to the word "employer" in section 124 then I would not apply that different meaning to "employer" in paragraph 1 of schedule 2 because the context provided by paragraph 3 otherwise requires.'

PAST EMPLOYERS

32.9   In many cases, regulations provide for an extended definition of employer for the purposes of the relevant regulations (or Act). This extended definition catches former employers if either:

- When they ceased to employ persons in the description of employment to which the scheme relates, the scheme had ceased to have active members (ie become frozen). The effect of this is that the last employers remain liable (otherwise a frozen scheme would have no employers and so no-one obliged to fund etc); or

- When they ceased to employ persons in the description of employment to which the scheme relates, the scheme continued to have active members (ie so the first limb does not apply) but the exiting company did not pay the debt due under s 75 (if there was one)[1].

1 This extended meaning (where any s 75 debt has not been paid) does not apply to scheme specific funding.

32.10   This can make former employers potentially still liable for scheme specific funding or the deficiency debt under s 75, PA 1995.

Employer Debt Regulations

32.11   Regulation 9 of the Employer Debt Regulations was substituted with effect from 6 April 2008 by SI 2008/731 and now provides as follows:

'9 Frozen schemes and former employers

(1)   In the application of section 75 of the 1995 Act to a scheme, subject to paragraph (3), references to employers include former employers.

(2)   For the purposes of this regulation—

(a)   a "former employer" means any person who employed persons in the description of employment to which the scheme relates but at the relevant time has ceased to do so;

(b)   in relation to a frozen scheme, "freezing event" means the event in consequence of which the scheme became a frozen scheme (this is subject to regulation 6A);

(c)   "relevant time" means in relation to a scheme which is not a frozen scheme, the applicable time, and in relation to a frozen scheme, the time of occurrence of the freezing event.

(3)   A person shall not be included as a former employer if—

    (a)   he is a defined contribution employer;

    (b)   before 19th December 1996, he ceased to be a person employing persons in the description or category of employment to which the scheme related and was not regarded as a "former participator" for the purposes of the 1996 Regulations by virtue of regulation 6 of those Regulations (ceasing to participate: transitional provision);

    (c)   at a time before the relevant time, when the scheme had not commenced winding-up and the scheme continued to have active members, he—

        (i)   on or after 19th December 1996 and before 6th April 1997, ceased to be a person employing persons in the description or category of employment to which the scheme related and was not regarded as a "former participator" for the purposes of the 1996 Regulations by virtue of regulation 6 of those Regulations (ceasing to participate: transitional provision);

        (ii)   on or after 6th April 1997 and before 6th April 2008, ceased to be a person employing persons in the description or category of employment to which the scheme related and one of conditions A to I is met;

        (iii)   on or after 6th April 2008 and before the applicable time, ceased to be a person employing persons in the description or category of employment to which the scheme related or an employment-cessation event or insolvency event occurs in respect of him and one of conditions A to I is met; or

    (d)   in relation to a frozen scheme, at a time on or after 6th April 2008, after the freezing event, when the scheme had not commenced winding-up and before the applicable time, he ceased to be a person employing persons in the description or category of employment to which the scheme related, or an employment-cessation event or insolvency event occurred in respect of him and one of conditions A to I is met.

(4)   In the application of regulation 6 to a frozen scheme which was a multi-employer scheme before the event as a result of which the scheme became a frozen scheme, in relation to a person who before the applicable time was a former employer under this regulation, an employment-cessation event shall be treated as having occurred where notice is given to the trustees or manager by such a person for the purposes of this paragraph.

(5)   A notice given for the purposes of paragraph (4) must specify the date on which the employment-cessation event is to be treated as having occurred, being a date not earlier than 3 months before the date on which the notice is given, and not more than 3 months after that date.

(6) Condition A is that as a result of the employment-cessation event, insolvency event or assumption of his liabilities by another person, no debt arose under section 75(2) or (4) of the 1995 Act (or, before 6th April 2005, under section 75(1) of that Act).

(7) Condition B is that no debt was treated as becoming due from him under section 75(2) or (4) of the 1995 Act (or, before 6th April 2005, under section 75(1) of that Act).

(8) Condition C is that a debt was treated as becoming due from him under section 75(2) or (4) of the 1995 Act (or, before 6th April 2005, under section 75(1) of that Act) and has been paid by him before the applicable time.

(9) Condition D is that in accordance with a withdrawal arrangement a debt that was treated as becoming due from him under section 75(4) of the 1995 Act and has been paid by him before the applicable time.

(10) Condition E is that in accordance with an approved withdrawal arrangement a debt was treated as becoming due from him under section 75(4) of the 1995 Act and has been paid by him before the applicable time.

(11) Condition F is that in accordance with a scheme apportionment arrangement a debt was treated as becoming due from him under section 75(2) or (4) of the 1995 Act and has been paid by him before the applicable time.

(12) Condition G is that in accordance with a regulated apportionment arrangement a debt was treated as becoming due from him under section 75(2) or (4) of the 1995 Act and has been paid by him before the applicable time.

(13) Condition H is that a debt was treated as becoming due from him and has not been paid solely because he was not notified of the debt, and of the amount of it, sufficiently in advance of the applicable time for it to be paid before that time.

(14) Condition I is that a debt was treated as becoming due from him under section 75(2) or (4) of the 1995 Act but at the applicable time it is excluded from the value of the assets of the scheme because it is unlikely to be recovered without disproportionate cost or within a reasonable time.

(15) For the purposes of paragraph (6), an "employment-cessation event" shall include circumstances where before 6th April 2005—

(a) section 75(1) of the 1995 Act applied when a scheme was not being wound-up, and

(b) an employer ceased to be a person employing persons in the description or category of employment to which the scheme related at a time when at least one other person continued to employ such persons.'

32.12   Para 3 of Sch 2 to the Scheme Funding Regulations is to similar effect in relation to a frozen scheme (but not an unfrozen scheme):

'3 Frozen or paid-up schemes

(1) In the application of Part 3 of the 2004 Act and these Regulations to a scheme which has no active members, references to the employer have

effect as if they were references to the person who was the employer immediately before the occurrence of the event after which the scheme ceased to
have any active members ("the freezing event").

(2)   A person shall cease to be treated as an employer under paragraph (1) if
after the freezing event he ceases to be treated as a former employer under
regulation 9 of the Occupational Pension Schemes (Employer Debt)
Regulations 2005.'

32.13   The change in para 3 is briefly discussed at para 61 in the judgment of
Morgan J in *Hearn v Dobson*.

Before its amendment, reg 9(1) of the Employer Debt Regulations used to
provide:

'In the application of Section 75 of the 1995 Act and these Regulations to a
scheme which has no active members, references to employers include every
person who employed persons in the description of employment to which the
scheme relates immediately before the occurrence of the event after which the
scheme ceased to have any active members.[1]'

1 To similar effect before 6 April 2008, see para 3 of Sch 2 to the Scheme Funding Regulations and
para 3 of Sch 5 to the MFR Regulations.

32.14   In an insolvency context, regulation 9 of the Employer Debt
Regulations is likely to apply at the time that the company enters insolvency,
because an assessment period will then start and have effect to freeze the scheme
while it continues – see PA 2004, s 133(5) and Chapter 28 (PPF: Assessment
period) above.

32.15   It is unclear if regulation 9 ceases to apply if (say) the scheme re-opens
and gains active members (eg if the assessment period ends because there is a
scheme rescue).

32.16   Regulation 9 of the Employer Debt Regulations also deems a former
employer to remain an employer even if it ceased to be an employer (ie the
applicable time occurred and it ceased to be a person employing persons in the
description of employment to which the scheme relates) at a time before the
scheme became a frozen scheme unless:

●   at that time the scheme was not being wound-up; and

●   the scheme continued to have active members (ie was not frozen); and

●   one of conditions A to I set out in reg 9 apply, principally that:

     ●   **A, B:** there was no debt due from the company at that time under s 75; or

     ●   **C:** the s 75 debt was paid before the applicable time; or

     ●   **D, E, F, G:** there was a withdrawal arrangement or apportionment
         arrangement under the Employer Debt Regulations and relevant
         amount due was paid before the applicable time; or

- **H:** the s 75 debt was not paid solely because the employer was not notified of it (and of the amount of it) sufficiently in advance of the applicable time for it to be paid before that time; or

- **I:** a s 75 debt arose, but is excluded from the assets of the scheme 'because it is unlikely to be recovered without disproportionate cost or within a reasonable time'[1].

1 Employer Debt Regulations, regulation 9(14) (reg 9(6) before the amendments made from 6 April 2008). This "unlikely to be recovered without disproportionate cost or within a reasonable time" wording mirrors the exclusion of such an asset for scheme specific funding purposes in regulation 3(1)(b) of the Scheme Funding Regulations and regulation 6(1)(b) of the MFR Regulations – see also para 33.97 below.

32.17   There are special rules for multi-employer sectionalised schemes – ie schemes with more than one employer which have separate independent sections with separated assets (eg industry-wide schemes)[1].

1 Employer Debt Regulations, reg 8.

PPF notices and Entry Rules

32.18   An 'employer' for the purpose of the PPF notification obligations in PA 2004, s 120 and 122 (see Chapter 28 above) includes a company which was an employer of active members in a scheme in the past if the company has continued to be treated as an employer for s 75 purposes – ie have a potential liability under s 75 to the scheme.

This flows from regs 1(4) and 1(5) of the PPF Entry Rules Regulations which expand the definition of employer in broadly (but not identically) the same way as applies under s 75.

32.19   Regulation 1(4) deals with schemes becoming frozen and is the same as reg 9(1) of the Employer Debt Regulations.

Regulation 1(4) states that it applies for the purposes of Part 2 of PA 2004. Conversely, reg 1(5) states that it only applies for the purposes of the PPF Entry Rules Regulations. It is not clear why there is a distinction or if, in practice, it matters.

32.20   Regulation 1(5) is broadly similar to reg 9(2) of the Employer Debt Regulations and deals with a situation where an employer has ceased to participate and a s 75 debt would have arisen.

The conditions in reg 1(5) are similar to conditions A to I in reg 9(2) of the Employer Debt Regulations outlined above, save that:

- Condition H in the Employer Debt Regulations does not apply in the PPF Entry Rules Regulations. This condition allows a company not to be deemed an employer if the s 75 debt has not been paid solely because the company was not notified of the debt sufficiently in advance to allow it to be paid. This is presumably excluded because it is not appropriate to apply it in relation to the PPF.

- Conditions D to G in the Employer Debt Regulations apply in a modified form in the PPF Entry Rules Regulations. These conditions deal with payment of a reduced s 75 debt under an apportionment arrangement or withdrawal arrangement.

    In the Employer Debt Regulations, it refers to payment of a relevant debt under that arrangement. In the PPF Entry Rules Regulations it refers to a legally enforceable agreement to reduce the debt (such a legally enforceable agreement outside an apportionment arrangement under the Employer Debt Regulations may well mean that the scheme is no longer an eligible scheme for PPF purposes – see Chapter 35 below dealing with compromises).

See also reg 1(2) and (3) of the Pensions Protection Fund (Multi-employer Schemes) (Modification) Regulations 2005 (SI 2005/441, as amended).

32.21 This is the view taken by the PPF – see the reference to a 'past employer' at para 2.1 on page 3 of the PPF Guidance for Insolvency Practitioners (April 2009).

See generally section 6.2 of the talk '*No room at the orphanage: some issues relating to PPF Entry*' given by Ian Greenstreet and Helen Butler to the APL in April 2009.

Summary of release conditions for former employers

32.22

Condition	Employer Debt Regulations, reg 9	PPF Entry Rules Regulations, reg 1(5)
No s 75 debt due on cessation	A or B	D
s 75 debt paid	C	A
s 75 debt reduced	D, E, F or G	B (debt became due, reduced by legally enforceable agreement, reduced amount paid)
s 75 not paid because company not told sufficiently in advance	H	Not applicable
s 75 debt arose, but 'unlikely to be recovered without disproportionate cost or within a reasonable time'	I	C

See also the appendix to the talk given by Ian Greenstreet and Helen Butler to the APL in April 2009 on '*No room at the orphanage: Some issues relating to PPF entry*'.

CHAPTER 33

Contributions to pension schemes

GENERAL POSITION

33.1   There is no general overriding legal requirement for an employer to contribute to any pension arrangement for its employees (save for payment of national insurance contributions, by way of contributions to the state pension scheme). The Pensions Act 2008 envisages imposing obligations (probably from April 2012) on employers to contribute to personal accounts.

33.2   Currently, stakeholder provisions apply. Under the current law, employers with more than five employees are obliged to have arrangements to nominate a stakeholder pension and to have payment arrangements available so that employees can direct contributions to be made to them out of pay (Welfare Reform and Pensions Act 1999). But no employer contributions to such arrangements are required.

It is envisaged that the stakeholder provisions will cease to apply when the personal accounts provisions under PA 2008 come into force.

33.3   An employer may enter into an arrangement with employees to establish or contribute to such pension arrangements and, if a contractual obligation, this will then be enforceable by the employees (or trustees), in the usual way, on the insolvency of the employer. Three areas should be noted:

(a)   Certain contributions owing by an employer to an occupational pension scheme are made preferential by virtue of category 4 of Sch 6 to the Insolvency Act 1986 – see Chapter 10 above. This category does not extend to any other claim for damages that the employee may have as a contractual matter. Such a claim would only be preferential to the extent to which it could be considered to be remuneration within category 5 of Sch 6 – see paras 10.63 to 10.68 above.

(b)   Certain unpaid contributions to an occupational pension scheme or a personal pension scheme are claimable from the National Insurance Fund under PSA 1993, s 124 (see Chapter 13 above). Again, such amounts are payable direct to the scheme and not to the employee. It may, perhaps, be the case that the employee could claim such an amount from the National

Insurance Fund under ERA 1996, s 184 if such contributions could be considered to be arrears of pay – see Chapter 13 above.

(c) Any amounts which the employer has deducted from wages or salary paid to the employee by way of contribution to the pension arrangement, but which the employer has not yet in fact paid to the relevant pension arrangement will probably, if amounts have been placed in a separate account or fund, be impressed with a trust – see eg *Re Chelsea Cloisters Ltd*[1], *Re Fleet Disposal Services Ltd*[2] and *Re Lewis's of Leicester Ltd*[3]. Contrast *Re ILG Travel*[4] where no separate account had in fact been set up[5] and *Re Holiday Promotions (Europe) Ltd*[6] where no intention could be shown to keep deposits separate. More recently see *Sendo International Limited*[7] and *Farepak Food & Gifts Limited*[8].

Trust assets fall outside the assets available to the other creditors of the insolvent employer through the insolvency practitioner – see also para 10.38 above.

Such a trust may arise by the employer seeking to comply with the requirements of the pensions legislation:

- Since 6 April 1997, where employers are responsible for paying benefits to pension scheme members (eg as paying agent for pension scheme trustees), they must generally hold the amount received in a separate account at a bank if it has not been paid within two business days – see reg 15 of the Occupational Pension Schemes (Scheme Administration) Regulations 1996 (SI 1996/1715).

- From 6 April 1997 to 2 April 2000 failure without reasonable excuse by an employer to pay the amount of such deducted employee contributions to the trustees of an occupational pension scheme before a prescribed date (generally by the 19th of the calendar month following the deduction) was a criminal offence[9].

Section 10 of the Welfare Reform and Pensions Act 1999 amended this from 3 April 2000 so that a failure to pay renders the employer liable to a civil penalty and requires the trustees to notify the Pensions Regulator (PA 1995, s 49(9)). A criminal offence remains: being knowingly concerned in the fraudulent evasion of the obligation imposed by PA 1995, s 49(8) – see paras 10.40 to 10.43 above.

1 (1981) 41 P & CR 98, CA.
2 [1995] 1 BCLC 345 (Lightman J).
3 [1995] 1 BCLC 428 (Robert Walker J).
4 [1995] 2 BCLC 128; [1996] BCC 21 (Jonathan Parker J).
5 On the issue of there being no trust if funds have not in fact been put aside or earmarked, see further the Privy Council in *Re Goldcorp Exchange Ltd* [1994] 2 All ER 806, 823 and Blackburne J in *Re TXU Europe Group Ltd* [2003] EWHC 3105, [2004] 1 BCLC 519, [2004] OPLR 323, [2004] PLR 175. See also *Re BA Peters plc* [2008] All ER (D) 392 (Jun) (Nicholas Strauss QC, sitting as a deputy judge of the High Court) and on appeal, *Moriarty v Various Customers of BA Peters Plc (in administration)* [2009] EWCA Civ 1604 and *Re Global Europe Trader Ltd* [2009] EWHC 602 (Ch), [2009] All ER (D) 297 (Mar).
6 [1996] BCC 671. See also *OT Computers Ltd (in administration) v First National Tricity Finance Ltd* [2003] EWHC 1010 (Ch); [2003] All ER (D) 118 (May) (Pumfrey J).

7 [2006] EWHC 2935; [2007] 1 BCLC 141 (Blackburne J).

8 [2006] EWHC 3272; [2006] All ER (D) 265 (Dec) (Mann J). Most recently see *Power v Revenue and Customs Commissioners: Re Farepak Food & Gifts* [2009] EWHC 2580; [2009] All ER (D) 286 (Oct) (Warren J).

9 PA 1995, s 49(8), and the Occupational Pension Schemes (Scheme Administration) Regulations 1996, SI 1996/1715, reg 16, as amended by SI 1997/768.
Directors, officers and others (potentially including an insolvency practitioner – see Chapter 8 above) can also be criminally liable if the failure occurred as a result of their consent, connivance or neglect – PA 1995, s 115.

33.4   In New Zealand in *MacIntosh v Fortex Group Ltd*[1], the Court of Appeal overturned the ruling by Gallen J[2] that a remedial constructive trust should be imposed on the assets of an insolvent employer which has failed to pay contributions to an occupational pension scheme.

1 [1998] 3 NZLR 17, NZ CA. Noted by David Brown in (1998) 14 Insolvency Law & Practice 334.
2 [1997] 1 NZLR 711 (Gallen J).

33.5   Similarly, in Canada, a constructive trust was refused by R A Blair J in *Attorney General of Canada v Confederation Life Insurance Company*[1] in relation to a failure by an insolvent employer to pay under an unfunded pension arrangement (a simple contractual pension promise).

1 (1995) 8 CCPB 1 (Blair J).

33.6   In Great Britain it is even less likely that a remedial constructive trust would be imposed by the courts. There are at least four reasons for this:

(a)   in Great Britain the courts have been more reluctant than the New Zealand courts to hold that an employer is in a fiduciary position with its employees – compare the comments of Robert Walker J in *National Grid v Laws*[1] with those of Cooke P in the New Zealand Court of Appeal in *Cullen v Pension Holdings Ltd*[2];

(b)   the courts have generally held that there can be no trust if funds have not in fact been put aside or earmarked, see further the Privy Council in *Re Goldcorp Exchange Ltd*[3] and Blackburne J in *Re TXU Europe Group Ltd*[4];

(c)   imposing a remedial constructive trust could be seen as an interference with the statutory scheme laid down by Parliament in the various provisions relating to contributions in the Pensions Act 2004 (scheme specific funding under Part 3) and previously in the Pensions Act 1995 (PA 1995) (including the minimum funding requirement under ss 56–61); and

(d)   a remedial constructive trust on an insolvent employer would also be a route to override the statutory priorities laid down by Parliament in the Insolvency Act - see the comments of Mummery LJ in *Re Polly Peck International plc (No 2)*[5].

1 [1997] PLR 157, [1997] OPLR 161 (Robert Walker J).
2 (1991) 1 NZSC 40,233 at 40,298, NZ CA.
3 [1994] 2 All ER 806, 823, PC.
4 [2003] EWHC 3105, [2004] 1 BCLC 519, [2004] OPLR 323, [2004] PLR 175, [2003] All ER (D) 326 (Dec) (Blackburne J).
5 [1998] 3 All ER 812, CA.

33.7   There may also be a contractual commitment on the employer to the trustees of an occupational pension scheme. Where there is an occupational pension scheme which has been established under trust (eg an Inland Revenue approved or, from April 2006, HMRC registered scheme) the employer may have entered into a commitment under the scheme's trust documents to the trustees of the scheme to make contributions.

Such a commitment is enforceable in the usual way as a contractual debt of the employer in the relevant insolvency proceeding. On the contractual point, see eg *MNOPF Trustees Ltd v FT Everard & Sons Ltd*[1].

For cases on the ambit of a contribution rule, see *Capital Cranfield Trustees Ltd v Pinsent Curtis*[2], *Allied Domecq (Holdings) Ltd v Allied Domecq First Pension Trust Ltd*[3] and *Alitalia-Linee Aeree Italiane SPA v Rotunno*[4].

1 [2005] EWHC 446; [2005] OPLR 315; [2005] PLR 225 (Patten J).
2 [2005] EWCA Civ 860; [2005] 4 All ER 449; [2005] OPLR 385, CA.
3 [2008] EWCA Civ 1084; [2008] All ER (D) 158 (Oct); [2008] PLR 425, CA.
4 [2008] EWHC 185 (Ch); [2008] All ER (D) 130 (Feb) (Henderson J).

33.8   However, it is relatively common for an employer establishing an occupational pension scheme to include provision in the pension scheme documentation for the employer to be able to terminate its liability to contribute to the scheme. A requirement for reasonable notice may be implied – see *Capital Cranfield Trustees Ltd v Pinsent Curtis*[1].

1 [2005] EWCA Civ 860; [2005] 4 All ER 449; [2005] OPLR 385, CA, per Smith LJ at para 32.

33.9   This, combined with a relatively common provision entitling the employer to wind up the scheme, would often have resulted in the past in there being no contractual claim against the employer either by the trustees or by the employee (but see para 2.30 above).

It would also be usual in such circumstances for the winding-up provisions in the pension scheme to provide for the trustees to use the assets of the scheme to secure benefits in a particular order of priority. To the extent that there are insufficient assets to secure particular levels of benefits, those benefits would abate proportionately – see Chapter 39 (Winding-up the pension scheme) below.

33.10   In these circumstances, although employees might expect that benefits of a particular level would be provided out of the pension scheme, in fact the employer could argue that it did not have a legal liability to ensure that the funding was provided to enable such benefits to be secured (relying on the express provision entitling it to cease to contribute, etc).

STATUTORY PROVISION ON FUNDING

33.11   As mentioned in Chapter 22 above, from 1997 provision was made in the Pensions Act 1995 to impose a debt obligation on the employer to provide a minimum level of funding for revenue approved occupational pension schemes:

- minimum funding requirement: the PA 1995, ss 56–61, imposed an obligation on employers (broadly) to maintain the funding of on-going schemes at a minimum level, set out in the regulations. This is called the 'minimum funding requirement' (MFR);

- debt on the employer: the PA 1995, s 75, imposed a debt obligation on employers when (broadly) the pension scheme started to wind-up or the employer entered liquidation or ceased to participate in the scheme.

33.12 These statutory obligations generally do not apply to money purchase pension schemes (ie those where all the benefits are money purchase). Separate provision is made for these schemes – see Chapter 38 (Money purchase schemes) below.

33.13 These provisions of PA 1995 were reviewed and strengthened by the Pensions Act 2004. Broadly:

(a) **Scheme specific funding (SSF):** This replaces the MFR with new funding provisions. Broadly the schedule of contributions is now fixed by agreement between the trustees and the employers (or fixed by the Pensions Regulator if agreement cannot be reached). There are savings for schemes where the trustees have an unfettered right to fix contributions. This replaces the MFR and applies from the first formal actuarial valuation with an effective date on or after 22 September 2005[1].

(b) **Employer debt (s75):** The statutory debt provisions in s 75 of the Pensions Act 1995 have been strengthened. In particular it now operates by reference to the amount considered to be necessary to secure benefits on a buy-out with an insurer.

(c) **PPF:** The Pension Protection Fund applies in some cases to take over eligible schemes and provide a protected level of benefits.

1 See the transitional provisions in Sch 4 to the Occupational Pension Schemes (Scheme Funding) Regulations 2005 (SI 2005/3377).

MINIMUM FUNDING REQUIREMENT (MFR)

33.14 The MFR was built around three processes:

(a) full actuarial valuations which needed to be undertaken at least once every three years, at which the MFR level was calculated and certified by the actuary[1]. The MFR Regulations prescribed the information that had to be provided from the valuation and the statements that had to be produced[2];

(b) agreement of a contribution schedule following each valuation[3] showing the amount of contributions payable by the company and by the members, and the dates they are due to be paid;

(c) annual reviews by the scheme actuary of the contribution schedule[4]; if there had been any changes (either within the scheme or externally) which the actuary considered would have adversely affected the funding of the scheme the contribution schedule may have needed to have been revised; if the approximate assessment revealed that the MFR level had fallen below 90%, a full actuarial valuation needed to be undertaken within six months of the date the actuary certified that the contributions were insufficient[5].

1 PA 1995, s 57(1)(a).
2 PA 1995, s 57(5).
3 PA 1995, s 58(3)(c).
4 PA 1995, s 57(1)(b).
5 PA 1995, s 57(4)(a).

33.15 For further details on the MFR requirements, see the second edition of this book and the book *The Guide to the Pensions Act 1995* by Freshfields (LexisNexis Tolley, 1995).

SCHEME SPECIFIC FUNDING (SSF)

33.16 The Pensions Act 2004 introduced a new funding regime, called 'scheme specific funding'. An overview is given below.

Part 3 of the Pensions Act 2004

33.17 Under Part 3 (ss 221 to 223) of the Pensions Act 2004 the minimum funding requirement (MFR) applicable under PA 1995 has been replaced with a scheme-specific funding requirement (SSF).

33.18 Much of the detail of the new SSF regime is set out in the Occupational Pension Schemes (Scheme Funding) Regulations 2005 (the 'Scheme Funding Regulations').

33.19 The Scheme Funding Regulations came into force on 30 December 2005. In addition to the Scheme Funding Regulations, the Pensions Regulator (tPR) has issued a code of practice. It also published (in May 2006) a statement entitled 'How the Pensions Regulator will regulate the funding of defined benefits'. This identified the approach that tPR intended to adopt in relation to implementing the new funding regime.

Timing for the scheme specific funding regime

33.20 The Scheme Funding Regulations provide that the new regime will apply to schemes with effect from the date of their first actuarial valuation after 22 September 2005. Until that time the MFR continued to apply to schemes. In practice, scheme valuations are normally required at intervals of no more than 3 years. This means that most schemes should have completed their first SSF valuation by now.

One aspect of the new regime applied to all relevant schemes immediately: a requirement to send pension scheme members an annual funding statement. The first one needed to have been issued before 22 September 2006.

Excluded schemes

33.21 Certain occupational schemes are excluded from the new regime, including schemes that provide only money purchase benefits (and insured death benefits) and unapproved schemes with fewer than 100 members (see Chapter 31 above).

Key features of the new SSF regime

Statutory funding objective (SFO)

33.22 Every relevant scheme will be subject to a statutory funding objective[1] (SFO): a scheme must have sufficient and appropriate assets to cover its 'technical provisions'.

The term 'technical provisions' is used in the EU IORP directive[2] as meaning, broadly, the amount of assets a scheme needs to hold now, on the basis of the actuarial methods and assumptions used, in order to pay its accrued benefits as they fall due in the future.

1 PA 2004, s 222.
2 The IORP Directive is the EU '*Directive on Institutions for Occupational Retirement Provision*' (2003/41/EC)

33.23 The Scheme Funding Regulations give more detail on how the technical provisions of a scheme are to be calculated.

33.24 A key change from the MFR legislation is that, under the Scheme Funding Regulations, trustees must determine (usually in agreement with the employer) the actuarial methods and assumptions to be used, having obtained advice from the scheme actuary (the MFR provisions set out a specific set of valuation measure).

The Scheme Funding Regulations provide that:

- an accrued benefits funding method must be used[1] (described in tPR's code of practice – see para 33.38 below); and

- in calculating the technical provisions the trustees must follow a set of principles (set out in the Scheme Funding Regulations) on actuarial assumptions, interest rates, mortality etc. The principles[2] require a large degree of 'prudence' to be used in, for example, choosing the actuarial assumptions and the discount rates (but unhelpfully prudence is not defined).

1 Scheme Funding Regulations, reg 5(2).
2 Scheme Funding Regulations, reg 5(2).

Statement of funding principles (SFP)

33.25   Within 15 months of the date of the first valuation under the new regime[1], the trustees must prepare a statement of funding principles (SFP). This is the written statement of their policy for ensuring that the statutory funding objective (SFO) is met[2].

The statement must record the methods and assumptions used in calculating the scheme's technical provisions and various other policy matters[3] (eg policy on cash equivalent transfer payments).

1 Scheme Funding Regulations, reg 6(2).
2 PA 2004, s 223(1)(a).
3 Scheme Funding Regulations, reg 6(1).

Actuarial valuations and reports

33.26   As under the MFR regime, actuarial valuations must be prepared at least every three years (every year if there is no intervening annual actuarial report)[1]. These must be based on a funding approach consistent with the strategy set out in the scheme's statement of funding principles and annual reports.

The Scheme Funding Regulations provide that actuarial valuations must contain the actuary's certification of the calculation of the technical provisions and the actuary's estimate of the solvency of the scheme[2].

1 PA 2004, s 224(1).
2 Scheme Funding Regulations, reg 7(4).

33.27   In addition to triennial valuations there must be annual actuarial reports[1]. Following each actuarial valuation or report, members and beneficiaries must be sent a summary funding statement[2].

1 PA 2004, s 224.
2. Occupational Pension Schemes (Disclosure of Information) Regulations 1996 (SI 1996/1655, as amended), reg 5(12ZA).

33.28   Actuarial valuations must be in place within 15 months of the effective date and reports must be in place within 12 months[1].

Transitional arrangements applied where a scheme's valuation had an effective date between 22 September 2005 and 29 December 2005. For such valuations the period was extended to 18 months.

1 PA 2004, s 224(4), and Scheme Funding Regulations, reg 7.

Recovery plan

33.29   If the valuation shows that the statutory funding objective is not met, the trustees must put in place a recovery plan (s 226, PA 2004), setting out the period over which the deficit is to be remedied. A copy of each recovery plan must be sent to tPR. These must similarly be in place within 15 months of the effective date of the actuarial valuation[1].

1 PA 2004, s 226, and Scheme Funding Regulations, reg 8.

33.30   tPR's code of practice (see para 33.38 below) includes some useful points for the trustees to take into account when considering the structure of a recovery plan, eg a shorter recovery period is likely to be appropriate if most of the members are already in receipt of pension or if there may be difficulty in pursuing an overseas employer.

In practice, tPR's view on funding is reinforced from time to time by statements it makes on funding issues – see for example its statement in June 2009 on 'Scheme funding and the employer covenant'[1].

1 http://www.thepensionsregulator.gov.uk/pdf/EmployerCovenantStatementJune2009.pdf

Schedules of contributions

33.31   Schedules of contributions for five-year periods (or longer if there is a longer recovery plan) must be in place within 15 months of the effective date of the actuarial valuation[1].

1 PA 2004, s 227, and Scheme Funding Regulations, reg 9.

33.32   tPR code of practice (see para 33.38 below) makes recommendations as to how the schedule should be structured in the interests of clarity and how certain items need not be included, provided an explanatory note appears (eg professional fees met directly by the employer). It specifically states that the PPF levy should be treated as an annual expense item, and if it forms part of the employer's overall contribution rate a note to this effect should be included, indicating the assumed annual amount of the levy.

Employer agreement/consultation?

33.33   The Pensions Act 2004 and the Scheme Funding Regulations provide that generally the trustees must agree with the employer the methods and assumptions to be used in the technical provisions (ie actuarial valuation) and each of the statement of funding principles, the recovery plan and the schedule of contributions[1]. Agreement must be obtained within 15 months of the effective date of the valuation[2]. See further para 33.70 below.

1 PA 2004, s 229.
2 Scheme Funding Regulations, reg 13.

33.34   But this requirement for employer consent does not apply where the relevant scheme trust deed gives the trustees unilateral power to determine the employer contribution rate with no power for the employer to suspend contributions. In those cases the trustees need only consult with the employer about each of these matters[1].

The requirement for agreement with the employer in relation to the statutory funding provisions still applies if, for example, it is currently the scheme actuary who fixes the employer contribution rate or if employers have the power to suspend their contribution obligation under the deed[2].

497

33.35   In *British Vita Unlimited v British Vita Pension Fund Trustees Limited*[3]
Warren J had to deal with the inter-relation between the scheme specific funding
regime under Part 3 of the Pensions Act 2004 with the terms of an express
funding rule in the scheme rules.

The new scheme specific funding regime (SSF) under the Pensions Act 2004
envisages that funding matters will be agreed between the trustees and the
employers (with the Pensions Regulator fixing in default of agreement).

This raises the question as to what happens if the scheme rules provide for a
different method of fixing contributions which can result in a higher rate being
set.

General views were that (unless the express saving applied) the trustee powers
were overridden by the statutory provision. But in *British Vita* Warren J held that
trustee powers remain and are not overridden by the SSF provisions in Part 3 of
PA 2004.

The facts of the case were that following the acquisition of British Vita by a
private equity purchaser, the trustees of two British Vita pension schemes sought
significant additional contributions based on valuing the schemes using more
conservative actuarial and investment assumptions than had been used in the last
formal valuations. The trustees purported to use their powers under the scheme
rules in making the demands.

The employer challenged the validity of the demands.

Warren J held that the demands had been validly made. In reaching his conclusion, he considered the new scheme funding regime:

1   The scheme funding legislation (Part 3 of the Pensions Act 2004 and the
     Scheme Funding Regulations) does not override scheme contribution rules.
     Instead, it provides a minimum basis. Trustees may therefore seek contri-
     butions at a higher level than required to meet the statutory funding objec-
     tive if their scheme rules allow.

2   A scheme contribution rule can only be overridden if it conflicts with the
     schedule of contributions requirements under the scheme funding legislation.

Until the first contributions schedule produced after the first Pensions Act 2004
valuation is in effect, the scheme contribution rule cannot as a matter of principle conflict with any of the requirements of the scheme funding legislation.

Warren J left open the question whether the scheme rule is overridden after the
first contributions schedule after the first Pensions Act 2004 valuation. This was
because the facts of the case allowed him to and because the first schedule may
be imposed by the Pensions Regulator so the Pensions Regulator 'may wish to
express views' requiring them to be joined to the proceedings.

The full implications of this decision remain to be seen.

In practice there may not be an issue if trustees (or a third party – e.g. the actuary)
are empowered under the scheme rules to fix the ongoing contributions. The
Scheme Funding Regulations contain an express provision reserving the trustees'
powers where trustees have a unilateral power under the scheme rules to fix contributions (and the employer has no power to reduce or suspend contributions).

However, the case is likely to be particularly relevant where, for example,
there is a provision in the rules allowing employers to suspend contributions.

Trustees may now seek to fix ongoing contributions in excess of the SSF contributions (at least before the employer exercises its suspension power).

The inter-relation of scheme funding rules with the statutory funding regime in Part 3 of PA 2004 continues to cause difficulties – see for example *Allied Domecq (Holdings) Ltd v Allied Domecq First Pension Trust Ltd*[4].

1 Scheme Funding Regulations, Sch 2, para 9(1).
2 Scheme Funding Regulations, Sch 2, paras 9(1)(b) and (5).
3 [2007] EWHC 953 (Ch); [2008] 1 All ER 37; [2008] ICR 1295, [2007] PLR 157 (Warren J).
4 [2008] EWCA Civ 1084; [2008] All ER (D) 158 (Oct); [2008] PLR 425, CA.

33.36   Where the scheme specific funding regime requires trustees to agree the funding rate with the employer, but they fail to reach agreement, the matter must be referred to tPR, which has the power to give directions including imposing a schedule of contributions for the scheme[1].

In order to determine whether the scheme specific funding regime changes the balance of power, employers and trustees need to look at the funding rules in their governing trust documentation.

1 PA 2004, ss 229(5) and 231.

33.37   A summary of the position is set out in tPR's Code of Practice 03:

Rules of the scheme	*Effect of legislation*
Trustees have, unrestrained by conditions, the power to determine the contribution rate and no other person has the power to reduce or suspend contributions.	Trustees are required to consult the employer but the employer's agreement is not required (Sch 2, para 9(1) to (3)). The code of practice recommends, however, that the trustees should seek to obtain the employer's agreement.
Trustees have, subject to conditions, the power to determine the contribution rate and no other person has the power to reduce or suspend contributions.	If the conditions are satisfied, trustees are required to consult the employer but the employer's agreement is not required (Sch 2, para 9(1) to (4) of). The code of practice recommends, however, that the trustees should seek to obtain the employer's agreement.
The contribution rate is determined by, or on the advice of, a person other than the trustees or the employer (usually the actuary).	Trustees must obtain the employer's agreement. They must take into account the recommendations of the other person on the method and assumptions for calculating the technical provisions and on the preparation of any recovery plan (regs 5(3)(b) and 8(2)(e); tPR must also take into account this other person's recommendations when exercising any of its Pt 3 powers, see s 231(2) and reg 14(1)).

Source: tPR Code of Practice 03: Funding defined benefits

Code of practice 03

33.38   The Pensions Regulator issued its code of practice 03 *Funding defined benefits* in early 2006. The code is available on its website[1].

Parts of the code of practice have already been referred to. The code is much more detailed than tPR's draft of March 2005.

It aims to summarise the requirements of the Scheme Funding Regulations as well as cross-refer to other codes of practice (eg notifiable events) where appropriate. It introduces a system of symbols, or flags, to indicate where the principle being set out is varied in certain cases (eg cross-border schemes, schemes with fewer than 100 members).

1 http://www.thepensionsregulator.gov.uk/pdf/codeFundingFinal.pdf

33.39   The code of practice recommends that the trustees put in place an action plan for the valuation process, taking into account all the steps which will need to be taken and the dates for completion of each step. It also emphasises the importance of record keeping, especially in relation to decisions made, and of employers and trustees providing each other with information and keeping an open dialogue.

33.40   The legislation contains numerous references to steps being taken within 'a reasonable period'. The code gives guidance on what constitutes a reasonable period', eg a recovery plan should be sent to tPR within ten working days, as should a report to tPR that the trustees and the employer have failed to reach agreement where required. A report to tPR of contribution failure should similarly be made within ten working days but where an immediate report is required, the trustees should make their initial report by telephone and follow it up in writing.

33.41   The Scheme Funding Regulations envisage that all the relevant documents (the SFO, the SFP, the valuation and the recovery plan) should be in place within 15 months (18 months in transitional cases) of the effective date of the scheme's actuarial valuation.

33.42   Multi-employer schemes will often have in place arrangements to nominate one employer to act for the others (eg on consultation and agreement).

tPR and regulation of scheme funding

33.43   The chart below gives an overview of the five commonly used measures of pension fund liabilities and their key features:

Valuation method	How assets are valued	How liabilities are valued	Main characteristics
Buy-out	Market value	Discounted at around gilt rate, most other assumptions very conservative Termination basis	Toughest measure, largest shortfall, highest cost, limited risk to pensioners Used in employer debt calculations under PA 1995, s 75

Valuation method	How assets are valued	How liabilities are valued	Main characteristics
FRS17/IAS19	Market value	Discounted at corporate bond rate, other assumptions best estimates Projected future salary basis for actives	Standard accounting measure, mandatory on face of accounts from 2005 onwards
MFR Minimum Funding Requirement	Market value	Discount rate takes account of equity returns in working lifetime, but not after retirement, other assumptions prescribed Termination basis	The weakest measure as its name implies
s 179 PPF Levy	Market value	Discounted at index linked gilt rate minus 0.5%, other assumptions best estimates Termination basis	Prescribed basis about buy-out, applied to PPF compensation level benefits
Ongoing funding basis	Usually market value	Various methods	
Projected future salary basis for actives	Stronger than MFR, many similar to FRS17 but weaker than buy-out		

Source: adapted from chart in tPR consultation document of 31 October 2005

33.44   The Pensions Regulator (tPR) finalised and published in May 2006 its statement 'How the Pensions Regulator will regulate the funding of defined benefits' (the '2006 Statement'). It was updated in September 2008. This is available on its website[1].

1 At www.thepensionsregulator.gov.uk/pdf/regulatorstatement.pdf

33.45   The 2006 Statement gives details on how tPR intends to monitor and investigate funding arrangements under the new statutory funding regime for defined benefit occupational pension schemes. It is a revised version of the consultation draft statement which tPR issued on 31 October 2005, taking account of comments from respondents to the consultation.

33.46 The 2006 Statement adds another layer of guidance on top of tPR's Code of Practice No 3, 'Funding defined benefits'.

tPR's general approach to scheme funding

33.47 tPR's statutory objectives include protecting the benefits of members of occupational schemes and reducing the risk of calls on the Pension Protection Fund (PPF)[1]. It may intervene in schemes where the trustees have failed to comply with their duties and if the funding of their scheme poses a risk to those statutory objectives.

1 PA 2004, s 5.

33.48 However, tPR's stated aim is that trustees and employers should work together without tPR's involvement. If tPR does become involved, it will use its statutory powers of intervention only if it considers it cannot achieve an equally good outcome by informal means, eg requesting more information and allowing a reasonable time for recommended steps to be taken. However:

> 'Trustees should not assume that the absence of any immediate regulatory inter-
> vention means that they satisfy the requirements of Pt 3 of PA 2004 or have set
> sufficiently robust provisions to adequately protect their members'.

33.49 The 2006 Statement makes the point that tPR's long-term objective is to strengthen scheme funding through effective implementation of the new regime. Defined benefit (DB) schemes are required to implement the new regime for valuations with effective dates falling on or after 22 September 2005. tPR hoped that by the end of 2009 all DB schemes subject to the SSF provisions in Part 3 of PA 2004 will have completed valuations and that those with a shortfall will have agreed a recovery plan which takes into account:

- prudent assumptions for the technical provisions; and

- appropriate recognition of risks to members taking account of what is reasonably affordable for employers: 'Our position is that the best means of delivering the members' benefits is usually for the scheme to have the continued support of a viable employer'.

33.50 tPR's general approach is therefore based on the following guiding principles:

- Protecting members.

- Scheme-specific approach, looking especially at:
  - the strength of the employer and its ability to eliminate a funding shortfall; and
  - the scheme's maturity (eg a new scheme with a strong employer could look risky on paper but not be so in reality).

- Risk-based intervention: focusing on the schemes that pose the greatest risk to members' benefits and to the PPF.

- Proportionate response: striking a balance between elimination of the shortfall and how quickly the employer can reasonably afford to eliminate it.

- Preventative: taking action where possible before risks materialise.

- Practicable: given resources and information available to tPR.

- tPR will act as a referee, not a player.

How tPR will identify schemes presenting the greatest risk

33.51   tPR notes that most DB schemes are likely to be underfunded, so it needs to prioritise those schemes that pose the greatest risk to its statutory objectives. It will identify these by means of triggers for intervention:

- technical provisions are not prudent;

- recovery plans are inappropriate; and

- non-agreement between trustees and employers.

33.52   tPR makes it clear that the triggers are not targets; they are 'only component parts in our regulatory toolkit and not the standards against which we will measure DB pension schemes'. (The only reference in the 2006 Statement to funding targets is that trustees of schemes still subject to the minimum funding requirement (MFR) should aim for funding targets higher than the MFR in the run-up to the first valuation under new regime.) The triggers will be kept under regular review.

How will tPR find out about schemes' funding levels?

33.53

- Reports under Part 3 of PA 2004, eg

  - by trustees under s 229 – failure to reach agreement on scheme funding; and

  - by actuary unable to certify calculation of technical provisions or schedule of contributions.

- Recovery plans submitted to tPR (PA 2004, s 226(6)).

- Notifiable event reports (PA 2004, s 69).

- Scheme returns.

- Requests for clearance.

- Trustee requests for guidance on funding plan proposals.

- Market intelligence.

Technical provisions trigger

33.54 A scheme's 'technical provisions' (the term taken from the EU Occupational Pensions Directive, IORP) means, broadly, the amount of assets a scheme needs to hold now, on the basis of the actuarial methods and assumptions used, to pay its accrued benefits as they fall due.

33.55 tPR's primary focus will be to ensure that the scheme's technical provisions have been calculated using methods and assumptions which are prudent given the scheme's circumstances.

33.56 tPR would make an initial assessment by comparing the s 179 (PPF risk-based levy valuation) and FRS17/IAS19 liabilities (IAS19 if available), regardless of which is higher.

33.57 It will then look at the strength of the employer covenant (including information from credit rating agencies) to assess if the trigger has come into operation.

33.58 The introduction of the technical provisions trigger represented a significant departure from the October 2005 consultation document, which instead referred to a funding target trigger and stated that tPR was likely to intervene if the funding level fell below 70 to 80 per cent of full buyout (which it said was the s 179 range). This was dropped. The new technical provisions trigger is less restrictive. tPR was at pains to emphasise that neither s 179 nor FRS17/IAS19 is a funding target. The revised approach involves looking at all the circumstances.

In its statement on 'Scheme funding and the employer covenant'[1] in June 2009, tPR stated that:

> 'At the current time, FRS17 is unlikely to represent an adequate level of prudence without further adjustment'.

1 http://www.thepensionsregulator.gov.uk/pdf/EmployerCovenantStatementJune2009.pdf

Recovery plan trigger

33.59 Under PA 2004 the recovery plan must set out the period over which the shortfall is to be met; this must be appropriate having regard to the nature and circumstances of the scheme. The code of practice states that 'trustees should aim for shortfall to be eliminated as quickly as employer can reasonably afford' – the future viability of the employer is important.

33.60 In its February 2009 statement to employers tPR said that where the employer and trustees agree to reschedule a recovery plan 'to maintain the long term health of the employer' a back-end loaded plan may be more appropriate than extending the plan length if there are short-term concerns over affordability to the employer. However if a new valuation shows a much larger scheme deficit 'a longer recovery plan length might be appropriate – remembering that the best outcome for scheme and employer is a viable sponsor that will continue to support the scheme'.

33.61   In June 2009 tPR said that its February 2009 statement sets out its position on agreeing recovery plans in general as well as instances where there might be a perceived need (eg because of the employer's financial difficulties) to renegotiate an already agreed plan.

33.62   tPR's 2006 Statement noted that triggers include:

- recovery period longer than ten years;

- recovery plan is significantly 'back-end loaded' (higher contributions towards the end of the period); and

- underlying assumptions, especially investment assumptions, appear inappropriate/unrealistic/over-optimistic.

33.63   The period in the 'longer than 10 years' trigger is not set in stone and in its February 2009 statement to employers, tPR said that to date it had seen and 'considered appropriate, recovery plans ranging in length from less than 1 year to over 20 years': tPR may also look at schemes where it believes that the employer can reasonably afford to pay off the shortfall more quickly, but in such cases it will focus its resources on schemes with weak or weakening employers. Furthermore, as noted in the Funding code of practice, in some circumstances a shorter recovery period is likely to be appropriate, eg if most members are pensioners.

33.64   When setting recovery plans, tPR's 2006 Statement states (para 3.22) that it expects envisages that trustees and employers will be able must show that they have taken:

- appropriate advice; and
- all available steps to minimise the risk of the funding position deteriorating further by:
  - adopting an investment policy 'strikes an appropriate balance between any upside potential of riskier asset classes whilst containing any downside risk'; and
  - achieving an appropriate balance between the cost of employer contributions going towards eliminating a shortfall and those going towards providing continued accrual of benefits.

33.65   If the employer is unable to pay contributions at the required level, tPR may require trustees and employers to consider modifying future accrual of benefits if they have not properly considered this option.

33.66   It is important to note that the technical provisions and recovery plan triggers are not to be used in isolation: tPR will look at the interaction between them.

tPR procedure

33.67 tPR will make a further assessment of the scheme's circumstances, to decide whether to intervene (informally or using statutory powers if necessary), including considering whether intervention is likely to protect the interests of the members and of the PPF.

33.68 Information likely to be requested includes the following (this is not an exclusive list):

- management accounts;
- employer's latest audited accounts plus updated information, eg budgets and forecasts, including projected cash flow;
- latest statement of investment principles;
- latest statement of funding principles;
- latest actuarial valuation and any actuarial report;
- trustee minutes;
- scheme rules; and
- where available, any independent reports or advice to trustees on matters such as scheme investments, financial strength of employer and use of contingent assets.

33.69 Factors tPR is likely to consider include:

- whether the trustees have taken appropriate advice;
- whether the trustees have considered all appropriate factors, including the code of practice;
- the assumptions used;
- the circumstances of the scheme and the employer, especially the employer covenant;
- the steps taken by the employer/trustees to mitigate the funding risk (eg modification of future accrual); and
- any contingent assets accepted by the trustees.

33.70 Guidance from tPR on the approach trustees are expected to take when considering the use of contingent assets in a scheme's funding strategy is available at www.thepensionsregulator.gov.uk/schemeFunding/contingentAssets/ index.aspx.

Special circumstances: additional considerations

33.71 Specific additional issues arise regarding certain types of scheme:

- employers subject to economic regulation (generally privatised industries):

    - effect of any periodic price review on the employer's ability to eliminate shortfall; and

    - franchise agreements (eg rail industry) – the outgoing franchisee will not necessarily be required to eliminate the shortfall before the end of the franchise term;

- multi-employer schemes:

    - whether industry-wide or for associated employers; and

    - whether investments are pooled or segregated;

- cross-border schemes:

    - requirement for full funding within two years means the recovery plan trigger cannot be used.

Non-agreement between trustees and employer

33.72 The new funding regime[1] requires trustees and employers to try to reach agreement on a number of issues, including:

- method and assumptions for the calculation of the technical provisions;

- content of the statement of funding principles;

- content of any recovery plan; and

- content of the schedule of contributions.

1 PA 2004, s 229. Modified for some schemes by the Scheme Funding Regulations (see in particular Sch 2, para 9).

33.73 If the statutory funding requirements are not met within the 15 month period, the trustees are potentially liable for a civil penalty unless they have taken all reasonable steps to secure compliance – see eg ss 223(4), 224(8), 226(7) and 227(8). In practice this means that trustees will want to show that they have taken reasonable steps to obtain agreement with the employer.

If trustees and employer are unable to reach agreement on these funding issues, tPR's code of practice indicates that trustees should show tPR that they have 'explored all reasonable avenues' eg alternative dispute resolution (ADR), mediation, and provide details of negotiations with the employer and of the reasons for non-agreement.

33.74 tPR may:

- give limited additional time to reach agreement on certain issues;

- suggest additional actuarial calculations; and

- suggest alternative dispute resolution (ADR).

33.75 If this still does not lead to agreement, Code of Practice 03 indicates that tPR may:

- require a skilled person's report, eg from the actuary regarding the calculations of the technical provisions using any methods and assumptions tPR specifies;

- modify future accrual of benefits;

- issue a direction as to the calculation of the technical provisions, indicating the method and assumptions to be used;

- direct how a recovery plan is to be drawn up, including its length;

- impose a schedule of contributions;

- issue a freezing order (stopping future accrual) while considering whether to order a scheme wind-up; and

- order a scheme wind-up.

Contribution failure report

33.76 Trustees must report to tPR and to the scheme members where a contribution failure is likely to be materially significant to tPR in the exercise of its functions[1]. Code of Practice 03 gives guidance on what is likely to be materially significant to tPR:

- the employer appears to be involved in fraudulent evasion of its obligation to pay members' pension deductions;

- there is reasonable cause to believe other dishonesty is involved;

- there is an immediate risk to members' benefits, eg pensions in payment normally met by the employer contribution;

- contributions remain unpaid 90 days after the due date (unless a one-off or infrequent administrative error then discovered and corrected);

- the employer appears not to have adequate procedures or systems in place for the payment of contributions and not to be taking adequate steps to rectify this; and the trustees conclude, after discussions with the employer, that there is for any reason no early prospect of contribution underpayments being corrected.

1 PA 2004, s 228(2).

33.77 tPR is likely to ask for an explanation from the employer. If it is not satisfied and intervenes, tPR may:

- issue an improvement notice regarding the unresolved procedural or system problems;

- impose a financial penalty on the employer if the improvement notice is ineffective or if a contribution failure appears to have been deliberate;

- recover unpaid contributions on behalf of the trustees if trustees are unable or unwilling to do it themselves;

- modify future accrual if the employer is unwilling or unable to pay contributions at the level required and the trustees and the employer are unable to agree themselves to such modification;

- issue a financial support direction;

- impose a freezing order if the employer appears unable or unwilling to continue to pay contributions at the level required; or

- in extreme circumstances, order a scheme wind-up where the employer is unwilling or unable to pay adequate contributions.

Contributions schedule in insolvency

33.78   A contributions schedule in place under the MFR provisions in PA 1995 will remain in place until a new contributions schedule under the SSF provisions in PA 2004 comes into force (see para 9 of Sch 4 to the Scheme Funding Regulations).

33.79   A contributions schedule under the SSF provisions in PA 2004 will cease to apply once the scheme enters winding-up (Scheme Funding Regulations, reg 17(1)(l) and see para 33.82 below and the table in Chapter 31 above). In practice if an assessment period starts all contributions are frozen while it continues (see PA 2004, s 133(3), discussed in Chapter 28 above and below).

33.80   Amounts shown in the contributions schedule are payable as debts by the employer. This applies both to:

- the contributions schedule under the MFR provisions – PA 1995, s 59(2); and

- the contributions schedule under the SSF provisions – PA 2004, s 228(3). This includes a schedule imposed by tPR under PA 2004, s 231 – see PA 2004, s 228(5).

33.81   In addition, failure by an employer to pay amounts due under a schedule of contributions under SSF renders the employer liable to a civil penalty from tPR under s 10 of PA 1995, if the failure is 'without reasonable excuse' – PA 2004, s 228(4)(b). There is no similar civil penalty on the employer for failing to pay amounts under an MFR schedule of contributions.

33.82   The obligation to pay future contributions under the schedule of contributions will terminate if the scheme starts to wind-up.

33.83　For an MFR schedule, regulation 28(4) of the MFR Regulations applies so that the schedule of contributions obligation in s 58, PA 1995 ceases to apply.

33.84　For an SSF schedule, reg 17(1)(l) of the Scheme Funding Regulations provides that Pt 3 of the Pensions Act 2004 does not apply to a scheme which starts to wind-up. This does not affect any rights or obligations arising before Pt 3 ceased to apply (reg 17(4)).

If the winding-up started after 30 December 2005 (the 'Commencement Date'), the exclusion of Pt 3 is dependent on the trustees obtaining before the end of each scheme year the actuary's estimate of the solvency of the scheme as at the end of the preceding scheme year (reg 18).

33.85　This cessation does not affect any 'rights or obligations arising' before Pt 3 ceased to apply – Scheme Funding Regulations, reg 17(4). For an MFR schedule the same applies under reg 28(5) of the MFR Regulations. This seems to mean amounts due and payable before the cessation.

33.86　Until the scheme starts to wind-up, the insolvent company (employer) will remain liable to pay any contributions outstanding under the contributions schedule even if (perhaps unusually) it transpired that the pension scheme is in surplus and did not require the further contribution (there is no provision providing for this debt to be cancelled if the scheme is in surplus).

The insolvent company could request a new actuarial valuation, following which the schedule of contributions will be revised (under PA 2004, s 227). However, it is unlikely that the trustees will be obliged to agree to such a new valuation (which in any event will take time). The company's alternative (if it has power) is to wind up the scheme (see Chapter 39 below). It will not be possible to start a scheme winding-up if the scheme is in an assessment period (PA 2004, s 135(2) and (3) and see para 28.34 above).

The obligation to contribute under the schedule of contributions ceases on the scheme winding up commencing (see para 33.82 above). The trustees' powers to prevent a winding up and continue as a closed scheme (see PA 1995, s 38 and Chapter 39 below) may then become relevant.

33.87　If the scheme has entered an assessment period, no further contributions are payable to the scheme while the assessment period lasts[1])), save for

- any due to be paid before the assessment period stated (ie the date of the relevant insolvency) or

- any s 75 debts or the obligations envisaged in PA 2004, s 143(5) (eg under contribution notices etc)[2].

This statutory freeze on contributions being paid lasts while the assessment period is in place. If the assessment period ends with the PPF Board not assuming responsibility for the scheme, any payment obligations falling due during the assessment period can revive[3] (see para 33.102 below).

1 PA 2004, s133(3).

2 Reg 14 of the PPF Entry Rules Regulations.
3 PA 2004, s 150(6) and reg 20 of the PPF Entry Rules.

33.88   If the company continues trading (and continues to employ scheme members) – eg in the case of an administration or receivership – payments under the schedule of contributions may continue to accrue against the company.

As a statutory claim (not arising under a contract), it seems (see Chapter 18 above) unlikely that this claim will be given priority as a 'qualifying liability' under an adopted employment contract under the provisions introduced by the Insolvency Act 1994 following the decision of the House of Lords in *Paramount Airways*[1].

1 [1995] 2 AC 394, HL – see Chapter 18 above.

33.89   However, the insolvency practitioner may still want to arrange for the company to continue to contribute to the pension scheme, depending on the circumstances.

33.90   This will not be possible during an assessment period (see Chapter 28 above), as the scheme will be frozen (and contributions are prohibited – see para 24.85 above).

If the assessment period ends (eg on a scheme rescue), continued accrual/contributions may be necessary in order to avoid the scheme trustees exercising a power to wind up the scheme which the insolvency practitioner may consider not to be desirable. For example it could give rise to industrial relations problems with the remaining employees (which the insolvency practitioner may be anxious to avoid on the grounds that the active co-operation of those employees is needed) or there may be the prospect of the sale of the business as a going concern together with the pension scheme.

33.91   Before 6 April 2005, the statutory debt on the employer provision in the PA 1995, s 75 applied only on a liquidation. From 6 April 2005, it now applies on all formal insolvencies (administration, administrative receivership etc), but as a contingent obligation – see Chapter 34 (Section 75) below.

33.92   The provisions in the PA 1995 dealing with the minimum funding requirement[1], including those relating to the schedule of contributions and serious underprovision, ceased to apply if the company concerned is the only employer or all the relevant employers also enter liquidation[2], but only if a debt under s 75 arises. If the scheme was sufficiently well funded so that a s 75 debt did not arise (less likely now that the debt is assessed on a buy-out basis), the MFR schedule of contributions would have continued in force.

1 PA 1995, ss 57–60.
2 MFR Regulations, reg 28(3).

33.93   In theory this left it open for the MFR schedule of contributions to continue to apply to a company in liquidation where (say) other participating employers are not in liquidation. However, in practice, the company in liquidation would have ceased to be subject to the schedule of contributions if it ceased to have any employees (it will cease to be an employer), but subject to the extended meaning of 'employer' (see Chapter 32 above).

Interest

33.94   There is no provision in the pensions legislation (or the relevant regulations) providing for interest to be payable by an employer on the debts arising under the MFR or SSF requirements. The Late Payment of Commercial Debts (Interest) Act 1998 does not apply as the debt does not fall within s 2 as by virtue of a contract for the supply of goods or services.

33.95   Interest may become payable if the employer enters liquidation[1]. In relation to periods before the employer went into liquidation this is only if the debt arises 'by virtue of a written instrument' or a written demand for interest has been made.

Similar provisions apply for proving interest in a post September 2003 administration[2].

1 See Insolvency Rules 1986 (SI 1996/1925), r 4.93.
2 See Insolvency Rules 1986 (SI 1996/1925), r 2.88 (as amended).

33.96   Amounts outstanding from an employer under the statutory debt provisions, including under the schedule of contributions or as a debt on the employer under s 75, do not count as employer-related investments (or employer loans) prohibited by PA 1995, s 40[1].

1 See Occupational Pension Schemes (Investment) Regulations 2005 (SI 2005/3378), reg 13(6), previously reg 6(7) of the 1996 Investment Regulations (SI 1996/3127).

Interrelationship of the SSF/MFR and the debt on the employer provisions

33.97   In some cases where the debt on the employer provisions in the PA 1995, s 75 start to apply (eg on liquidation of all employers or when a scheme starts to wind up), the debt elements of the MFR or SSF provisions (ie the schedule of contributions and any liability in relation to a serious underprovision) cease to apply for the future[1].

33.98   In other cases the debt elements of the SSF or MFR provisions could continue to apply even though a debt has arisen under s 75 (eg one employer enters liquidation, the others do not). In practice however, in this situation the company concerned may cease to be an employer and so the schedule of contributions provisions will cease to apply in an ongoing sense, subject to the deeming provision in the relevant regulations, if the company was the last active employer (or one of them)[2].

1 MFR Regulations, reg 28(3) and (4); Scheme Funding Regulations, reg 17(1)(l).
2 Scheme Funding Regulations, Sch 2, para 3, and MFR Regulations, Sch 5, para 3 – see para 32.9 above.

33.99 Any debt due from the employer under the schedule of contributions (but unpaid) is excluded as an asset of the scheme for the purpose of assessing the MFR or SSF funding level or the statutory deficit under s 75 only to the extent that any amount is 'unlikely to be recovered without disproportionate cost or within a reasonable time'[1] – see also para 32.16 above.

1 MFR Regulations, reg 6(1)(b); Scheme Funding Regulations, reg 3(1)(b); Employer Debt Regulations reg 5, in particular reg 5(6)(c).

33.100 The scheme specific funding obligations cease (see Chapter 31 above) if:

- the scheme is the subject of a scheme failure notice under ss 122 or 130 of PA 2004 (Scheme Funding Regulations, reg 17(1)(k)); or

- the scheme starts to wind-up (Scheme Funding Regulations, reg 17(1)(l)), subject to the trustees obtaining the actuary's estimate of the solvency of the scheme on an annual basis (reg 18).

This cessation does not affect any rights or obligations arising before the cessation – reg 17(4).

33.101 Over and above this, if there is a relevant insolvency event applicable to the employer in relation to an eligible scheme, an assessment period will start. This means that no contributions can be paid to the scheme (PA 2004, s133(3)), save:

- for those that have fallen due to be paid before the beginning of the assessment period; or

- in prescribed circumstances.

33.102 The PPF Entry Rules Regulations[1] prescribe that contributions payable by a employer under s 75 can be paid. Regulation 14 of the PPF Entry Rules Regulations allows an employer to pay further contributions where those contributions relate to:

(a) all or any part of that employer's liability for any debt due from him to the scheme under s 75 of PA 1995 which has not yet been discharged; and

(b) the value of an asset of the scheme arising from a debt or obligation referred to in s 143(5)(a) to (d) of PA 2004 (Board's obligation to obtain valuation of assets and protected liabilities).

1 The Pension Protection Fund (Entry Rules) Regulations 2005 (SI 2005/590, as amended).

33.103 Section 143(5) relates to statutory obligations on an employer under various provisions, including s 75 PA 1995 and under contribution notices, financial support directions or restoration orders issued by the Pensions Regulator under PA 2004.

33.104 In practice this means that if the scheme has not started to wind-up before the insolvency event (and the assessment period starts), no amounts are payable under scheme specific funding or s 75 while the assessment period continues.

This statutory freeze on contributions being paid lasts while the assessment period is in place. what happens at the end of the assessment period depends on what happens to the scheme:

If the assessment period ends:	
• with the scheme entering the PPF (on the issuing of a transfer notice under s 160, PA 2004):	All the assets and liabilities of the scheme transfer to the PPF and the scheme is treated as having been wound up immediately after the date of the transfer notice – s 161(2), PA 2004.
	In practice there seems no scope for the payment obligations under the schedule of contributions for the period from the start of the assessment period to the transfer date to revive and become payable.
• with the PPF Board not assuming responsibility for the scheme and the scheme winding-up eg if the scheme is funded above the level needed to secure the PPF protected benefits – PA 2004, s 132(2)(iii) and (4)(iii):	The scheme must usually start to wind up (s 154, PA 2004) if not already winding-up (see para 39.27 below). This winding up is treated as beginning immediately before the start of the assessment period (ie usually at the date of the company insolvency) – s 154(6), PA 2004.
	This means that any obligations under the schedule of contributions to make payments after the start of the assessment period (which were frozen during the assessment period under s 133(3), PA 2004) will not revive retrospectively because of the exclusion of the scheme from the scheme specific funding provisions under reg 17(1)(k) of the Scheme Funding Regulations (see para 33.98 above).

• with the PPF Board not assuming responsibility for the scheme and the scheme not winding-up	The schedule of contributions will spring back into effect for amounts due after the end of the assessment period.
(eg if the insolvency practitioner serves a rescue notice and this has been approved by the PPF under s 123, PA 2004 and become binding under s 124):	The benefits from the start of the assessment period (usually the company insolvency date) and any payment obligations falling due during the assessment period can revive – s 150(6), PA 2004 and reg 20 of the PPF Entry Rules.
	Reg 20 makes this revival conditional on the member paying any outstanding unpaid member contributions under the schedule of contributions within a year of the end of the assessment period (or 28 days before the date of a request by the member to put his benefits into payment) – reg 20(2).
	If the member contributions are paid, employer contributions under the schedule of contributions then become payable for the missing period – reg 20(3). This revival only applies to amounts due under the schedule of contributions – s 150(7), PA 2004.

33.105 Although the debt due under s 75 is deemed for insolvency law purposes to arise immediately before the insolvency event occurs (s 75(4A)), it is contingent on either a scheme failure notice being issued or the scheme starting to wind-up – PA 1995, s 75(4C) and see Chapter 34 below.

33.106 A scheme which is an eligible scheme for PPF purposes will usually enter an assessment period on an insolvency event occurring. This means that if the scheme is not already winding-up, the scheme cannot then start to wind-up while the assessment period applies (PA 2004, s 135(2)), unless:

• the PPF validates it – PA 2004, s 135(9); or

• the winding-up is under an order of the Pensions Regulator – PA 2004, s 135(3).

But this contingent approach does not apply if:

• the insolvency event is a members' voluntary winding-up (MVL); or

• the scheme has already started to wind-up before the insolvency event.

For multi-employer schemes where only one employer enters insolvency – see Chapter 36 (Multi-employer schemes) below.

CHAPTER 34

Debt on employer: s 75

34.1 Section 75 of the Pensions Act 1995 imposes a statutory debt on an employer in relation to a relevant occupational pension scheme. Section 75 was substantially modified by the Pensions Act 2004. The underlying 2005 regulations also made substantial changes. They are the Occupational Pension Schemes (Employer Debt) Regulations 2005 (SI 2005/678 as amended)

34.2 Section 75 came into force on 6 April 1997, with any debt set to be calculated using liabilities calculated on the MFR basis. The level of this statutory debt has gradually been increased, mainly by changes to the underlying regulations. The method of calculating the amount of a scheme's benefit liabilities has now moved, in a number of steps so that, from 2 September 2005, the buy-out basis applies.

34.3 See para 33.43 above for a chart giving an overview of the differences between the various different measures for pension fund liabilities.

34.4 This move to a buy-out debt obligation on employers has been a fundamental shift in the legal relationship of employers with the occupational pension schemes.

DEVELOPMENT OF s 75

34.5

Relevant date on or after	Scheme winding-up	Employer enters liquidation	Employer in other formal insolvency (eg administration or administrative receivership)	Employment-cessation event
6 April 1997	MFR[1]	MFR[1]	N/A	MFR[1]

Relevant date on or after	Scheme winding-up	Employer enters liquidation	Employer in other formal insolvency (eg administration or administrative receivership)	Employment-cessation event
19 March 2002	Buy-out for pensioners MFR for others[2]	MFR	N/A	MFR
11 June 2003	Buy-out[3]	MFR	N/A	MFR
15 February 2005	Buy-out	Buy-out[4]	N/A	MFR
6 April 2005	Buy-out[5]	Buy-out[5] (contingent)[6]	Buy-out[5] (contingent)[6]	MFR
2 September 2005	Buy-out	Buy-out (contingent)[6]	Buy-out (contingent)[6]	Buy-out[7]

1 PA 1995, s 75, and Deficiency Regulations 1996 (SI 1996/3128).
2 Amendment by SI 2002/380.
3 Amendment by SI 2004/403. Applies if scheme winding-up after 11 June 2003, employer not already in liquidation and 'relevant time' is after 15 March 2004.
4 Amendment by SI 2005/72.
5 Changes to s 75 made by PA 2004 and Employer Debt Regulations 2005 (SI 2005/678).
6 If scheme is not already winding-up, debt is contingent (save for an MVL) until scheme failure notice is issued or subsequent winding-up (PA 1995, s 75(4C), as amended) – see para 34.27 below.
7 Moved to buy-out by amendments made from 2 September 2005 by SI 2005/2224.

34.6   Section 75 of the Pensions Act 1995 was a re-enactment (with only minor variations[1]) of the previous statutory provision.

The original statutory debt obligation was in the Social Security Pensions Act 1975, s 58B, which was inserted by the Social Security Act 1990 and came into force on 29 June 1992 (see SI 1992/1532). Section 58B was later consolidated into the Pension Schemes Act 1993 as s 144. The section was re-written as part of the consolidation process.

1 There were major changes in the underlying regulations.

34.7   Section 75, as originally enacted in PA 1995, provided a statutory liability on an employer to make up deficiencies on a winding up either of the scheme or of the employer or on the employer ceasing to have any active members in the scheme.

34.8   The effect of s 75 was modified by the Occupational Pension Schemes (Deficiency on Winding Up etc) Regulations 1996, SI 1996/3128, (the Deficiency Regulations 1996). These came into effect on 6 April 1997 (subject to some transitional provisions effective from 19 December 1996). The Deficiency Regulations 1996 contained substantial changes from the previous regulations.

34.9   Section 75 was substantially modified, with effect on and from 6 April 2005 by the Pensions Act 2004 and the Employer Debt Regulations. In particular the trigger events were expanded to cover the entry by an employer into a relevant insolvency process eg administration or administrative receivership (previously neither of these were a s 75 trigger, only liquidation was an insolvency trigger).

34.10   In the meantime from 2003 to 2005 the underlying regulations had changed to provide for debts in many cases to be calculated on the buy-out basis (see the chart at para 34.5 above).

34.11   Generally s 75 and the Deficiency Regulations 1996 only applied if the 'applicable time' (ie employer liquidation or scheme winding up) occurred after 5 April 1997[1]. Similarly, if the scheme commenced winding up before 19 December 1996, s 75 and the Deficiency Regulations 1996 do not apply[2]. If an employer ceased to participate in a scheme between 19 December 1996 and 6 April 1997, the transitional provisions in reg 6 of the Deficiency Regulations 1996 can apply.

1 Deficiency Regulations 1996 (SI 1996/3128), reg 1(4).
2 Deficiency Regulations 1996, reg 1(5).

34.12   In relation to situations where s 75 does not apply (eg a scheme winding-up before 19 December 1996), the previous statutory provisions in the PSA 1993, s 144 remain applicable[1].

1 See Deficiency Regulations 1996, reg 13 and Pensions Act 1995 (Commencement No 10) Order 1997, SI 1997/664, reg 11(3).

Non-preferential debt

34.13   Basically, s 75 is designed to provide a simple debt obligation on an employer. The obligation is without prejudice to any other right or remedy which the trustees of an occupational pension scheme may have[1] and it is expressly provided that a debt due by virtue only of s 75 is not to be regarded as a preferential debt for the purposes of the Insolvency Act 1986[2].

1 PA 1995, s 75(7), (not changed by PA 2004).
2 PA 1995, s 75(8), (not changed by PA 2004). See Chapter 10 (Pensions as a preferential debt) above further on this.

34.14   Section 75 and the relevant regulations raise many questions. It remains to be seen how the particular issues that arise will be resolved, either in future court cases or in further legislation.

SCHEMES TO WHICH s 75 APPLIES

34.15 The liability under s 75 arises only if the scheme satisfies the tests below.

(a) If there is an occupational pension scheme (as defined in the Pension Schemes Act 1993, s 1 – see para 2.60 above). No liability arises under s 75 in the case of a personal pension scheme.

(b) The scheme must not generally be a 'money purchase' scheme (but see Chapter 38 (Money purchase schemes) below for further details).

(c) Section 75 (unlike PSA 1993, s 144) refers to the debt as being due to the 'trustees or managers' of the scheme. Accordingly it seems that s 75 could apply to schemes which are not set up under trust (eg simple contractual promises or statutory schemes). In practice, s 75 now does not apply to unregistered (before 6 April 2006, unapproved) schemes, which will exclude most simple contractual promises. The PSA 1993, s 144 seemingly only applied if the occupational pension scheme had been established under trust, given that s 144(1) referred to a debt as being due from the employer to the trustees of the scheme. Thus, s 144 did not apply where there were no trustees (ie a simple contractual promise).

(d) The scheme must not be excluded from s 75 by reg 4 of the Employer Debt Regulations[1]. The categories of schemes excluded by reg 4 are almost identical to those excluded from eligibility for entry into the PPF by reg 2 of the PPF Entry Rules (see Chapter 31 (Scope of main pensions legislation) above.).

1 Previously reg 10 of the Deficiency Regulations 1996 (which was very similar to the exclusion from the MFR in reg 28 of the 1996 MFR Regulations).

WHEN DOES A DEBT UNDER S 75 ARISE?

34.16 The debt under s 75 on a company is triggered in five cases:

(1) if it is an employer, over the period from the date of winding up of the pension scheme to the date of a 'relevant event'[1] in relation to the company[2];

(2) if it is an employer, on the occurrence of a 'relevant event'[1]. Normally this will be on the company going into a formal insolvency (eg liquidation, administration or administrative receivership), whether or not the scheme is being wound up[3];

(3) in a multi-employer scheme which is not being wound up, on the occurrence of an 'employment-cessation event' ie the company ceasing to be 'an employer employing any persons in the description or category of employment to which the scheme relates at a time when at least one other person continues to employ such persons[4];

(4)   after it has ceased to be an employer, on an event within (1) or (2) occurring
      – ie the scheme being wound up or the employer entering relevant insol-
      vency – if it has been deemed to have remained an employer for this
      purpose under reg 9 (Frozen schemes and former employers) of the
      Employer Debt Regulations[5]; and

(5)   if a multi-employer scheme is frozen (so no debt arises at the freezing time,
      but the last employers remain liable as former employers), an employment-
      cessation event arises if the former employer gives notice to the trustees[6].

It is to be noted that the 'applicable time' in event (1) above is a period, while in
the other cases it is a single point of time.

If there is a deficiency, the relevant debt obviously can only be demanded by
the scheme trustees from the employer once its amount has been fixed and certified (see below). This will generally be some time after the effective date of the
calculation – the 'applicable time' (the trustees and the actuary will need some
time to work out the asset and liability position).

But the better view is that the actual debt arises (eg for limitation purposes –
see also para 34.80 below) at the applicable time, even though it has not been calculated no demand has been made. There are some comments that are to the contrary by Sir Andrew Morritt V-C in *Phoenix Venture Holdings Ltd v Independent
Trustee Services Ltd*[7], but these were not essential for his decision and are best
viewed as limited to the actual rule being construed. Warren J in *L v M Ltd*[8] left
the point open, but seems to have had doubts about the approach in *Pitmans*.

The Pensions Regulator has power to issue a direction to trustees that they
should not seek to enforce a debt arising under s 75, pending recovery of a debt
due under a contribution notice – PA 2004, ss 41(4) and 47(4).

1 The term 'relevant event' is defined in s 75(6A) to include an insolvency event (see para 27.6
   above), an MVL and an application or notice to enter the PPF under PA 2004, s 129, (only available in limited circumstances where no normal insolvency event can occur – see para 27.12
   above).
2 PA 1995, s 75(2), as amended by PA 2004.
3 PA 1995, s 75(4), as amended by PA 2004.
4 Employer Debt Regulations, reg 6, as amended from 6 April 2008 by the Occupational Pension
   Schemes (Employer Debt and Miscellaneous Amendments) Regulations 2008 (SI 2008/731).
5 See paras 32.9 above and 34.17 below.
6 Employer Debt Regulations, reg 6(4), as amended from 6 April 2008 by the Occupational
   Pension Schemes (Employer Debt and Miscellaneous Amendments) Regulations 2008
   (SI 2008/731).
7 [2005] EWHC 1379 (Ch), [2005] All ER (D) 325 (May) (Sir Andrew Morritt V-C) at para [52].
8 [2006] EWHC 3395 (Ch); [2007] PLR 11 (Warren J) at paras [40] and [58]– see also Chapter 35
   below.

Former employers

34.17   Regulation 9 of the Employer Debt Regulations deems former employers to remain as employers (and hence potentially liable for the deficiency debt
under s 75). Former employers are persons who used to employ persons in the
description of employment to which the scheme relates, but at the relevant time
have ceased to do so. The relevant time is either:

- the applicable time for the s 75 debt calculation (if the scheme is not frozen); or

- the occurrence of the freezing event (if the scheme is a frozen scheme).

A scheme is a frozen scheme if it has ceased to have any active members (ie members in pensionable service – see PA 1995, s 124(1)) – reg 2(1).

In some cases a former employer is excluded as counting as a former employer under reg 9:

(a) if the company is a 'defined contribution employer'[1] – ie an employer where all the liabilities under the scheme are liabilities for money purchase benefits or supplementary benefits on death (see further Chapter 29 for a discussion of money purchase concepts); or

(b) if the scheme has become a frozen scheme – ie has no active members (ie members in pensionable service – see PA 1995, s 124(1)) and the company was (in effect) an employer at the freezing event (ie employed persons in the description (or, before 6 April 2008, category) of employment to which the scheme relates immediately before the scheme ceased to have any active members)[2]; then the company will be deemed to remain a former employer unless before a scheme winding up starts a s 75 event occurs (ie an employment cessation event or an insolvency event) and one of conditions A to I (see below) is met – ie (broadly) the relevant debt is paid; or

(c) if the company ceased to be a person employing persons in the description or category of employment to which the scheme relates on or after 6 April 1997 and before the applicable time and[3]:

(i) at that time the scheme was not being wound-up and continued to have active members; and

(ii) one of conditions A to I below is met:

Conditions A to I[4] are outlined below (see Chapter 32 above for a comparison with the equivalent PPF events):

- **A, B:** there was no debt due from the company at that time under s 75; or

- **C:** the s 75 debt was paid before the applicable time; or

- **D, E, F, G:** there was a withdrawal arrangement or apportionment arrangement under the Employer Debt Regulations and relevant amount due was paid before the applicable time; or

- **H:** the s 75 debt was not paid solely because the employer was not notified of it (and of the amount of it) sufficiently in advance of the applicable time for it to be paid before that time; or

- **I:** a s 75 debt arose, but is excluded from the assets of the scheme 'because it is unlikely to be recovered without disproportionate cost or within a reasonable time'[5].

1 Employer Debt Regulations, reg 9(3)(a).
2 Employer Debt Regulations, reg 9(3)(d).
3 Employer Debt Regulations, reg 9(3)(c). See further Chapter 32 above.
4 Regs 9(6) to 9(14).
5 Employer Debt Regulations, regulation 9(14) (reg 9(6) before the amendments made from 6 April 2008).
   This 'unlikely to be recovered without disproportionate cost or within a reasonable time' wording mirrors the exclusion of such an asset for scheme specific funding purposes in regulation 3(1)(b) of the Scheme Funding Regulations and regulation 6(1)(b) of the MFR Regulations and also for s 75 asset purposes in regulation 5(4)(b) of the Employer Debt Regulations – see paras 32.16 above and 34.35 below.

34.18   There are special rules for multi-employer schemes (ie schemes with more than one employer) which have separate independent sections with separated assets (eg industry-wide schemes)[1].

See the discussion of these provisions in Chapter 32 (Who is an employer under the pensions legislation?) above.

1 Employer Debt Regulations, reg 8.

WHEN DOES A SCHEME START TO WIND UP?

34.19   In deciding when a scheme starts to wind up, s 124(3A) to (3E) of PA 1995 apply[1]. These sections provide generally for the time of winding up to be as follows:

(a)   if winding-up is under a requirement or power in the rules, the time fixed in the rules, or if no time is fixed by the rules, the time chosen by the trustees (or other person with the power under the scheme rules) 'as the time for which steps for the purpose of winding-up are to be taken' – s 124(3B) and (3D);

(b)   if there is a postponement of a winding-up, either under a scheme power or the statutory power in PA 1995, s 38 (see Chapter 39 below), the date of winding up is also delayed – s 124(3C). This means there would be no s 75 debt trigger under s 75(2);

(c)   winding up by order of the court or the Pensions Regulator (under PA 1995, s 11) takes effect as envisaged in the relevant order or when it comes into force – s 124(3A).

1 As inserted by the Child Support, Pensions and Social Security Act 2000 from 1 April 2002. See previously, to similar effect, the Occupational Pension Schemes (Winding Up) Regulations 1996 (SI 1996/3126).

34.20   This timing is subject to ss 28, 154 and 219 of PA 2004:

●   Section 28 back dates the effect of a winding-up order made by the Pensions Regulator under s 11 of PA 1995 if the order is made during a period during which a freezing order (under PA 2004, s 23) has effect. The winding-up is deemed to have started when the freezing order took effect – s 28(2)(a);

- Section 154 back dates a winding-up of a scheme where an assessment period comes to an end but the scheme is not taken over by the PPF because the scheme has sufficient assets to meet the PPF protected liabilities (but a scheme rescue is not possible). In such a case, the scheme must generally be wound-up (s 154(1)(a) and (12)) and the winding-up is back-dated to immediately before the assessment period started (ie the insolvency event) – s 154(6);

- Section 219 backdates a winding-up of an eligible scheme if a qualifying insolvency event (defined in s 127 – see Chapter 27 above) has occurred in relation to the employer and the scheme starts to wind-up after that event but before a scheme failure notice or withdrawal notice has become binding. The winding-up is backdated to the date of the qualifying insolvency event.

WHAT IS A RELEVANT EVENT?

34.21   The insolvency trigger in s 75(4), PA 1995 (as amended by PA 2004) is the occurrence of a 'relevant event'. Under PA 1995 before the changes introduced by PA 2004, this event was limited to a liquidation. The changes introduced by PA 2004 now result in this being extended to most forms of corporate insolvency.

34.22   The term 'relevant event' is defined in s 75(6A) as:

- An 'insolvency event'- s 75(6A)(c). The term 'insolvency event' has the same meaning as in PA 2004, s 121 – see s 75(6C)(a) – and cover liquidations, administrations etc – see para 27.6 above,

- A relevant application under s 129 of PA 2004 (only available in limited circumstances where no normal insolvency event can occur –see para 27.12 above) – s 75(6A)(b); or

- A voluntary winding-up with a declaration of solvency under IA 1986, s 89 – ie a members' voluntary liquidation (MVL) – s 75(6A)(c).

- An MVL is not within the list of events which otherwise count as an insolvency event in s 121 of PA 2004 (see para 27.6 above in relation to the PPF), but is specifically included as a s 75 trigger by s 75(6A)(c).

34.23   If an MVL is later:

(a)   stayed indefinitely (a stay for a 'limited period' does not count – Employer Debt Regulations, reg 17); or

(b)   converted into a CVL by a meeting of creditors under IA 1986, s 95,

then, for the purposes of s 75, the MVL (and any s 75 debt arising) is treated as if it had never arisen – s 75(6D). The aim is presumably to allow the later conversion to trigger a new s 75 debt (ie the exclusion in s 75(4)(e) will not apply).

34.24   Any relevant event occurring before the relevant company became an employer in relation to the scheme is ignored – s 75(6C)(c).

34.25   Under PA 1995 before the changes introduced by PA 2004, the insolvency event in s 75(4) used to refer to the liquidation of a 'company'. This term was not defined in PA 1995 or PSA 1993 (compare the definition in PA 1995, s 22(3) in relation to the appointment of independent trustees, discussed in Chapter 30 above).

Accordingly, it was not particularly clear whether old s 75 applied to all corporate bodies. It would seem clear that a company incorporated under the Companies Act 1985 (or its predecessors) was within the section. However, it was less clear whether corporate bodies not incorporated under Companies Acts (eg statutory corporations, industrial and provident societies etc) and corporations incorporated overseas (ie outside Great Britain) were within the meaning of 'company' for these purposes. In other contexts, the courts have held that the term company does not extend to include bodies corporate generally – see the Court of Appeal in *Gardiner v London Borough of Merton*[1] and the Northern Ireland Court of Appeal in *Halsey v Fair Employment Agency*[2].

1 [1980] IRLR 472, CA.
2 [1989] IRLR 106, NI CA.

34.26   The changes made by PA 2004 have resolved this issue. All insolvency proceedings within s 121 of PA 2004 will trigger the s 75 provisions. The listed events in s 121 (and the regulations) relate to formal insolvency proceedings under IA 1986.

Events outside IA 1986 (eg an overseas liquidation) are not a relevant event – see Chapter 40 (Overseas employees and insolvencies) below.

CONTINGENT DEBT

34.27   If the debt is arising by virtue of an insolvency event occurring in relation to an employer, s 75(4A) deems the debt to arise 'immediately before the occurrence of the current event'.

34.28   This provision that the debt is calculated at the latest at the date of the relevant insolvency follows the general rule that provable debts must be assessed at that time (see Chapter 16 above). In *Bishopsgate Investment Management Ltd v Homan*[1], Vinelott J at first instance refused to allow a claim for a shortfall to be increased to reflect increased costs (caused by changed annuity rates) after the date of deemed liquidation, following *Re Lines Bros Ltd*[2] on this.

This is consistent with the argument that the amount of the s 75 debt is the figure as certified by the scheme actuary – see the discussion at para 34.40 below of the decision of Lewison J in *Cornwell v Newhaven Port & Properties Ltd*[3] .

1 [1994] PLR 179 (Vinelott J), at page 193.
2 [1982] Ch 17, CA.
3 [2005] EWHC 1469, [2005] OPLR 277, [2005] PLR 329 (Lewison J). Discussed at an APL Caselaw Forum on 26 September 2006 led by Nigel Burroughs.

34.29   In *Gleave v Board of the Pension Protection Fund; sub nom Re Federal-Mogul Aftermarket UK Ltd*[1], David Richards J considered a dispute on how to value a s 75 claim as part of a company voluntary arrangement (CVA) of the T&N group of companies.

The CVA required the claims to be determined and admitted as at 1 October 2001[2]. The s 75 claims only arose on the cessation of participation of the relevant companies on 13 July 2004 and the amounts were certified by the actuary (under s 75) in March 2006[3].

The CVA supervisors argued that this meant that the s 75 debts were contingent as at the CVA record date and so (on general liquidation principles), this meant that the amount of the debt fell to be estimated by them. They proposed to adopt different mortality and other assumptions compared to those adopted by the actuary, resulting in a smaller claim.

This was rejected by David Richards J who held that the amount of the s 75 debt as later emerged in March 2006 was a conclusive factor to be taken into account when seeking to quantify the claim. The 'hindsight' principle, as explained by the Privy Council in *Wight v Eckhardt Marine Gmbh*[4] applied. David Richards J held (at para [24]) that:

'The subsequent quantification of the liability is equally a matter which renders certain what was previously uncertain, particularly in a case such as the present where a debt does not arise as a matter of law except through a certified mechanism, in this case the certificate and apportionment of the scheme actuary.'

1   [2008] EWHC 1099 (Ch); [2008] BPIR 846; [2008] All ER (D) 287 (May); [2008] PLR 237 (David Richards J). See Stuart Firth and Stephen Davies QC 'Clearing up the mess: applying the basic principles of insolvency law' (2009) 22 Insolvency Intelligence 117
2   Judgment para [15].
3   Judgment para [12].
4   [2003] UKPC 37; [2004] 1 AC 147 (PC) and see Chapter 16 (Carrying on business – provable debts) above.

34.30   If the scheme is not being wound up immediately before the insolvency event (excluding an MVL) then, under PA 1995, s 75(4C), the debt is contingent on:

● a scheme failure notice being issued, or

● the commencement of the winding up of the scheme.

Section 75(4C) only applies where the current event was an insolvency (PA 1995, s 75(4B)). So the contingency approach seems not to apply where the liability arises because of an employment-cessation event even though this operates by deeming an additional event into s 75(4) – see reg 6(1)(d) of the Employer Debt Regulations 2005.

34.31   The net effect seems to be that any debt arising because of the insolvency event (not the employment-cessation event) is contingent. This was a new provision in the amendments to s 75 made by PA 2004.

Valuation of a contingent debt may be difficult. The deeming provision in s 75(4A) should mean that the debt can still be proved in the relevant insolvency process even though it is contingent – see para 34.28 above and Chapter 16 (Carrying on business – provable debts) above. This leads to questions about how it would be valued in the insolvency proceedings – see para 34.28 above.

If the s 75 trigger is an insolvency, then it is likely that an assessment period will start at the insolvency event date (see Chapter 29 above). It is not possible for a winding-up to start during the assessment period unless tPR agrees – see section 135, PA 2004.

A winding-up as a scheme is a separate s 75 trigger – see s 75(2). This trigger gives the trustees power to designate the time for the debt to be fixed, provided it is before any later relevant event which occurs – a relevant event is an insolvency event under s 75(6A).

The winding- up trigger in s 75(2) however only applies if the conditions in (a) and (b) of s 75(3) are met.

The condition in s 75(3)(b) is that no members' voluntary winding-up has occurred after 5 April 2005 (the appointed day) and ending with the commencement of the scheme winding-up.

The condition in s 75(3)(a) involves either (i) or (ii) being satisfied. The condition in (a)(i) is that no 'relevant event' (ie an insolvency event or a notice under PA 2004, s 129 – where the PPF can act without an insolvency event) has occurred in the period from 5 April 2005 (the appointed day) to the date of commencement of the winding-up of the scheme. If there is (say) an administration (after the appointed day) then that means that this condition will not be satisfied.

The condition in (a)(ii) is where there has been such a relevant insolvency event but before the scheme started to wind-up a cessation notice has been issued in relation to the scheme and become binding.

A cessation notice is a withdrawal notice under PA 2004, s 130(3) – ie where a scheme rescue has occurred – see s 75(6B)(b).

In practice this means that:

- A s 75 event by virtue of the company entering administration would be the binding event unless a cessation notice is issued before the scheme starts to wind-up.

  – Obviously the issue of a cessation notice will mean that the original insolvency s 75 debt under s 75(4) will stop being contingent – s 75(4C).

  – Presumably the rationale is this means there is no need for the later winding-up of the scheme to trigger a new s 75 debt.

- Conversely, if the cessation note is issued (and becomes binding) before the scheme starts winding-up (and it becomes binding), this would mean that:

  – The original contingent s 75 debt attributable of the administration will not actually apply (because the contingency set out in s 75(4C) will not apply. But

  – The later winding-up will itself trigger a new separate s 75 claim.

34.32 If contingent, the debt is not payable until the contingency occurs. The rationale for this provision is presumably that the insolvency event will force the insolvency practitioner to look at the scheme and decide whether or not a scheme rescue will be possible.

If it is possible, then there seems to be little reason to trigger the s 75 debt on the insolvency (it would remain subject to a later trigger if the scheme wound-up or an employment-cessation event occurred) and there would be little point in enforcing a s 75 debt until the destiny of the scheme is known (see PA 2004, s 133 and Chapter 28 (PPF assessment period) above).

AMOUNT OF THE DEBT

34.33   The amount of the debt due under s 75 is based on the value by which the scheme's liabilities at the applicable time (ie the effective date of the calculation – see para 34.16 above) exceeds the value of its assets – see s 75(2) and (4).

34.34   For this purpose, the value of both a scheme's liabilities and its assets are to be determined, calculated and verified by a prescribed person in a prescribed manner – s 75(5). The relevant regulations are the Employer Debt Regulations. These regulations were amended with effect on and from 6 April 2008 by the Occupational Pension Schemes (Employer Debt and Miscellaneous Amendment) Regulations 2008[1].

For this purpose regs 5(18) and 6(8) provide that:

(i)   the liabilities are determined by the trustees and

(ii)   then the amount of relevant scheme liabilities needs to be calculated and verified by the actuary – ie the individual acting as the statutory scheme actuary[2] appointed by the scheme trustees under the PA 1995, s 47(1)(b).

1 SI 2008/731.
2 If there is no statutory actuary (because the PA 1995, s 47 does not apply to the scheme) the actuary must be authorised by the trustees for this purpose – see the definition of 'actuary' in reg 2(1) of the Employer Debt Regulations.
The scheme actuary appointed under s 47(1)(b) must be a fellow of the Institute or Faculty of Actuaries or otherwise approved by the Secretary of State – reg 4(1)(b) of the Occupational Pension Schemes (Scheme Administration) Regulations 1996 (SI 1996/1715).

34.35   Under reg 5 of the Employer Debt Regulations:

(a)   **assets:** the value of the scheme's assets are to be determined, calculated and verified by the trustees (reg 5(1)), ignoring:

(i)   amounts treated as invested in contravention of the employer-related investment provisions in PA 1995, s 40 – reg 5(4)(a) (see further para 34.52 below); and

(ii)   amounts treated as a debt due under s75 or s228 (schedule of contributions) which are unlikely to be recovered without disproportionate cost or within a reasonable time – reg 5(4)(b). This ties in with Condition I in reg 9(14) as to when a former employer is to be treated as remaining an employer (see paras 32.16 and 34.17 above); and

(iii) any rights under an insurance policy where it appears appropriate to the actuary to exclude them – reg 5(4)(c). This may be intended to cover earmarked pre-1997 insurance policies that still retain some priority on a winding up of a scheme under PA 1995, s 73 (see para 39.46 below). The corresponding liabilities are ignored under reg 5(9)(a) (although there seems to be a cross referencing error in the regulations). If insurance policies are included as an asset, their value is that which the actuary considers appropriate – reg 5(6)(b); and

(iv) assets representing the value of any rights to money purchase benefits – reg 5(4)(d). The corresponding liabilities are ignored under reg 5(9)(b); and

(v) assets representing transfer amounts are treated as remaining with the transferring scheme until received by the receiving scheme – last paragraph of reg 5(4). The same applies to corresponding liabilities – reg 5(10)(a).

(b) **relevant accounts:** assets are those attributable to the scheme in the relevant accounts (defined in reg 2(1) as the scheme's audited accounts complying with PA 1995, s 41)) – reg 5(4) and are valued as shown in the relevant accounts (less the external liabilities – reg 4(6). This seems to mean that scheme assets not shown in the accounts cannot (save as noted in (c) below) be included – eg (say) the benefit of a guarantee or contingent asset or potential receipts from a contribution notice issued by the Regulator.

(c) **withdrawal arrangement:** if the scheme is not winding up and there has been a withdrawal arrangement or an approved withdrawal arrangement, amount B (the amount payable by the relevant guarantors – see reg 6C and Schedule 1A) is treated as an asset, provided the trustees are reasonably satisfied that the guarantor have sufficient resources to be likely to pay amount B – reg 5(15). The amount is determined by the trustees and calculated by the actuary – reg 5(16).

(d) **updated asset assessment:** in the case of an employment-cessation event, an updated asset assessment can be used to work out the assets if the trustees so decide (having consulted the scheme employers) – reg 5(5). An 'updated asset assessment' is defined in reg 2(1) as an update (whether or not audited) of the value of the scheme assets indentified in the most recent relevant accounts received by the trustees which is prepared by the trustees and estimates any alteration in asset values where the trustees consider appropriate.

(e) **deduct external liabilities:** a net asset figure is needed, ie 'external liabilities' are deducted. These are liabilities shown in the relevant accounts (or updated asset statement) – reg 5(7) – but ignoring benefit liabilities to members.

(f) **liabilities:** liabilities are to be determined by the trustees and then calculated by the actuary – reg 5(2) – as being the liabilities to provide benefits to members (or survivors) – reg 5(8) – assuming that all pensionable service has ceased – reg 5(10)(b), excluding some insurance policies and liabilities representing rights to money purchase benefits – reg 5(9).

(g) **Ignore limit by reference to assets** in determining the value of the scheme's liabilities, any provision of the scheme rules (as defined in PA 2004, s 318) which limits the amount of its liabilities by reference to the amount of its assets is to be disregarded – PA 1995, s 75(6).

This provision is clearly designed to overcome any provision in the terms of the pension scheme which provides for abatement of the liability of the pension scheme (ie the trustees) on a winding up.

(h) **buy-out cost:** the amount of the liabilities in respect of pensions and other benefits is to be calculated and verified by the actuary on a buy-out basis – Ie the amount required to purchase matching annuities with an insurer (as described in PA 1995, s 74(3)(c)) – reg 5(11).

The actuary has to estimate the cost of buying the relevant annuities on terms the actuary considers consistent with those in the available market or, if this is not practicable, in such manner as the actuary considers appropriate in the circumstances – reg 5(12).

(i) **expenses:** liabilities must include an estimate by the trustees of the likely costs of winding-up the scheme (excluding annuity costs) – reg 5(13).

(j) **updated actuarial assessment:** in the case of an employment-cessation event, an updated actuarial assessment can be used to work out the liabilities if the trustees so decide (having consulted the scheme employers) – reg 5(14). An 'updated actuarial assessment' is defined in reg 2(1) as an update of the actuary's estimate of the solvency of the scheme as shown in the latest actuarial valuation under PA 2004, s 224, updated to the applicable time by the actuary's assessment of changes between the valuation date and the applicable time and of the matters in regs 7(6)(a)(i) and (ii) of the Scheme Funding Regulations (ie the cost of purchasing annuities and likely winding-up expenses)

34.36 Before 6 April 2008, the unamended version of the Employer Debt Regulations were different (this remains relevant for transitional cases[1] – eg if the scheme started to wind-up before that date). They used to provide, in reg 5, that the actuary must determine the debt:

(a) on the general assumptions specified in reg 3(2) and (3) of the MFR Regulations[1], ie on the basis of actuarial guidance note GN27[2];

(b) subject to (f) and (g) below, in accordance with regs 4 to 8 of the MFR Regulations;

(c) subject to (d) below, in so far as the guidance in actuarial guidance note GN27 applies as respects regs 3(2) and (3) and 4 to 8 of the MFR Regulations, in accordance with that guidance;

(d) in accordance with the guidance given in actuarial guidance note GN19[3] so far as that guidance applies for the purposes of the Employer Debt Regulations;

(e) where, in the Employer Debt Regulations (or in the MFR Regulations as applied by reg 5), there is a reference to the value of any asset or the amount of any liability being calculated or verified in accordance with the opinion of the actuary or as he thinks appropriate, the actuary must comply with any relevant provision in the guidance in GN27 or, as the case may be, GN19 in making that calculation or verification;

(f) reg 6(1)(b) of the MFR Regulations had effect with the addition at the end of the words 'and any amount treated as a debt due to the trustees or managers of the scheme under s 75(2) or (4) by virtue of the valuation in question'. The effect of this is not very clear (what is the 'valuation' it refers to? Presumably the intention is that the debt which will fall due from the employer under s 75 by reason of this actuarial certification will not be counted as an asset. Any previous debts which have already been certified and have fallen due will remain available as an asset unless they are 'unlikely to be recovered without disproportionate cost or within a reasonable time' – see Chapter 13 above); and

(g) in its application for the purposes of reg 5 of the Employer Debt Regulations in a case where the applicable time falls after the scheme has begun to be wound up, reg 6(1) of the MFR Regulations had effect with the addition after sub-paragraph (c) of the words:

> 'and for the purposes of sub-paragraph (a), regulation 5(1)(a) of the Occupational Pension Schemes (Investment) Regulations 1996 (exclusion of employer-related investments over five per cent of current market value) shall be disregarded'.

1 See the transitional provisions in Reg 2 of the Occupational Pension Schemes (Employer Debt and Miscellaneous Amendments) Regulations 2008 (SI 2008/731).
2 The MFR Regulations remained in force for this purpose – see para 19 of Schedule 4 to the Scheme Funding Regulations
3 GN19 was substantially repealed for deficiency calculations from 5 April 2008 as no longer being necessary. According to version 4.9 of GN19, 'The reason for the change of application is that the legislation relevant in these circumstances no longer needs to be supplemented by an actuarial guidance note.'

34.37   The effect of (g) above seemed to be that in the case of a scheme winding up any employer-related investment that did not contravene the PA 1995, s 40 only because it does not exceed five per cent of the scheme's assets is disregarded as an asset—see also para 4.2 of GN19. See the further discussion at para 25.52 below.

If such an investment would not contravene s 40 for another reason (eg it was first made before 9 March 1992 and is unquoted shares[1]) then it seemed that it could remain as an asset for both MFR purposes and the Deficiency Regulations at least until 5 April 2007 – see para 34.52 below for problems this can cause.

This may not apply after 5 April 2007 when the transitional period ended and these assets were required to be excluded for MFR purposes (MFR Regulations, reg 6(2)) and hence for the purposes of the old (pre 2008) Employer Debt Regulations as well.

The limitation in (g) did not apply if the s 75 debt has to be calculated at some other time when there is no scheme winding up, eg in a multi-employer scheme if one employer enters liquidation or ceases to employ any active members.

1 See Occupational Pension Schemes (Investment) Regulations 1996, SI 1996/3127, reg 7.

34.38   The amount of the liabilities of a scheme (but not, seemingly, the value of the assets) which are to be taken into account for the purposes of s 75(2) and (4) must be certified by the scheme actuary in the form set out in Sch 1 to the Employer Debt Regulations – regs 5(18) and 6(8).

34.39   It seems that the amount certified by the scheme actuary may be difficult for any party to challenge.

34.40   In *Cornwell v Newhaven Port & Properties Ltd*[1], Lewison J held that an employer was not entitled to challenge a certificate that had been issued by the scheme actuary. Nor was the employer entitled to require the actuary to disclose details of how he had calculated the certified amount. This was not an insolvency case.

This may be a pragmatic solution to the evidential difficulties of settling the s 75 debt. Its calculation is by no means simple, both:

- In calculating the total deficiency for the whole scheme (eg how are the liabilities calculated?, how is the cost of buying out estimated?); and

- In a multi-employer schemes, how is the amount of this debt divided amongst the individual employers (this depends on the scheme's ability to attribute liabilities to individual employers).

1 [2005] EWHC 1469; [2005] OPLR 277; [2005] PLR 329 (Lewison J). Discussed at an APL Caselaw Forum on 26 September 2006 led by Nigel Burroughs.

34.41   However, *Cornwell* is difficult to reconcile with the decision of Sir Andrew Morritt V-C in *Pitmans Trustees Ltd v Telecommunications Group Plc*[1]. Morritt V-C held that a s 75 debt certificate was void where it was shown that it had been calculated by the actuary on a mistaken basis, in that case where the trustees had tried to move to a gilts matching policy for investment, but had failed to consult properly with the employer as required by the legislation. This failure to consult had the result that the relevant statement of investment principles had not been adopted properly and so the s 75 certificate based on it was invalid as well.

1 [2004] EWHC 181; [2005] OPLR 1; [2004] PLR 213 (Morritt V-C).

34.42   If the employer is a company in liquidation or administration, any s 75 debt can only in practice be proved by a proof of debt, in the liquidation or administration. The Insolvency Rules 1986 provide that the liquidator[1] or administrator[2] may call for documents or other evidence to be produced as part of such a claim. The liquidator or administrator can also require an affidavit to be sworn verifying the debt claim[3].

This could provide a power for an administrator or liquidator to obtain evidence from the trustee or actuary about how any s 75 certificate had been calculated. This would give more scope for challenge.

It seems likely that the actuary or trustees owe a duty of care to the affected parties (eg employers and members) to get the certified amount right. So there could be a liability (e.g. in negligence or for breach of statutory duty) on the actuary.

1 Insolvency Rules 1986, rr 4.75(3), 4.76.
2 Insolvency Rules 1986, r 2.72(2).
3 Insolvency Rules 1986, rr 2.73, 4.77.

34.43   In *Gleave v Board of the Pension Protection Fund; sub nom Re Federal-Mogul Aftermarket UK Ltd*[1], David Richards J commented (at para [30]):

> 'One of the triggering events for a liability under section 75 is the liquidation of the employer. In that event the debt is taken to arise immediately before the liquidation: section 75(2). In a liquidation, it would therefore be deemed to be a present but unascertained debt. Nonetheless, section 75, read both on its own and as modified for multi-employer schemes by the Deficiency Regulations, clearly requires the process of ascertainment and apportionment to be undertaken by the scheme actuary and his conclusions will be binding on the liquidator, subject only to such rights of challenge as would be available to any employer.'

Cornwell was not cited in the judgment.

1 [2008] EWHC 1099 (Ch), [2008] BPIR 846, [2008] All ER (D) 287 (May), [2008] PLR 237 (David Richards J). See also para 34.28 above.

MONEY PURCHASE BENEFITS

34.44   There was no express exclusion in old s 75 of the position in relation to money purchase assets or benefits. Money purchase schemes were and are excluded – see s 75(1)(a) and Chapter 38 below.

A scheme which is generally a defined benefit or final salary scheme may also provide some money purchase benefits, for example in respect of additional voluntary contributions.

Assets representing the value of any rights to money purchase benefits and the relevant liabilities are now expressly excluded from the s 75 calculations – Employer Debt Regulations, regs 5(4)(d) and 5(9)(b) (as amended in April 2008).

34.45   Section 75(6) provides that liabilities should be calculated disregarding any provision in the scheme rules that limits the amount of its liabilities to the amount of its assets. A money purchase benefit is generally in practice calculated by reference to the value of the matching asset.

The better view (under the old provisions) was that did not mean that money purchase benefits/assets should be included in s 75 calculation. The better view was that a money purchase benefit is not, as such, limited by reference to the value of assets, but is rather calculated by reference to the value of the assets. Accordingly, it was appropriate to assume that money purchase benefits did not give rise to any debt under s 75 (it would in any event be difficult to see how the liability in respect of money purchase benefits could be calculated if not by reference to the value of the assets).

34.46 Changes in 2005 to the MFR Regulations clarified the position and meant that money purchase assets and liabilities were excluded for the purposes of the MFR (and hence for s 75 purposes pre April 2008).

Reg 6(1)(d)[1] of the MFR Regulations excluded assets representing the value of any rights in respect of money purchase benefits under the scheme rules. Money purchase liabilities were, in effect excluded by virtue of reg 7. This refers to the liabilities being taken into account as being those mentioned in s 73(4) of the Pensions Act 1995[2]. This section (as amended by PA 2004) excludes money purchase liabilities – see the definition of 'liabilities' in s 73(10).

1 Regulation 6(1)(d) was inserted from 31 August 2005 by the Occupational Pension Schemes (Winding Up) (Modification for Multi-employer Schemes and Miscellaneous Amendments) Regulations 2005, SI 2005/2159.
2 See the substitution made from 6 April 2005 by the Occupational Pension Schemes (Winding up etc) Regulations 2005, SI 2005/706.

Guidance note GN19

34.47 The Institute and Faculty of Actuaries jointly issued in March 1997 a revised version of the mandatory guidance note, GN19. This was updated when version 4.7 was issued on 2 September 2005. GN19 was later taken over by the new Board for Actuarial Standards (BAS).

GN19 no longer applies (although there is provision in reg 5(17) of the Employer Debt Regulations for the actuary to apply any relevant BAS standards). Version 4.9 of GN19 states[1]:

> 'Version 4.9 of GN19 is introduced to clarify the application of GN19. In particular, GN19 will no longer apply in relation to any scheme that started to wind-up on or after 1 December 2008. The reason for the change of application is that the legislation relevant in these circumstances no longer needs to be supplemented by an actuarial guidance note.
>
> *Application*
>
> GN19 is not applicable in respect of:
>
> (i)   wind-up calculations for schemes that started to wind up on or after 1 December 2008; or
>
> (ii)   deficiency calculations for schemes where the deficiency is being calculated as at a date after 5th April 2008.'

34.48   GN19 used to specify how an actuary should act when approving a method of calculating a scheme's assets and liabilities as envisaged in the Employer Debt Regulations. The revised version of GN19 was stated to apply from 6 April 2005 (the previous versions will apply before then). Previous versions were stated only to apply to the United Kingdom (it is unclear whether this was intended to impose a geographical limitation on the schemes to which GN19 applies over and above any limitation implicit in the operation of ss 144 or s 75 itself).

34.49   It is important to note (and indeed the note to the certificate in Sch 1 to the Employer Debt Regulations and before that in the Deficiency Regulations 1996 requires the actuary to point this out to the scheme trustees) that the amount of the s 75 debt may not represent the amount of cash required by the scheme to secure all the benefits in the scheme by purchasing insurance policies

This was particularly the case where the debt was calculated on the MFR basis. Under the Deficiency Regulations 1996 this note read (emphasis mine):

> 'The valuation of the amount of the liabilities of the scheme does <u>not</u> reflect the cost of securing those liabilities by the purchase of annuities, if the scheme were to have been wound up on the date as at which the valuation is made.'

34.50   The current note in the certificate in Sch 1 to the Employer Debt Regulations reads (emphasis mine):

> 'The valuation of the amount of the liabilities of the scheme <u>may</u> not reflect the actual cost of securing those liabilities by the purchase of annuities if the scheme were to have been wound up on the date as at which the valuation is made.'

34.51   If the scheme is being wound up on the date as at which the valuation is made, the actuary must modify the note at the end of the certificate by omitting the words from 'if the scheme' onwards[1].

1 See note in the form of the certificate in Sch 1 to the Employer Debt Regulations. Previously (before the April 2008 amendments) this change was in Employer Debt Regulations, reg 5(5) and the Deficiency Regulations 1996, reg 3(2).

EMPLOYER-RELATED INVESTMENT

34.52   The question of valuing any employer-related (self) investment is difficult. If (say) the scheme owns shares in the employer, the value of those shares might (in extreme circumstances) depend on the level of the debt obligation owed under s 75, which would itself depend on the value of the shares! Obviously a circularity occurs.

34.53   There is a similar problem if there is already a debt outstanding from the employer to the pension scheme outside the statutory liability under s 75 – such as an unpaid contribution or a loan previously made from the scheme to the employer (but note that loans to an employer have in most cases been prohibited since April 1997 – see PA 1995, s 40 and the Occupational Pension Schemes (Investment) Regulations 2005 – see para 34.55 below).

34.54   The actuary and the trustees must either:

(a)   ignore the value of the employer's debt when calculating the value of the assets of the scheme. This seems, in the absence of statutory provision to allow it, to be unjustified as it ignores the value of what is an asset.

In addition an element of 'double proof' would arise as the scheme would be proving in the liquidation for both the original debt and the liability under s 75, which to a degree represent the same debt. This is not allowed in a liquidation as a matter of general insolvency law. In *Re Oriental Commercial Bank, ex p European Bank*[1], Mellish LJ stated that 'There is only to be one dividend in respect of what is in substance the same debt' – see also *Re Fenton*[2], *Barclays Bank plc v TOSG Trust Fund*[3] and *Re Glen Express Ltd*[4].

In *Bishopsgate Investment Management Ltd v Homan*[5], Vinelott J at first instance refused (at page 194) to allow trustees to have a 'double dipping claim' ie to claim from the employer in relation to a shortfall in scheme assets both under a provision in the scheme and under the SSPA 1975, s 58B (the predecessor of the PA 1995, s 75). This would infringe the rule against double proofs or double dividends in an insolvent winding up. The point was not raised in the Court of Appeal; or

(b)   try to assess the value of the debt. If the employer is insolvent then the value attributable to the debt will be less than 100 pence in the pound, but must reflect the likely amount to be recovered, presumably by way of dividend in the insolvency.

The problem with this is that the amount which is likely to be recovered may well depend on the amount of the liability owed to the pension scheme under s 75. The circularity problem arises again.

1 (1871) LR 7 Ch App 99 at 103, CA.
2 [1931] 1 Ch 85, CA.
3 [1984] AC 626, HL.
4 [2000] BPIR 456; 19 October 1999 (Neuberger J).
5 [1994] PLR 179 (Vinelott J).

34.55   Since April 2008, the Employer Debt Regulations now provide simply that assets treated as invested in contravention of the employer-related investment provisions in PA 1995, s 40 are ignored – reg 5(4)(a). This is subject to reg 5(15) which provides that any Amount B due under a withdrawal arrangement under the Employer Debt Regulations (see Chapter 35 below) can still count as an asset.

As mentioned above (see para 34.36(g) above), before April 2008 the MFR Regulations and the Employer Debt Regulations contained some provisions expressly excluding the value of some employer-related investment (as defined in PA 1995, s 40, and the Occupational Pension Schemes (Investment) Regulations 2005 (SI 2005/3378)):

(a) Resources invested in contravention of s 40 are ignored[1]. This will catch all employer-related loans[2] and other investment if over five per cent of the scheme's assets[3], subject to transitional provisions.

(b) After 6 April 2007, employer-related loans are excluded even if allowed under the transitional provisions in the Investment Regulations 1996[4].

(c) After a scheme has started to wind up, the five per cent limit in reg 5(1)(a) of the Investment Regulations is to 'be disregarded'[5]. The effect of disregarding reg 5(1)(a) is that all employer-related investment, save for employer-related loans within reg 5(1)(b), should be counted. The effect of disregarding reg 5(1)(a) seems to be that all such investment is allowed – it is no longer limited by reg 5(1) and so would no longer contravene s 40 – see s 40(1) containing the main requirement that a scheme complies with any 'prescribed restrictions'. This is certainly how the Institute and Faculty of Actuaries read this provision in the past – see para 3.2 of GN19 (ver 4.7).

1 MFR Regulations, reg 6(1)(a).
2 Investment Regulations 2005, reg 12(1)(b).
3 Investment Regulations 2005, reg 12(1)(a).
4 MFR Regulations, reg 6(2).
5 See reg 5(7) of the (pre 2008) Employer Debt Regulations (previously reg 3(4) of the Deficiency Regulations 1996).

MULTIPLE CERTIFICATES?

34.56 No provision is made in s 75 or the Employer Debt Regulations as to the position if the value of the assets or liabilities changes. Clearly the value of an asset can vary from day to day, as can the value of a liability (ie the costs of securing a particular pension will vary as the prices of gilts or equities or the rates quoted by insurance companies vary from day to day). Some liabilities may be difficult to assess, for example, is there an equalisation liability under Art 141 of the EU Treaty (formerly Art 119 of the Treaty of Rome)? – see para 39.69 below.

34.57 The second edition of this book (2000) argued that, although there is no express provision to this effect in s 75 or the Employer Debt Regulations, it would seem to be a more reasonable interpretation of these provisions that the amount of debt owing by the employer can reduce (or increase) from day to day as s 75 certificates are issued until the debt is finally discharged or until a relevant insolvency event (see para 34.22) occurs. For example, if there is a deficit on initial winding up of the scheme, but this is subsequently eliminated as a result of increase in an asset's value, it would seem appropriate for the debt due from the employer also to be extinguished.

34.58   Conversely, the second edition argued that it would also seem to be possible (at least before a relevant insolvency event) for the trustees to issue a second s 75 certificate – eg if the position of the scheme worsens since the first certificate.

There has now been some judicial comment that such multiple certificates are probably not possible. Although not strictly needed for the relevant decision in any of the cases, the judges have commented that only single certificates are allowed.

34.59   In 2002 in *Bradstock Group Pension Scheme Trustees Ltd v Bradstock Group*[1], Charles Aldous QC (sitting as a deputy High Court judge) held:

> 'A question arose as to whether by reason of the reference to "any time" in Section 75(3) a trustee could serve more than one deficit notice whilst the Scheme was in the course of winding up and before the employer went into liquidation. If so, the issue was whether it could be said that more than one debt could arise in the future which trustees could not fetter their right to enforce by compromising it in advance. It may take a considerable time to complete the winding up. Even if not strictly a separate debt, could it be said that trustees cannot compromise a Section 75 debt as the amount might vary during the course of the winding up because of changed financial circumstances affecting the size of the deficit? Could it be said that trustees cannot deprive themselves of the right to serve a further notice?
>
> I am inclined to the view that the reference to "any time" merely enables the amount of the shortfall to be determined by the actuary at any time within the course of the winding up, but once determined and certified it is no longer open to issue a second certificate at a later date. If it had been open to serve further certificates one would expect to see a mechanism providing for recalculation of the deficit, both upwards and downwards, from time to time during the winding up to take account of changed conditions. However, I am aware that some specialists take a different view. The point was not argued out before me. It is unnecessary for me to decide this as the answer here lies in the terms of Section 15 Trustee Act, which permits trustees to compromise both accrued and prospective liabilities, at least where one of those liabilities has arisen or is about to arise in the circumstances set out above.'

1 [2002] OPLR 281; [2002] ICR 1427; [2002] PLR 327 Charles Aldous QC (sitting as a deputy High Court judge).

34.60   Later, in 2004 in *Pitmans Trustees Ltd v Telecommunications Group plc*[1], Sir Andrew Morritt V-C held:

> 'What is the consequence of the failure to consult?
>
> [66] I have quoted the definition of "applicable time" contained in s 75(3) in para 25 above. There has been no relevant insolvency event as described in s 75(4). Accordingly the period in which the applicable time must occur commenced with the winding up of the Plan on 28 May 2002 and is still running. Roxspur contends that the Trustees may only select one point of time within that period for the ascertainment of the amount of the debt. The Trustees submit that they can select as many points of time within that period as they think fit, giving

credit for sums paid in response to earlier notices, so as to pick up any increase in liability due to a decline in the value of the assets. They rely on s.6 of the Interpretation Act 1978 for the proposition that in the absence of a contrary context the single includes the plural. They also rely on the reference to "any time" in sub-s (3)(a).

[67] If a relevant insolvency event, as defined in s 75(4), occurs then only one point of time is applicable namely the moment immediately before the occurrence of that event. Similarly in the case of a multiplicity of employers under a scheme which is not being wound up the definition substituted by reg 4(3)(b)(i) of the Deficiency Regulations allows only one point of time, namely the moment immediately before an employer ceases to participate in the scheme. Further there are no provisions for the revaluation of a certificate in the light of subsequent events, regulating how often trustees may require the debt to be ascertained by the Actuary, or taking account of previous demands or payments. In these circumstances it would be odd if the reference to "any time" in s 75(3)(a) allowed more than one point of time within the period from the commencement of the winding up of the scheme to the occurrence of a relevant insolvency event. Accordingly I am inclined to agree with the views of Mr Charles Aldous QC sitting as a deputy High Court judge in *Bradstock Group Pension Scheme Trustees Ltd v Bradstock Group plc* [2002] PLR 327 para 16.

[68] But, I do not think it is necessary to reach a final conclusion in this case either. The failure to consult vitiated both the adoption of the revised Statement of Investment Principles and the Actuary's certificate. It follows that the debt on which the Trustees rely has not been established in accordance with s 75(5) and their claim must be dismissed. The unsuccessful attempt to recover the debt as at 31 May 2003, the valuation date for the purposes of the invalid Certificate, cannot amount to an irrevocable election to claim as at that date so as to preclude a proper valuation and valid certificate at a later date during the permitted period. I see nothing to exclude a claim based on such a certificate.'

1 [2004] EWHC 181 (Ch); [2005] OPLR 1; [2004] PLR 213 (Morritt V-C).

TRUSTEES AND TIMING

34.61 The trustees may have three separate ways of affecting the level of debt that arises under s 75:

(a) On a scheme winding-up they choose the effective date at which any deficiency is calculated. Multiple certificates are arguably not possible (see above). Conversely, if the relevant trigger event is an insolvency event or an employment-cessation event, the effective date for the deficiency calculation is fixed (as the insolvency date or date of cessation);

(b) For s 75 debts based on the MFR position, the level of the relevant liability under the MFR Regulations could often have been increased if the trustees choose to amend the scheme's statement of investment principles (under PA 1995, s 35) to move to a gilts matching strategy (see para 3.14 of GN 27). The trustees must consult the employers about the Statement of Investment Principles[1], but the employer has no veto – PA 1995, s 35(5).

It was to avoid this risk that the administrators of the employer company in *Re T&N Ltd (No 1)*[2] went to court to get confirmation that they would be acting properly if they arranged for the subsidiaries to stop participating before the trustees had the opportunity to switch to a gilts matching strategy (and so increase the then debt under s 75). David Richards J allowed this.

Similarly in *Pitmans Trustees v The Telecommunications Group*[3], the trustees were concerned that the employer may be about to go into liquidation. They wanted to move to a gilts matching policy before that happened.

(c)   In cases where the s 75 debt was generally calculated on the same basis as the minimum funding requirement (MFR), the statutory overriding priority order on a scheme winding up gave (for a scheme winding-up starting before 6 April 2005) first priority to benefits in payment (or secured by an insurance policy entered into before 6 April 1997). The amount to be allocated to secure this level of benefits was the greater of the MFR amount and the amount calculated under the scheme's rules (often the cost of buying insurance company annuities[4]). The cost of buying insurance company annuities will usually have been more than the MFR liability. This left the possibility of the trustees deciding to buy insurance company annuities to buy out pensioners and only claiming the s 75 deficit after this (but it is unclear if this would have been a proper exercise of their powers[5]). This may have resulted in a higher debt than would have applied before the buy-out.

In *Easterly Ltd v Headway plc*[6], Sir Andrew Morritt C seemed to allow a similar strategy to be adopted by trustees (if they had the relevant powers under the scheme). This was upheld by the Court of Appeal: *Eastearly Ltd v Headway plc*[7].

In effect the proposal by the trustees was to act in a way that should increase the amount of the s 75 debt payable by the (solvent) employer. This was a winding-up which started before 2003, so the s 75 debt was assessed using the MFR calculation of liabilities. The trustees' proposal was to use the available assets to buy out a proportion of the members' benefits. This would leave the scheme with no assets and the remaining liability for the proportion of the benefits not bought out. This would result in a higher s 75 debt than would be otherwise payable.

Lord Neuberger noted this effect at para [7] of his judgment:

'The nature and alleged effect of this proposed Arrangement is most easily appreciated by reference to an example given below by Mr Simmonds QC, who appears for the Trustee:

"A. Assume the Scheme has assets of £10m and liabilities calculated at (a) £20m on the full buy-out basis and (b) £15m on the prescribed section 75 basis.

B. If the Trustee adopts the conventional approach and collects the section 75 debt before buying out members' benefits, the Employer will be liable to pay the £5m section 75 shortfall and there will remain a £5m deficit on buyout.

C. If the Trustee adopts the partial buy-out route, it will apply the £10m assets in buying out half (i.e. 10/20) of the Scheme liabilities [- stage one]. The Trustee will then fix an "applicable time" for section 75 purposes. At that time the Scheme's liabilities on the prescribed section 75 basis will be £7.5m (i.e. 50% of £15m because half of the liabilities are bought out at stage one) and the assets will be nil. The section 75 debt is therefore £7.5m rather than £5m [- stage two]. The Trustee will collect this and will accordingly have an extra £2.5m available to meet the remaining buy-out cost of £10m [- stage three].

D. The difference in outcome is accounted for by the fact that, under the partial buy-out route, the liabilities discharged at stage one are effectively valued on the buy-out basis rather than on the prescribed section 75 basis.'

But this strategy is of much less relevance following the switch to using buy-out levels to fix s 75 liabilities (see Lord Neuberger at para 2 of the note at the end of the judgment, refusing leave to appeal to the House of Lords).

1 Occupational Pension Schemes (Investment) Regulations 2005 (SI 2005/3378), reg 2(2)(b). This requirement was formerly in PA 1995, s 35(5)(b) (before its amendment by PA 2004).
2 [2004] EWHC 1680(Ch); [2004] OPLR 343; [2004] PLR 351 (David Richards J).
3 [2004] EWHC 181(Ch); [2005] OPLR 1; [2004] PLR 213 (Morritt V-C).
4 See PA 1995, s 73 and Occupational Pension Schemes (Winding Up) Regulations 1996 (SI 1996/3126), reg 4(5) and see Chapter 39 below.
5 See for example Patten J in *Re T&N, Alexander Forbes Trustee Services v Jackson* [2004] EWHC 2448 (Ch); [2004] OPLR 391; [2004] PLR 33 at para 36 and in *Hearn v Bell* [2004] EWHC 2803 (Ch); [2004] 90 PBLR at para 21.
6 [2008] EWHC 2573; [2008] All ER (D) 305 (Oct); [2009] PLR 1 (Sir Andrew Morritt C).
7 [2009] EWCA Civ 793; [2009] All ER (D) 251 (Jul); [2009] PLR 279, CA.

34.62 It is clear that the s 75 debt that arises if there is an insolvency trigger under s 75(4) is assessed as at the date of the insolvency. Section 75(4)(a) refers to where 'the value of the assets of the scheme is less than the amount at that time of the liabilities of the scheme' – i.e. immediately before the relevant event (i.e. the liquidation or administration etc) occurs. Similarly s 75(4A) provides that the debt is, for the purposes of the law relating to insolvency as it applies to the employer, deemed 'to arise immediately before the occurrence of the current event'.

As noted above, the relevant s 75 debt arising under s 75(4) is stated to be contingent on either (a) a scheme failure notice being issued and becoming binding or (b) the scheme starting to wind-up. If (say) a scheme failure notice is issued (presumably by the IP and accepted by the PPF). This means that the relevant s 75(4) debt would cease to be contingent under s 75(4C), but it obviously remains unquantified until its amount is fixed (and presumably certified by the scheme actuary).

Regulation 5 of the Employer Debt Regulations 2005 (SI 2005/678, as amended by SI 2008/731), as amended with effect from 6 April 2008, deals with how assets and liabilities are to be calculated for the purposes of s 75. As noted above, it provides that the assets of the scheme are to be valued and the amount of the liabilities determined and calculated by reference to the same date – reg 5(3).

There is provision for a 'updated asset assessment', but this can only be used if there is an employment cessation event – reg 5(5).

The trustees fix the value of the assets of the scheme. This is to be 'the value given to those asset in the relevant accounts… less…. the amount of the external liabilities' – reg 5(6)(a). There are special provisions for rights under an insurance policy.

Similar provisions apply for the purpose of assessing 'external liabilities' as been the amount shown in the net assets statement in the relevant accounts – reg 5(7)(a).

The liabilities of the scheme are fixed by the trustees, with the actuary then fixing then calculating and verifying the amount – regs 5(8) and 5(11). The amount of the liabilities is fixed as being an estimate of 'the cost of purchasing annuities' – reg 5(11). The actuary estimates this cost under reg 5(12) as being:

- 'the cost of purchasing the annuities on terms the actuary considers consistent with those in the available market and which he considers would be sufficient to satisfy the scheme's liabilities in respect of pensions and other benefits'; or

- otherwise an appropriate estimate.

ASSETS

The assets (and external liabilities) to be used for the calculation of the amount under s 75(4) are those as provided under reg 5(4) – ie the assets attributable to the scheme in the relevant accounts.

The term 'relevant accounts' is defined as 'the audited accounts for the scheme that comply with the requirements imposed under s 41 of the 1995 Act (provision of documents to members)'. In practice this means the usual accounts of the scheme. Part of the checks by the PPF in the assessment period will be the production of a new set of audited accounts up to the day before the start of the assessment period (ie the day before the insolvency event)

The only assets to be included are therefore those 'attributable to the scheme in the relevant accounts' – reg 5(4) and are to be valued at 'the value given to those assets in the relevant accounts' – reg 5(6)(a).

This would seem a little odd, if the latest relevant accounts are some time before the relevant insolvency date (and date for assessing the s 75 debt). However in practice it is a requirement that the s 143 valuation required when the scheme enters the PPF assessment period (see below) requires an updated set of audited accounts to be produced as at the day before the insolvency event.

The value of the assets will, we assume, in the main be the market value of the relevant investments – eg their market value (if listed) or surrender value etc. for pooled investments. Presumably in practice there is not a generally an issue in terms of how this is calculated (although trustees may want to use the offer price rather than the higher bid price given that they would have to sell the assets).

There could be difficulties in assessing the value of some contingent assets. For example if the trustees had a claim against a third party and it was unclear how much would be realised for that claim. The intention of the regulations seems to be to fix the value of the asset by reference to the value shown in the accounts. Accordingly the relevant accounting standards are presumably relevant here.

The structure of s 75 and the debt claim seems to be that it is not in fact possible to adjust asset calculations (or indeed liability calculations) to reflect later events or more information. Once the s 75 debt has been certified, that is the relevant debt. It seems to be the appropriate debt payable by the employer (including in an insolvency) even if it proves to be too high or too low by reference to subsequent events. This is the thrust of the decisions in *Cornwell v Newhaven Port & Properties Ltd*[1] and *Gleave v PPF*[2] (see para 34.40 above).

BENEFIT LIABILITIES

The scheme's benefit liabilities need to be calculated at the same date as the assets – reg 5(3), ie they need to be calculated by reference to the insolvency date.

This means that the value of the scheme liabilities (i.e. the estimate of the cost of purchasing annuities) needs to be by reference to buy-out conditions as at the date of the administration.

It has been argued that reg 5(11) begs the question of how the actuary is to perform that estimate and that the actuary is allowed to use up to date annuity rates (ie after the insolvency date) to convert the scheme liabilities into a capital annuity cost. It seems to us that the better view is that the regulations (and PA 1995) require that the calculations and estimate etc. must be based conditions as at the relevant s 75 calculation date – ie the date of the insolvency. There are various reasons for this:

- the amount assessed is clearly to be as at the insolvency date. There is no ability to taking account of later variations (eg later variations and asset values, interest rates etc). It is not appropriate that one element of the calculation (annuity rates) should be variable.

- as a separate matter, even if the s 75 debt were paid in full, no interest is payable on the calculation (unless interest is paid in the insolvency, which would be very unusual). So even if the s 75 debt were paid in full it would not necessarily secure all the benefits (because it was paid late there would be no investment return).

- if the full s 75 debt is not paid, then it is very unlikely that the scheme will be sufficiently well funded so that all the benefits can be paid in any event.

- the estimated annuity rates could of course vary either way after the insolvency calculation date. They could improve (in the sense of reducing the liability), depending on market conditions.

- the whole thrust of s 75 is to fix the date at which the calculations are to be performed. No discretion is given to the trustees to choose instead a different date for working out the s 75 amount (contrast the position under s 75(2) where there is a scheme winding-up outside insolvency). There seems no scope for giving a discretion to the trustees to choose the relevant date for fixing amounts.

In effect, there is some tension here between the aim of the pensions legislation in having a fixed amount payable (eg the *Gleave* case) and the more flexible approach adopted by the insolvency legislation in allowing debts to be contingent until contingencies have in fact been fulfilled (ie adjusting up and down the claim for dividend purposes).

It seems likely that the actuary owes duties to both the scheme and the employer in relation to fixing the amount of the s 75 debt. If he were to underestimate in a fashion that is negligent, it seems to us that he would be liable in damages to the scheme as a result. Conversely, if he overestimates the amount of the debt, he seems to us likely that he would owe a duty of care to the employer (under *Hedley Byrne*[3] principles) in relation to any amount overpaid.

1 [2005] EWHC 1469; [2005] OPLR 277; [2005] PLR 329 (Lewison J).
2 [2008] EWHC 1099 (Ch); [2008] BPIR 846; [2008] All ER (D) 287 (May) (David Richards J).
3 *Hedley Byrne & Co Ltd v Heller & Partners Ltd* [1964] AC 465, HL.

EMPLOYER REORGANISATIONS

34.63   There is no express exclusion from the obligation under s 75 covering the position where there is a reorganisation of the employer's pension arrangements. Thus, the debt relating to the deficit still arises even if the employer is setting up a new scheme in exactly the same position as the old scheme (and taking a transfer of assets from the old scheme) and where the liabilities of the old scheme are being assumed by a different scheme which is properly funded (and has no deficit) after the transfer of assets from the old scheme. However, it would seem arguable that no deficit in fact arises in these circumstances.

The Employer Debt Regulations (as amended in April 2008) include specific provision for modifying the s 75 debt in some circumstances, though an apportionment arrangement or a withdrawal arrangement. There is also provision for a 'relevant transfer deduction' in some cases (see the discussion in Chapter 35 below).

The DWP has said that it is considering changes to the s 75 provisions to deal with intra group changes. A consultation paper was issued by the DWP in September 2009.

Similarly, there is no provision dealing with the position where, after the employer has in fact discharged the debt arising under s 75 in relation to a deficit, the deficit subsequently is reduced or extinguished. There is no express right of subrogation given to the employer in these circumstances and it seems that the 'surplus' arising is to be held on the terms of the pension scheme.

INTEREST

34.64   There is no provision in the pensions legislation (or the relevant regulations) providing for interest to be payable by an employer on the debts arising under s 75. The Late Payment of Commercial Debts (Interest) Act 1998 does not apply as the debt does not fall within s 2 as by virtue of a contract for the supply of goods or services.

Interest may become payable if the employer enters liquidation[1]. In relation to periods before the employer went into liquidation this is only if the debt arises 'by virtue of a written instrument' or a written demand for interest has been made.

Similar provisions apply for proving interest in a post September 2003 administration[2].

Amounts outstanding from an employer under the statutory debt provisions, including under the schedule of contributions or as a debt on the employer under s 75, do not count as employer-related investments (or employer loans) prohibited by the PA 1995, s 40[3].

1 See Insolvency Rules 1986, SI 1996/1925, r 4.93.
2 See Insolvency Rules 1986, SI 1996/1925, r 2.88 (as amended).
3 See Occupational Pension Schemes (Investment) Regulations 2005 (SI 2005/3378), reg 13(6), previously reg 6(7) of the 1996 Investment Regulations (SI 1996/3127).

MULTIPLE EMPLOYERS

34.65   Where the scheme applies to more than one employer (as is common for HMRC registered pension schemes which can apply to a group of companies), the obligation under s 75 is modified by reg 6 of the Employer Debt Regulations (as amended in April 2008 by SI 2008/731). A multi-employer scheme is defined as one with more than one employer (reg 2(1) of the Employer Debt Regulations) – eg if:

- there is more than one employer of persons in pensionable service; or

- there is more than one company counting as an employer, including under the former employer provision in reg 9 (see para 32.16 above).

34.66   In such a multiple employer case, reg 6(1) modifies s 75 to provide:

- that a cessation of participation is a trigger event for a s 75 debt obligation as an 'employment-cessation event' – reg 6(1)(d); and

- how to calculate the s 75 debt payable by each employer (ie how to divide the total s 75 deficiency for the scheme among the employers) – reg 6(2).

An 'employment-cessation event' is defined in reg 2(1) as occurring on the date on which an employer has ceased to employ at least one person who is an active member of the scheme.

This only applies if there is such a cessation at 'a time when at least one other employer (who is not a defined contribution employer) continues to employ at least one active member of the scheme'.

34.67   Before April 2008, reg 6(2) used to provide that the amount of the total s 75 deficiency due from each employer was:

- the amount as apportioned by the rules of the scheme – reg 6(2)(b), or

- if the rules do not provide for this, an amount which, in the opinion of the actuary (after consultation with the trustees), is the 'amount of the scheme's liabilities attributable to employment with that employer bears to the total amount of the scheme's liabilities attributable to employment with the employers' – reg 6(2)(a).

34.68 Regulation 6(2)(b) was not very well worded. But the ability of the rules to deal with apportionment seemed to be clear from reg 16 (see below). Warren J held in *L v M Ltd*[1] that the old reg 6(2)(b) had this effect, holding:

> 'Following from that distinction between a valuation difference at the designated time on the one hand and the debt equal to that difference which only arises following its ascertainment, what reg 6(2)(a) provides is not for the ascertainment of an employer's share of the debt but of an employer's share of the difference and it provides a formula for doing so. Similarly, although reg 6(2)(b) refers to debt it clearly means difference, and I can see no reason why the scheme should not provide a formula which can be applied to the difference as of the designated time e.g. if there are two employers, the formula could be an equal division of the difference. Or it could be of a specified amount e.g. the first £1 or £25 million to be apportioned to one employer and the balance to the other. If trustees are given a discretion about how to ascertain that difference I do not see why, in principle, they should not be able to determine how to do so prior to the ascertainment of the amount provided that the enabling power is expressed in appropriate language to achieve that end, although the actual apportionment might not be effected until the valuations were complete.'

1 [2006] EWHC 3395 (Ch); 27 October 2006, [2007] PLR 11 (Warren J) – see also Chapter 35 below.

34.69 The Employer Debt Regulations were amended in April 2008 (by SI 2008/731) in an attempt to clarify the position on apportionment of liabilities for the purpose of working out s 75 debts. Various changes were made:

- The exiting employer's s 75 debt is now calculated as its 'share of the difference' ie defined in reg 2(1) as the employer's share of the total difference between the value of the assets and the amount of the liabilities of the scheme. This amount is now calculated as its 'liability share' unless an alternative is agreed – reg 6(2).

- The 'liability share' is similar to the default allocation mechanism under the former regime and it is based on working out a fraction (the 'liability proportion'): ie the liabilities attributable to employment with the exiting employer divided by the liabilities attributable to employment with all remaining employers.

- This amount is now determined by the trustees (rather than the actuary under the former regime) after consulting the actuary and the relevant employer.

34.70 In the absence of a scheme provision, the apportionment was (before April 2008) made by the scheme actuary, acting in accordance with actuarial guidance note GN19[1]. GN19 dealt (in para 4.7) with the apportionment to an individual employer.

The current position is similar (but now set out in the Employer Debt Regulations). The liability share is the liability proportion of the total difference between the assets and the liabilities.

The 'liability proportion' is defined in reg 2(1) as 'K' divided by 'L' where:

K is the amount of the scheme's liabilities attributable to the employer and

L is the amount of the scheme's liabilities attributable to all employers (ie all current employers and former employers deemed to remain employers under reg 9).

This can, as before, be summarised as being on the following basis:

$$\textit{Total scheme deficiency} \times \frac{\textit{employer's liabilities}}{\textit{all employers' liabilities}}$$

For this purpose:

Total scheme deficiency	is the overall deficiency in respect of the entire scheme (para 4.4 of GN19). This includes an arbitrary percentage provision for the expenses of winding up the scheme);
employer's liabilities	are the value of the scheme's liabilities (excluding any provision for expenses) in respect of employees and former employees of that employer;
all employers' liabilities	means the value of the scheme's liabilities (excluding any provision for expenses) in respect of employees and former employees of all those who count at that time as employers for the purposes of s 75.

1 Employer Debt Regulations, reg 4(5), before amendment by SI 2008/731.

34.71 Under reg 6(5)(b) of the Employer Debt Regulations (as inserted in April 2008), where trustees are:

- unable to determine exact liabilities attributable to the exiting employer; or

- can do so only at disproportionate cost,

the amended regulations give guidance as to how liabilities should be allocated. This is useful where, for example, the employer has not kept detailed records of intra-group transfers.

Under the new rules in reg 6(4), if reg 6(5) applies:

- if the exiting employer was the last employer of a person, all liabilities of that person are attributed to that employer;

- liabilities in respect of any member which cannot be attributed to any employer are attributed in a 'reasonable manner' to one or more employer (which may or may not include the exiting employer); and

- if the trustees are unable to determine whether the exiting employer was the last employer and liabilities cannot be attributed to any employer, those liabilities are not attributed to any employer (i.e. they become 'orphan' liabilities).

34.72 From April 2008, there are four express options under the revised Employer Debt Regulations[1] for modifying what would otherwise be a section 75 debt:

(1)   Scheme Apportionment Arrangement (SAA)

(2)   Regulated Apportionment Arrangement (RAA)

(3)   Withdrawal Arrangement (WA)

(4)   Approved withdrawal arrangement (AWA)

These arrangements are discussed in more detail in Chapter 35 below. There is a good discussion of these arrangements in the talk given by Ian Greenstreet and Louise Howard '*Employer debt: a better regime?*' to the APL summer conference in 2008.

1 Employer Debt Regulations, reg 6(2), as modified by the Occupational Pension Schemes (Employer Debt and Miscellaneous Amendments) Regulations 2008 (SI 2008/731).

EFFECT OF ALLOCATING LIABILITIES

34.73 The effect of the default allocation mechanic under the Employer Debt Regulations is to make it clear that (unlike the situation in relation to the predecessor of s 75, PSA 1993, s 144) all the statutory deficiency for the whole scheme is allocated among the current employers.

If the scheme includes orphan liabilities – ie liabilities for employees of a company which no longer participates (and is no longer an employer for the purposes of s 75) – the 'total scheme deficit' will be calculated including the liability to those members.

Conversely, this liability (to orphan members) will not be included in the 'liability proportion ie in either the 'employer's liabilities' or the 'all employers' liabilities' (as described in para 34.70 above).

Example:

Say: Scheme assets: £80m, buy-out liabilities: £100m

●   Total scheme deficit £20m – scheme is 20% under funded

Say: 4 current employers – liabilities in respect of each employer £10m each

●   So £60m orphan liabilities (£100m – £40m)

If one employer leaves:

●   Relevant percentage = 25% (ie 10m/40m)

●   Exiting employer debt = £5m (25% of £20m)

NOT 20% of £10m (= £2m)

34.74 It is clear from the Employer Debt Regulations (like under the Deficiency Regulations 1996) that a deficiency debt can arise in a multi-employer scheme in relation to one employer only.

34.75 This was a change from the position under the PSA 1993, s 144. If an employer enters a relevant insolvency process (including an MVL) or ceases to be 'a person employing persons in the description or category to which the scheme relates' (see the discussion of this phrase in Chapter 32 above) then if this is prior to the scheme winding up (or all the employers entering insolvency) a deficiency debt arises in relation to that employer only (and not the others) – Employer Debt Regulations, reg 6(1)).

34.76 It seems that this debt obligation on the employers is a several obligation, ie one employer is not (subject to what is said below) liable for any deficiency debt of another employer. Where employees have moved between employers but stayed within a group and stayed in the same scheme, it seems that (eg formerly under para 4.7 of GN19) the liability of each employer relates only to the period of service of the employee with the employer alone, ie not to periods of employment with a previous employer in the group.

However, this is only for the purpose of calculating the proportion of the total debt. As outlined in para 34.73 above, the employer can then be liable for a proportion of the scheme's liabilities which do not apply to any current employer.

If the records are unclear, it is also possible that the trustees may use their power under new reg 6(4)(c) to apportion liability on to the last employer etc – see para 34.71 above.

34.77 There is also no provision in s 75 or the Employer Debt Regulations dealing with what happens after an employer has contributed its share of the deficiency to the scheme. If one or more of the other employers defaults in payment of its share of the deficiency, there will still be a deficit in the scheme and this could leave it open (if liquidation has not occurred) for a further debt obligation to arise on all remaining employers. This could perhaps be avoided if some statutory provision had been made for attribution of the amount received by the trustees towards providing the benefits of the employees of the employer concerned. However, there is no such provision in s 75 or the Employer Debt Regulations. A partial winding-up rule, if there is one in the rules of the scheme, may provide a form of allocation (see Chapter 36 below).

34.78 This problem under s 75 is less than that which arose under s 144. Under s 75, an employer will cease to be an employer (and hence liable for any debt) once (in effect) it ceases to participate in the scheme. This is subject to the provision in the Employer Debt Regulations deeming an employer to remain as an employer for the purposes of s 75 until any relevant deficiency debt has been paid[1].

1 Employer Debt Regulations, reg 9 – see para 34.17 above.

Cessation by one employer – finding out the debt

34.79   One difficulty that an employer will face if it ceases to participate in a multi-employer scheme is knowing whether a debt will actually arise under s 75 at the time it ceased to participate.

34.80   Sections 75(2) and 75(4) as amended by PA 2004 are clearer than the previous section 75 in providing that a debt falls due when the relevant event occurs. Obviously the debt cannot be enforced until it has been calculated and certified in accordance with the Employer Debt Regulations, but it seems that the debt arises earlier – no actual demand from the trustees seems to be necessary (this could relevant for any statutory limitation period)See also para 34.16 above.

This means that an employer remains potentially liable even though it is unaware that a debt obligation has arisen. There is no statutory power for the employer to force the trustees to confirm whether or not a deficiency could have arisen (and trustees may be reluctant to give any confirmation about this in the absence of a full valuation by the actuary and in view of the compromise issues under reg 2(2) of the PPF Entry Rules Regulations – see Chapter 35 below).

34.81   If the scheme was underfunded on the MFR basis at the last full valuation or annual solvency check, the trustees were, under the MFR Regulations obliged to carry out a new MFR actuarial valuation on an event occurring in a multi-employer scheme that could trigger a debt under s 75 – see MFR Regulations, reg 13.. Only three months was given for this (unless the applicable time coincided with a normal valuation date, in which case six months was given).

There is no equivalent obligation under the scheme specific funding legislation. The revised Employer Debt Regulations (post April 2008) include specific provision for the trustees/actuary to be able to use updated asset and actuarial assessments if the trustees so decide (having consulted the employers) – see para 34.35 above.

If a cessation by one employer is material, the trustees may exercise their general power to revise the recovery plan etc – Scheme Funding Regulations, reg 8(5).

GRACE PERIOD

34.82   The April 2008 amendments to the Employer Debt Regulations also introduced a provision allowing a 'grace period' in some circumstances – see reg 6A. This only applies if:

- there is a multi-employer scheme and an employment-cessation event occurs (ie it cannot apply if there is another s 75 trigger such as a scheme winding-up or insolvency event); and

- the exiting employer gives notice to the trustee. This notice must be given on or before the employment-cessation event or after the employment-cessation event provided it is given 'as soon as possible' and in any event not later than one month after.

If such a notice is given the s 75 debt does not arise. Instead the employer is given a period of grace of up to one year and is treated as if it continued to employ an active member in the scheme.

34.83　This period of grace ends either:

(a)　when the employer employs an active member; or

(b)　when the employer gives notice to the trustees or the period of one year expires or an insolvency event occurs in relation to the exiting employer.

Under (a) the original employment-cessation event is treated as if it never happened.

Under (b) the period of grace is treated as if it had not applied. This means that the s 75 debt as at the original cessation date will then become due and enforceable in the usual way.

The grace period provision seems to be designed to allow employers to deal with temporary loss of active members (eg in a seasonal business) without a s 75 debt arising.

TAX RELIEF

34.84　Section 199 of the Finance Act 2004 applies in relation to HMRC registered schemes to deem contributions made by an employer under PA 1995, s 75, as contributions under the pension scheme. This means that tax relief will be available – FA 2004, s 196. The term 'employer' for this purpose includes a former employer – FA 2004, s 279(1).

In addition, payments under s 75 are deemed to be paid on the last day that the relevant trade, profession, business or vocation of the employer was carried on – FA 2004, s 199(4).

These provisions were derived from ICTA 1988, s 592(6A), which was added by the Finance Act 1993.

34.85　Section 199 only refers to payments under PA 1995, s 75. However, it probably has effect in relation to amounts paid under previous enactments in the same way. This is on the basis that s 75 is a re-enactment of PSA 1993, s 144, and so s 17(2)(a) of the Interpretation Act 1978 applies to construe the reference to s 75 to be one to s 144 as well. Section 592(6A) only referred to s 144.

Section 592(6A) only applied to payments made after 27 July 1993 – see the Finance Act 1993, s 112(6).

34.86　It seems implicit from section 199 that any deficiency payments made by the employer after its business has ceased under some provision other than s 75 (eg a provision of the pension scheme itself) may not have been thought eligible for tax relief. Presumably, the argument would be that such payments were not made wholly and exclusively for the purposes of the trade – see Income and Corporation Taxes Act 1988, s 74(1)(a).

34.87   However, post-cessation payments are now generally allowed as a tax deduction where they are made to employees under a pre-existing contractual or statutory obligation – see the Revenue Interpretation issued in February 1999 following the decision of the Privy Council in *IRC v Cosmotron Manufacturing Co Ltd*[1]. In principle there seems no reason why this should not cover deficiency debts due to pension scheme trustees as well (whether under statute or under a term of the scheme)[2].

The position is discussed in HMRC's Business Income Manual at page BIM46040 – Specific deductions: registered pension schemes: wholly & exclusively: cessation of a trade[3].

1 [1997] 1 WLR 1288; [1997] STC 1134, PC.
2 See the comments in the HMRC Business Income Manual at BIM 38315. On the web at http://www.hmrc.gov.uk/manuals/bimmanual/BIM38315.htm
3 http://www.hmrc.gov.uk/manuals/bimmanual/BIM46040.htm

CLAIMS OVER THE s 75 LEVEL – SCHEME RULES

34.88   In some cases, scheme rules may give a contractual funding claim to trustees that is greater than the s 75 debt. For example if the scheme funding rule provides for the employer to pay enough fully to fund all benefits, this may then result in a bigger claim than under s 75 (for example to cover a change in the asset or liability position after an insolvency date, but before the scheme actually winds up).

This would only be claimable in the employer's insolvency if:

(a)   the contribution obligation survived the winding-up of the scheme –see for example *Re K & J Holdings Ltd; Capital Cranfield Trustees Ltd v Pinsent Curtis (a firm)*[1], where a contribution rule was terminated by notice from the employer; and

(b)   the scheme ends up winding-up outside the PPF. If it were to be taken over by the PPF, the scheme will be deemed to have started winding-up at the start of the assessment period (see para 33.104 above) and any funding claim under the rules would be likely to be the same as the s 75 debt and so caught by the rule against double proofs. In addition, contributions (other than those under s 75) cannot be paid during an assessment period – PA 2004, s 133(3) and see para 28.34 above.

An element of 'double proof' would arise if the scheme would be proving in the liquidation for both the funding rule debt and the liability under s 75, which to a degree represent the same debt. This is not allowed in a liquidation as a matter of general insolvency law. In *Re Oriental Commercial Bank, ex p European Bank*[2], Mellish LJ stated that 'There is only to be one dividend in respect of what is in substance the same debt' – see also *Re Fenton*[3], *Barclays Bank plc v TOSG Trust Fund*[4] and *Re Glen Express Ltd*[5].

In *Bishopsgate Investment Management Ltd v Homan*[6], Vinelott J at first instance refused (at page 194) to allow trustees to have a 'double dipping claim' ie to claim from the employer in relation to a shortfall in scheme assets both under a provision in the scheme and under the SSPA 1975, s 58B (the predecessor of the PA 1995, s 75). This would infringe the rule against double proofs or double dividends in an insolvent winding up. The point was not raised in the Court of Appeal.

If these conditions are met, then it may be possible for a contractual debt claim to be made in addition to any s 75 claim, but this will depend on whether or not such a power could be construed as surviving a scheme winding-up – see *Re ABC Television Ltd Pension Scheme*[7], *Jones v Williams*[8] and *Leadenhall Independent Trustees Limited v Welham*[9].

1 [2005] EWCA Civ 860, [2005] 4 All ER 449, [2005] ICR 1767
2 (1871) LR 7 Ch App 99 at 103, CA.
3 [1931] 1 Ch 85, CA.
4 [1984] AC 626, HL.
5 [2000] BPIR 456; 19 October 1999 (Neuberger J).
6 [1994] PLR 179 (Vinelott J).
7 [1989] PLR 21 (Foster J). See also para 39.68 below.
8 [1989] PLR 21 (Knox J).
9 [2004] OPLR 115 (Park J).

SECTION 75 DEBTS – SUMMARY

34.89

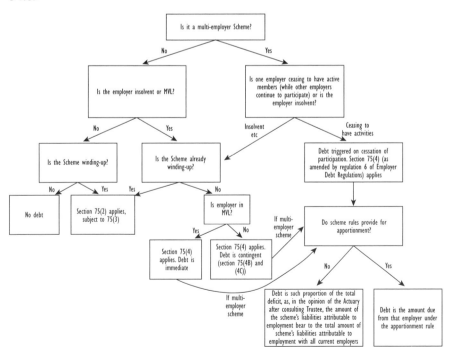

CHAPTER 35

Modifying or compromising the s 75 debt

CHANGING THE s 75 DEBT

35.1   The debt that would otherwise arise under s 75 can be affected in various ways:

- In the case of a multi-employer scheme by modifying the liability share by the use of an allocation arrangement or withdrawal arrangement – reg 6(2), Employer Debt Regulations. These were briefly discussed in the previous Chapter, but more detail is given below.

- by use of the 'relevant transfer deduction' – this is also discussed below; or

- by a compromise of the debt – this is also discussed below.

ALLOCATION ARRANGEMENTS AND WITHDRAWAL ARRANGEMENTS

35.2   A statutory debt is triggered under s 75 of the Pensions Act 1995 on participating employers in the Fund in various events, including the cessation of participation of an employer or a winding-up of the Fund.

35.3   As outlined in the previous chapter, under reg 6 of the Employer Debt Regulations, the calculation of any s 75 debt triggered in those circumstances where there is a multi-employer scheme involves:

(1)   the trustees and the scheme actuary calculating the deficiency for the whole scheme on a notional buy-out basis.

(2)   the total amount of this debt being allocated among the employers (including any exiting company).

35.4   Broadly the allocation is the amount decided by the trustees (after consulting with the actuary) as being the 'liability share' – ie the 'liability proportion' of the total scheme deficit.
   The 'liability proportion' is K divided by L, where:

- K is 'the amount of the scheme's liabilities attributable' to the employer (under reg 6(4)), and

- L is the liabilities attributable to employment with all the employers.

In effect, a percentage of the scheme's total buy-out deficit (for all members, including 'orphan' members whose service does not relate to a current employer) is allocated to each employer. This is the default rule under the legislation – reg 6(2) of the Employer Debt Regulations.

35.5   This has the result that calculating the allocation of liabilities between participating employers can be very difficult, as it requires significant historic information to be available in respect of the membership of the scheme to assess what liabilities are 'attributable to employment with' that employer.

35.6   From April 2008, there are four express options under the revised Employer Debt Regulations[1] for modifying what would otherwise be a section 75 debt:

(1) Scheme Apportionment Arrangement (SAA)

This replaces the previous provision in the original Employer Debt Regulations allowing for allocation under the scheme rules provisions and allows trustees to consent to the exiting employer paying the 'scheme apportionment arrangement share', which can be less than the default 'liability share'. This new arrangement also needs to be reflected on the face of the rules. The remaining employers must be able to meet the 'funding test' (see below).

(2) Regulated Apportionment Arrangement (RAA)

This is similar to a SAA but is only relevant where the trustees are of the opinion that there is reasonable likelihood of the scheme entering an assessment period for the PPF in the next 12 months or an assessment period has already started. It requires a notice of approval to be issued by the Pensions Regulator and the PPF must not object to the proposal. Unlike the other three arrangements, there is no requirement that the 'funding test' be met.

(3) Withdrawal Arrangement (WA)

This is similar to the approved withdrawal arrangement under the former (pre April 2008) Employer Debt Regulations, but it does not require Pensions Regulator approval. Trustees can agree with an employer that a lower debt than the s 75 debt is payable, but the amount paid must not be less than the amount calculated based on the scheme funding deficit (rather than the buy-out deficit). The difference is payable (on a fixed or floating basis) at some stage in the future by a third party (ie a 'guarantor) who is either another employer(s) in the scheme or a third party.
    The 'funding test' must be met (see below) and the trustees must be satisfied the guarantor(s) have sufficient financial resources to be likely to be able to pay the guaranteed amount when required.

(4) Approved withdrawal arrangement (AWA)

This option requires Pensions Regulator agreement but can be used where the exiting employer proposes to pay less than the scheme funding amount share of the debt. The Pensions Regulator must be satisfied that it is reasonable to approve the arrangement, having regard to such matters as it considers relevant, including:

- the potential effects of the employment-cessation event on the method or assumptions for calculating scheme's technical provisions;

- the financial circumstances of the proposed guarantor;

- the amount of the liability share (if it had applied);

- the amount of the AWA share; and

- the effect of the proposed AWA on the security of members' benefits.

- the 'funding test' must be met (see below).

There is a good discussion of these arrangements in the talk given by Ian Greenstreet and Louise Howard *'Employer debt: a better regime?'* to the APL summer conference in 2008.

1 Employer Debt Regulations, reg 6(2) as modified by the Occupational Pension Schemes (Employer Debt and Miscellaneous Amendments) Regulations 2008 (SI 2008/731).

Funding test

35.7   For an SAA, WA and AWA, the funding test will need to be met. The funding test does not apply for an RAA.

To meet the 'funding test', the trustees must be reasonably satisfied that when the arrangement takes effect, the remaining employers will be reasonably likely to be able to fund the scheme so that it will have sufficient and appropriate assets to cover its technical provisions (taking account of any change in the technical provisions[1] necessary as a result of the arrangement) – reg 2(4A).

Trustees may consider the test met if, in their opinion, the remaining employers are able to meet the relevant payment as they fall due under the schedule of contributions, taking account of any revision necessary – reg 2(4C).

With an SAA[2], trustees must also be reasonably satisfied that the effect of the SAA will not be to adversely affect the security of members' benefits as a result of:

- a material change in legal, demographic or economic circumstances that would justify a change to the method or assumptions used in the last calculation of the scheme's technical provisions; or

- a material revision to an existing recovery plan.

1 Although there is no definition in the Employer Debt Regulations, the definition of a scheme's 'technical provisions' in PA 2004 will apply – ie its estimated actuarial liabilities for scheme specific funding purposes – PA 2004, s 222(2) – see para 33.22 above.
2 See Employer Debt Regulations, reg 2(4A)(b).

35.8   The expression 'reasonably satisfied' is not defined further in the Employer Debt Regulations. It seems to envisage a factual test being satisfied. One problem is that third parties will not be able to know definitively if the trustees have actually so satisfied themselves (even if they say so in the arrangements, this is presumably not definitive).

In order to be 'reasonably satisfied' about the funding test, it seems that the Trustee must:

(a)   actually hold that view; and

(b)   be satisfied that it has evidence that the facts are sufficient to induce that belief or opinion in a reasonable person.

There are, as yet, no decided court decisions on the funding test under the Employer Debt Regulations. But this analysis fits with the legislation and various Australian decisions (on similar wording) say this: *ING Funds v ANZ*[1] referring to *Gypsy Jokers Motorcycle Club v Commissioner of Police*[2] and *George v Rockett*[3] where all seven members of the High Court said (at page 112):

> 'When a statute prescribes that there must be 'reasonable grounds' for a state of mind – including suspicion and belief – it requires the existence of facts which are sufficient to induce that state of mind in a reasonable person.'

It is not sufficient, the High Court said (at page 113), for the decision-maker to act 'parrot-like' upon the bald assertion of an informant. The decision-maker must be 'satisfied that there are sufficient grounds reasonably to induce the state of mind'.

1 (2009) NSWSC 243; (2009) 27 ACLC 423 (Barrett J) at para [102].
2 (2008) HCA 4, High Court.
3 [1990] HCA 26; (1990) 170 CLR 104, High Court.

35.9   In practice, in an insolvency situation it may be relatively difficult for the trustees to reach the conclusion that they are reasonably satisfied that the funding test is met (given the insolvent status of one or more relevant companies).

Allocation mechanic

35.10   Before April 2008, many employers and trustees had amended scheme rules to provide for an alternative allocation mechanism to ensure that minimal or reduced debts are triggered on employers ceasing to have active members, usually attributing responsibility to the principal company or other employers continuing to participate in the scheme. This was allowed under the original Employer Debt Regulations, before their amendment in April 2008.

35.11   In the 2006 case of *L v M Ltd*[1] (see para 34.68 above) Warren J confirmed that agreeing in advance to allocate the s 75 debt in this way would not prejudice the scheme's eligibility for the Pension Protection Fund.

This approach is no longer possible under the new regulations as they introduce other options for dealing with a section 75 debt (such as the SAA).

There were transitional provisions for schemes which had introduced such a rule[2]. An existing apportionment rule can continue to apply in relation to a specific trigger event (eg an employment-cessation event) which occurred before 6 April 2009 (ie a year from when the amending regulations came into force) where:

- an agreement between the employer and trustees is entered into before, on or within 12 months after 6 April 2008 (ie up to 5 April 2009) on the basis that a scheme's apportionment rule will apply after the 6 April 2008 in relation to a specific employment-cessation event, or in relation to a debt arising as a result of the commencement of winding-up of the scheme;

- the scheme's apportionment rule was in force before 14 March 2008; and

- the transaction to which the agreement related was considered before that date by the managing body (eg the board of directors of a company[3]) of at least one of the parties to the agreement or of a connected or associated person[4] of such a party.

1 [2006] EWHC 3395 (Ch); [2007] PLR 11 (Warren J) – see also para 34.68 above and Chapter 35 below.
2 See Occupational Pension Schemes (Employer Debt and Miscellaneous Amendment) Regulations 2008 (SI 2008/731), reg 2(7), (8).
3 Reg 2(9)(b).
4 The Insolvency Act definition of 'connected' and 'associated' applies here – see Occupational Pension Schemes (Employer Debt and Miscellaneous Amendment) Regulations 2008 (SI 2008/731), reg 2(9)(c) incorporating the definitions in PA 1995, s 123. See further Chapter 41 (Who is connected or associated?) below.

35.12 Under the amended Employer Debt Regulations, it is clear that an apportionment can be included in rules prospectively – ie before the debt arises.

Before the April 2008 changes, modifying a s 75 debt after it has arisen (ie after it has been certified by the actuary, or perhaps after the relevant s 75 event has occurred) through a scheme rule change, ran the risk that it could have resulted in the scheme ceasing to be eligible for the PPF (see below). This point was left open by Warren J in his decision in *L v M Ltd.*

35.13 The April 2008 changes also clarified that a modification before the beginning of an assessment period through a scheme apportionment arrangement, a regulated apportionment, a withdrawal arrangement or an approved withdrawal under the modified Employer Debt Regulations does not prejudice the scheme's eligibility to enter the PPF – see the PPF Entry Rules, reg 2(4)[1].

1 As modified by the Occupational Pension Schemes (Employer Debt and Miscellaneous Amendments) Regulations 2008 (SI 2008/731).

Trustee modification power

35.14 Under the original 2005 Employer Debt Regulations, if a scheme 'could not be modified for the purpose of making provision' for the apportionment of the debt between employers under reg 6(2)(a), the trustees are given, in reg 16, a statutory power to amend the scheme (without any need for employer consent) to provide for the apportionment of the statutory debt[1]. It seems clear that this power only applied if there is no suitable amendment power in the scheme already (which must be uncommon).

A wider interpretation would have been to allow the trustees to use the power if, for some reason, the existing amendment power is wide enough but cannot be exercised, eg because the relevant employer's consent is needed but refused. But this wider interpretation seems wrong (contrast the wider power given in PA 1995, s 65, allowing trustees to modify schemes to comply with the sex equality provisions, including where consents cannot be obtained).

1 PA 1995, s 68(2)(e), and Employer Debt Regulations, reg 16.

35.15 Under the new (post April 2008) Employer Debt Regulations, reg 16 was amended to become more widely drafted and seemed on its face to give trustees a unilateral power to amend scheme rules:

> 'for the purposes of making provision for an employer's share of the difference for the purposes of regulation 6(2) [the provision setting out SAAs, RAs, WAs and AWAs] to be apportioned in a different proportion from that which would otherwise apply by virtue of the liability share'.

This would have been a significant shift in the balance of power, allowing (in effect) trustees to allocate s 75 debts amongst employers as they see fit. This would seem an odd result, particularly given it was in a section of the regulations headed 'Supplementary'.

35.16 This interpretation (of a unilateral trustee power) was not clear. The contrary view seemed better – that employer agreement is required for the exercise of a SAA, because:

- the definition of SAA requires 'the trustees or managers consent to' the arrangement under the scheme rules. It would seem odd if trustee consent is required to an act they have the power to make unilaterally;

- the exclusion from the funding test in regulation 6B(2)(b) for SAAs applies where, 'at the date of the *agreement* the scheme had commenced winding up …' [*emphasis added*], envisaging an agreement between the employer and trustees for a SAA.

35.17 In any event, the Government moved to amend regulation 16 again, shortly after the new regulations came into force on 6 April 2008. Regulation 16 was amended[1] so that it now states:

> 'The trustees of such a trust scheme, after consulting such employers in relation to the scheme as they think appropriate, may by resolution modify the scheme for the purposes of making provision for an employer's share of the difference for the purposes of [regulation 6(2)(a) or (b)] to be attributed in a different proportion from that which would otherwise apply by virtue of the liability share.'

The cross reference now to regs 6(2)(a) or (b) means that this power only refers to a scheme apportionment arrangement share or a regulated apportionment arrangement share and the relevant definitions envisage a need for employer consent[2]. The explanatory note to the amending regulations states:

> 'Regulation 2(2) amends the definition of 'scheme apportionment arrangement' in regulation 2(1) of the 2005 Regulations so as to provide that the employer, or in an applicable case any employer to whom all or part of the employer's liability has been apportioned, must consent to the arrangement.'

1 Occupational Pension Schemes (Employer Debt – Apportionment Arrangements) (Amendment) Regulations 2008 (SI 2008/1068) with effect from 15 April 2008.

Effect of apportioning liabilities

35.18 Generally the four arrangements specified in reg 6(2): SAA, RAA, WA and AWA, envisage:

(a)   the amount of the s 75 debt payable by the exiting employer is changed; and

(b)   another person agrees to pick up the liability of the exiting employer – this can be either:

- a fixed liability (eg the third party agree to pay a fixed amount if a relevant trigger event occurs) – this is a fixed amount because it is not affected by later changes in the funding position of the scheme; or

- a floating liability – ie the third party agrees to be responsible for a future s75 debt as if the employees of the exiting employer had been employees of the third party – this is a floating amount because the amount of the debt will depend on the later position of the scheme (eg if the scheme were to be fully funded on a s 75 basis at the later trigger date, no further debt would be payable).

35.19 Before the April 2008 changes, reg 6(2)(b) of the Employer Debt Regulations, allowed for an alternative allocation where the scheme rules provide it. Provided that the scheme's amendment power permitted it, it was possible to make a scheme amendment to provide for an express allocation for the purposes of reg 6(2)(b).

35.20 But care needed to be taken with the wording – see *Re Phoenix Venture Holdings Ltd (Company No 2692 of 2005), Phoenix Venture Holdings Ltd v Independent Trustee Services Ltd*[1] where Morritt V-C held that the allocation attempted was not actually allowed under the amended terms of the scheme.

1 [2005] EWHC 1379; [2005] PLR 379; [2005] All ER (D) 325 (May) (Morritt V-C).

Pensions Regulator role

35.21 In practice the employer and the trustees are likely to want to consider whether or not to seek advance clearance for any arrangements from the Pensions Regulator (see Chapter 37 below).

35.22   At a technical level, the main purpose of entering into an SAA is to prevent all or part of a potential s 75 debt that would otherwise be payable by the exiting employer from becoming due and so this could potentially allow the Pensions Regulator to issue a contribution notice on connected or associated persons who are party to the relevant act.

35.23   However the Guidance on clearance[1] issued by the Pensions Regulator indicates that clearance is not necessary where the section 75 debt arises in circumstances in which there is no net reduction of employer covenant, e.g. say where there is a consolidation of several employers within the employer group, provided that all employer assets and their pension liabilities transfer (see paragraphs 70 to 71 of the Guidance).

1 See the Regulator's website: www.thepensionsregulator.gov.uk/guidance/clearance/index.aspx.

35.24   Agreeing to a scheme allocation arrangement (SAA) or withdrawal arrangement (WA) is not a notifiable event (requiring a written notification to tPR) under the usual set of notifiable events – see Chapter 29 above. The better view is that it does not fall within the event relating to a decision which results in a debt not being paid in full.

Where an SAA is entered into *after* an employment cessation event, this is expressly made a notifiable event for trustees under the Employer Debt Regulations[1] (as amended with effect from 6 April 2008 by amending regulations[2]). The amending regulations introduced a new notifiable event in relation to SAAs[3] which applies where the SAA is entered into on or after the employment-cessation event.

Conversely, an SAA entered into before the employment-cessation event is *not* a notifiable event, either under the new express event or under the general set of notifiable events.

1 The Occupational Pension Schemes (Employer Debt) Regulations 2005 (SI 2005/678 as amended).
2 The Occupational Pension Schemes (Employer Debt and Miscellaneous Amendment) Regulations 2008 (SI 2008/731).
3 Employer Debt Regulations, Sch 1B, para 2.

35.25   Regulation 2(1)(a) of the 2005 Notifiable Events Regulations deals with notification by the trustees and is as follows:

> '(a) any decision by the trustees or managers to take action which will, or is intended to, result in any debt which is or may become due to the scheme not being paid in full.'

Regulation 2(2)(a) of the 2005 Notifiable Events Regulations deals with notification by the employers and is in identical terms (save that it refers to a decision by, and action of, the employer) as follows:

> '(a) any decision by the employer to take action which will, or is intended to, result in any debt which is or may become due to the scheme not being paid in full.'

In both cases, the term 'debt' includes a contingent debt – see regulation 1(2).

35.26   Despite the width of these provisions, an SAA entered into before the employment-cessation event is not a notifiable event because, although the s 75 debt payable on an employment cessation event is probably a 'contingent debt' within the Notifiable Events Regulations, s 75 (and the Employer Debt Regulations) define what this s 75 debt is.

If the necessary circumstances are satisfied, the debt will be the amount payable under an SAA (defined in the Employer Debt Regulations as the scheme apportionment arrangement share (SAA amount)). If the intention is that the SAA amount (which is the s 75 debt) will be paid in full, this means that the decision to enter into the SAA will not result in any 'debt' which is 'not being paid in full' and therefore, no notification to tPR by the Trustee or the employer would be required.

This view is consistent with and supported by the addition (in April 2008) of the specific notifiable event for trustees under the Employer Debt Regulations trustees to notify an SAA entered into on or after the 'applicable time' (ie the employment cessation event).

Effect of an arrangement

35.27   It was therefore possible to amend the scheme to change the allocation of the s 75 debt between the scheme's employers.

An insolvent company may desire this as a way of achieving a larger sale price (say) for a subsidiary.

35.28   See for example *Re T&N Ltd (No1)*[1] where the insolvent company (in administration) went to court to get confirmation that it and the insolvency practitioner would be acting properly if they arranged for the subsidiaries to stop participating before the trustees had the opportunity to switch to a gilts matching strategy (and so increase the then debt under s 75). David Richards J allowed this.

1 [2004] EWHC 1680(Ch); [2004] OPLR 343; [2004] PLR 351 (David Richards J).

35.29   An allocation mechanism could achieve this by allocating the s 75 liabilities so that the resulting s 75 debt applicable to the subsidiary on an employment-cessation event is reduced or a fixed amount.

35.30   Such an allocation of liabilities to the remaining employers can result in:

(a)   a lower s 75 debt arising on the cessation of participation of an employer (while other employers remain participating); and

(b)   the remaining employers ultimately bearing the entire cost of the liabilities at some later time, if and when it is required to pay a s 75 debt (eg on the scheme winding up).

35.31   In practice, before April 2008 insertion of an allocation provision was likely to require the consent of the trustees (depending on the scheme's amendment power).

563

Following the April 2008 changes, the consent of the trustees (and satisfaction of the funding test) is required for these arrangements

In order to comply with their fiduciary duties under trust law, the trustees would need to have good grounds for agreeing to this. They are likely to want to be able to justify a change that resulted in the liability to pay the bulk of any s 75 debt being deferred to a later time, rather than triggered at the time of a cessation of participation (eg on a the disposal) of an employer.

PENSIONS REGULATOR

35.32   Making a scheme amendment to introduce an allocation mechanism for the s 75 debt could potentially be viewed as an avoidance mechanism having a purpose of reducing the s 75 debt payable or reducing the recovery by the scheme of any s 75 debt. This could lead to the Pensions Regulator considering whether to exercise its powers under the Pensions Act 2004 to issue contribution notices and financial support directions (see Chapter 37 below).

35.33   In practice, the employer will want (jointly with the trustees) to consider whether or not to seek clearance from the Pensions Regulator in relation to any proposed allocation amendment.

35.34   In any event, the entry into an SAA, WA or AWA before the relevant employment-cessation event has occurred does not look to be a notifiable event (to the Regulator) under the Pensions Regulator (Notifiable Events) Regulations 2005 (as a decision <u>not</u> to take action which may result in a debt which may become due to the scheme not being paid in full) – see above).

PENSION PROTECTION FUND

35.35   A further concern for the trustees in relation to the introduction of an express allocation provision would be whether that could prejudice the protection available to the pension scheme under the PPF.

35.36   Under reg 2(2) of the Pension Protection Fund (Entry Rules) Regulations 2005, a scheme will cease to be eligible for PPF protection where, at any time:

> 'the trustees or managers of the scheme enter into a legally enforceable agreement the effect of which is to reduce the amount of any debt due to the scheme under Section 75 of the 1995 Act which may be recovered by, or on behalf of, those trustees or managers.'

35.37   Regulation 2(4) of the PPF Entry Rules Regulations was amended effect from 6 April 2008 by amending regulations[1]. The amended reg 2(4) clarifies that where before the beginning of an assessment period in relation to the scheme any of an SAA, RAA, WA or AWA under the Employer Debt Regulations are is place, the scheme is not excluded from PPF eligibility under reg 2(2).

1 The Occupational Pension Schemes (Employer Debt and Miscellaneous Amendment) Regulations 2008 (SI 2008/731), reg 18.

35.38 The issue arose before April 2008 as to whether reg 2(2) technically could apply on the trustees agreeing to an apportionment mechanism in the rules in relation to the s 75 debt.

Under the amendment power in a typical scheme, both the principal employer and the trustees would need to be a party to any deed of amendment introducing an allocation mechanism. As this would be a legally binding agreement, the trustees will be concerned to ensure that this does not affect the pension scheme's position as an eligible scheme under reg 2(2).

There were strong arguments that reg 2(2) did not (before April 2008) apply to an apportionment provision put in place before any s 75 debt has actually arisen (i.e. before an employment-cessation event). The effect of the apportionment does not reduce the amount of any debt due and payable. The PPF had confirmed that it agreed with this in principle.

35.39 In addition, in a 2006 case, *L v M Ltd*[1], Warren J held that such a provision does not stop the scheme from being an eligible scheme for the PPF. Warren J decided that reg 2(2) is not triggered, at least if the allocation provision is inserted before the debt arises (eg before an employment-cessation event).

1 [2006] EWHC 3395 (Ch); (2006) 27 October; [2007] PLR 11 (Warren J).

35.40 In *L v M Ltd* Warren J held:

'95. The Pension Proposal in the present case results in a legally enforceable agreement which operates to alter the apportionment provisions which take place on the winding up of the Scheme. It is an agreement which will be made before any triggering event giving rise to a debt under either Section 75 or Section 75A of [sic] the Employer Debt Regulations has occurred. At that time, there will be no debt then presently due to the Trustees. In my judgment, the Pension Proposal does not constitute an agreement the effect of which "is to reduce the amount of any debt due to the Scheme". That phrase indicates, I consider, a temporal requirement that the debt is due at the time of the agreement. It is not enough that the agreement has the effect of reducing a debt which will (or even may) become due as the result of a triggering event in the future.

96 Whether a debt can be due before it is quantified is not a question I need to answer nor, therefore, do I need to say whether the decision in Phoenix1 governs the meaning of regulation 2(2). I do not consider that regulation 2(2) is to be read as if it refers to a legally enforceable agreement the effect of which is or will or may in the future be to reduce a debt which is or will, or may in the future become due and payable (although I do not dismiss the possibility that it may include an agreement made when the debt has fallen due for quantification eg when the scheme commences winding up.'

1 *Phoenix Venture Holdings Ltd v Independent Trustee Services Ltd* [2005] EWHC 1379; [2005] PLR 379; [2005] All ER (D) 325 (May) (Morritt V-C).

35.41   Warren J also confirmed that a scheme rule which prospectively appor-
tions s 75 liabilities is within reg 6(2)(b) of the Employer Debt Regulations:

> '36 Following from that distinction between a valuation difference at the desig-
> nated time on the one hand and the debt equal to that difference which arises only
> following its ascertainment, on the other, what regulation 6(2)(a) provides is not
> for the ascertainment of an employer's share of the debt but for the employer's
> share of the difference and it provides a formula for doing so.
>
> 37 Similarly, although regulation 6(2)(b) refers to "debt" it clearly means 'differ-
> ence', and I can see no reason why the scheme should not provide a formula
> which can be applied to the difference as of the designated time. For instance if
> there are two employers, the formula could be an equal division of the difference
> or it could be of a specified amount, for instance, providing for the first £1 or £25
> million to be apportioned to one employer and the balance to the other. If trustees
> are given a discretion about how to ascertain that difference I do not see why, in
> principle, they should not be able to determine how to do so prior to the ascer-
> tainment of the amount provided that the enabling power is expressed in appro-
> priate language to achieve that end, although the actual apportionment might not
> be effected until the valuations were complete.'

Pre 2008 AWA

35.42   A further option before April 2008 would have been to include the allocation rule change in an approved withdrawal arrangement (AWA) under the
Employer Debt Regulations. Regulation 2(2) of the PPF Entry Rules Regulations
did not apply if old reg 2(4) applied. This stated (before April 2008):

> '(4) Paragraph (2) above shall also not apply in relation to an eligible scheme
> where, before the beginning of an assessment period in relation to the scheme, a
> prescribed arrangement is in place pursuant to regulations made under
> Section 75A of the 1995 Act (debt due from the employer in the case of multi-
> employer schemes)'.

The relevant prescribed arrangement was an AWA under the Employer Debt
Regulations.

35.43   So if the allocation rule change formed part of an AWA, it would definitely fall outside of reg 2(2). But the other conditions for an AWA would still
have to be met. In particular the requirement that the Pensions Regulator considers that the entry into the AWA makes it 'more likely' that the relevant debt will
be paid (Employer Debt Regulations, Sch 1A, para 2(3)(b)).

RELEVANT TRANSFER DEDUCTION

35.44   The Employer Debt Regulations also include a provision allowing the
amount of a s 75 debt that would otherwise arise on a 'departing employer' to be
reduced if there is a 'relevant transfer.

The term 'departing employer' is defined[1] as an employer who is a cessation employer out of a multi-employer scheme or an employer in respect of whom an insolvency event has occurred.

If a notice is given to the trustees, the amount of the departing employer's liabilities is to be reduced by the 'relevant transfer deduction', provided the relevant transfer takes place within the 12 months following the applicable time – reg 6(7).

The effect is that the s 75 debt can be reduced. The amount of the reduction reflects the amount of liabilities transferred to another scheme, less the amount of asses accompanying the transfer. So if the assets are less than the relevant s 75 liability, a deduction will follow.

The amount of the deduction is calculated by reference to the 'relevant transfer liabilities' – defined[1] as the 'liabilities attributable to the departing employer that are transferred'. This does mean that it seems that the deduction only relates to liabilities directly attributed to the departing employer and so cannot deal with any increased s 5 debt payable because of the effect of orphan liabilities.

This seems odd, but there has not yet been any caselaw on this issue. It would require a purposive interpretation by a court to allow a sensible full deduction.

1 Definition of 'departing employer' in Employer Debt Regulations, reg 2(1) (as amended).
2 Definition of 'relevant transfer liabilities' in Employer Debt Regulations, reg 2(1) (as amended).

SUMMARY OF ARRANGEMENTS

35.45

	Withdrawal Arrangement	*Approved Withdrawal Arrangement*	*Scheme Apportionment Arrangement (SAA)*	*Regulated Apportionment Arrangement*
Regulations	6C, Sch 1A	7	See definition 6B	See definition 7A
Funding Test?	Yes Employer must pay an amount equal to or greater (not less) than amount A	Yes Employer must be paying *less* than Amount A	Yes UNLESS: 1. SAA share higher than liability share and employer can afford to pay SAA share or	Not needed

	Withdrawal Arrangement	*Approved Withdrawal Arrangement*	*Scheme Apportionment Arrangement (SAA)*	*Regulated Apportionment Arrangement*
			2. Scheme in wind-up and SAA share is lower than liability share and employer could not pay liability share and can pay SAA share The funding test that applies here is different	
Trustee Consent?	Trustees must be satisfied guarantors can pay amount B	Trustees must notify Regulator that funding test is met		(unless assessment period has commenced)
Regulator approval required?	X	Must be reasonable	X	Must be reasonable
PPF approval required?	X	X	X	Must not object
Timing	Any	Any	Any	Any – however this option is only appropriate where assessment period has commenced or is likely to.
Notes	Funding test - when arrangement takes effect, remaining employers will be reasonably likely to be able to fund the scheme/will have sufficient and appropriate assets to cover technical provisions.		Arrangement under scheme rules	Arrangement under scheme rules

SECTION 75 COMPROMISES

Powers of trustees to compromise

35.46 Trustees of a scheme have an implied power to compromise or settle the statutory debt arising under s 75 or to allow time for payment – see Trustee Act 1925, s 15, as modified by the Trustee Act 2000 and the comments of Robert Walker J (as he then was) in *National Grid v Laws*[1] and Charles Aldous QC in *Bradstock Group Pension Scheme Trustees Ltd v Bradstock Group*[2] – see below.

1 [1997] PLR 157 (Robert Walker J) at 179 (para 103).
2 [2002] EWHC 651, [2002] ICR 1427, [2002] OPLR 281 (Charles Aldous QC sitting as a deputy judge of the Chancery Division).

35.47 In practice however, it will often be difficult to see why the trustees would be acting properly in not enforcing the debt. Enforcing the debt will often mean that the members of the pension scheme are better off. The scheme has more assets (and hence greater security for members' benefits) if the debt is paid.

35.48 If there are members of the scheme still in employment with the relevant employers, it is possible that the trustees will be able to consider the interests of those members in having continued employment as a factor in deciding whether or not to enforce the debt.

35.49 But there may be circumstances where the employer can offer more (as a full and final settlement of its liabilities to the scheme) than would be recovered by the scheme if the employer were to enter insolvency (eg as in *Bradstock*).

The trustees would need to be able to satisfy themselves that they would be acting properly if they were to agree to such a compromise. In particular they will almost always need financial advice and will often seek approval from the Pensions Regulator or the Court.

The Pensions Ombudsman has in his determination[1] of a complaint by Mr Symons rejected a complaint made by a member in relation to a compromise entered into by trustees with an employer, apparently after advice form the scheme's actuary, solicitor and independent advisor.

1 Determination involving Mr R H Symons, 14 February 2008 (S00048).

35.50 In its December 2008 'Abandonment of defined benefit pension schemes' guidance[1] (first issued in May 2007), tPR states that the 'overriding message' is that it:

> 'expects trustees' starting point to be that any arrangement that breaks the link with the existing employer may not be in members' interests, unless the full section 75 debt (the full amount necessary to insure members' benefits with a regulated insurer) is paid, or unless the scheme remains supported by an employer of substance and is suitably compensated for any change in the employer's covenant. Trustees must consider the situation with great care' but that any proposal or arrangement'.

tPR does however comment that any proposal or arrangement 'must be considered on its individual merits'

1 Available on tPR's website: www.thepensionsregulator.gov.uk

35.51   Trustees owe a duty of care to exercise such care and skill as is reasonable in the circumstances, having regard in particular:

(a)   to any special knowledge or experience that the trustee has or holds himself out as having, and

(b)   if the trustee acts as trustee in the course of a business or profession, to any special knowledge or experience that it is reasonable to expect of a person acting in the course of that kind of business or profession.

Trustee Act 2000, s 1(1).

35.52   In *Bradstock Group Pension Scheme Trustees Ltd v Bradstock Group plc*[1], Charles Aldous QC (sitting as a deputy judge) held that trustees could validly compromise the s 75 debt in some circumstances (broadly where the debt had arisen or was about to arise).

1 [2002] EWHC 651, [2002] ICR 1427, [2002] OPLR 281 (Charles Aldous QC sitting as a deputy judge of the Chancery Division).

35.53   There was previously some uncertainty about whether a trustee could compromise a debt arising under s 75 of the Pensions Act 1995. This was on the basis that it should not be possible to contract out of the statutory funding provisions or the statutory debt arising under s 75.

35.54   However, the decision in *Bradstock* confirmed that, whilst it is not possible to contract out of the statutory funding provision (previously the MFR requirements and now the SSF requirements) nor in advance to contract out of the requirements of s 75, it is possible for trustees to compromise a debt arising under s 75 once it has arisen. Further, on the facts of *Bradstock*, it seems that a compromise agreement entered into in advance which envisages the s 75 debt being triggered and compromised in short order is allowed.

35.55   The trustees in the *Bradstock* case had entered into a compromise agreement with the employing company under which the parties agreed that (subject to court approval) the scheme would be wound up and the s 75 debt then triggered would be compromised. This was approved by the judge.

35.56   *Bradstock* was followed by Neuberger J (as he then was) in *Re Owens Corning Fibreglass (UK) Ltd*[1], holding that an application for court approval could be made without appointing representative beneficiaries or even telling the members (although Neuberger J made it clear that he would generally expect members to be informed and have the opportunity to make submissions).
    See also *Hearn v Bell*[2]; *Re T&N Ltd (No 2)*[3] and *Re T&N (No 3)*[4].

1 [2002] PLR 323 (Neuberger J).
2 [2004] 90 PBLR; [2004] EWHC 2803 (Ch) (Patten J).
3 [2004] 78 PBLR; [2004] EWHC 2361 (Ch) (David Richards J).
4 [2005] 30 PBLR; [2004] EWHC 2448 (Ch) (Patten J)

PPF IMPLICATIONS

35.57   The PPF points out in its summary on eligible schemes that eligibility can be lost if there is a debt compromise. This is a reference to regulation 2(2) of the PPF Entry Rules Regulations. As amended, this provides that:

> 'an occupational pension scheme which would be an eligible scheme but for this paragraph is not an eligible scheme where, at any time, the trustees or managers of the scheme enter into a legally enforceable agreement . . . the effect of which is to reduce the amount of any debt due to the scheme . . . under Section 75 of the 1995 Act which may be recovered by, or on behalf of, those trustees or managers.'

35.58   Regulation 2(2) is clearly designed to reduce the risk of the PPF ending up with responsibility for providing protected benefits under a scheme with only a reduced ability of the scheme (or the PPF) to recover the statutory debt due from the employer under s 75 of the Pensions Act 1995 – see Chapter 34 (Section 75) above.

35.59   Clearly the effect of reg 2(2) of the PPF Entry Rules Regulations is that a scheme ceases to be eligible if the trustees enter into a compromise agreement on the same lines as in *Bradstock*.

35.60   A compromise on *Bradstock* lines will be a 'legally enforceable agreement the effect of which is to reduce the amount of any debt due to the scheme under s 75 of PA 1995 which may be recovered by, or on behalf of, those trustees'.

35.61   It is not absolutely clear whether the entry by trustees into a compromise on *Bradstock* lines will make the scheme ineligible even if it occurred before the coming into force of the Pensions Act 2004 (on 6 April 2005).

Regulation 2(2) states that it applies to such an agreement 'at any time'. It could be argued that applying this to compromises in the past is to give retrospective effect to the legislation (which the courts often presume legislation does not do). But this seems unlikely as the test is prospective – it applies at the time of the qualifying insolvency event – ie on or after 6 April 2005 – see Chapter 27 (PPF) above.

35.62   Regulation 2(2) does refer to a 'legally enforceable agreement' and to one which has effect to 'reduce the amount of any debt due to the scheme under Section 75'. This points towards the regulation only applying at the time that a s 75 has fallen due and payable. There are two reasons for this:

- The reference to a 'legally enforceable agreement' looks to be intended to take account of the comments in *Bradstock* that a legally binding compromise can only affect a s 75 debt at the time it becomes due (see above); and

- The reference to a debt being 'due' points to one which is due and payable (rather than still contingent and only potentially due).

35.63 To give reg 2(2) an expanded meaning would be potentially to catch schemes which have not entered into a formal compromise at all, but instead have carried out normal scheme transactions (eg a transfer of members or change in investments) which later are seen to have effect to have reduced the ultimate s 75 debt. For example, an agreement between the trustees and the employer for the employer to pay an additional contribution will usually be a 'legally binding agreement' and will have effect to reduce the s 75 debt that may later become payable.

35.64 It would be bizarre if this could be held to result in reg 2(2) applying and so the scheme ceasing to be eligible for the PPF.

35.65 As noted above, in 2006 Warren J in *L v M Ltd*[1] upheld a narrow view of the operation of reg 2(2). Warren J held that a s 75 debt apportionment provision does not stop the scheme from being an eligible scheme for the PPF. Warren J held that reg 2(2) is not triggered, at least if the allocation provision is inserted before the debt arises (eg before an employment-cessation event).

1 [2006] EWHC 3395 (Ch); (2006) 27 October; [2007] PLR 11 (Warren J).

35.66 In *L v M Ltd* Warren J held (emphasis mine):

'95. The Pension Proposal in the present case results in a legally enforceable agreement which operates to alter the apportionment provisions which take place on the winding up of the Scheme. It is an agreement which will be made before any triggering event giving rise to a debt under either Section 75 or Section 75A of [sic] the Employer Debt Regulations has occurred. At that time, there will be no debt then presently due to the Trustees. In my judgment, the Pension Proposal does not constitute an agreement the effect of which 'is to reduce the amount of any debt due to the Scheme'. That phrase indicates, I consider, a temporal requirement that the debt is due at the time of the agreement. It is not enough that the agreement has the effect of reducing a debt which will (or even may) become due as the result of a triggering event in the future.

96 Whether a debt can be due before it is quantified is not a question I need to answer nor, therefore, do I need to say whether the decision in *Phoenix*[1] governs the meaning of regulation 2(2). I do not consider that regulation 2(2) is to be read as if it refers to a legally enforceable agreement the effect of which is **or will or may in the future be** to reduce a debt which is **or will or may in the future become** due and payable (although I do not dismiss the possibility that it may include an agreement made when the debt has fallen due for quantification e.g. when the scheme commences winding up'.

1 *Phoenix Venture Holdings Ltd v Independent Trustee Services Ltd* [2005] EWHC 1379; [2005] PLR 379; [2005] All ER (D) 325 (May) (Morritt V-C).

EXPRESS EXCEPTIONS

35.67 There are various express exceptions to reg 2(2) set out in reg 2(3) and (4). If one of the conditions is met, these can allow a scheme to remain an eligible scheme even if there is an agreement reducing the amount of a s 75 debt. The conditions are if:

- the agreement is entered into before the start of an assessment period[1], but the assets of the scheme exceed the value of its PPF liabilities (and the actuary has given an estimate of this to the PPF Board, which has determined to validate the estimate and statement)[1] – reg 2(3)(a), (5)–(7); or

- the agreement is entered into before the start of an assessment period[2], but is 'part of an arrangement under s 895 of the Companies Act 2006'[3] (formerly s 425 of the Companies Act 1985) – reg 2(3)(b); or

- the agreement is entered into after the beginning of an assessment period (or a further assessment period) but by the PPF Board – reg 2(3)(c); or

- before the beginning of an assessment period in relation to the scheme, an SAA, RAA, WA or AWA is in place – see para 35.30 above. Before April 2008, this referred to 'a prescribed arrangement is in place pursuant to regulations made under s 75A of the 1995 Act (debt due from the employer in the case of multi-employer schemes)' – reg 2(4). The relevant 'prescribed arrangement' was an approved withdrawal arrangement (AWA) under the Employer Debt Regulations 2005. An AWA had to be approved by the Pensions Regulator and the scheme trustees. Note that the effect of reg 2(4) could be that an SAA or AWA etc has the effect of making the scheme an eligible scheme even if the relevant agreement relating to s 75 is unconnected with the SAA or AWA etc.

Regulations 2(2) to (7) apply separately to each section of a segregated scheme – reg 2(9).

1 The actual mechanics of this process are quite tricky.
2 An assessment period starts on the date of a qualifying insolvency event – see PA 2004, s 132(2).
3 Companies Act 1985, s 425 was replaced by Companies Act 2006, s 895 when the 2006 Act came into force on 1 October 2009.

35.68 Decisions by trustees or employers with a view to taking action which will or are intended to result in a debt being payable to the scheme not being paid in full are events that must be notified to the Pensions Regulator.

See PA 2004, s 69, and the Pensions Regulator (Notifiable Events) Regulations 2005 (SI 2005/900), reg 2(1)(a) and (2)(a). See Chapter 29 (Notifiable events) above.

35.69 If an employer of a defined benefit pension scheme suffers a formal 'insolvency event' (for example enters into administration) and enters the PPF's assessment period 'the rights and powers of the scheme trustees are exercisable by the PPF' – PA 2004, s 137. Amongst other things this allows the PPF to agree to compromise the debt an employer owes to the scheme.

35.70 The PPF may in some circumstances be in a better position than trustees to engage in a restructuring. This is because the PPF can accept a sizable equity stake in the employer whereas trustees cannot invest more than 5% of the scheme's assets by value of the shares in their employer (or an associate). Furthermore a compromise by the PPF will not later bar the scheme from transferring to the PPF – PPF Entry Rules, reg 2(3)(c).

35.71 In a distressed restructuring creditors often agree to a debt for equity swap to avoid a prolonged and value destructive insolvency process. The PPF's ability to compromise a s 75 debt in exchange for accepting an equity stake in the employer in effect allows it to act as any other creditor.

35.72 The PPF first agreed to take equity in July 2005 in the Heath Lambert administration. The Heath Lambert scheme had a £210m deficit. There have been a number of cases where the PPF has acted in a similar way (see the paper '*Restructuring a pension scheme*' by Alastair Lomax, Pippa Read and Graham Frost at the R3 18th Annual conference 2008).

35.73 The PPF has commented that its decisions to compromise or remove a pensions debt is, on the face of it, contrary to one of the purposes of the Pensions Act 2004 ie 'to stop employers dumping their pensions'.

Therefore the PPF has formally stated (in its guidance for insolvency practitioners and official receivers – revised April 2009 version) that it will *only* ever participate in a restructuring or rescue if:

- insolvency is inevitable and the scheme receives consideration which is significantly better than the dividend that would be received if the company went into an ordinary insolvency (ie the scheme will be better off);

- what is offered is fair given what the other creditors and shareholders are to gain as a consequence of the rescue (for example, the insolvency return might be £0 and the PPF is offered £500,000 in respect of a £100 million pension debt. However, the expectation is that post the restructuring, the irrecoverable bank debt of £100 million would become fully recoverable over time because the pension debt is no longer in the company. In such a case, the PPF would seek to extract a suitable 'price' from the bank for allowing it the opportunity of getting its money back over time);

- the scheme is given 10% of the equity where the future shareholders are not currently involved with the company and 33% if the parties are currently involved;

- the Pensions Regulator would *not* be able to issue a contribution notice/financial support direction which would generate more money for the scheme than the deal the PPF has negotiated;

- the Pensions Regulator is prepared to clear the deal; and

- the other party pays both the PPF's and the trustees' legal fees for documenting and executing the deal.

The PPF comments that its willingness to reduce or remove the debt 'can mean the defined benefit pension scheme is much better off than it would have been if the business was simply left to fail'. In effect it is making a commercial decision.

SCHEME RESCUE

35.74   A compromise agreed with the PPF after an assessment period has started can be a scheme rescue event for PPF purposes (see Chapter 28 above). The term 'scheme rescue' is defined in reg 9 of the PPF Entry Rules Regulations. In relation to a corporate employer it means:

'(i)   the company has been rescued as a going concern and the employer:

(aa) retains responsibility for meeting the pension liabilities under the scheme, and

(bb) has not entered into a binding agreement with the PPF to reduce the amount of the s 75 debt;'.

CHAPTER 36

Multi-employer schemes: PPF and s 75

36.1 This Chapter looks at the position in relation to pensions should one member of a group get into financial difficulties and enter insolvency proceedings (administration, liquidation etc).

36.2 This assumes that the company has current employees and that they are active members of the group pension scheme. The company participates in the group pension scheme but is not its principal employer (or sponsor).

36.3 The terms of the group scheme may envisage that if the company ceases to participate, then there is a mandatory requirement for the trustees to segregate part of the assets of the scheme and establish a separate part in relation to the company and any members attributable to the company.

This Chapter looks at the pensions issues that arise.

There is a good discussion of the issues here in the paper '*No room at the orphanage: some issues relating to PPF Entry*' given by Ian Greenstreet and Helen Butler to the APL in April 2009.

PENSIONS ISSUES

36.4 To a degree the pensions issues can depend on the timing of events. There may be a distinction depending on whether:

- the company ceases to participate before it enters a formal insolvency; or

- the insolvency precedes such a cessation.

36.5 Another relevant issue is whether the scheme continues to have employers participating after the company ceases to participate (eg did the scheme convert to frozen before such cessation).

36.6 This Chapter looks at issues that arise in relation to:

- The employer debt under s 75 of the Pensions Act 1995;

- Winding-up of the scheme;

- Entry of the scheme (or part) into the PPF.

SECTION 75

36.7 As outlined above in Chapter 34, cessation of participation in the scheme by an employer (eg ceasing to have any employees who are active members in the scheme) will trigger a debt under s 75 of the Pensions Act 1995 on the company, if at least one other employer continues to participate and continues to have active members. The cessation will be a 'employment-cessation event' within reg 6 of the Employer Debt Regulations 2005.

36.8 There may be a timing issue here. If the withdrawal happens first and is followed by an insolvency event, both seem to be trigger events under the multi-employer parts of the Employer Debt Regulations. Regulation 6(1)(d) amends s 75(4)(a) to refer both to an insolvency event (a 'relevant event') and an employment-cessation event.

36.9 Unless the cessation employer has paid the relevant s 75 debt occurring by virtue of the cessation of participation, then it will be deemed to be still an employer (see reg 9) in most cases (see para 32.16 above).

36.10 The same position seems to arise if the insolvency event precedes the cessation of participation. Section 75(4)(d) and (e) do attempt to deal with multiple relevant events. But they are expressly dis-applied in such a multi-employer context by reg 6(1)(f) of the Employer Debt Regulations.

PARTIAL WINDING-UP RULE?

36.11 A partial winding-up involves the assets and liabilities of a set of members in the scheme being, in effect split into a separate fund, which is then probably wound up. Such a partial winding-up depends on the rules of the scheme. Some schemes do not provide for such a partial winding-up. Others do, in particular if an employer in a multi employer scheme ceases to participate.

There used to be a view that the Inland revenues practice notes for tax approval of schemes mandated such a rule being included, but at least in recent years, there was not an issue in getting approval for a scheme without such a partial winding-up provision.

There is a good discussion of the partial winding-up issues in two APL talks:

- The talk by Duncan Buchanan 'Partial Wind up Rules – honoured in their breach?' given in February 2008 on partial winding-up;

- Followed by the paper 'No room at the orphanage: some issues relating to PPF Entry' given by Ian Greenstreet and Helen Butler in April 2009.

36.12 If the scheme did not provide for a partial winding-up, then the calculation of the amount of the debt under s 75 would follow the usual rules (reg 6).

But where the scheme requires a partial winding-up different rules may apply under the relevant PPF Regulations.

PPF: NO REQUIREMENT TO HAVE A PARTIAL WINDING-UP

36.13   Clearly the trustees would need to consider whether they have any other power to wind-up the scheme etc.

36.14   Assuming that they do not (or decide not to wind-up), then they would seek to enforce the s 75 debt in the usual way and look to the remaining employers in relation to on-going funding (and any ultimate s 75 debt). This is the equivalent to the 'last man standing' approach mentioned in the PPF guidance.

36.15   The insolvency practitioner would have to issue relevant notices under PA 2004, ss 120 and 122, to the PPF, tPR and trustees etc. These then have to be copied-on by the trustees to all the other scheme employers[1].

1 See the modifications made to ss 120 and 122 of PA 2004 by reg 62(1) and (2) of the Pension Protection Fund (Multi-Employer Schemes) (Modification) Regulations 2005, (SI 2005/441, as amended).

36.16   The PPF guidance to trustees states as follows[1]:

No requirement for partial wind-up

The Pension Protection Fund considers the section, not the whole pension scheme, as for a single employer section, but only if all the section's participating employers have entered insolvency and the insolvency event is in relation to the last employer of that section – the last man standing approach.

The process is similar to that of single employer sections but with two main differences:

- An insolvency event in respect of one of the section's participating employers is only a qualifying insolvency event, one that triggers the start of an assessment period, if all the other participating employers have already entered insolvency proceedings; and

- The Pension Protection Fund must only approve a pension scheme status notice when they receive a notice in respect of all the section's employers. When all notices are received, the Pension Protection Fund decides whether to approve the last notice.

There may be circumstances where, following insolvency events for one or more employers, there remains a solvent employer. If that employer then withdraws from the scheme and pays its section 75 debt (leaving only insolvent employers), trustees should make an application for the Board of the Pension Protection Fund to assume responsibility for the scheme. [Section 129 Pensions Act as amended by the Pension Protection Fund (Multi-employer Schemes) (Modification) Regulations 2005]

---

1 See the PPF website: http://www.pensionprotectionfund.org.uk/index/trustee_guidance/detailed_ trustee_guidance/tg_overview/tg_multi-employer.htm#04

36.17 Although this part of the guidance refers to sections, similar rules apply where it is a non-segregated pension scheme.

36.18 This approach outlined in the guidance seems to follow from the provisions of reg 64(1)(b) of the PPF Multi-employer Regulations[1]. This regulation modifies s 127(3) of PA 2004 by re-defining the term 'qualifying insolvency event'. This is redefined so that it only occurs if:

- all the employers enter an insolvency proceeding or
- the relevant employer is the last one, with insolvency events having occurred in relation to all the others and 'an insolvency practitioner is still required by law to be appointed to act in relation to them'.

1 The Pension Protection Fund (Multi-Employer Schemes) (Modification) Regulations 2005 (SI 2005/441, as amended).

36.19 Under PA 2004, s 132 an assessment period only starts if a qualifying insolvency event occurs. Section 132 is modified in relation to this sort of scheme by reg 66 of the PPF Multi-Employer Regulations. The effect is that a qualifying insolvency event needs to occur in relation to an employer. Because of the modification of s 127(3) by reg 64, this would mean it has to be an insolvency event in relation to the last employer remaining.

36.20 If the other employers remain solvent, this means that the s 75 debt arising on the cessation employer (either in relation to the employer–cessation event or the insolvency event) will be enforceable in the usual way. The scheme will not enter an assessment period.

36.21 If the debt is arising by virtue of an insolvency event occurring in relation to the cessation employer, PA 1995, s 75(4A) deems the debt to arise 'immediately before the occurrence of the current event' (different rules apply if it is an MVL).

36.22 Again if the scheme is not being wound up immediately before the insolvency event (excluding an MVL) under PA 1995, s 75(4C), the debt is contingent on:

- a scheme failure notice being issued, or
- the commencement of the winding up of the scheme.

36.23 Sub-Section 75(4C) only applies where the current event was an insolvency (s 75(4B)). So the contingency approach seems not to apply where the liability arises because of an employment-cessation event even though this operates by deeming an additional event into s 75(4) – see reg 6(1)(d) of the Employer Debt Regulations.

36.24   So the net effect seems to be that any debt arising because of the insolvency event (not the employment-cessation event) is contingent. This was a new provision in the amendments to s 75 by PA 2004.

36.25   If contingent the debt is not payable until the contingency occurs. The rationale for this provision is presumably that the insolvency event will trigger the start of an assessment period in relation to the scheme and there would be little point in enforcing a Section 75 debt in relation to the scheme until the destiny of the scheme is known (see PA 2004, s 133). Valuation of a contingent debt may be difficult.

The deeming provision in s 75(4A) should mean that the debt can still be proved in the relevant insolvency process even though it is contingent (this leads to questions about how it would be valued)[1].

1 See Chapter 34 above.

Phoenix case

36.26   The position in relation to the entering into the PPF of a scheme that does not provide for a partial winding-up in a situation where not all employers enter insolvency was considered by Sir Andrew Morritt V-C in *Phoenix Venture Holdings Ltd v Independent Trustee Services Ltd*[1]. The decision was given on 20 May 2005 (the date is relevant because of later amendments to the regulations).

1 [2005] EWHC 1379 (Ch); [2005] PLR 379 (Morritt V-C).

36.27   Under that scheme, five out of the six employers had entered formal insolvency proceedings. The trustees were concerned that the effect of regs 62 and 64 in the PPF Multi-employer regulations was that unless the final company also entered insolvency this scheme may not be able to fall within the PPF. The concerns are outlined at paras 34 to 42 of the judgment.

36.28   The trustees' concern apparently was that if the last company ceased to be an employer without an insolvency event occurring, then there would need to be further insolvency events in relation to the other employers if the PPF was to assume responsibility for the scheme – see para 37.

36.29   This was disputed by the company. It pointed out that the insolvency event still had to be contemporaneous or simultaneous for all employers and pointed to s 121(3) and reg 61(2)(a). The company contended that the company could cease to be an employer without an insolvency event having occurred in relation to it. If this happened it argued (para 39):

> 'it would be the case that all employers will have sustained an insolvency event and any previous impediment to the Scheme being considered for admission of the PPF would have disappeared'.

36.30   The company also contended that even if the trustee submission was right there would only need to be one insolvency event in relation to one of the employers (eg conversion of a CVL into a compulsory liquidation).

Morritt V-C however was reluctant to decide the issues raised – see para 42.

36.31   Morritt V-C held that the apportionment attempted by the trustee (an attempt to get a bigger debt on the sixth company and so drive it into winding that up) was invalid under its terms.

36.32   This meant that Morritt V-C did not have to consider other arguments raised by the sixth company. The company claimed that the purpose of the apportionment was to 'drive it into insolvency so that the scheme might qualify for acceptance by the PPF' (para 65). The sixth company argued that this was a collateral purpose and so invalidated the apportionment etc. Similarly, the company argued that the trustee decision was based on a mistake of law namely the extent to which an insolvency was needed to enable the PPF to takeover the scheme (para 67).

36.33   Morritt V-C did not decide these points but considered that both raised serious issues which would require a full trial, first to establish the point of law and then to investigate the issue. These issues meant that there was a bona fide dispute on substantial grounds as to the existence of the relevant debt. That of itself was sufficient to justify the injunction against presentation of a winding-up petition.

REQUIREMENT TO HAVE A PARTIAL WIND-UP

36.34   The PPF guidance for trustees[1] (March 2005) summarised the position at paragraphs 5.1.16 and 17:

> **Requirement for partial wind-up**
>
> In this type of section when a participating employer becomes insolvent, the pension scheme trustees must create a new section for that employer's assets and liabilities, known as the 'segregated part' in regulations.
>
> Essentially, a new single employer section is formed and is handled in a similar way to the single employer process. There are two differences:
>
> - A valuation of the entire section is necessary; and
>
> - Once it is clear that the Pension Protection Fund must assume responsibility for the segregated part, where the binding valuation shows assets less than the protected liabilities and a pension scheme rescue is not possible, a second valuation is needed. This is because the Pension Protection Fund is assuming responsibility for a proportion of the section's assets and it is important to take into account any changes to the value of those assets during the assessment period[2].

1 See the PPF website: http://www.pensionprotectionfund.org.uk/index/trustee_guidance/ detailed_trustee_guidance/tg_overview/tg_multi-employer.htm#04

2 This reference to an additional valuation seems to come through regs 58 and 59 of the PPF Multi-employer Regulations, modifying s 160 of, and adding a new s 160A into PA 2004.

36.35 For PPF purposes, a scheme which currently is non-segregated but has a requirement for partial winding-up is covered by Part 5 of the PPF Multi-employer Regulations (regs 45 to 60).

DEEMED TIMING OF SEGREGATION

36.36 Regulation 45(2) applies where an insolvency event occurs and:

> 'the requirement in the scheme rules for the trustees or managers of the scheme to segregate such part of the assets of the scheme as is attributable to the scheme's liabilities to provide pensions or other benefits to or in respect of the pensionable service of some or all of the members by reference to an employer in relation to the scheme ('the segregation requirement') would be triggered when an employer in relation to the scheme ceases to participate in the scheme'.

36.37 If this condition is met then under Reg 45(2) the segregation requirement is: 'deemed to have been triggered immediately after the occurrence' of the insolvency event and

> 'a segregated part of the scheme shall be deemed to have been created for and in respect of any period after the occurrence of that event where a withdrawal event within the meaning of Section 149(2) of the Act has not occurred in relation to the segregated part.'

This raises some issues in relation to how the s 75 debt is calculated.

36.38 If there are orphan members of the scheme (not applicable to the exiting employer), then the normal rule would be that the s 75 debt payable by the exiting employer will include a proportion of the share of the orphan liabilities (absent any specific apportionment rule under reg 6(2)(b) of the Employer Debt Regulations – see Chapter 26 above).

36.39 But if the scheme has been segregated before the s 75 trigger event occurs, then presumably the s 75 debt will only relate to those employees or members who have entered the segregated part.

36.40 The position could get even more complicated if the segregated part only refers to (say) active current employees while leaving behind pensioners and deferred members.

36.41 Assuming all relevant members do actually move into the segregated part, then the net effect would be to reduce the s 75 debt by envisaging that the exiting employer (here the cessation employer) may only have a debt to the segregated part (ie in respect of its own employees or former employees and not in relation to orphans).

36.42   So does the deeming wording in reg 45(2) mean that the segregation is deemed to have taken place before the debt arises? Does the deeming apply for s 75 purposes as well as the PPF[1].

1 Note that the PPF Multi-employer Regulations are not purported to be made under any power in s 75.

36.43   The deeming is stated to occur 'immediately after' the insolvency event. Conversely, the s 75 debt seems to arise when the insolvency event occurs – s 75(4) – and, indeed, is deemed for insolvency purposes to arise immediately before the occurrence of the insolvency event – s 75(4A).

36.44   Conversely, if the cessation had occurred before the insolvency event, then it seems possible that the s 75 debt would be calculated in the normal way (ignoring the segregation on the basis this occurs after the cessation event). One alternative analysis would be that the segregation is deemed to occur at the same time as the cessation event and therefore should be reflected in the s 75 debt.

36.45   Once the segregated Section has been set up, it is treated broadly under Pt 5 of the PPF Multi-employer Regulations as though it were a separate section. So the Section would enter the PPF process in the normal way.

36.46   Notice would have to be given by the insolvency practitioner of the exiting cessation company (PA 2004, ss 120 and 122) and this would trigger an assessment period in relation to the segregated part.

CHAPTER 37

tPR: Moral hazard powers

THE PURPOSE OF THE MORAL HAZARD PROVISIONS

37.1   The moral hazard provisions in the Pensions Act 2004, ss 38 to 57, are aimed at discouraging the abuse of corporate structures to avoid pensions liabilities. The timing of the introduction of these provisions was tied to the creation of the Pension Protection Fund (PPF).

37.2   The Pensions Act 2008 made significant changes to these powers, in particular gave tPR a an extended power to issue contribution notices under a new 'material detriment' test. These changes are discussed below.

37.3   The PPF is modelled on the Pension Benefit Guaranty Corporation (PBGC) in the US and is established to compensate defined benefit pension scheme members if the employer becomes insolvent and the pension scheme is underfunded. It is funded by a levy on defined benefit pension schemes (see Chapter 27 above).

37.4   The moral hazard provisions are intended to reduce the risk of employers dumping their pension liabilities on the PPF, and consequently to keep the levy cost of the PPF commercially sustainable. Protection of the PPF is one of the objectives of the Pensions Regulator[1].

1 PA 2004, s 5.

37.5   The moral hazard provisions consist of two separate mechanisms that can be used by the Pensions Regulator (tPR) to seek to make third parties liable to plug pension scheme deficits:

* contribution notices (CNs); and

* financial support directions (FSDs).

37.6   The intention behind FSDs is to ensure that there is adequate financial support from all group and connected entities for an ongoing pension scheme. tPR is likely to use its powers to seek to ensure that those entities with resources provide suitable backing to prevent a pension scheme from being unable to meet its liabilities.

37.7   In contrast, a CN is more likely to be used as a means of dealing with pension scheme liabilities that have crystallised.

37.8   As at the time of writing, tPR does not seem to have issued a single CN and only two FSDs (both involving Sea Containers)[1]. Instead tPR's policy seems to be to use the threat of CNs or FSDs to achieve a negotiated settlement.

1 See Sea Containers: reasons for the determination – June 2007 (ref: TM222/ TM1495). Available on tPR's website: www.thepensionregulator.gov.uk

37.9   In the *Sea Containers* case tPR issued two FSDs against a Bermudan company in US Chapter 11 proceedings. The FSDs were issued on 5 February 2008 in relation to two pension schemes, both in deficit, belonging to Sea Containers' UK subsidiary (for more information on this case see the discussion below on reasonableness).

37.10   A report in 2007 by the National Audit Office said that tPR had 'not yet felt the need to use its enforcement powers widely considering it more proportionate to use the threat of powers to influence the desired behaviour'[1].

1 National Audit Office report – The Pensions Regulator: Progress in establishing its new regulatory approach (26 October 2007).

37.11   In a July 2009 webcast on scheme funding, tPR commented that it had nearly used its enforcement powers on a number of occasions but had been able to avoid public proceedings because the relevant parties had offered last minute concessions.

This statement is given force by media reports in September 2008 which claimed that tPR had asked Duke Street Capital (a private equity owner) to plug the deficit of a pension scheme a year after it had sold a business with that pension scheme. tPR did not publish a determination in respect of Duke Street Capital (presumably it had been able to avoid pursuing formal proceedings).

37.12   tPR's guidance on the moral hazard provisions (and on obtaining clearance from tPR) was issued in April 2005. tPR reissued a revised version of this clearance guidance in March 2008 (and again updated it in June 2009 to reflect changes made by the Pensions Act 2008)[1].

1 Available on tPR's website: www.thepensionregulator.gov.uk

Contribution notices (CNs)

37.13   tPR is able to issue a CN under either:

- the 'main purpose'; or

- (from April 2008) the alternative 'material detriment' test,

(if it considers it reasonable to do so) to require a person 'connected with' or 'associated to' an employer to contribute up to the whole of the pension scheme deficit.

37.14   tPR can specify that the recipient of the notice must pay either the whole or a specified part of the deficit. The act or failure to act must have occurred on or after 27 April 2004 and within six years of the notice. The relevant person must have been connected to or associated with an employer in that same period.

37.15   Under the 'main purpose' test tPR is broadly able to issue a CN if tPR considers that a person has deliberately acted or deliberately failed to act (or knowingly assisted in that act or deliberate failure to act) with the main purpose of avoiding or reducing pension liabilities (PA 2004, s 38).

37.16   The Pensions Act 2008 (PA 2008) removed the requirement for tPR to prove that a person did not act in 'good faith' before it can issue a CN under the 'main purpose' test. However, this change only has effect from 14 April 2008 so this defence is available for CNs issued in respect of acts or failures to act that took place before that date.

37.17   PA 2008 gave tPR a new additional power to issue a CN under the 'material detriment' test. tPR is able to issue a CN under this alternative test if an act or failure to act has, in its opinion, detrimentally affected in a material way the likelihood of accrued scheme benefits being received (PA 2004, ss 38 and 38A). As with CNs issued under the main purpose test, tPR is only be able to issue a CN if, in its view, it is 'reasonable' to impose a CN on that person.

37.18   This new power to issue CNs under the 'material detriment' test can be used in relation to acts or failures to act that occur on or after 14 April 2008 (PA 2008, Sch 9, para 15).

37.19   tPR appears to have been given this new power as a response to the government's concern about the emergence of new business models for managing pension liabilities, which, among other features, may reduce the security provided by a pension scheme's sponsoring employer. The government cited non-insured alternatives to the traditional insurance buy-out solution for defined benefit pension schemes as examples of such arrangements. As the government perceives them, such business models threaten risks for pension scheme members while generating profits from those schemes for those businesses. However, the proposed amendments have the potential to have an effect on a much broader range of transactions than ones involving such arrangements.

37.20   The government commented that this new material detriment test requires a before-and-after comparison of the effect of the act (or failure to act) based only on the circumstances prevailing at the time. There is no requirement on tPR to show that the detrimental effect on scheme benefits was a main purpose of an act or failure to act (as is required under the 'main purpose test').

37.21   Clearly, a test based on material detriment could potentially be satisfied in a very wide range of circumstances, putting persons at risk of liability under

CNs despite the lack of any intention to avoid liabilities to pension schemes. For example, an employer could invest resources in a flawed business strategy or in a manner that loses money. Simply by weakening the financial position of the employer, this decision could be interpreted as satisfying the material detriment test.

37.22 In response to this concern, the government and tPR have introduced the following safeguards to provide reassurance that this new power will not be used in 'normal business transactions':

- a defence to the material detriment test (PA 2004, s 38B);

- additional 'reasonable' conditions that tPR is required to consider before it exercises its powers (see below for discussion on the importance of reasonableness;

- a code of practice stating when tPR expects to use its new powers; and

- 'illustrative examples' issued by tPR providing examples of circumstances it may use its new powers[1].

1 The illustrative examples and code are available on tPR's website: www.thepensionsregulator.gov.uk

Financial support directions (FSDs)

37.23 Under PA 2004, s 43, tPR may direct (if it considers it reasonable to do so) that associated and connected persons must put financial support in place to meet the pension liabilities of an employer where:

- the employer is a service company (that is, a company in a group whose turnover derives solely from amounts charged for the provision of the services of its employees to the group); or

- the employer is found to be 'insufficiently resourced' to fund pension liabilities – i.e. did not have sufficient assets to meet 50% of the section 75 debt in relation to the scheme and at that time there:

  - was a connected or associated person who did have sufficient resources; or

  - there were two or more persons who were connected with each other and their combined resources are sufficient.

37.24 The financial support must remain in place for the life of the scheme. It can be given by way of a guarantee of scheme liabilities, or in such other ways as are prescribed.

37.25 tPR can specify that the recipient of an FSD must put financial support in place in respect of either the whole or a specified part of the scheme deficit.

37.26 tPR is able to 'look-back' and issue an FSD if the relevant circumstances existed any time within two years of the directions (provided that this is on or after 6 April 2010)[1]. The relevant person must have been connected to or associated with an employer in that same period.

The period was originally one year, but this was extended to two years by amending regulations in 2009[2] (with a transitional period to 2010).

1 The Pensions Regulator (Financial Support Directions etc) Regulations 2005 (SI 2005/2188), reg 5.
2 See the Pensions Regulator (Miscellaneous Amendment) Regulations 2009 (SI 2009/617) amending reg 5 of the FSD Regulations.

Bulk transfers

37.27 If the requirements for issuing CNs or FSDs are satisfied in relation to a pension scheme (the initial scheme) and the accrued rights of at least two person who were members of the initial scheme are transferred to another pension scheme (the transferee scheme), tPR will be able to issue CNs or FSDs in relation to the transferee scheme.

37.28 The power for tPR to issue FSDs and CNs in relation to the transferee scheme were inserted into the PA 2004 by the PA 2008[1] and has effect on and from 14 April 2008[2].

1 See new ss39A, 39B, 43A and 43B inserted into PA 2004.
2 PA 2008, para 15(3) of Sched 9.

Relevant schemes

37.29 The moral hazard powers only apply in relation to schemes which are not money purchase schemes and are not of a prescribed description[1]. The relevant regulations are:

● For CNs, the Pensions Regulator (Contribution Notices and Restoration Orders) Regulations 2005, SI 2005/931;

● For FSDs, the Pensions Regulator (Financial Support Directions etc) Regulations 2005, SI 2005/2188.

1 PA 2004, s 38(1), for CNs and PA 2004, s 43(1) for FSDs.

37.30 The FSD Regulations prescribe that the same schemes exclusions apply as those set out in the CN regulations[1]. The CN Regulations prescribe[2] broadly the same exclusions as apply for s 75 purposes – see Chapter 31 (Scope of the main pensions legislation) above.

1 FSD Regulations (SI 2005/2188), reg 3.
2 CN Regulations (SI 2005/931), reg 3.

How will tPR know where to look?

37.31 tPR will not normally be alerted to troubled pension schemes by its own investigations but by a combination of the following.

- information supplied by a member or trustee to tPR

- notification by the trustees if there is a failure to pay contributions under the schedule of contributions on time (and this is material) (PA 2004, s 228(2) – see para 33.74 above).

- the duty imposed on persons who are closely connected to a pension scheme (for example, trustees, auditors and other advisers) to notify tPR as soon as reasonably practicable (ie whistleblow) if they believe that a duty, imposed by virtue of an enactment or rule of law, relevant to the administration of the scheme has not been or is not being complied with and the failure to comply is likely to be of material significance to tPR in the exercise of any of its functions (PA 2004, s 70 – see Chapter 29 above).

- the duty imposed on trustees, employers and advisers to make reports to tPR if certain prescribed events occur, eg any breach of a banking covenant by the employer, (before April 2009) a significant change in the employer's credit rating or a decision by a controlling company to relinquish control of the employer (PA 2004, s 69 – see Chapter 29 above).

- information supplied to tPR in support of an application for a clearance statement (see below for a discussion of clearance statements).

WHOM DO THE MORAL HAZARD PROVISIONS AFFECT?

Connected persons and associates

37.32 A CN or an FSD, broadly speaking, may be issued against persons who are (or have been in the relevant period) connected to or associated with the employer of a pension scheme.

37.33 The terms 'connected person' and 'associate' are imported from ss 249 and 435 of the Insolvency Act 1986. This is a double-edged sword: on the one hand, these are terms with which those in the insolvency field are familiar; however, anyone who is familiar with them will know how complicated and broad they are – see Chapter 41 (Who is connected or associated) below.

37.34 The position at present can be summarised as follows:

- where there is a corporate employer, an individual (including a director and his relatives) cannot be issued with an FSD[1];

- an individual eg a director (including a shadow director) and his relatives can be issued with a CN if tPR considers it reasonable – this will depend on a number of factors, including any benefit derived by the individual from the relevant company[2];

- parent companies are potentially liable to be issued with a CN even if they merely omit to prevent the steps taken by a participating employer that lead to a weakening of the employer's ability to fund its pension scheme (for example, delays in making contributions); and

• shareholders are potentially liable for a CN or FSD if they are associated with a director or have a large stake (more than one-third of voting rights) in a participating employer (directly or indirectly)[3].

For a fuller discussion on 'Who is connected or associated' – see Chapter 41 below.

1 PA 2004, s 43(6).
2 PA 2004, s 38.
3 Definition of 'associate' and 'control' in IA 1986, s 435(6) and (10).

37.35   There is power for regulations to be issued in respect of partnerships and limited liability partnerships (PA 2004, s 57). None have yet been issued.

Insolvency practitioners

37.36   Limited carve-outs relating to who can be issued a CN offer some protection to IPs who may have been party to an act or failure to act with the main purpose of avoiding pension liabilities. These carve outs were introduced after representations were made while the Pensions Bill was passing through Parliament. In addition, David Richards J in *Re T&N (No 1)*[1] commented that the IP in that case (see para 37.11 above) was acting in good faith (and so potentially outside the then draft legislation).

1 [2004] EWHC 1680 (Ch); [2004] OPLR 343; [2004] PLR 351 (David Richards J).

37.37   To fall within the carve-out, the IP must have been 'acting in accordance with his functions as an insolvency practitioner'[1]. It seems that this will include an IP acting in relation to another company (eg a parent company) as well as an IP over the employer.

1 PA 2004, s 38(3)(c).

37.38   For the purposes of the carve-out, an insolvency practitioner means a liquidator, provisional liquidator, administrator, administrative receiver or nominee or supervisor under a voluntary arrangement[1].

1 PA 2004, s 38(11), cross referring to IA 1986, s 388.

37.39   It does not apply to fixed charge receivers or Law of Property Act 1925 receivers[1] (see para 4.23 above) who, depending on the nature of their appointment (for example, if over a controlling interest in the shares of an employer), may be exposed to liability for CNs.

1 See the comments made by the Financial Markets Law Committee in their paper issued in December 2005 on the issue of receivers (see Issue 104) on their website: http://www.fmlc.org/papers/Issue104PA.pdf. This was updated in a letter dated 7 February 2007 (also on their website). The DWP responded in October 2009 saying that it was not persuaded that a change in the law on this was appropriate (see the FMLC website).

37.40   There is no equivalent specific carve-out for insolvency practitioners for FSDs for two reasons:

- First, there is no prospect of an FSD being issued against an IP where the relevant employer is a body corporate – PA 2004, s 43(6).

- Second, as the risk only arises for an IP if he or she is an associate of an individual employer (ie he or she is related to the employer), professional rules of conduct ought to prevent an IP from taking an appointment over an individual employer to whom he or she is related. However, care should be exercised where an appointment is taken over a person (for example, a sole trader or partnership) who is an associate of an individual employer.

Nominee directors

37.41   The position of 'nominee' directors, that is, persons appointed to the boards of companies to represent the interests of private equity investors, must also be carefully considered (see also Chapter 41 below).

37.42   As mentioned above, tPR has the power to issue CNs (but generally not FSDs) against individual directors. This will most likely be in situations where the director has knowingly assisted in or been party to an Act or deliberate failure to act. To protect themselves from personal liability directors will need to be fully apprised of the financial circumstances of the companies to which they are appointed, and carefully consider the impact of their actions or omissions on the ability of the pension scheme to meet its liabilities.

37.43   Directors' and officers' (D&O) insurance cover, if available, could be sought to cover this risk and any pre-existing cover would need to be carefully reviewed to ensure that the risk of incurring liability under a CN is not excluded.

37.44   Those appointing the director may also be at risk, for example if they have given an indemnity to the director or if the nominee is also an employee or director of the appointor (because the appointor will then be an associate of the employer). As one of the matters tPR is to consider when determining whether it is reasonable to impose liability on a person is that person's financial circumstances, those with 'deep pockets' may find themselves especially at risk.

Company 'doctors'

37.45   Company 'doctors' who are brought in to assist a company in financial difficulties may face potential liability under the moral hazard provisions. Their liability is likely to be limited to CNs; FSDs will only be a concern if the employer is an individual, non-corporate entity (which is rare given the nature of restructurings involving company doctors). The risk arises if a company doctor is appointed to the board of directors (for example, as chief restructuring officer) or takes an equity stake.

37.46 They will, however, have the protection afforded by the requirements of reasonableness. In particular tPR is required to consider 'the likelihood of 'relevant creditors' being paid and the extent to which they are likely to be paid' when deciding whether to issue a CN. In debates on the Pensions Bill 2008 the Lord McKenzie (a government minister) commented that[1]:

> 'First, where a company doctor has to make hard decisions in an attempt to save a company, these factors would protect the position of a company doctor who had to cause detriment to a pension scheme, which, in the particular circumstances, was reasonable in the context of the outcome for other creditors. Secondly, the regulator would need to take into account that, in some circumstances, decisions must necessarily be rapid, as the noble Lord has indicated, and perfect data to inform the decision may not be available. Provided that the company doctor has behaved reasonably and has not, for example, wilfully ignored available information or recklessly taken risks that a reasonable company doctor would not have taken, I believe that members of organisations such as R3 and the Institute for Turnaround should take significant comfort from these provisions.'

1 See statement by Lord McKenzie, Hansard House of Lords, 3rd committee sitting, report stage, column 1584, 29 October 2008.

37.47 Furthermore D&O insurance, if available, could be sought to cover this risk and any pre-existing cover should be reviewed.

External Investors

37.48 tPR is able to issue CNs against persons who it is of the opinion 'was a party to an act or a deliberate failure to act' that satisfies either the 'main purpose' test or 'material detriment' test.

If an investor received a substantial payment (for example dividends) from an employer participating in a pension scheme which weakens the ability of the employer to financially support the pension scheme the investor may potentially be seen as a 'party to the act' and at risk of a CN.

37.49 However, a person that is a party to the act or failure to act will only be at risk of a CN if they are connected or associated with the employer. For example due to a large shareholding in an employer (or associated with a director of an employer).)

A person (for example a private equity owner) that owns shares in an a company that receives payment from the employer is unlikely to be seen as a party to an 'act or failure' to act solely on the basis that they received an indirect benefit from the payment.

37.50 There is no requirement for an 'act or failure' to act to have occurred in relation to an FSD. tPR is able to issue an FSD where an employer is insufficiently resourced or a service company. Therefore receipt of a payment from the employer by an investor is not an issue in the same way as for CNs. However, the investor may still be at risk if they are connected or associated with an employer of the pension scheme.

37.51 PA 2004, s 52 also gives tPR a separate power to 'claw back' an asset if given as a gift or if the party received it at a significant undervalue.

Insolvent companies

37.52 The PA 2004 does not expressly prevent tPR from using its moral hazard powers against companies that have entered into formal insolvency. Furthermore, tPR has issued FSDs against Sea Containers at a time when the company was in Chapter 11 US bankruptcy proceedings.

However, it is not clear whether in practice tPR would be able to enforce its powers given the moratorium on enforcement or proceedings under IA 1986 – see Chapter 5 (Insolvency moratorium) above for discussion on this point.

Overseas companies

37.53 The fact that a company is incorporated in foreign jurisdiction does not, as a matter of English law, prevent tPR from serving a FSD or CN against it (if it is connected or associated with the employer).

37.54 tPR maintains the public position that it will be able to enforce a CN or FSD outside the UK (particularly within other EU member states). Furthermore the only confirmed case of tPR using its powers has been against Sea Containers, a Bermudan Company in Chapter 11 US bankruptcy proceedings.

37.55 However, it is less clear whether tPR would be able to enforce an FSD or CN in a foreign court if a person refused to comply with the FSD or CN. tPR was not required to enforce the FSDs in Sea Containers because the company and trustees agreed a settlement, which was approved by the United States Bankruptcy Court for the District of Delaware[1].

1 [2008] PLR 413. Its decision is available at: www.deb.uscourts.gov/Opinions/2008/ seacontainers.06.11156.memorandum.order.pdf

37.56 The amount stated in the CN 'is to be treated as a debt due to the trustees ... of the scheme' (PA 2004, s 40(3)), which the trustees (alternatively tPR or PPF on their behalf) can enforce.

37.57 This statutory debt can be pursued through the civil courts but it is still how an overseas jurisdiction will react to a judgment debt, which derives from a decision made by tPR.

37.58 Parties would need to consider the reciprocal enforcement agreements, such as a Brussels Conventions and Lugano Convention, any bilateral agreements entered into between the UK and another country or whether the local law permits enforcement.

37.59 It may be difficult to enforce a judgment relating to CN in a foreign court, especially under the Brussels and Lugano convention which only apply to 'civil' and 'commercial' matters. It is arguable that actions by tPR or trustees to enforce such a debt are not civil or commercial matters as they are brought created by virtue of a power given to tPR as a public authority acting in the exercise of its powers under the PA 2004. Ultimately this will be decision for the foreign court.

THE IMPORTANCE OF REASONABLENESS

37.60 A CN or FSD can only be issued where tPR considers it reasonable to do so. PA 2004 prescribes[1] a number of matters that tPR must consider in determining reasonableness for this purpose. It is largely a factual question whether it is reasonable for tPR to issue a CN or FSD.

1 PA 2004, ss 38(7) and 43(7).

37.61 Many of the reasonableness factors are similar for FSDs and CNs, however it may be more difficult for tPR to issue a CN than to issue an FSD. This is because tPR is required to consider additional factors for CNs issued under either 'main purpose' or 'material detriment' test that it is not required to consider when deciding whether to issue an FSD. There is also a second set of reasonableness factors that tPR will be required to consider before it can issue a CN under the 'material detriment' test (but not the 'main purpose' test).

The reasonableness factors are summarised below.

Factors relevant in determining 'reasonableness'

37.62

Financial support Directions and Contribution Notices
• The relationship that person has or had with the employer, including whether the person has 'control' of the employer.
• The value of any benefits received directly or indirectly by that person from the employer (or in the case of CNs, any benefit the person is entitled to receive from either the employer or under the scheme).
• Any connection or involvement the person had or has had with the pension scheme.
• The person's financial circumstances.
• Other matters prescribed in regulations (as yet none have been).
Contribution notices (issued under either the main purpose or material detriment test)
• The degree of involvement of the person to whom the CN would be addressed.
• The relationship that person has or had with the employer, including whether the person has 'control' of the employer.

- Any connection or involvement the person had or has had with the pension scheme.

- The purposes of the Act or failure to Act (including whether a purpose was to prevent or limit loss of employment)

- The likelihood of relevant creditors being paid and the extend to which they are likely to be paid.

- The person's financial circumstances.

- Other matters prescribed in regulations (as yet none have been).

Contribution notices (issued only under the material detriment test)

- The value of the assets or liabilities of the scheme.

- The effect of a person's act, or failure to act, on the value of those assets and liabilities.

- The obligations of any person to the scheme.

- Effect of an act, or failure to act, on any persons' obligation to provide funding to the scheme (including whether the act or failure causes the country or territory in which any of those obligations would fall to be enforced to be different).

- The effect of an act, or failure to act, on any person's ability to discharge those obligations.

- Other matters prescribed in regulations (as yet none have been).

37.63 Of particular interest is the requirement for tPR to consider the 'likelihood of relevant creditors being paid and the extent to which they are likely to be paid'.

The government stated in debates on the Pensions Bill that the purpose of this condition was to reduce concerns of the pension schemes becoming a 'super creditor' in insolvencies[1]. The implications of this reasonableness factor have already been discussed in relation to company doctors (see above discussion).

1 See the government's October 2008 response to the consultation on' Amendments to the anti-avoidance measures in the Pensions Act 2004'.

CLEARANCE STATEMENTS

37.64 PA 2004 contains a formal clearance procedure[1] whereby parties can seek from tPR a statement that their proposed transaction will not fall foul of the moral hazard provisions.

1 PA 2004, ss 42 and 46.

37.65 For the clearance to be of any value, full disclosure must be made by the parties seeking it. Board papers in particular are likely to be of importance. A clearance can be set aside if the circumstances described in the application are not the same as those arising and this is material – PA 2004, ss 42(5) and 46(5). In addition it is a criminal offence knowingly or recklessly to provide false or misleading information to tPR in relation to an exercise of its functions – PA 2004, s 80(1)(c).

CHALLENGING TPR'S DECISION

37.66 Persons who are affected by a determination of tPR (for example, persons against whom a CN or an FSD has been issued) and who wish to challenge it can refer the determination to the Pensions Regulator Tribunal[1].

1 PA 2004, ss 102 to 106.

37.67 The Pensions Regulator Tribunal, which was also created by PA 2004, has the power to confirm, vary or revoke determinations made by tPR. Persons who wish to challenge tPR must act quickly: references to the Tribunal must be made within 28 days of the relevant determination.

37.68 Parties can also appeal the Pensions Regulator Tribunal's decision on a point of law to the Court of Appeal (and eventually the House of Lords or, from October 2009, the Supreme Court).

37.69 As a matter of principle there is nothing to prevent a determination of tPR being the subject of judicial review proceedings. However, judicial review is a remedy of last resort and therefore the applicant must first exhaust all other available remedies. It is likely to be difficult to obtain permission to apply for judicial review of a determination of tPR.

AMOUNT OF LIABILITY UNDER A CN OR FSD

37.70 If tPR successfully uses its moral hazard powers, it has discretion on the amount to specify under the FSD or CN (PA 2004, ss 39, 45 and 48). It can specify a sum that may be either the whole or part of the employer's liability to the scheme under a s 75 debt (or estimated s 75 debt if not yet due).

37.72 Legislation does not say how tPR should exercise its discretion but in Parliamentary debates on the Pensions Bill 2008 a government minister commented that if tPR issues a CN it 'would then be bound to act reasonably in its assessment of how much of this sum should be payable by the party to the transaction' and not simply target a person because they have 'deep pockets'[1].

1 See statement by Lord McKenzie, Hansard House of Lords, 3rd committee sitting, report stage, column 1585, 29 October 2008.

37.73 In assessing the sum specified under a CN that is issued under the material detriment test, the minister commented that tPR would, for example, have to consider:

- the benefit they received;

- the history of the person's involvement with the scheme;

- whether there were any other parties to the act;

- whether the person was an individual who merely acted as an agent for a corporate entity that was a party to the act;

- any other purposes of the act which may have made a person's actions reasonable in the circumstances;

- the position of the scheme after the act.

37.74   The minister made the above statement in reference to CNs issued under the material detriment test. However, some of the factors mentioned may also be relevant for CNs issued under the main purpose test or FSD.

37.75   The minister's statement does not have the force of law and tPR is not obliged to act in accordance with it.

THE IMPACT OF THE MORAL HAZARD PROVISIONS ON RESTRUCTURING AND INSOLVENCY

37.76   When the financial condition of an employer is precarious, the fact that the potentially greater buyout debt under PA 1995, s 75, is triggered by the commencement of formal insolvency proceedings may have a bearing on a director's decision to continue to trade. The directors might conclude that, properly having regard to the interests of the company's general body of creditors, it is in the best interests of the creditors as a whole for the company to avoid formal insolvency proceedings so that those claims are not diluted by a claim made by the pension scheme that is valued on the buyout basis.

37.77   The combined effect of s 75 and the accounting standards FRS17 and IAS 19 (which requires companies to show any scheme deficits on their balance sheet) has been to increase the prominence of defined benefit schemes that are in deficit or are underfunded. This may further differentiate the financial stability of employers that contribute to defined benefit pension schemes from those that do not.

37.78   This may have two consequential effects on the insolvency and restructuring market:

- First, companies that have a primary liability (that is, as employer) to defined benefit schemes that are in deficit on a buyout basis may be forced to restructure or, in the worst-case scenario, commence insolvency proceedings. At the very least, such companies may find it harder and more costly to raise debt.

- As a consequence, tPR may consider issuing FSDs and CNs to other companies within the group. This may lead to a second raft of corporate restructurings and failures, caused by the overburdening of companies' cash flow and balance sheets as a result of their financial obligations under FSDs and CNs.

Impact on restructurings

37.79   Restructurings need to be planned carefully if they are to avoid triggering a buyout debt under s 75 or the risk of participants being issued with CNs or FSDs. In particular, care must be taken where it is proposed as part of a restructuring that employees be transferred, companies wound up or value extracted from the group (for example, by way of payment of a dividend or the grant of security). This will be an issue even where the company's pension scheme has no deficit on an ongoing basis because tPR is concerned with ensuring there is potential funding for the (much) higher buyout basis required under statute.

37.80   There are, however, some steps that can be taken to minimise the moral hazard risk.

- **Purpose:** purpose is a key requirement for tPR to issue a CN under the 'main purpose' test. Parties will be concerned to take care in minuting the purpose of decisions that might weaken the strength of the participating employer's ability to fund the pension scheme. Purpose will be assessed with the benefit of hindsight. Past experience with insolvency and tax legislation is that it is notoriously difficult to assess.

- **Defence to the 'material detriment test':** If an act or failure to act was 'materially detrimental' the legislation provides a defence against a CN being issued if the necessary steps have been taken. Broadly, the defence will be available to a person that considered the effect of an act on the scheme benefits, took all reasonable steps to eliminate or minimise the risk and in light of prevailing circumstances it was reasonable to conclude that an act was not materially detrimental to scheme benefits. Again directors should take care minuting decisions to make it easier to later rely on this statutory defence;

- **Clearances:** where a restructuring involves, or might affect the financial position of, a participating employer of a defined benefit pension scheme, the parties to the restructuring will need to consider seriously the need to seek a clearance statement prior to completion. The need for full disclosure of the details of the proposed transactions can be time consuming and costly; however, a failure to do so may render the clearance worthless. Clearance may be difficult to obtain where there is a short deadline, eg 24 hours. Furthermore, tPR often requests information regarding the specific deal, and will not give clearance on a broader basis to confirm that the directors are doing the right thing, making it difficult to obtain clearance if the deal is continuously changing.

- **Use of formal restructuring tools:** schemes of arrangement under s 895 of the Companies Act 2006 (formerly Companies Act 1985, s 425) and company voluntary arrangements (CVAs) under Part I of the Insolvency Act 1986 may be used to implement a restructuring proposal. A scheme and a CVA can bind trustees of a defined benefit pension scheme to a compromise of the pension scheme debt if the trustees are parties to it[1].

  However, the decision by scheme trustees to seek to compromise a pension scheme debt gives rise to a duty on the employer and the scheme trustee to notify tPR of the proposed compromise (PA 2004, s 69). This might lead to a review of the proposed transaction by tPR. Unless a clearance notice is obtained in respect of the compromise it is possible that tPR might issue a CN or FSD in respect of any deficit[2].

  In addition, trustees will be concerned not to exclude their scheme from the potential of entry into the PPF. If there is a legally enforceable agreement which has the effect of reducing a s 75 debt (eg a compromise of a scheme debt) the scheme might also be excluded from the scope of the PPF[3]. This does not apply to a s 895 scheme of arrangement[3].

- **Alternatives to compromising a pensions debt:** recent years have seen parties in distressed restructurings implementing innovative proposals where the trustees agree to a lower pensions deficit (with clearance from tPR) without compromising a pensions debt[4].

  For example, in the restructuring of Polestar, the UK printing company that was formerly part of Robert Maxell's group, the trustees agreed to apportion the s 75 debt to a new ringfenced company outside Polestar. This was to ensure that Polestar could not be made liable for the pension scheme deficit in the future. tPR cleared this apportionment.

  In exchange for the trustee agreement a payment of £45m was paid into the pension scheme over 12 years. Although the pension scheme deficit on a buy-out basis was estimated to be £300m this was still a positive result for the pension scheme given that as an unsecured credit it would have received zero dividend had Polestar become insolvent[5].

  Although it would have been more straightforward for the trustees to compromise the s 75 debt this would have risked the scheme being excluded from the scope of the PPF.

- **Involving the PPF:** if the scheme enters into an assessment period the PPF is able to compromise the scheme debt on behalf of the pension scheme. This is discussed in para 35.66 above.

1 See *Re T&N Ltd* [2006] EWHC 1447 (Ch), [2006] Lloyd's Rep IR 817 (David Richards J).
2 See reg 2(2) of the Pension Protection Fund (Entry Rules) Regulations 2005 (SI 2005/590 as amended), and the discussion in Chapter 35 above.
3 For examples of restructurings since 2005 taking account of pensions liabilities see the paper by Alastair Lomax, Pippa Read and Graham Frost at the R3 18th Annual Conference 2008.
4 See reg 2(3)(b) of the PPF Entry Rules Regulations.
5 For a description of the restructuring of Polestar see the article by Richard Tett and Chris Howard: '*Insolvency, Banking and Finance: International Rescue*' in Legalweek, 8 February 2007.

Impact on formal insolvencies and members' voluntary liquidations

37.81   tPR cannot issue a CN to an insolvency practitioner unless, in being a party to an act or a deliberate failure to act with the main purpose of avoiding pension liabilities, that insolvency practitioner was not acting in accordance with his functions as an insolvency practitioner[1].

1 PA 2004, s 38(3)(c).

37.82   Provided therefore that an administrator or liquidator is properly carrying out his officeholder functions there should be little risk of personal liability.

This sits well with the approach taken by David Richards J in *Re T&N (No 1)*[1], decided in July 2004. On the administrator's application for directions, it was held that the administrators' primary duty to act in the best interests of creditors justified their decision to withdraw associated participating companies from the T&N group pension scheme even though to do so would put the scheme into deficit on a buyout basis (although, crucially, at the time of withdrawal the buyout liability had not been triggered).

1 [2004] EWHC 1680(Ch); [2004] OPLR 343; [2004] PLR 351 (David Richards J). See also para 35.11 above.

37.83   Although there is no express carve-out for insolvency practitioners in respect of FSDs, this is unlikely to be problematic. This is because tPR is not entitled to issue an FSD against an individual if the relevant employer is a body corporate (see para 37.24 above). If the employer is an individual, an FSD may be issued against an insolvency practitioner, but only if he or she is an associate of the employer (for example, the husband, wife or relative of that employer).

37.84   The relatively strong position of insolvency practitioners may mean that we see more pre-packaged sales out of formal insolvencies where previously the cost of appointing an insolvency officeholder outweighed the benefits.

37.85   However, it should be noted that tPR has shown some hostility towards the use of pre-packaged administration sales. In March 2009 it exercised its powers under the Pensions Act 1995 to appoint an independent trustee to the Graphex Limited Pension and Life Assurance Scheme[1]. Amongst other things tPR commented that proposals by the employer's directors to 'strip out certain assets' from the principal employer and then buy-back the remaining assets through a pre-packaged arrangement but leaving behind the pension liabilities posed a risk to the scheme members and PPF.

1 Final Notice 31 March 2009: The Graphex Limited Pension and Life Assurance Scheme (Case ref: TM6511). See the tPR website: www.thepensionsregulator.gov.uk

37.86   In this case tPR had received evidence that the employer was technically insolvent although trading legally. It was not clear why tPR felt that the proposals posed a risk to scheme members and the PPF over and above the risk of employer insolvency already present.

37.87 When used as a restructuring tool, the issues highlighted above will apply equally to members' voluntary liquidations (MVLs). Indeed, as a result of the impact of the increased buyout liability on pension scheme deficits and FRS17/IAS19 there may be a reduction in the use of MVLs. In particular, in group situations where the group has an underfunded pension scheme,s directors of non-participating companies may find it difficult to satisfy themselves that the company is and will continue to be solvent in view of the risk of a CN or an FSD being issued against the company. For the same reason, parent companies that would typically offer some support to such a company may be increasingly reluctant to do so. One option may be to seek a clearance from tPR.

CHAPTER 38

Money purchase schemes

38.1   Much of the pensions legislation is concerned with funding and liabilities and so does not apply to 'money purchase schemes'. The term 'money purchase' is used in the pensions legislation. An equivalent term (but not used in the UK legislation) is 'defined contribution' or 'DC'.

38.2   The relevant exclusions include:

- the PPF;

- scheme specific funding and the MFR;

- the debt obligations under PA 1995, s 75.

38.3   The term 'money purchase scheme' is defined for the purposes of PA 2004[1] and PA 1995[2] in s 181 of the Pension Schemes Act 1993 as an occupational pension scheme under which all the benefits that may be provided are money purchase benefits. Some regulations also go on to deem a scheme to be a money purchase scheme even if some death benefits are not money purchase benefits – see below.

1 See PA 2004, s 318(1).
2 See PA 1995, s 214(5).

38.4   The term money purchase benefits is defined in s 181 of PSA 1993 as meaning:

> 'benefits the rate or amount of which is calculated by reference to a payment or payments made by the member or by any other person in respect of the member and which are not average salary benefits.'

38.5   Money purchase schemes are to be contrasted with a defined benefit scheme – eg a 'final salary' or career average scheme where all or some benefits are calculated by reference to a final level of salary or remuneration.

38.6   In a money purchase scheme, the risk (and reward) of the underlying investments and annuity rates feed through directly to the benefits. In practice this means that the rights of the members are calculated by reference to an underlying selection of investments (the choice of which, between various available funds often rests with the member). The ultimate fund generated is then used by the trustees to purchase an annuity with an insurer when the benefits start to be payable. So, unlike a defined benefit schemes (ie a scheme which is not solely money purchase) broadly the employer and the trustees have no investment risk (other than in relation to safeguarding of assets etc).

38.7   This matching of the benefits with the underlying assets is commonly a feature of the operation of money purchase schemes, but is not expressly required by the definition in PSA 1993, s 181. However, in *Aon Trust Corp Ltd v KPMG*[1] the Court of Appeal held that such a matching of assets with liabilities is a requirement for a schemes to be categorised as being money purchase.

1 [2005] EWCA Civ 1004; [2006] 1 WLR 97; [2006] 1 All ER 238. For a good discussion of the difficulties raised by this decision, see the paper by Paul Newman '*Should money purchase schemes exist?*' given at the APL annual conference in November 2008.

38.8   Jonathan Parker LJ held:

'[167] Looking no further for the moment, therefore, the scheme would appear to lack the basic characteristics of a money purchase scheme (using that expression for the moment in a colloquial as opposed to a statutory sense) as identified in part 3 of this judgment. In the first place, the requisite direct relationship between contributions and benefits is broken by the introduction of actuarial factors (see [159], above). As Mr Ham succinctly put it at the conclusion of his submissions (see [147], above), in the case of a money purchase scheme you do not need an actuary. Secondly, by including the powers in cll 8.4 and 8.5 the scheme not only recognises but positively caters for a continuing mismatch between assets and liabilities.

[168] However, the overall appearance of the scheme (on its true construction) is not necessarily determinative of the question whether it is a "money purchase scheme" in the statutory sense. I therefore turn to the relevant statutory provisions (but leaving s 67 of the 1995 Act on one side for the moment).

[169] As noted earlier (see [40]–[42], above) an occupational pension scheme is a "money purchase scheme" if "all the benefits that may be provided are money purchase benefits": ie benefits the rate or amount of which is calculated by reference to [contributions] and which are not average salary benefits' (see s 181(1) of the 1993 Act).

[170] I turn first to the question whether either of the two elements in the pension benefit as prescribed by r 7.2, that is to say the standard pension benefit and any bonuses declared in exercise of the cl 8.4 power are, on analysis, 'calculated by reference to' contributions within the meaning of that definition.

[171] In my judgment the inclusion in the first stage of the calculation process of the actuarial factors to which I referred earlier is fatal to such a contention. The expression "calculated by reference to" means, in my judgment, "calculated only by reference to", in the sense that the benefit in question must be the direct product of the contributions (that being the basic characteristic of a money purchase scheme, as that expression is commonly understood: see part 3 above). Neither the standard pension nor bonuses fall within that category.

[172] Support for this strict interpretation of the definition of 'money purchase benefits' is, in my judgment, to be found in s 56 of the 1995 Act itself. As noted earlier (see [46], above) it is implicit in that Section that a provision in the scheme which is designed to achieve automatic equilibrium between assets and liabilities by limiting the amount of the scheme's liabilities by reference to its assets is not in itself enough to render the scheme a 'money purchase scheme': for if it were, s 56 would not apply to it. Yet the inclusion of such a provision in a scheme would, on the face of it, inevitably produce a situation in which benefits (liabilities) would be calculated by reference to contributions (assets). As indicated in para [53], above, the same considerations apply in relation to s 75.

[173] Accordingly, I respectfully agree with Sir Andrew Morritt V-C that neither of the two components of the pension benefit prescribed by r 7, that is to say the standard pension and any bonuses declared under cl 8.4, is a 'money purchase benefit'. It follows that in my judgment (and leaving aside s 67 of the 1995 Act) the answer to question 31 is: No.'

1 Question 3 asked whether 'the scheme is a money purchase scheme within PSA 1993?'

38.9   However, in *Bridge Trustees Ltd v Yates and others*[1], Sarah Asplin QC (sitting as a deputy judge in the High Court) rejected arguments made by the First Defendant that certain benefits were not money purchase benefits because of the use of actuarial factors, the way investment returns were applied to the members' interests, the existence of balance of cost provisions and salary related elements.

In coming to her judgment Sarah Asplin QC distinguished the KPMG case for the following reasons:

'[129]However, in my judgment, the rules of the Scheme are materially different from those under consideration in the KPMG case which was described by counsel as a CARE scheme, in the form often referred to as a 'building block' scheme. The actuarial factors in that case were an integral part of the calculation of the benefits provided under the scheme and could be described as defining the benefits provided. Jonathan Parker LJ described the tables at paragraph 156 of his judgment in the following way:

"The tables were designed to show 'the amount of pension 'secured by' (which must connote 'attributable to' a contribution of £1 in respect of each successive year of the member's life until age 65."

[130] It was accepted that the structure of that scheme, ('the KPMG Scheme'), was vastly different from the one under consideration here. In the KPMG scheme, standard benefits were calculated by multiplying total contributions for each period, paid at a specified rate, by a figure set out in a table. The multiplier was the product of actuarial assessment of factors such as future investment returns, inflation and mortality. Thereafter, bonuses were added according to a formula, if there was a surplus on the fund as a whole and the sum was decreased if a deficit was revealed.

[131] To put the matter another way, the contributions secured for the member, an annual pension, the amount of which was determined by the application of multipliers which were based upon actuarial factors. Thus, pension payable for

each year of membership was defined by application of the multipliers and therefore, the actuarial assumptions, to the contributions.

[132] The Scheme [in the present case], however, does not include provisions of this type by which the extent of the benefit to be provided in respect of each year in which contributions were made could be determined. In the case of the Scheme, the 'pot' whether it be the Member's Interest or VIP Interest, remains just that until it has to be applied in the provision of such benefits as the Member selects. Only at the stage at which a pension is selected, are actuarial factors used purely as a means of conversion from 'pot' to pension. The actuarial factors did not define the benefit in the way that the tables in the KPMG case did but were merely a tool to effect their conversion.

[133] In this regard, it is also relevant in my judgment, that the reference to conversion factors to which I was referred [see para 53], which appeared in the 1992 version of a guide for members, expressly stated that the terms offered for the conversion, "will vary from time to time to reflect market conditions" and were only provided to give members an idea of current rates. This is altogether different from the exercise being undertaken in the KPMG case in order to determine the amount of benefit to which a member was entitled in any year, depending upon his age, gender and other factors. In the Scheme, the factors applied were subject to variation dependent upon current market rates, but as Mr Orton states in his second witness statement, were intended to provide the Member with a better deal than if an annuity were purchased which would include the inevitable profit margin for the provider.

[134] Therefore, I consider that the KMPG case can be distinguished from the circumstances under consideration here. Accordingly, I reject Mr Newman's submission that the application of actuarial factors is inevitably fatal to the contention that the benefits arising from the Member's Interest and/or the VIP Interest are money purchase benefits.

[135] Furthermore, in my judgment it should make no difference whether the Trustee secures such benefits by means of "internal annuitisation" or purchases an annuity in the market, whether in its own name or that of the Member. I accept Mr Stallworthy's submission that to make such a distinction would create insupportable anomalies and leave the question of whether a benefit was money purchase in nature unanswered until the benefit was actually secured. Such uncertainty cannot have been intended and I reject Mr Newman's submission that that very uncertainty renders all such benefits incapable of falling within the definition of money purchase benefits. If that were the case, all such benefits would have to fall outside the definition even if ultimately, an annuity was purchased in the market.

[136] Equally, I reject Mr Newman's assertion that the manner in which the investment returns are calculated under the notional Guaranteed Interest Fund means that the benefits arising from the Member's Interest cannot be calculated "only" by reference to the contributions and therefore, satisfy the construction placed upon the expression by Jonathan Parker LJ in paragraph 171 of his judgment in the KPMG case.

[137] Despite the fact that the final rate of return to be applied to the Member's Interest is arrived at by the addition of a bonus percentage to the initial conservatively declared rate, in my judgment, it is merely a rate of return nevertheless. The

mechanism by which the rate is arrived at is just that. The fact that one is required to have regard to returns on other funds over a number of years in order to determine the percentage to be applied is merely a product of the fact that the investment is only notional in the first place. In my judgment, its application does not prevent the benefits from being a direct product of the contributions.

[138] Furthermore, the application of the bonus percentage in order to arrive at the investment return for the Guaranteed Interest Fund, envisaged in rule 3.1.1 (c)(c) of Schedule 3, can be distinguished from the bonus regime under consideration in the KPMG case. In that case, if an actuarial valuation relating to the assets and liabilities of the entire scheme, revealed a surplus, the trustees had power to reduce contributions or increase benefits by the declaration of bonuses. In my judgment this is entirely different from the arrival at a percentage investment return on a notional fund by reference to the performance of a variety of investments.

[139] Next, I turn to the existence of the provisions referred to by both Mr Newman and Mr Stallworthy as "balance of cost" provisions. The respective rules are contained in rule 2.3 of Schedule 3 in respect of MoneyMatch and at rule 3.1 of Schedule 4 in respect of VIP. They are both similar in form. The provision in Schedule 4 is applicable to Final Pay benefits and Mr Stallworthy says it should be confined to them. In my judgment, given the heading 'Ordinary contributions', rather than VIP Contributions and the reference to rule 4, which itself refers to contributions to be recorded in an MFR schedule where applicable, it is possible to confine the application of the provision to the Final Pay benefits. However, this is not true of rule 2.3 of Schedule 3 which applies to MoneyMatch. In this regard, I accept Mr Stallworthy's submissions that the provision caters for the situation in which the process of internal annuitisation has caused a strain upon the Fund.

[140] In any event, I do not consider the existence of the "balance of cost" provisions to be fatal to the characterisation of benefits arising from a Member's Interest or VIP Interest as money purchase benefits. Mr Newman conceded that the existence of such provisions was not considered determinative in the KMPG case.'

1 [2008] EWHC 964 (Ch); [2008] All ER (D) 17 (May) (Sarah Asplin QC sitting as a deputy judge of the High Court).

38.10 It is to be noted that in order for a scheme to qualify as a money purchase scheme, all of the benefits (other than death benefits) must be money purchase. If even a few of the benefits are salary related the scheme will not be a money purchase scheme.

DEATH BENEFITS

38.11 It is common for schemes which are mainly money purchase also to provide death benefits payable on a member's death in pensionable service based on the member's final salary (eg a lump sum and/or a spouse's pension). These benefits are commonly insured (and the employer undertakes to provide any additional funding needed). These schemes are broadly money purchase, but would not strictly fall within the definition.

38.12   Accordingly various regulations exclude schemes which contain death benefits (ie in the same way as a 'pure' money purchase scheme) even if it includes death benefits that are not money purchase (eg a lump sum life benefit or a pension to a spouse or dependant). In relation to PA 1995, there is a power to do this is in PA 1995, s 125(2).

38.13   Relevant regulations doing this include:

● Employer Debt Regulations, reg 2(1);

● Scheme Funding Regulations, reg 17(1)(j), but only if the death benefits are secured by insurance policies or annuities;

● MFR Regulations, reg 28(1)(f), but there must be no accrued rights within the scheme (other than for money purchase benefits). This means that the exclusion does not apply to a scheme which provides salary-related death benefits for members who die having left pensionable employment; and

● PPF Entry Rules Regulations, reg 2(1)(h), but again there must be no accrued rights within the scheme (other than for money purchase benefits); and

● Contribution Notices Regulations 2005 (SI 2005/931), reg 3(h), but again there must be no accrued rights within the scheme (other than for money purchase benefits).

38.14   Regulation 2 of the Occupational and Personal Pension Schemes (Miscellaneous Amendments) Regulations 1997 (SI 1997/786), also provides generally that:

> 'Schemes providing salary-related death benefits
>
> 2 . Part I of the Pensions Act 1995 applies to any occupational pension scheme under which all the benefits that may be provided other than death benefits are money purchase benefits as if every reference in that Part to a money purchase scheme included such a scheme.'

38.15   The exemptions in the MFR Regulations, the PPF Entry Rules Regulations and the Contribution Notices Regulations all refer to no member having any accrued rights (defined in PA 1995, s 124(2)).

38.16   In effect a scheme where benefits (whether lump sum or pension to spouse or dependants or both) are only payable if a member dies in pensionable service will be exempt (there will be no accrued rights because s 124(2) defines these on the assumption that a member has left pensionable service). Conversely, if salary-related benefits are payable if a member dies as a pensioner or deferred member, there will be accrued rights and the exemption will not apply.

MONEY PURCHASE SCHEMES: DEBT ON EMPLOYER

38.17   The Employer Debt Regulations[2] apply the debt provisions in s 75 in a limited way to money purchase schemes (which for this purpose includes schemes which also provide death benefits). These regulations deem a debt to arise on an employer in relation to such a scheme in the following circumstances:

(a) **criminal reduction:** if there is a criminal reduction in the scheme assets[3] which could otherwise trigger a claim on the Pension Compensation Board under PA 1995, s 81; and

(b) **levy payments:** to reimburse the scheme the amount of any levy paid to the Registrar of Occupational Pension Schemes under PSA 1993, s 175, as substituted by PA 1995, s 165[2].

1 Regs 10 to 13.
2 Employer Debt Regulations, reg 10.
3 Occupational and Personal Pension Schemes (General Levy) Regulations 2005 (SI 2005/626), reg 3(1) or (2).

38.18   In both of the above cases the debt:

(a) arises whether or not the scheme is in winding-up and whether or not the employer has entered insolvency; and

(b) only arises if there are insufficient 'unallocated assets' to meet the relevant claim.

38.19   For this purpose unallocated assets are defined as assets which are not allocated assets. The term allocated assets is defined in as assets which have been specifically allocated for the provision of benefits to or in respect of members (whether generally or individually) or for the payment of the scheme's expenses – reg 10(4) of the Employer Debt Regulations.

38.20   A 'criminal reduction' is a reduction which is attributable to an act or omission which constitutes an offence prescribed for the purposes of s 81(1)(c) of PA 1995[1] (or, in the case of an act or omission which occurred outside England and Wales or Scotland, would constitute such an offence if it occurred in England and Wales or in Scotland). Such prescribed offences are offences involving dishonesty (including an intent to defraud)[2].

1 The Employer Debt Regulations still refer to s 81(1)(c) of the PA 1995, although that section has been repealed and replaced from 1 September 2005 by s 182 of PA 2004.
2 See Occupational Pension Schemes (Fraud Compensation Payments and Miscellaneous Amendments) Regulations 2005 (SI 2005/2184), reg 3, replacing Occupational Pension Schemes (Pensions Compensation Provisions) Regulations 1997 (SI 1997/665), reg 3.

38.21   The Employer Debt Regulations also deal with valuation of scheme assets (reg 11), attribution of liabilities in multi-employer schemes (reg 12) and in relation to a scheme with no active members, treating former employers as continuing to be deemed employers[1] (reg 13).

1 Similar in effect to reg 9(1) – see para 32.10 above.

MONEY PURCHASE SCHEMES: PAYMENT SCHEDULE

38.22   The provisions of PA 2004 and PA 1995 dealing with scheme specific funding and the minimum funding requirement[1] do not, for obvious reasons, apply to money purchase pension schemes[2] nor to schemes that would be money purchase but for providing death benefits[3].

1 Part 3 of PA 2004 and PA 1995, ss 56–61.
2 See PA 2004, s 221(1)(a) and PA 1995, s 56(2)(a).
3 Scheme Funding Regulations, reg 17(1)(j), and MFR Regulations, reg 28(1)(f).

38.23   However, PA 1995, s 87, provides that the trustees of a money purchase scheme must secure that there is 'prepared, maintained and from time to time revised' a payment schedule showing:

(a)   the rates of contribution payable towards the scheme both by the employer and active members;

(b)   the amounts payable towards the scheme by the employer in respect of expenses likely to be incurred in the scheme year[1]; and

(c)   the due dates for payments of such contributions.

1 Occupational Pension Schemes (Scheme Administration) Regulations 1996 (SI 1996/1715) (the 'Scheme Administration Regulations'), reg 18.

38.24   The schedule must give separate details for each employer and the active members[1]. This obligation does not apply to various money purchase schemes, including those which are not registered with HMRC and s 615(6) schemes, provided they have less than 100 members[2].

1 Scheme Administration Regulations, reg 19.
2 Scheme Administration Regulations, reg 17, as amended by SI 2005/2426. The inclusion of schemes that have 100 or more members even if they are not registered with HMRC presumably flows from the requirement in the Directive on Institutions for Occupational Retirement Provision (the 'IORP Directive') that funding is dealt with – see Chapter 31 above.

38.25   Section 87(4) envisages that the relevant matters to be shown in the payment schedule must:

(a)   be determined as provided for in the scheme, or in default;

(b)   be agreed between the employer and the trustees, or in default;

(c)   be determined by the trustees.

38.26   In practice, many money purchase schemes merely leave the rate of contributions to be agreed between the employer and the individual member rather than the trustees and the employer. Given this, the role for the trustees in agreeing a contribution schedule will in may cases be limited. But, the Section seems aimed at ensuring that trustees know what is agreed between the employer and individual members so a composite schedule of contributions can be prepared and be monitored by the trustees.

38.27   In view of the importance of the prompt making of payments to money purchase schemes, the obligation to produce a payment schedule is reinforced by PA 1995, s 88(1) which provides that trustees must notify the Pensions Regulator and the members of the scheme if payments have not been paid by the due date, provided the trustees have reasonable cause to believe that the failure is likely to be of material significance to the Pensions Regulator[1]. The timescale for these notices is set out in reg 21 of the Occupational Pension Schemes (Scheme Administration) Regulations 1996.

1 Guidance on this has been issued by the Pensions Regulator. See Code of Practice 05: 'Reporting late payment of contributions to occupational money purchase schemes', available on the web at www.thepensionsregulator.gov.uk.

38.28 PA 1995, s 88(2), makes it clear that any amounts on the payments schedule left unpaid (including member's contributions) are a debt due from the employer. These provisions mirror those applicable to salary-related schemes contained in PA 1995, s 59 and PA 2004, s 228.

38.29 Trustees are liable to civil penalties[1] if they fail to take all reasonable steps to secure compliance in the setting up of the payment schedule or in failing to make a report of failure to pay before the due date[2].

1 PA 1995, s 10.
2 PA 1995, ss 87(5) and 88(4).

38.30 In addition, the employer itself is liable to a civil penalty under PA 1995, s 10, if it fails to make payments on or before the due date shown in the schedule[1]. There is no defence if any payment failure was with a reasonable excuse.

This is similar to the penalty under PA 2004, s 228(4)(b), on an employer who fails without reasonable excuse to make a payment required under the schedule of contributions under scheme specific funding for a non-money purchase scheme (there was no equivalent penalty under the MFR regime).

1 PA 1995, s 88(3).

38.31 There is also a potential criminal penalty if employee contributions deducted from pay by the employer are not paid by the 19th of the following month—see paras 10.40 and 33.3 above. From 6 April 1997 to 3 April 2000 the Pensions Act 1995 made it a criminal offence for an employer to fail, without reasonable excuse, to pay the amount of such deducted employee contributions to the trustees of an occupational pension scheme[1].

Directors, officers and others (potentially including an insolvency practitioner[2]) can also be criminally liable if the failure occurred as a result of their consent, connivance or neglect[3].

1 Section 49(8) of the Pensions Act 1995 and reg 16 of the Occupational Pension Schemes (Scheme Administration) Regulations 1996, SI 1996/1715, as amended by SI 1997/768.
2 See Chapter 8 above.
3 Pensions Act 1995, s 115 and see Chapter 8 above.

38.32 Since 3 April 2000[1] only fraudulent evasion has been criminal and not also a simple negligent failure. It is currently an offence, under s 49 of the Pensions Act 1995, for a person knowingly to be concerned in the fraudulent evasion of this duty by an employer.

1 When the amendments made by s 10 of the Welfare Reform and Pensions Act 1999 came into force.

38.33   Employers will need to have ensured that they have appropriate authority (under Pt 2 of the Employment Rights Act 1996, formerly the Wages Act 1986) to deduct amounts due from active members to the scheme (even if these are voluntary contributions etc). If for any reason member contributions are not paid by the due date then they become a debt on the employer even if they were direct obligations of the employee to the scheme.

INDEPENDENT TRUSTEES

38.34   The independent trustee obligations in PA 1995 (see Chapter 30 above) now apply to money purchase schemes in the same way as to non-money purchase schemes.

38.35   This includes the obligation to give notice to the PPF, the Pensions Regulator and the trustees under PA 1995, s 22(2B). The Pensions Regulator will have a discretion to appoint an independent trustee. Contrast *Polly Peck International plc v Henry*[1] where Buckley J rejected an application by the insolvent employer to appoint a new independent trustee (who's fee would then be payable out of the fund).

1 [1999] PLR 135, [1999] 1 BCLC 407 (Buckley J) and see para 26.33 above.

PPF/TPR NOTIFICATIONS

38.36   The requirement under PA 2004, ss 120 and 122 (see Chapter 28 above) to notify the PPF of the appointment of an insolvency practitioner and scheme rescue etc, applies to a money purchase scheme. This is because the notification obligations apply whether or not the scheme is an eligible scheme. A pure money purchase scheme is not an eligible scheme – PA 2004, s 126(1)(a).

38.37   The obligation to notify the Pensions Regulator about various notifiable events (PA 2004, s 69 – see Chapter 29 above) does not apply in relation to a money purchase scheme as it is not an eligible scheme – PA 2004, ss 69(2) and 126(1)(a).

38.38   The obligation to notify the Pensions Regulator about material breaches of law (PA 2004, s 70 – see Chapter 29 above) does apply to money purchase schemes.

CHAPTER 39

Winding up the pension scheme

39.1   If a company participates in an occupational pension scheme there will usually be an express provision dealing with the effect on the scheme of the liquidation of the company or of the company's failure to pay contributions (if due) or otherwise to comply with the terms of the scheme.

39.2   If the company which has entered insolvency proceedings is just a participating employer in a centralised scheme (ie not the sponsor or establisher of the scheme, usually called the principal company or principal employer), then its insolvency will usually only trigger the cessation of its participation, perhaps with a partial winding up of the scheme in respect of the company and its employees.

39.3   If the insolvent company is the principal company for the purposes of the scheme then a winding up of the whole scheme may be triggered.

39.4   It is common for the winding-up provisions in the scheme documentation to provide that a liquidation of the principal company will automatically cause the winding up of the scheme (unless provision is made for a substitution of the principal company, for example on a reconstruction).

39.5   Warner J in *Mettoy Pension Trustees Ltd v Evans*[1] held that a winding-up clause that referred to the principal company 'going into liquidation' was only triggered by the making of the winding-up order, not the presentation of a petition.

   If (more unusually) a winding-up clause refers to the making of an administration order, this may not apply to an out of court administration – see *William Hare Ltd v Shepherd Construction Ltd*[2]. But note that there is a saving for pre-15 September 2003 contracts in Enterprise Act 2002, Sch 17, para 1.

1 [1991] 2 All ER 513 at 544 (Warner J).
2 [2009] EWHC 1603 (TCC); [2009] All ER (D) 01 (Sep) (Coulson J).

39.6   As mentioned above (see Chapter 28), the entry of an eligible scheme into an assessment period for PPF purposes will mean that any scheme power cannot be used to start the winding-up of the scheme unless the PPF agrees (PA 2004, s135).

39.7 The Pensions Regulator also has a power to order the winding-up of an occupational pension scheme – see PA 1995, s 11. This power can be exercised in some circumstances during an assessment period, if the Regulator considers it necessary to ensure that the scheme's PPF protected liabilities do not exceed its assets (or the excess is minimised) – PA 1995, s 11(3A), as inserted by PA 2004.

39.8 Conversely, a receivership or administration would not commonly automatically trigger the winding up of the scheme. However, this may be triggered if the insolvency practitioner arranges for the company to exercise a winding up power under the scheme's winding-up provision or if one of the other triggering events such as cessation of contributions or failure to comply with the terms of the scheme occurs.

39.9 In *Air Jamaica v Charlton*[1] the Privy Council held that the employer had triggered the winding up of a pension scheme (under a provision which allowed the employer to discontinue the scheme) when it ceased to pay contributions (even without a formal resolution of the board of directors of the employer).

1 [1999] 1 WLR 1399 at p1410, PC.

WHEN AND HOW DOES WINDING UP OCCUR?

39.10 Some or all of the following circumstances are commonly expressly included in the documentation of pension schemes as winding-up events:

(a) if the principal employer terminates its liability to contribute to the scheme by giving notice in writing to the trustees (often a minimum notice period is required);

(b) if the principal employer enters liquidation or, less commonly, ceases to trade (and there is no other body corporate willing to take over its responsibility);

(c) if the scheme becomes insolvent[1] and the trustees resolve to wind up;

(d) if the principal employer breaches a provision of the scheme and the trustees resolve to wind up; or

(e) if the principal employer or, less commonly, the trustees resolve.

The Pensions Regulator has a power to order a winding up of a pension scheme under PA 1995, s 11.

1 See the article by Suzannah White 'Insolvency as a wind-up trigger: a useful tool?' in (2004) 101 Pension Lawyer 19 on whether the covenant of the employers to pay to the scheme can be considered as an asset for these purposes.

WHEN DOES A SCHEME START TO WIND UP?

39.11 In deciding when a scheme starts to wind up, s 124(3A) to (3E) of PA 1995 apply[1]. These sections provide generally for the time of winding up to be as follows:

(a) if winding-up is under a requirement or power in the rules, the time fixed in the rules, or if no time is fixed by the rules, the time chosen by the trustees (or other person with the power under the scheme rules) 'as the time for which steps for the purpose of winding-up are to be taken' – s 124(3B) and (3D);

(b) if there is a postponement of a winding-up, either under a scheme power or the statutory power in PA 1995, s 38 (see below), the date of winding up is also delayed – s 124(3C);

(c) winding up by order of the court or the Pensions Regulator (under PA 1995, s 11) takes effect as envisaged in the relevant order or when it comes into force – s 124(3A).

This timing is subject to ss 28, 154 and 219 of PA 2004:

● Section 28 back dates the effect of a winding-up order made by the Pensions Regulator under s 11 of PA 1995 if the order is made during a period during which a freezing order (under s 23, PA 2004) has effect. The winding-up is deemed to have started when the freezing order took effect – s 28(2)(a);

● Section 154 back dates a winding-up of a scheme where an assessment period comes to an end but the scheme is not taken over by the PPF because the scheme has sufficient assets to meet the PPF protected liabilities (but a scheme rescue is not possible). In such a case, the scheme must generally be wound-up (s 154(1)(a) and (12)) and the winding-up is back-dated to immediately before the assessment period started (ie the insolvency event) – s 154(6);

● Section 219 back dates a winding-up of an eligible scheme if a qualifying insolvency event (defined in s 127 – see Chapter 27 above) has occurred in relation to the employer and the scheme starts to wind-up after that event but before a scheme failure notice or withdrawal notice has become binding. The winding-up is backdated to the date of the qualifying insolvency event.

1 As inserted by the Child Support, Pensions and Social Security Act 2000 from 1 April 2002. See previously, to similar effect, the Occupational Pension Schemes (Winding Up) Regulations 1996 (SI 1996/3126).

Timeframe for winding up

39.12 In their joint statement on winding up[1], tPR, PPF and FAS set out the relevant time frame in which they expect parties to complete the key activities in a winding up. The key activities include serving a debt on the employer, securing pensioner benefits and conducting a final actuarial valuation. The guidance states that:

- schemes should complete the key activities as soon as practicably possible and at least within two years from 30 June 2008 if the scheme is outside the PPF and already winding up;

- schemes should complete the key activities within two years from the date of wind up if the scheme is outside the PPF and commences winding up after 30 June 2008;

- there will be very limited exceptions to these time frames; and

- trustees of ongoing schemes should consider the steps that could be taken in advance of a scheme wind up.

The joint statement comments that issuing directions will be tPR's principal means of enforcements. Other powers referred to are the removing or appointing trustees, publishing information and taking action for failure to provide the regulator with registrable information about starting or completing winding up.

1 Available on tPR's website www.thepensionsregulator.gov.uk

Partial and total winding up

39.13   Where a pension scheme provides for more than one employer to participate, the Inland Revenue practice notes (applicable before 6 April 2006) used to envisage that it required that exempt approved schemes include a provision dealing with a cessation of participation (PN 21.6 of IR 12) eg where there has been the sale of a subsidiary.

Commonly this involves a segregation of part of the scheme's assets and a partial winding up of that part of the scheme in relation to the employer that is ceasing to participate. However, the trend in more modern schemes was to avoid such a partial winding up. The inclusion of a partial winding-up provision can impact on the PPF position – see Chapter 36 above.

There is a good discussion of the partial winding-up issues in two APL talks:

- The talk by Duncan Buchanan 'Partial Wind up Rules – honoured in their breach?' given in February 2008 on partial winding-up;

- Followed by the paper 'No room at the orphanage: some issues relating to PPF Entry' given by Ian Greenstreet and Helen Butler in April 2009.

Impact of the winding-up rule

39.14   The position on winding up is central to the underlying pensions 'promise' of a scheme. The following are key issues:

(a) commonly, employers reserved the right in the scheme documents to discontinue pension arrangements or contributions (see para 33.8 above);

(b) the security of the accrued pension promise would then depend on the level of the scheme's funding and the priority under the trust deed given to the member's benefits; and

(c) even if the employer is clearly solvent, one factor that the trustees used to need to keep in mind will be the possibility of the employer winding up the scheme and starting again with a new arrangement.

39.15 The move to a statutory debt under PA 1995, s 75 of the employers based on the buy-out liability (see Chapter 34 above) has meant that the ability of solvent employers to terminate and wind-up the scheme has become more restricted (unless they are content to pay the debt).

Priorities on winding up

39.16 A statutory priority order applies on winding up for most HMRC registered salary-related schemes (see para 39.45 below).

39.17 Schemes which are contracted-out on a salary-related basis were required, before 6 April 1997, under PSA 1993, s 23 to provide a priority on winding up to guaranteed minimum pensions (GMPs) and state scheme premiums etc.

39.18 Subject to this, after realising the assets it was possible, before 6 April 1997, for schemes to provide that all benefits were to have an equal degree of priority if there is a deficiency. However, it was common to provide for some benefits to rank ahead of others.

39.19 Benefits on a money purchase basis attributable to members' voluntary contributions were often dealt with separately (see para 34.46 above). The following was a comparatively common order for the other benefits:

(a) pensions and other benefits in payment together with benefits payable to those over normal pension age and still in service;

(b) GMPs and accrued rights to GMPs and state scheme premiums;

(c) deferred pensions and other benefits for early leavers;

(d) deferred pensions and other benefits for scheme members still in service when the winding up began as if they had left service then;

(e) trustee or employer discretion (perhaps with the other's consent) to augmentation of benefits within the old Inland Revenue limits as applied to the scheme (including mandatory LPI increases to pensions in payment if there is to be any surplus refund); and

(f) payment of any remaining surplus to the employers.

39.20 Since 6 April 1997, an overriding statutory priority order has applied under PA 1995, s 73. See para 39.45 below.

30.21 Where the assets attributable to voluntary contributions by members were segregated and provide benefits on a money purchase basis, it was common that these assets are separated out from the winding up and used only to provide the AVC benefits. This is now the effect of the statutory provisions in PA 1995, s 73, following PA 2004.

39.22 Winding up of a scheme can be a difficult process for trustees and for employers. It is outside the scope of this book to try to deal with the issues in much depth.

39.23 Winding-up of a scheme triggers a number of obligations on the trustees:

(a) to notify HMRC and (if contracted-out) the National Insurance Contributions Agency (formerly the Contributions Agency of the DSS);

(b) to deal with the Pension Protection Fund (PPF)[1];

(c) to notify the members and the Pensions Regulator[2];

(d) to consider if there is any statutory deficiency under the PA 1995, s 75 which becomes a debt payable by the employers;

(e) to decide whether or not to run as a closed scheme;

(f) to decide how to secure benefits based on the winding-up rule;

(g) if there is a surplus, to look at any power of augmentation of benefits for members or return of surplus to the employer.

1 The PPF publishes a guide for trustees on its website – www.pensionprotectionfund.org.uk
2 Winding-up an eligible scheme during any recovery period specified in the scheme's recovery plan for scheme specific funding purposes used to be a notifiable event to the Pensions Regulator under PA 2004, s 69 – see reg 8(8) of the Scheme Funding Regulations and Chapter 29 above.

RUNNING AS A CLOSED SCHEME – PENSIONS ACT 1995, s 38

39.24 In some cases, particularly larger schemes, the trustees may consider it to be more in the interests of the members if the scheme continues to operate (and to pay benefits) instead of being wound up (with benefits bought out with an insurance company). This is because it can often be relatively expensive for a scheme to buy-out benefits, when compared with the expected actuarial cost within the scheme.

39.25 Running as a closed scheme, with no employer available to take any investment risk, is not a simple decision for trustees. Before 1997, it also depended on whether or not the scheme made express provision for it to be run on as a closed scheme instead of being wound up.

39.26 PA 1995, s 38 enables trustees to allow a scheme to continue even in circumstances where the scheme rules require the scheme to be wound up. There are various exemptions[1], including money-purchase schemes (ignoring death benefits) or schemes which are not registered with HMRC under the Finance Act 2004. Regulations have exempted schemes such as small self-administered schemes, for which power to run on would be of less value[2].

1 See the Occupational Pension Schemes (Winding Up) Regulations 1996 (SI 1996/3126), reg 10(1) as amended.
2 See para 39.38 below.

39.27 Entry of a scheme into an assessment period has the effect of freezing it in any event. The scheme cannot start to wind-up unless the PPF agrees (see PA 2004, s 135(2) and Chapter 28 above).

39.28 An exit from an assessment period with no scheme rescue is possible if the scheme has sufficient assets to meet its PPF protected liabilities – PA 2004, s 132(2)(iii) and (4)(iii). If this happens:

- once PA 2004, s 153 came into force (on 6 April 2007[1]), if the scheme is unable to obtain a full buy-out quotation, the trustees must apply to the PPF for authority to continue as a closed scheme (PA 2004, s 153(2)). The application must be made within an 'authorised period' ie six months[2]; and

- if no such application is made (or it is determined), the scheme must start to wind-up (PA 2004, s 154(1)). Section 38 does not then apply[3].

1 See the Pensions Act 2004 (Commencement No 10 and Saving Provision) Order 2006 (SI 2006/2272).
2 PA 2004, s 153(7), applying s 151(6) and reg 24(3) of the PPF Entry Rules Regulations.
3 PA 1995, s 38(4), inserted by PA 2004. See also on s 154, paras 33.104 and 34.20 above.

39.29 Section 38 broadly only applies where a 'relevant employer debt event' has occurred. This requires a relevant event for s 75 purposes to have occurred and for the provisions of the scheme to require the scheme to be wound up as a result[1].

1 See the Occupational Pension Schemes (Winding Up) Regulations 1996 (SI 1996/3126), reg 10(1)(a), (2), as amended, discussed at para 39.38 below.

39.30 The purpose of s 38 is to avoid trustees having to wind up a scheme where this would not be in the interests of the beneficiaries. An example of this might be where they were unable to purchase annuities or might consider the time to be unfavourable.

39.31 By allowing schemes to run on the aim is that the trustees of a scheme should be able to discharge their liabilities gradually as and when they crystallise. The trustees will be able to determine that the scheme should continue as a frozen scheme only if they conclude that this would be a proper use of the power balancing the interests of the beneficiaries of the scheme.

39.32   Section 38 also allows the trustees to decide:

(a)   that no new members are to be admitted to the scheme; and

(b)   to limit its continuing operation so that no new benefits are to accrue to or in respect of members.

But it does not allow the trustees to determine that benefits are not to be increased.

39.33   However, s 38 will only apply to give trustees power to defer a winding up which would otherwise take place. If the principal employer had reserved the power to make the scheme paid-up (and frozen) ie to terminate future contributions, to close the scheme to new entrants and to terminate the accrual of future pensionable service, then this power remains unaffected by s 38.

39.34   Section 38 does, though, override the principal employer's powers and discretions in two important areas:

(a)   if the principal employer has not reserved the right to make the scheme paid-up, but only the right to wind up, then the trustees will be able to over-ride this; and

(b)   in any event, the trustees will be able to defer a winding up which an employer had planned, potentially leaving the employer liable to meet any increased deficit that flows as a result, eg under the deficiency provisions in s 75.

39.35   Trustees will need to consider the issues carefully and take advice before exercising their powers under s 38. The implications of deferring winding up and operating as a closed scheme are many.

For example, the priority position of members will alter as more benefits enter payment (and so increase in statutory and common scheme priority). This point has been addressed in the relevant regulations. Trustees are empowered to make a modification to schemes to fix the time for settling priority of liabilities on winding up[1]. This power may be exercised by resolution to modify the scheme with a view to fixing or providing for the fixing of the time when the paragraph in the PA 1995, s 73(3), into which the liability in respect of any person falls, is to be determined. In effect, this is a power to fix the date at which a person is treated as a pensioner instead of a deferred member.

1 Occupational Pension Schemes (Winding Up) Regulations 1996 (SI 1996/3126), reg 5.

39.36   This applies for the purposes of the PA 1995, s 73(2) and (3) or of any priority rule of the scheme. For this purpose a 'priority rule' means a rule of the scheme requiring the trustees to apply the assets of the scheme on a winding up in satisfying the amounts of certain liabilities to or in respect of members before other such liabilities[1].

1 Occupational Pension Schemes (Winding Up) Regulations 1996 (SI 1996/3126), reg 5(3).

39.37 The power is only available in the event of a determination (whether in pursuance of s 38 or otherwise) that the scheme is not for the time being to be wound up, despite rules otherwise requiring it to be so.

39.38 The time fixed by the trustees must be:

(a) on or after the date of the resolution and of any such determination to defer winding up; and

(b) before the date on which the scheme begins to be wound up.

39.39 PA 1995, s 38(3) excludes money purchase schemes, and allows for regulations to exclude some other schemes, from s 38. The schemes excluded (under reg 10 of the Occupational Pension Schemes (Winding Up) Regulations 1996 (SI 1996/3126) are:

(a) any scheme in relation to which no relevant employer debt event has occurred;

(b) a scheme in respect of which any Minister of the Crown has given a guarantee or made any other arrangements for the purpose of securing that the assets of the scheme are sufficient to meet its liabilities;

(c) a scheme which provides relevant benefits, but is neither an approved scheme nor a relevant statutory scheme;

(d) a s 615(6) scheme (if the trustees are not authorised to operate in other EU states);

(e) a scheme with less than two members;

(f) a small, self-administered scheme which is an approved scheme;

(g) a scheme, the only benefits provided by which (other than money purchase benefits), are death benefits; or

(h) a relevant lump sum retirement benefits scheme.

See Chapter 31 (Scope of the main pensions legislation) above for descriptions of the other categories mentioned here.

A scheme which the trustees are required to wind-up (or continue to wind-up) under PA 2004, s 154(1) (ie following an assessment period – see para 39.28 above) is also excluded from the ambit of s 38 – s 38(4) (as inserted by PA 2004).

39.40 For the purposes of s 38(3), a relevant employer debt event has only occurred in relation to a scheme if (apart from s 38 or any other power to defer winding up the scheme) the rules of the scheme require the scheme to be wound up as a result of a relevant insolvency event having occurred in relation to any person who immediately before the event occurred was an employer in relation to the scheme.

For this purpose

(a) the PA 1995, s 75(6A) (definition of relevant insolvency events) applies as it applies for the purposes of s 75 (disregarding any modifications of that section); and

(b) in the case of a scheme which has no active members, the reference to an employer is to the person who was the employer immediately before the occurrence of the event after which the scheme ceased to have any active members.[1]

1 Occupational Pension Schemes (Winding Up) Regulations 1996 (SI 1996/3126), reg 10(2).

39.41 A 'small self-administered scheme' is a scheme within reg 2(1) of the Retirement Benefits Schemes (Restriction on Discretion to Approve) (Small Self-administered Schemes) Regulations 1991[1], ie a retirement benefits scheme where (a) some or all of the income and other assets are invested otherwise than in insurance policies; (b) a scheme member is connected with: (i) another scheme member, or (ii) a trustee of the scheme, or (iii) a person who is an employer in relation to the scheme; and (c) there are fewer than 12 scheme members.

Other terms used above have the same meanings as in relation to the exclusions from scheme specific funding and s 75 – see Chapter 31 (Scope of the main pensions legislation) above.

1 Occupational Pension Schemes (Winding Up) Regulations 1996, SI 1996/3126, reg 10(3).

39.42 If the trustees decide to run a scheme as a frozen or closed scheme instead of winding-up (eg under a provision in the scheme rules or under PA 1995, s 38 – see para 39.24 below), then any winding-up is postponed (so no trigger under s 75(2)) – see PA 1995, s 124(3C).

SCHEME WINDING UP – FURTHER ISSUES

39.43 A full review of the provisions relating to scheme winding up is outside the ambit of this book.

39.44 But two further provisions in PA 1995 are of importance:

(a) s 73 contains an overriding order of priority on winding up; and

(b) s 74 contains overriding statutory powers for the trustees of a scheme being wound up to be able to discharge liabilities by the purchase of insurance etc.

39.45 Both sections are modified by the:

● Occupational Pension Schemes (Winding Up) Regulations 1996 (SI 1996/3126) (the '1996 Regulations'); and

● Occupational Pension Schemes (Winding Up etc) Regulations 2005 (SI 2005/706) (the '2005 Winding-up Regulations').

39.46 Section 73 applies to (broadly) the same schemes as are not excluded from s 75. See Chapter 31 above and reg 3 of the 2005 Winding-up Regulations.

39.47 A brief summary of the statutory priority order (applicable to a scheme winding up starting on or after 6 April 2005) is set out below:

(a) benefits secured by pre-1997 insurance contracts

Entitlement to payment of a pension or other benefit has arisen and is secured by an insurance policy (entered into before 6 April 1997) which may not be surrendered (or whose surrender amount is less than the liability secured)

(b) liability for benefits up to the PPF protected level (if not within (a));

(c) liability for benefits attributable to voluntary contributions (if not within (a) or (b))

(d) any other liability.

39.48 Benefits which are money purchase are outside the s 73 priority order, together with the assets representing them[1]. This means that they will in practice be provided in full.

It can be a complex area as to how to categorise members – eg as pensioners or not. This is beyond the scope of this book, but see *Foster Wheeler Ltd v Hanley*[2]; *Trustee Solutions Ltd v Dubery*[3]; *Alexander Forbes Trustee Services Ltd v Clarke*[4] and *Bestrustees v Stuart*[5].

1 See the definitions of 'assets' and 'liabilities' in s 73(10).
2 [2009] EWCA Civ 651; [2009] All ER (D) 82 (Jul), CA.
3 [2007] EWCA Civ 771; [2008] 1 All ER 826, [2008] ICR 101, CA.
4 [2008] EWHC 153 (Ch); [2008] All ER (D) 41 (Feb) (Henderson J).
5 [2001] EWHC 549 (Ch); [2001] PLR 283 (Neuberger J).

39.49 Section 74 contains an overriding power for trustees to discharge liabilities on a winding-up by:

(a) a transfer to another occupational pension scheme;

(b) a transfer to a personal pension;

(c) purchase of an annuity from an insurance company; or

(d) subscription to other prescribed arrangements.

39.50 Generally, the arrangements must satisfy the requirements prescribed in regs 6 to 9 of the Occupational Pension Schemes (Winding Up) Regulations 1996 (SI 1996/3126).

SURPLUSES

39.51 On a winding-up of a final salary (ie defined benefit) pension scheme a surplus may well arise; that is, the assets of the scheme will exceed those needed to fund the benefits promised to and in respect of members on a non-discretionary basis. Usually there will be a discretion given to use this surplus to increase benefits to members (within former Inland Revenue limits), with any funds remaining being returned to the employer (this has been a requirement since 1970 for Inland Revenue approved schemes). Whether an insolvency practitioner can get access to any surplus (by way of a refund to the company) raises difficult issues depending on the construction of the trust documents.

Surpluses usually arise only in relation to a final salary scheme (as opposed to a money purchase scheme, where a surplus would arise only in limited circumstances, for example in relation to members who left with less than two years' qualifying service).

39.52 A surplus can arise on a winding up of a final salary scheme because the scheme will have been funded on an on- going basis, (making allowance for anticipated future salary increases, and perhaps assuming fewer early leavers than has in fact occurred). This was more common in the past than it is now.

39.53 Scott J (as he then was) gave a good analysis in *Davis v Richards & Wallington Industries Ltd*[1]:

> 'The 1975 scheme . . . was one in which each employee's pension entitlement was based on the level of his or her final salary. In the nature of things an individual's salary tends to rise during the course of his or her employment, both by reason of annual salary rises and by reason of promotion. In any one year, an employee's 5 per cent contribution to the fund would be based on the salary for that year, but the funding of the expectant pension on retirement would be based on the expected higher level of the salary at the time of retirement. The employer's contribution in each year would be based on an actuarial calculation of the sum necessary to fund a pension based on that higher salary level. So where a pension scheme based on final salary levels terminates, there will almost inevitably be a surplus. Each employee who is under retirement age will be entitled to benefits payable in the future but based on his or her salary at the date of termination. But the funding of the benefits and the employer's contributions before the termination date will have been based on the higher level of his or her expected final salary. So on the termination there is bound to be a surplus in the fund.
>
> One of the options open to an employee of the group when leaving his or her employment with less than five years' qualifying service was, subject to certain specified limits, to have a refund of his or her contributions to the scheme. Both before and after the execution of the definitive deed a number of employees availed themselves of this option. Their contributions were refunded to them. But, of course, the contributions paid on their behalf by their employers remained in the scheme and enhanced the size of the surplus.'

1 [1990] 1 WLR 1511 at 1528 (Scott J).

39.54 However, such discontinuance surpluses have, in practice, recently tended to get smaller. This is a result of a combination of factors including:

● reduced investment return,

- the abolition of tax credits relating to advanced corporation tax,

- increased statutory benefits in deferment and retirement,

- possible liability to equalise benefits between males and females (see below) and

- increased cost of securing benefits by the purchase of insurance policies.

Tax on refunds

39.55   There is a tax at 35% payable on surplus payments out of a registered pension scheme – Finance Act 2004, ss 177 and 207.

39.56   This replaced from 6 April 2006 a similar tax charge (originally at 40%, but reduced by Finance Act 2001, s 74(2) to 35% for payments made after 11 May 2001) under ICTA 1988, s 601 on any refunds to an employer out of a pension scheme which is, or has been, Inland Revenue approved.
This is a stand-alone tax which cannot be off-set against other tax losses.

Is there really a surplus?

39.57   The liabilities of the scheme may be greater than those set out in the scheme documentation. This is because of statutory provisions which may be applicable with overriding effect. These:

- used to include provision for limited price indexation of increases to pensions in payment (see below) and

- still include equalisation of benefits between the sexes (see below).

Limited price indexation increases to pensions

39.58   It was originally intended that the Social Security Act 1990, s 11(1) would insert into SSPA 1975 a new s 58A (now PSA 1993, ss 102 to 108) which would require limited price indexation (LPI) of pensions when they come into payment from final salary schemes (ie increases to pensions when they come into payment of 5 per cent per annum or the increase in the retail prices index, if less). This provision never came into force.

39.59   However, the Social Security Act 1990, s 11(3) (which came into force on 17 August 1990 – see SI 1990/1446) provided that in the meantime no payment can be made out of the resources of a scheme to an employer unless the scheme provides for pensions when they come into payment to be given LPI increases. This was subject to various exemptions (see SI 1990/1530 and SI 1991/4) but there was no exemption applicable to the winding up of the scheme or an employer. Section 11(3) was later consolidated as PSA 1993, s 108(1).

39.60   Sir Donald Nicholls V-C held in *Thrells Ltd (1974) Pension Scheme v Lomas*[1], that s 11(3) required LPI increases to be given, as from the date on which any payment was made to the company, in relation to all pensions payable (or prospectively payable) under the scheme on the date the company went into liquidation (in this case 28 November 1984); that is, it was not possible to avoid the obligation under s 11(3) by arranging for the buy-out or transfer of all members of the scheme before any refund to the company.

1 [1992] OPLR 21 (Nicholls V-C).

39.61   PA 1995, s 76 now provides that where a tax-registered scheme is winding up and the scheme rules allow a payment to be made to the employer, excess assets can be paid to the employer provided certain specified conditions are met. The conditions which must be satisfied under s 76(3) are:

(a)   the liabilities of the scheme have been fully discharged;

(b)   the power to distribute assets to any person other than the employer has been exercised or the decision not to use it was taken;

(d)   members must be notified in accordance with prescribed requirements of the intention to make a payment from surplus to the employer. These are set out in regs 15 to 17 of the Occupational Pension Schemes (Payment to Employers) Regulations 2006, SI 2006/802.

39.62   The condition, formerly in s 76(3)(c), that LPI pension increases be given was deleted by PA 2004 with effect from 6 April 2006.

39.63   Section 76 is the 'winding-up equivalent' of PA 1995, s 37, which deals with payments to employers out of ongoing schemes.

39.64   Regulation 15 of the 2006 Regulations requires that two notices (at least two months apart, with the second at least three months before any power to pay the employer is exercised) have been sent to members giving details of the assets of the scheme and how it is proposed they be distributed. The members must also be informed of their right to make representations to the Pensions Regulator.

39.65   Members have a right to ask the Pensions Regulator to intervene where they believe the trustees have not complied with the statutory requirements.

39.66   Section 76 does not allow the trustees to refuse to make a refund of surplus on a winding up if that is required by the provisions of the scheme. If, for example, a scheme's winding-up rule provides that, after all benefits had been received, any remaining assets must be paid to the employer (subject to the employer's discretion to allow augmentation of benefits), s 76 would not prevent a return of surplus under this rule. It merely requires compliance with the conditions set out in it. Guidance from Opra on s 76 (and s 77 – see below) was given in Opra Note 3 'Payment of Surplus – Opra's role' issued in June 1998.

ASSETS REMAINING AFTER WINDING UP: POWER TO DISTRIBUTE (PA 1995, S 77)

39.67   PA 1995, s 77 used to give trustees power on a winding-up to augment benefits (subject to Inland Revenue limits) if they would otherwise pass to the Crown as bona vacantia. Section 77 was however repealed from 6 April 2006 (when the tax changes under the Finance Act 2004 came into force – these removed the old tax Revenue limits on benefits that could be paid out of an approved scheme).

39.68   A problem could occur in some older schemes where there is an express prohibition on refunds to employers and on amendments to allow such refunds—see the case of *Re ABC Television*[1]. However, this is now more unlikely following the decision of the Privy Council in *Air Jamaica v Charlton*[2] to the effect that a resulting trust will often be implied.

1 [1989] PLR 21 (decided in 1973).
2 [1999] 1 WLR 1399, PC. See also *Scully v Coley* [2009] UKPC 29, PC.

EQUALISATION OF BENEFITS – THE *BARBER* DECISION

39.69   The scheme documents may provide for benefits to differ between male and female employees. This has commonly been the case as occupational schemes have often followed the practice of the state pension scheme and provided for a normal retirement age of 60 for women and 65 for men. Such discrimination on the basis of sex was permitted by the relevant UK Acts of Parliament and EC Directives dealing with equality between the sexes.

39.70   However, in *Barber v Guardian Royal Exchange*[1], the European Court of Justice (ECJ) held that pension rights constituted 'pay' and hence discrimination on the grounds of sex contravenes what is now article 141 of the EU Treaty (formerly art 119 of the Treaty of Rome). However, the decision was expressly stated not to be retrospective and so not to apply to benefits relating to the period before the date of the judgment, 17 May 1990. This means there is an existing, directly enforceable requirement for pension schemes to give equal benefits to male and female employees (eg if a female has a right to retire at age 60 with an unreduced pension, a male must be given the same right). It was unclear whether the equalisation obligation is enforceable against scheme trustees (and hence overrides the terms of the scheme documentation) or just against the employer.

1 [1990] ECR I-1889; [1990] 2 All ER 660, ECJ.

39.71   There have been a number of subsequent decisions of the ECJ in this area, in particular *Coloroll Pension Trustees v Russell*[1].

1 [1994] ECR I-4389; [1994] IRLR 586, ECJ.

39.72   The statutory position in the UK is set out in PA 1995, ss 62–66 (which came into force on 1 January 1996) and the Occupational Pension Schemes (Equal Treatment) Regulations 1995, SI 1995/3183. These require:

(a) full equalisation of benefits back to 17 May 1990 (the date of the decision of the ECJ in Barber); and

(b) equal access to schemes without limit, save for any national time limit on claims.

39.73 Problem areas remain (where further liability could be imposed on schemes), including guaranteed minimum pensions provided in relation to service between 17 May 1990 and 5 April 1997 were not equalised. In practice this means that contracted-out schemes will continue to have unequalised benefits. Commonly, schemes are not dealing with GMP equalisation before a winding up.

39.74 However, the PPF has decided[1] that trustees of schemes (with members with GMPs accrued on or after 17 May 1990) entering into an assessment period will have to consider GMP inequalities when determining the compensation members would be entitled to if the scheme entered the PPF. The PPF believes that trustees can either:

- determine whether a comparator exists for each member and, where does, calculate an equalised amount of PPF compensation allowing for difference in GMP formula; or

- amend the scheme rules to achieved equalisation for GMPs (without determining whether a comparator exists).

In coming to its view the PPF stated that it had 'received advice from its Counsel (Andrew Simmonds QC) that it must adjust compensation to make up for inequalities between men and women caused by their GMP entitlement, where there is a comparator.'

Although the PPF's view on equalising GMPs only applies to trustees of schemes entering into an assessment period, this view may become influential in the wider debate on equalising GMPs.

1 See the PPF's 'Consultation on the requirement under Section 171 of the Pensions Act 2004 to equalise compensation to allow for differences in the GMP formula' – April 2008

OTHER HIDDEN LIABILITIES/BENEFIT CHANGES

39.75 It may be that the stated benefits under the scheme provisions are under or indeed over stated. This could result from:

- ineffective amendments made in the past – see eg *Walker Morris Trustees v Masterson*[1] where Peter Smith J held that some longstanding benefit improvements had not been validly made (because the actuarial advice required under the amendment rule did not seem to have been obtained) and the Australian case of *ING Funds Management v ANZ Nominees*[2] where Barrett J held that a requirement that the responsible entity reasonably con-

siders the change will not adversely affect members' rights' was not satisfied and so the change was ineffective.

- Failure to comply with over-riding legislation – eg sex discrimination provisions (see above) or the other discrimination legislation (eg age).

- Invalidity applying to employer consents – eg In *Gibb v Maidstone and
  Tunbridge Wells NHS Trust*[3], Treacy J reversed a decision by an NHS Trust
  to give the former Chief Executive an 'irrationally generous' compensation
  payment on loss of office. Treacy J commented that in assessing the amount
  of compensation, the non-executive director's 'personal views coloured
  their approach, which was one of wishing to be generous'. The *Gibb* case
  concerned an NHS Trust which, as a public body, was required to exercise
  its powers within the statutory limits and in the public interest in a way that
  is 'reasonable' (ie 'decisions should take into account relevant considerations and exclude irrelevant considerations').

1 [2009] EWHC 1955(Ch); [2009] All ER (D) 38 (Aug) (Peter Smith J).
2 [2009] NSWSC 243; (2009) 27 ACLC 423 (Barrett J).
3 [2009] EWHC 862 (QB); [2009] IRLR 707, [2009] All ER (D) 209 (Apr) (Treacy J).

SURPLUS: WHO HAS THE DISCRETION?

39.76   Having resolved the issue as to whether there is a surplus, the insolvency
practitioner will need to consider whether advantage can be taken of provisions of
the pension scheme relating to refunds on a winding up of the scheme. This will
depend on the wording of the winding-up provision dealing with augmentation of
benefits to members (subject to Inland Revenue limits) out of the surplus before
any refund to employers is made. There are three common alternatives:

(a)   surplus to be allocated at the discretion of the trustees alone (this will
       become a discretion of the independent trustee);

(b)   discretion to be exercised by the trustees with the consent or approval of the
       principal company; or

(c)   augmentation only at the request or option of the principal company.

39.77   Section 73(5) of PA 1995 used to provide that if any person other than
the trustees has the power to apply the assets of the scheme in respect of pensions
or other benefits then the power passed to the trustees. The better view was that
the Section did not override any power (or need for consent) given to the
employers. Instead s 73(5) was best seen as designed to be able to direct sanctions against trustees if the priority order in s 73 was not followed[1].

In any event s 73(5) has now been repealed and not included in the new substituted s 73 under PA 2004.

1 See further para 30.57 of *The Guide to the Pensions Act 1995* (Tolley Publishing, 1995).

39.78   In some (unusual) circumstances it can be a difficult question of interpretation of the trust deed as to whether any discretions (or requirement of

consent) given to the principal company are vested in it in a fiduciary capacity (in which case they will, where the PA 1995, s 25(2)(b) applies (see para 30.80 above), pass to any independent trustee appointed by the Pensions Regulator).

39.79 Usually it is to be anticipated that such requirements for consent will not be fiduciary, although they may be subject to good faith duties (the duty not to Act capriciously) as laid down in *Imperial Group Pension Trust Ltd v Imperial Tobacco Ltd*[1] – see further paras 17.12 and 26.7 above.

1 [1991] 2 All ER 597 (Browne-Wilkinson V-C).

39.80 Most powers and discretions of a company in relation to a pension trust are beneficial. Thus, a power to agree with the trustee to augmentations of benefits or to amendments to a scheme will almost always be a beneficial power – see *Imperial Group Pensions Trust Ltd v Imperial Tobacco Ltd*[1], *Mettoy Pension Trustees Ltd v Evans*[2] and *Re Courage Group's Pension Schemes*[3].

Similarly in Australia – see *Lock v Westpac Banking Corpn*[4] and *Ansett Australia Ground Staff Superannuation Plan Pty Ltd v Ansett Australia Ltd*[5].

1 [1991] 2 All ER 597 at 604 (Browne-Wilkinson V-C).
2 [1991] 2 All ER 513 at 551 (Warner J).
3 [1987] 1 All ER 528 at 544 (Millett J).
4 (1991) 25 NSWLR 593; [1991] PLR 167 (Waddell CJ in Eq).
5 [2002] VSC 576 (Warren J.

39.81 However, exceptionally employer powers may be fiduciary, depending on the circumstances. In 1991 in *Mettoy Pension Trustees Ltd v Evans*[1] for example, a power of the company to consent to augmentations in a winding-up was held by Warner J to be fiduciary. However this was in the unusual circumstances that the previous provisions had vested this augmentation power in the trustees and there was no evidence that the trustees had considered the implications of the change when agreeing to amend the scheme.

In 1997 in *National Grid v Laws*[2] Robert Walker J (who had been one of the counsel involved in *Mettoy*) commented (at page 177) that:

> 'Had *Imperial Tobacco*[3] been decided earlier and been cited in *Mettoy*, Warner J might possibly have come to a different conclusion as to whether the employer's power should be classified as fiduciary.'

See further the discussion of *Mettoy* at para 30.82 above.

1 [1991] 2 All ER 513 (Warner J).
2 [1997] PLR 157; [1997] OPLR 161 (Robert Walker J).
3 *Imperial Group Pensions Trust Ltd v Imperial Tobacco Ltd* [1991] 2 All ER 597 (Browne-Wilkinson V-C).

39.82 In 2008 in *Bridge Trustees Ltd v Noel Penny (Turbines) Ltd*[1] Judge Purle QC (sitting as an additional Judge of the High Court) followed *Mettoy* and held that a power to distribute surplus given to the employer was a fiduciary power. He further held that the purpose of the statutory regime was to remove from the employer the power to distribute a surplus. This meant that the court could appoint a new trustee to exercise the power (the company had ceased to be in receivership, so the obligation under the Pensions Act 1995 to have an independent trustee – see Chapter 30 (Independent trustee obligations) below – had ended).

Judge Purle QC stated that:

> 'Para 11 Under the [previous] statutory regime, where an independent trustee is acting, any power which the scheme confers on the employer (otherwise than as trustee of the scheme), and which is exercisable by him at his discretion but only as trustee of the power, may be exercised only by the independent trustee: Pensions Act 1995 as amended, section 25(2)(b). Similar provisions applied to the earlier legislation: see, for example, section 57D(5) of the 1975 Act as amended. In the light of the decision of Warner J in *Mettoy Pension Trustees Ltd. v Evans* [1990] 1 WLR 1587, it is doubtful whether an insolvency practitioner could exercise the employer's rights even without these statutory bars, as the power is not an asset of the employer distributable amongst its creditors, but a fiduciary power: p. 1616F. The point is nevertheless reinforced by these provisions, and the conferring of that power on the independent trustee clearly needed legislative input.
>
> Para 15 It is evident that the statutory policy is to remove from an insolvent company the power to determine the destination of a pension surplus, once an insolvency practitioner has been appointed. The duties of an insolvency practitioner are to get the best result for creditors, and that is obviously inconsistent with the exercise of a fiduciary power in favour of a class which includes the employer company as one only of its objects. That observation seems to me to apply with equal force once an insolvency practitioner has ceased to act, but the insolvency remains. The pressure on the directors to have recourse to the fund to relieve the company's own difficulties (having regard to what they may erroneously perceive or be advised to be their duties as directors) may be too much to resist. At the other extreme, the directors may, as disaffected ex-employees and members of the Scheme, be tempted to apply the whole of the surplus for their own benefit. Either way, the need for an independent person to exercise the power is obvious.
>
> Para 18 It is contended by Mr. Rawlings for the Claimant that the power of determining the destination of the surplus is clearly a fiduciary power, and, as the Defendant is required to make a selection among the specified objects, that power can fairly be described as a trust power. It is a power which the Defendant is bound to exercise in some way and has no discretion not to exercise. I agree.'

Judge Purle QC's comments that the employer's power in relation to surplus could be seen as fiduciary seems odd (see paras 39.75- 39.77 above) and need to be treated with care. The company did not appear and was not represented before the court.

1 [2008] EWHC 2054 (Ch); [2008] PLR 345, (22 August 2008) (Judge Purle QC sitting as an additional Judge of the High Court).

39.83   In *Scully v Coley*[1] the Privy Council dealt with an appeal from the courts in Jamaica concerning the destination of a surplus on the winding-up of a pension scheme that had been established by Gillette. The main thrust of the decision concerns the meaning of who is a member of the scheme, but the Privy

Council also briefly commented on the nature of employer's powers. Lord Collins gave the judgment and commented (at para [47]):

> '47   The final question is whether the provision that the allocation by the Administrator under Rule 12(c) is 'subject to the approval of [Gillette]' gives Gillette a fiduciary power to withhold approval, with the consequence (say the respondents) that the trustees could make no allocation, which would then be left to the court: *McPhail v Doulton* [1971] AC 424 at 457.
>
> 48 This question was raised in argument before Brooks J and the Court of Appeal, but was not the subject of decision. On this point the Board is satisfied that the appellants are right. The argument between the parties was centred on the question whether the power was a fiduciary power, and their Lordships were referred to several cases on the distinction between a power in relation to which the duty of the employer was limited to a duty of good faith and a power in respect of which the employer was a fiduciary and which was to be exercised solely in the interests of the objects of the power: *Icarus (Hertford) Ltd v Driscoll* [1990] PLR 1; *Mettoy Pension Trustees Ltd v. Evans* [1990] 1 WLR 1587; *Imperial Group Pension Trust Ltd. v. Imperial Tobacco Ltd.* [1991] 1 WLR 589; *Re William Makin & Son Ltd* [1992] PLR 177; *British Coal Corp v British Coal Staff Superannuation Scheme Trustees* [1994] ICR 537 (overruled on other grounds in *National Grid Co plc v Mayes* [2001] UKHL 20, [2001] 1 WLR 864 (HL)).
>
> 49 The question is not primarily whether the power is a fiduciary power (as the respondents say) or an administrative power (as the appellants say), since there is no necessary contrast between the two. In *Weinberger v Inglis* [1919] AC 606 (a decision which it would now be impossible to justify on the facts: the General Purposes Committee of the Stock Exchange was held entitled to exclude British naturalised subjects of German origin from membership) the power to admit persons to membership was held (at 640) to be both an administrative power and a fiduciary power. The real question is what is the purpose for which the power was granted. It is not necessary to decide in what circumstances Gillette could withhold approval of allocation under Rule 12(c). The reason is that their Lordships are satisfied that the power to withhold approval could not be used to alter the allocation to the "then Members" and thereby to vary the Rules. There is already an express power in Rule 12(a) to change, modify or discontinue the Plan at any time. Gillette has not done so, and their Lordships consider it difficult (as the Board did in *Air Jamaica Ltd v Charlton* [1999] 1 WLR 1399, at 1411) to see how the Plan could lawfully be amended once it had been discontinued. Gillette has been kept informed at all times of the intentions of the Administrator and of the trustees, and is a party to these proceedings. Gillette's failure to withhold approval cannot be regarded as a refusal to exercise a trust power so as to give the court the power to vary the provisions for allocation.'

Unfortunately, the decision of the Privy Council does not give much guidance as to the reason why the employer in that case (Gillette) could not withhold its consent to the use of the surplus to increase benefits for members.

1 [2009] UKPC 29, PC.

39.84   Trustees exercising a trust power do so in a fiduciary capacity (ie they must generally act for a proper purpose – often in the best interests of the beneficiaries of the trust).

39.85 It is a difficult question as to whether it is proper for trustees to take account of how the surplus has arisen (ie who provided the funding of the scheme) and the fact that the employer is probably a residuary beneficiary (as required by the Inland Revenue since 1970 for approved schemes). The argument is that the employees/beneficiaries have received all the benefits to which they are entitled and that in a balance of cost scheme (such as that described by Scott J (as he then was) in *Davis v Richards & Wallington Industries*[1] any surplus represents overfunding by the employer.

1 [1990] 1 WLR 1511 (Scott J) – see para 39.53 above.

39.86 However, there is an argument that the primary purpose of the scheme is to provide benefits for the employees/beneficiaries and not the employer. This would lead to the conclusion that trustees should give more weight to the interests of the members, as opposed to the employer, perhaps only refunding amounts to the employer if it were not possible to increase benefits for members (eg because of Inland Revenue limits).

39.87 Some guidance is given by Sir Donald Nicholls V-C (as he then was) in *Thrells Ltd (1974) Pension Scheme v Lomas*[1]. In this case the company was the sole trustee and the liquidator had arranged for its powers to be surrendered to the court (the requirement to appoint an independent trustee under SSPA 1975, s 57C did not apply because the company entered liquidation before s 57C came into force). Sir Donald Nicholls V-C decided that the court would exercise the discretion to increase benefits in the manner in which a reasonable trustee could be expected to act, having regard to all the material circumstances. These circumstances included the position of the employer. Nicholls V-C listed the material circumstances as including:

(i)   the scope of the power;

(ii) the purpose of the power;

(iii) the source of the surplus;

(iv) the size of the surplus and the impact of the Social Security Act 1990, s 11(3) (see above);

(v)   the financial position of the employer; and

(vi) the needs of the members of the scheme.

As a result Nicholls V-C decided that the surplus, after securing LPI increases on pensions in payment (see above) should be used to provide LPI increases on deferred pensions, with the remaining balance (about half the surplus) being paid to the company to benefit its creditors.

1 [1992] OPLR 22 (Sir Donald Nicholls V-C).

39.88 The legal position on this issue is probably that the trustees have been given the discretion and that it would be very difficult to challenge the exercise of their discretion. *Mettoy Pension Trustees Ltd v Evans*[1] indicates that such a challenge will only succeed if the trustees have acted improperly or have considered matters which they should not have considered or have failed to consider matters which they should have considered and that this has caused them to reach a decision which they would not otherwise have reached.

1 [1991] 2 All ER 513 (Warner J) and later cases, such as *Edge v Pensions Ombudsman* [2000] Ch 602; [1999] 4 All ER 546, CA.

39.89   *Thrells* indicates that it is proper for the trustees to consider the interests of the employer (as a beneficiary) in exercising this discretion. Similarly Hart J in *Alexander Forbes Trustee Services Ltd v Halliwell*[1].

More recently in *Foster Wheeler Ltd v Hanley*[2] Arden LJ in the Court of Appeal commented that providing windfall benefits to certain members in excess of their *Barber* rights was 'unfair to the company and potentially unfair to other members'.

This suggests that courts construing scheme rules and trustees exercising their powers in the future may have to also consider the interest of the employer and not just scheme members.

This is another clear move away from the notion that trustees should be mainly concerned with looking after the interests of the scheme members and should ignore the interest of employers, unless this potentially has an adverse effect on members.

See generally the author's article '*Trustees' duties to employers: the scope of the duty of pension trustees*'[1].

1 [2003] EWHC 1685; [2003] OPLR 355 (Hart J).
2 [2009] EWCA Civ 651; [2009] All ER (D) 82 (Jul), CA.
3 (2006) 20 Trust Law International 21.

39.90   Any amount which is found to be repayable to the insolvent company will be an asset of the insolvent company and, in effect, come under the control of the relevant insolvency practitioner. In the case of a receiver this will depend on the terms of the security document (charge or debenture) under which the receiver is appointed, but this will usually extend to cover future property (such as an interest in any refund under a pension scheme), even property arising after the subsequent liquidation of the company. The trustees are obliged to deduct tax at 35% before making any payment (see para 39.55 above).

39.91   Care may be needed if the pension scheme contains a provision entitling the trustee to forfeit a benefit if any attempt is made to assign the benefit. It is possible that such a provision could apply not only to benefits otherwise payable to individual members, but also to any employing company. The appointment of a receiver usually operates as crystallisation of the floating charge in the relevant security document into a fixed charge which possibly operates on an equitable assignment of the assets within the charge. The appointment of a liquidator does not operate as an assignment but beneficial ownership of the company's assets does cease to rest in the company – see *IRC v Olive Mills Ltd*[1] and *Ayerst v C & K (Construction) Ltd*[2].

1 [1963] 1 WLR 712 (Buckley J).
2 [1976] AC 167, HL – see also para 41.41 below.

39.92 It is unlikely that the provisions of ss 91 to 94 of PA 1995 prohibiting assignment and forfeiture are applicable to the potential benefit to an employer. They are intended to deal with benefits payable to or in respect of a member.

39.93 Section 91(1) refers to where a 'person' is 'entitled, or has an accrued right to a pension'. An employer will usually be within the meaning of 'person' (see the Interpretation Act 1978) and the term 'pension' is widely defined to include any benefit payable under the scheme – PA 1995, s 94(2). However, the better view is that these provisions should be limited to benefits payable to or in respect of members even though they are not expressly so restricted.

39.94 The terms of the scheme often give the discretion over any surplus to the trustees but require them to consult with the employer. In this case, it is probably an implication that such consultations are entered into in good faith. For a discussion of the consultation obligation (in relation to the statutory obligation to consult about a statement of investment principles) see Sir Andrew Morritt V-C in *Pitmans Trustees Ltd v Telecommunications Group plc*[1].

A consultation obligation could be interpreted as requiring the trustees to give reasons why they have reached a particular decision. This would be contrary to the usual position (that trustees are not obliged to give reasons) – see the decision of the Court of Appeal in *Re Londonderry's Settlement*[2], applied in a pensions context by Rattee J in *Wilson v Law Debenture Corpn plc*[3]. More recent caselaw indicates that this position on giving reasons may be moving.

1 [2004] EWHC 181 (Ch); [2005] OPLR 1; [2004] PLR 213 (Morritt V-C).
2 [1965] Ch 918, CA.
3 [1995] OPLR 103 (Rattee J).

39.95 The book, *The Law of Occupational Pension Schemes* by Nigel Inglis-Jones QC refers (at para 12–34) to an unreported decision of Sir Nicolas Browne-Wilkinson V-C in *Re Laker Airways Pension and Life Assurance Scheme*[1] as authority that once consultation has taken place, and due weight has been given to the relevant representations made, the discretion of the trustees is unfettered.

1 23 July 1986, unreported.

CHAPTER 40

Overseas employees and insolvencies

40.1   Cross border (ie non-UK) employment and pensions issues can arise in insolvencies. Perhaps the main examples are where:

- a UK company enters a UK insolvency process, but has employees based outside the United Kingdom; or

- a UK company enters an overseas insolvency process, either with employees in the UK or overseas; or

- a non-UK company with employees in the UK enters an insolvency process outside the UK; or

- a non-UK company with employees in the UK enters an insolvency process in the UK; or

- a non-UK company with employees outside the UK enters an insolvency process in the UK.

UK COMPANY AND INSOLVENCY PROCESS – OVERSEAS EMPLOYEES

40.2   Where a UK company enters a UK insolvency process, but has employees based outside the United Kingdom, the usual rules for dealing with the employees will apply.

There will, however be a potential conflict of laws between the English law[1] of the insolvency and the laws of the place where the employee works. At one end of the spectrum will be where (say) the contract of employment is governed by the overseas law and the employee was hired and worked there. Generally, the governing law of the employment relationship is irrelevant for purposes of ERA 1996[2]. But in the case mentioned, there is little real connection with the UK and so the law governing the employment relationship will be the overseas law and the UK employment legislation will not apply.

There may be cases where this is not so clear (eg pilots who work out of several bases, individuals hired by UK embassies etc).

The position of such employees was considered by the House of Lords in

Lawson v Serco Ltd[3], dealing with the territorial impact of the UK's employment legislation in such cases.

1 This Chapter does not deal with Scottish or Northern Ireland law.
2 ERA 1996, s 204.
3 [2006] UKHL 3; [2006] 1 All ER 823, HL. For a later application of these principles, see e.g. *Burke v The British Council* [2006] All ER (D) 205 (Dec), EAT.

40.3 As a matter of principle, the claims and rights of such overseas employees should be dealt with in the UK insolvency in the same way as for UK employees. An analogy can be drawn with the extra-territorial effect of the insolvency provisions dealing with transactions at an undervalue – see the decision of the Court of Appeal in *Re Paramount Airways Ltd*[1] (cited by the House of Lords in *Lawson v Serco*[2]).

1 [1993] Ch 223, CA.
2 [2006] UKHL 3; [2006] 1 All ER 823; [2006] IRLR 289, HL. and see para 13.26 above.

40.4 Claims of the overseas employees will be claimable in the usual way in the UK insolvency. If the overseas law would give rise to a different legal claim compared to the UK equivalent, in principle it is the overseas claim that is provable (assuming it is legally binding).

40.5 In practice, issues may arise in relation to the impact of the overseas law (e.g. does it grant a stay on legal proceedings to a UK liquidator or administrator in the same way as English law? – this will depend on the overseas law and the degree to which it assists a UK IP).

In relation to employees and pensions, one issue is how the applicable UK insolvency principles apply in cases where the employment relationship (ie the employment contract and applicable employment legislation) is governed by the overseas law. Dealing with these in turn:

Insolvency effect	Impact of overseas employment
1. Effect of insolvency on employment Does the appointment of the IP terminate employment? (eg a court liquidator)	This looks primarily to be a contractual issue and so should be governed by the overseas law (subject to the decision of the UK insolvency practitioner eg to arrange for the company to terminate employment anyway).
2. Preferential debts· • wages and salary/ holiday pay	See Chapters 9 and 10 above. There is no reason why overseas employees should not be preferential creditors. The £800 limit will apply – claims not in sterling are converted using the exchange rate at the insolvency date – rules 2.86 and 4.91, Insolvency Rules 1986 and *Re Lines Bros Ltd* [1983] Ch 1, CA.

Insolvency effect	Impact of overseas employment
• statutory claims (eg pay for time off under ERA 1996 or a protective award under TULRCA 1992)	The statutory claims seem unlikely to apply. There does not seem to be room for the courts to extend this by analogy to the equivalent claim under the overseas laws. But see *Re MG Rover Espana SA* noted below.
• occupational pensions	Preferential debt only applies if due to an 'occupational pension scheme' as defined in s 1, PSA 1993. This term now (since the changes made by PA 2004 from September 2005) excludes a scheme established outside the UK but in another EU member state (see Chapter 2 above).
3. National Insurance Fund Payment by the Secretary of State:	ECJ case law is unclear, but obligation will fall on UK even for overseas employees, unless a branch or 'activities' overseas – see the ECJ in *Mosbaek*, *Everson* and *Holmqvist* (discussed in Chapter 12 above).
• arrears of pay /holiday pay	There is no reason why overseas employees should not claim. The cap on a week's pay will apply (unclear how claims not in sterling are converted).
statutory claims (eg statutory minimum notice, basic award for unfair dismissal etc)	The statutory claims seem unlikely to apply. There does not seem to be room for the courts to extend this by analogy to the equivalent claim under the overseas laws.
4. Carrying on business:	There is no reason why overseas employees should not be covered in the same way as UK.
• insolvency expenses	It may be that the insolvency expenses issue (see Chapter 17 above) can depend on whether or not there is a moratorium against legal proceedings (which may not apply in the overseas jurisdiction).
• adoption of employment contracts	The adoption provisions in IA 1986 are not limited to UK employees. *Re Antal* [2003] 2 BCLC 406 (noted above in Chapter 18) is an example involving whether adoption would affect missing French employees of an English company.

639

Insolvency effect	Impact of overseas employment
5. TUPE	TUPE 2006 only applies to a transfer of an undertaking or business 'situated immediately before the transfer in the United Kingdom'- reg 3(1)(a).
6. PAYE and NI	The normal cross border rules on UK taxes will apply. Overseas law may impose an obligation on the IP to pay overseas equivalents.
7. Pensions ● IP powers	See the chart in Chapter 31. IP powers to control overseas trusts etc will depend on the law of the scheme
● PPF	Schemes with a main administration outside the UK are outside the PPF
● Section 75, PA 1995	s 75 does not apply to schemes which are not UK tax registered. So unlikely to apply to an overseas pension scheme.
● tPR moral hazard powers	tPR moral hazard powers (CNs and FSDs) do not apply to schemes which do not have (and never have had) UK tax registration (see Chapter 37 above). So unlikely to apply to an overseas pension scheme.

PRIORITY ORDER – PREFERENTIAL DEBTS

40.6   In administrations there seems to be some power for the courts to approve actions of administrators in relation to overseas claims (particularly of employees) if to do would be in the interest of the administration (as opposed to just paying creditors). This is under the power in para 66 of Schedule B1 to the Insolvency Act 1986 for administrators to make payments if they 'think it likely to assist achievement of the purpose of the administration'.

40.7   In *Re MG Rover Espana SA*[1], Judge Norris QC allowed an English administrator appointed over overseas companies to make payments to overseas employees that would be outside the priority order under English law.

He held that para 66 of Schedule B1 to the Insolvency Act 1986 permitted an administrator to depart from the strict ranking of claims if he thought it likely to assist achievement of the broader purpose of administration[2]. In this case there was a concern that the overseas employees would otherwise seek to wind-up the overseas companies, resulting in them ceasing to be able to trade (together with the other group companies) and so reducing the prospects for saving the businesses as a going concern.

1   [2006] EWHC 3426; [2005] BPIR 1162; [2006] BCC 599 (Judge Norris QC). Noted in
        (2005) 21 Insolvency Law & Practice 91. Also cited as *Re MG Rover Belux SA/NV* [2006]
        EWHC 3618 (Ch) (29 March 2006),
2   *Re Mount Banking Plc* (Unreported, 25 January 1994), *Re WBSL Realisations 1992 Ltd*
        [1995] BCC 1118 and *Re TXU UK Ltd (In Administration)* [2002] EWHC 2784; [2003]
        2 BCLC 341 applied.

40.8   Similarly, in *Re Collins & Aikman Europe SA*[1], Lindsay J authorised the English-appointed administrators of a group of companies to be able to carry out assurances they had given to some creditors to respect some provisions of the laws of other European jurisdictions even though they differed from English law (the law of the main proceedings).

Lindsay J authorised this using the general powers in para 66 of Schedule B1. The administrators had given oral assurances to some creditors to avoid the risk of them issuing proceedings in any of the countries where a relevant company had an establishment. The assurance was that their financial positions in as creditors under the relevant local law would as far as possible be respected in the English administration.

1 [2006] EWHC 1343; [2007] 1 BCLC 182; [2006] BCC 861 (Lindsay J).

UK COMPANY – OVERSEAS INSOLVENCY

40.9   A UK registered company may be placed in an insolvency process outside the UK. This is now more likely to occur than before under the various cross border insolvency provisions, in particular under:

● the EC Regulation on Insolvency Proceedings 2000 (EC 1346/2000), for proceedings in another EU state; or

● the Cross-Border Insolvency Regulations 2006 (SI 2006/1030) dealing with the application of the Uncitral model law on cross border insolvency.

These provisions are complex (and outside the scope of this book). Broadly they allow for cross border insolvencies and can involve an insolvency process in one country of a company incorporated in another.

For further detail see Roy Goode *Principles of Corporate Insolvency* (Sweet & Maxwell, 2005) and Look Chan Ho *Cross border insolvency: a commentary on the UNCITRAL Model Law* (Globe Publishing 2006).

40.10   In such cases, the overseas insolvency law will tend to govern proof and enforcement of claims etc, subject to any insolvency proceedings being opened in the UK. The relevant UK employment laws will, as the law of the Member State applicable to the contract of employment, apply to the UK employees[1].

Under the EC Regulation, the overseas proceedings will apply in the UK, including whether there is a stay on other proceedings (article 4). Secondary proceedings can be opened in the UK, but these can only be winding-up proceedings (ie presumably a liquidation)[2].

In secondary proceedings, UK rules on set-off will apply as a substantive rule of English law – see article 4 of the EC Regulation and *Re Bank of Credit and Commerce International SA (No 10)*[3].

1 See article 10 of the EC Regulation.
2 See article 3(3) of the EC Regulation and the comment in *Re MG Rover Espana SA* [2006] EWHC 3426; [2005] BPIR 1162; [2006] BCC 599 (Judge Norris QC) at para 9.
3 [1997] Ch 213, 246 (Sir Richard Scott V-C)

40.11 There will be impacts (outside the immediate insolvency regime) in the UK of an overseas insolvency, including on:

• claims on the national insurance fund;

• transfer of liabilities under TUPE; and

• the impact on any UK pension schemes (in particular will an assessment period start?).

NATIONAL INSURANCE FUND

40.12 As mentioned in Chapter 13 above, the government guarantee out of the national insurance fund can extend to employers which are companies incorporated outside Great Britain. However, in order for a claim to be made, the company must, under, ERA 1996, s 183 (and s 166(5)), have entered insolvency proceedings within Great Britain.

Following the decision of the ECJ in *Everson*[1] and the amendments made to the 1980 Employment Insolvency Directive by Directive 2002/74/EC, it seems that this requirement could contravene article 9 of the Employment Insolvency Directive – see Chapters 12 and 13 above. This requires Member States to ensure that decisions taken in insolvency proceedings in other Member States are taken into account when determining the employer's state of insolvency for the purposes of the Directive (see para 12.4 above).

1 [1999] ECR I-8903; [2000] IRLR 202 (Case C-198/98), ECJ.
2 Article 4 of the EC Regulation.

40.13 The fact that making a winding-up order in England and Wales will enable employees to make claims under these sections may be a ground on which a winding-up petition may be granted against a company incorporated outside Great Britain (see *Re Eloc Electro-Optieck and Communicatie BV*[1]).

This may require a secondary winding-up proceeding in the UK, which may not be in the general interest of the insolvency proceedings – see the comments of Judge Norris QC in *Re MG Rover Espana SA*[2], and Lindsay J in *Re Collins & Aikman Europe SA*[3].

1 [1982] Ch 43 (Nourse J).
2 [2006] EWHC 3426; [2005] BPIR 1162; [2006] BCC 599 (Judge Norris QC).
3 [2006] EWHC 1343; [2007] 1 BCLC 182; [2006] BCC 861 (Lindsay J).

SECONDARY LIQUIDATION – FRUSTRATING MAIN PROCEEDINGS?

40.14 It has been pointed out that a secondary liquidation could frustrate the primary proceedings[1] – for example if there was a Dutch administration as the main proceeding, employees in the UK may want to try to put the company into a UK insolvency process in order to be able to claim on the National Insurance Fund or put the pension scheme into the PPF.

But where the EC Regulation on Insolvency proceedings applies, the only secondary proceeding available is a liquidation[2] (see para 40.10 above). A liquidation would mean that the company needed (in general) to cease trading and so may not be consistent with the trading aspirations of the Dutch administrator in the main proceedings.

1 See for example Gerard McCormack, '*Jurisdictional Competition and Forum Shopping in Insolvency Proceedings*' [2009] CLJ 169 at page 195.
2 See article 3(3)of the EC Regulation and the comment in *Re MG Rover Espana SA* [2006] EWHC 3426; [2005] BPIR 1162; [2006] BCC 599 (Judge Norris QC) at para 9.

40.15 This does seem to be an unfortunate effect of the legislation. The point could be resolved if the UK legislation, both for the National Insurance Fund (ERA 1996) and the PPF (PA 2004) was amended to recognise overseas insolvencies.

40.16 In *Re Nortel Networks SA*[1] Patten J granted an application by English administrators for the court to issue letters of request to courts throughout the EU asking for the English administrators to be told of any application for secondary proceedings to be opened and to allow the administrators to make submissions if any such application was made.

Patten J noted that the administrators had already obtained an order from Blackburne J 'authorising the Joint Administrators in their discretion to make payments out of their assets to employees and preferential creditors of the relevant Companies corresponding to the amounts they would receive in the event that secondary insolvency proceedings were to be commenced in other Member States'[2].

1 [2009] EWHC 206 (Ch); [2009] All ER (D) 128 (Feb) (Patten J). Discussed by Adam Al-Attar in '*Using and losing secondary proceedings*' (2009) 22 Insolvency Intelligence 76.
2 Presumably in line with Lindsay J's decision in *Re Collins & Aikman Europe SA* [2006] EWHC 1343.

40.17 Patten J noted the obligation in article 31 of the EC Regulation on Insolvency Proceedings 2000 for any liquidator in secondary or ancillary proceedings to co-operate with the liquidator in the main proceedings. But he noted that cooperation may not be enough, given that the appointment of a secondary liquidator may harm the prospects in the English administration. Patten J held:

'12. But for this obligation to be effective it is obviously desirable for the court dealing with an application to open secondary insolvency proceedings to be provided with the reasons why such proceedings might have an adverse impact on the main proceedings. An example of the advantage of permitting the Joint Administrators in English main proceedings to be heard in relation to the opening

643

of secondary proceedings in another Member State can be found in the decision of the Court of Appeal of Versailles in *Rover France SAS* [2006] I.L.Pr. 32. The court in its judgment at paragraphs 44-47 said this:

"44. The Advocate General requests the Court to apply the Regulation in its entirety, and therefore to open secondary insolvency proceedings pursuant to Art 27.

45. However, the opening of secondary insolvency proceedings is only desirable if it is purposeful, which the applicant must demonstrate.

46. Messrs Lomas and Hunt, in their official capacity [as joint administrators appointed by the English High Court], argue without contradiction that the insolvency proceedings are progressing without difficulty, and that they are preserving the interests of all concerned; they hold that single proceedings permit continuation of activity, and hence sale of vehicles over a longer period, and allow coordination of these sales operations throughout the territory of Europe; in their eyes secondary insolvency proceedings would multiply costs and formalities to no purpose.

47. It does not appear to be demonstrated that the opening of secondary insolvency proceedings would offer advantages in this case, in particular by improving the protection of local interests or the realisation of assets."

The application to open secondary proceedings was therefore refused.'

40.18   Patten J also considered that the right for the insolvency practitioner to apply for a stay of the secondary proceedings (under article 33) was not enough. He commented:

'13. There is, of course, provision under Article 33(1) of the EC Regulation for the court which has opened the secondary proceedings to stay the process of liquidation at the request of the liquidator in the main proceedings subject to suitable measures being taken to guarantee the interests of creditors in the secondary proceedings. This would therefore halt the realisation of assets located in the State of the secondary proceedings. But it would not prevent the continuation of winding-up proceedings in the Member States in which each of the Companies is incorporated (see *Re Collins & Aikman*, Higher Regional Court of Graz, 20 October 2005, 3 R 149/05, reported in NZI 2006 vol 11 p.660) and the effect of the commencement and continuation of such proceedings is likely to be to cause the relevant Company to cease to trade save for the purposes of winding up. The Joint Administrators take the view that the continuation of trading is necessary in order to achieve the re-organisation of the Nortel Group which is planned.'

WILL A UK COURT AGREE TO A SECONDARY LIQUIDATION?

40.20   It may well be the case that relevant parties (e.g. employees or trustees) seek to wind-up a company in the UK so that this will operate as a trigger under the relevant UK statutes, either:

- for a section 75 debt to arise or the relevant pensions scheme to be able to enter the PPF; or

- for a claim to be made on the National Insurance Fund.

40.21   It is clear that such an ancillary benefit for an employee is sufficient to found a winding-up petition and the making of a winding-up order by the court (even if the company has no assets itself within the jurisdiction)– see *Re Eloc Electro-Optieck and Communicatie BV*[1]. The petitioners may need to give an indemnity to the Official Receiver for any liability or cost he may incur in acting as liquidator – see the last paragraph of the judgment.

This operates to satisfy the general rule that a creditor's petition will be dismissed unless the creditor can show that he will have a tangible benefit from liquidation – *Re Crigglestone Coal Co Ltd*[2].

1 [1982] Ch 43 (Nourse J).
2 [1906] 2 Ch 327 (Buckley J).

40.22   However, it is clear that the decision of the court whether or not to grant a winding-order is discretionary – IA 1986, s 125(1). See also *Re P & J Macrae Ltd*[1].

Generally the rule is that a winding-order will follow if a creditor has standing and the company is insolvent unless there is some reason why it should not. The burden of arguing against is with the company as to why an order should not be made – *Re Lummus Agricultural Services Ltd*[2]. The objectors also need to give reasons (at least if otherwise an order would be made) – see *Re J D Swain*[3] and *Re Television Parlour plc*[4].

1 [1961] 1 WLR 229, CA.
2 [2001] 1 BCLC 137; [1999] BCC 953 at pages 956 and 957 (Park J).
3 [1965] 1 WLR 909, CA.
4 (1988) 4 BCC 95 (Peter Gibson J).

40.23   Having said that, in the case of a multi-national insolvency, it may well be the case that the company (acting (say) through the equivalent of an administrator) wishes to continue to trade, taking the view this is in the best interests of the creditors as a whole. In this case, it seems likely that the UK court will need to balance:

- the arguments of the overseas insolvency practitioner (to continue to trade etc);

against

- the interests and desires of the UK employees (to put the relevant pension scheme into the PPF or make a claim on the national insurance fund).

As mentioned above, a secondary winding-up proceeding in the UK may not be in the general interest of the insolvency proceedings – see the comments of Judge Norris QC in *Re MG Rover Espana SA*[1], and Lindsay J in *Re Collins & Aikman Europe SA*[2].

This may be a reason why the court may refuse to make a winding-up order or may adjourn the application. It is clear that a creditor seeking a winding-up order is exercising, in effect, a class right belonging to all the creditors – see Buckley J in *Re Crigglestone Coal Co Ltd*[1].

1 [2006] EWHC 3426; [2005] BPIR 1162; [2006] BCC 599 (Judge Norris QC).
2 [2006] EWHC 1343; [2007] 1 BCLC 182; [2006] BCC 861 (Lindsay J).
3 [1906] 2 Ch 327 (Buckley J).

40.24 For example in Australia a winding up application was adjourned, the where the evidence was that the creditors have a better prospect of payment without winding up. In *Re Presha Engineering (Aust) Pty Ltd*[1], Murphy J acknowledged that an adjournment may be justified: 'in exceptional circumstances where there would be better prospects existing for the creditors as a whole if the company were allowed to trade on than there would be if the company were wound up.'

Generally the cases indicate that in disputed winding-up cases (not involving overseas element) the wishes of the majority in number of value of the creditors will be extremely important and will normally prevail – *Re Crigglestone Coal Co. Ltd*. But this is not simply a headcount of value or number – see for example *Re ABC Coupler & Engineering Co Ltd*[2].

See also *Re P & J Macrae Ltd*[3]; *Re Southard & Co Ltd*[4]; *Re Vuma Ltd*[5]; *Re Falcon RJ Developments Ltd*[6] and *Re Lummus Agricultural Services Ltd*[7].

For other cases see *Re Television Parlour plc*[8]; *Re HJ Tomkins & Son Ltd*[9]; *Re Leigh Estates (UK) Ltd*[10] and *Re Demaglass Holdings Ltd*[11].

1 (1983) 1 ACLC 675 at 677 (Murphy J).
2 [1961] 1 WLR 243 (Pennycuick J).
3 [1961] 1 WLR 229, CA.
4 [1979] 1 WLR 546 at page 550, CA.
5 [1960] 1 WLR 1283, [1960] 3 All ER 629, CA.
6 [1987] BCLC 437 at pages 440 to 446 (Vinelott J).
7 [1999] BCC 953 (Park J).
8 (1988) 4 BCC 95 (Peter Gibson J).
9 [1990] BCLC 76 (Hoffmann J).
10 [1994] BCC 292 (Richard Sykes QC, sitting as a deputy High Court judge).
11 [2001] 2 BCLC 633 (Neuberger J).

40.25 There is some case law saying that court may refuse a UK winding-up order if it was more convenient for a winding-up order to be made in another jurisdiction. The Court of Appeal so held in *Re Harrods (Buenos Aires) Ltd*[1].

Generally such a forum non-conveniens argument may now be inconsistent with article 2 of the EC Judgments Regulation[2] (formerly the Brussels Convention) – see the decision of the ECJ in *Owusu v Jackson*[3] – but the Regulation does not apply to insolvency proceedings[4].

1 [1992] Ch 72, CA.
2 Council Regulation 44/2001/EC.
3 [2005] QB 801, case C-281/02, ECJ.
4 See Article 1.2(b).

40.26 There does not seem to be a direct case where the interests of the employees have been weighed directly against the interests of other creditors generally such as would apply here.

In *Re Leigh Estates*[1], Richard Sykes QC (sitting as a deputy High Court judge) refused to grant a winding-up petition where the bulk of creditors opposed the petition and where the petitioner council wanted a winding-up because it considered it more likely that this would make the receiver liable for rates. The process of realisation would be disturbed. Depending on the facts, there looks to be a direct analogy here with employees or trustees.

1 [1994] BCC 292 (Richard Sykes QC, sitting as a deputy High Court judge).

40.27   In some cases, the court may be prepared to grant an adjournment instead of making winding-up orders straight way.

In *Re Bank of Credit and Commerce International SA*[1], the Bank of England presented a winding-up position in relation to BCCI under the Banking Act 1987.

The majority share holders (supported by the provisional liquidators) sought a substantial adjournment of the winding-up position to further investigate the position of BCCI and whether or not a partial rescue could be achieved.

The Bank of England resisted such an application for further adjournment, partly on the basis that the UK depositors would not enjoy the benefits of the Deposit Protection Scheme under the Banking Act 1987 until a winding-up order was made. Obviously this bears similarities with the position of employees and pension schemes.

1 [1992] BCLC 570; [1992] BCC 83 (Sir Nicolas Browne-Wilkinson V-C).

40.28   Sir Nicolas Browne-Wilkinson V-C (as he then was) commented:

> 'It is the interests of the depositors as a whole which I believe this court ought to consider. Though it can, and should, take into account particular classes of creditors, no class such as the sterling depositor in this country can have the right to stand in the way of what otherwise might be in the interests of the creditors of BCCI as a whole. I am bound to say that the case put forward by the Bank of England seems to be putting undue stress on the interests of English sterling creditors at the expense of other creditors. The truth of the matter, as far as I can see, is that if any substantial recovery is to be made by the creditors of BCCI as a whole, worldwide, the best and possibly the only hope is the restructuring proposals which may be put forward by the government of Abu Dhabi. To stand in the way of that possibility is not to serve the interests of the depositors of this company viewed as a whole but to approach the matter on an insular basis.'

In this case, Sir Nicolas Browne-Wilkinson V-C granted a substantial (six months) adjournment of the winding-up petition. It is easy to see that a judge could reach a similar view in relation to an employee/trustee claim in these circumstances.

Browne-Wilkinson V-C commented:

> 'The second point to be investigated was the position of the employees of BCCI in this country whose future during a prolonged adjournment would be very difficult. They were not entitled to redundancy payments until a winding-up order was made, nor would the provisional liquidators necessarily be in a position to continue their employment.
>
> The third matter to be considered was the position of sterling depositors in England. Under the deposit protection scheme established by the Banking Act

1987, on the making of a winding-up order depositors would be entitled to receive payment of up to 75% of their loss to a maximum of £15,000. The effect of a prolonged adjournment of a winding-up petition would be that those depositors would not be entitled to receive their compensation under the scheme. Those three matters seemed to me matters directly relevant to the question whether or not to grant the adjournment sought by the majority shareholders with a view to investigating the position and possibly putting forward a scheme for a partial or total rescue of BCCI could be worked out.

The matter now comes back to me and proposals have been put forward to deal with all three of those matters.'

Browne-Wilkinson V-C then outlined the proposals that had been put forward by the provisional liquidators to deal with these creditors and went on:

'It was, therefore, rather to my surprise that I found the Bank of England opposing the application now made by the majority shareholders to adjourn the hearing until 2 December, to enable first the whole complicated situation within BCCI and its associates to be investigated and, secondly, having done that to see whether there can be put forward proposals for a partial or total restructuring and refinancing of BCCI.

The provisional liquidators, and in particular the commissaire appointed by the Luxembourg court, are in discussion with the majority shareholders. The provisional liquidators support the adjournment and consider a period of four months as an appropriate and necessary period in order for the research to take place.

The grounds of opposition by the bank are stated in an affidavit that has been sworn. The first ground is that the small depositors who would be entitled to 75% of their deposits up to £15,000 under the statutory scheme should get that full amount under the interim proposal being put forward by the majority shareholders. The bank has not proved willing itself to contribute any cash towards that objective.

Secondly, it is said that BCCI is insolvent. That has not been proved though I am very far from saying it is untrue. But the very purpose of this adjournment is to lead to a position where the court does not at this stage investigate the truth or falsity of the allegations made. The bank feels that it is its responsibility to look after the position of the small depositors. It is said that the provision of less than the full maximum £15,000 casts doubts over the willingness of the majority shareholders to make funds available for a rescue. It is said that the bank is concerned, in a case where the most serious allegations of widespread fraud are made against the conduct of BCCI, that the winding up should proceed and that the necessary investigations should take place. Finally, it is said that there are no firm proposals put forward by the majority shareholders as to the terms on which any rescue could be effected.

Two small depositors also oppose the adjournment. It is not clear to me that they themselves are actually prejudiced by it, since I understood them to be depositors of under £2,000. But their position is the same as that put forward by the Bank of England, namely they think they would do better, like other small depositors, if there were an immediate winding up.

I have no hesitation in rejecting the Bank of England's grounds for opposing an adjournment. This case raises, and will continue to raise, enormous problems.

BCCI is a Luxembourg bank; it is not an English bank. As I understand it, if a winding up goes forward the assets of BCCI worldwide will be applicable for the creditors of BCCI worldwide. The attempt to put a ring fence around either the assets or the creditors to be found in any one jurisdiction is, at least under English law as I understand it, not correct, and destined to failure. I believe the position will prove to be the same in most other countries and jurisdictions. It is a matter of profound regret to me that there is no international convention regulating international insolvency. This case, I hope, if it does nothing else may concentrate people's minds on the necessity for such a convention. What we do have are some rather dated rules of private international law which will regulate the disposal of the assets in the event that no rescue scheme is possible. It will require the most difficult and complicated attempts at co-operation between the different national jurisdictions which I hope will be forthcoming. I am told that such co-operation is already forthcoming from at least three other jurisdictions including Abu Dhabi itself with a view to co-ordinating what is an overwhelmingly difficult problem given the absence of any international structure whether the case is dealt with by way of winding up or by schemes of arrangement, my present understanding is that all assets worldwide will have to be taken into account, as will all creditors. It is for that reason primarily that I am quite unable to accept the Bank of England's grounds for objecting to an adjournment in this case.

One aspect of their objection concentrates on the position of those creditors who are sterling creditors of branches in this country who will, to the extent that I have tried to indicate, be worse off than if an immediate winding-up order were to be made. They number, at the most, some 9,000 creditors. The evidence before me states there are 1.25m depositors of BCCI worldwide. It is the interests of the depositors as a whole which I believe this court ought to consider. Though it can, and should, take into account particular classes of creditors, no class such as the sterling depositor in this country can have the right to stand in the way of what otherwise might be in the interests of the creditors of BCCI as a whole. I am bound to say that the case put forward by the Bank of England seems to be putting undue stress on the interests of English sterling creditors at the expense of other creditors. The truth of the matter, as far as I can see, is that if any substantial recovery is to be made by the creditors of BCCI as a whole, worldwide, the best and possibly the only hope is the restructuring proposals which may be put forward by the government of Abu Dhabi. To stand in the way of that possibility is not to serve the interests of the depositors of this company viewed as a whole but to approach the matter on an insular basis.

I entirely accept the point made by the bank that if the allegations made are true, BCCI has been conducted in a way which is scandalously fraudulent and it would be in the public interest to put an end to it. Weighing that, and taking it into account, I am influenced by the fact that no question of further fraudulent dealing by BCCI in this country can occur in the interim. There are provisional liquidators in charge of the operation. The risk of perpetuation of that fraud in day-to-day dealings in the future is non-existent. Accordingly, though I can well understand the desire of the Bank of England to demonstrate that banks conducted in the way they allege BCCI has been conducted cannot survive, I do not believe that it is essential in the immediate interests either of the public or the depositors that that should be demonstrated at this stage.'

TUPE

40.29   TUPE 2006 will apply if there is a transfer of a business by the insolvent company (see Chapters 19 to 24 above). But TUPE 2006 only applies to a transfer of an undertaking or business 'situated immediately before the transfer in the United Kingdom' – reg 3(1)(a). Equivalent provisions should apply in other EU states in order to comply with the EU Acquired Rights Directive (ARD) that underlies TUPE.

40.30   If there is an overseas insolvency, the special provisions in regulations 8 and 9 of TUPE 2006 dealing with insolvencies may apply. The DTI guidance issued in June 2006 (in URN 06/1368) commented that if there were insolvency 'proceedings in other jurisdictions, where a relevant transfer occurs in Great Britain', the position in relation to TUPE would depend on whether the overseas proceedings are 'analogous to bankruptcy proceedings' (ie whether or not the exclusions in regulation 8(6) or 8(7) can apply).

PENSIONS

40.31   As outlined above in relation to the PPF and section 75 of the Pensions Act 1995, entry of an employer into an 'insolvency event' triggers various pensions events for an eligible UK pension scheme, including:

- entry into an assessment period in relation to the PPF (Part 2 of the Pensions Act 2004 – see Chapter 28 above); and

- a contingent debt becoming payable under the PA 1995, s 75 (see Chapter 34 above)

For these purposes the Pensions Act 2004, s 121 applies for the purposes of determining whether an insolvency event has occurred. A similar test arises under PA 1995, s 22 in relation to the power for the Pensions Regulator to appoint an independent trustee of the pension scheme (see Chapter 30 above).

Under the Pensions Act 2004, s 121(3) various insolvency events are listed. These are expanded by Regulation 5 of the Pension Protection Fund (Entry Rules) Regulations 2005 (SI 2005/590).

The statutory list in and under ss 121(2) to (5) is definitive – see s 121(6).

40.32   The definition of an 'insolvency event' in and under s 121 relates to only to insolvency proceedings under the Insolvency Act 1986 and so does not include overseas insolvency proceedings. This could be an issue in some insolvencies as the trustees of the pension scheme may be keen to force an insolvency event so that the scheme can enter the Pension Protection Fund (PPF).

As noted above in relation to the National Insurance Fund, this may require a secondary winding-up proceeding in the UK (which may not be in the general interest of the insolvency proceedings – see the comments of Judge Norris QC in *Re MG Rover Espana SA*[1], and Lindsay J in *Re Collins & Aikman Europe SA*[2]) – see para 40.14 above.

The list of schemes able to enter the PPF (under PA 2004, ss 128 and 129) was extended from 1 April 2009 by the Pension Protection Fund (Miscellaneous Amendments) Regulations 2009[3] to include an 'EEA Credit Institution' and an 'EEA Insurer' (broadly such institutions established in the EEA, but outside the UK). – see Chapter 27 above. The explanatory notes to the amending statutory instrument clarify that this change was made because such institutions cannot enter a UK insolvency proceeding:

> 'Any institution which is an overseas company but is also an European Economic Area ("EEA") credit institution (or a UK branch of one) or EEA insurer is currently unable to apply to the UK courts under section 221 of the Insolvency Act 1986. This means that an EEA credit institution and insurer can only be wound-up under the laws of the country where its head office is located. Because of this, the pension schemes of European Economic Area ('EEA') credit institutions and insurers cannot be taken over by the PPF. Regulation 2(2), (3) and (4) of these Regulations therefore makes provision, by amending the Entry Rules Regulations, so that such schemes may make an application to the Board of the PPF.'

1 [2006] EWHC 3426; [2005] BPIR 1162; [2006] BCC 599 (Judge Norris QC).
2 [2006] EWHC 1343; [2007] 1 BCLC 182; [2006] BCC 861 (Lindsay J).
3 SI 2009/451.

40.33 See generally section 10.1 of the talk 'No room at the orphanage: some issues relating to PPF Entry' given by Ian Greenstreet and Helen Butler to the APL in April 2009.

CHAPTER 41

Who is 'connected' or 'associated'

41.1   Under the Insolvency Act 1986[1] transactions involving connected persons or associates can give rise to particular considerations. Liquidators or administrators can challenge or reverse certain transactions which involved the insolvent company and took place before the formal insolvency[2]. If the transaction was in favour of a connected person then the onus of proof may be reversed and transactions completed up to two years prior to insolvency may be open to challenge. A transaction entered into by a liquidator with an associate may be set aside by the court.

Establishing whether a party to a transaction is connected or associated can therefore be very important. But the statutory tests are wide-ranging and complex. This Chapter[3] looks at the issues that can arise in deciding whether or not a person is 'connected' or 'associated' under the definition of these terms as used in ss 249 and 435.

1 All statutory references in this Chapter are to the Insolvency Act 1986 unless stated otherwise.
2 See generally the usual works on insolvency law. In particular the book 'Vulnerable Transactions in Corporate Insolvency', edited by John Armour and Howard Bennett (Hart Publishing, 2003).
3 See further the paper given by the author at the annual conference of the Association of Pension Lawyers in November 2008.

THE IMPACT OF DEALINGS WITH CONNECTED PERSONS AND ASSOCIATES

41.2   Some of the situations in which it can be important to identify connected persons and associates within the IA definitions:

(a) Reversible transactions

Transaction at an undervalue

A transaction at an undervalue arises where a company makes a gift or otherwise enters into a transaction on terms that the company receives no consideration or enters into a transaction for a consideration the value of which, in money or money's worth, is significantly less than the value, in money or money's worth, of the consideration provided by the company – s 238(4).

The court can set aside transactions entered into by the company at the 'relevant time' – s 238(2). The 'relevant time' is a period of two years ending with the onset of insolvency, whether or not the party was connected – s 240. The company must be unable to pay its debts at the time of the transaction or become unable to do so as a result – s 240(2). Where the transaction was with a connected person[1], there will be a presumption of such insolvency (so the burden of proof is reversed).

1 Note that for the purposes of s 238, certain of the presumptions which arise in respect of connected parties do not arise where a person is connected by reason of only being an employee of the company which has entered into the transaction at an undervalue or given a preference.

Preferences

A company gives a preference to a person if:

(a) that person is one of the company's creditors or a surety or guarantor for any of the company's debts or other liabilities; and

(b) the company does anything (or suffers anything to be done) which has the effect of putting that person into a position which, in the event of the company going into insolvent liquidation, will be better than the position he would have been in if that thing had not been done – s 239(4).

The company must have 'desired' to prefer the creditor, surety or guarantor (s 239(5)). Where the transaction was with a connected person[1] the burden of proof is reversed: there is a rebuttable presumption that the company intended to put that connected person (other than an employee) in a better position – s 239(6).

The transaction must have taken place within the 'relevant time'. For a connected person this will be a period of two years ending with the onset of insolvency, for anyone else it will be a period of six months ending with the onset of insolvency – s 240(1).

As with transactions at an undervalue, the company must be unable to pay its debts at the time of the transaction or become unable to do so as a result – s 240(2). But unlike transactions at an undervalue, there is no presumption of insolvency where the preference was to a connected person.

1 Note that for the purposes of s 239, certain of the presumptions which arise in respect of connected parties do not arise where a person is connected by reason of only being an employee of the company which has entered into the transaction at an undervalue or given a preference.

Invalid floating charges

A floating charge on a company's undertaking or property is invalid except to the extent of the aggregate of:

(a) the value of so much of the consideration for the creation of the charge as consists of money paid, or goods or services supplied, to the company at the same time as, or after, the creation of the charge; and

(b) the value of so much of that consideration as consists of the discharge or reduction, at the same time or after the creation of the charge, of any debt of the company; and

(c) the amount of interest payable on the amount falling within paragraph (a) or (b);

if it was made within the 12 months ending with the onset of insolvency and at the time the floating charge was created, the company was unable to pay its debts within the meaning of s 123 or becomes unable to pay its debts as a consequence of the charge – s 245.

Two differences apply where the charge is created in favour of a connected person. It will be invalid if made up to two years prior to the onset of insolvency (rather than 12 months) and there is no need to show that the company was insolvent at the time or became insolvent as a result.

(b) Transactions by liquidators etc

A transaction entered into by a liquidator with an associate of the liquidator can be set aside by the court[1]. The same applies to a transaction by a trustee in bankruptcy[2]. A trustee in bankruptcy has to give notice to the creditors' committee (if there is one) if there is to be a disposal of any property to an associate of the bankrupt[3].

1 Rule 4.149, Insolvency Rules 1986 (SI 1986/1925, as amended).
2 Rule 6.147.
3 S 314(6), Insolvency Act 1986.

(c) Voluntary arrangements

Where there is a voluntary arrangement, whether corporate or individual:

● The proposal must state how those creditors who are associates of (or connected with) the debtor are to be treated[1];

● The statement of affairs must include details of debts owed to or by associates of (or persons connected with) the debtor[2];

● Votes of any creditors who are connected with the debtor must be left out of account in counting votes for resolutions of creditors[3].

1 Rules 1.3(2)(c)(ii) for a CVA and rule 5.3(2)(c)(ii) for an IVA, Insolvency Rules 1986.
2 Rule 1.5(2)(e) for a CVA, rule 5.8(3)(e) for an IVA.
3 Insolvency Rules 1986, rr 1.19(4) and 5.18(4).

(d) Creditors' committees

A member of a creditors' committee or any associate of a member must not acquire assets out of the estate or receive any profit from the administration or receive out of the debtor's assets any payment for services given or goods supplied[1]. But this does not stop such transactions with a relevant sanction.

1 Insolvency Rules 1986, rr 4.170(1)(a) and (c) and 6.165(1).

(f) Moral hazard provisions of the Pensions Act 2004

The terms 'connected' and 'associated', as defined in IA 1986, are incorporated into the Pensions Act 2004. A financial support direction may be issued to an employer or a company[1] who is 'connected' with or 'an associate of' an employer if certain conditions are met. (A financial support direction may only be made where the regulator considers that it is 'reasonable' for the regulator to do so. There are a number of factors that the regulator needs to consider in deciding this, including the relationship of the party with the employer; the value of any benefits received; the involvement with the pension scheme; and the financial circumstances of the associate.)

1 Unlike contribution notices, FSDs can generally only be issued against companies – see PA 2004, s 43(6) and para 28.18 above.

THE RATIONALE BEHIND THESE PROVISIONS

41.3   The Cork Report (the Report of the Review Committee on Insolvency Law and Practice[1]) into reform of the insolvency legislation recommended that special provisions apply in relation to connected persons and suggested that these be defined to include related individuals and companies with common substantial shareholdings. Thus the report stated (at para 1033):

> 'If the law of insolvency is to reflect the social and economic conditions of modern society and is to be accepted as fair and just by the general public, then it cannot treat husband and wife, or persons living together as man and wife or other closely connected persons, as if they were unrelated parties accustomed to deal with each other at arm's length. Nor can it treat companies which are members of the same group, or other closely associated companies, as if they were wholly unrelated. Special relationships call for special provisions to be made.'

1 Cmnd 8558 (1982), chairman Sir Kenneth Cork.

INTERPRETATION OF THE TERMS 'CONNECTED' AND 'ASSOCIATED'

41.4   They are quite complicated definitions. Often they refer to other concepts (eg 'director', 'shadow director', 'officer') which are themselves the source of some difficulty. As the statutory provisions are detailed, one case at least (and there are not vast numbers of cases on these provisions) suggests that the courts are unwilling to take a purposive approach when determining whether or not a person falls within the definitions – see *Re Thirty-Eight Building Limited*[1].

1 [1999] 1 BCLC 416; [1999] OPLR 319 (Hazel Williamson QC). See also para 6.32 above

41.5   There is in a general rule that there no chain principle: merely because A is associated with B, and B is associated with C, does not necessarily mean that A is associated with C. This is reasonable – otherwise in practice just about everyone one in the world would ultimately end up associated with everyone. But common control does make a chain. And the definition of 'connected' allows an onward link if a person is associated with a director: if A is associated with B and B is a director of C, then A is connected with C (s 249 – see below). Much, of course, turns on the detail.

WHO IS CONNECTED?

41.6

---

s 249 'Connected' with a company

For the purposes of any provision in this Group of Parts, a person is connected with a company if—

(a)   he is a director or shadow director of the company or an associate of such a director or shadow director, or

(b)   he is an associate of the company;

and 'associate' has the meaning given by section 435 in Part XVIII of this Act.

A person: a person for the purposes of this test (and all of the other tests referred to in this article) can be an individual, a company or a body of unincorporated persons[1]. Note that a person can be connected only with a company – not with an individual.

A company: the term 'company' is not defined in s 249. Section 251 used to state that terms defined in Companies Act 1985, Part 26 apply for this purpose (but this provision was repealed from 1 October 2009, with transitional savings). Section 735 of the Companies Act 1985 is in Part 26 and defines a company as 'a company formed and registered under this Act or an existing company' (although this does not apply if the contrary intention appears). This suggests, although untested, that the operation of s 249 should be restricted to companies incorporated under the Companies Acts. But it seems more likely that the courts would construe the term 'company' in s 249 more widely. Section 435, which defines 'associate' expressly extends 'company' to include any body corporate including overseas companies (see s 435(11)) and the transaction at an undervalue provisions apply to overseas transactions (see *Re Paramount Airways Ltd²*), so there seems not good reason not to extend s 249 similarly.

Various cases have considered whether other insolvency provisions apply to a corporate body not incorporated under the Companies Acts – *Re International Bulk Commodities Ltd³* (receiver appointed over an overseas company could be an administrative receiver), *Re Dallhold Estates (UK) Pty Ltd⁴* (appointment of an administrator following a request from an Australian court) and *In the matter of Dairy Farmers of Britain Limited⁵* – but none have addressed this issue.

An associate: the use of the term 'associate' within the definition of connected means that the terms must be considered along side one another. Associates are considered more fully below.

1 Interpretation Act 1978, s 5, Sch 1.
2 [1993] Ch 223 (CA).
3 [1993] Ch 77 (Mummery J).
4 [1992] BCLC 621; [1992] BCC 394 (Chadwick J).
5 [2009] EWHC 1389 (Henderson J).

COMMON DIRECTORSHIPS, EMPLOYERS AND EMPLOYEES

Common directorships

41.7   There is a limited chain here. If a company has directors (including non-executive directors) who are also directors of another company, those companies will be connected. Thus, for example, if B is a director of A and also a director of C, this will mean that A is connected with C. This has potentially odd results. It means that all companies sharing just one common director are connected for these purposes even though there is no other link (e.g. common shareholding or transactions etc).

41.8   The Court of Appeal in Singapore (where the statutory provisions are similar) addressed this issue in the context of an unfair preference claim in *Show Theatres Pte Ltd v Shaw Theatres Pte Ltd¹* and commented:

> '21 We were mindful that this ruling could have some repercussions in view of the corporate practice in Singapore, where it is a common phenomenon to see a person sitting on the boards of several companies. We do not, however, see anything seriously objectionable in the construction we have given. All it means is that whenever two companies have a common director or common directors, they are to be treated as 'connected with' each other. In this regard, it is vitally important to bear in mind the clear objective behind ss 98 to 101. What is prescribed in those sections is a scheme for the protection of creditors generally. It underscores the need for transparency. Because of the connection due to common directorship, a payment to a 'connected' company made within the period of two years prior to the liquidation of the company is presumed to be made in unfair preference and it is for the 'connected' company to rebut that presumption. It is right, and not unfair, to assume that a director exercises influence within the company.'

1 [2002] SGCA 42; [2002] 4 SLR 145, Singapore CA.
   The judgment is on the web at http://app.supremecourt.gov.sg/default.aspx?pgID=1136

Employers and employees

41.9   Persons are connected with a company if they are associates of a director or shadow director of the company. Associates include any person whom a person employs or by whom he is employed – s 435(4).

41.10   If company A employs someone (not a director) – say Mr X – and Mr X is also a director of another company B, this means that A is connected to B (because A is connected with Mr X) but B is not (absent anything else) connected with A. (Although C is connected with Mr X because he is a director of C, the connection into company A does not apply because Mr X is not a director of company A.)

41.11   The employers of any director will be connected with that company. For example, a bank or venture capital fund that has nominated one of its employees to be a director of a company (perhaps to protect their interests as minority shareholder) will be connected with that company. The director is also connected with the company.

41.12   If the director was nominated by the Bank/Venture Capital Fund but not its employee, the Bank/Venture Capital Fund would not be connected or associated with the company (unless there was another connection – eg it had acted as a shadow director).

41.13   Any director or other officer of a company is treated as an employee of that company (s 435(9)). Thus in this structure the director is treated as being an employee of Company A and is an associate of Company A. Company A is therefore an associate of a director of Company B, so Company A is connected with Company B. For the same reasons, Company B is connected with Company A.

41.14   Company A is an associate of its employee. Company A is therefore an associate of a director of Company C, so Company A is connected with Company C. However, Company C is not connected with Company A.

SHADOW DIRECTORS AND DE FACTO DIRECTORS

41.15   The terms director, shadow director and de facto director are difficult. There has been a fair amount of case law on what they actually mean (mainly in other contexts)[1].

   Section 251[2] defines a director to include any person occupying the position of director, by whatever name called (ie a de facto director).

Section 251[3] also defines a shadow director as a person in accordance with whose directions or instructions the directors of the company are accustomed to act (but a person is not deemed a shadow director by reason only that the directors act on advice given by him in a professional capacity).

1 See further *State for Trade and Industry v Deverell* [2001] Ch 340, CA; *Re Mea Corporation Ltd: Secretary of State for Trade and Industry v Aviss* [2006] EWHC 1846 (Ch); [2007] 1 BCLC 618 (Lewison J); *Secretary of State for Trade and Industry v Hollier* [2006] EWHC 1804 (Ch); [2007] BCC 11 (Etherton J) and '*Examining Company Directors through the Lens of De Facto Directorship*' by Chris Noonan and Susan Watson [2008] JBL 587.
2 The definition in CA 1985, s 741(1) (to become CA 2006, s 250) is the same.
3 The definition in s 741(2), CA 1985 (to become CA 2006, s 251) is the same, save that it excludes parent companies.

41.16 The Court of Appeal in *Secretary of State for Trade and Industry v Deverell*[1] considered the statutory definition of shadow director and held[2] that:

- The definition should not be strictly construed.

- The purpose of the legislation was to identify those, other than professional advisers, with real influence in the corporate affairs of the company. But it is not necessary that such influence should be exercised over the whole field of its corporate activities.

- Whether any particular communication from the alleged shadow director, whether by words or conduct, is to be classified as a direction or instruction must be objectively ascertained by the court in the light of all the evidence.

- Non-professional advice may come within that statutory description. The proviso excepting advice given in a professional capacity appears to assume that advice generally is or may be included. Moreover the concepts of 'direction' and 'instruction' do not exclude the concept of 'advice' for all three share the common feature of 'guidance'.

- It is not necessary to show that in the face of 'directions or instructions' from the alleged shadow director the properly appointed directors or some of them cast themselves in a subservient role or surrendered their respective discretions.

1 [2001] Ch. 340; [2000] 2 All ER 365.
2 [2001] Ch. 340; [2000] 2 All ER 365 at pages 375/376 (para 35).

41.17 It seems that a one-off direction is not enough – there must be a course of conduct (see Lewison J in *Re Kilnoore: Unidare v Cohen*[1]). Control of just one director on a multi-member board does not look to be enough[2], but control of a majority of the board (or of the active board) may be enough. In *Ultraframe (UK) Ltd v Fielding*[3], Lewison J held that a person at whose direction a governing majority of the board was accustomed to act was capable of being a shadow director.

1 [2005] 3 All ER 730 at page 739 (para 36). See also the article by Look Chan Ho 'Connected Persons and Administrators' Duty to Think: Unidare v Cohen' (2005) Journal of International Banking and Regulation , Vol 20, issue 11.

2 See *Re Unisoft Group Ltd (No 3)* [1994] 1 BCLC 609, 620 (Harman J) and *Lord v Sinai Securities Ltd* [2004] EWHC 1764 (Ch) at para [27]; [2005] 1 BCLC 295, 303 (Hart J).
3 *Ultraframe (UK) Ltd v Fielding; Northstar Systems Ltd v Fielding* [2005] EWHC 1638 (Ch); [2005] All ER (D) 397 (Jul); [2007] WTLR 835, Lewison J. at para [1272]. Discussed by D.D. Prentice and Jenny Payne in 'Directors' fiduciary duties' (2006) 122 LQR 558-565.

Application of s 251

41.18   The definitions in s 251 apply to 'this Group of Parts' – ie including s 249, but *not* s 435. Thus, while de facto directors and shadow directors are clearly connected, it is arguably less clear whether they are associates. In the IA itself the fact that s 251 does not apply to s 435 probably does not matter, because the term associate is used in the reversible transaction provisions in sections 238 to 245 (which are in the same Group of Parts as s 251). But this drafting problem could be an issue where (as in pensions legislation[1]) s 435 is being used outside the IA. This does not seem to have been raised as an issue in any case so far. In practice a judge might decide that this was a drafting slip and construe s 435 as though the interpretation provision in s 251 applied to it as well. It seems likely that, in construing the definitions of both 'connected' and 'associated', the term 'director' includes a 'shadow director' or a 'de facto director'. But there is scope for doubt here.

   (Furthermore in practice a shadow director is likely to 'control' the company and so be associated with it under the test in s 435(10)(a) discussed below.)

1 For example the moral hazard powers under Part 1 of the Pensions Act 2004, employer-related investment under Pensions Act 1995, s 40, independent trustee on insolvency under Pensions Act 1995, s 23(3)(b), pension provision following a TUPE transfer under Pensions Act 2004, s 257.

WHO IS AN ASSOCIATE?

41.19   The term 'associate' is defined exhaustively in section 435. It is important both because it is used in insolvency legislation in its own right (for example the court can set aside transactions entered into by a liquidator with an associate) and because it is used within the definition of connected.

Individuals

41.20   An individual is a natural person, and the term will *not* include a company or body corporate. See for example Mann J in *Jasmine Trustees Ltd v Wells & Hind (a firm)*[1], a decision on section 37 of the Trustee Act 1925.

1 [2007] EWHC 38 (Ch); [2007] 1 All ER 1142 (Mann J).

Spouses and reputed spouses

41.21   In this article, the term 'spouse' covers a husband or wife or civil partner[1], a former husband or wife or civil partner, and a 'reputed' husband or wife.

1 The sections were amended from December 2005 to include civil partners under the Civil Partnership Act 2004 on the same basis as husbands and wives.

41.22   The use of the term 'reputed' is quite odd. In *Smurthwaite v Simpson-Smith (No 2)*[1] Judge Rich QC held that something more than living together was needed: there also needed to be a holding out or reputation of marriage. In this case Miss Williams was cohabiting with the bankrupt but had not married him or adopted his name, nor was any of their friends or neighbours under the impression that they were married. Judge Rich held that she was not a reputed wife for the purposes of s 435.

1 [2006] BPIR 1483; [2005] All ER (D) 275 (Apr) (Judge Rich QC, sitting as a deputy High Court Judge).

Relatives of individuals and their spouses

41.23   A person is an associate of an individual if that person is:

1   the individual's spouse;

2   a 'relative' of the individual;

3   the spouse or former spouse of a 'relative' of the individual; or

4   the spouse or former spouse of a 'relative' of the individual's spouse or former spouse.

41.24   A person is a 'relative' of an individual if he is that individual's brother, sister, uncle, aunt, nephew, niece, lineal ancestor or lineal descendant – s 435(8). This does not extend to more distant relations than a niece or nephew (eg a cousin or a great niece). But it does extend to lineal ancestors or descendants – eg great grandparents or great grandchildren.

41.25   Under s 435(8) any relationship of half blood is treated as relationship of whole blood, the stepchild or adopted child of any person is treated as his child and an illegitimate child is treated as the legitimate child of his mother and reputed father.

41.26   All of the people shown below, **plus their current and former 'spouses'**[1], would be 'associates' of the individual. There is no age limit: all children are connected even if adults[2].

1 Including civil partners and reputed spouses as noted above.
2 Contrast the references to infant children in the Companies Act 2006 – eg s 253 – or in the Companies Act 1985 – eg ss 328 and 346(3)(a).

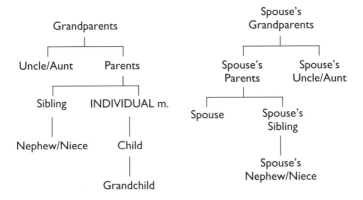

Companies

41.27 As discussed above, references to companies in s 435 include overseas companies and catch any body corporate – s 435(11). As to limited liability partnerships (LLPs) see the separate section below.

41.28 A company is an associate of another company:

(a) if one company controls the other company; or

(b) if the same person has 'control' of both; or

(c) if a person (A) has control of one and persons who are associates of A, or A together with persons who are his associates, have control of the other; or

(d) if a group of two or more persons has control of each company, and the groups either consist of the same persons or could be regarded as consisting of the same persons by treating (in one or more cases) a member of either group as replaced by a person of whom he is an associate.

(s 435(6) and (7))

WHAT IS 'CONTROL'?

41.29 Clearly establishing whether two companies are associated therefore turns on the meaning of control.

Section 435(10)

(10) For the purposes of this section a person is to be taken as having 'control' of a company if:

(a) the directors of the company or of another company which has control of it (or any of them) are accustomed to act in accordance with his directions or instructions, or

---

> (b) he is entitled to exercise, or control the exercise of, one third or more of the voting power at any general meeting of the company or of another company which has control of it;
>
> and where two or more persons together satisfy either of the above conditions, they are to be taken as having control of the company.

Person having control contrasted with shadow directors

41.30   Part (a) of this definition is obviously similar to the definition of a 'shadow director' in s 251. But, as Antony Zacaroli QC points out in Chapter H5 of the book 'Insolvency'[1], there are two differences between the definitions:

1 Looseleaf edited by Segal, Totty and Moss (Sweet & Maxwell). See para H5-03.

41.31   *Professional advisers:* the definition of shadow director in s 251 states that 'a person is not deemed a shadow director by reason only that the directors act on advice given by him in a professional capacity'. Section 435(10)(a) does not include this exception. This leaves open the potential that professional advisers may be taken to have 'control' in some circumstances even though they only give advice.

41.32   *All or some of the directors:* the definition of shadow director in s 251 refers to 'a person in accordance with whose directions or instructions the directors of the company are accustomed to act'. But s 435(10) requires that 'the directors of the company or of another company which has control of it (*or any of them*) are accustomed to act in accordance with his directions or instructions'[1].

The words 'or any of them' do not appear in s 251 and are difficult here. Anthony Zacaroli takes the view that they render s 435(10)(a) 'far wider' than s 251 and that a person will control a company if just one director is accustomed to act in accordance with his instructions or directions. So there could be significant scope for a 'nominee' director giving rise to control (even if the majority of directors are not 'controlled' and so the controller is not a shadow director[2]).

This seems to be an odd result. If right, then the 'controller' would not have control of the board (or a majority), but only of one director. A single director is not himself (or herself) treated as having control of the company[3]. So why should a person who gives directions to one director be treated as having control?

1 Contrast also the controlling interest definition in s 823, CA 2006, stating that a person is taken to be interested in shares if a body corporate is interested in them and 'the body or its directors are accustomed to act in accordance with his directions'. The words underlined are clearer in not referring to a single director, but of course s 435(10) is drafted differently.

2 See *Re Unisoft Group Ltd (No 3)* [1994] 1 BCLC 609, 620 (Harman J) and *Lord v Sinai Securities Ltd* [2004] EWHC 1764 (Ch) at para [27]; [2005] 1 BCLC 295, 303 (Hart J) and Lewison J at para [1270] in *Ultraframe (UK) Ltd v Fielding; Northstar Systems Ltd v Fielding* [2005] EWHC 1638 (Ch); [2005] All ER (D) 397 (Jul); [2007] WTLR 835; as to nominee directors, see later.

3 A director is not, as such, treated as associated with his fellow directors and so they do not, in my view, as such have control as a group under s 435(6) (absent some other association – eg if they were all related). See further the discussion below on directors of holding companies.

41.33 An alternative interpretation would be to construe the words 'or any of them' as applying not to 'the directors of the company', but to control of the directors of any of (i) 'the company' or (ii) 'another company which has control of it'. This view is more consistent with the Court of Appeal decision in *Secretary of State for Trade and Industry v Deverell*[1] in relation to the statutory definition of shadow director that the purpose of the legislation was to identify those, other than professional advisers, with real influence in the company's corporate affairs. (As against this, however, the second limb of the definition of 'control' in s 435(10)(b) only requires a one-third shareholding, not a majority.)

1 [2000] 2 All ER 365, CA.

41.34 In *Re a debtor (No 87 of 1993) (No 2)*[1] Rimer J viewed 'control' of just one director (although the points raised above were not discussed) as falling within s 435(10)(a). The case dealt with a challenge to an arrangement in a bankruptcy and one issue was whether a creditor, Stylemoney Limited, was an associate of the debtor under s 435. Rimer J held that it was, apparently on the basis that the debtor gave instructions to his wife who was one of the directors. But Rimer J did not discuss whether s 435(10)(a) only requires control of one director. The earlier part of the judgment shows that he seems to have been ready to conclude that the debtor was a de facto director anyway, based on the debtor's involvement in the company. Furthermore Rimer J suspected that the debtor's remuneration from Stylemoney had deliberately been left uncertain with a view to avoiding the risk that Stylemoney might become an associate by reason of being the debtor's employer. So Rimer J's conclusions may have turned on the particular facts of this case.

1 [1996] 1 BCLC 63 (Rimer J).

41.35 *Nominee directors:* this debate is relevant in the context of nominee directors. Investors are often given power to appoint one or more persons to the board of directors of a company. Could this make the appointor connected or associated with the company?

If the nominee is associated with the appointor (eg is an officer, employee or director of the appointor – ss 435(4) and(9)), then s 249 will mean that the appointor is connected with the company.

As discussed above, even if the nominee director is accustomed to act in accordance with the directions of the appointor, it seems unlikely that this would make the appointor a shadow director (and hence connected to the company). The definition of shadow director suggests that more than one director would have to act in accordance with the directions. It may be, however, that this is enough to give the appointor control of the company.

Voting power – Unidare case

41.36 In the 2005 case of *Re Kilnoore Ltd (in liquidation), Unidare plc v Cohen*[1], which involved a shareholder holding shares on a bare trust for a third party, Lewison J held that the use of the phrase *'voting power'* in s 435, rather than '*voting rights*' in Companies Act 1985, ss 736 and 736A (see now CA 2006, s 1159) was significant. He thought this gave him 'some encouragement to look to the economic reality of the case'. He noted:

> 'A registered shareholder who holds his shares on a bare trust under which he is required to cast his vote in accordance with the directions of the beneficial owner might be said to have voting rights, but I do not consider that in any real sense he can be said to have voting power'.

However, the application of this case may be limited. Lewison J was influenced by the fact that the parties intended the shares to be transferred – they just had not completed all the necessary steps at the time.

1 [2005] 3 All ER 730; [2005] EWHC 1410 (Ch); [2005] All ER (D) 12 (Jul).

Aggregation of people?

41.37   The wording at the end of s 435(10) is also difficult. There is as yet no reported British case law on it. Taken literally it would allow aggregation of any small shareholdings to get over the one-third threshold. Thus it could be argued that since the shareholders in any company together control the exercise of more than one-third of the votes, they are to be treated as individually as having control. But this seems to be the wrong result. Logically it seems that something more than this must needed – some degree of association between the two or more persons whose shareholdings in the company are being aggregated – see for example the group references in s 435(6).

41.38   Anthony Zacaroli seems to take the contrary view, stating[1] in a footnote to a description of the control test in s 435(10)(a) that 'where there are two or more persons who together fulfil…[the test in s 435(10)(a)] then they are each associates of the company'[2]. This is difficult to understand (given that s 435(10) deals with control, not associate status), but indicates that he favours a more several approach.

1 Chapter on 'associated and Connected Persons' in 'Insolvency ' looseleaf (Sweet & Maxwell).
2 Footnote 2 on page H5/2.

41.39   In *Show Theatres*[1], the Singapore Court of Appeal commented on what seem to be identical provisions in the context of a preference claim where the insolvent company (Show Theatres) had repaid a loan to its two shareholders (both companies) before entering liquidation. One shareholder held 75% of the shares, the other 25%[2]:

> '28 … If two companies, X and Y, both receive repayments from the insolvent company, and between them they exercised 1/3 or more of the voting power of the latter company, then by virtue of the proviso[3] they are deemed to be associates of the latter. And if X and Y were to hold 100% of the voting power in the insolvent company the proviso should apply to the situation with even greater force. All the more so where it was clear that the two companies … had acted in concert in getting their loans repaid by the insolvent company. This

would be wholly in line with the scheme to render void payments made in unfair preference.

29 Accordingly, this would be a further basis to hold that [the two shareholders] were companies 'connected with' Show Theatres.'

Strictly, this conclusion was obiter (the Singapore Court of Appeal had already held that the shareholders were connected under the common directorship provisions – see above), but it gives an indication of the potential breadth of the aggregation wording. It is noticeable that the Court of Appeal pointed to the fact that the two shareholders were acting in concert and that both received repayments of their loan at the same time.

1 *Show Theatres Pte Ltd v Shaw Theatres Pte Ltd* [2002] SGCA 42; [2002] 4 SLR 145 (Singapore CA) mentioned above.
2 See para [4] of the judgment.
3 Identical to the aggregation wording at the end of s 435(10) in the UK.

What is the effect if a company enters into an insolvency process?

41.40 Does entry of a company into an insolvency process impact on its relationship with others in the group – eg do they cease to be associated?

41.41 *Liquidations:* the normal rule (for example for tax purposes) is that on a liquidation the beneficial ownership of the assets of the company moves away from the company to be held on a form of statutory trust (controlled by the liquidator) – see *Ayerst (Inspector of Taxes) v C&K (Construction) Ltd*[1]. If the tax rule were to be applied to assessing connection or association, this could mean that subsidiaries of the insolvent company would cease to be controlled by (or associated with) it. Shareholders in the insolvent company would seem still to control it (as they hold the voting power even though shareholder meetings may be uncommon in a liquidation).

But the Employment Appeal Tribunal has recently taken a view that liquidation of one employer company does not break the link of being an associated employer under employment law – see *Da Silva v Composite Moldings & Design Limited*[2].

1 [1976] AC 167 (HL). See the discussion at paras 4.6 to 4.15 *Taxation in Corporate Insolvency and Rescue* by Anthony Davis (6th edition, Bloomsbury Professional, 2009).
2 [2008] UKEAT/0241/08.

41.42 *Administrations:* it is unclear if the same beneficial ownership position would apply in relation to administrations. The Revenue indicated in 1990 that they would not normally regard an administration order as affecting the beneficial ownership tests relating to the various group relationships of a parent company. But the position could be said to have changed following the changes made in 2003 by the Enterprise Act 2002 to the administration regime in IA 1986: Anthony C R Davis comments in *Taxation in Corporate Insolvency and Rescue* that there are features of the reformed regime, such as the power to make distributions under IA 1986, Sch B1, para 65 and to dissolve the company under IA 1986, Sch B1, para 84, which bring it closer to liquidation where indisputably beneficial ownership is lost[1].

1 See the discussion at paras 4.16 to 4.21 *Taxation in Corporate Insolvency and Rescue*. Anthony Davis goes on to state that his view is that admninistration does not automatically have the effect that the company loses beneficial ownership of its assets, 'although there may come a point in some administrations where this does occur'.

41.43 *Receiverships:* receiverships have for tax purposes been treated as different to liquidations, with beneficial ownership of assets remaining with the company. See *English Sewing Cotton Co v CIR*[1] where the Master of the Rolls stated (albeit obiter) that 'It has never been suggested to my knowledge, and it cannot be suggested on principle, that the appointment of a receiver by a mortgagee affects the beneficial ownership of the shares'.

1 [1947] 1 All ER 679 (CA). See the discussion at pages 52 and 53 of '*Tolley's Taxation in Corporate Insolvency*'.

Associates within groups of companies

41.44 It follows that most companies in a group will be associates of each other and hence connected parties.

41.45 Example of associated companies:

Companies A, B, C and D are all 'associates'. Subsidiary E is an 'associate' of Companies A, B D and C.

Company A: X owns one third of the voting stock of Companies A and B. Therefore X has control of Company A and Company B. As the same person has control of both companies, Company A and Company B are associates[1].

Company D: X owns one third of the voting stock of Company A, which in turn owns one third of the voting stock of Company D. X has control of Company A and Company A has control of Company D. Therefore, X has control of Company D – s 435(10)(b). Because X has control of each of Company D, Company A and Company B, all three companies are associates of each other. Company C would also be an associate of A, B and D (see below).

Company E: Company A owns one third of the voting stock of Company D, which in turn owns one third of the voting stock of Company E. Company A has control of Company D and Company D has control of Company E. Therefore, Company A has control of Company E.

X has control of one-third of the votes in Company A and so s 435(10)(b) applies in that X 'controls the exercise of one-third or more of the voting power at any general meeting of …. another company [ie Company A] which has control of' Company E. So X controls Company E and is associated with Company E.

Company A, Company D and Company E are associates of each other. Companies A and B and Company D are associates of X (see below). Company A and Company D both have control of Company E. Therefore, as Company A and Company D are associates of X and X also has control of Company B, Company B and Company E are associates.

Company C: no one individual has control of the company. However, as Y and Z together hold over one third of the voting power together they together they have control of the company. As they are both 'associates' of X, Company C is an associate of Companies A and B and Subsidiaries D and E because X has control of these companies. However, as Y and Z are not associates of each other, they are probably not themselves associates of Company C (see discussion of s 435(10) above).

Companies associated with individuals

1 For an example of this, see *Clements (liquidator of HHO Licensing Ltd) v Henry Hadaway Organisation Ltd* [2007] EWHC 2953 (Ch); [2008] 1 BCLC 223 (Peter Leaver QC sitting as a Deputy Judge of the High Court).

41.46 A company is an associate of another person if that person has control of it or if that person and persons who are his associates together have control of it.

41.47 Examples of companies associated with individuals:

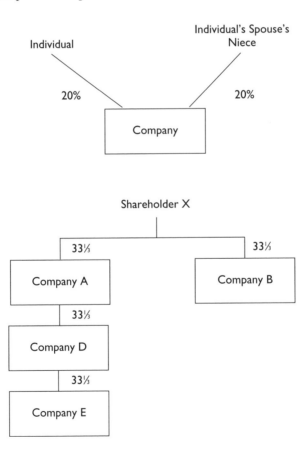

The individuals are associates of one another, because they are relatives. Together they exercise one third or more of the voting power of the company, therefore together they control the company. Because they are associates who together control the company, the company is an associate of each of them – s 435(7).

X is an associate of Company A, Company B and Company D and Company E.

X has control of Companies A and B because he is entitled to exercise one third of the voting power. Company A is entitled to exercise one third of the voting power of Company D, therefore Company A has control of Company D – s 435(10)(b). X has control of Company A which has control of Company D – s 435(10)(b), therefore X has control of Company D.

As X has control of Company A, Company B and Company D they are associates of X.

X has control of one-third of the votes in Company A and so s 435(10)(b) applies in that X 'controls the exercise of one-third or more of the voting power at any general meeting of …. another company [ie Company A] which has control of' Company E. So X controls Company E and is associated with Company E.

Director in Holding Company – associated with subsidiaries?

41.48   What is the position if an investor (*Investor*) has a minority stake (less than one-third voting power) in a company (*Holding Company*) and perhaps appoints a director of the Holding Company? The other shareholders are not associated with the Investor but there may be a shareholder agreement. Is the Investor connected with or an associate of a subsidiary (*Subsidiary*) of the Holding Company?

41.49   Clearly the Holding Company is an associate of the Subsidiary because it controls the Subsidiary. It is much less clear whether the Investor would be considered to be connected or associated with the Subsidiary. The analysis is as follows:

(a)   The Investor will be connected with the Holding Company if any of the directors of the Holding Company are associated with the Investor (eg officers, employees or directors of the Investor). This can be common. But merely because the Investor is connected with the Holding Company, does not mean that the Investor is associated with the Holding Company. So, if this is the only link, the Investor is not associated with companies controlled by the Holding Company and so is not connected or associated with the Subsidiary.

(b)   If the Investor had control of the Holding Company, it would also have control of the Holding Company's subsidiaries (s 435(10)(b)) and so would be associated with those subsidiaries – s 435(7). But the Investor will often not have control of the Holding Company since control generally requires the Investor either becoming (in effect) a shadow director or being entitled to exercise or control the exercise of one third or more of the voting power at any general meeting of the company.

(c) If the Investor were associated with the Holding Company (eg an individual who is also a director of the Holding Company[1]), it seems unlikely that it would be treated as associated with the Subsidiary as well. Section 435(7) says that a company is an associate of another person if 'that person and persons who are his associates together have control of it'. Given that the Holding Company has control of the Subsidiary, it does not seem appropriate to treat the Investor as 'together' with the Holding Company having control of the subsidiary. It seems more likely that these words are meant to catch the situation where the addition of the associates together is needed to show control.

(d) It would seem wrong to apply a further 'chain principle': if A is associated with B and B controls C, this should not mean that A is associated with C by reason of s 435(7). Thus while the Investor is only connected with the Holding Company under s 249 (and not associated under s 435), it seems clear that section 435(7) will not apply.

(e) There is an argument that the Investor's relationship with the other investors could mean that the Investor is in fact associated with the Holding Company as well. The problem here is once again the wording at the end of s 435(10) and whether some degree of association is needed between the two or more persons whose shareholdings in the Holding Company are being aggregated with the Investor.

1 In practice it is difficult to see how a corporate investor would be an associate of the Holding Company absent it having control of the Holding Company (or control higher up the shareholding).

Partners – s 435(3)

41.50   A person is an associate of any person with whom he is in partnership – s 435(3)[1]. A person is also an associate of the spouse or a relative (each as defined above) of any individual with whom he is in partnership. This association does *not* extend to relatives of the partner's spouse or spouses (or former spouses etc) of a relative or spouse of the partner. Former partners do not continue to be associated (contrast former spouses – see s 435(8)). But persons remain partners for this purpose even though their partnership has ceased carrying on business, while they are winding up the partnership's affairs – see Sir Francis Ferris in *Goel v Pick*[2] referring to Partnership Act 1890, s 38.

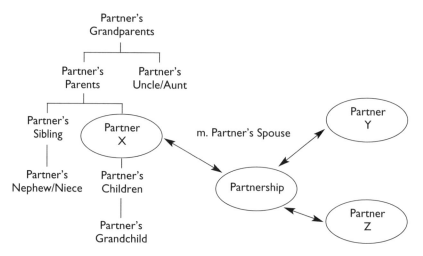

Partners Y and Z will be associates of partner X. Partners Y and Z will also be associates of Partner X's spouse and all of Partner X's 'relatives' as shown in the diagram. Partners Y and Z will *not* be associates of the relatives of Partner X's spouse or the spouses of Partner X's 'relatives'.

This is an extension compared to the position of a company director. A director is not (without more) treated as associated with his or her fellow directors (or their spouses/relatives).

1 For example, in *Re Scientific Investment Pension Plan, Clark v Hicks* [1992] OPLR 185; [1992] PLR 213 (Mervyn Davies J), it was noted that a solicitor would be allowed to continue to act as an independent trustee on insolvency (under SSPA 1975, s 57C, now PA 1995, s 22) if he was a sole practitioner and he (or perhaps his employees) provided services to the scheme, but not if he was in partnership – because he would then be associated with his other partners.
2 [2007] 1 All ER 982; [2006] EWHC 833 (Ch) at paras [28] to [30].

41.51   A Scottish firm[1] is an associate of any person who is a member of it – s 435(3).

1 A Scottish firm, unlike an English partnership, is deemed to have a separate personality from its partners – see s 4(2), Partnership Act 1890. An LLP under the Limited Liability Partnerships Act 2000 is a corporate body with legal personality separate from its members – see s 1(2).

Limited liability partnerships (LLPs) – s 435(3A)

41.52   Partnership does not seem for the purpose of s 435(3) to include members of a LLP established under the Limited Liability Partnerships Act 2000. Instead the Limited Liability Partnerships Regulations 2001[1] provide for modified provisions in the IA 1986 to apply to LLPs (see reg 5). These include modifications to ss 249 and 435.

1 SI 2001/1090.

41.53   Broadly the effect of the modifications is to treat an LLP in the same way as a company, with the members being treated as directors; and to treat the members in the same way as partners.

41.54   Shadow directors are treated as including 'shadow members', defined (in reg 2) in identical terms to that used for a shadow director (save referring to a member instead of a director) ie a person in accordance with whose directions or instructions the members of the LLP are accustomed to act (but so that a person is not deemed a shadow member by reason only that the members of the LLP act on advice given by him in a professional capacity).

41.55   A new section 435(3A) provides that a member of a LLP is an associate of that LLP, every other member of that LLP and the spouse or relative of every other member of that LLP. This is an extension compared to the position of a company director. A director is not (without more) treated as associated with his or her fellow directors (or their spouses/relatives).

Trustees – s 435(5)

41.56   A person in his capacity as trustee of a trust (other than certain specified types of trusts including pension schemes and employees' share schemes (as defined in the Companies legislation[1])) is an associate of another person if the beneficiaries of the trust include, or the terms of the trust confer a power that may be exercised for the benefit of, that other person or an associate of that other person – s 435(5)[2]. This is presumably designed to cover certain trust relationships where the insolvent person or his or its associates could benefit from the trust.

1 See CA 2006, s 1166, formerly CA 1985, s 743.
2 There is a similar provision in CA 2006, s 252(2)(c), formerly s 346(2)(c) and (3)(b) of the Companies Act 1985 ('Connected persons' etc).

41.57   So a trustee is an associate of a company if the beneficiaries include the company or an associate of the company (eg a director, officer or employee). Thus a trustee of (say) a family trust for the benefit of a relative of a director of a company is associated with that director and so connected with that company. Similarly if the company is a trustee, it is associated with each of the beneficiaries of the trust (and their associates).

EMPLOYEES/ DIRECTORS/ OFFICERS – s 435(4) AND (9)

41.58   As mentioned above, a person is an associate of any person whom he employs or by whom he is employed – s 435(4). A director or other officer of a company is treated as employed by that company – s 435(9). The term 'officer' is not defined in the IA for the purposes of s 435[1]. The definition in s 1173 of the Companies Act 2006[2] is likely to be used as the closest analogy and provides that officer includes a director, manager or secretary. There is some difficulty with this definition: it is inclusive, not exclusive and leaves it open as to who is a 'manager'. There is a good summary of the issue in Butterworths Insolvency Law at para 10.152, quoting Lindley LJ in *Re Western Countries Steam Bakeries* *and Milling Co.*[3], that 'to be an officer there must be an office, and an office imports a recognised position with rights and duties annexed to it.... it would be an abuse of words to call a person an officer who fills no such position either de jure or de facto, but who happens to do some of the work which he would have to do if he were an officer in the proper sense of the word'[4].

1 IA 1986, s 251 used to incorporate defined terms from the Companies legislation. But s 251 only applied for 'this Group of Parts', which does not include s 435 – see discussion above in the section 'Shadow directors and de facto directors'.
2 Formerly CA 1985, s 744.
3 [1897] 1 Ch 617, CA.
4 See also *Re London and General Bank* [1895] 2 Ch 166 and *Mutual Reinsurance Co Ltd v Peat Marwick Mitchell* [1997] 1 BCLC 1.

41.59 Butterworths goes on to point out that the expression 'manager' was considered in *Re a Company No 009966 of 1979*[1]. Butterworths also comments[2] that auditors are generally officers (*Re London and General Bank*[3], but that bankers, solicitors and other professional advisers are not, as such, officers: *Re Imperial Land Co of Marseilles, Re National Bank*[4] (and see also s 219(3), IA, which draws a distinction between an officer and an agent).

1 [1980] Ch 138 at 144.
2 At para 10.1254.
3 [1895] 2 Ch 166.
4 (1870) LR Eq 298.

41.60 It seems likely that a director (Mr A) of a company (B) which is itself a director of another company (C) is not an officer of that company, ie Mr A is not an officer of company C – see the Court of Appeal in *Masri v Consolidated Contractors International Co SAL*[1] discussing the meaning of 'officer' in another context.

1 [2008] EWCA Civ 876; [2008] 2 CLC 126 at para [20].

WHO IS NOT CONNECTED OR ASSOCIATED?

41.61 In the absence of any other potential connection or association, it is possible to point to some people who are not connected or associated (without more) in relation to a company: advisors, bankers, lawyers, contracting parties (eg the purchaser of a business from the company), creditors, pension scheme trustee advisors.

SHARE MORTGAGES

41.62 Could a person (*security holder*) holding the benefit of a mortgage or charge over all the issued shares[1] in a company (eg a bank or security trustee) become 'connected with' or an 'associate of' the company solely by virtue of having that charge because it could in some sense be said to have 'control' over the voting power in the company conferred by the shares?

1 Control of over one-third of the votes is all that is needed. But in many cases the charged shares will be of a subsidiary, so will all be charged.

41.63 It may be a feature of the security that the security holder will have a mortgage or charge over shares of the borrower (or other companies in the group). This could be:

- a legal mortgage (ie with the shares transferred into (and registered in) the name of the security holder or its nominee); or

- an equitable mortgage or charge (where the shares remain registered in the name of the parent, but a security document has been signed and blank transfers and/or a power of attorney given to the security holder).

41.64 Some comfort may be available from Lewison J's judgment in *Unidare*[1] discussed above (that the use of the phrase '*voting power*' in s 435, rather than '*voting rights*' in Companies Act 1985, ss 736 and 736A was significant). However, as mentioned, the application of this case may be limited since Lewison J was influenced by the fact that the parties intended the shares to be transferred – they just had not completed all the necessary steps at the time.

1 [2005] 3 All ER 730; [2005] EWHC 1410 (Ch); [2005] All ER (D) 12 (Jul).

Equitable mortgage

41.65 Where the security is equitable (rather than legal), the security holder (mortgagee) will not be the registered holder of the securities. If in addition the terms of the charge make it clear that the mortgagor (parent) can exercise the voting rights attached to the shares unless and until (say) an event of default occurs or is declared, it seems likely that until such an event of default occurs the mortgagee is not 'connected with' or an 'associate of' the company. This is on the basis that there is no current entitlement – and s 435(10) uses the present tense, ie 'he is entitled to exercise, or control the exercise of, …. the voting power' – before the occurrence of an event of default.

41.66 Once an event of default is declared, the security document may provide that the mortgagee/security holder becomes entitled to exercise, or control the exercise of, one third or more of the voting power at any general meeting. On such exercise, the mortgagee will fall within the net of association. It is therefore important to ensure that the voting rights are not *automatically* triggered on the occurrence of an event of default where it may have unintended consequences (for example in the context of the moral hazard pensions legislation).

Legal mortgage

41.67 The same analysis can be applied to a legal mortgage (where the security holder or its nominee will become registered holder of the shares) if there is provision in the mortgage document dealing with exercise of voting rights by the mortgagor/parent. Here the security holder will be the person registered as the holder of the shares and so the one prima facie entitled to exercise the voting and other rights attached to the shares (articles of association generally envisage that companies can ignore any other interests in shares – see eg regulation 5 of 1985 Table A[1]). But the legal mortgagee/security holder, although the registered holder of shares, will not be entitled to exercise, or control the exercise of the voting power. It will only be on an event of acceleration that the mortgagee will become entitled to or control the exercise the voting power of the shares.

1 See also s 360, CA 1985 and s 126, CA 2006.

Ability to declare an event of default/acceleration?

41.68   The position is more difficult if the mortgagee/security holder becomes entitled to declare an event of default. It could be argued that this power to declare an event of default means that the mortgagee/security holder is entitled to control voting rights[1]. Antony Zacaroli does so in the footnote to para H5-03 in the looseleaf book 'Insolvency'[2], commenting that the taking of blank transfers may be said to give control, but that taking a charge over shares in a holding company would not give control over shares in a subsidiary.

This may well be too cautious (it is difficult to see why, if the security holder has control over the parent, it does not have control of the subsidiary). It would be safest for the security document expressly to restrict voting rights with a security holder until an actual default had been declared by it.

1 See Insolvency (Sweet & Maxwell) (edited by Segal, Totty and Moss) at page H5/3.
2 (Sweet & Maxwell) (edited by Segal, Moss and Totty) .

41.69   Care must also be taken to ensure that there are no circumstances which might suggest that the security holder could be viewed as a shadow director of the company.

CHAPTER 42

Pre pack administrations – employee and pension issues

42.1 A practice has grown up, comparatively recently, for businesses to be placed into administration (or receivership) and for the business assets and trade then to be sold under a previously organised arrangement.

42.2 Statement of Insolvency Practice 16 (SIP 16) issued by R3 effective from 1 January 2009 defines a 'pre pack' as:

> 'an arrangement under which the sale of all or part of a company's business or assets is negotiated with a purchaser prior to the appointment of an administrator, and the administrator effects the sale immediately on, or shortly after, his appointment.'

42.3 The essence of a pre pack is that an onward sale will have been structured and made ready before the administrators are appointed. Court cases have indicated that the administrators have power to agree to such an immediate sale – see eg *DKLL Solicitors v Revenue and Customs*[1] and *Re Transbus International Limited*[2].

But administrators will need to be careful that they are not seen as mere ciphers and that they independently check that such a sale is the best that can be achieved in the relevant insolvency.

The courts will consider the implications of a pre-pack sale when deciding whether or not to grant an administration order – see *Re Kayley Vending Limited*[3].

1 [2007] EWHC 2067 (Ch); [2008] 1 BCLC 112, [2007] All ER (D) 68 (Mar) (Andrew Simmonds QC sitting as a deputy judge of the High Court).
2 [2004] EWHC 932 (Ch); [2004] 2 All ER 911, [2004] 1 WLR 2654, [2004] 2 BCLC 550 (Lawrence Collins J)
3 [2009] EWHC 904 (Ch) (Judge David Cooke).

42.4 Because of criticisms of the swiftness and lack of transparency of the process, SIP 16 sets out a fairly extensive regime of disclosure by administrators. The aim is that administrators should be in a position to justify that the sale as part of the pre pack was in fact the best way of maximising returns for creditors.

42.5 A pre pack will possibly involve a sale to an entity in which the existing directors have an interest or in which a secured creditor has an interest. As such, some criticism is sometimes made that the individual directors (who may have been responsible for the insolvency of the company) are benefitting out of the pre pack sale. The converse argument is that the sale is intended to maximise recoveries for creditors of the company – particularly in situations where a more extended sale process could erode customer or employee confidence and so reduce the proceeds received. This may be the best offer available.

42.6   For further discussion of the general position on pre packs see chapter 10 in the book by Vanessa Finch *'Corporate Insolvency Law'* (2nd Edn, Cambridge, 2009), the article by Mark Hyde and Iain White in (2009) Law and Financial Market Review 134 and the article by Sandra Frisby in (2009) 4 Journal of International Banking and Financial Law 198.

42.7   In relation to employees and pension schemes, pre packs have no special status but apply the principles outlined in the chapters above. There is no express mention of employees or pension schemes in SIP 16.

42.8   Generally there will be a transfer of the business from the insolvent company to the purchasing entity (Newco). If there is a pension scheme in the old company, this will usually be left behind in the insolvent company.

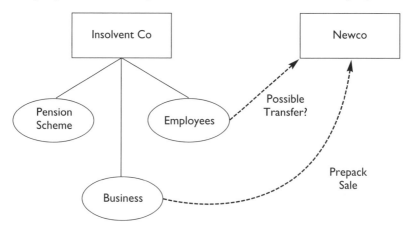

This raises two issues relevant for this chapter:

(a)   impact on employees;

(b)   impact on the pension scheme.

EMPLOYEES

42.9   One key question is whether or not the transfer of the business from the insolvency company to the new entity will amount to a transfer of business regulated by TUPE. As a matter of general law, generally such a transfer would clearly fall within TUPE as being a transfer of a business. The main question that arises is whether or not a transfer by a company in administration in these circumstances falls outside TUPE because of the 'terminal insolvency' provisions in Regulation 8(7) –see Chapter 20 (TUPE 2006 – terminal and non-terminal insolvencies) above.

42.10   In January 2009 the EAT in *Oakland v Wellswood (Yorkshire) Limited*[1] held that a transfer, immediately after the appointment of administrators, was on the facts of that case a 'terminal insolvency' proceeding within reg 8(7) in that there was a liquidation of the assets of the insolvent company. This decision is discussed more fully in Chapter 20 above.

The decision of the EAT is contrary to the guidance that had previously been given by the DTI, but it seems difficult to distinguish such a pre pack administration from a liquidation. In both cases, immediately following the appointment of the insolvency practitioner, the business is transferred and all that the insolvent company retains are cash assets.

The Court of Appeal gave judgment on appeal in the *Oakland* case at the end of July 2009[2], but refused to deal with the reg 8(7) point and decided the case based on the continuity of employment provisions in ERA 1996. Moses LJ in the Court of Appeal stated:

> '10. This court was thus furnished with full written submissions from the Secretary of State on the point and also a full skeleton on the point from Ms Toman [counsel for Mr Oakland]. Supplied with that, it was not surprising perhaps that Mummery LJ gave leave, and for my part I would wish to emphasise that there are strong grounds for thinking that both the Employment Tribunal and the Employment Appeal Tribunal took the wrong approach to their construction both to the Article 5 of the Directive and to Regulation 8.'

And later:

> '17 In those circumstances, adopting the wisdom of Rix LJ, it would seem to me most unwise for us to give a binding pronouncement on the correctness or otherwise of the contention that administration necessarily excludes the application of regulation 8(7). I would only, for my part, wish to emphasise that that is a strongly arguable point, and the only reason I agree that it should not be resolved today is that the Secretary of State is not here and, since the Wellswood (Yorkshire) Limited Administration, Newco, is in the process of being liquidated almost as we speak, and therefore has no representation here today, it would be unwise to reach and pronounce upon any definitive conclusion. Expressing regret that that cannot be done today, I would allow this appeal.'

If some of the assets are retained by the insolvent company or a business is carried on, then it will be much more unlikely that the insolvency will be treated as a terminal insolvency within reg 8(7). For example, in *Marra v Express Gifts Ltd*[3] in January 2009, the ET considered the EAT decision in *Oakland* and held that on the facts reg 8(7) did not apply where there was a transfer out of an administration. This case involved a transfer of some only of the insolvent company's assets and was made some 22 days after the insolvent company had entered administration. The insolvent company also seems to have carried on some business after the transfer.

1 UKEAT/0395/08; [2009] IRLR 250, EAT.
2 [2009] EWCA Civ 1094, CA.
3 [2009] BPIR 508; ET case 2401065/08, ET.

Current position

42.11 The chart below summarises the position depending on whether or not Oakland is followed in the future. An analysis of the legal position follows.

Legal issue	If Oakland followed – ie prepack sale is out of a terminal insolvency so reg 8(7) applies	If Oakland **not** followed – ie prepack sale is out of a non-terminal insolvency so reg 8(6) applies
Automatic transfer under TUPE, reg 4	No	Yes
Newco can choose which employees to offer to hire	Yes	No (subject to power to dismiss)
Transferring employees have continuity of employment	Yes	Yes
Automatic unfair dismissal if dismissal by reason of the transfer (unless ETO) – TUPE reg 7	No	Yes
Newco inherits past liabilities	No, unless contractually agreed	Yes (save for pensions) and NI fund claims excluded under reg 8
Newco can offer changed terms and conditions of employment	Yes, unless contractually agreed	No – TUPE reg 4(4), unless new reg 9 applies
Parties required to inform and consult about the transfer	Yes	Yes
Insolvent Co required to pass employee information to Newco	Yes	Yes
Transferring employee can claim statutory redundancy from insolvent company?	Probably	No (no dismissal because of statutory novation under TUPE, reg 4)
Employee unreasonably refusing transfer offer can claim statutory redundancy from Insolvent Co?	Probably	No
Insolvent Co potentially obliged to consult on dismissals (under TULCRA)	Yes re all employees depending on numbers (and potential 'special circumstances' defence)	Yes re non-transferring employees depending on numbers (and potential 'special circumstances' defence)
Newco obliged to offer future pensions to transferring employees under PA 2004?	Yes	Yes

If *Oakland* followed

42.12 If the decision of the EAT in *Oakland* is followed, the transfer to Newco will be treated as a terminal insolvency and so reg 8(7) of TUPE 2006 will apply. This means that regs 4 and 7 of TUPE 2006 do not apply – ie there is no automatic transfer of relevant employees to Newco. Regulation 4 deals with the 'Effect of relevant transfer on contracts of employment' and reg 7 deals with 'Dismissal of employee because of relevant transfer'.

But there will still be a business transfer. So it seems that the other provisions of TUPE 2006 will apply if they are not directly dependent on there being a transfer under reg 4 of TUPE.(ie need to consult, need to provide information to Newco). The business transfer to Newco is arguably still a 'relevant transfer' under reg 3 to which the other provisions of TUPE (ie excluding regs 4 and 7) can apply.

See the discussion in the article by Richard Parr 'The rescue culture and TUPE'[1] (written before the Court of Appeal decision in *Oakland*).

The impact on a pre pack is discussed below.

1 (2009) 22 Insolvency Intelligence 91.

42.13 **Automatic transfer:** There is no automatic transfer of relevant employees from the insolvent company to Newco. Under reg 8(7), reg 4 of TUPE does not apply. This means that Newco can decide whether or not it wants to make offers of employment to some or all of the relevant employees;

42.14 **Past liabilities:** Those employees who transfer will not necessarily have Newco pick up any pre-existing liabilities. This depends upon the terms of the transfer and the terms offered by Newco. Any claims relating to their previous employment do not transfer automatically (because reg 4 of TUPE does not apply), so therefore should remain with the transferring (insolvent) company. This could include issues such as unpaid wages, discrimination claims etc.

It may be that a term of the transfer could be that the insolvent company looks for Newco to take over the responsibility for all such claims as a matter of contract (conversely the employees may look for this as part of the job arrangements). There may be an issue for the administrators here in that potentially the amount payable to the insolvent company by Newco may reduce if Newco is accepting such claims.

42.15 **Inform and consult:** It seems likely that the requirement to inform or consult employees (or their representatives) under regs 13 to 15 of TUPE (see Chapter 21 above) still applies. There is case law that the consultation obligation under TUPE applies whether or not there is in fact a transfer – see the EAT in *Banking Insurance and Finance Union v Barclays Bank plc*[1] and in *South Durham Health Authority v UNISON*[2] and para 16.41 above.

1 [1987] ICR 495, EAT.
2 [1995] ICR 495; [1995] IRLR 407, EAT.

42.16 **Employee liability information:** the obligation under reg 11 of TUPE 2006 to pass on employee liability information to the transferee (here Newco) –

see Chapter 21 above – applies in relation to persons assigned to the relevant organised grouping of resources or employees that is the subject of a relevant transfer. So this obligation seems to apply to the employees who could actually transfer.

But in practice it seems odd that any liability could apply to the insolvent company in relation to employees who do not in fact transfer. And in relation to employees who do transfer, there is no transfer of liability under TUPE (reg 4 does not apply) so the practical worth of the employee information for Newco may be small (the date of start of continuous service will be relevant – see below). So it may be that if there were a claim under this provision, then any liability (award of compensation) is reduced by the tribunal below the standard £500 per employee under its discretionary power to reflect what it considers to be just and equitable –TUPE 2006, reg 12(5).

42.17   Continuity of employment: Any employees who do transfer will have continuity of employment for statutory purposes under ERA 1996, s 218(2) – see the Court of Appeal in Oakland and para 20.22 above. It is clear that a transfer of an undertaking can be made by a company in insolvency – see *Teesside Times Ltd v Drury*[1], and *Thomsons Soft Drinks Ltd v Quaife*[2], cases on continuity of employment under EPCA 1978 (now consolidated into ERA 1996).

1 [1980] ICR 338, CA.
2 8 June 1981, EAT.

42.18   Redundancy payment by insolvent company?: It would seem that any employees who do transfer to Newco can still claim a redundancy payment against the insolvent company. Although ERA 1996, s 138 excludes statutory redundancy payments (subject to trial period provisions) where there is a suitable offer of employment, this only extends to offers by the employer or an 'associated employer' (references in s 138 to re-engagement by the employer include re-engagement by an associated employer – s 146). The term 'associated employer' only includes those under common control with the insolvency company (which Newco probably will not be) –ERA 1996, s 231.

The predecessor to ERA 1996, EPCA 1978 did include provisions dealing with the position of redundancy payments on a business transfer –EPCA 1978, s 94. But this section was repealed in August 1993[1] (presumably on the basis that TUPE then covered the position , so the section was no longer needed) and so no equivalent provision appears in the consolidating ERA 1996.

Employees who do transfer and who are paid a redundancy payment may reduce any potential future statutory redundancy rights – see ERA 1996, s 214. But this is a complex area – see eg *Secretary of State v Lassman*[2], *Senior Heat Treatment v Bell*[3], and the discussion in *Harvey on Industrial Relations and Employment Law* at paras E299 to E326. See also para 20.32 above.

1 By the Trade Union Reform and Employment Rights Act 1993.
2 [2000] IRLR 411, CA.
3 [1997] IRLR 614, EAT.

42.19   Different employment terms offered by Newco?: Newco can offer different terms and conditions of employment – the prohibition under reg 4(4) of

TUPE on changes in terms and conditions of employment by reason of a transfer does not apply (because reg 8(7) disapplied reg 4).

In *Oakland* it seems that pay for one employee was reduced. This was not part of the dispute however.

42.20 Pensions for transferring employees: The pension provisions in the Pensions Act 2004 apply if there is 'relevant transfer' within the meaning given by TUPE. This means that these provisions apply in relation to any employee who actually transfers (even if such transfer is not under reg 4 of TUPE). See Chapter 24 (TUPE: pension liabilities) above for a description of the obligations.

Non-transferring employees

42.21 Non-transferring employees: Any employees who do not receive offers or do not transfer will presumably be made redundant by the insolvent company. They will presumably be dismissed and will have the usual claims against the insolvent company (wrongful dismissal, redundancy, unfair dismissal etc.);

- Any dismissal (whether by the insolvent company or Newco) will not be automatically unfair (in the absence of an ETO reason) under reg 7 of TUPE even if the dismissal is caused by the transfer. Regulation 7 is disapplied by reg 8(7).

- If an employee is offered a job by Newco before the end of his or her employment with the insolvent company, it seems that he or she does not lose any claim for a statutory redundancy payment even if the offer is unreasonably refused. Although ERA 1996, s 141 contains restrictions on the right to a statutory redundancy payment where an offer of re-engagement is unreasonably refused, this only applies to such offers made by the employer or an associated employer (see ERA 1996, s 146 and para 42.18 above), which probably will not (depending on the facts) cover Newco.

- Such an employee may be unable to claim significant damages for wrongful dismissal or unfair dismissal by the insolvent company on the basis that he or she has failed to mitigate the loss by accepting the new contract of employment with the Newco (assuming this is no less favourable than the existing contract). But note potentially the impact of the loss of pension rights.

If Oakland not followed

42.22 Conversely, if the EAT in *Oakland* were not followed and TUPE were held to apply, the usual TUPE rules will be applicable (see Chapters 19 to 24 above). Broadly:

- all relevant employees assigned to the business should transfer under TUPE in the usual way;

- terms and conditions are more difficult to vary, although new Regulation 9 (see Chapter 20 above) may assist;

- all liabilities will transfer, save for those within reg 8(6).

- the information and consultation obligations would apply in relation to the TUPE transfer.

- the usual rules under TUPE on transfer of liability for employees dismissed by the transferring company even before the transfer will apply – see Chapter 23 above.

Failure to comply with TUPE obligations

42.23   In practice it may well be that the insolvent company does not comply with the information and consultation obligations (on the grounds of secrecy etc.) arising both under TUPE (see Chapter 23 above) and in relation to any redundancies under TULRCA 1992 (see Chapter 7 above).

Hence there may be a liability under the relevant provisions of TUPE. This is a joint and several liability on both transferor (the insolvent company) and the transferee (Newco) – see reg 15(9) of TUPE (this was a change made by TUPE 2006).

The insolvent company may seek to obtain a contractual indemnity from Newco in relation to such liability. However, it is thought that such a contractual arrangement is, in fact, invalidated by TUPE on the basis that it is not possible to have a contractual provision that contravenes TUPE – see reg 18.

The BIS Guidance on TUPE states[1]:

> 'Q. Can the transferor and the new employer agree between themselves that this information should not be provided by contracting-out of the requirement?
>
> A. No. There is no entitlement to contract-out of the duty to supply employee liability information because that would disadvantage the employees involved.'

It would be possible for a third party (eg a shareholder in Newco) to give an indemnity to the transferring company. In practice, any claim brought by employees would be likely to be made against Newco (as, presumably, a solvent entity) rather than against the insolvent company as transferor.

It does not seem that the joint and several liability of Newco is limited only to any failure in relation to employees who transfer to Newco. Newco's liability could extend to employees who do not transfer (if those employees are affected by the transfer).

1 Q&A on page 21. See http://www.berr.gov.uk/files/file20761.pdf: 'Employment rights on the transfer of an undertaking: a guide to the 2006 TUPE regulations for employees, employers and representatives' (June 2009).

42.24   The 'special circumstance' defence (see Chapter 7 above) to any failure to inform and consult (both in relation to the transfer and any redundancies) could, perhaps, be available if the insolvency (and so the transfer) was urgent and unexpected. But even here there will be an obligation to inform/consult as much as possible.

Failing to inform and consult by reason of a desire to keep the proposals confidential is unlikely to amount to enough (at least on its own) to allow the special circumstances defence to be available. See para 7.37 above.

42.25   A failure by those controlling the insolvent company to disclose their plan is not enough to allow the special circumstances defence to apply – see reg 15(6) of TUPE and TULCRA 1992, ss 188(7) and 193(7) and para 7.36 above. If the prepack was not instigated by the insolvent companies directors or shareholder but (say) by its creditors, it may well be arguable that they were not the controllers (directly or indirectly) of the insolvent company, so the special circumstances defence may potentially apply. This is untested.

PRE-PACKS AND IMPACT ON EXISTING PENSION SCHEMES

42.26   The position of the pension scheme as, often, a material unsecured creditor of the insolvent company needs to be considered.

42.27   The Pensions Regulator may be concerned that the position of the pension scheme has potentially been prejudiced by a sale as part of a pre pack. It, and the trustees of the pension scheme, could seek to bring claims against some or all of the relevant parties.

42.28   In practice, given that the pension scheme is normally an unsecured creditor, it may be difficult for the trustees (or the Pensions Regulator) to succeed in an action against (say) the directors or the administrators to the effect that the sale in the pre pack was somehow improper. The administrators and the directors will no doubt have taken due advice and considered that given the insolvent position of the company itself, the pre pack represented the best way of realising value for creditors generally. So to that extent they may well have taken account of the position of the pension scheme.

To an extent, a more difficult balancing exercise may be involved where the effect of the pre pack sale is that most of the other unsecured creditors are transferred and retained by the Newco. This could happen (say) where good will of customers was important for the business of Newco and employees also were needed to be transferred. The administrators would need to be able to show that their decision to sell, on these terms, was a proper one and balanced the interests of all the relevant creditors.

42.29   The Pensions Regulator has various powers to be able to make third parties who are connected or associated with the employer liable in certain circumstances for pension debts. As discussed above (see Chapter 37 above), the powers to issue contribution notices or financial support directions could be relevant here. In practice, FSDs cannot be issued against individuals where there is a corporate employer. In addition, contribution notices cannot be issued against insolvency practitioners acting in accordance with their powers – see PA 2004, s 33(3)(c) and para 37.37 above. Given this, the Regulator's powers may be relevant:

(a) if there are other companies in the same group as the insolvent company (eg if a subsidiary is transferred as part of the business); or

(b) if a contribution notice could be issued against (say) the directors personally.

42.30 In practice, it may well be that the directors would seek to show that the pre pack was in fact the best way of seeking to maximise recovery by creditors. However, it is not inconceivable that the Pensions Regulator (tPR) could seek to bring claims against individual directors, particularly if it saw them as having been responsible (by way of an act or omission) for the relevant insolvency. The Regulator's powers in this area were expanded by the Pensions Act 2008 – see Chapter 37 (tPR – Moral hazard powers) above.

42.31 This may point towards a need for clearance from the Pensions Regulator, although this would need to be balanced against a need for secrecy and/or speed as part of the pre pack.

42.32 However, it should be noted that tPR has shown some hostility towards the use of pre-packaged administration sales. In March 2009 it exercised its powers under s 7 of the Pensions Act 1995 to appoint an independent trustee to the Graphex Limited Pension and Life Assurance Scheme[1]. Amongst other things tPR commented that proposals by the employer's directors to 'strip out certain assets' from the principal employer and then buy-back the remaining assets through a pre-packaged arrangement but leaving behind the pension liabilities posed a risk to the scheme members and PPF.

1 Final Notice 31 March 2009: The Graphex Limited Pension and Life Assurance Scheme (Case ref: TM6511). See the tPR website: www.thepensionsregulator.gov.uk

42.33 In this case tPR had received evidence that the employer was technically insolvent although trading legally. It was not clear why tPR felt that the proposals posed a risk to scheme members and the PPF over and above the risk of employer insolvency already present.

42.34 The Scheme is then likely to enter a PPF assessment period (see Chapter 28 above).

42.35 There are perhaps three scenarios:

● No recovery for unsecureds if a liquidation (eg security held by a bank)

   – issue is one mainly for bank

● Some recovery for unsecureds if a liquidation sale of business in pre pack (net of employee liabilities assured under TUPE) likely to realise more than in a liquidation

   – pre pack looks to be easy to justify

● Some recovery for unsecureds if a liquidation – could be more than is available in a pre pack (save for employees)

    – more difficult balancing exercise for the administrators. Need to balance the interests of the unsecured creditors generally with any creditors (eg employees?) who may be better off under the pre-pack.

Index

[all references are to paragraph number]